Mesopotamian Commentaries on the Diagnostic Handbook Sa-gig

Cuneiform Monographs

Editors

VOLUME 49/2

The titles published in this series are listed at *brill.com/cumo*

Mesopotamian Commentaries on the Diagnostic Handbook Sa-gig

Edition and Notes on Medical Lexicography

By

John Z. Wee

BRILL

LEIDEN | BOSTON

The Library of Congress Cataloging-in-Publication Data is available online at http://catalog.loc.gov
LC record available at http://lccn.loc.gov/2019048168

Typeface for the Latin, Greek, and Cyrillic scripts: "Brill". See and download: brill.com/brill-typeface.

ISSN 0929-0052
ISBN 978-90-04-41755-7 (hardback)
ISBN 978-90-04-41756-4 (e-book)

This book is printed on acid-free paper and produced in a sustainable manner.

Printed by Printforce, the Netherlands

For My Mom and Dad

Contents
(Two Volumes)

1. Knowledge and Rhetoric in Medical Commentary

Preface XIII
Acknowledgements XV
List of Figures XVIII
Medical Text Labels and Abbreviations XIX
Format and Translation Issues XXVI
Glossary XXXIV

CHAPTER ONE
Introduction to the Sa-gig Commentaries

1.1.1 **The Situatedness of Commentaries** 5

1.1.2 **The Diagnostic Handbook Sa-gig and Its Serialization** 22
1.1.2.1 The Title Sa-gig 23
1.1.2.2 Magician Interest and *Esagil-kīn-apli's Manifesto* 26

1.1.3 **Serialized Variants and Their Interpretation** 36

1.1.4 **The Presentation of Alternatives in Text Series and Commentaries** 54
1.1.4.1 Commentary Tablet Formats 55
1.1.4.2 Commentary Equation and Base Text 62
1.1.4.3 Inflected Comments in Base Text Contexts 68

CHAPTER TWO
Commentary and Scholastic Rhetoric

1.2.1 **Commentary Designations and Scribal Actors** 88
1.2.1.1 "Glossary" (*ṣâtu*) 90
1.2.1.2 "Oral Lore" (*šūt pî*) 102
1.2.1.3 "Readings" (*malsûtu*) 106
1.2.1.4 "Questionings" (*maš'altu*) 113

I.2.1.5 "From the Mouth of the *Ummânu*-scholar" (*ša pî ummâni*) 119
I.2.1.6 Patterns of Commentary Designations 136

I.2.2 Textual Sources of Authority 143
I.2.2.1 Lexical Text Citations 144
I.2.2.2 Narratival Intertextuality 161

I.2.3 Forms of Argumentation 184
I.2.3.1 Two-Member Arguments 184
I.2.3.1.1 *Identification of Logographic Meanings* 185
I.2.3.1.2 *Identification of Syllabic Values* 190
I.2.3.1.3 *Clarification of Homophonic Meanings* 194
I.2.3.1.4 *Identification of Lexical Derivation* 200
I.2.3.1.5 *Definition by Synonymous Referents* 206
I.2.3.1.6 *Definition by Antonymy* 209
I.2.3.1.7 *Definition by Long Description* 213
I.2.3.1.8 *Symbolic Correspondence* 218
I.2.3.2 Multiple Member Arguments 221
I.2.3.2.1 *A:B:A:C Argument Types* 225
I.2.3.2.2 *A:B(:A):C Argument Types* 238
I.2.3.2.3 *A:B:C Argument Types* 244
I.2.3.2.4 *B:A':B:C Argument Types* 251
I.2.3.2.5 *Other Concatenated Arguments* 261
I.2.3.2.6 *Analyses of Logographic Forms* 265
I.2.3.2.7 *Analyses of Syllabic Forms* 269
I.2.3.3 Single Member Arguments 277

I.2.4 Exemplar and License in Scholastic Hermeneutics 281

CHAPTER THREE
Commentary and Medical Knowledge

I.3.1 Epistemic Progression in Medical Practice and Texts 291
I.3.1.1 The Therapeutic Tradition 292
I.3.1.2 Structuring the Diagnostic Handbook 316
I.3.1.2.1 *Sa-gig Chapters I to III—Framing Time* 317
I.3.1.2.2 *Sa-gig Chapters IV to V—the Stage for Therapy* 336

I.3.1.2.3 *Sa-gig Chapter VI—Other Bodies* 350
I.3.1.2.4 *Commentary Interest in Sa-gig Chapters* 353

I.3.2 **Harmonizing Texts and Phenomena** 356
I.3.2.1 Knowledge Assumptions in Topic Choice 356
I.3.2.2 The Pericope and Omissions from Topics 370
I.3.2.3 Comment Choice and Argument as Pretext 391

I.3.3 **Habits of Use and the Cuneiform Handbook** 410

Conclusion

Scholasticism and the Boundaries for Interpretation 427

Appendix One: Embedded Variants in the Diagnostic Handbook Sa-gig 433
Appendix Two: Transliterations of Medical Texts 440
Bibliography 449
Index of Excerpts (Two Volumes) 486

II. Mesopotamian Commentaries on the Diagnostic Handbook Sa-gig

Preface XIII
Acknowledgements XV
Medical Text Labels and Abbreviations XVIII
Format and Translation Issues XXV

PART ONE
Edition of the Sa-gig Commentaries

II.1.1 **Commentary Sa-gig 1A** 5
(Tablet AO 17661)

II.1.2 **Commentary Sa-gig 1B** 29
(Tablet W 22307/6 = IM 74357; ed. *SpTU* I, 27)

II.1.3 **Commentary Sa-gig 1C** 57
(Tablet W 22307/24 = IM 74374; ed. *SpTU* I, 28)

II.1.4 **Commentary Sa-gig 1D** 66
(Tablet W 22666/1c; ed. *SpTU* V, 256)

II.1.5 **Commentary Sa-gig 1–3** 72
(Tablet S.U. 51/70; ed. *STT* II, 403)

II.1.6 **Commentary Sa-gig 3A** 101
(Tablet W 22307/71; ed. *SpTU* I, 29)

II.1.7 **Commentary Sa-gig 3B** 107
(Tablet BM 43854 + 43938)

II.1.8 **Commentary Sa-gig 3C** 117
(Tablet BM 55491)

II.1.9 **Commentary Sa-gig 4A** 124
(Tablet W 22307/60 + 79 + 80 (+) 75; ed. *SpTU* I, 30)

II.1.10 **Commentary Sa-gig 4B** 139
(Tablet BM 66965 + 76508)

II.1.11 **Commentary Sa-gig 4C** 158
(Tablet BM 40837 + 41252)

II.1.12 **Commentary Sa-gig 5** 170
(Tablet W 22307/16; ed. *SpTU* I, 31)

II.1.13 **Commentary Sa-gig 7A** 184
(Tablet W 22307/2; ed. *SpTU* I, 32)

II.1.14 **Commentary Sa-gig 7B** 195
(Tablet W 22307/10; ed. *SpTU* I, 33)

II.1.15 **Commentary Sa-gig 7Ca** 201
(Tablet BM 48727 + 48741)

II.1.16 **Commentary Sa-gig 7Cb** 207
(Tablet BM 48729)

II.1.17 **Commentary Sa-gig 7Cc (?)** 210
(Tablet BM 49044)

II.1.18 **Commentary Sa-gig 10 & 11** 213
(Tablet DT 87)

II.1.19 **Commentary Sa-gig 13+** 225
(Tablet GCBC 766; ed. *GCCI* II, 406)

II.1.20 **Commentary Sa-gig 14** 236
(Tablet W 22307/20; ed. *SpTU* I, 36)

II.1.21 **Commentary Sa-gig 18** 261
(Tablet BM 66873)

II.1.22 **Commentary Sa-gig 19** 269
(Tablet W 22307/32; ed. *SpTU* I, 38)

II.1.23 **Commentary Sa-gig 21 & 22a** 283

II.1.24 **Commentary Sa-gig 23** 307
(Tablet RMC 193)

II.1.25 **Commentary Sa-gig 29** 313
(Tablet BM 38375)

II.1.26 **Commentary Sa-gig 34** 316
(Tablet W 22730/2; ed. *SpTU* II, 39)

II.1.27 **Commentary Sa-gig 36** 323
(Tablet W 22307/23 + 74; ed. *SpTU* I, 39)

II.1.28 **Commentary Sa-gig 39** 330
(Tablet W 22311; ed. *SpTU* I, 40)

II.1.29 **Commentary Sa-gig 40A** 340
(Tablet W 22308a; ed. *SpTU* I, 41)

II.1.30 **Commentary Sa-gig 40B** 348
(Tablet W 22307/73; ed. *SpTU* I, 42)

PART TWO
Commentary Notations

II.2.1 **Disjunction Sign** 356

II.2.2 **"The Case of / Where" (*ša*)** 364

II.2.3 **"Which It Said" (*ša iqbû*)** 370

II.2.4 **"As in" (*libbû*)** 380

II.2.5 **"Complement to" (IGI / *pāni*)** 388

II.2.6 **"(Points) to" (*ana*)** 394

II.2.7 **"The Usual (Meaning)" (*kayyān*)** 398

II.2.8 **Other Notations** 401

Photographs 403
Bibliography 437
Index of Excerpts (Two Volumes) 474

Preface

The two volumes on *Knowledge and Rhetoric in Medical Commentary* (CM 49/1) and *Mesopotamian Commentaries on the Diagnostic Handbook Sa-gig* (CM 49/2) in the Cuneiform Monographs (CM) series represent companion studies on one of the most abstruse textual genres from ancient Mesopotamia.

Knowledge and Rhetoric in Medical Commentary (§1) is intended for historians interested in the ancient history of medicine or the history of interpretation. Whereas straightforward English translations suffice in making most ancient texts accessible to the modern reader, the commentary genre presents special difficulties, because of the way it relies on unusual word choices, proof-texting, as well as intricate turns of logic, in order to manipulate the rules of language and script in service to commentators' arguments. For the reader willing or eager to understand these challenging texts, the volume helps by providing a convenient glossary defining key terms, maintains a consistent translation of individual Akkadian words and expressions into English, divides the main text into bite-sized sections amply illustrated by excerpts, and explains linguistic artifices as lucidly as possible without under-representing their complexity.

The three chapters in this volume explore the dynamic between knowledge and rhetoric in the production of medical commentary. Chapter One (§1.1) introduces the Diagnostic Handbook Sa-gig as the product of text serialization, with special attention to the situatedness of its ancient commentaries, and how their written forms mimic long-established practices of editing and reading serialized texts. Chapter Two (§1.2) observes how commentators' self-fashioning as experts of diverse disciplines is expressed in the scholastic rhetoric of Sa-gig commentaries, whose tablet labels evoke contexts of scribal education, and which display intertextuality involving a variety of lexical, astronomical, religious, magic, and literary texts, while employing patterns of argumentation that resist categorization within any single branch of knowledge. Such recurring features functioned also as cognitive shortcuts—the validity of whose reasoning did not have to be repeatedly proven, but could simply be taken for granted. Chapter Three (§1.3) recounts Sa-gig's historical significance as a move from older to newer ways of defining the field of medicine, which mirrors the progression from earlier to later stages of medical pedagogy evident in its commentaries. In their choices and omissions of topics and comments, commentators sought to harmonize atypical language and ideas in the Diagnostic Handbook with conventional ways of perceiving and describing the sick body in existing therapeutic recipes, so that scholastic rhetoric—supposedly universal and unfettered to any particular discipline—served in fact as a pretext for affirming current forms of medical knowledge.

Mesopotamian Commentaries on the Diagnostic Handbook Sa-gig (§11) adopts the more traditional form of an Assyriological monograph, with philological and bibliographical detail for specialists in cuneiform studies. The two parts of this volume elucidate the cuneiform primary sources of the Sa-gig commentaries. Part One (§11.1) contemplates the issues involved in translating ancient commentarial logic into English forms and modern typesetting, while illustrating how these issues may be addressed in a cuneiform edition, translation, and notes on medical lexicography for thirty Sa-gig commentary tablets and fragments. Part Two (§11.2) clarifies the meanings of various technical notations recurring in commentaries on Sa-gig and other cuneiform genres.

Acknowledgements

These volumes had their origin in my 2012 dissertation on the Diagnostic Handbook Sa-gig and its cuneiform commentaries, but evolved significantly after years spent thinking over and endeavoring to inhabit the logical processes and language choices of the ancient authors. Over these years, many helped shape my intellectual growth as a historian of ancient science and medicine, to whom I remain deeply grateful. Here, I voice my acknowledgements particularly of those who contributed in more direct ways to the creation of these volumes.

Among my teachers at Yale, first thanks goes to my *Doktorvater* Eckart Frahm, of whose profound knowledge, nuanced scholarship, and gentle friendship I am recipient, and whose wise counsel and encouragement continue to help me navigate the waters of academia. Benjamin Foster made sure class times were always happy times, and inspired me to think big ideas, to turn a fresh eye to old problems, and to love my calling as a lifelong student of the humanities. To Kathryn Slanski, I owe the illumination of countless lines of Akkadian text, a model for teaching with carefulness and clarity, and a warm interest in my personal and academic life.

Frahm's book on *Origins of Interpretation* (2011) provided a preliminary list of Sa-gig commentaries that laid the foundation for my work. Hermann Hunger displayed a remarkably intuitive grasp of commentarial logic already in his *editio princeps* of the Uruk commentaries, and Andrew George his rich insight into the layers of intertextuality for commentaries on Sa-gig Tablet 1. Any improvements in understanding these texts, on my part, represent heights achieved only on the shoulders of giants like these. Marten Stol combed through my dissertation and returned fourteen priceless pages filled with observations, amendments, and pure musings. Characteristic of his generosity in our interactions over a decade, Markham Geller shared results from his own unpublished research, and showed an admirable openness in seriously deliberating even viewpoints and interpretations that differed from his own. Uri Gabbay carefully read my early commentary editions and notes and sent me his insights and articles. While visiting the British Museum in early summer of 2013, Christopher Walker liberally provided me with a list of Sa-gig and other commentaries gathered from his own studies, giving me a head start in mulling over these manuscripts, including several that would be announced only years later through Yale's Cuneiform Commentaries Project (CCP).

From Stefan Maul I received hospitality and memorable lessons in cuneiform epigraphy during my yearlong stay at Heidelberg (2008–2009), as well as permission to consult the Geers copy (notebook N 39) of Tablet DT 87 (§11.1.18). Ulrike Steinert offered valuable help by collating readings in the difficult tablet *STT* 403 (§11.1.5) from Istanbul, while Geller allowed me to look at his transcription and hand copy of the joints BM 43854+43938 (§11.1.7). Christopher Woods shared with me tablet photos and his own readings of the lexical composition Igituh, which he prepared for the *Materialien zum sumerischen Lexikon* series. I am grateful to Hunger and Margarete van Ess for permission to use tablet photos from the Uruk excavations, to Ulla Kasten and Elizabeth Payne for those from the Yale Babylonian Collection (§11.1.19), and to Joseph Shemtov for those from the John Frederick Lewis Collection of the Free Library of Philadelphia (§11.1.23). While most commentary tablets from the British Museum were photographed by me, I thank Jonathan Taylor for later sending me photos of tablets that were unavailable when I visited—all by courtesy of the Trustees of the British Museum.

At Yale, I benefitted from Samuel K. Bushnell (2010–2011) and Teaching (2007–2012) Fellowships, and a Landesstiftung Baden-Württemberg Scholarship (2008–2009) that funded my stay at Heidelberg. Later, I was fortunate to receive support for my work from a Provost's Career Enhancement Postdoctoral Scholarship (2012–2014) at the University of Chicago, and subsequently, from research funds provided by the university's Oriental Institute and College. Above all, the astonishing diversity of expertise in the Oriental Institute compelled me to broaden my perspective on ancient studies and the kinds of questions to ask of my work, so as to situate it within larger agenda in the humanities and social sciences. I thank Christopher Woods, Theo van den Hout, and Robert Biggs—the best of mentors during my early days at the Oriental Institute—as well as Rebecca Hasselbach-Andee and Matthew Stolper, whose lively conversations illumined various topics in these volumes. From Biggs and Van den Hout, I received also gifts of many weighty tomes on Mesopotamian medicine, astronomy, and scholarship, which line my office shelves as monuments of their generosity.

I thank the editors of the Cuneiform Monographs series for their oversight of this project and their prompt responses to my concerns and queries, as well as the staff at Brill Academic Publishers for their meticulous efforts in seeing these volumes to print. Special acknowledgement is due to Katelyn Chin, who was my liaison at Brill from the very beginning in 2012, and who showed unfailing optimism and patience that these manuscripts would one day come to fruition.

On a personal note, I am grateful to my dear mother, Chiam Siew Beng, for her years of love and friendship, and who has been a refreshing fount of strength in support of my academic interests and life choices. To my mother and my fondly remembered late father, Wee Titt Hock, I dedicate these volumes.

John Z. Wee
8 April 2019

Medical Text Labels and Abbreviations

The Diagnostic Handbook Sa-gig is attested today in numerous tablets and fragments that need to be joined together and restored in composite cuneiform text editions. Base text manuscripts consulted by ancient commentators, in fact, not infrequently bear readings that differ from those in Sa-gig manuscripts preserved today. In some cases, these are readings we might not even anticipate in the Diagnostic Handbook were it not for quotations in ancient commentaries. Obviously then, when we refer to an entry in a commentator's base text by means of its equivalent position in modern composite editions of Sa-gig, we do so only as convenient shorthand.

In my two volumes, individual entries of the Diagnostic Handbook are designated primarily by the prefix "Sa-gig," followed by tablet and entry numbers in Heeßel (2000), (2001/2002), and (2010), Scurlock and Andersen (2005), and Scurlock (2014). Since entries edited by Scurlock (on Sa-gig 3–14, 36–37, and 40) are composite ones that do not reflect variations in orthography or vocabulary among different tablet copies, I often include together in parentheses the corresponding entry numbers in Labat's *editio princeps* and tablet drawings (1951), particularly in footnotes and the notes of §11.1 where they would not clutter the main text. Along with lists of source manuscripts in Heeßel (2000: 139–146, etc.) and Scurlock (2014: 705–712), these will be helpful for scholars intending to consult readings from particular manuscripts, or from older and even recent publications that continue to cite pagination in Labat (1951). References to Labat's publication *Traité akkadien de diagnostics et pronostics médicaux* (1951) typically appear as the acronym *TDP*, followed by the page number and the pertinent entry or line number found on that page. In my volumes, I employ the non-italicized prefix "TDPT"—which stands for "*TDP* Tablet"—followed by tablet and entry numbers as supposed by Labat. The list below displays how these labels deviate from those of the "Sa-gig" prefix, most significantly in the way Sa-gig 16, 36, and 37 were earlier mistaken as TDPT 15, 35, and 36 respectively.

Tablet 1 of the Diagnostic Handbook appeared in antiquity in two main versions with different ordering of entries. In accordance with George (1991: 138–139), I employ the label "Sa-gig S1" for the "standard version" from the Neo-Assyrian city of Dūr-Šarrukēn and from the Babylonian cities of Nippur, probably Babylon, and Uruk—including the base text for the Uruk commentary Sa-gig 1D that dates from Late Achaemenid to Early Hellenistic times. The label "Sa-gig U1" is used for the "variant version" from Uruk—including the base texts of Comm. Sa-gig 1B and 1C in the Late Achaemenid period, and likely also the base text of Comm. Sa-gig 1–3 from Neo-Assyrian Ḫuzirīna.

Often, I provide a string of references to medical texts in increasing order of tablet numbers, wherein colons separate tablet numbers from line numbers, commas separate different line numbers, and semicolons separate different tablet or column numbers. In a given string (read left to right), the prefix to any numbered label is the nearest prefix encountered when one traces the string backwards (right to left) from the point of interest. My adoption of a system (prefix "Sa-gig") that coincides in numbering with those by other authors is primarily for the reader's convenience, and does not necessarily indicate assent with these authors' readings and reconstructions of the text.

MSS C, D, F in George (1991: 142–145)	=	Sa-gig S1: 1–51		
		Sa-gig U1: 1–43	=	TDPT 1: 1–43
Heeßel (2001/2002: 28–40)	=	Sa-gig 2: 1–82b	=	TDPT 2: 1–83
		Sa-gig 3: 1–11		
		Sa-gig 3: 12–123	=	TDPT 3: 3–113
		Sa-gig 4: 1–71	=	TDPT 4 obv. 1–71
		Sa-gig 4: 87–142	=	TDPT 4 rev. 1–57
		Sa-gig 5: 1′–17′	=	TDPT 5 B1 1–17
		Sa-gig 5: 37′–48′	=	TDPT 5 E1 3–14
		Sa-gig 5: 51′–60′	=	TDPT 5 C2 2–11
		Sa-gig 5: 61′–67′	=	TDPT 5 D2 1–7
		Sa-gig 5: 67′–79′	=	TDPT 5 E2 1–13
		Sa-gig 5: 81′–98′	=	TDPT 5 F3 1–18
		Sa-gig 5: 102′–126′	=	TDPT 5 G 3–27
		Sa-gig 6: 1–36	=	TDPT 6 obv. 1–36′
		Sa-gig 6: 82″–109″	=	TDPT 6 rev. 19′–47′
		Sa-gig 7 A obv. 1–32	=	TDPT 7: 1–32
		Sa-gig 7 B obv. 1′–17′	=	TDPT 7: 40′–56′
		Sa-gig 7 B rev. 1–17	=	TDPT 7: 57′–73′
		Sa-gig 7 A rev. 1′–17′	=	TDPT 7: 76′–91′
		Sa-gig 8: 1–25	=	TDPT 8: 1–25
		Sa-gig 9: 1–79	=	TDPT 9: 1–79
		Sa-gig 10: 1–54	=	TDPT 10 obv. 1–54
		Sa-gig 10 B rev. 1–18	=	TDPT 10 rev. 1–18
		Sa-gig 11: 1–56	=	TDPT 11 obv. 1–56

		Sa-gig 11 rev. 1–60	=	TDPT 11 rev. 1–60
		Sa-gig 12: 1–26	=	TDPT 12 i 1–17
		Sa-gig 12: 57″–63″	=	TDPT 12 ii 52′–58′
		Sa-gig 12: 64″–108″	=	TDPT 12 iii 1–45
		Sa-gig 12: 109″–134″	=	TDPT 12 iv 1–27
		Sa-gig 13: 4–58	=	TDPT 13 i 5′–59′
		Sa-gig 13: 59–111	=	TDPT 13 ii 1–53
		Sa-gig 13: 112–159	=	TDPT 13 iii 2–47
		Sa-gig 13: 162–181	=	TDPT 13 iv 11′–30′
		Sa-gig 14: 1–31	=	TDPT 14 i 1–31
BAM VII/49 i 1′–22′	=	Sa-gig 14: 32–69	=	TDPT 14 i 32–69
BAM VII/49 i 23′–27a′	=	Sa-gig 14: 70–78		
BAM VII/49 i 27b′–ii 36′	=	Sa-gig 14: 79–145	=	TDPT 14 ii 7–73
		Sa-gig 14: 146–167	=	TDPT 14 iii 1–22
		Sa-gig 14: 168′–173′	=	TDPT 14 iii 35′–40′
BAM VII/49 iii 2′–18′	=	Sa-gig 14: 174′–197′	=	TDPT 14 iii 41′–64′
BAM VII/49 iii 19′–26′	=	Sa-gig 14: 198′–206′		
BAM VII/49 iii 27′–37′	=	Sa-gig 14: 207′–220′	=	TDPT 14 iv 1′–14′
		Sa-gig 14: 221′–227′	=	TDPT 14 iv 15′–21′
BAM VII/49 iv 2′–12′	=	Sa-gig 14: 228′–247′	=	TDPT 14 iv 22′–46′
		Sa-gig 14: 248′–254′	=	TDPT 14 iv 47′–53′
BAM VII/49 iv 18′–24′	=	Sa-gig 14: 255′–266′	=	TDPT 14 iv 54′–65′
Heeßel (2000: 150–275)	=	Sa-gig 15–23		
Heeßel (2000: 278–340)	=	Sa-gig 26–30		
Heeßel (2000: 342–374)	=	Sa-gig 31 and 33		
		Sa-gig 36: 1–115	=	TDPT 35: 1–115
		Sa-gig 37: 1–21	=	TDPT 36: 1–21
		Sa-gig 40: 1–122	=	TDPT 40: 1–122
		Sa-gig 40: 123		

For the majority of Sa-gig commentary tablets edited in §II.1 and quoted in Excerpts throughout the two volumes, I reset the numbering of lines at the top of obverse (labeled “obv.”) and reverse (labeled “rev.”) sides of the tablet. Where the top is damaged, numbering begins from the first (partially) preserved line, and line numbers are accompanied by the prime symbol (′). For some tablets, however, their popularly cited *editiones principes* or hand copies are based on line numbers that run continuously from obverse to reverse sides. In such cases, I retain the customary numbers to avoid confusion, indicating lines on the obverse with the label “obv.,” but those on the reverse with the label "line(s)" instead of "rev." Lines of text preserved in the commentaries below are labeled as follows:

Comm. Sa-gig 1A	"obv. 1–27" on the obverse, and "lines 28–52" on the reverse
Comm. Sa-gig 1–3	"obv. 1–32" on the obverse, and "lines 33–55" on the reverse
Comm. Sa-gig 5	"obv. 1–21" on the obverse, and "lines 22–41" on the reverse
Comm. Sa-gig 10 & 11	"obv. 1–11" on the obverse, "rev. 1′–10′" on the reverse, and "rev. 11′" on the top edge
Comm. Sa-gig 13+	"obv. 1–9" on the obverse, "lines 10–12" on the bottom edge, and "lines 13–17" on the reverse
Comm. Sa-gig 19	"obv. 1–22" on the obverse, and "lines 23–37" on the reverse

Below are diagnostic tablets that may have served as precursors to the Diagnostic Handbook, or that exhibit different diagnostic traditions:

2 NB 336	Spurious label for 2N-T 336 (= IM 57947), corrected by unpublished catalog information from Richard Zettler in Rutz (2011: 295 n. 7).
2N-T 336	Incorrectly labeled as "2 NB 336" and edited by Labat (1956: 119–130).
BM 47687+48517	"Poor Man's *TDP*" in Finkel (1988: 153, 158–159, Fig. II).
CBS 3424(A)	Heeßel (2000: 99–100).
CBS 3831	Rutz (2011: 305–307).
CBS 12580	Rutz (2011: 301–305).
KBo VII	Otten (1954).
KBo VII, 13	Fincke (2011b: 475–476).
KBo XIV	Güterbock (1963).
KBo XXXVI	Wilhelm (1991).
KUB XXXVII	Köcher (1953).
LB 2126	TLB II/21 (= van Dijk 1957); edited by Geller (2001–2002: 73–74).
MS 2670	No. 15 in George (2013: 85–89)
Msk 74122a	No. 694 in Emar VI/1 (= Arnaud 1985: 301); Emar VI/4 (= Arnaud 1987: 315–316).

Msk 74127a	No. 695 in Emar VI/1 (= Arnaud 1985: 321); Emar VI/4 (= Arnaud 1987: 317).
Ni. 470	Kraus (1987: 194–206).
StBoT XXXVI	Wilhelm (1994).
STT 89	Gurney and Finkelstein (1957: vol. 1, no. 89); edited by Abusch (1987: 63, lines 38–42); Stol (1993: 91–98, lines 103–214).
VAT 10235	Heeßel (2010: 171–177, 179); earlier published as KAR 211.
VAT 10748	Heeßel (2010: 178–181); partial duplicate of VAT 10235.
VAT 10886	Heeßel (2010: 184–186).
VAT 11122	Heeßel (2010: 181–184).
VAT 12385	Heeßel (2010: 186–187).

Therapeutic texts are attested from too great a variety of sources to be all enumerated here, but a majority are readily accessible as cuneiform copies in Campbell Thompson's *Assyrian Medical Texts from the Originals in the British Museum* (*AMT*) and the publication series Die babylonisch-assyrische Medizin in Texten und Untersuchungen (*BAM*). For ease of consultation, I prefer to use *AMT* and *BAM* prefixes for these tablets, instead of their museum sigla and numbers.

AMT	Campbell Thompson (1923).
BAM	Hand copies of tablet manuscripts are numbered consecutively across Volumes I–VI of Köcher (1963–1980), and so only the manuscript number and not the volume number is cited here.
BAM VII	Geller (2005). Note the exception of *BAM* VII/49, whose contents belong to the Diagnostic Handbook rather than to the therapeutic genre.
BAM X	Geller and Panayotov (2019).
BAM XI	Johnson (2020).

Bibliographical, archaeological, and museum abbreviations mostly follow those listed in Volume 20 (U and W) of the *Chicago Assyrian Dictionary* (*CAD*) vii–xxxii. Below are some of the more common abbreviations in this volume or ones that differ from *CAD* abbreviations.

5*R*	*The Cuneiform Inscriptions of Western Asia, Vol. V* by Rawlinson (1884)
Aa	Lexical series á A = *nâqu* in *MSL* XIV
AHw	*Akkadisches Handwörterbuch* by von Soden (1959–1981)
AO	Tablets in the collections of the Musée du Louvre
BM	Tablets in the collections of the British Museum
CAD	*The Assyrian Dictionary of the Oriental Institute of the University of Chicago*. Chicago: The Oriental Institute of the University of Chicago, 1956–2011
CBT	*Catalogue of the Babylonian Tablets in the British Museum*
CCP	Cuneiform Commentaries Project (2013–2018): http://ccp.yale.edu/
CDA	*A Concise Dictionary of Akkadian* by Black, George, and Postgate (2000, 2nd corrected printing)
CDLI	Cuneiform Digital Library Initiative: http://cdli.ucla.edu/
CT	*Cuneiform Texts from Babylonian Tablets in the British Museum*. London
DT	Tablets in the collections of the British Museum
EAE	Astronomical omen series *Enūma Anu Enlil*
GAG	*Grundriss der Akkadischen Grammatik* by von Soden (1995, 3rd ed.)
GCCI	*Goucher College Cuneiform Inscriptions*, by Dougherty (1923–1933)
GKAB	Geography of Knowledge in Assyria and Babylonia Project (2007–2012): http://oracc.org/cams/gkab/
HALOT	*The Hebrew and Aramaic Lexicon of the Old Testament* by Koehler, Baumgartner, Stamm, et al. (1994–2000)
Hg.	Lexical commentary Ḫ̮AR-gud or, more precisely, Mur-gud
Hh.	Lexical series Ḫ̮AR-ra = *ḫ̮ubullu* or, more precisely, Ur_5-ra = *ḫ̮ubullu*
HKL	*Handbuch der Keilschriftliteratur* (1967–1975)
LKU	*Literarische Keilschrifttexte aus Uruk* by Falkenstein (1931)
LTBA	*Die lexikalischen Tafelserien der Babylonier und Assyrer in den Berliner Museen* by Matous (1933) and von Soden (1933)
MSL	Materialien zum sumerischen Lexikon
MZL	*Mesopotamisches Zeichenlexikon* (2nd revised ed., 2010)
PNAE	*Prosopography of the Neo-Assyrian Empire*
PSD	*Pennsylvania Sumerian Dictionary*. Pennsylvania: University of Pennsylvania, 1984–

RLA	Reallexikon der Assyriologie und Vorderasiatischen Archäologie
RMC	Rare Manuscript Collections at Cornell University Museum, USA
SpTU	*Spätbabylonische Texte aus Uruk*
STT	*The Sultantepe Tablets*, by Gurney, Finkelstein, and Hulin (1957/1964)

Other abbreviations adopted in this volume include:

coll.	collated
Comm. Sa-gig x	Commentary or Commentaries on the Diagnostic Handbook Tablet(s) x
ed.	edited (by), editor(s), or edition
fig(s).	figure(s)
incl.	includes
MA	Middle Assyrian
MS(S)	manuscript(s)
NA	Neo-Assyrian
OB	Old Babylonian
obv.	obverse
p(p).	page(s)
pl(s).	plate(s)
rev.	reverse
s.v.	sub verbo ("under the word," i.e., under the dictionary entry)
var.	variant
§	siglum to chapters/parts and sub-divisions of these two volumes: CM 49/1 (= §I) and CM 49/2 (= §II) of the Cuneiform Monographs (CM) series

Format and Translation Issues

Format of Volumes §1 and §11.2

Headings of excerpts allow only concise references to specific Sa-gig commentary entries, and I indicate with each such heading the relevant section of my *Edition of the Sa-gig Commentaries* (§11.1), under which the reader may find the commentary text in full, along with tablet and bibliographical information. A convenient list of each commentary tablet's field and/or museum number, as well as abbreviations of commonly cited *editiones principes*, is included as part of the *Contents* page for §11.1. For readers without immediate access to my second volume (§11), a sense of how individual commentary entries appear as part of larger blocks of text may be obtained by referring to Excerpts 340–344. Cuneiform transliterations and English translations in excerpts appear in continuous linear text—except in cases where I discuss *Commentary Tablet Formats* (§1.1.4.1), where effort is made to reflect in typesetting the ancient text's appearance in columns and indented lines on the physical tablet. To save space, entries from lexical lists and serialized compilations may be presented as continuous text such as "(47) nam-dub-sar = scribal art, (48) eme-gir_{15} = Sumerian, (49) ka-ka-si-ga = syllable sign" (Excerpt 120), with the number of each line specified in parentheses for easy reference. Line divisions occurring naturally at the tablet's edge are marked by using a single slant line (/) in transliterations, but are unmarked in translations. Horizontal lines intentionally etched across the tablet by the ancient scribe are either replicated in print, or labeled in transliterations and translations as {*line divider*}. Text restored to damaged portions of the manuscript are represented within [square brackets], which however never interrupt the spelling of a translated English word.

Format of Edition of the Sa-gig Commentaries (§11.1)

In order to foreground commentators' motivations and knowledge assumptions, I adopt a two-column format, where brief remarks are interpolated with translations. In the left column, each new commentary entry is introduced by a reference in bold print to the base text commented on, such as **Sa-gig 3: 15**, **Sa-gig U1: 39b (S1: 4)**, ***Sa-gig 40: 5**, or ***Sa-gig 7**. The 'base text' refers to the *manuscript* methodically studied by the commentator (§1.1.4.2), and base text readings quoted in commentaries can differ from other manuscript copies that are preserved and available to us today. It bears repeating that these references in bold indicate textual positions in modern composite editions of Sa-gig, which may not always accurately reflect forms in the commentator's manuscript, but which nonetheless serve as convenient shorthand. I make clear note of cases where there are detectable discrepancies of orthography or content between base text manuscripts and our modern editions.

The use of an asterisk (*) in references like ***Sa-gig 40: 5** and ***Sa-gig 7** indicates that the topic of the commentary entry does not correspond exactly to forms in available Sa-gig manuscripts, though enough of the context is preserved for us to be certain of the Sa-gig Tablet or even line number that is commented on. The asterisk is occasioned in cases where damage to the Sa-gig or commentary tablet makes their connection less sure, where the commentator seems to have relied on a base text manuscript that differs from those available to us today, or where the commentator intentionally deviated from base text forms in order to express a *Single Member Argument* (§1.2.3.3). For the sake of clarity, a short portion of the version preserved in manuscripts today is sometimes quoted along with its reference—e.g., ***Sa-gig 40: 111—"his IGI.2 are suffused(?),"** which corresponds to what is written in the commentary tablet as "His IGI.MEŠ are suffused(?)."[i]

The remainder of the left column consists of short explanations of the commentator's argument and/or possible motivations in his choice of commentary topics. The two-column format articulates my view that such information, external to the commentary tablet itself, is indispensable for a proper understanding of the commentator's craft. To give an example, Comm. Sa-gig 4A contains what appears at first glance to be a rather superfluous entry involving unremarkable terms: "'It shakes.' To shake *means* to tremble."[ii] The Akkadian topic "it shakes," however, occurs rarely and only as a description of the patient's temple. On the other hand, the comment "to tremble" is a more general Akkadian synonym applicable to many other parts of the human body, and which was in fact a favorite explanation recurring in several commentaries. Seen in this light, the commentary entry represents a reasonable effort to clarify a less common medical description and to explain it in a way congruent with other known body behaviors. While the use of descriptors such as 'rare,' 'unusual,' and 'less common' admittedly reflects my own subjective impressions

i Comm. Sa-gig 40B, rev. 5′ (§11.1.30).

ii Comm. Sa-gig 4A, obv. 9 (§11.1.9). See also [*ra-ʾ-bu*] : *sa-la-*⌊*ḫu*⌋, "[To shiver] *means* to tremble" in Comm. Sa-gig 3B, rev. 3 (§11.1.7).

of the frequency of lexical or grammatical items in the medical literature,[iii] I endeavor to validate such impressions by providing substantial lists of medical text references on the said item(s) in my Notes. Future discoveries and publications of additional medical texts may fine-tune our understanding of the nuances of particular arguments, but my hope is that the larger picture of commentators' motivations and audience assumptions will remain credible.

Moving on to another example in Comm. Sa-gig 5, for instance, we seem to detect nothing more than a straightforward lexical equation: "'ŠID' *means* limbs."[iv] The full significance of this entry, again, cannot be appreciated until we realize that the term "limbs" is almost always represented in the Diagnostic Handbook as the logogram UB.NIGIN, and only in the base text here (Sa-gig 5: 89′) as the logogram ŠID. In other words, the commentator was affirming that the word in the base text should in fact be understood as ŠID—meaning "limbs"—even though its deviation from conventions in medical writing appeared to cast doubt on this interpretation. Furthermore, it is significant that the explanatory comment "limbs" is not expressed logographically as UB.NIGIN—as is typical of the Diagnostic Handbook—but syllabically as *minâtu* as is typical of therapeutic texts. Choices of topics and comments can tell us much about knowledge assumptions shared by the commentator and his audience, revealing technical vocabularies, orthographies, and concepts current among particular groups of medical practitioners and professionals. The rhetorical pattern here is one repeatedly noted in the left column: Commentators on Sa-gig often chose topics that differed from basic medical language of the kind used in therapeutic texts—even if these topics were common in Sa-gig itself—and chose comments that were typical of descriptions of the sick body in therapeutic texts. This is a phenomenon whose implications I discuss extensively in §1.3.

The right column contains my English translation of the Sa-gig commentary, with each statement beginning with its line number(s) in the commentary tablet written in parentheses. Double inverted commas (i.e., quotation marks) are reserved for words or expressions actually cited in ancient times from a base text or from another source, but no quotation marks are used for individual components (e.g., KI and ud, or A and gur) or dictionary forms (e.g., *talālu*) that result from analyzing cited logograms (e.g., "KI.UD.BI") or syllabic spellings (e.g., "*agurru*" or "*uttatallil*"). I also omit quotation marks in the few instances

iii To avoid sounding repetitive, my Notes and remarks are not always explicit that such descriptors refer to frequencies only within 'medical texts' or the 'medical literature,' but this should be understood as the context of my two volumes.

iv [Š]ID : *mi-na-a-tú* (Comm. Sa-gig 5, line 28 in §11.1.12).

of 'single member arguments' (§1.2.3.3) where, in the position we expect to find a cited topic, we find instead a different written form of the commentator's own choosing. Where modern references in the Notes to these English translations already employ double inverted commas, the portions quoted in antiquity appear within single inverted commas instead—e.g., "'It is puckered' *means* it is broken up."

Translation Issues in Volumes §I and §II

The thoughtful reader may be concerned that I do not render base text topics in a consistent way, sometimes translating them into English, sometimes leaving them as logograms (e.g., SAG.GIŠ.RA), sometimes expressing their normalized Akkadian forms (e.g., *ittenenbiṭū*), and sometimes even separating out their component signs (e.g., *rík-su*, ma-rak(/šal), *i-ta-na-áš-šá-a*). While such translation decisions can be subjective and may at times reflect uncertainties in reading, my overriding principle is to prioritize the clarity of the commentator's larger argument over that of individual lexical items.

In cases where the commentator appears to be giving lexical definition to a less familiar logogram or syllabic form, this less familiar term is not translated into English: for example, "'SAG.GIŠ.RA' (*means*) to smite" and "'*ittenenbiṭū*' *derives from the dictionary root* to have cramps."[v] For the latter example, a translation such as "'(his innards) keep having cramps' *derives from the dictionary root* to have cramps" would inaccurately appear as a tautology: If one were already certain that *ittenenbiṭū* means "keep having cramps," there would be altogether no need for the commentator to identify its verbal derivation—i.e., "*derives from the dictionary root* to have cramps." Other written forms were of interest, because they could be suspected of multiple meanings or were likely to be misread, and I have tried to reflect the ambiguity experienced by ancient audiences. For example, in my translation "'[His belly] *i-ta-na-áš-šá-a* [to] vomit' *means* his belly rises to vomit," my depiction of the individual syllables *i-ta-na-áš-šá-a* (from the verb *našû*, "to rise") illustrates their possible confusion with orthographies like *i-ta-na-áš* (Sa-gig 22: 25, 28; from the verb *âšu*, "to retch") that appear in similar contexts of vomiting, and which therefore would have prompted the commentator to clarify the form.[vi]

v Comm. Sa-gig 39, obv. 2–3 (§II.1.28) and Comm. Sa-gig 4B, obv. 9 (§II.1.10) respectively.

vi Comm. Sa-gig 7B, rev. 2′–3′ (§II.1.14). Again, a translation such as "'[His belly] keeps rising/heaving [to] vomit' *means* his belly rises to vomit" obscures the commentator's motivation for choosing to comment.

I am well aware that such translation methods may create difficulties for readers who are unfamiliar with cuneiform signs or Akkadian words. In my *Edition of the Sa-gig Commentaries* (§11.1), even when terms are left untranslated in the *right* column to better reflect the logic of an argument, I supply English translations of these terms as remarks in the *left* column. On the other hand, there are times when topic and comment both need to be translated into English, in cases where audiences were expected to have known the meanings of the individual words involved, but had to be instructed in their nuances for specific situations. An example would be the entry "'His ka is pressed down, he will die.' To press down *means* to become palsied. To press down *means* to twitch."[vii] It is unlikely that the commentator's audience was ignorant of the meaning of the common verb "to press down" (*ṣapāru*). Rather, the commentator was concerned to express the range of meanings possible for the ambiguous body part "ka"—i.e., whereas "palsy" was the likely reason for medical descriptions of pressed down "mouth" (logogram KA) and lips, "twitching" indicated similar behavior by the "nose" (cuneiform sign ka as logogram KIR_4).

By not translating logograms into English, I follow the usual practice by other scholars, which recognizes that commentators tend to treat logograms as written symbols requiring syllabic—and verbal—explication. This, however, does not necessarily imply a precise one-to-one relation between a logogram topic and its syllabic comment. As a matter of fact, lexical lists frequently pair the same logogram with several different Akkadian syllabic forms, or the same Akkadian syllabic term with different logograms.[viii] At times, the particle *ša* ("in the case of / where") appears explicitly to introduce the prescribed context within which a particular "logogram–syllabic term" pair is valid (§11.2.2). Our commentaries, moreover, employ B:A′:B:C and B:C:B:A′ arguments (§1.2.3.2.4–5) that propose a connection between a cognate of the base text topic (A′) and another syllabically written term (C), on the basis that both may be expressed by the same logogram in position B.

One way of distinguishing a logogram from its Akkadian syllabic form might be to express the logogram in terms of its etymology, such as "GIŠ. dUTU (Sum.: 'tree of Šamaš') : plane tree."[ix] Such translation strategies, however, raise the question whether the commentator was proposing alternative names or identifications for the same object, or whether he was clarifying a single name or identity label. To complicate matters, it is not always clear if etymology figured consciously in the popular usage of a term or in the commentator's argument,

---

vii Comm. Sa-gig 39, obv. 12 (§11.1.28).

viii See Excerpts 392–393 in §11.2.2.

ix GIŠ dUTU : *dul-bi* (*CTMMA* II, 69 = MMA 86.11.109, obv. 2) in Finkel (2005: 280–281).

or whether some logograms were simply treated as frozen symbols of Akkadian expressions. In this edition, I have generally refrained from etymological translations of logograms, except in cases where the analysis of logographic forms (§1.2.3.2.6) is clearly a part of the argument.

Transliterations of vocabulary and grammar in the Sumerian language are expressed with expanded character spacing (e.g., šag$_4$ íb-ba-dab$_5$-e-ne ĝe). Cuneiform signs functioning as Akkadian syllables are transliterated in italicized lowercase letters (e.g., *a-ga-nu-til-la-a*), while those functioning as logograms (word signs) of Akkadian words appear in non-italicized uppercase letters (e.g., SIG$_4$.AL.ÙR.RA, A.GA, and TI.LA), according to conventions in John Huehnergard's *A Grammar of Akkadian* (2011). While it is true that logographic values depicting Akkadian words and particles are historically indebted to Sumerian vocabulary and grammar, a clear distinction between Sumerian and Akkadian meanings becomes important in commentarial argumentation. For example, whereas one commentator interpreted the writing al-du as a fossilized form AL.DU essentially identical to the common Akkadian logogram DU "to move" (Comm. Sa-gig 4A), other commentators gave weight to the stative sense of the Sumerian prefix al- and therefore shunned this straightforward explanation that involved movement (Comm. Sa-gig 4B and 4C).[x] Furthermore, commentarial arguments sometimes require discussion about a cuneiform sign without affirming its role either as a logogram or as a syllable sign. I have chosen to depict such cases in unitalicized lowercase (e.g., gur$_4$, aš-*tenû*, and si-*gunû*) or to use circumlocutions such as "the cuneiform sign for ŠIKA" and "the logogram for 'pig' (ŠÁḪ) is the same cuneiform sign as the logogram for 'youth' (ŠUL)." Terms cited from lexical texts that are not in syllabic Akkadian are also mostly rendered in unitalicized lowercase. While many of such readings have values reminiscent of logograms of Akkadian words, ancient commentators seem at times to be cognizant of distinctions between the two, preserving lexical forms such as ki-šá-ra, which, as they would have been aware, differed from familiar logograms such as KI.ŠÁR.(RA)—meaning "all" (*kiššatu*).[xi]

Two slant lines (/ ... /) are used to enclose rough approximations of how terms were pronounced. The pronunciation */makutu/*, for instance, could refer either to the noun *makūtu* ("pole") or to the verbal adjective *makûtu*

x Comm. Sa-gig 4A, obv. 2–3 (§11.1.9). The signs al-du were interpreted syllabically as *al-ṭù* (from the root *wašāṭu*, "to become stiff") in Comm. Sa-gig 4B, obv. 9–10 (§11.1.10) and Comm. Sa-gig 4C, obv. 4′ (§11.1.11).

xi The writing ki-šá-ra comes from a version of Erimhuš v, 46. See Note on Comm. Sa-gig 36, rev. 10′ (§11.1.27).

("lacking").[xii] Such pronunciations do not always appear with cuneiform orthography that accurately reflects the vowel lengths or verbal accentuation of the words pronounced. Thus, *ḫa-bu-ú* refers to the pronunciation */ḫabu/* that can express not only the verb *ḫabû* ("to draw up water"), but also the verb *ḫâbu* ("to consecrate").[xiii] In other words, the writing *ḫa-bu-ú* with its long final vowel does not technically depict the verb *ḫabû* ("to draw up water"), but represents the abstract pronunciation */ḫabu/* + an additional nominal ending *-u*, in much the same way that Akkadian sign names such as *ubû* (the sign aš or aš-*tenû*) and *anšû* (the sign for ANŠE) also appear with a long final vowel.[xiv] While modern linguistic convention presents phonemic transcriptions within slant lines and phonetic transcriptions within square brackets, my general use of slant lines for the approximate pronunciations of terms does not express a firm or consistent decision whether the values enclosed are always phonemic or phonetic. In any case, it would be inappropriate to use square brackets here for phonetic transcriptions, since it is the Assyriological convention that square brackets enclose readings restored in damaged texts.

Ancient commentators and modern scholars sometimes make arguments based on the visual appearance of cuneiform graphs (i.e., written symbols). Such arguments are roughly illustrated in my Notes using the Unicode Cuneiform font (TTF) "Assurbanipal" for Neo-Assyrian signs, which was designed by Sylvie Vanséveren and generously made available freely to the scholarly community. I do not mean to imply that cuneiform graphs printed in my volumes precisely replicate sign-forms on Sa-gig commentary tablets, which reflect idiosyncrasies in hand-writing by different scribes, and which are mostly written in Neo-/Late Babylonian script that can differ slightly from the Neo-Assyrian signs.

Depictions of commentarial arguments such as A:B(:A):C, A:B:C, and B:A′:B:C, among other patterns, reflect my own system of shifting sigla that I discuss more extensively and illustrate in § 1.2.3.2. Whereas specific positions in an argument can be represented by varying sigla—depending on how much of the argument is recorded or preserved in ancient texts, or excerpted for purposes of modern discussion—these sigla shift in such a way as to maintain

xii Comm. Sa-gig 21 & 22a, obv. 2 (§ 11.1.23).

xiii Comm. Sa-gig 1B, obv. 21′ (§ 11.1.2).

xiv For the sign names *ubû* and *anšû*, see Comm. Sa-gig 1B, rev. 25 (§ 11.1.2) and Comm. Sa-gig 7A, rev. 13 (§ 11.1.13) respectively. Sign names are often Akkadianized by adding the endings *-u* or *-a*. Gong (2000: 42–51); cf. Gong (2003: 2–19). In other instances, sign names may be represented without these endings, again analogous to the way pronunciations like */makutu/* may be written simply as *ma-ku-tu*$_4$ (Comm. Sa-gig 21 & 22a, obv. 2 in § 11.1.23) without an additional *-u* ending.

the same logical relationships among the positions. The siglum A is reserved exclusively for the base text topic, while comments are depicted alphabetically as B, C, D, E, and so on, in the order they appear within the argument being considered. Cognates such as A′ and B′ with the prime symbol (′) most frequently represent the dictionary forms of their antecedents (in this case, A and B), and can also denote variations on their antecedents' inflection, orthography, or sign value. By designating, say, A′ as a 'cognate' instead of just another comment, its relationship to its antecedent (A) is emphasized for purposes of further argumentation.

PART ONE

Edition of the Sa-gig Commentaries

This volume explores professional uses of medical language in ancient Mesopotamia, through an examination of commentators' motivations in their choices and omissions of language, in commentaries on the Diagnostic Handbook (Sa-gig).[1] The thirty commentary tablets and fragments edited in this volume represent an accumulation of sources, preliminarily listed by Eckart Frahm in his catalog on *Babylonian and Assyrian Text Commentaries* (2011), in addition to those identified and brought to my attention in 2013 by Christopher Walker, Curator at the British Museum, and yet others later discovered by staff and other contributors at Yale's digital Cuneiform Commentaries Project (CCP).[2] For the most part, I retain or build upon the labels assigned by Frahm, who designated Sa-gig commentaries according to the tablet number of their Sa-gig base text, in contrast to commentaries on therapeutic tablets that are grouped together based on their archaeological provenance.[3] At only two points do I deviate from Frahm's labels—the commentaries designated as "Sa-gig 13 and 12/14(?)" and "Sa-gig 21 and 21a" by Frahm occur here as "Comm. Sa-gig 13+" (§11.1.19) and "Comm. Sa-gig 21 & 22a" (§11.1.23) respectively.

Absent from my edition are two texts, which have been proposed as Sa-gig commentaries, but which Frahm considered instead to be Uruk Therapeutic Comm. 8 (*SpTU* 1, 55) and Comm. 10 (Scheil 1916: 137–138).[4] While certain expressions in these two commentaries appear promising, the fragmentary nature of commentary or base text prevents us from identifying them

1 The volume extends my proposals in §1.3.2 on medical lexicography, by providing detailed supporting evidence from the Sa-gig commentaries, and represents more than an anthology of texts.

2 Digital Resources are indicated by their permanent CDLI, GKAB, and CCP numbers and are often based on previously published work by scholars in Printed Editions/Hand Copies—both kinds of secondary sources are listed at the beginning of my edition of each commentary text. In addition, at relevant points in the Notes, particular interpretations and collations original to digital contributors are credited, according to the record online when last accessed on 1 July 2017. To avoid cumbersome repetition in the Notes, I do not generally highlight individual points of interpretation original to my edition of the Sa-gig commentaries in a 2012 dissertation and later adopted by others, since the present volume represents an updated revision based on my dissertation.

3 Frahm (2011a: 220–229, §7.4.1.1). In particular, I follow Frahm's 2011 print publication in labeling the tablet BM 43854+43938 as "Comm. Sa-gig 3B," though its label seems to have been later confused in the digital project as "CCP 4.1.3.C," while another tablet (BM 55491) appearing in my volumes as "Comm. Sa-gig 3C" corresponds to "CCP 4.1.3.B."

4 Frahm (2011a: 234). These tablets are identified online as commentaries on "Therapeutic (eyes, neck, tendons)? Or Sa-gig (3)?" (CCP 4.2.K) and "Sa-gig 13 (?)" (CCP 4.1.13.A) respectively.

unambiguously with the Diagnostic Handbook.[5] Although the laconic reference to "questionings (*maš'altu*) of Sa-gig" in a small Assur catalog (*BAM* 310) may point to the rare attestation of a Sa-gig commentary from the north, the identity of such a work is uncertain.[6] Finally, though the cuneiform fragment K 19769 was earlier suspected to be a "commentary to SA.GIG(?)," it has since been joined with K 22038 and considered as possibly part of Sa-gig itself.[7]

---

5 Note, for example, SA.MEŠ + *i-nu-uš-šu* (*SpTU* I, 55: 13′) in Sa-gig 3: 94 (TDPT 3: 85); the form ^{na_4}KIŠIB (*SpTU* I, 55: 11′) in the Diagnostic Handbook Sa-gig 4: 20; 10: 22–25; 21: 16′; *rabbiš* (Scheil (1916) 138 rev. 13, 15) in Sa-gig 13: 138 (TDPT 13 iii 27; noted in *CAD* R, 15).

6 *maš-al-a-te šá* SA.GIG (*BAM* 310 obv. 3–4).

7 Fincke (2003/2004: 143); Fincke, Database of Babylonian Nineveh Texts, last accessed on 1 July 2017.

Commentary Sa-gig 1A

Provenance:	Nippur
Period:	Achaemenid (Enlil-bēlšunu appears in documents dated 424–410 BCE)
Names:	"*Imgida*-tablet of Enlil-bēlšunu ... [son] of Ninurta-nāṣir ... descendant of Absummu the Sumerian"
Script:	Neo-/Late Babylonian
Typology:	*ṣâtu* 7c in Frahm (2011a: 54–55)
Field/Museum No.:	AO 17661 (Musée du Louvre, France)
Photos:	Plate 1 (obverse) and Plate 2 (reverse)
Printed Hand Copy:	*TBER*, 56–57; Durand (1979: 156–157)
Printed Edition:	Durand (1979: 153–170); George (1991: 137–163, MS a); Wee (2012: 500–514)
Digital Resources:	CDLI P461308; CCP 4.1.1.A.b (printed hand copies digitized by Frahm, Frazer, and Jiménez 2013; photos by Wagensonner)
Discussion:	Labat (1954: 40); Leichty (1973: 83); Durand (1979: 153–170); Cavigneaux (1982: 231–240); Oelsner (1982: 94–95); George (1991: 137–163, MS a) and (2013: 62); Joannès (1992: 89 n. 20); Finkel (*NABU* 1993/15), (2014a: 311–312), and (2014b: 321–323); Geller (1995: 53) and (2010a: 141–144); Heeßel (2000: 95–96 n. 103; 132, 139 (1. Tafel MS a)); Frahm (2002: 85 n. 47, 92 n. 88), (2010c: 171), and (2011a: 54 n. 242, 92, 95–96, 221–223, 291 n. 1384, 294, 299 n. 1428, 303–304); Böck (2009b: 391 n. 36); Genty (2010a: 365–366) and (2010b: 9 n. 52, 16 n. 65, 26); Wee (2012: 500–514), (2016b: 149–150), and (2017: 241, 256); Gabbay (2015: 356 n. 42) and (2016: 342–343, see references to George 1991 MS a); Schmidtchen (2018: 327 n. 40)
Pericope:	At least Sa-gig S1: 1–49

Transliteration

Obverse

1) [DIŠ] ⸢*e*⸣-[*nu-ma* K]A.PIRIG *ana* É ^{lu_2}GIG DU-*ku* : KA.PIRIG : *a-ši-*[*pu*]

2) [PIRI]G : *nam-ri* : pirig-gal : pirig-gal-e-ne : pirig-gal-abzu : *nu-ú*[*r* GAL-*ú*]

3) [*nu-ú*]*r-šú-nu* ⟨GAL-*ú*⟩ : *nu-úr* GAL-*ú šá ap-si-i* : DIŠ *ina* SILA ŠIKA *zaq-pa* IGI GIG [BI]

4) *na-qud* NU TE-*šú* : $^{\text{še-ek}}$ ⟨šika⟩-al-ús-sa *iš-ḫi-il-ṣu* : *ḫaṣ-bat-*⸢*tu*$_4$⸣ : al-ús-sa *d*[*i-i-šú*]

5) *l*[*ìb-b*]*u-u it-te-eḫ-pi kar-pi ḫa-aṣ-bu-um-ma* ⸢*im-tu-ut*⸣ [LÚ ...]

6) $^{\text{še-ek}}$ŠIKA : *ḫaṣ-bi* : *la-lu-ú* : *ma-ri* : DIŠ KI.UD.BI IGI N[AM.ERIM$_2$ DAB-*s*]*u*

7) *lu-u* ⸢*šá*⸣ *ana* SISKUR *mi-ḫir lu-u šá ana* ^{d}U.GUR *lu-u šá ana ḫi-s*[*u-ú-ti* GAR-*nu* (?)]

8) *lìb-bu-ú ina* KI.UD.BI-*šú* NIDBA.MEŠ DINGIR.MEŠ GAL.MEŠ *uq-*[*tar-ra-bu* (?)]

9) *šá* KI ^{d}U.GUR *kaš-kaš* DINGIR *na-ram* ^{d}*Nin-men-na šá ina* NAM.E[RIM$_2$.BÚR.RU.D]A

10) E-*ú* : KI.UD.BI : KI : *áš-ri* : ud : *el-lu šá-niš* KI.UD.BI : u[d : *eb-b*]*u*

11) DIŠ SIG$_4$.AL.ÙR.RA IGI : *šá ina ḫur-šá-an i-tu-ru* : A : *me-e* : GUR : *ta-a-ri šá-ni*[*š* MUNUS.PEŠ$_4$]

12) A : *ma-ri* : gur$_4$(KÌR) : *ka-ra-ṣi* : *šá-niš* A : *ma-ri* : *gur* : *na-*[*šu-ú*]

13) *šal-šiš ḫa-ban-na-nu* : A : *me-e* : gur : *m*[*a-l*]*u-ú* : DIŠ ŠÁḪ G[E$_6$ IGI]

14) *šá ana dum-qí u lum-nu* E-*ú* : $^{\text{su-ul}}$ šáḫ : *le-e-bu* : BA.ÚŠ *šá-niš* [PAP.ḪAL.MEŠ-*m*]*a* TIN-*uṭ*

15) *ki-i* GIG *dan-na-at i-mu-ru* TIN-*uṭ ki-i dan-na-at la* [IGI] ÚŠ [*lìb-b*]*u-u*

16) DIŠ ŠÁḪ *ana ùr-ši* É LÚ KU$_4$ *a-sìr-tu*$_4$ *ana* É LÚ KU$_4$: *a-*⸢*sìr*⸣*-t*[*u*$_4$: *e-se-r*]*u*

17) NAM.ERIM$_2$ *ma-la ina*(!) SA.GIG : DIŠ *ba-ri-*BA.ÚŠ IGI x[... *a-ga-nu-til-la-*]*a* :(!)

18) *ár-kát la ba-la-ṭu* : *šá-niš a-ga-nu-til-la-a* : ⸤SA$_5$⸥ *me-e* : x[... *m*]*e-e*

19) DIŠ GU$_4$ ⸢SA$_5$⸣ IGI GIG BI ^{d}DÌM.ME DAB-*su* : *ma-ar-tu*$_4$ *šá* [^{d}*A-nim* x]x

20) *šá* DINGIR.⸢MEŠ GAL.MEŠ E⸣-*ú* : DIŠ GU$_4$ SI-*šú* ŠUB-*ma* IGI : *šá-*[*niš* DIŠ GU$_4$ *ru-pu-uš-t*]*u*$_4$(!)

21) *is-su-ku* : *šá-*⸢*niš* DIŠ *ru*⸣*-pu-*⸢*uš-tu*$_4$⸣ ŠUB-*ma i-m*[*u-ur* : SI : *qar-nu*]

22) SI : *ru-pu-uš-tu*$_4$: ⸢ŠUB : SI *na-di-i*(?)⸣ [*lìb-bu-ú ki-i* GU$_4$]

23) SI-*šú ú-šap-pi-lu* : *ana* SAḪAR(?) *šá-*x[...]

24) *lu-u ki* GU$_4$ *ik-ki-pu-ú-ma* S[I-*šú*(?) ...]

25) *is-sa-al-la-a*ʾ-[*m*]*a* : LÍL : *s*[*i-li-tu* ...]

26) *ik-tap-pi-lu* : *šá a-*⸢*ḫa-meš*⸣ x[... EME$_3$ *pa-an* GIG]

27) ANŠE *pa-an mu-tú šá-kin lì*[*b-bu-ú* ...]

Reverse

28) DIŠ ⸢ANŠE RA⸣-*su* : GÌR RA(!).RA : *ra-ḫa-ṣu* : GÌR : *še-e-pi* : R[A : *ma-ḫa-ṣu*]

29) *šá-niš* ^{d}Ud-dè-anše : Ud-da : ^{d}IŠKUR : DIŠ DINGIR *saḫ-ḫi-ri* IGI : *lu-u* ^{d}[x x]

30) *lu-u Ur-gu-la-a lu-u* ^{d}*Gaz-ba-ba* : *šá-niš Un-na-niš-šú* : ^{d}MAR.T[U]

31) ^{lu_2}an-na-ba-ti : lú-^{giš}kéš-da : nin-nun-gal-e-ne : *eš-⸢še⸣-bu-u*

32) *ri-kis* ^{d}*Na-ru-du* : DIŠ *maḫ-ḫa-a* IGI ŠU ^{d}MAŠ : ^{lu_2}G[UB.BA : *ma*]*ḫ-⸢ḫu⸣-u*

33) ^{d}Lugal-i-bí-gub-ba : ^{d}MAŠ : ^{lu_2}an-dib-ba-ra : ní-⸢zu⸣-ra-a[ḫ : kur-gar-r]a

34) ^{lu_2}an-sal-la : *maḫ-ḫu-u* : *a-ḫur-ru-u* : *kur-ga-ra-u* : [*a*]*s-s*[*in-nu*]

35) DIŠ *suk-ku-ku* IGI ŠU ^{d}U.GUR : KI ^{mul}KA.DU$_8$.A *a-li*[*d u*]*q-q*[*u-u*]*q*

36) *šá-niš suk-ku-uk* : *iz-bi* GEŠTUG.2-*a-šú ki-la-at-ta-an* B[A.RA BÙ]R(!).MEŠ(!)

37) *mi-qit-tu*$_4$ *dúr*$_{du-ur}$*-giš-lu-ú* GÁL-*ši* : *dúr-giš-lu-ú* : d[ur-giš(?)]-⸢lam NIBRU^{ki} (?)⸣

38) *dúr-giš-lu-ú* : NIBRU^{ki}-*ú* : *áš-šú* ^{d}U.GUR : DIŠ ^{lu_2}BA.A[N.ZU] IGI ⸢ŠU ^{d}MAŠ⸣

39) ^{lu_2}BA.AN.ZU : *pe-su-ú* : *ku-ru-ú* : ^{lu_2}BA.AN.ZU : *pe-ḫu-u*

40) G[I]G.TIL.LA : *pe-su-ú* : *šu-ú-lu* ⸢: *šu*⸣-*ul-la-nu*

41) DIŠ [Á] 15-*šú iz-qut-su* : *šá zi-iq-tu*$_4$: ⸢*šá*⸣ [Á] 15-*šú ana* ^{lu_2}MAŠ.MAŠ *i-zaq-qí-⸢tú⸣*

42) DIŠ [^{giš}GIGI]R IGI ŠU ^{d}15 : ^{giš}GIGIR *šá* SAG : $^{[gi]š}$GIGIR *šá* LUGAL : ŠU ^{d} ⸢15⸣

43) [MUL *š*]*á ina lìb-bi* ^{mul}GIGIR : ^{d}*Dili-bat* : DIŠ ^{giš}GAG.SI.LÁ IGI

44) ⸢^{giš}GAG.SI⸣.LÁ *šá* ^{lu_2}*kab-tu* : ^{giš} ⸢MAR.GÍD⸣.DA : *e-req-⸢qu⸣*

45) *šá-niš ta*[*l-l*]*ak-tu*$_4$: DIŠ ^{giš}GABA.GÁL.LA : ⸢*pi-it-nu* ^{giš}MAR.GÍD.DA(?)⸣

46) *šá* 1-*en* ANŠE.KUNGA *u lu-u* 1-*en* ANŠE.x[...]x x[x]

47) SA.GIG : *ri-kis mur-ṣu šá-niš n*[*ap-har mur-ṣu* ...]

---

48) *ṣa-a-tú šu-ut* KA *u maš-a-a-al-tú šá* KA *um-man-nu šá* ŠÀ

49) DIŠ *e-nu-ma* KA.PIRIG *ana* É GIG DU-*ku* DUB.1.KAM É[Š.GÀ]R ⸢SA.GIG⸣

50) NU AL.TIL DIŠ NA *ana* É ^{lu_2}GIG DU-⸢*kam-ma* SÚR.DÙ^{mušen}⸣ [*ana* 15]-*šú* DIB-*iq*

51) IM.GÌ.DA $^{m.d+}$*En-líl*-EN-*šú-nu* ^{lu_2}MAŠ.MAŠ [A $^{m.d}$]⸢*Nin-urta-na*⸣-*ṣir*

52) ^{lu_2}KUL.LUM $^{d+}$*En-líl* A ^{m}AB.SUM.MU ⸢*šu-me-ru*$_6$⸣-*u*

Translation

Incipit-title of Sa-gig 1	(Obv. 1) "[Whenever] the KA.PIRIG-healer goes to the sick man's house."
Sa-gig S1: 1 (U1: 1) The magician-healer is one who "speaks" (ka) what is "bright" (PIRIG), i.e., his spoken diagnosis illumines the identity of the patient's malady.	(1) "KA.PIRIG" *means* magician. (2) PIRIG *means* bright.
This bilingual list is quoted to support the preceding assertion that PIRIG *means* "bright."	(2–3) "pirig-gal, pirig-gal-e-ne, *and* pirig-gal-abzu *mean* [great] light, their ⟨great⟩ light, *and* great light of the Apsû *respectively*."
Sa-gig S1: 2 (U1: 2) The following arguments prove the link between the potsherd and the patient's critical condition.	(3–4) "If he sees a potsherd (ŠIKA) standing upright in the street, [that] sick man is critically sick; One must not approach him."
Evidence #1: The writing šika-al-ús-sa "(pot)sherd" includes the idea of being "trampled down" (al-ús-sa), thus implying the sick man's "death."	(4) ⟨šika⟩-al-ús-sa (*means*) sherd *or* potsherd. (4) al-ús-sa (*means*) trampled down.
Evidence #2: This quotation from a compilation of bilingual proverbs compares man's wellbeing to the integrity of a pot, in line with the tradition that man was fashioned from clay.	(5) As in, "Pot has been broken into potsherd, and [Man] has died."
Evidence #3: The cuneiform sign for ŠIKA has these alternative meanings, which	(6) ŠIKA *means* potsherd *or* prime of life *or* son.

suggests that a broken "potsherd" portends harm to the sick man's vitality or virility.

Sa-gig S1: 3 (U1: 3)

(6) "If he sees the KI.UD.BI, an oath-curse [has seized] him."

KI.UD.BI is a cultic installation, whose different functions are described here.

(7) Whether (the KI.UD.BI) is one that is [set up] for a sacrificial offering, that is, for the god Nergal or for [commemoration (?)].

This quotation from Nam-erim$_2$-búr-ru-da shows that KI.UD.BI is associated with Nergal. It also supports the omen in Sa-gig S1: 3 that KI.UD.BI implies an "oath-curse" (NAM.ERIM$_2$) has seized the sick man.

(8–10) As in, "On his KI.UD.BI, the meal-offerings of the great gods have been [brought near (?)]," which *refers to* "Nergal the almighty god, beloved of the goddess Ninmenna," which it said in Nam-erim$_2$-búr-ru-da (Incantations to Undo Oath-Curses).

Analysis of Logograms #1: KI.UD.BI is analyzed as a "pure place."

(10) "KI.UD.BI."
(10) KI *means* place. ud *means* pure.

Analysis of Logograms #2: KI.UD.BI is analyzed as a "cleansed place."

(10) Secondly, "KI.UD.BI."
(10) ud *means* cleansed.

Sa-gig S1: 4 (U1: 39b)
agurru "kiln-fired brick" is analyzed as A + gur, where A is the logogram for either "water" or "son." The commentator argued that the following objects or persons have the same omen significance as the "kiln-fired brick."

(11) "If he sees a kiln-fired brick" *refers to*:

Analysis of Logograms #1:
GUR typically functions as the logogram for the verb “to return.” Logograms A + GUR refer to “one who returned (from) water,” i.e., one who returned from the river ordeal.

(11) One who returned from the river ordeal.
(11) A *means* water.
(11) GUR *means* to return.

Analysis of Logograms #2a:
gur$_4$ is the same sign as GIR$_8$ or KÌR, which is the logogram for the verb “to pinch off.” Logogram A + sign gur$_4$ refers to “one who will pinch off a son (from her body?),” i.e., a pregnant woman.

(11) Secondly, [a pregnant woman].
(12) A *means* son.
(12) The cuneiform sign gur$_4$ *means* to pinch off.

Analysis of Logograms #2b:
/*gur*/ is the pronunciation of the logogram GUR$_{17}$ or GÙR meaning “to carry.” Logogram A + /*gur*/ refers to “one who carries a son,” i.e., a pregnant woman.

(12) Secondly, A *means* son.
(12) /*gur*/ *means* to carry.

Analysis of Logograms #3:
The graph (i.e., written symbol) gur (𒄥) visually resembles the graph si (𒋛), which has the logographic meaning (SI) “to become full.” Logogram A + graph gur refers to “that which is full of water,” i.e., a water vessel.

(13) Thirdly, a water vessel.
(13) A *means* water.
(13) The graph gur (𒄥) *means* to become full.

Sa-gig S1: 6 (U1: 9)
The base text includes both positive and negative prognoses, implying that the “pig” can be a good or ill omen.

(13) “If [he sees] a black pig (ŠÁḪ),”
(14) which it said for good or ill.

“Pig” as ill omen:
SUL, which denotes deadly *li’bu*-sickness, is the same cuneiform sign as ŠÁḪ “pig.”

(14) The cuneiform sign šáḫ as the logogram SUL *means* *li’bu*-sickness, *which means* he will die.

"Pig" as good omen:
(Prognosis in entry Sa-gig S1: 6)

(14) Secondly, "[he will get into dire straits], and he will live."

***Sa-gig S1: 7 (U1: 10)—"that sick man will live, hardship seizes him"**
ŠÁḪ "pig" (𒂠) is the same sign as ŠUL "youth" (𒂠), which has the same meaning as another logogram GURUŠ "youth" (𒄨), which is the same sign as KALA "hard" (𒄨). Thus, the pig is a portent for hardship.

(15) If the sick man sees hardship, he will live. If he does not see hardship, he will die.

Quotation from *Šumma ālu* XLIX, 41′ may suggest that "pig" and "female captive" had the same divinatory significance, but more likely validates the link between "pig" and the prognosis of "dire straits."

(15–16) As in, "If a pig enters a man's bedroom, a female captive will enter the man's house."

The idea of being held "captive" portended the sick man's "confinement (to the bed)" (*esēru*), which represented the commentator's interpretation of the prognosis "he will get into dire *straits*" in the base text Sa-gig S1: 6 (U1: 9).

(16) "Female captive" *refers to* [confinement (*esēru*)],

Furthermore, a play on the homophones *esēru* ("confinement") and *esēru* ("to press for payment due") portrays sickness as a divine act to settle unfulfilled "oath" promises.

(17) (*which refers to*) any oath-curse in the Diagnostic Handbook Sa-gig.

***Sa-gig S1: 9 (U1: 12)—ŠÁḪ GÙN.A "a dappled pig"**
"Dappled things" (*barimāt*) are indicated by the writing *ba-ri*-BA.ÚŠ(*imât*), which imply the interpretation "it is seen (*bari*), he

(17) If he sees dappled things (*bari–imât*) ...

will die (*imât*)." The "dappled" pig therefore portends the sick man's death.

Sa-gig S1: 9 (U1: 12)
aganutillâ is analyzed as the logograms A.GA "future" + NU "without" + TI.LA "life."

(17–18) "… [*aganutillâ*-sickness]" *refers to* a future without life.

This resembles a quotation from the Old Babylonian *List of Diseases* 117e (*MSL* IX, 79).

(18) Secondly, "*aganutillâ*-sickness" *means* full of water. …

Sa-gig S1: 14–15 (U1: 17–18)
Is the "red ox" (*alpa sāma*) here compared to the "Bull of Heaven" (GU$_4$.AN.NA analyzed as *alap šamê*) in *Gilgamesh* VI, 92–150, where Ištar (like the *lamaštu*-demoness here) appears as Anu's daughter who is antagonistic to man?

(19) "If he sees a red ox, the *lamaštu*-demoness has seized that sick man."

(19–20) Daughter of [the god Anu] … of the great gods, which it said.

Sa-gig S1: 16 (U1: 19)

(20) "If he sees an ox throw (ŠUB) its horn (SI)."

The language here echoes and alludes to the description that Bull of Heaven "ejects drool" in *Gilgamesh* VI, 126.

(20–21) Secondly, [if] he sees [an ox] "ejects [drool]" or throws up drool.

The commentator argued that, whether the observed ox throws its "horn" or its "drool," the same ominous meaning is intended.

(21–22) ["SI" *means* horn.]
(22) "SI" *means* drool.
(22) "ŠUB" *means* to throw "SI" (i.e., whichever of the above meanings it may have).

These lines seem to contain descriptions involving an ox and its SI, presumably in contexts where SI could mean either "horn" or "drool."

(22–23) [As in, "When an ox] lowers its SI" *means* to the dust(?) …

(24) Or, "when an ox butts and [its SI (?)] …"

Sa-gig S1: 21 (U1: 23)

(25) "He will become ill."

(25) LÍL *means* [illness]. ...

Sa-gig S1: 22 (U1: 24)—"If he sees a donkey mounting a jenny, that patient and death are interwined"

(25–26) "... they are intertwined" *refers to* the case where ... one another.

The commentator verified the base text by identifying the jenny with the sick man and the donkey with death.

(26–27) [The jenny is complement to the sick man.] The donkey is complement to death.

Support for this interpretation may involve wordplay between "death" (*mūtu*) and the "husband" (*mutu*) who mounts his wife.

(27) As in, ...

Sa-gig S1: 26 (U1: 27)

(Line 28) "If a donkey kicks (RA) him."

In medical texts, RA often means "to strike" rather than "to kick."

(28) GÌR RA.RA *means* to kick.
(28) GÌR *means* foot.
(28) RA [*means* to strike].

The divinatory significance of a kicking donkey is extended to include stormy weather, because the storm-god's name ^{d}Ud-dè-anše involves the element ANŠE "donkey." Also, *raḫāṣu* "to kick, devastate" very often describes the storm-god's floods.

(29) Secondly, ^{d}Ud-dè-anše *or* Ud-da *refers to* the storm-god Adad.

Sa-gig S1: 30 (U1: 37a)

(29) "If he sees a prowling god."

The commentator explained this omen about a "prowling god," so that it referred not only to some invisible divine or demonic being, but also to beings that are more readily observable, such as cultic

(29–30) Either [...], Urgula, or Gazbaba.

(30) Secondly, Unnānîššu *or* Amurru.

persons like the "shaman" and "(man-of)-the-knot of Narudu," and perhaps star constellations like Leo (Urgula), i.e., the prowling lion.

(31–32) (Thirdly), "^{lu_2}an-na-ba-ti *or* lú-^{giš}kéš-da : nin-nun-gal-e-ne, *which means* shaman (*or*) (man-of)-the-knot of Narudu *respectively*."

Sa-gig S1: 31 (U1: 30)

(32) "If he sees an ecstatic, Hand of the god Ninurta."

The /gub-ba/ element in their names links "an ecstatic" to "the god Ninurta."

(32) ^{lu_2}GUB.BA *means* "an ecstatic."
(33) ^{d}Lugal-i-bí-gub-ba *refers to* the god Ninurta.

This quotation resembling the lexical list Erimhuš III, 169–172 extends the omen's applicability to other cultic persons associated with the "ecstatic."

(33–34) "^{lu_2}an-dib-ba-ra, ní-zu-ra-aḫ, [kur-gar-ra], *and* ^{lu_2}an-sal-la *refer to* ecstatic, catamite, cultic performer, *and* male cultic prostitute *respectively*."

Sa-gig S1: 32 (U1: 39)

(35) "If he sees a deaf man, Hand of the god Nergal."

This horoscope links the god Nergal's constellation (^{mul}Ka-du$_8$-a) to muteness and deafness, as expressed by its elements: ka "speech" + DU$_8$.A "dispersed."

(35–36) "(If a child) is born under the constellation ^{mul}Ka-du$_8$-a (Cygnus), he will be mute; secondly, deaf."

This is a quotation from the omen series *Šumma izbu* IV, 38.

(36–37) "(If) both ears of an anomaly [do not have ear-holes], the downfall of Durgišlû will occur."

This association is proposed in the *Principal Commentary to Šumma izbu* IV, 38, as well as attested in the lexical text Erimhuš V, 21–22.

(37) "Durgišlû *or* Dur-giš-lam(?) (*refers to*) the city of Nippur(?)."

Nippur's downfall is associated with Nergal, who is perhaps identified with Erra and his destruction of cities in the *Erra Epic*. The absence of ear-holes and, hence, deafness is therefore connected to Nergal.

(38) "Durgišlû *refers to* the city of Nippur," because of the god Nergal.

Sa-gig S1: 33 (U1: 38b)
To show the link between ^{lu_2}BA.AN.ZU and the god Ninurta (^{d}MAŠ), the element BA.AN is interpreted as a reference to the sign bán with its logographic value MAŠ "half."

(38) "If he sees a ^{lu_2}BA.AN.ZU, Hand of the god Ninurta."

BA.AN.ZU refers to one whose stature is "half" (bán) that of a normal "man" (ZA).

(39) ^{lu_2}BA.AN.ZU *means* stunted *or* dwarf.

BA.AN.ZU refers to one who has only "half" (bán) his "wits" (ZU).

(39) ^{lu_2}BA.AN.ZU *means* half-witted.

Though the ancient distinctions between these terms are uncertain, the "gnome" and "pygmy" are also relevant to this omen due to their associations with the "stunted."

(40) GIG.TIL.LA *means* stunted, gnome, *or* pygmy.

Sa-gig S1: 36 (U1: 31)
The omen can mean that the magician's right arm stings him (i.e., gives him a "stinging pain"), or someone else's right arm points at the magician—with the root *zaqātu* encompassing various ideas involving a "sting" or a "point."

(41) "If his right [arm] (performs the action of) *izqut* to him" *refers to* the case of a stinging pain (*ziqtu*),

(41) *or* the case where (some) one's right [arm] points (*izaqqit*) at the magician.

Sa-gig S1: 46 (U1: 40b)

(42) "If he sees a [chariot], Hand of the goddess Ištar."

As subsequent omens in the base text deal with other chariot-like vehicles, it was important here to specify the kinds of "chariots" that refer to Ištar.

(42) A chariot of the chief *or* a chariot of the king *refers to* Hand of the goddess Ištar.

In this visual argument, Dilibat (Venus) is contained inside the constellation Chariot (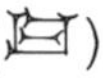), by considering its inner contents either (I) as the sign aš()-*tenû* whose non-*tenû* portion is the syllable sign *dili* that alludes to Dilibat, or (II) as a "single" (DILI) cuneiform sign bat () that once again refers to Dilibat.

(43) [The star] inside the constellation Chariot (Northern part of Taurus) *refers to* Dilibat (Venus).

Sa-gig S1: 47 (U1: 41)
The idea of defining "chariot"-like vehicles by the status of their passengers may have been inspired by assonantal links between *narkabtu* "chariot" and *kabtu* "the honored, dignitary."

(43–44) "If he sees a carriage" (*refers to*) the carriage of a dignitary.

Sa-gig S1: 48 (U1: 42a)

(44) "^{giš}MAR.GÍD.DA" *means* cart.
(45) Secondly, wagon.

Sa-gig S1: 49 (U1: 42b)

(45–46) "If (he sees) a ^{giš}GABA.GÁL.LA" *refers to* the box of a cart, which a single mule or a single donkey(?) ...

***Colophon of Sa-gig Tablet 1**
An effort to make the title of the Diagnostic Handbook SA.GIG conform to its definition in *Esagil-kīn-apli's Manifesto* as "a bundling together (SA) of sickness (GIG)," i.e., a compilation on "all (SA) sickness (GIG)."

(47) "SA.GIG" *refers to* the bundling together of sickness.

(47) Secondly, all [sickness] ...

(Colophon)

(48–49) Glossary (including) oral lore and questionings from the mouth of the *ummânu*-scholar on the contents of "Whenever the KA.PIRIG-healer goes to the sick man's house," Tablet 1 of the series Sa-gig.

Incipit-title of Sa-gig 1

(50) Unfinished (and continued with) "If the person goes to the sick man's house, and a falcon passes by at his [right]."

Incipit-title of Sa-gig 2

(51–52) *Imgida*-tablet of Enlil-bēlšunu the magician, [son] of Ninurta-nāṣir, temple-brewer of Enlil, descendant of Absummu the Sumerian.

Notes

Intro—A parallel edition of Commentaries Sa-gig 1A, 1B, and 1C has been provided by George (1991: 137–168). As he observed, tablet 1 of the Diagnostic Handbook appeared in two main versions with different ordering of entries. In my edition, "Sa-gig S1" is employed as prefix for the "standard version" from Dūr-Šarrukēn, Nippur, and probably Babylon, which includes the base text for Comm. Sa-gig 1A. "Sa-gig U1," on the other hand, is used as prefix for the "variant version" from Uruk (including the base texts for Comm. Sa-gig 1B and 1C), as well as from Ḫuzirīna (see Note Intro to Comm. Sa-gig 1–3). Yet another Uruk commentary (Comm. Sa-gig 1D) was published by von Weiher (*SpTU* v, 256) in 1998, which, interestingly, adhered to the contents and arrangement of Comm. Sa-gig 1A, rather than those of the other Uruk Commentaries Sa-gig 1B and 1C. Readers should consult George's comments and references alongside my edition and notes, which will focus mainly on differences in our interpretations, the commentator's use of rhetoric, as well as the significance of vocabularies and concepts in the context of medical practice. A comparison of readings on the tablet of Comm. Sa-gig 1A (see recent photos in Plates 1–2) with those in Durand's hand copies (*TBER*, 56–57; Durand 1979: 156–57) suggests that the tablet surface suffered from flaking damage in the interim, so that several cuneiform signs along the edges of preserved lines on obverse and reverse sides have been worn away.

Obv. 1–3—// Comm. Sa-gig 1C, obv. 1–2. Associations between PIRIG and cognates of *namāru* occur in the lexical texts Aa III/3, 81 (*MSL* XIV, 334); Aa III/4, 68 (*MSL* XIV, 340); Idu II, 219 (*CAD* N II, 347). See also *The Weapon Name Exposition*, where PIRIG = *namru* (lines 21, 24, 25) in Livingstone (1986: 54). As a diagnostician, the magician is depicted as KA.PIRIG, because he "speaks" (ka) what is "bright" (PIRIG), i.e., his spoken diagnosis illumines the identity of the patient's malady.

Obv. 4—// Comm. Sa-gig 1B, obv. 1′–2′ // Comm. Sa-gig 1C, obv. 3–4 (main Note) on connections to ^{giš}gišimmar-al-ús-sa ("trampled (date-palm)") in Hh. III, 303 (*MSL* V, 118).

Obv. 5—// Comm. Sa-gig 1B, obv. 3′ and 4′–5′ (main Notes) on the quotation here from a compilation of bilingual proverbs and allusions to the creation of humankind from clay.

Obv. 6—The three meanings here relate to the sign ŠIKA in various ways: (I) The logogram ŠIKA (𒆷) stands for *ḫaṣbu* ("potsherd"). (II) ŠIKA is the same sign as the logogram LA (𒆷), which means *lalû* ("prime of life"). See the equation $^{\text{la-a}}$ LA = *lalû* in the lexical texts Aa III/4, 63 (*MSL* XIV, 340); Ea III, 184 (*MSL* XIV, 311); S^{b} I, 204 (*MSL* III, 114). (III) Neither ŠIKA nor LA is explicitly linked in the lexical tradition with *māru* ("son"), which implies here that the vitality in "prime of life" is to be measured in terms of virility, i.e., one's ability to bear or beget children. The need for this definition becomes clear after some thought: While commentary arguments like this endeavor to make the omen more relevant by expanding its range of possible referents, the omen would quickly lose its weight if its referents are too common—as in cases of persons in their "prime of life," or those who have or are "a son." In other words, the person who qualifies as an omen here is restricted to one known to the healer as having many sons. Reading the signs *ma-ri* (obv. 6) as *ba-ri* ("collationé" by Cavigneaux 1982: 232 n. 7) seems less probable.

Obv. 8–10—// Comm. Sa-gig 1B, obv. 8′–10′. The description of Nergal in these lines occurs also in a Šu-íl-la prayer to Nergal. See King (1896: 87, no. 27, line 4); Mayer (1976: 479, "Nergal 2," line 4); Durand (1979: 158); George (1991: 154). See Note on Comm. Sa-gig 1B, obv. 8′–10′ for my interpretation of the additional qualifier NAM.ERIM$_2$ *mál i-na* SA.GI[G] (obv. 9′) as "*concerning* any oath-curse in (the Diagnostic Handbook) Sa-gig."

Obv. 11–13—// Comm. Sa-gig 1B, rev. 21–23. This is one of the most vivid illustrations of argumentation by analysis of syllabic forms (§1.2.3.2.7).

According to the base text Sa-gig S1: 4 (U1: 39b), the healer's sighting of a kiln-fired brick en route to the patient's house was a negative portent that the patient would die. This ominous significance of the "kiln-fired brick" (*agurru*) was extended also to other persons and objects that could be defined by the components a + gur.

Obv. 11—// Comm. Sa-gig 1B, rev. 21–22. The components of *agurru* ("kiln-fired brick") are interpreted as the logogram A ("water") + the logogram GUR ("to return"), referring to "one who returned (from) water," i.e., the river ordeal. George (1991: 147, 154) proposed that "the brick is seen to be a man who has evaded risk of death in rejecting the river-ordeal, and the inference is taken that the exorcist's patient will die in his place," but the logic more likely runs in the opposite direction: It was the healer's sighting of a man returning from the river ordeal that constituted an omen equivalent to the sighting of a kiln-fired brick. Gabbay (2017: 78) understood the situation as a positive one involving "the granting of a new life, in the case of the person who survived the river ordeal." Although the meaning of "returning" (*târu*) from a river ordeal is admittedly disputed, the options seem to be negative for the accused—referring either to his refusal to undergo the ordeal and therefore accepting liability for punishment, or to his failure to clear the ordeal. See, for example, Postgate (1976: 160); Frymer-Kensky (1977: 385–387, 394–399, 521–522); van Soldt (2003–2005: 126 §4.4; 128 §8); as summarized in Faist (2014: 190); cf. Kataja (1987: 66); Oelsner, Wells, and Wunsch (2003: 495–496).

Obv. 11–12—// Comm. Sa-gig 1B, rev. 22. This is the first of two analyses ascribing to a pregnant woman the same ominous significance as a kiln-fired brick: The components of *agurru* ("kiln-fired brick") are interpreted as the logogram A ("son") + the cuneiform sign gur$_4$ (as the logogram GIR$_8$ or KÌR for *karāṣu*, "to pinch off"), referring to the pregnant woman as "one who will pinch off a son (from her body?)." Note the lexical support for GIR$_8$ as the logographic value: $^{\text{gi-[r]i(?)}}$ lagab = *ka-ra-ṣu šá* IM (Aa I/2, 27 in *MSL* XIV, 208); $^{\text{gi-ri-in}}$ lagab = MIN (= *ka-ra-ṣu*) *šá ṭi-di* (Antagal III, 144 in *MSL* XVII, 155). In Comm. Sa-gig 1B, rev. 22, however, the commentator's gloss $^{\text{ki-ir}}$ gu[r$_4$(KÌR) : *ka-ra-ṣ*]*a* suggests that the logographic value was KÌR. In any case, despite phonological similarities with GIR$_8$ and KÌR, the term GUR$_4$ does not appear in lexical texts as the logogram of *karāṣu* ("to pinch off"). On the contrary, there are strong indications that commentators themselves did not consider gur$_4$ (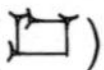) logographic: If they did, there would have been no reason to deviate from the consistent use of the cuneiform sign gur (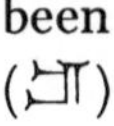) in other analyses of Comm. Sa-gig 1A (obv. 11–13) and Comm. Sa-gig 1B (rev. 21–23), since the very next argument (Comm. Sa-gig 1A, obv. 12; Comm. Sa-gig 1B, rev. 23) illustrates that the sign gur could be employed to designate any logogram with the value /gur/, such as GUR$_{17}$ (), GÙR (), and GUR$_4$ (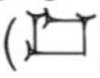). The term *karāṣu* ("to pinch off") commonly describes the process in which mother-goddesses "pinch off" clay to create human forms. See, for example, the creation of Enkidu by the goddess Aruru in the Standard Babylonian *Epic of Gilgamesh* I, 102 (George 2003: 544; cf. Comm. Sa-gig 1B, obv. 4′–5′), as well as the creation of humankind by ^{d}*Zulummaru* in Lambert (1960: 88–89, line 277). Admittedly, though, it is the god Ea who does the "pinching" at other times (Lambert 1970: 43, section III, lines 25–26). The imagery, in fact, is already implied in Comm. Sa-gig 1A, obv. 5; Comm. Sa-gig 1B, obv. 2′–5′ where man's wellbeing is compared to the integrity of a (clay) pot. Such narratives, however, tend to portray creation from clay as an alternative to the usual process of reproduction and birth, typically in situations where the creature formed (i.e., Enkidu or the first humans) does not have a precedent. The commentary argument here, therefore, is remarkable in the way it associates "pinching off" with a "pregnant woman," as if the human mother performs an act of creation similar to that of mother-goddesses. This association clarifies a misunderstanding involving the expression *šà*-ŠÀ-*šà* NITA : *i-kar-ri-iṣ* (Sa-gig 36: 1 (TDPT 35: 1)), about which Stol (2000: 194) has remarked: "The verb *karāṣu* means 'to break off' and the cognate *kirṣu* means 'abortion.' Is this an abortion by cutting up the foetus, embryotomy (Hebrew *ḥātak*)?" The commentarial context here makes the interpretation of *karāṣu* as an act of abortion unlikely.

Obv. 12—// Comm. Sa-gig 1B, rev. 23. This is the second of two analyses ascribing to a pregnant woman the same ominous significance as a kiln-fired brick: The components of *agurru* ("kiln-fired brick") are interpreted as the logogram A ("son") + the pronunciation /*gur*/ (of the logogram GUR$_{17}$ or GÙR for *našû*, "to carry"), referring to the pregnant woman as "one who carries a son." For lexical attestations of GUR$_{17}$ () as the logogram for *našû*, see S^{b} I, 304 (*MSL* III, 123); *MSL* II, 141 C rev. ii 15′ (Proto-Ea); Ea IV, 205 (*MSL* XIV, 363); cf. *MZL*, no. 470. Alternatively, the logogram ÍL that commonly expresses *našû* occasionally occurs with the value GÙR (). See $^{gu-ru}$ GÙR = *na-šu-ú* (Nabnitu K, 139 in *MSL* XVI, 146); i-ši-gùr-ru = *na-áš ša*-⌜*lum-ma*⌝-[*ti*] (Izi V, 66 in *MSL* XIII, 162); *MZL*, no. 493 (Kapital II) where gùr may be related to ga$_6$ (cf. Waetzoldt, *NABU* 1992/16).

Obv. 13—The components of *agurru* ("kiln-fired brick") are interpreted as the logogram A ("water") + the graph gur ( confused or conflated with the similar graph  of the logogram SI for *malû*, "to become full"), referring to "that which is full of water," i.e., a water vessel. In another unrelated text, for example, Hunger (1968: 124, no. 424, line 4) has noticed the confusion of "SI für GUR" in a depiction of the verb *târu* ("to return").

Obv. 13–14—// Comm. Sa-gig 1B, obv. 13′. The equation su-ul SUL(šáḫ) = *le-e-bu* is attested also in the lexical text Aa VIII/3, 23 (*MSL* XIV, 507). In Comm. Sa-gig 4A (obv. 8) and Comm. Sa-gig 19 (obv. 9 and 10), I understand the writing *le-e-bu* to denote the noun *lēbu* ("*li'bu*-sickness") rather than the verb *le'ēbu* ("to infect, said of *li'bu*-sickness"), because the term equated with *le-e-bu* is the noun "*zi'pu*-sickness." I extend the same interpretation to the writing *le-e-bu* in this commentary and Comm. Sa-gig 1B (obv. 13′). For discussion on the sickness *li'bu*, see Stol (2007a: 11–12). The commentator's interest in the significance "for good or ill" of the base text omen (Sa-gig S1: 6 (U1: 9)) may have been motivated by its surprising prognosis: PAP.ḪAL.MEŠ-*ma* TI ("He will get into dire straits, and he will become healthy"). Among the occurrences of the verb *šupšuqu* ("to get into dire straits"; *CAD* P, 235–236 s.v. *pašāqu*) in the Diagnostic Handbook (Sa-gig 3: 97 (TDPT 3: 88); Sa-gig 10 B rev. 14; 13: 91, 129 (TDPT 13 ii 33; iii 18); Sa-gig 16: 57′; 19/20: 118′, 119′), there are several negative outcomes (Sa-gig 13: 91 MS B (TDPT 13 ii 33); Sa-gig 16: 57′; 19/20: 119′) and no unambiguously positive ones (cf. the embedded variants GAM : TIN of Sa-gig 13: 91 in Scurlock 2014: 106). The disjunction sign after BA.ÚŠ in the transliteration by George (1991: 146) is absent in Durand's hand copy (*TBER*, 56).

Obv. 15–17—// Comm. Sa-gig 1B, obv. 14′–15′. The point of interest here is the base text prognosis "(the sick man) will get into dire straits" (Sa-gig U1: 9 (S1: 6)). Using a quotation from *Šumma ālu* XLIX, 41′ (Freedman 2017: 78), the commentator showed that the "pig" is a portent for a "female captive." This notion of being held "captive," in turn, alluded to the sick man's "confinement (to the bed)," expressing the manner in which the commentator thought the sick man would get into "straits" (Š stem of *pašāqu*, "(G) to become narrow, constricted"; *CAD* P, 235–236). See Note on Comm. Sa-gig 1B, obv. 8′–10′ for the affirmation that remedies for "any oath-curse (as a verdict) in the Diagnostic Handbook Sa-gig" are available from the corpus of Nam-erim$_2$-búr-ru-da incantations. Though there is no mention of Nam-erim$_2$-búr-ru-da here, the same expression "any oath-curse in the Diagnostic Handbook Sa-gig" (obv. 17) reveals a play on the homophones "to enclose, confine" (*esēru* B in *CAD* E, 334–335) and "to press for payment due" (*esēru* A in *CAD* E, 332–334). Diagnostic verdicts involving oath-curses defined sickness as the result of unfulfilled oath promises that were being called up for reckoning. Accordingly, the patient's "confinement" (*esēru*) to the sick bed indicated that the gods were "pressing for payment" (*esēru*) for violated oaths, a transgression that needed to be absolved by the performance of apotropaic Nam-erim$_2$-búr-ru-da incantations.

Obv. 17—Instead of the signs ŠÁḪ GÙN.A ("a dappled pig") in existing manuscripts of Sa-gig S1: 9 (U1: 12), the commentator conveyed the idea of "dappled things" by writing *ba-ri*-BA.ÚŠ(*imât*). See Cavigneaux (1982: 238). This is probably an example of argumentation by 'single member argument' (§1.2.3.3), where the commentator intentionally deviated from base text forms in order to express his own interpretation of the text. The signs *ba-ri*-BA.ÚŠ(*imât*) could be understood as "it is seen (*bari*), he will die (*imât*)," thereby depicting the "dappled" pig as a portent of the sick man's death.

Obv. 17–18—// Comm. Sa-gig 1B, obv. 19′. The sickness *aganutillâ* is analyzed as A.GA (*arkatu*, "future") + NU (*lā*, "without") + TI.LA (*balāṭu*, "life"), referring to the fatality of the sickness that ensures "a future without life." Associations between A.GA and *arkatu* occur in the lexical texts Emesal Voc. III, 72 (*MSL* IV, 33); Antagal G, 221 (*MSL* XVII, 227); Hh. VII A, 31 (*MSL* VI, 86).

Obv. 18—The statement that "'*aganutillâ*-sickness' *means* full of water" resembles a quotation from the Old Babylonian (OB) *List of Diseases* 117e (*MSL* IX, 79): [a-ga]-la-til-la = MIN (= *ma-la-a me-e*). George (1991: 148–149) restores the end of this line as a.g[a : SA$_5$ *šá m*]*e-e* ("a.ga [= 'to be full of] water'"), but perhaps we should restore one of two other entries that share the same description "full of water" in the OB *List of Diseases*: [a-mu]d-a-sè-ke = *ma-la-a me-e* (line 117d) or [a-š]à-ga-si = MIN (= *ma-la-a me-e*) (line 117f).

Obv. 19–20—The topic in obv. 19 seems to be cited from a base text that conflated the protasis "If he sees a red ox" in Sa-gig S1: 14 (U1: 17) with the apodosis "the *lamaštu*-demoness has seized that sick man" in Sa-gig S1: 15 (U1: 18). Alternatively, the conflation may represent an error made by the scribe of this commentary. What seems to be a quotation in obv. 19–20 is unfortunately damaged. One wonders, however, if the commentator referred here to the 'Bull of Heaven' episode in the Standard Babylonian *Epic of Gilgamesh* VI, 92–150 (George 2003: 624–629), which is alluded to also in the following commentary entry (obv. 20–24), and where Ištar (like the *lamaštu*-demoness here) appears as the daughter of the god Anu who is antagonistic towards man. Was the "Bull of Heaven" (read not as *alû*, but as the individual components of GU$_4$.AN.NA = *alap šamê*) compared to the "red ox" (*alpa sāma*) in the Sa-gig base text? See also Comm. Sa-gig 1B, obv. 25′ where the title "Daughter of the god Anu" is ascribed to the *lamaštu*-demoness, as part of an argument connecting this demoness with "heat."

Obv. 20–24—// Comm. Sa-gig 1B, obv. 30′. The expression *rupuštu issuku* ("(he sees an ox) eject drool"; lines 20–21) here echoes the language of *Epic of Gilgamesh* VI, 126 (George 2003: 626–627): GU$_4$.AN.NA *ana pānīšu issuka rupušta* ("the Bull of Heaven ejected drool at his face"). This *Gilgamesh* passage would have been fresh on the commentator's mind, if it had indeed been referred to in the preceding lines (obv. 19–20). Obv. 22–23 possibly describes the "horn" of an ox scattering "dust," a behavior considered ominous in *STT* 73 lines 136–137 (Reiner 1960: 35).

Obv. 25–27—cf. Comm. Sa-gig 1B, rev. 9 // Comm. Sa-gig 1C, rev. 1′. The commentator asserted that the mounted jenny is complement (*pān*) to the sick man, while the donkey is complement (*pān*) to death, so that the scene portrayed the sick man held in the firm grasp of death. For the commentary notation IGI / *pān*(*i*) ("complement to") and its derivation from the depiction of reciprocals in cuneiform mathematics, see §II.2.5. Because of damage to obv. 25–27, however, we are uncertain how the commentator proceeded to prove his claims. One possible interpretation would involve wordplay between "death" (*mūtu*) and the "husband" (*mutu*) who mounts his wife. As a matter of fact, several have already posited such wordplay for the myth of *Nergal and Ereshkigal*, where Ereshkigal, who expresses her intention to kill Nergal, ends up as his spouse. See, for example, Bottéro and Kramer (1989: 458); Dalley (1989: 181 note 2); Izre'el (1997: 57 note 27). I would suggest that this wordplay was operative also in literary tropes involving "death" in the bedroom: *mūtu ina bēt eršēya iḫlula ḫillūtu* ("then to our bedroom stealthy Death did creep"; K 890, rev. 20) in *Elegy for a Woman Who Died in Childbirth*, translated by George (2010: 211, 213); *ina bīt mayyālīya ašib mūtu* ("in my bed-chamber Death does abide") in *Epic of Gilgamesh* XI, 245 (George 2003: 718). For possibly the opposite situation where the woman does the mounting, see [DIŠ ... D]AM-*sà ir-kab* (K 9169, line 9′) in Oppenheim (1969: 157). An alternative interpretation might be to compare the donkey to the deadly *Anzû*-bird, as in the case of Comm. Sa-gig 7A, rev. 12–13: "Death is complement to ^{d}IM.DUGUD.MUŠEN, (*which means*) *Anzû*-bird, *which sounds like* anšû (𒀲), *which is the sign name for* donkey (ANŠE)."

Lines 28–29—// Comm. Sa-gig 1B, rev. 10 // Comm. Sa-gig 1C, rev. 3′ // Comm. Sa-gig 1D, rev. 1′–4′. The commentator extended the divinatory significance of a kicking donkey to include stormy weather as well, based on one of the names of the storm-god Adad (^{d}Ud-dè-anše), which seems to involve the element ANŠE ("donkey"). ^{d}Ud-dè-x forms of Adad's name appear in the lexical list An = *Anum* III, 224–227 (Litke 1998: 141). For the suggestion that ANŠE here is a "pun" on UG (= *ūmu* "storm"), see Lambert's note in Durand (1979: 170). Another link to the storm-god is not as explicitly stated: the verb *raḫāṣu*, which denotes the donkey's action of "kicking," is also very frequently used to describe "devastation" caused by the floods of the storm-god (*CAD* R, 69–72).

Lines 29–32—// Comm. Sa-gig 1B, rev. 13–17 // Comm. Sa-gig 1C, rev. 4′ // Comm. Sa-gig 1D, rev. 4′–6′. The commentator's intention here was to explain the omen about a "prowling god" (Sa-gig S1: 30 (U1: 37a)), so that it referred not only to some invisible divine or demonic being, but also to beings that are more readily observable, such as cultic persons and perhaps star constellations. A detailed explanation of the divine and human beings mentioned in lines 29–32 is provided by George (1991: 158–160). It is not entirely clear that Urgula in this commentary refers to the constellation Leo (i.e., the prowling lion), instead of an actual lion or even a person afflicted with a certain disease (*CAD* U/W, 216 s.v. *urgulû* §2). Although an astral context is more definite for the parallel entry in Comm. Sa-gig 1B (rev. 15, 17) and perhaps also 1C (rev. 4′), Urgula there is identified with Latarak in accordance with the lexical entry Hg. A I, 203 (Vedeler 2002: 45; listed as Hg. B II, 194 in *MSL* VI, 143 without actual attestation in recension B), and Latarak is not unambiguously synonymous with Leo in astronomical contexts. Nonetheless, if the "seeing" of star constellations is taken at face value, it provides indirect evidence of at least some instances of night visits to the patient made by the healer. George (1991: 158) connects the "knot of Narudu" (lines 31–32) to "a ritual in which the *kurgarrû* and *assinnu* tie on (*rakāsu*) a head-gear of the goddess Narudu as part of a cultic performance (*RAcc.* p. 115, 7; cf. *LKU* 51, obv. 18; the head-gear is a *tillû*, 'sash', which may have been used as a mask: so *CAD* A/2, p. 341; K, p. 558)." The Neo-/Late Babylonian sign in line 31 resembles kéš rather than sar, and the Akkadian *rikis* ("knot"; line 32) certainly reflects the logogram KÉŠ. On the other hand, note the equation lú sar-da = *ma-ḫu-ú-um* in lexical text OB Lu, C_3 line 14 (*MSL* XII, 194), as well as the writing munus-mú(sar)-da in Charpin (1983/1984: 107); Sommerfeld (1985: 506). It is possible that the similar signs kéš and sar were confused at some point. George (1991: 150) enclosed the disjunction sign of lú-^{giš}kéš-da : nin-nun-gal-e-ne within curly brackets {}. As I argue in §II.2.1.3, however, this disjunction sign may actually play a role in clarifying the syntax of this long expression, grouping together the signs lú-^{giš}kéš-da ("man-of-the-knot") as a reference to the "ecstatic" (*maḫḫû*), a profession closely related to the "shaman" (*eššebû*; line 31).

Lines 32–34—// Comm. Sa-gig 1B, rev. 10–11 // Comm. Sa-gig 1D, rev. 7′–9′. The quotation in lines 33–34 resembles a section in the lexical list Erimhuš III,

169–172 (*MSL* XVII, 51): [lú]gub-b[a-ra] = *mu-[u]ḫ̮-ḫ̮u-[ú]*, ní-zu-ra-⸢aḫ̮⸣ = *zab-b[u]*, kur-[gar-r]a = *kur-ga-ru-u*, [lú]an-sal-la(!) = *as-sin-nu*. For Ninurta's name [d]Lugal-i-bí-gub-ba (line 33), see note by Lambert in Durand (1979: 170). George (1991: 160) examined the variations between Erimhuš and this commentary. Peled (2014: 283–297) argued that *assinnu* denoted an effeminate figure in contrast to the masculine *kurgarrû*.

Lines 35–38—// Comm. Sa-gig 1B, rev. 20–21 // Comm. Sa-gig 1D, rev. 9′–13′. The quotation in lines 35–36 evidently comes from a horoscope related to *TCL* VI, 14 = AO 6483, rev. 32 (Sachs 1952: 67): [mul]UD.KA.DU$_8$.A *È-a uq-qú-uq* : *su-ku-uk*. See comments in George (1991: 160). The name [mul]UD.KA.DU$_8$.A is explained as "the roaring storm" (*u$_4$-mu na-ʾ-ri*), according to the analysis UD ("storm"; *CAD* U/W, 153–154 s.v. *ūmu* §2a–d) + KA.DU$_8$.A ("mouth spread open") in the *List of Stars and Deities* (5*R* 46 No. 1, line 43 in Wee 2016a: 162–163, 166 note xviii). In the cited horoscope and in this commentary, however, the name seems to have been analyzed as ka ("speech") + DU$_8$.A ("spread out," i.e., "dispersed"), and hence related to muteness and deafness. Cygnus is associated with the god Nergal in the astral composition Mul-apin I, i 28 (Hunger and Steele 2019: 35; cf. Hunger and Pingree 1989: 26, 138). I follow George's restoration of B[A.RA BÙ]R(!).MEŠ(!) at the end of line 36, though these signs are difficult to make out in Durand's hand copy (*TBER*, 57), and completely worn away on the tablet itself. The quotations in lines 36–38 are from the omen series *Šumma izbu* IV, 38 and its *Principal Commentary*. See Leichty (1970: 70, 216, line 140); De Zorzi (2014: 440, line 15; 446, IV 38). Similar associations are also attested in the lexical text Erimhuš V, 21–22 (*MSL* XVII, 67): dur-giš-lam-ma = *dur-giš-lam*, nibru[ki] = *ni-ip-pu-ru-ú*. Though "the significance of the name of Nippur *Durgišlam* (Sum. Dur-gišlam) in respect of Nergal is unknown" (George 1991: 160), it is possible that Nippur's downfall here was imagined in connection with the destruction of cities by the god Erra (identified with Nergal) described in the *Erra Epic*. See, for instance, the claim that "Ešarra (Enlil's temple at Nippur) is at your (Erra's) disposal" (*Erra Epic* IIID, 7 in Cagni 1969: 102–103).

Lines 38–40—// Comm. Sa-gig 1B, rev. 17–19 // Comm. Sa-gig 1C, rev. 6′ // Comm. Sa-gig 1D, rev. 13′–14′. Hallo (1969: 66–70) interpreted the Sumerian Proverb 1.66 ("in the city of the lame (AD$_4$), the halt (BA.ZA) is courier") as a version of the saying *luscus praefertur caeco, sic undique fertur* ("Better one-eyed than entirely blind"), whereby AD$_4$ denotes a condition of the legs more severe than BA.ZA. He thought that commentary explanations of BA.AN.ZA as "short" (*kurû*) mean "with one leg shorter than the other"; *contra* the translation "In the city of cripples, the dwarf is the runner" (*PSD* B, 22). See also Hallo (1990: 207) and various publications by Alster (1995:

1–6), (1997: 18, 347–348), (2005: 325), and (2006: 56, Proverb i 17). Admittedly, stunted legs are a feature of dwarfism, but the term BA.AN.ZA also appears outside the context of proverbs to denote more general conditions of dwarfism (e.g., ḪAŠḪUR BA.ZA, "dwarf apple tree"). See Couto-Ferreira (2009: 359–360). Interestingly, the term *ḫuzzû* ("lame (man)"), employed as comment in Comm. Sa-gig 1–3, obv. 19, appears in none of the four commentaries above (Comm. Sa-gig 1A–D). Instead, the key to the logic here is most explicitly expressed in Comm. Sa-gig 1B, rev. 18: "BA.AN *means* half." In other words, the element BA.AN in ^{lu_2}BA.AN.ZU was interpreted as a reference to the sign bán with its logographic value MAŠ "half." ^{lu_2}BA.AN.ZU therefore depicts a "stunted" man whose stature is "half" (bán) that of a normal "man" (ZA), or a "half-witted" man who has only "half" (bán) his "wits" (ZU). For the meaning of ZA as "man," see lexical texts S^b I, 7 (*MSL* III, 96); Ea I, 20 (*MSL* XIV); za = *a-me-lu* eme-suḫ-a (V.A.Th. 244, iv 3 in Reisner 1894: 163); [$^{za-a}$ z]a = ⸢*a*⸣-*me*-[*lu*] = [ζ]α α[υελ(?)] (BM 34781 + 35154, obv. 7 in Geller 1997: 74). The entry BA.AN.ZA || *pe-es-su-u* // *ku-ru-u* appears also in the *Principal Commentary to Izbu* I, 54 (Leichty 1970: 212, line 23; De Zorzi 2014: 340, line 23) without further explication, and one wonders if the logic here was applicable there as well. In what may be a graphic argument (Comm. Sa-gig 18, rev. 6′), the commensurable forms *bamat* ("half") and 1-*át* ("one") are juxtaposed, so that the element *bam-* (interpreted as bán, 𒑏) would therefore appear visually as a bisected form of the written symbol 1 (𒁹).

Line 41—// Comm. Sa-gig 1D, rev. 15′–16′. George (1991: 151) understood this line as: "'If his right [arm] hurts him'—the reference is to a sharp pain; alternatively, ['If] the exorcist's right arm begins to hurt him.'" Even without specifying whose "right arm" it is, however, the natural assumption is that it belongs to the KA.PIRIG-healer (i.e., "magician / exorcist"), and not the sick man. Omens in Sa-gig Tablet 1 all occur en route to the sick man's house, and the sick man has not yet been encountered. Thus, the first mention of the "right [arm]" already refers to the healer's own body part. Furthermore, it seems awkward to translate the syntax of 15-*šú ana* ^{lu_2}MAŠ.MAŠ (line 41) as "the exorcist's right arm." There are several clues that the crux of interpretation here lies with the verb *zaqātu*. First is the comment *šá zi-iq-*tu_4 ("the case of a stinging pain") that does little more than employ a cognate form of the topic *iz-qut-su* ("stings him"). Second is the writing *i-zaq-qí-*⸢*tú*⸣, which deviates from the expected Durative form *izaqqatu*. In my translation, I understand the form *zaqātu* as also having the meaning "to point," likely related to its usual meaning "to sting" (i.e., "to jab with a point"). Note the entry *zaqātu* II "spitzig sein, spitz zulaufen" (*AHw*, 1513), though this meaning is only attested in Stative or Infinitive verb forms. The meaning "to point" is also evident in the adjective *zaqtu* ("pointed"; *CAD* Z, 63–64), which can describe weapons, teeth, horns, and barbs. This interpretation explains the value of the cognate noun *ziqtu*, which typically takes meanings involving "stinging," as a means to differentiate between *zaqātu* ("to sting"; see examples in Salin 2017: 36–39) and *zaqātu* ("to point"). The atypical theme vowel in *izaqqit* (instead of *izaqqat*) may suggest some confusion with the Stative *zaqit*, or reflect the poor attestation of the meaning "to point" (*zaqātu*) elsewhere in the Durative form. I translate the statement ⸢*šá*⸣ [Á] 15-*šú ana* ^{lu_2}MAŠ.MAŠ *i-zaq-qí-*⸢*tú*⸣ as "the case where (some)one's right [arm] points at the magician." Notice that the commentator Enlil-bēlšunu referred to the "magician" healer of Sa-gig as *āšipu* in obv. 1 and as ^{lu_2}MAŠ.MAŠ here, suggesting that the two forms were interchangeable in his view.

Lines 42–43—// Comm. Sa-gig 1B, rev. 23–25 (main Note) // Comm. Sa-gig 1C, rev. 9′ on the visual argument that Dilibat (Venus) is contained within the constellation Chariot (𒇀), by considering its inner contents either as the sign aš(𒀸)-*tenû* whose non-*tenû* portion is the syllable sign *dili* that alludes to Dilibat, or as a "single" (DILI) cuneiform sign bat (𒁁) that once again refers to Dilibat.

Lines 43–44—The idea of defining "chariot"-like vehicles by the status of their passengers may have been inspired by assonantal links between *narkabtu* "chariot" and *kabtu* "the honored, dignitary."

Line 46—The logographic element transliterated as KÚNGA in George (1991: 152, §49a) corresponds to KUNGA(šú.mul) in *MZL*, no. 872.

Line 47—It is probable that the title of the Diagnostic Handbook Sa-gig originally expressed similar meanings as the term *sakikku* ("medical sign" or "symptom"; logogram SA.GIG). Commentators, however, often alluded to the definition of Sa-gig provided by Esagil-kīn-apli (chief scholar and editor of Sa-gig) in his Manifesto: "Sa-gig is a compilation of sickness (*rikis* GIG) and a compilation of distress" (lines A 65–66, B 28′ in Finkel 1988: 148; cf. Wee 2015a: 251–255). In order to make the title SA.GIG conform to this definition as a compilation of "all sickness," its components were analyzed as SA + GIG ("sickness"), with the element SA interpreted as *riksu* ("binding, bundling together, compilation") or "all" (*napḫaru, kiššatu*). The interpretation relied on an artful semantic shift from the literal meaning of the logogram SA ("strands"), to the idea of "bundling together" (i.e., "strand-ing," behaving as strands do), to the notion that diverse items were bundled together in a comprehensive group (i.e., "all"). In addition to this commentary entry, see Comm. Sa-gig 5, lines 33–34; Comm. Sa-gig 36, rev. 9′. Some commentaries take this meaning of SA ("all") yet another step further, by extending it to situations involving actual body parts such as "all (SA) of his temple"

(Comm. Sa-gig 4A, obv. 5) and "all (SA) of his feet" (*SpTU* 1, 84 obv. 19). For more discussion on Esagil-kīn-apli and his status in later times as scribal ancestor of the magician (*āšipu*) profession, see §1.1.2.1–2.

Line 51—Enlil-bēlšunu appears in documents dated to 424–410 BCE. See Joannès (1992: 89 n. 20); Jursa (2005: 111) in Frahm (2011a: 221 n. 1033). Instead of the reading ^{lu_2}MAŠ.MAŠ [TUR (?)] ⸢A-*šú šá* ^{m}*na*(?)⸣-*ṣir* ("[*junior*] exorcist, son of Nāṣir") by George (1991: 152, Colophon a), I read ^{lu_2}MAŠ.MAŠ [A $^{m.d}$]⸢*Nin-urta-na*⸣-*ṣir* ("the magician/exorcist, [son] of Ninurta-nāṣir") as suggested in Frahm (2011a: 221, 303).

Line 52—George (1991: 162) argued that "by these late scribes the adjective *Šumerû* was employed as a learned term for 'the Nippurian.'" In the same vein, a therapeutic commentary from Nippur mentions "^{m}lú-dumu-nun-na the Sumerian" (11N-T3, line 55 in Civil 1974: 333).

Commentary Sa-gig 1B

Provenance:	Uruk (Warka), Area U18, Level v; Same findspot and consignment (W 22307) as Comm. Sa-gig 1C, 5, 7A, 7B, and 19 suggests library of Anu-ikṣur
Period:	Late Achaemenid
Names:	Colophon not preserved
Script:	Neo-/Late Babylonian
Field/Museum No.:	W 22307/6 = IM 74357 (National Museum of Iraq)
Photos:	Plate 3 (obverse), Plate 4 (reverse), Plate 5a (bottom edge), and Plate 5b (right edge)
Printed Edition/Hand Copy:	*SpTU* I, 27 (= Hunger 1976: 34–37); George (1991: 137–163, MS b); Wee (2012: 515–532)
Digital Resources:	CDLI P348448; GKAB P348448 (edition digitized by Clancier 2009); CCP 4.1.1.B (printed hand copies digitized by Frahm, Frazer, and Jiménez 2013)
Discussion:	*SpTU* I, 27 (= Hunger 1976: 34–37); Schramm (1979: 123); Cavigneaux (1982: 231–240); Powell (1987: 483–484); George (1991: 137–163, MS b) and (2013: 62); Finkel (*NABU* 1993/15) and (2014a: 311–312); Wiggermann (1993: 235) and (2000: 236–238); Streck (1999: 51); Heeßel (2000: 132, 139 (1. Tafel MS b)); Frahm (1999: 79 n. 30), (2002: 85–86), (2010c: 171), and (2011a: 38, 80–81, 92–93, 95–98, 103–104, 109, 221–223, 233, 291, 303); Bilbija (2008: 20–21 n. 7); Geller (2010a: 141–144); Genty (2010a: 368); Weszeli (2011: 100); Wee (2012: 515–532), (2014a: 29 n. 48), (2015a: 281–282), and (2016b: 149–150, 200 n. 166); Gabbay (2012: 289–290), (2014: 339), (2016: 342–343, see references to George 1991 MS b), and (2017: 77–79); Steinert (2017: 300–301 n. 50)
Pericope:	At least Sa-gig U1: 2–42b

 | DOI:10.1163/9789004417564_003

Transliteration

Obverse

1′) [...] ⸢x *na mu* x x x⸣ [...]

2′) [...] *ú-pat-tíq* ^{d}*É-a pa-ḫa-r*[*u-ma*]

3′) [*it-te-eḫ-pi k*]*ar-pat ḫa-ṣa-bu-um-ma im-tu-ut* LÚ *e-ṣi-*⸢*id*(?)⸣ [...]

4′) [...] *i-de* ALAM *ṭi-ṭi* LÚ-*ut-tì* : *ṭi-iṭ-ṭi ik-t*[*a-ri-iṣ*]

5′) [*it-ta-d*]*i i-na* EDIN : *i-na* EDIN $^{m.d+}$*En-ki-dù ib-ta-n*[*i qu-ra-du*]

6′) [KI.UD.BA : *a-ša*]*r* SISKUR$_2$ GABA.RI : KI.UD.BA : *a-šar te-b*[*i-ib-ti*]

7′) [tam-(ma ?) : t]am-ma : tam-tam-ma : *ta-lim* : *qa-a-pi te-bi-i*[*b-ti*]

8′) [*ina* KI.UD.BA-*šú* K]AŠ.SAG NIDBA DINGIR.MEŠ GAL.MEŠ *uq-ta-*[*rab*]

9′) [*šá ina* NAM.E]RIM$_2$.BÚR.RU.DA : NAM.ERIM$_2$ *mál i-na* SA.GI[G]

10′) [E-*ú* : *ú*]-*za-bal-ma i-kaš-ma* : *zu-ub-bu-lu* : *ka-a-ša lìb-bu-ú*

11′) [*i-kab-bi-i*]*t-ma* : gá-gá : *za-ba-lu šá* ⸢*mur-ṣu*⸣ : ŠU.SI 15-*šú* GAL-*ti ik-kip*

12′) [U : *ú-ba*]-*nu* : U : *qa-ab-ru* : DIŠ ⸢ŠÁḪ GE$_6$⸣ IGI GIG BI ÚŠ *šá-niš uš-ta-pa-šaq-ma* TIN

13′) [$^{šu-ul}$ šáḫ] : *dan-nu* : ŠUL : ^{lu_2}GURUŠ : ŠÁḪ [: (?)] *šá-ḫu-u* : šáḫ : *le-e-bu*

14′) [*lìb-bu-u*] DIŠ ŠÁḪ *ana qé-re-eb* ⸢*ur-ši* KU$_4$-*ub*⸣ *a-si-ir-ti* [*ana*] É EN-*šú* ⸢KU$_4$⸣-*ub*

15′) [*šá ina* DIŠ URU] *ina* SUKUD-*e* GAR-*in a-si-ir-ti šá* E-*ú e-sér* ^{lu_2}GIG

16′) [*ki-i* ^{lu_2}GI]G ^{munus}KALA.GA IGI TIN *ki-i* ^{munus}KA[LA.G]A NU IGI BA.ÚŠ *šá-niš ki-i*

17′) [GIG *na-qu-d*]*u a-na* 3 U$_4$-*mu* ⸢*ki-i*⸣ *la na-*[*a*]*q-du ana* ITI 3 ÚŠ : DIŠ ŠÁḪ GÙN IGI *šá* E-*ú*

18′) [šáḫ-z]é-da-s[ur-ra :] *bu-ri-ia-a-mu šá zu-mur-šú ki-ma ṭi-me uṣ-ṣu-ru*

19′) [*a-ga-nu*]-*til-*⸢*la*⸣-*a* ⸢*ár-kát la*⸣ *ba-še-e* : *a-ga-n*[*u-ti*]*l-la-a* : *šá ár-kat-su la* TIN

20′) [*a-ga-nu-ti*]*l-la-a ma-ak-*⸢*kur* DINGIR.MEŠ⸣ *la qa-a-tu-u* : A : *me-e*

21′) [Í]L : *ḫa-bu-ú* ⸢*šá*⸣ A.MEŠ ⸢: *šá* NÍG.GA (?)⸣ : *ma-ak-kur šá-niš* ÍL : *na-šú-u*

22′) [x x x x] : x x [x] x x x *za-bil me-e šá me-e a-na ḫa-bé-e*

23′) [x x x]x x-*ta*(?)-*šá* ⸢x :⸣ DIŠ GU$_4$ BABBAR IGI GIG BI ŠU!(ma) ^{d}MAŠ : *ina ú-re-e* GU$_4$

24′) ⸢^{d}*Nin-urta im-ri u-ta-ra* (?)⸣ NÍG.GIG ^{d}*Nin*(!)-*urta* GU$_4$ GÙN IGI GIG BI

25′) [^{d}DÌM.M]E DAB-*s*[*u* :] ⸢^{d}DÌM⸣.ME : *um-mu* D[UMU.MU]NUS ^{d}60 : ME : *um-mu*

26′) [*ina* NAM.ERIM$_2$]-*šá* (?) BA.ÚŠ : NA[M :] *mu-u-tu*$_4$: ERIM$_2$: *rag-gu* $^{ḫe\text{-}pí_2}$

27′) [*mu-ut r*]*ag-gu* BA.ÚŠ : GÙN : *ba-ra-mu šá* E-[*ú*] *ki-ma nim-ri tuk-ku*(!)-*pa*

28′) [ELLAG$_2$.MEŠ-*šá* :] ^{d}DÌM.ME.MEŠ giš-ḫur : sag-ba(!) : sag(!)-dingir

29′) [mu-dingir-ra : *i-siq*(?)-*t*]*u*(?) [: *m*]*a-*[*mi-t*]*ú* ⸢*ḫur-šá*⸣-*an* : *ni-iš* DINGIR.MEŠ

30′) [...] x SI : *ru-pu-uš-ti*

Reverse

1) [...] *šu-ú-ru* : ^{giš}APIN

2) [... IGI.ḪU]Š(?) *né-kel-mu-u* : IGI : *i-ni*

3) [HUŠ : *ez-zu* (?) ... IG]I.ÍL : *né-kel-mu-u* : *šá in-šú*

4) [... *a-ḫ*]*a*(?)*-a iš-šu-*⸢*ku*(?) : *né-kel-mu-u*⸣ : *a-ma-ri šá ze-e-e-ri*

5) [DIŠ GU$_4$ *ik-ki*]*p-šú* GIG BI *na-qud* NU TE-*šú šá iq-bu-ú ina* ŠÀ *šá* GU$_4$: *al-pi* : GU$_4$: *e-ṭém-mu*

6) [DIŠ SI GU$_4$ IG]I GIG BI ÚŠ : SI : *qar-nu* : SI : *nu-úr* : SI : *šá-ru-ru*

7) [*lìb-bu*]-⸢*ú*⸣ *šá-ru-ru-šú im-qu-tu* : ANŠE EME$_3$ U$_5$*-ma* IGI GIG BI

8) [*mu-tú*] *u šu-ú ik-tap-pi-lu* : la-ga : ANŠE : la-ga : *la nap-ṭu-*[*r*]*u* :

9) [*kit-pu-lu pa*]*-ni* ANŠE *šá-niš pa-ni* MUŠ ŠU DAM NA *lìb-bu-ú a-na* DAM NA TE-*ḫe*

10) [ANŠE RA-*s*]*u* : ANŠE *ir-ḫi-is-su* : RA : *ma-ḫa-ṣu* : *maḫ-ḫa-a* IGI ŠU ^{d}*Nin-urta*

11) [$^{\text{lu}_2}$GUB.B]A : *maḫ-ḫu-u* : ^{d}Lugal-ba-$^{\text{gu-ub}}$gub$_4$-ba : ^{d}*Nin-urta* : NAM.TAR : *mur-ṣu šá-niš* NAM.TAR

12) [*mu-tú* (?) : ^{t}]$^{\text{ug}_2}$NÍG.DARA$_2$ ŠU.LÁL : *ú-la-a-pa su-u-nu* : NÍG.DARA$_2$: *ú-la-pa* : ŠU : *ú-ba-nu*

13) [LÁL : *ka-m*]*u-u* : ⸢ù⸣-ma : ù-na : igi-ḫuš : DINGIR *saḫ-ḫi-ra* : ^{d}*Gaz-ba-ba*

14) [...] x *še-e-ḫu* bad é me : *ina* GAŠAN-*ia*$_5$(mu) ^{d}ZUEN ^{d}INNIN ⟨É⟩.AN.NA

15) [*u* ^{d}*Gaz-ba*]*-ba iq-ta-bi šá-niš* ^{d}*La-ta-ra-*⸢*ak*⸣*-a šal-šiš* ^{d}*Un-na-ni-ši*

16) [^{d}MAR.TU ^{d}]MAŠ.TAB.BA *šá* E-*ú* : ^{mul}MAŠ.TAB.BA *šá* IGI-*et* ^{mul}SIPA.ZI.AN.NA

17) [GUB.MEŠ-*z*]*u* ^{d}LÚ.LÀL *u* ^{d}*La-ta-ra-ak-a* : $^{\text{lu}_2}$BA.AN.ZA IGI ŠU ^{d}*Nin-urta*

18) [BA.AN.ZA : *p*]*e-su-u* : *ku-ru-u* : BA.AN.ZA : BA.AN : *mi-šil*

19) [ZA : *a-m*]*e-lu* : ^{d}*Šad-da-ri* : ^{d}*Nin-urta* : *šá-da-ri* : *mi-šil*

20) [DIŠ *suk-ku-k*]*u* IGI : ŠU ^{d}U.GUR : KI ^{mul}UD.KA.DU$_8$.A Ù.TU *uq-qu-uq*

21) [*suk-ku-k*]*u* : DIŠ SIG$_4$.AL.ÙR.RA IGI GIG ÚŠ : SAG.UŠ *šá-niš* LÚ *š*[*á ina ḫur-šá-a*]*n i-tu-ra*

22) [A : *me-e*] : GUR : *ta-a-*⸢*ra šal*⸣*-šiš* MUNUS.PEŠ$_4$: A : *ma-ru* : $^{\text{ki-ir}}$gu[r$_4$(KÌR) : *ka-ra-ṣ*]*a*

23) [*šá-niš*] ⸢A⸣ : *ma-ri* : *gur* : *na-šú-u* ⸢:⸣ DIŠ ^{giš}GIGIR IGI GIG BI ŠU ^{d}*Iš*$_8$*-tá*[*r* : ^{giš}GIGIR]

24) [*nar-kab-t*]*u*$_4$: $^{\text{mul.giš}}$GIGIR : ^{d}*Dili-bat* : ^{MIN} GIGIR : *nar-kab-tu*$_4$: x[...]

25) [^{d}]⸢15⸣ MUL.MEŠ : ^{MIN} GIGIR : *nar-kab-tu*$_4$: *ú-bu-u* : *di-l*[*i* : ^{d}*Dili-bat*]

26) [*šá-niš* Ú].BU : BÁN 3 SILA$_3$: Ú.BU : 15 : ^{d}15 : ^{giš}GAG.SI.[LÁ : ^{giš}GAG]

27) [*šu-kur*]*-ri* : *si* : *a-gal-lu*$_4$: L[Á :] *ra-ka-su* : ^{giš}M[AR.GÍD.DA : *e-riq-qu*]

28) [*šá-niš a-r*]*i-ik-tu*$_4$ *šá maḫ-rat-su*(!) ^{giš}GIGIR *ù* EGIR-*su* x[...]

29) [...]x $^{\text{ḫe-pi}_2}$ *šá* 1-*en ú-ma-ma* ⸢*ṣa*⸣-[*an-du* ...]

30) [... $^{\text{ḫe-pi}_2}$ ^{e}]$^{\text{š-šu}_2}$ *i-g*[*ab-* ...]

Translation

***Incipit-Title of Sa-gig 1**

(Obv. 1) ["Whenever the KA.PIRIG-healer goes to the sick man's house."] ...

(1′–2′) ...

***Sa-gig U1: 2 (S1: 2)**

(2′) "Ea the potter moulded."

Several literary quotations here reflect the tradition that man was fashioned from clay, thus supporting the omen's reasoning that the integrity of a clay pot is symbolic of man's wellbeing. "Pot [has been broken] ..." is cited from a compilation of bilingual proverbs.

(3′) "Pot [has been broken] into potsherd, and Man has died."

(3′) "The harvester(?) of ...
(4′) knows ... a clay figure of humankind."

This quotation is from *Gilgamesh* I, 102–103.

(4′–5′) "She pinched off clay (and) [threw it] down into the steppe. In the steppe, she created [the hero] Enkidu."

Sa-gig U1: 3 (S1: 3)

KI.UD.BA is a cultic installation.

(6′) ["KI.UD.BA" *means*] place of sacrificial offering.

KI.UD.BA is analyzed as a "place" (KI) of "cleansing" (ud).

(6′) That is, "KI.UD.BA" *means* place of cleansing.

This quote from a version of lexical text Erimhuš I, a29–31, shows that "cleansing" can be expressed by tam (same sign as ud), and that KI.UD.BA also denotes the "place" (KI) of a "close brother" or "trust."

(7′) "[tam-(ma ?)], tam-ma, *and* tam-tam-ma *mean* close brother, to entrust, *and* cleansing *respectively*."

This quotation from Nam-erim$_2$-búr-ru-da supports the omen in Sa-gig U1: 3 (S1: 3) that KI.UD.BA implies an "oath-curse" (NAM.ERIM$_2$) has seized the sick man.

(8′–10′) "[On his KI.UD.BA], premium beer, the meal-offering of the great gods has been brought near," [which it said in] Nam-erim$_2$-búr-ru-da (Incantations to Undo

Oath-Curses), *concerning* any oath-curse in the Diagnostic Handbook Sa-gig.

Sa-gig U1: 3 (S1: 3)
The basic meaning of *zubbulu* is "to carry, deliver," and the commentator felt the need to clarify its derived nuance "to carry on," i.e., "to tarry on" in the context of sickness.

(10′) "It will carry on" (*means*) it will tarry on.
(10′) To carry on *means* to tarry on.

Since gá-gá denotes both *kabātu* "to become severe" and *zabālu* "to carry," a sickness described as *zubbulu* "carries on" due to its "severity."

(10′–11′) As in the fact that [it will become severe] *means* gá-gá, *which means* to carry (on), in the case of sickness.

Sa-gig U1: 4 (S1: 42)
The shared logogram U connects "finger" and "grave," thus supporting the omen's prediction that a stubbed thumb portends death.

(11′) "He stubs his right thumb."

(12′) [U *means*] finger.
(12′) U *means* grave.

Sa-gig U1: 9 (S1: 6)

(12′) "If he sees a black pig (ŠÁḪ), that sick man will die. Secondly, he will get into dire straits, and he will live."

ŠÁḪ "pig" (𒂄) is the same sign as ŠUL "youth" (𒂄), which has the same meaning as another logogram GURUŠ "youth" (𒆗), which is the same sign as KALA "hard" (𒆗).

(13′) [The cuneiform sign šáḫ as the logogram ŠUL] *means* hard (KALA),
(13′) (since) ŠUL *means* youth (GURUŠ).

The "pig" as an omen of what is "hard" more properly reflects the diagnosis "hardship will seize him" in the next base text entry Sa-gig U1: 10 (S1: 7) on the white pig. The commentator was concerned only with the meaning of "pig" (ŠÁḪ), without regard for its color.

Also, the "hardship" suffered takes the form of SUL "*li'bu*-sickness" (the same sign as ŠUL and ŠÁḪ).

(13′) ŠÁḪ *means* "pig."
(13′) šáḫ (as the logogram SUL) *refers to li'bu*-sickness.

Quotation from *Šumma ālu* XLIX, 41′ may suggest that "pig" and "female captive" had the same divinatory significance, but more likely validates the link between "pig" and the prognosis of "dire straits."

(14′) [As in,] "If a pig enters into the interior of the bedroom, a female captive will enter [into] her master's house,"

(15′) [which (it said) in (the terrestrial omen series) *If a City*] *is Situated on a Height.*

The idea of being held "captive" portended the sick man's "confinement (to the bed)," which represented the commentator's interpretation of the prognosis "he will get into dire *straits*" in the base text Sa-gig U1: 9 (S1: 6).

(15′) The female captive, which it said, (*refers to*) the sick man's confinement.

***Sa-gig U1: 10 (S1: 7)—"that sick man will become healthy : hardship will seize him"**
These variants were not treated as alternative prognoses, but alternative descriptions of the same situation, i.e., for the sick man to become healthy is to be seized by hardship.

(16′) [If] the sick man sees hardship, he will become healthy. If he does not see hardship, he will die.

***Sa-gig U1: 11 (S1: 8)—"that sick man will die in three months : in three days"**
A different approach was adopted for these variants, both of which were considered valid in limited and mutually exclusive situations: Death "in three days" applied to those who

(16′–17′) Secondly, "if [the sick man] is critically sick, he will die in three days. If he is not critically sick, in three months."

were critically sick, while death in three months concerned those not critically sick.

Sa-gig U1: 12 (S1: 9)
This omen applies also to the *buriyāmu*-pig, whose name is a cognate of the word "dappled" (*burrumu*).

(17′) "If he sees a dappled pig," which it said,
(18′) šáḫ-zé-da-sur-ra [*means*] a *buriyāmu*-pig, whose body is patterned like yarn.

Sa-gig U1: 12 (S1: 9)
aganutillâ is analyzed as the logograms A.GA "future" + NU "without" + TIL "existence."

(19′) "*aganutillâ*-sickness" (*means*) a future without existence.

aganutillâ is analyzed as the logograms A.GA "future" + NU "without" + TI.LA "life."

(19′) "*aganutillâ*-sickness" *means* one whose future is without life.

aganutillâ is analyzed as the logograms A.GA "gods' property" + NU "without" + TIL "completion."

(20′) "*aganutillâ*-sickness" (*means*) the gods' property without completion.

The following argument shows that A.GA can substitute for NÍG. GA "property," when this property pertains to the gods.

(20′) A *means* water.

The two verbs below can be equated due to their homophony (/*ḫabu*/), and because both are expressed by the same logogram ÍL "to raise":

(21′) ÍL *means* /*ḫabu*/

ḫabû means "to draw up (i.e., raise) water."

(21′) in the case of water,

ḫâbu means "to consecrate" (i.e., raise in consecration) the gods' property.

(21′) *or* in the case of NÍG.GA (?), *which means* property.

Thus, "water" (logogram A) can replace "thing" (logogram NÍG) when the property indicated by NÍG.GA belongs to the gods, so that the resulting form A.GA means "gods' property."

Whatever the other functions of ÍL, the commentator may also have attempted a link to the following omen in Sa-gig U1: 13 (S1: 10) on pigs "raising" their tails.

(21′) Secondly, ÍL *means* to raise.
(22′–23′) ... water-bearer, who to draw water ...

Sa-gig U1: 15 (S1: 13)
The following quotation is not certain, but it seems intended to support the omen's connection of "ox" and "Ninurta."

(23′) "If he sees a white ox, that sick man (suffers from) Hand of the god Ninurta."

There may be a play on the signs MUR.GU$_4$ ("fodder") as UR$_5$(mur) GU$_4$ ("oracle of ox").

(23′–24′) "In the ox's stall, [the god Ninurta replenishes the fodder (?)]," (*which refers to*) a taboo of Ninurta.

Sa-gig U1: 18 (S1: 15)

(24′–25′) "(If) he sees a dappled ox, [the *lamaštu*-demoness] has seized that sick man."

"Daughter of the god Anu" refers to the "*lamaštu*-demoness" (^{d}DÌM.ME), the element ME of whose name was identified with "heat" according to the lexical text Izi E, 11.

(25′) "The *lamaštu*-demoness" *refers to* heat,

(25′) (*or*) daughter of the god Anu,

(25′) *or* ME, *which means* heat.

***Sa-gig U1: 18 (S1: 15)**

(26′) "He will die [by her oath-curse (?)]."

NAM.ERIM$_2$ "oath-curse" is analyzed as NAM "death" + ERIM$_2$ "wicked."

(26′) NAM [*means*] death.
(26′) ERIM$_2$ *means* wicked. *break*

(27′) He will die [the death of] the wicked.

Sa-gig U1: 18 (S1: 15)
This quote from the *Lamaštu* Incantation Series II, 37 validates the omen that links the "dappled" ox with the *lamaštu*-demoness and her "spotted" lateral parts.

(27′) "GÙN" *means* to become dappled.

(27′–28′) (According to) that which it said:
"[Her lateral parts (lit. kidneys)] are spotted like a leopard."

This quote from the lexical text Erimhuš VI, 80–83 extends the omen's applicability by listing other items or events that may be associated with the *lamaštu*-demoness.

(28′–29′) *Lamaštu*-demonesses (*refer to*) "giš-ḫur, sag-ba, sag-dingir, (*and*) [mu-dingir-ra], [*which mean* engraved pattern(?),] oath-(curse), river ordeal, *and* (oath by) the gods' life *respectively*."

Sa-gig U1: 19 (S1: 16)—"he sees an ox throw its horn"
SI is the logogram for "horn" and "drool," so this omen also applies to the case where an ox throws up drool.

(30′) ... "SI" *means* drool.

***Sa-gig U1: 19 (S1: 16) ?**
Perhaps an argument to link *šūru* "bull" and the "*šūrû* farm-implement," based on their similar pronunciation.

(Rev. 1) ... /*šuru*/ *refers to* a plow.

Sa-gig U1: 20 (S1: 17)—"If an ox glares at him"

(2) ... IGI.ḪUŠ(?) *means* to glare at.

(2) IGI *means* eye.
(3) [HUŠ *means* furious. (?)] ...

(3–4) IGI.ÍL *means* to glare at, *which refers to* one whose eye bites(?) another(?) ...

(4) To glare at *means* to look, in the case of hatred.

Sa-gig U1: 21 (S1: 18)
The sick man's critical condition and impending death is implied by the symbolism of the same logogram GU_4 that can mean "ox" or "ghost."

(5) "[If an ox butted] him, that sick man is critically sick, one must not approach him," which it said.
(5) Implicit in that "GU_4" *means* ox, (and) "GU_4" *means* ghost.

Sa-gig U1: 22 (S1: 19)

(6) "[If he] sees [an ox's horn (SI)], that sick man will die."

SI denotes an object that is long and narrow, such as an ox's "horn" or a "ray" of light.

(6) "SI" *means* horn.
(6) "SI" *means* light.
(6) "SI" *means* rays.

An ox's horn that is detached and "fallen off" (*maqātu*) the animal is compared to "diminished" (*maqātu*) light rays, which allude to the failing sight of a dying man.

(7) As in, its rays diminished.

Sa-gig U1: 24 (S1: 22)

(7–8) "(If) he sees a donkey mount a jenny, that sick man and [death] are intertwined."

Reference to the ANŠE.LA.GU equid.

(8) la-ga *means* "donkey."

la-ga is analyzed as *lā* "not" + GÁ "to release" (Proto-Aa). The jenny held in the donkey's firm grasp becomes an omen that the sick man will "not be released" from impending death.

(8) la-ga *means* not to become released.

kitpulu "to become intertwined" more often describes a snake's behavior, which has negative implications for the sick man.

(9) [To become intertwined] is complement to a donkey; secondly, it is complement to a snake.

Sa-gig U1: 25 (S1: 23)
Diagnoses of the type “Hand of X” typically depict X (often a deity, demon, ghost, or sorcerer) as an *agent* that actively brings about the illness; not merely as a *reason* for the illness, as “Hand of (another) man’s wife” would imply.

(9) “Hand of (another) man’s wife.”

For illicit sexual relations, this is a more idiomatic expression than “Hand of (another) man’s wife.”

(9) As in, “He approached (another) man’s wife (for sex).”

Sa-gig U1: 27 (S1: 26)
In medical texts, RA often means “to strike” rather than “to kick.”

(10) “[A donkey (performs the action of) RA to] him” *means* a donkey kicks him.

(10) RA *means* to strike.

Sa-gig U1: 30 (S1: 31)

(10) “(If) he sees an ecstatic; Hand of the god Ninurta.”

The /gub-ba/ element in their names links “an ecstatic” to “the god Ninurta.”

(11) ^{lu_2}GUB.BA *means* “an ecstatic.”
(11) ^{d}Lugal-ba-gub$_4$-ba *refers to* the god Ninurta.

Sa-gig U1: 34 (S1: 39)

(11) “NAM.TAR” *refers to* sickness.
(11–12) Secondly, “NAM.TAR” (*refers to*) [death (?)].

Sa-gig U1: 37b (S1: 44)
^{tug_2}NÍG.DARA$_2$ ŠU.LÁL is analyzed here as “the rag that binds the finger,” referring to finger wrappings worn by manual laborers to protect against abrasions or blisters. This association with human manual activity explains the omen’s verdict: “Hand of Humankind.”

(12) “^{tug_2}NÍG.DARA$_2$ ŠU.LÁL” *means* rag cloth.

(12) NÍG.DARA$_2$ *means* rag.
(12) ŠU *means* finger.
(13) [LÁL *means*] to bind.

These items seem to come from a lexical list, but it is uncertain how they fit into the commentator's argument.

(13) "Outbreak of divine anger, to become overbearing, to glare at."

Sa-gig U1: 37a (S1: 30)

The commentator explained this omen about a "prowling god," so that it referred not only to some invisible divine or demonic being, but also to star constellations like Leo (i.e., the prowling lion), which are more readily observable.

(13) "Prowling god" *refers to* Gazbaba.

(14–15) … "Among Bēltīya, Sîn, Bēlet-Eanna, [and Gazbaba]," it said.

(15) Secondly, Latarak.

(15–16) Thirdly, Unnānîši, [Amurru], the Twins.

Quotation from the astral compendium Mul-apin I, ii 3–4.

(16–17) (According to) that which it said: "The Twins who [stand] opposite Sipazianna (Orion) are Lulal and Latarak."

Sa-gig U1: 38b (S1: 33)

To show the link between ^{lu_2}BA.AN.ZA and the god Ninurta (^{d}MAŠ), the element BA.AN is interpreted as a reference to the sign bán with its logographic value MAŠ "half."

(17) "(If) he sees a ^{lu_2}BA.AN.ZA; Hand of the god Ninurta."

(18) [BA.AN.ZA *means*] stunted *or* dwarf.

BA.AN.ZA refers to one whose stature is "half" (bán) that of a normal "man" (ZA).

(18) BA.AN.ZA *consists of*
(18) BA.AN, *which means* half, *and*
(19) [ZA, *which means*] man.

(19) Šaddari *refers to* the god Ninurta.
(19) *šá-da-ri means* half.

Sa-gig U1: 39a (S1: 32)

(20) "[If] he sees [a deaf man]; Hand of the god Nergal."

This horoscope links the god Nergal's constellation (^{mul}(Ud)-ka-du$_8$-a) to muteness and deafness, as expressed by its elements: ka "speech" + DU$_8$.A "dispersed."

(20–21) "(If a child) is born under the constellation ^{mul}Ud-ka-du$_8$-a (Cygnus); he will be mute [(*or*) deaf]."

Sa-gig U1: 39b (S1: 4)

(21) "If he sees a kiln-fired brick, (that) sick man will die."

Interpretation #1:
"Kiln-fired brick" is plainly understood.

(21) The usual (meaning).

Next, *agurru* "kiln-fired brick" is analyzed as A + gur, where A is the logogram for either "water" or "son." The commentator argued that the following persons have the same omen significance as the "kiln-fired brick."

Interpretation #2:
GUR typically functions as the logogram for the verb "to return." Logograms A + GUR refer to "one who returned (from) water," i.e., one who returned from the river ordeal.

(21) Secondly, the man who returned [from the river] ordeal.
(22) [A *means* water.]
(22) GUR *means* to return.

Interpretation #3a:
gur$_4$ is the same sign as GIR$_8$ or KÌR, which is the logogram for the verb "to pinch off." Logogram A + sign gur$_4$ refers to "one who will pinch off a son (from her body?)," i.e., a pregnant woman.

(22) Thirdly, a pregnant woman.
(22) A *means* son.
(22) The cuneiform sign gur$_4$ as the logogram KÌR [*means* to pinch] off.

Interpretation #3b:
/*gur*/ is the pronunciation of the logogram GUR17 or GÙR meaning "to carry." Logogram A + /*gur*/ refers

(23) [Secondly], A *means* son.
(23) /*gur*/ *means* to carry.

to "one who carries a son," i.e., a pregnant woman.

Sa-gig U1: 40b (S1: 46)

(23) "If he sees a chariot, that sick man (suffers from) Hand of the goddess Ištar."

The following arguments demonstrate that the constellation "Chariot" (Northern part of Taurus) is associated with "Dilibat" (Venus), which represents Ištar.

(23–24) ["^{giš}GIGIR" (*means*)] chariot.
(24) The constellation ^{giš}GIGIR *refers to* Dilibat (Venus).

Argument #1:
This argument probably names Dilibat (Venus) as "Ištar of the stars."

(24–25) *Ditto* (i.e., the constellation) GIGIR *means* Chariot (Northern part of Taurus). ... Ištar of the stars.

Argument #2a:
According to Comm. Sa-gig 1A and 1C, "the star inside the constellation Chariot *refers to* Dilibat (Venus)." This is a visual argument, whereby the inner contents of the graph gigir (𒄋) "chariot," which resemble the sign bat (𒁁), are interpreted as a reference to Dilibat.

(25) *Ditto* (i.e., the constellation) GIGIR *means* Chariot (Northern part of Taurus).

What resembles the sign bat (𒁁) within the graph gigir (𒄋) "chariot" is actually the sign aš(𒀸)-*tenû*, which is the "*ubû*-sign" that serves as logogram for the "*ubû*-measure." Since signs like aš-*tenû* are classified by their non-*tenû* portion, the sign within the graph gigir is technically aš(𒀸), which has the syllabic value *dili*.

(25) The *ubû*-sign *refers to* the syllable sign *dili*, [*which refers to* Dilibat (Venus).]

Argument #2b: Another way to link the "*ubû*-sign" (inside the graph gigir) with Ištar is by metrological equivalence: 1 *ubû* = 1 *sūtu* 3 *qû* = 15 *qû*.	(26) [Secondly], an *ubû*-measure *means* 15 *qû*-measures.
Ištar's name is written as ${}^{\text{d}}$15, hence her association with the number 15.	(26) An *ubû*-measure *refers to* the number 15, *which refers to* the goddess Ištar.
Thus, the complex of ideas involving the *ubû*-measure validate the omen connecting the "chariot" with Ištar.	
Sa-gig U1: 41 (S1: 47)	(26) "${}^{\text{giš}}$GAG.SI.LÁ."
${}^{\text{giš}}$GAG.SI.LÁ "carriage" is analyzed as "(a vehicle for which) an ass is bound to the (carriage) peg."	(26–27) [${}^{\text{giš}}$GAG (*means*)] (carriage) peg. (27) /*si*/ *means* ass. (27) LÁ *means* to bind.
Sa-gig U1: 42a (S1: 48)	(27) "${}^{\text{giš}}$MAR.GÍD.DA" [*means* cart.]
${}^{\text{giš}}$MAR.GÍD.DA "cart" includes the element GÍD.DA "long."	(28) [Secondly], long (cart), whose front (resembles) a chariot and whose rear ...
***Sa-gig U1: 42b (S1: 49)—${}^{\text{giš}}$GABA.GÁL.LA**	(29) ... ${}^{\textit{break}}$ to which a single animal is harnessed ... (30) ... ${}^{\textit{new [break]}}$ ...

Notes

Obv. 1′–2′—// Comm. Sa-gig 1A, obv. 4 // Comm. Sa-gig 1C, obv. 3–4 (main Note) on connections to ${}^{\text{giš}}$gišimmar-al-ús-sa ("trampled (date-palm)") in Hh. III, 303 (*MSL* V, 118). George (1991: 146) restored these lines as [...].⌜x.na *mu-ú-tu*(!) :⌝ ${}^{\text{g}}$[${}^{\text{iš}}$GIŠIMMAR.AL.ÚS.SA] / [*di-i-šú* ...].

Obv. 3′—// Comm. Sa-gig 1A, obv. 5. The quotation in this line was initially thought to be from "a bilingual account of the early history of mankind (unpublished BM, courtesy Finkel; the Sumerian of this line is lost)"

(George 1991: 153); but later joins revealed the manuscript to be a compilation of bilingual proverbs (Finkel *NABU* 1993/15). Where we would expect *amēlūtu* ("humankind"), this commentary has LÚ (obv. 3′), but George suggested reading LÚ-⟨*tu*⟩. The parallel expression in Comm. Sa-gig 1A, obv. 5 is damaged and can shed no light on the reading. We should be open to the possibility that the commentator did not cite his source precisely, choosing instead to adapt its form so that the quotation more clearly applied to a single "human" individual, i.e., the sick man.

Obv. 4′–5′—The quotation in these lines is from the Standard Babylonian *Epic of Gilgamesh* I, 102–103. See George (2003: 544). For negative implications of potsherds, possibly linked to traditions in which humankind is fashioned from clay, see Cavigneaux (1982: 232–236); George (1991: 152–154); Steinert (2017).

Obv. 6′–7′—// Comm. Sa-gig 1A, obv. 6ff. // Comm. Sa-gig 1C, obv. 5–6. The logogram SISKUR appears in Comm. Sa-gig 1A, obv. 7, whereas SISKUR$_2$(siskur.siskur) occurs here and in Comm. Sa-gig 1C, obv. 5. All three are rendered as SISKUR in George (1991: 146). The quotation in obv. 7′ seems to come from the lexical passage Erimhuš I, a29–31 (*MSL* xvii, 14–15), with the initial equation restored as [NÍG.Ú].RUM = *ta-li-mu* by George (1991: 154), based on a hand copy by Cavigneaux (1980: 260). However, I assume that the version of Erimhuš I, a29 (*MSL* xvii, 14) cited in Comm. Sa-gig 1B and 1C appears not as [NÍG.Ú.RUM] = *ta-lim* (George 1991: 146–147, §3b–c), but as [tam-(ma ?)] = *ta-lim*, following readings attested in other lexical texts Aa III/3, 50 (*MSL* xiv, 333); Lu Excerpt II, 188 (*MSL* xii, 109), since the element tam (𒌓) was crucial for the explanation of ud (𒌓, the same cuneiform sign) in these commentarial arguments concerning KI.UD.BA.

Obv. 8′–10′—// Comm. Sa-gig 1A, obv. 8–10 where the KI.UD.BA is related specifically to the god Nergal, by citing descriptions occuring also in a Šu-íl-la prayer to this deity. Here in Comm. Sa-gig 1B, the disjunction sign after [NAM.E]RIM$_2$.BÚR.RU.DA (obv. 9′) is visible in the tablet's photo and indicated in Hunger's text edition (*SpTU* I, 27), but omitted from Hunger's hand copy and by George (1991: 146). Moreover, we find the additional qualifier NAM.ERIM$_2$ *mál i-na* SA.GI[G] (obv. 9′). George (1991: 154) thought this expression referred "to a subsection of the (Nam-erim$_2$-búr-ru-da) genre dealing with the treatment by incantation of physical ailments (SA.GIG) that were considered to have been induced by curse." Instead, I understand the term SA.GIG as the title of the Diagnostic Handbook. The mention of contents "[in] Nam-erim$_2$-búr-ru-da (Incantations to Undo Oath-Curses), *concerning* any oath-curse in the Diagnostic Handbook Sa-gig" refers to the fact that the "oath-curse" (NAM.ERIM$_2$) frequently appears in diagnostic verdicts of Sa-gig (as it does in the base text Sa-gig U1: 3 (S1: 3) here), remedies for which are available from the corpus of Nam-erim$_2$-búr-ru-da incantations. This interpretation is supported by the mention of NAM.ERIM$_2$ *ma-la ina*(!) SA.GIG ("any oath-curse in the Diagnostic Handbook Sa-gig") elsewhere at Comm. Sa-gig 1A, obv. 17, in a context that makes no explicit reference to Nam-erim$_2$-búr-ru-da.

Obv. 10′–11′—// Comm. Sa-gig 1C, obv. 7. The expression *uzabbal* ("it will carry on") appears as the prognosis in Sa-gig 12: 19, 21 (TDPT 12 i 14a, 15a); Sa-gig 14: 2, 13, [33], 41, [44] (similarly numbered entries in TDPT 14 i); Sa-gig 14: 159, 254′ (TDPT 14 iii 14; iv 53′); *BAM* 578 iii 5; iv 44; *AMT* 12/12: 4′. The basic meaning of *zabālu* (G stem) and even *zubbulu* (D stem) is "to carry, deliver" (*CAD* Z, 1), with the derived nuance of *zubbulu* best translated by the analogous English idiom: "to carry on (said of a sick person or sickness)." The comment here (*kâšu*, "to tarry on") seems to have been a preferred explanation that is used also for *dalāpu* ("to linger") in Comm. Sa-gig 13+ (obv. 3) and possibly in a commentary on *Šumma ālu* (*CT* 41, 33 [rev. 8]). I accordingly made the restorations GIG-*su ú-zab-bal* ⸢*i*⸣-[*ka-áš*] (Comm. Sa-gig 14, obv. 1) and *ú-zab-bal-ma* / [*i-kaš-ma*] (Comm. Sa-gig 34, obv. 5–6). On the basis of Comm. Sa-gig 1C, obv. 7, I restore obv. 10′–11′ as *lìb-bu-ú* / [*i-kab-bi-i*]*t-ma* : gá-gá : *za-ba-lu šá* ⸢*mur-ṣu*⸣ ("As in the fact that [it will become severe] *means* gá-gá, *which means* to carry (on), in the case of sickness"), even though the more typical rhetorical structure would be * gá-gá : *ka-ba-tu* : gá-gá : *za-ba-lu šá mur-ṣu* (* "gá-gá *means* to become severe. gá-gá *means* to carry (on), in the case of sickness"). In any case, the commentator here relied on the following lexical equations: [$^{\text{ga-a}}$ gá] = *ka-ba-tum* (Aa IV/4, 65 in *MSL* XIV, 385); [gá]-gá = MIN (= *zu-ub-bu-*[*lu*]) *šá* GAB[A] (Antagal D, 53 in *MSL* XVII, 203); gá-gá = *ṣu-ub-bu-lu* (Antagal III, 140 in *MSL* XVII, 155). Since gá-gá denotes both *kabātu* ("to become severe") and *zabālu* ("to carry"), a sickness that "carries on" (*zubbulu*) is a "severe" one.

Obv. 11′–12′—Because the terms "finger" and "grave" may each be represented by the logogram U, they are symbolically associated in support of the base text Sa-gig U1: 4 (S1: 42): "If he (the healer) stubs the thumb of his right hand, that sick man will die within seven days." The restoration [*ú-ba*]-*nu* instead of [*u-ba*]-*nu* (George 1991: 150) may be preferable, in view of the orthography *ú-ba-nu* (rev. 12) later in the same tablet. The logogram U expresses *qabru* ("grave") in the lexical text Aa II/4, 31 (*MSL* XIV, 281).

Obv. 13′—The signs šaḫ (𒋚) and šáḫ (𒂅) are very similar in their Neo-/Late Babylonian forms. Where George has transliterated ŠAḪ as the logogram for "pig," I prefer the value ŠÁḪ (cf. *CAD* Š I, 102 s.v. *šaḫû*), in anticipation of how this commentarial argument relies on alternative values (ŠUL and SUL) of the sign šáḫ. I understand the logic here as follows: [$^{\text{šu-ul}}$ šáḫ] : *dan-nu* : ŠUL : $^{\text{lu}_2}$GURUŠ ("[The cuneiform sign šáḫ as the logogram ŠUL] *means* hard (KALA), (since) ŠUL *means* youth (GURUŠ)"). This argument is somewhat unusual, since it immediately affirms that the "pig" (ŠÁḪ) is an omen of "hardship" (KALA), before systematically working through the steps of logic that lead to this conclusion. It is instructive to compare this argument to the extended A:B:C argument (§1.2.3.2.3) of Comm. Sa-gig 7A, rev. 12–13, which may be summarized as *p* ("death") ↔ *q* ("*Anzû*-bird") ↔ *r* (ANŠE, "donkey"), thereby proving that a patient who sounds like a donkey will die. In similar fashion, the argument in Comm. Sa-gig 1B might have been presented as * *p* ("pig," 𒋚) ↔ *q* ("youth," 𒋚) ↔ *r* ("youth," 𒂄) ↔ *s* ("hard(ship)," 𒂄). Instead, the order of elements inscribed on the tablet expresses the rhetorical structure: *p* ↔ *s*, since *q* ↔ *r*. It is also important to notice that, while everything discussed above is nested under the citation (obv. 12′) of base text Sa-gig U1: 9 (S1: 6) on the black pig, the connection between "pig" and "hardship" more properly belongs to the prognosis "hardship will seize him" in the next base text entry Sa-gig U1: 10 (S1: 7) on the white pig. Later in obv. 16′–17′, the alternative prognoses "he will die in three months : in three days" that belong to Sa-gig U1: 11 (S1: 8) on the red pig, similarly, are portrayed as a "second" (*šanîš*) explanation for the prognoses in Sa-gig U1: 10 (S1: 7) on the white pig. The laxity with which separate Sa-gig entries are assumed to convey similar meanings is aligned with the nature of the commentator's argument here, which is concerned only with the divinatory significance of a "pig" (ŠÁḪ), while ignoring any implications of its color.

Obv. 13′—// Comm. Sa-gig 1A, obv. 13–14 (main Note) on the logogram SUL for deadly "*li'bu*-sickness," which is the same sign as ŠÁḪ ("pig").

Obv. 14′–15′—// Comm. Sa-gig 1A, obv. 15–17 (main Note) on the use of a quotation from *Šumma ālu* XLIX, 41′ (Freedman 2017: 78) where the "pig" is an omen for a "female captive," so that the "pig" in Sa-gig likewise portends the sick man's "confinement (to the bed)." Comm. Sa-gig 1A includes an additional argument—absent in Comm. Sa-gig 1B—that is based on homophony between *esēru* ("confinement") and *esēru* ("to press for payment due").

Obv. 16′–17′—// Comm. Sa-gig 1C, obv. 9–10. These commentary entries provide insight into the inconsistent ways that commentators made sense of embedded variants. The base texts are "If he sees a white pig, that sick man will become healthy : hardship will seize him" (Sa-gig U1: 10 (S1: 7)), and "If he sees a red pig, that sick man will die in three months : in three days" (Sa-gig U1: 11 (S1: 8)). As I discuss at length in §1.1.3, because editors of serialized texts were unaware of the contexts in which independent variants developed, they often chose to preserve different readings of what they considered the same text entry as embedded variants, such as "he will become healthy : hardship will seize him." In Comm. Sa-gig 1B, these variants were not treated as alternative prognoses, but alternative descriptions of the same situation, i.e., for the sick man to become healthy is to be seized by hardship, and the absence of hardship becomes indicative of impending death. A different interpretive approach was adopted for the variants "in three months : in three days." Instead of affirming one time reference at the expense of the other, commentators considered both valid in limited and mutually exclusive situations: Death "in three days" applied to those who were critically sick, while death in three months concerned those not critically sick. As remarked above (Note on obv. 13′), prognoses in Sa-gig U1: 10 (S1: 7) on the white pig are connected via the notation "secondly" (*šanîš*) to those in Sa-gig U1: 11 (S1: 8) on the red pig. For an analogous use of "secondly" (*šanîš*) to incorporate a second base text topic into an existing argument, see Comm. Sa-gig 4C, rev. 10′: [IGI.2-*šú u-rat-ta*] ⌜: DÙ :⌝ [*re-tu-u* : DÙ : *za-q*]*a-pu* : DÙ : GUB-*zu šá-niš* ⌜DUL⌝.D[UL ...], "[**'He fixes in place his eyes** (base text Sa-gig 4: 109).'] DÙ *means* [to fix in place]. [DÙ *means*] to protrude. DÙ *means* to stand (still). Secondly (*šanîš*), **'DUL.DUL'** (base text Sa-gig 4: 111) ..."

Obv. 17′–18′—// Comm. Sa-gig 1C, obv. 11. Note the equation *bur-ma-mu* = MIN (= *šá-ḫu-u*) in the lexical text Malku v, 48 (Hrůša 2010: 399); šáḫ-zé-da-bar-sur-ra = MIN (= *bur-ma-mu*) in Hh. xiv, 164 (*MSL* viii/2, 20). This creature has been identified as a "porcupine" in *CAD* B, 330; *AHw*, 140; Landsberger (1934: 104). For problems in the identification of zé-da as "porcupine," see Foster and Salgues (2006: 285–286).

Obv. 19′—The sickness *aganutillâ* is analyzed as A.GA (*arkatu*, "future") + NU (*lā*, "without") + TIL (*bašû*, "existence"), referring to the "nonexistent future" of one stricken with this fatal sickness. See following Note for lexical connections between A.GA and *arkatu*.

Obv. 19′—// Comm. Sa-gig 1A, obv. 17–18. The sickness *aganutillâ* is analyzed as A.GA (*arkatu*, "future") + NU (*lā*, "without") + TI.LA (*balāṭu*, "life"), referring to the fatality of the sickness that ensures "a future without life." Associations between A.GA and *arkatu* occur in the lexical texts Emesal Voc. iii, 72 (*MSL* iv, 33); Antagal G, 221 (*MSL* xvii, 227); Hh. vii A, 31 (*MSL* vi, 86).

Obv. 20′–21′—The sickness *aganutillâ* is analyzed as A.GA (*makkūr ilī*, "property of the gods") + NU (*lā*, "without") + TIL (*qatû*, "completion"), implying that the sickness results from failure to complete an act or promise of consecrating what properly belongs to the gods. The meaning ascribed to

A.GA has no lexical basis and needed to be demonstrated. The commentator argued that the verbs *ḫabû* ("to draw up water"; *CAD* Ḫ, 19) and *ḫâbu* ("to consecrate, i.e., the gods' property"; *CAD* Ḫ, 20–21) could be equated, since they were roughly homophones of each other, and since both supposedly could be expressed by the same logogram ÍL ("to raise"). The "raising" of water, therefore, was deemed comparable to the "raising" of property (in consecration to the gods), implying that the logogram A ("water") could replace the logogram NÍG ("thing") in the expression NÍG.GA ("property") when the "property" under consideration pertains to the gods—so that the resulting form A.GA means "gods' property." One wonders whether the link between "property" (*makkūru*) and "water" could have been encouraged by the false cognate *makāru* ("to irrigate"; *CAD* M I, 125–126).

Obv. 23′–24′—The beginning of obv. 24′ is very damaged. The statement has been restored as *ina ú-re-e* GU$_4$ / ⸢^{d}⸣*Nin-urta* ⸢*im*(?)-x-x⸣-*ra* NÍG.GIG ^{d}*Nin*(!)-*urta* ("'in the ox's stall Ninurta …': taboo of Ninurta") by George (1991: 148–149, fig. 5, MS b obv. 23′–24′). Many of these signs are scarcely visible on the tablet's photo, and I very tentatively base my interpretation on the sign traces in George's hand copy: *ina ú-re-e* GU$_4$ / ⸢^{d}*Nin-urta im-ri u-ta-ra* (?)⸣ NÍG.GIG ^{d}*Nin*(!)-*urta* ("In the ox's stall, [the god Ninurta replenishes the fodder (?)]," (*which refers to*) "a taboo of Ninurta."). Note the description of Ninurta "who has water given to the animal pen" (*mušašqû tarbaṣi*) in the *Myth of Anzu* I, 6 (Vogelzang 1988: 30, 40, 73; Foster 2005a: 562), as well as the discussion of Ninurta as fertility god in Al-Rawi and Black (2000: 31–39). Another possible translation would be "in the stall of Ninurta's ox, one replenishes the fodder." Either way, the ox in view may refer to a animal particularly devoted for sacrifice to the god, i.e., an "anathema" or "taboo" (NÍG.GIG = *ikkibu*, obv. 24′). The quotation seems intended to demonstrate the logic of the omen, which relates the observation of a white "ox" to the god Ninurta. One wonders, moreover, whether a closer connection can be detected via wordplay between the terms MUR.GU$_4$ (= *imrî*, "fodder") and UR$_5$(mur) GU$_4$ (= *têret alpi*, "oracle of ox"), as well as among the terms *urê* GU$_4$ ("stall of ox"), *urre* GU$_4$ ("daytime ox"), and GU$_4$ BABBAR ("white ox"). Finally, note the stipulation in the *Offering Bread Hemerology* that, on the 7th day of the month Tašrītu (VII), "one should not ride in a boat; it is taboo to Ninurta." Livingston (2013: 137, lines 32–33).

Obv. 25′—The element ME from ^{d}DÌM.ME ("*lamaštu*-demoness") is identified with "heat" (*ummu*), based on a tradition reflected in the lexical entry [me] = *um-mu* (Izi E, 11 in *MSL* XIII, 186). Note that *um-mu* in this lexical text (Izi E, 11) has been understood instead as "mother" (*ummu*) in *CAD* U/W, 120. In the view of Wiggermann (2000: 238), the argument here "is based on a widely spread method of verbal analysis, in which the meaning of the isolated elements reveals the hidden nature of the named phenomenon ... as a mythological figure, she [Lamaštu] is the (frustrated) mother (*ummu*), who poisons instead of nurtures, and the (rejected) daughter (*martu*) of Anu, who rebels instead of obeys. As a pathogenic agent, Lamaštu is fever (*ummu*; i.e., heat) and bile (*martu*), the reverse evil variants of what she is not, a good mother and a good daughter." In this commentary entry, ME functions not as a grammatical appendage, but as an independent lexical item. The same is assumed in another argument based on the analysis of *meḫra* ("incident") as ME ("*lamaštu*-demoness") + *ḫâra* ("to espouse") (Comm. Sa-gig 40A, obv. 6).

Obv. 26′—I tentatively follow the restoration [*ina* NAM.ERIM$_2$]-*šá* (?) BA.ÚŠ (?) ("He will die [by her oath-curse (?)]") by George (1991: 148–149), which, if correct, conflates and paraphrases the embedded variants of the diagnosis: "The *lamaštu*-demoness has seized that sick man : an oath-curse has seized him; he will die soon" (Sa-gig U1: 18 (S1: 15)).

Obv. 27′–28′—The quotation here is from the *Lamaštu* Incantation Series II, 37, translated "The small of her back is speckled like a leopard" by Farber (2014: 168–169, 230); cf. Myhrman (1902: 170, i 37). This source had already been identified by Hunger (*SpTU* I, 27) and George (1991: 156). The argument confirms the link between the *lamaštu*-demoness with "spotted" lateral parts (lit. kidneys) and the "dappled" ox, as suggested by the omen in Sa-gig U1: 18 (S1: 15). Association between *tukkupu* ("to cover with spots") and *barāmu* ("to become dappled") also occurs in the lexical text Antagal D, 115–116 (*MSL* XVII, 204). The "spottedness" of the creature *nimru* may suggest its identity as a "leopard" (Landsberger 1934: 77) or another type of panther. Along similar lines, I understand the beginning of an Old Assyrian *Lamaštu* incantation (Kt 94/k, 821 obv. 1–4) as follows: *e-za-at pu-ul-ḫa-at* / *i-lá-at na-ma-ra-at* / *ba-ar-ba-ra-tum* / *ma-ra-at A-ni-im* ("She is fierce. She is fearsome. She is a goddess. She is a leopard (*nammarat*). The daughters of Anu are she-wolves."), where "leopard" is not *nimru* but *nammar*, a word attested also in the description of Enkidu as "a mule on the run, donkey of the uplands, leopard (Sultantepe MS e: *nam-mar* // Nineveh MS R: *nim-ru*) of the wild" (*Epic of Gilgamesh* VIII, 50 in George 2003: 654–655). *Contra* "elle est éblouissante" (Michel 1997: 59, 62); "(she is) glaringly bright" with *nammarat* "explained as based on a hitherto unattested intensifying adjective *nammarum*; for this meaning of the formation **parras*, see GAG §55m a III β" (Farber 2014: 148–149, 201 n. 15). The expression *nammarat* became confused as *amurrât* ("she is an Amorite woman") in an Old Babylonian (and probably also Ugaritic) version(s) of the incantation, and as *namurrat* ("she is one of awesome brightness"; cf. *CAD* N I, 254) in Standard Babylonian copies.

Obv. 28′–29′—This is a quotation from the lexical text Erimhuš VI, 80–83 (*MSL* XVII, 83), with the restoration of its first entry as giš-ḫur = *i-*⸢*siq*(?)*-tú*(?)⸣ suggested by George (1991: 156). Among the four items in the list, "engraved pattern" (giš-ḫur) relates to the variegated designs of the "dappled" ox (obv. 24′) or the *lamaštu*-demoness's "spotted" kidneys (obv. 27′–28′), while sag-ba ("oath-(curse)") refers back to NAM.ERIM$_2$ ("oath-curse") that occurs several times in the preceding lines. The lexical list, therefore, seems to represent an attempt at widening the scope of the omen's applicability, by exploring the range of items or events that could also be associated with the *lamaštu*-demoness.

Obv. 30′—// Comm. Sa-gig 1A, obv. 20–24 (main Note) on the extension of divinatory significance from an ox's "horn" (SI) to include also its "drool" (SI).

Rev. 1—The signs *šu-ú-ru* : ^{giš}APIN have been read as "bull; plough" by George (1991: 149), apparently referring to the term *šūru* B ("bull"; *CAD* Š III, 369), in line with the omen Sa-gig U1: 19 (S1: 16) that "an ox throw its horn." The term ^{giš}APIN ("plow"), however, suggests that *šu-ú-ru* may refer to the "*šūrû* farm-implement" (*CAD* Š III, 370), even though the orthography does not reflect the final long vowel. Perhaps the argument (unfortunately broken) includes an attempt to associate "bull" with the "*šūrû* farm-implement," based on their similar pronunciation /šuru/.

Rev. 3–4—I tentatively read *šá in-šú* / [... *a-ḫ*]*a*(?)*-a iš-šu-*⸢*ku*(?) ("one whose eye bites(?) another(?) ..."), though it is tempting to see the signs *iš-šu* as a form of *našû* (ÍL). Perhaps also relevant is this bilingual statement on the evil eye: lú igi-ḫul-gál-e igi-ḫuš ba-an-ši-íb-íl-la = *šá i-nu le-mut-tú ez-zi-iš ik-kel-mu-šú* ("he at whom the evil eye glared angrily"). See Borger (1967: 5, line 36).

Rev. 5—The syllable signs here are *e-ṭém*(gim)*-mu*, not *e-ṭem*(dim)*-mu* (rev. 5) as rendered by the typo in the printed edition *SpTU* I, 27; George (1991: 148). GU$_4$ as the logogram for *eṭemmu* and *alpu* occurs in the lexical text Idu II, 215–216 (*CAD* E, 397; *CAD* A I, 364). The commentarial equations here also appear in a therapeutic commentary (*SpTU* I, 49 obv. 16) identified as "Readings (*malsûtu*) of Anu-ikṣur." See Frahm (2011a: 233); cf. Finkel (2014a: 309–311).

Rev. 6–7—Association of the terms *qarnu, nūru,* and *šarūru* occurs in the lexical text S^{a} Voc. N, 1′–4′ (*MSL* III, 66; restored in *CAD* Q, 134 s.v. *qarnu*, lexical section). For the connection between "horn" and "ray" (by means of their shared logogram SI) as a feature of the bovine imagery of celestial bodies, see Wee (2014a: 29). For numerous examples of "diminished" rays expressed by the verb *maqātu* (lit. "to fall"), see *CAD* Š II, 141 s.v. *šarūru* §2′. The omen "if he sees an ox's horn (SI)" at Sa-gig U1: 22a (S1: 19) comes at the very end of a section on ox omens (Sa-gig U1: 15–22a (S1: 12–19)), and it must denote something more than the mere sight of the horn attached to the rest of the ox. In my view, the omen refers to a horn that is detached from the ox, perhaps due to an accident, and that has "fallen" on to the ground. This situation would represent a closer parallel to the description of light rays that have "diminished" (< *maqātu*, lit. "fallen"). That the verb *maqātu* ("to fall") does not denote merely the act of "lowering" the horns is evident from Sa-gig U1: 19 (S1: 16), where the verb *nadû* serves this purpose. In short, an ox's horn that is detached and "fallen off" (*maqātu*) the animal is compared to "diminished" (*maqātu*) light rays that allude to the failing sight of a dying man.

Rev. 8—For ANŠE.LA.GU and other equid names, see *CAD* K, 492 s.v. *kūdanu* (concluding remarks). Durand (1979: 161 n. 28) suggested that the equation la-ga = *lā napṭuru* results from analyzing la-ga as the negative particle *lā* + gab(DU$_8$ = *paṭāru*). Another possibility, which I adopt here, is to appeal to lexical equations like GÁ = *pa-ṭa-*⌜*rum*⌝ in *MSL* XIV, 101: 728: 10′ (Proto-Aa).

Rev. 9—// Comm. Sa-gig 1C, rev. 1′; cf. Comm. Sa-gig 1A, obv. 25–27. George (1991: 149) rather cryptically translates "a donkey's face (*pāni*), alternatively, a snake's face (*pāni*)." For the commentary notation IGI / *pān*(*i*) ("complement to") and its derivation from the depiction of reciprocals in cuneiform mathematics, see §II.2.5. I restore rev. 9 as [*kit-pu-lu pa*]-*ni* ANŠE *šá-niš pa-ni* MUŠ ("['To become intertwined'] is complement to a donkey; secondly, it is complement to a snake.") For numerous instances in which *kitpulu* describes intertwining snakes, see K 12851:[6′] (*CT* 11, 35); Recip. Ea Section F, 15′ (*MSL* XIV, 532); *CT* 38, 10: 27; 11: 44; 34: 20′; *CT* 39, 14: 24; K 8038, 2′ (*CT* 40, 24); *KAR* 384 obv. 4; 389 obv. [ii 18]; *STT* 321 i 11′. The fear and danger associated with snakes made "intertwining" an inauspicious omen, even if enacted by a donkey and a jenny during sexual intercourse.

Rev. 9—// Comm. Sa-gig 1C, rev. 2′. The logogram NA ("man") is used in Comm. Sa-gig 1B, rev. 9, in contrast to LÚ ("man") that appears in Sa-gig S1: 23 and probably in Sa-gig U1: [25] and Comm. Sa-gig 1C, rev. [2′] as well. The verdict "Hand of (another) man's wife" takes a form that is stereotypical for the Diagnostic Handbook: "Hand of X," wherein X (often a deity, demon, ghost, or sorcerer) represents an *agent* that actively brings about the illness. Implied here is the fact that the patient's illicit affair with "(another) man's wife" is the *reason* for his suffering, not that this "(other) man's wife" somehow becomes an agent of the ailment. In fact, reasons for sicknesses are typically introduced not by ŠU ("Hand of"), but by MU ("because (of)").

See, for example, [MU *k*]*i-gul-lim u áš-tam-me* ("[because of] the place of destruction(?) and tavern") from Sa-gig 3: 42 (TDPT 3: 33) as cited in Comm. Sa-gig 1–3, line 41; and MU KI MUNUS *ina* KI.NÁ KUR ("because he is encountered with a female in bed") in Sa-gig 3: 100–104 (TDPT 3: 91–95); Sa-gig 18: 21–23; cf. Note on Comm. Sa-gig 14, obv. 23–24. As his explanation, the commentator reworded the topic ("Hand of (another) man's wife") into an expression more idiomatic in the Diagnostic Handbook, i.e., "He approached (another) man's wife (for sex)" (cf. Sa-gig 17: 32). In Comm. Sa-gig 7Ca, obv. 5′–6′, the topic "He fornicated with his mother" is reformulated as a similar idiom: "He approached his mother (for sex)." See also "he approached his sister (for sex)" at Sa-gig 12: 125″ (TDPT 12 iv 17), and "he approached the *ēntu*-priestess of his god (for sex)" at Sa-gig 7 A obv. 20 (TDPT 7: 20); Sa-gig 13: 23 (TDPT 13 i 24′); Sa-gig 14: 134, 137–139 (TDPT 14 ii 62, 65–67). See also Note on Comm. Sa-gig 4A, obv. 14–15 where I discuss other similar statements in the Diagnostic Handbook that ascribe sickness to a variety of illicit heterosexual relations.

Rev. 10—// Comm. Sa-gig 1A, lines 28–29 (main Note) // Comm. Sa-gig 1C, rev. 3.

Rev. 10–11—// Comm. Sa-gig 1A, lines 32–34 (main Note) // Comm. Sa-gig 1D, rev. 7′–9′. For Ninurta's name ^{d}Lugal-i-bí-gub-ba (line 33), see note by Lambert in Durand (1979: 170).

Rev. 11–12—The base text here is Sa-gig U1: 34 (S1: 39), but George (1991: 150–151, section 31b) seems to have mistaken it for Sa-gig U1: 30 (S1: 31). His restoration [*mu-tú* (?)] (rev. 12) was possibly motivated by lexical associations in Antagal III, 63, 65 (*MSL* XVII, 152); *LTBA* II, 2: 264. Other possible restorations suggested by lexical texts include *di-ḫu-*[*ú*] and *šimtu* (Izi Q, 275–276 in *MSL* XIII, 221), *mukīl rēš lemutti* (Antagal III, 64 in *MSL* XVII, 152), and *pulḫu* (*LTBA* II, 2: 62).

Rev. 12–13—// Comm. Sa-gig 1C, rev. 4′–6′. The restoration [LÁL : *ka-m*]*u-u* (rev. 13) was suggested by George (1991: 150), though the verb *kamû* ("to capture, bind") is more often expressed by LAL (*CAD* K, 128–129). George has also translated ^{tug_2}NÍG.DARA$_2$ ŠU.LÁL as "soiled towel" and its comment *ulāpa sūnu* as "sanitary towel," perhaps influenced by the comment *ulāpi luʾʾu* ("dirty towel") in Comm. Sa-gig 1C, rev. 5′. The dictionary entries *CAD* S, 388–390, and *CAD* U/W, 71–72, do not help much in pin-pointing the function of the cloth/rag under consideration. In Comm. Sa-gig 1B, the analysis of ^{tug_2}NÍG.DARA$_2$ ŠU.LÁL as "the rag that binds the finger" does not seem to fit the description of a sanitary towel. Instead, I interpret this item as some kind of hand or finger wrapping, perhaps worn as protection against abrasions or blisters by those engaged in manual labor. Such an item would naturally become dirty and worn out with use, and one can easily imagine the magician encountering discarded finger wrappings or frayed pieces of the fabric en route to the patient's house. The association of finger wrappings with human manual activity validated the omen's verdict in Sa-gig U1: 37b (S1: 44): "Hand of Humankind" (ŠU NAM.LÚ.U_{18}.LU).

Rev. 13—The enumerated items ⸢ù⸣-ma : ù-na : igi-ḫuš (rev. 13) most likely represent a comment on Sa-gig U1: 37b (S1: 44), since they are followed by the topic from an adjacent omen in the base text, i.e., Sa-gig U1: 37a (S1: 30). While these items seem to derive from a lexical list, the quotation here lacks equivalents in syllabic Akkadian. Note the lexical equations ù-ma = *ir-nit-tú*, ù-na = *ka-da-ru*, ù-igi-bar-ra = *da-la-pu* (Lu Excerpt II, 80–82 in *MSL* XII, 106); ù-ma, ù-ma du-du, ù-na (Proto-Izi I, 475–477 in *MSL* XIII, 32). It is tempting to see igi-ḫuš (= *nekelmû*) cited in this commentary as a substitute for ù-igi-bar-ra = *da-la-pu* ("to stay awake"), though lexical evidence for such a substitution is wanting. The terms "outbreak of divine anger" (ù-ma = *irnittu*), "to become overbearing" (ù-na = *kadāru*), and "to glare at" (igi-ḫuš = *nekelmû*) are all expressions of hostility, though it is uncertain how they fit into the commentator's argument here.

Rev. 13–17—// Comm. Sa-gig 1A, lines 29–32 (main Note) // Comm. Sa-gig 1C, rev. 4′ // Comm. Sa-gig 1D, rev. 4′–6′ on defining the omen's "prowling god" (Sa-gig S1: 30 (U1: 37a)) not only as some invisible being, but also as star constellations or cultic persons, which are more readily observable. The quotation in rev. 16–17 comes from the astral compendium Mul-apin I, ii 3–4: DIŠ mulMAŠ.TAB.BA *šá ina* IGI-*et* mulSIPA.ZI.AN.NA GUB.MEŠ-*zu* dLÚ.LÀL *u* d*La-ta-ra-ak* (Hunger and Steele 2019: 39). Lulal and Latarak here were identified as "π^3 and π^4 Orionis?" by Hunger and Pingree (1989: 31, 138); cf. Hunger and Pingree (1999: 273–274). Gössmann (1950: 89 no. 234; 92 no. 246) had earlier identified Lulal as Betelgeuse (α Orionis) or $\alpha\beta$ Columbae, and Latarak as Bellatrix (γ Orionis) or θ Eridani.

Rev. 17–19—// Comm. Sa-gig 1A, lines 38–40 (main Note) // Comm. Sa-gig 1C, rev. 6′ // Comm. Sa-gig 1D, rev. 13′–14′ on the analysis of lu₂BA.AN.ZU as a "stunted" man whose stature is "half" (bán) that of a normal "man" (ZA), or a "half-witted" man who has only "half" (bán) his "wits" (ZU). The reference to Ninurta in rev. 19 comes from the following entry in a god-list (K 4339, iii 10 = *CT* 25, 12): d*Šad-da-ri* = MIN (= d*Nin-urta*). The equation *šá-da-ri* : *mi-šil* remains puzzling.

Rev. 20–21—// Comm. Sa-gig 1A = lines 35–38 (main Note) // Comm. Sa-gig 1D, rev. 9′–13′ on the god Nergal's association with deafness, based on the analysis of his constellation mulUD.KA.DU_8.A (Cygnus) as ka ("speech") + DU_8.A ("spread out," i.e., "dispersed").

Rev. 21–23—// Comm. Sa-gig 1A, obv. 11–13. This is one of the most vivid illustrations of argumentation by analysis of syllabic forms (§1.2.3.2.7). According to the base text Sa-gig S1: 4 (U1: 39b), the healer's sighting of a kiln-fired brick en route to the patient's house was a negative portent that the patient would die. This ominous significance of the "kiln-fired brick" (*agurru*) was extended also to other persons and objects that could be defined by the components a + gur.

Rev. 21—The commentary notation *kayyān* ("the usual (meaning)" is discussed in §11.2.7.

Rev. 21–22—// Comm. Sa-gig 1A, obv. 11 (main Note) on the analysis of *agurru* as the logogram A ("water") + the logogram GUR ("to return"), referring to "one who returned (from) water," i.e., the river ordeal.

Rev. 22—// Comm. Sa-gig 1A, obv. 11–12 (main Note) on the first of two analyses comparing the kiln-fired brick (*agurru*) to a pregnant woman: The logogram A ("son") + the cuneiform sign gur_4 (as the logogram GIR_8 or KÌR for *karāṣu*, "to pinch off") refers to the pregnant woman as "one who will pinch off a son (from her body?)."

Rev. 23—// Comm. Sa-gig 1A, obv. 12 (main Note) on the second of two analyses comparing the kiln-fired brick (*agurru*) to a pregnant woman: The logogram A ("son") + the pronunciation /*gur*/ (of the logogram GUR_{17} or GÙR for *našû*, "to carry") refers to the pregnant woman as "one who carries a son." The syllable signs here are *na-šú-u* (rev. 23), not *na-šu-u* as rendered by the typo in George (1991: 146).

Rev. 23–25—// Comm. Sa-gig 1A, lines 42–43 // Comm. Sa-gig 1C, rev. 9′. This lengthy argument was intended to validate the connection between "chariot" and the goddess Ištar in the omen Sa-gig U1: 40b (S1: 46). I understand the writing as ^{MIN}GIGIR in rev. 24 and 25, referring to the term earlier in rev. 24: $^{mul.giš}$GIGIR ("the constellation Chariot"). George (1991: 150–151, 161 note 46) identified this constellation with Auriga, but I follow the view of Hunger and Pingree (1989: 137) and (1999: 271) that it comprises the northern portion of Taurus. As a matter of fact, Auriga ("The Crook") and the "Chariot (of Enmešarra)" are addressed in separate sections (§12 and §14) in a Late Babylonian astral commentary on *Marduk's Address to the Demons* (BM 47529+47685, rev. 11–13 and 15, discussed in Wee 2016a: 157–158 and 159 respectively). For the epithet "Ištar of the stars" (rev. 25) in association with Dilibat, see attestations in *CAD* K, 47 s.v. *kakkabu* §1c. George must be credited for recognizing the visual argument in these Sa-gig commentary entries, even though I differ from him in my interpretation of its details. The key to the argument is most explicitly expressed in Commentaries Sa-gig 1A (line 43) and 1C (rev. 9′): "(The star) inside the constellation Chariot

(^{mul}GIGIR) *refers to* Dilibat (Venus)," which alludes to the written contents of cuneiform graph gigir (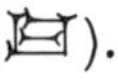). According to George (1991: 161 note 46), "in the third millennium the sign for 'chariot' could be written with lagab×u (gigir$_2$) rather than with lagab×bad (gigir) ... Though it later fell out of use in conventional orthography, the sign gigir$_2$(lagab×u) was preserved in the lexical tradition ..., and so was known to scholars in the first millennium. Thus the chariot, orthographically the sign u enclosed within a square box, is taken by our commentary to depict pictographically Ištar residing as the star Dilibat within the constellation Auriga [*sic*]." This interpretation was adopted also by Frahm (2002: 85–86) and (2011a: 80–81). I would argue, however, that the visual argument involved not the archaic graph gigir (), but its first millennium one () concurrent with the Sa-gig commentaries, as evident from mention of the "*ubû*-sign" (aš-*tenû*). In other words, the inside of gigir (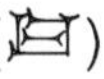) that resembles the sign bat () was considered by this commentator to be actually the sign aš()-*tenû*. Since signs like the latter were classified in ancient lexical lists by their non-*tenû* portion, the sign inside the "Chariot" () was technically aš(), which has the syllabic value *dili* that alludes to Dilibat. For lexical support interpreting the graph gigir as (I) lagab×aš-*tenû* as well as (II) lagab×bad, see Gong (2000: 153). Thus, instead of the reading $^{u_2\text{-}bu}$UBU$_x$(u) : *di-l*[*i-pat*] ("ubu = Dilipat"; Comm. Sa-gig 1B, rev. 25) by George (1991: 150–151), I read *ú-bu-u* : *di-l*[*i* : ^{d}*Dili-bat*] ("The *ubû*-sign *refers to* the syllable sign *dili*, [*which refers to* Dilibat]"). Notice that my proposal avoids the problem of the absent divine determinative in George's restoration *di-l*[*i-pat*] (rev. 25), when compared with ^{d}*Dili-bat* in rev. 24. The syllabic value *dili* of the sign aš is attested in the lexical text Ea II, 56, 204 (*MSL* XIV, 249, 256). The sign aš-*tenû* as a logogram for the "*ubû*-measure" occurs in Ea II, 200 (*MSL* XIV, 256); Ea II Assur MA Excerpt, iii 6′, 9′ (*MSL* XIV, 261); *MSL* XIV, 124, no. 9 (BM 54720) line 483 (Proto-Aa). For the long final vowel of sign names like *ú-bu-u* (rev. 25), see also *an-šu-ú* (for ANŠE, "donkey") in Comm. Sa-gig 7A, rev. 13. In contrast to the lengthy argument here, those in Comm. Sa-gig 1A (lines 42–43) and 1C (rev. 9′) are much shorter and make no mention of the *ubû*-sign. Though we are probably correct to assume some kind of visual argument in these other commentaries as well (see above), we might reasonably question whether the logic here precisely applied elsewhere. In addition to the argument in Comm. Sa-gig 1B, which interprets the inner contents of the constellation Chariot () as the sign aš()-*tenû* (> the sign aš as syllable sign *dili* alluding to Dilibat), Comm. Sa-gig 1A and 1C may also have understood these contents to comprise a "single" (DILI) cuneiform sign bat (), once again referring to Dilibat (Venus) and the goddess Ištar.

Rev. 26—As an additional step unique to Comm. Sa-gig 1B, the commentator argued that 1 *ubû*-measure (whose logogram is the *ubû*-sign = aš-*tenû*) comprised 15 *qû*-measures. Note the reading from a metrological table cited in George (1991: 161; Esagil Tablet, *Babylonian Topographical Texts*, no. 13 = *TCL* VI, 32 rev. 9): 50 *mu-šar* = $^{\text{u-bu}}$ aš = BÁN 3 SILA_3 ("50 *mušaru* = 1 *ubû* = 1 *sūtu* 3 *qû*"). Because the writing for "Ištar" (^{d}15) includes the number 15, the *ubû*-sign inside the graph gigir (
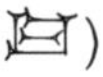
) was indicative of the role played by the "chariot" (^{giš}GIGIR) as an omen of the goddess Ištar. See also Comm. Sa-gig 4A, obv. 12 where the goddess Ištar (^{d}15) is associated with the number 15, which in turn serves as the logogram for the "right (side)."

Rev. 27—I follow the restoration [*šu-kur*]-*ri* by Hunger (*SpTU* I, 27); cf. [*sa-par?*]-*ri* in George (1991: 150). /*si*/ is the pronunciation of a logogram for "ass," according to the lexical equations: $^{\text{si-i}}$ ù = *agālu* in Diri II, 131 (*MSL* XV, 126); cf. the restoration $^{\text{s[i]}}$ [ù] = [*a-ga-lu*] in Antagal F, 44 (*MSL* XVII, 214).

Commentary Sa-gig 1C

Provenance:	Uruk (Warka), Area U18, Level v; Library of Anu-ikṣur
Period:	Late Achaemenid
Names:	"[Tablet of] Anu-ikṣur, descendant of Šangû-Ninurta"
Script:	Neo-/Late Babylonian
Typology:	Perhaps *ṣâtu* 6b in Frahm (2011a: 53)
Field/Museum No.:	W 22307/24 = IM 74374 (National Museum of Iraq)
Photos:	Plate 6 (reverse) and Plate 7a (right edge)
Printed Edition/Hand Copy:	*SpTU* 1, 28 (= Hunger 1976: 37); George (1991: 137–163, MS c); Wee (2012: 533–538)
Digital Resources:	CDLI P348449; GKAB P348449 (edition digitized by Clancier 2009); CCP 4.1.1.C (printed hand copies digitized by Frahm, Frazer, and Jiménez 2013)
Discussion:	*SpTU* 1, 28 (= Hunger 1976: 37); Cavigneaux (1982: 231–240); George (1991: 137–163, MS c) and (2013: 62); Heeßel (2000: 132, 139 (1. Tafel MS c)); Frahm (2002: 85–86) and (2011a: 53 n. 231, 92, 222–223, 291); Bilbija (2008: 20–21 n. 7); Clancier (2009: 50, 52, 55, 71, 265, 281); Geller (2010a: 141–144); Wee (2012: 533–538) and (2015a: 280–282); Gabbay (2014: 352) and (2016: 342–343, see references to George 1991 MS c)
Pericope:	At least Sa-gig U1: 1–9 and 22–42b

Transliteration

Obverse

1) [...] : KA.[PIRIG : *a-ši-pu* ...]
2) [...]-*zu* : K[A ...]
3) [$^{\text{še-ek}}$ŠIKA.AL.Ú]S.SA [: *iš-ḫ*]*i*-⸢*il*⸣-[*ṣ*]*u* ⸢: x x⸣ [...]
4) [...] : *mu-ú-tu* : ^{giš}GIŠIMMAR.AL.ÚS.⸢SA :⸣ [*di-i-šú*]
5) [KI.UD.BA : KI] SISKUR$_2$ GABA.RI : KI.UD.BA : *a-šar te-b*[*i-ib-ti*]
6) [tam-(ma ?) : ta]m-ma : tam-tam-ma : *ta-lim* : *qa-a-pi* : *te-bi-i*[*b-t*]*i*

 | DOI:10.1163/9789004417564_004

7) [*ú*]-⸢*za-bal-ma*⸣ [: *i-k*]*ab-bit-ma* : gá-gá : *za-ba-lu šá m*[*ur-ṣ*]*u*
8) [DIŠ ŠÁḪ GE$_6$ IGI *u*]*š-ta-pa-áš-šaq*!(ka)-*ma* : *i-dan-n*[*in-m*]*a*
9) [DIŠ ŠÁ]Ḫ ⸢SA$_5$⸣ [IGI GIG B]I *a-na* ITI.⸢3⸣.KAM : *ana* U$_4$.[3.KAM ÚŠ *š*]*á* E-*ú*
10) [*ki*]-*i* ⸢*na*⸣-*a*[*q-du ana* 3 U$_4$-*mu*] ⸢*ki-i*⸣ *la na-aq-d*[*u ana*] ⸢3⸣ ITI ÚŠ
11) [DIŠ ŠÁḪ GÙN.A IGI *šá* E-*ú* šáḫ-zé]-⸢da-sur⸣-ra : *b*[*u-ri-i*]*a-mu*

Reverse
1′) [... *kit-pu-lu pa-ni* ANŠE *š*]*á-niš* ⸢*pa-ni*⸣ [MUŠ]
2′) [ŠU DAM LÚ *lìb-bu*]-*ú a-na* DAM LÚ T[E-*ḫi*]
3′) [DIŠ ANŠ]E ⸢RA⸣-*su* : RA : *ra-ḫa-ṣi* : RA : *ma-ḫa-*⸢*ṣi*⸣
4′) [DIN]GIR(!) *saḫ-ḫi-ra* : ^{d}*La-ta-ra-ak-a* : ^{tug_2}NÍG.DARA$_2$ ŠU.LÁL
5′) *ú-la-pi lu-*⸢*ʾu*⸣*-ú* : ŠU.LÁL : *lu-ʾu-ú*
6′) ŠU.LÁL : *lu-up-pu-ut-tu*$_4$: ^{lu_2}BA.AN.ZI : *pe-su-ú mi-šil* LÚ
7′) SIG$_4$.AL.ÙR.RA IGI GIG BI ÚŠ *aš-šum* ÙR : *šá-rap* : ÙR : *ṣa-ra-pa*
8′) ⸢AD$_6$⸣ IGI GIG BI TI-*uṭ* : *šá-al-ma-ti lìb-bu-ú pu-ú-ḫu* IGI
9′) [DIŠ ^{giš}GIGIR] IGI GIG BI ŠU ^{d}15 *ina* ŠÀ *šá* ^{mul}GIGIR : ^{d}*Dili-bat*
10′) [^{giš}MAR.GÍD.D]A : *a-ri-ik-tu*$_4$: GABA.GÁL.LA : *pi-it-nu*
11′) [*šá-niš* GABA.GÁ]L.LA : *ka-lu-ú lìb-bu-ú* GABA IGI [...]

12′) [DIŠ NA *ana* É GIG D]U-*ma* SÚR.DÙ^{mušen} *ana* 15-*šú* DIB[-*iq*]
13′) [*ṣa-a-tú ù šu-ut* KA] *šá* KA [U]M.ME.A *šá* DIŠ U$_4$-⸢*ma*⸣ *ana* É GIG K[A.PIRIG DU-*ku*]
14′) [*mál-su-ut* $^{m.d}$*Anu-ik*]-*ṣur* A ^{lu_2}SANGA-^{d}*Nin-urta* ^{1}[^{u_2}MAŠ.MAŠ ...]

Translation

***Incipit-title of Sa-gig 1**

(Obv. 1) ["Whenever the KA.PIRIG-healer goes to the sick man's house."]

Sa-gig U1: 1 (S1: 1)

(1–2) "KA.PIRIG" [*means* magician.] ...

Sa-gig U1: 2 (S1: 2)
The following arguments prove the link between the potsherd and the patient's critical condition.

(3) šika-al-ús-sa [*means*] sherd. ...

The writing šika-al-ús-sa "(pot)sherd" includes the idea of being "trampled down" (al-ús-sa), thus implying the sick man's "death."

(4) ... *means* death.

(4) [giš]gišimmar-al-ús-sa *means* [trampled (date-palm)].

Sa-gig U1: 3 (S1: 3)
KI.UD.BA is a cultic installation.

(5) ["KI.UD.BA" *means* place] of sacrificial offering.

KI.UD.BA is analyzed as a "place" (KI) of "cleansing" (ud).

(5) That is, "KI.UD.BA" *means* place of cleansing.

This quote from a version of lexical text Erimhuš I, a29–31, shows that "cleansing" can be expressed by tam (same sign as ud), and perhaps that KI.UD.BA also denotes the "place" (KI) of a "close brother" or "trust."

(6) "[tam-(ma ?)], tam-ma, *and* tam-tam-ma *mean* close brother, to entrust, *and* cleansing *respectively*."

Sa-gig U1: 3 (S1: 3)
The basic meaning of *zubbulu* is "to carry, deliver," and the derived meaning of *zubbulu* as "to carry on (said of sickness)" required clarification.

(7) "It will carry on" [*means*] it will become severe.

Since gá-gá denotes both *kabātu* "to become severe" and *zabālu* "to carry," a sickness described as *zubbulu* "carries on" due to its "severity."

(7) gá-gá *means* to carry (on), in the case of sickness.

Sa-gig U1: 9–10 (S1: 6–7)
The prognosis "he will get into dire straits" from an omen about a black pig (Sa-gig U1: 9) is equated with the prognosis "hardship will seize him" from an omen about a white pig (Sa-gig U1: 10).

(8) "[If he sees a black pig], he will get into dire straits" *means* it will become hard.

Sa-gig U1: 11 (S1: 8)	(9) "[If he sees a] red pig, [that sick man will die] in three months : in [three] days," which it said.
	(10) If he is critically sick, he will die [in three days]; if he is not critically sick, [in] three months.
Sa-gig U1: 12 (S1: 9)	(11) ["If he sees a dappled pig," which it said,]
This omen applies also to the *buriyāmu*-pig, whose name is cognate to the word "dappled" (*burrumu*).	(11) šáḫ-zé-da-sur-ra *means* a *buriyāmu*-pig.
Sa-gig U1: 24 (S1: 22) *kitpulu* "to become intertwined" more often describes a snake's action, which has negative implications for the sick man.	(Rev. 1′) [To become intertwined is complement to a donkey]; secondly, it is complement to a [snake].
Sa-gig U1: 25 (S1: 23) Diagnoses of the type "Hand of X" typically depict X (often a deity, demon, ghost, or sorcerer) as an *agent* that actively brings about the illness; not merely as a *reason* for the illness, as "Hand of (another) man's wife" would imply.	(2′) ["Hand of (another) man's wife."]
For illicit sexual relations, this is a more idiomatic expression than "Hand of (another) man's wife."	(2′) [As in,] "He approached (another) man's wife (for sex)."
Sa-gig U1: 27 (S1: 26)	(3′) "[If a donkey] kicks (RA) him."
In medical texts, RA often means "to strike" rather than "to kick."	(3′) "RA" *means* to kick. (3′) "RA" *means* to strike.

Sa-gig U1: 37a (S1: 30)
The commentator explained this omen about a "prowling god," so that it referred not only to some invisible divine or demonic being, but also to Latarak (perhaps understood as the prowling lion constellation Leo), which is more readily observable.

(4′) "Prowling god" *refers to* Latarak.

Sa-gig U1: 37b (S1: 44)
^{tug_2}NÍG.DARA$_2$ ŠU.LÁL is analyzed in the parallel Comm. Sa-gig 1B entry as "the rag that binds the finger," referring to finger wrappings worn by manual laborers to protect against abrasions or blisters. This association with human manual activity explains the omen's verdict: "Hand of Humankind."

(4′–5′) "^{tug_2}NÍG.DARA$_2$ ŠU.LÁL" (*means*) dirty rag.

(5′) ŠU.LÁL *means* dirty.
(6′) ŠU.LÁL *means* soiled.

Sa-gig U1: 38b (S1: 33)
This argument shows the link between ^{lu_2}BA.AN.ZA and the god Ninurta (^{d}MAŠ). BA.AN is interpreted as BÁN, which is the same sign as MAŠ "half." BA.AN.ZI refers to one whose stature is "half" (MAŠ) that of a normal "man" (ZA).

(6′) "^{lu_2}BA.AN.ZI" *means* stunted (*or*) half a man.

Sa-gig U1: 39b (S1: 4)
SIG$_4$.AL.ÙR.RA "kiln-fired brick" includes the notion, not only of "(brick) firing" (ÙR), but also of "burning" (ÙR) in general, which implies the death of the sick man.

(7′) "(If) he sees a kiln-fired brick, that sick man will die."

(7′) Because ÙR *means* to burn.
(7′) ÙR *means* to fire (brick).

Sa-gig U1: 40a (S1: 35)
The form *šalmāti* is the plural of both *šalamti* "corpse" and *šalimti* "well-being," so that observing a "corpse" becomes an omen for "well-being."

(8′) "(If) he sees a corpse, that sick man will live."

(8′) *Šalmāti.*

The commentator explained the apparent contradiction of the corpse as a good omen, by describing it as a substitute for what the patient would otherwise have suffered.

(8′) As in, he sees a substitute.

Sa-gig U1: 40b (S1: 46)
In this visual argument, Dilibat (Venus) is contained inside the constellation Chariot (𒄀), by considering its inner contents either (I) as the sign aš(𒀸)-*tenû* whose non-*tenû* portion is the syllable sign *dili* that alludes to Dilibat, or (II) as a "single" (DILI) cuneiform sign bat (𒁁) that once again refers to Dilibat.

(9′) "[If] he sees [a chariot], that sick man (suffers from) Hand of the goddess Ištar."

(9′) (The star) inside the constellation Chariot (Northern part of Taurus) *refers to* Dilibat (Venus).

Sa-gig U1: 42a (S1: 48)
^{giš}MAR.GÍD.DA "cart" includes the element GÍD.DA "long."

(10′) "^{giš}MAR.GÍD.DA" *means* long (cart).

Sa-gig U1: 42b (S1: 49)

(10′) "GABA.GÁL.LA" *means* box (of a cart).

The element GÁL.LA sounds like *kalâ* "to hold back."

(11′) [Secondly,] "GABA.GÁL.LA" *means* to hold back.

This seems to be an argument involving the logogram GABA "chest."

(11′) As in, … chest …

(Colophon)

Incipit-title of Sa-gig 2

(12′) "[If the person] goes [to the sick man's house], and a falcon passes by on his right."

Incipit-title of Sa-gig 1

(13′) [Glossary including oral lore] from the mouth of the *ummânu*-scholar on "Whenever the KA.PIRIG-healer [goes] to the sick man's house."

(14′) [Readings] of Anu-ikṣur, descendant of Šangû-Ninurta, [magician] …

Notes

Obv. 1–2—// Comm. Sa-gig 1A, obv. 1–3 (main Note) on the magician as KA.PIRIG.

Obv. 3–4—// Comm. Sa-gig 1A, obv. 4 // [Comm. Sa-gig 1B, obv. 1′–2′]. The commentators had in view the lexical equation ^{giš}gišimmar-al-ús-sa = *di-i-šú* ("trampled (date-palm)") in Hh. III, 303 (*MSL* V, 118), and, here, the fragmentary statement […] : *mu-ú-tu* ("… *means* death"; obv. 4) may derive from another nearby equation ^{giš}gišimmar-al-ug$_5$-ga = *mi-i-tum* (Hh. III, 301 in *MSL* V, 118; translated "dead date-palm" in *CAD* M II, 140).

Obv. 5–6—// Comm. Sa-gig 1A, obv. 6ff. // [Comm. Sa-gig 1B, obv. 6′–7′ (main Note) on my argument that the version of Erimhuš I, a29 (*MSL* XVII, 14) cited in these commentaries appears not as [NÍG.Ú.RUM] = *ta-lim* (George 1991: 146–147, §3b–c; cf. 154), but as [tam-(ma ?)] = *ta-lim.*

Obv. 7—// Comm. Sa-gig 1B, obv. 10′–11′ (main Note) on *zubbulu* ("to carry on (said of a sick person or sickness)") as derivative of the basic meaning "to carry, deliver" and its attestations in medical texts, as well as *kâšu* ("to tarry on") as the preferred explanation in several commentaries.

Obv. 8—See Note on Comm. Sa-gig 1B, obv. 13′ for how prognoses of different Sa-gig omens on black, white, and red pigs were conflated together, as if the color of the pig was of no divinatory significance. Here, the commentator at least equated the prognosis "he will get into dire straits" from an omen about a black pig (Sa-gig U1: 9 (S1: 6)) with the prognosis "hardship will seize him" from an omen about a white pig (Sa-gig U1: 10 (S1: 7)). It is less certain whether such an equation was achieved via the complex reasoning that is explicit in Comm. Sa-gig 1B, obv. 13′: ŠÁḪ "pig" (𒂄) is the same sign as ŠUL "youth" (𒂄), which has the same meaning as another logogram GURUŠ "youth" (𒆗), which is the same sign as KALA "hard" (𒆗).

Obv. 9–10—// Comm. Sa-gig 1B, obv. 16′–17′ (main Note) on the inconsistent ways in which commentators resolved embedded variants, such as "he will become healthy : hardship will seize him" (Sa-gig U1: 10 (S1: 7)) and "in three months : in three days" (Sa-gig U1: 11 (S1: 8)).

Obv. 11—// Comm. Sa-gig 1B, obv. 17′–18′ (main Note) on the "dappled pig" of Sa-gig U1: 12 (S1: 9) as a *buriyāma*-pig, based on Hh. XIV, 164 (*MSL* VIII/2, 20) and other lexical texts. I include a disjunction sign after [šáḫ-zé]-⸢da-sur⸣-ra (obv. 11), visible in George's hand copy (fig. 4) but absent from his transliteration (George 1991: 148).

Rev. 1′—// Comm. Sa-gig 1B, rev. 9 (main Note) on how "intertwining," which is typical of dangerous snakes, represents an inauspicious omen, even when enacted by a donkey and a jenny during sexual intercourse.

Rev. 2′—// Comm. Sa-gig 1B, rev. 9 (main Note) on the inappropriateness of the expression "Hand of (another) man's wife," which implies the *agent* rather than only the *reason* for illness, as well as its reformulation into a more idiomatic statement "he approached (another) man's wife (for sex)."

Rev. 3′—// Comm. Sa-gig 1A, lines 28–29 (main Note) // Comm. Sa-gig 1B, rev. 10.

Rev. 4′—// Comm. Sa-gig 1A, lines 29–32 (main Note) // Comm. Sa-gig 1B, rev. 13–17 // Comm. Sa-gig 1D, rev. 4′–6′ on defining the omen's "prowling god" (Sa-gig S1: 30 (U1: 37a)) not only as some invisible being, but also as star constellations or cultic persons, which are more readily observable.

Rev. 4′–6′—// Comm. Sa-gig 1B, rev. 12–13 (main Note) on ^{tug_2}NÍG.DARA$_2$ ŠU.LÁL as "the rag that binds the finger," which refers to hand or finger wrappings worn by manual laborers to protect against abrasions or blisters, thus validating the verdict "Hand of Humankind" of the omen in Sa-gig U1: 37b (S1: 44).

Rev. 6′—// Comm. Sa-gig 1A, lines 38–40 (main Note) // Comm. Sa-gig 1B, rev. 17–19 // Comm. Sa-gig 1D, rev. 13′–14′ on the analysis of ^{lu_2}BA.AN.ZU as a "stunted" man whose stature is "half" (bán) that of a normal "man" (ZA), or a "half-witted" man who has only "half" (bán) his "wits" (ZU).

Rev. 7′—For the meaning of *ṣarāpu* as "to fire (brick)," see *CAD* Ṣ, 102–103 s.v. *ṣarāpu* A §1b.

Rev. 8′—The form *šalmāti* can serve as the plural of *šalamti* ("corpse") or *šalimti* ("well-being"), so that observing a "corpse" becomes an omen for "well-being." Since it seemed contradictory that a corpse would be a good omen, the commentator felt the need to explain that the corpse served as a "substitute" for the fate the patient would otherwise have experienced.

Rev. 9′—// Comm. Sa-gig 1A, lines 42–43 // Comm. Sa-gig 1B, rev. 23–25 (main Note) on the visual argument that Dilibat (Venus) is contained within the constellation Chariot (𒄀), by considering its inner contents either as the sign aš(𒀸)-*tenû* whose non-*tenû* portion is the syllable sign *dili* that alludes to Dilibat, or as a "single" (DILI) cuneiform sign bat (𒁁) that once again refers to Dilibat.

Rev. 13′–14′—I am uncertain of the restoration [*maš-a-a-al-tú*] (rev. 13′) and [DUB $^{m.d}$*Anu-ik*]-*ṣur* (rev. 14′) by George (1991: 152), because other Sa-gig commentaries with Anu-ikṣur's name seem to have the designations "Glossary including oral lore from the mouth of the *ummânu*-scholar" and "Readings of Anu-ikṣur." See Comm. Sa-gig 5, lines 40–41; Comm. Sa-gig 7A, rev. 14–15; Comm. Sa-gig 7B, rev. 8′–9′; Comm. Sa-gig 19, lines [34, 36]. I tentatively restore [*ṣa-a-tú ù šu-ut* KA] (rev. 13′) and [*mál-su-ut* $^{m.d}$*Anu-ik*]-*ṣur* (rev. 14′) while acknowledging that the proposed signs may not all fit into the space at the beginning of the line. See also Frahm (2011a: 53 n. 231, 222).

Rev. 14′—George (1991: 139–140) suggested that either Commentaries Sa-gig 1C and 1B were written by Anu-ikṣur and his brother Rīmūt-Anu respectively, or that Comm. Sa-gig 1B "was a relic of [their] father's (Šamaš-iddin's) schooldays." Frahm (2011a: 223) cautioned us not to discount the possibility that "both tablets were written by Anu-ikṣur, who has, in fact, left us two different commentaries on Sa-gig 7."

Commentary Sa-gig 1D

Provenance:	Uruk (Warka), Area U18, Level II; May belong to library of Iqīšāya
Period:	Late Achaemenid–Early Hellenistic
Names:	Colophon not preserved
Script:	Neo-/Late Babylonian
Field/Museum No.:	W 22666/1c (National Museum of Iraq)
Printed Edition/Hand Copy:	*SpTU* V, 256 (= von Weiher 1998: 73); Wee (2012: 539–542)
Digital Resources:	CDLI P348843; GKAB P348843 (edition digitized by Clancier 2009); CCP 4.1.1.A.a (printed hand copy digitized by Frahm, Frazer, and Jiménez 2013)
Discussion:	*SpTU* V, 256 (= von Weiher 1998: 73); Heeßel (2000: 139 (1. Tafel MS d)); Frahm (2002: 85 n. 47) and (2011a: 221, 223, 291, 294); Genty (2010a: 367); Clancier (2009: 399); Wee (2012: 539–542); Finkel (2014a: 311–312) and (2014b: 321–323); Gabbay (2016: 59 n. 233, 74 n. 323, 100–101)
Pericope:	At least Sa-gig S1: 26–36

Transliteration

Reverse

1′) [...]x *m*[*u*(?) ...]

2′) [... DIŠ ANŠE RA-*su* : GÌ]R RA.R[A]

3′) [*ra-ḫa-ṣu* : GÌR : *še-e-pi* : RA : *ma-ḫa-ṣ*]*u šá-niš* Ud-dè-an-an[še]

4′) [Ud-da : ^{d}IŠKUR : DIŠ DINGIR *saḫ-ḫi-ri* IGI ...]x *be-let* DINGIR.MEŠ *lu-ú*

5′) [^{d}*Gaz-ba-ba* : *šá-niš*] *Un-na-niš*(!)-*šú* : ^{lu_2}an-né-ba-t[i]

6′) [lú-^{giš}kéš-da : nin-nun-gal-e]-⸢ne⸣ : *eš-še-bu-ú* : *ri-kis* ^{d}*Na-r*[*u-du*]

7′) [DIŠ *maḫ-ḫa-a* IGI ŠU ^{d}MAŠ : ^{l}]^{u_2}GUB.BA *maḫ-ḫu-ú* : Lugal-ba-gub-ba

8′) [^{d}*Nin-urta* : ^{lu_2}an-dib-ba-ra :] ⸤ní-zu⸥-ra-aḫ : kur-gar-ra : LÚ ^{d}*Gu-la*

9′) [*maḫ-ḫu-u* : *a-ḫur-ru-u* : *kur-ga-ra*(/*ru*)-*u* : *a*]*s-sin-ni* : *suk-ku-ka* IGI

10′) [ŠU ^{d}U.GUR : KI ^{mul}KA.DU$_8$.A *a-lid uq-q*]*u-qu šá-niš suk-ku-ku*

 | DOI:10.1163/9789004417564_005

11′) [*iz-bi* GEŠTUG.2-*a-šú* *ki-la-at-ta-an* BA.RA BÙR.MEŠ Š]UB-*ti* *dúr-giš-lu-ú*
12′) [GÁL-*ši* : *dúr-giš-lu-ú* : dur-giš-lam NIBRU^{ki} : *dú*]*r-giš-lu-ú*
13′) [NIBRU^{ki}-*ú* : *áš-šú* ^{d}U.GUR : DIŠ ^{lu_2}BA.AN.ZU IGI ŠU ^{d}MAŠ ^{lu_2}BA. AN.ZU : *pe-su-ú* : *k*]*u-ru-ú*
14′) [^{lu_2}BA.AN.ZU : *pe-ḫu-u* : GIG.TIL.LA : *pe-su-ú* : *šu-ú-lu* :] *šu-ul-la-nu*
15′) [DIŠ Á 15-*šú* *iz-qut-su* : *šá zi-iq-tu*$_4$: *šá* Á 15-*šú* *ana*] ⌞^{lu_2}MAŠ.MAŠ⌟
16′) [*i-zaq-qí-tú* ...]

Translation

***Sa-gig S1: 26 (U1: 27)**

The divinatory significance of a kicking donkey is extended to include stormy weather, because the storm-god's name ^{d}Ud-dè-anše involves the element ANŠE "donkey." Also, *raḫāṣu* "to kick, devastate" very often describes the storm-god's floods.

(Rev. 1′–2′) ... ["If a donkey kicks (RA) him."]

(2′–3′) GÌR RA.RA [(*means*) to kick.]

(3′) [GÌR *means* foot.]
(3′) [RA *means* to strike.]

(3′–4′) Secondly, ^{d}Ud-dè-an-anše (*or*) [Ud-da *refers to* the storm-god Adad.]

Sa-gig S1: 30 (U1: 37a)

The commentator explained this omen about a "prowling god," so that it referred not only to some invisible divine or demonic being, but also to star constellations or cultic persons such as the "shaman" and "(man-of)-the-knot of Narudu," which are more readily observable.

(4′) ["If he sees a prowling god."]

(4′–5′) ... Lady of the gods or [Gazbaba].

(5′) [Secondly], Unnānîššu.

(5′–6′) (Thirdly), "^{lu_2}an-na-ba-ti (*or*) [lú-^{giš}kéš-da : nin-nun-gal-e-ne], *which means* shaman *or* (man-of)-the-knot of Narudu *respectively*."

Sa-gig S1: 31 (U1: 30)

(7′) ["If he sees an ecstatic, Hand of the god Ninurta."]

The GUB.BA element in their names links "an ecstatic" to "the god Ninurta."

(7′) ^{lu_2}GUB.BA (*means*) "an ecstatic."
(7′–8′) Lugal-ba-gub-ba (*refers to*) [the god Ninurta].

This lexical list extends the omen's applicability to other cultic persons associated with the "ecstatic." Instead of ^{lu_2}AN.SAL.LA for "male cultic prostitute," the apparent writing LÚ ^{d}*Gu-la* "man of the goddess Gula" may attempt to define this profession in relation to Gula.

(8′–9′) "[^{lu_2}an-dib-ba-ra], ní-zu-ra-aḫ, kur-gar-ra, *and* LÚ ^{d}*Gu-la* (*refer to*) [ecstatic, catamite, cultic performer,] *and* male cultic prostitute *respectively*."

Sa-gig S1: 32 (U1: 39a)

(9′–10′) "(If) he sees a deaf man; [Hand of the god Nergal]."

This horoscope links the god Nergal's constellation (^{mul}Ka-du$_8$-a) to muteness and deafness, as expressed by its elements: ka "speech" + DU$_8$.A "dispersed."

(10′) ["(If a child) is born under the constellation ^{mul}Ka-du$_8$-a (Cygnus);] he will be mute; secondly, deaf."

This is a quotation from the omen series *Šumma izbu* IV, 38.

(11′–12′) "[(If) both ears of an anomaly do not have ear-holes], the downfall of Durgišlû [will occur]."

This association is proposed in the *Principal Commentary to Šumma izbu* IV, 38, as well as attested in the lexical text Erimhuš V, 21–22.

(12′) ["Durgišlû *or* Dur-giš-lam *refers to* the city of Nippur."]

Nippur's downfall is associated with Nergal, who is perhaps identified with Erra and his destruction of cities in the *Erra Epic*. The absence of ear-holes and, hence, deafness is therefore connected to Nergal.

(12′–13′) "Durgišlû (*refers to*) [the city Nippur," because of the god Nergal].

Sa-gig S1: 33 (U1: 38b)
To show the link between ^{lu_2}BA.AN.ZU and the god Ninurta (^{d}MAŠ), the element BA.AN is interpreted as a reference to the sign bán with its logographic value MAŠ "half."

(13′) ["If he sees a ^{lu_2}BA.AN.ZU, Hand of the god Ninurta."]

BA.AN.ZU refers to one whose stature is "half" (bán) that of a normal "man" (ZA).

(13′) [^{lu_2}BA.AN.ZU *means* stunted *or*] dwarf.

BA.AN.ZU refers to one who has only "half" (bán) his "wits" (ZU).

(14′) [^{lu_2}BA.AN.ZU *means* half-witted.]

Though the ancient distinctions between these terms are uncertain, the "gnome" and "pygmy" are also relevant to this omen due to their associations with the "stunted."

(14′) [GIG.TIL.LA *means* stunted, gnome, *or*] pygmy.

Sa-gig S1: 36 (U1: 31)
The omen can mean that the magician's right arm stings him (i.e., gives him a "stinging pain"), or someone else's right arm points at the magician—with the root *zaqātu* encompassing various ideas involving a "sting" or a "point."

(15′) ["If his right arm (performs the action of) *izqut* to him" *refers to* the case of a stinging pain (*ziqtu*),]

(15′–16′) [*or* the case where (some)one's right arm points (*izaqqit*) at] the magician. …

Notes

Rev. 1′–4′—// Comm. Sa-gig 1A, lines 28–29 (main Note) // Comm. Sa-gig 1B, rev. 10 // Comm. Sa-gig 1C, rev. 3′ on how the divinatory significance of a kicking donkey is extended to include stormy weather as well, based on one of the names of the storm-god Adad (^{d}Ud-dè-anše), which seems to involve the element ANŠE ("donkey"). The signs here are Ud-dè-an-an[še] (rev. 3′), not U$_4$.DÈ.an[še] as rendered by the typo in the printed edition *SpTU* v, 256.

Rev. 4′–6′—// Comm. Sa-gig 1A, lines 29–32 (main Note) // Comm. Sa-gig 1B, rev. 13–17 // Comm. Sa-gig 1C, rev. 4′ on defining the omen's "prowling god" (Sa-gig S1: 30 (U1: 37a)) not only as some invisible being, but also as star constellations or cultic persons, which are more readily observable. Also, see Note on Comm. Sa-gig 1A (lines 29–32) for my proposal that lú-^{giš}kéš-da is a reference to the "ecstatic" (*maḫḫû*). Here, the preserved writing [...]x *be-let* DINGIR.MEŠ ("... Lady of the gods"; rev. 4′) may be interpreted in several ways: (I) It may relate to the divine name in the damaged end of Comm. Sa-gig 1A, rev. 29. Judging by the tablet (see Plate 2), the damaged portion seems to contain only one or two signs. (II) It may represent an interpretation of the name Urgula (Leo), in which the /gula/ element is understood as Gula the goddess of healing, who is then addressed as "Lady of the gods." In fact, considering that this commentary otherwise adheres closely to the text of Comm. Sa-gig 1A, the position of "Lady of the gods" here corresponds well to that of "Urgula (Leo)" in Comm. Sa-gig 1A. (III) It may refer to either "Bēltīya" or "Bēlet-Eanna" (^{d}INNIN ⟨É⟩.AN.NA) in Comm. Sa-gig 1B, rev. 14. One wonders if, especially with the omission of the sign É in the latter, the writing ^{d}INNIN(*Bēlet*) ⟨É⟩.AN(𒀭).NA could have been confused as *Bēlet* DINGIR(𒀭).MEŠ. Against this view, however, is the fact that this commentary (Comm. Sa-gig 1D) follows the text of the Comm. Sa-gig 1A, rather than Comm. Sa-gig 1B. In rev. 5′, the correct reading is *Un-na-niš*(!)*-šú*, not érin.me *na-man*(!)*-šá* as rendered in the printed edition *SpTU* V, 256.

Rev. 7′–9′—// Comm. Sa-gig 1A, lines 32–34 // Comm. Sa-gig 1B, rev. 10–11. The quotation in lines 33–34 resembles a section in the lexical list Erimhuš III, 169–172 (*MSL* XVII, 51): $^{\text{lu}_2}$gub-b[a-ra] = *mu-*[*u*]*ḫ-ḫu-*[*ú*], ní-zu-ra-⸢aḫ⸣ = *zab-b*[*u*], kur-[gar-r]a = *kur-ga-ru-u*, $^{\text{lu}_2}$an-sal-la(!) = *as-sin-nu*. George (1991: 160) examined the variations between Erimhuš and this commentary. If von Weiher's hand copy in *SpTU* V, 256 is accurate, the signs at the end of rev. 8′ are not $^{\text{lu}_2}$an-sal-la (𒇽 𒀭 𒊩 𒆷) as expected, but LÚ ^{d}*Gu-la* (𒇽 𒀭 𒄖 𒆷) ("man of the goddess Gula"). Given the great similarities in writing, the variation can easily be attributed to scribal confusion, though it is also possible that the "male cultic prostitute" (*assinnu* = $^{\text{lu}_2}$an-sal-la) was intentionally defined in this context of sickness as "man of the (healing) goddess Gula." Peled (2014: 283–297) argued that *assinnu* denoted an effeminate figure in contrast to the masculine *kurgarrû*. For Ninurta's name ^{d}Lugal-i-bí-gub-ba (rev. 7′–8′), see note by Lambert in Durand (1979: 170).

Rev. 9′–13′—// Comm. Sa-gig 1A = lines 35–38 (main Note) // Comm. Sa-gig 1B, rev. 20–21 on the god Nergal's association with deafness, based on the analysis of his constellation ^{mul}UD.KA.DU$_8$.A (Cygnus) as ka ("speech") + DU$_8$.A ("spread out," i.e., "dispersed"), as well as an omen that ascribes to Nergal the downfall of Durgišlû (Nippur) portended by a birth anomaly without ear-holes (*Šumma izbu* IV, 38). The signs in rev. 11′ are [Š]UB-*ti*, not [Š]UB-*di* as rendered by the typo in the printed edition *SpTU* v, 256. Restoring the mostly damaged rev. 13′ on the basis of Comm. Sa-gig 1A results in an unusually long line, and it is possible that either NIBRU^{ki}-*ú* ("the city Nippur") or *áš-šú* ^{d}U.GUR ("because of the god Nergal") was omitted here in Comm. Sa-gig 1D.

Rev. 13′–14′—// Comm. Sa-gig 1A, lines 38–40 (main Note) // Comm. Sa-gig 1B, rev. 17–19 // Comm. Sa-gig 1C, rev. 6′ on the analysis of ^{lu_2}BA.AN.ZU as a "stunted" man whose stature is "half" (bán) that of a normal "man" (ZA), or a "half-witted" man who has only "half" (bán) his "wits" (ZU).

Rev. 15′–16′—See Note on Comm. Sa-gig 1A, line 41 for the commentator's interpretation of the root *zaqātu* as encompassing various ideas involving a "sting" or a "point."

Commentary Sa-gig 1–3

Provenance: Ḫuzirīna (Sultantepe)
Period: Neo-Assyrian (7th century BCE)
Names: Colophon absent
Script: Neo-Assyrian

Field/Museum No.: S.U. 51/070 (Ankara Archaeological Museum, Turkey)
Printed Hand Copy: *STT* II, 403 (= Gurney and Hulin 1964)
Printed Edition: Wee (2012: 543–561)
Digital Resources: CDLI P338717; CCP 4.1.1.D (printed hand copies digitized by Frahm, Frazer, and Jiménez 2013)
Discussion: von Soden (1966: 563) and (1977: 29); Landsberger (1967b: 24); Leichty (1973: 83); Civil (1987: 50); Mayer and van Soldt (1991: 114); Stol (1991–1992: 47 n. 36), (1998: 348), and (2007a: 9 n. 15, 11 n. 24); Kouwenberg (1997: 411) and (2010: 311 n. 90); Böck (2000a: 75 n. 372) and (2010: 79 n. 183); Heeßel (2000: 133, 139 (1. Tafel MS e), 140 (2. Tafel MS a), 141 (3. Tafel MS a)), (2001/2002: 43 n. 51, 44 n. 61, 45–46), and (2010a: 161 n. 36); Scurlock and Andersen (2005: 806, see references to *STT* 403); Worthington (2009: 134); Reynolds (2010: 302); Genty (2010b: 11, 16, 18, 19 with typo: "STT 406"); Frahm (2010a: 171), (2011a: 108, 223–224, 272, 333 n. 1589), and (2014: 327); Wee (2012: 543–561), (2015a: 261–263, 267–268), and (in press: §G); Scurlock (2014: 25–28 (various notes), 43 n. 86, 93 n. 63, 356 n. 2); Salin (2015: 322); Jiménez and Schmidtchen (2017: 217 n. 8, 223, 225); Couto-Ferreira (2017: 63); Steinert (2018: 267 n. 67)
Pericope: At least Sa-gig 3: 5–88

Transliteration

Obverse

1) [x]x ba || du ta a [x]
2) ˡᵘ²BA.⌈AN⌉.ZU || *ḫu*-⌈*zu*⌉-[*ú*]
3) GABA.⌈GÁL⌉.LA || *su-nu-ša-t*[u_4]

 | DOI:10.1163/9789004417564_006

4) *za-mu-ú* || ⌜*si-ip*⌝-*pu*
5) *na-ṣa-bu* || ^{giš}*pi-sa-an-nu*
6) *zi-i-bu* || *ḫa-ru-ḫa-a-a*
7) *a-ri-bu* || *qa-rib maṣ-ḫa-a-ti*
8) [*k*]*a-ṣa-a-ti* || *ki-ma* ^{d}UTU ŠÚ
9) [M]UŠ.[D]ÍM.[GU]RUN.NA || *iṣ-ṣu-ʾu*
10) [*aš-q*]*u-la-*lu_4 || *il-ʾa-ta* ^{d}UTU
11) [*ḫa-*]*mi-tú* || *ne-ni-gal-li*
12) [*bi*]*r-ṣu* || *kak-ka-bu*
13) [EN.NU]N.BAR.RA!(ṣi) || *ma-ṣar-ti ba-ra-ri-ti*
14) [EN.NU]N.ZALAG$_2$!(sig$_5$).GA || *ma-ṣar-ti na-*^{ma}*mari*$_x$(A)-*ti*
15) [x]x lu || *a-ši-pu*

---

16) [*ne*]-*ʾ-a* || ⌜*x-x*⌝-*ú*
17) KÚM ⌜*la ḫa-ḫa-šá* (?)⌝ || KÚM ⌜*la dan*⌝-*nu*
18) *bir-*⌜*ti*⌝ Á.2-*šú* || *bi-rit* MAŠ.SILA$_3$.MEŠ-*šú*
19) ŠÀ-*šú i-ta-na-ší*(si) || Š[À]-*šú ana* BURU$_8$ *e-te-ni-la-a*
20) [*ḫ*]*e-ḫe-en* KIR$_4$-*šu* || *ṣe*$_x$(si)-*nu-ni-tu*$_4$ *šá* KIR$_4$-*šu*
21) [*šu-r*]*u-ʾ-*⌜*šu*⌝ || *a-ga-pi* IGI.2-*šú*
22) [*ši-bit*] SAG.DU-*šú paṭ-rat* ÚŠ || SAG.DU-*šú* TAG.MEŠ
23) [*ú-ru*]-*uḫ* SAG.DU-*šú bé-*[*e-er*] || *bé-ri-it-tú šá* SAG.DU-*šú mar-ṣa-at*
24) [*ú-ru*]-⸤*uḫ*⸥-*šu bé-e-er* || DILIB$_2$(ka×šid) *ú-ru-uḫ* DILIB$_2$ *a-la-tú*
25) [------------]------------------------------ || ÚḪ *ul i-la-ʾ-ut*
26) [*kal-li* SAG].DU-*šú saḫ-rat* || SÍG SAG.DU-*šú saḫ-rat*
27) [pé(/bi)-ret(/rit) SAG.]DU-*šú sa-mi* || SÍG SAG.DU-*šú sa-ma-at*
28) [SÍG SAG.DU-*š*]*ú se-pat* ÚŠ || SI *se-pu-u* SI *e-né-šú* SÍG SAG.DU-*šú in*$_4$(en)-*qúr*
29) [...] x || *su-uḫ-si*
30) [...]x || pa qu ru šu
31) [*i-ṭa-mu*] || *i-da-al*
32) [*ú-kan-na-an*] || *ú-qa-ab-bar*

Reverse

33) [... || ...]*x-šú*
34) [... || ...]x *a-ki-im-ma*
35) [... || *i*]*t-ta-*[*n*]*a-ad-la-aḫ*
36) [ŠÀ-*šú* GAZ.MEŠ-*šú* ||] ⌜*i*⌝-*bu-ut-su*
37) [a-lagab] || *ḫu-ṭa-*[*r*]*u ù* GÚ.ZI

38)	[-----------------------------------]------------	‖ GIDRU [*s*]*a-a-*⌊*ru*⌋ *ḫu-ṭa-ru*
39)	[-----------------]------------------------------	‖ *sa-ma-li* GÚ.ZI
40)	[KI.SIKIL.B]ÀN.DA	‖ *ba-tul-tu*
41)	[MU *k*]*i-gul-lim u áš-tam-me*	‖ *ke-ze-ru u ḫa-rim-tu*
42)	⌈*ú*⌉*-rap-pad*	‖ *ú-par-rad*
43)	*ina* DU$_{11}$.DU$_{11}$*-šú it-te-né-ep-rik-ku*$_8$(gu)	‖ *ina* DU$_{11}$.DU$_{11}$*-šú ib-ta-nak-ki*
44)	*lu-ʾ-tu*$_4$	‖ *kiš-pu*
45)	*ana ma-al-taq*(/*tak*)*-ti*	‖ *a-na la-ta-ki*
46)	*lu-ʾ-a-ti*	‖ *la-ʾa-šu*
47)	ŠE U.MEŠ*-šú*	
	TA GABA!(mu) *ap-pat* ŠU.SI.MEŠ*-šú*	‖ EN SAG *ṣu-ur-ri-šu*
48)	[Ḫ]ÁŠ-⌊*su*⌋ KALA*-an*	‖ KI.TA LI.DUR *er*!(sa)*-ri* SILIM
49)	[Š]U.2*-šú* GÌR.2*-šú* [KÚ]M*-šu*	‖ ŠU.2*-šú* GÌR.2*-šú ka-ṣi*$_x$(si)*-a*
50)	ŠU.2*-šú* GÌR.2*-šú tar-ṣa-šu*	‖ [ŠU.2*-šú* GÌR.2*-šú*] ⌊*šag-ga*⌋
51)	*i-ta-na-zu*	‖ *ik-k*[*il*]-⌈*lu*⌉ ŠUB.ŠUB*-di*
52)	MÚD *i-ta-na-ḫu*	‖ MÚD *ú-qa-ʾa*
53)	MÚD *i-ḫa-ḫu*	‖ MÚD *i-qe-ʾe*
54)	*ú-šam-šá*	‖ *an-ni-*⌈*mi*(?)⌉*-šu* Ù *né-*⌈*eḫ*⌉*-ḫu* ŠUB
54b)	--	‖ ⌈*la*⌉ *i-*⌈*na-al*(?)⌉
55)	KÚM*-šú mit-ḫar*	‖ DÙ SU*-šu ṣa-bit*

Translation

(Obv. 1) …

Sa-gig U1: 38b (S1: 33)

(2) "^{lú_2}BA.AN.ZU" *refers to* a lame man.

Sa-gig U1: 42b (S1: 49)

(3) "GABA.GÁL.LA" *refers to sunnušātu*-carts(?).

Sa-gig 2: 3

(4) "Outer corner" *refers to* wall edge.

Sa-gig 2: 6

pisannu "gutter" has been described as a wooden version of *naṣṣabu* "drain pipe."

(5) "Drain pipe" *refers to* (wooden) gutter.

Sa-gig 2: 7

(6) "The *zību*-vulture" *refers to* the *ḫarruḫāya*-vulture.

Sa-gig 2: 13
In lexical texts, these bird names are not linked with each other, but both are associated with the *ḫaḫḫuru*-raven.

(7) "The *āribu*-raven" *refers to* the *qārib maṣḫâti*-raven.

Sa-gig 2: 48
The explanation implies continuity of the regions beneath western and eastern horizons.

(8) "Early morning" *refers to* when the sun is (still) set.

Sa-gig 2: 48
The *pizallūru*-gecko is a larger or more decorated version of the *iṣṣû*-gecko.

(9) "The *pizallūru*-gecko" *refers to* the *iṣṣû*-gecko.

Sa-gig 2: 51
ašqulālu denotes an atmospheric phenomenon of sorts.

(10) "*ašqulālu*" *refers to* the exultation of the sun-god Šamaš.

Sa-gig 2: 61

(11) "The *ḫamītu*-wasp" *refers to* the *nenigalli*-insect.

Sa-gig 2: 72
The commentator may have understood the omens about "a flash" in Sa-gig 2: 72–75 to be the continuation of preceding omens (Sa-gig 2: 63–71) on shooting stars.

(12) "A flash" *refers to* a (shooting) star.

Sa-gig 2: 72
The typical writing is EN.NUN.AN.USAN, and EN.NUN.BAR.RA has been influenced by the syllabic values of *barārītu* "evening watch."

(13) "EN.NUN.BAR.RA" *means* the evening watch.

Sa-gig 2: 74
The correct sign $ZALAG_2$ was confused with SIG_5(= $igi.zalag_2$). It is

(14) "EN.NUN.SIG_5.GA (mistake for EN.NUN.$ZALAG_2$.GA)" *means* the morning watch.

uncertain if the commentator was trying to correct this error from his base text, or if the error originated with the commentator himself.

***Sa-gig 2**

(15) … *refers to* the magician.

***Sa-gig 3: 5—"his temples are *ne-eḫ-a*"**

(16) "(His temples) are *neʾā*" *means* …

***Sa-gig 3: 6—"his temples are hot la(-)ḫa-aḫ-šá"**
The damaged topic seems to have been understood as KÚM *lā ḫaḫḫaš* "non-*ḫaḫḫaš* heat," which is explained by the description "non-strong heat" that appears in some therapeutic texts.

(17) "Non-*ḫaḫḫaš* heat (?)" *means* non-strong heat.

Sa-gig 3: 9
"Between his arms" is explained more precisely as "between his shoulders." The "shoulder" occurs rarely in the Diagnostic Handbook, but is common in therapeutic texts.

(18) "Between his arms" *means* between his shoulders.

Sa-gig 3: 13 (TDPT 3: 4)
The statement "his belly (*libbu*) keeps rising (< *našû*)" uses terms that are cognate to the theme of "(sexual) arousal" (*nīš libbi*) in the base text. The commentator, however, interpreted this statement as the common medical description of the patient's belly heaving to vomit.

(19) "His belly keeps rising" *means* his belly keeps coming up to vomit.

Sa-gig 3: 15 (TDPT 3: 6)
ḫeḫēn occurs rarely in the Diagnostic Handbook and not in therapeutic texts. The explanation here may be

(20) "*ḫeḫēn* of his nose" *refers to* *ṣenunītu* of his nose.

inspired by the Asakku-monster's description in *Lugale* VI, 33 as "*ṣennītum* (= *ṣenunītu*?) whose issue from the nose is unpleasant."

Sa-gig 3: 22 (TDPT 3: 13)
In the Diagnostic Handbook, *šu-ru-ʾ* appears along with other similar forms, at least some of which denote the "eyebrows" (*šuʾru*).

(21) "His *šu-ru-ʾ*" *refers to* the flaps of his eyes.

Sa-gig 3: 24 (TDPT 3: 15)
paṭāru often describes "slack" body parts, but the commentator explained that it means "split" here and describes a fissure in the head.

(22) "[The seam of] his head (is) *paṭrat*, he will die" *means* his head is touched (i.e., breached).

Sa-gig 3: 27 (TDPT 3: 18)
The commentator may have understood the unusual verb *bēr* as cognate to *berittu* "in-between area > partition," perhaps denoting a bald spot where the hair is "parted."

(23) "The *uruḫḫu*-hair of his head (is) *bēr*" *means* the partition of his head is sick.

Sa-gig 3: 28 (TDPT 3: 19)

(24) "His *uruḫḫu*-hair is parted (*bēr*)."

The commentator probably wished to associate the loss of "*uruḫḫu*-hair" (DILIB$_2$) with the medical condition of not "swallowing" (DILIB$_2$) spittle.

(24) DILIB$_2$ (*means*) "*uruḫḫu*-hair."
(24) DILIB$_2$ (*means*) to swallow.

(25) He does not swallow spittle.

Sa-gig 3: 32a (TDPT 3: 23a)
The rare term *kalli* SAG.DU (lit. "bowl of head") does not appear in therapeutic texts. The commentator argued that this body part itself is not "curved," but serves as a metonym for its "curved" or "curled" hair.

(26) "[The bowl] of his head is curved" *means* the hair of his head is curved (i.e., curled).

Sa-gig 3: 32b (TDPT 3: 23b)
The signs are not to be read as *bi-rit* "within" but *pé-ret* "hair (of)," even though the feminine noun *peret* "hair" disagrees in gender with the masculine verb *sami* "is faltering" in the base text. "Faltering" hair is described elsewhere as hair that is "lacking" or "spread (thin)."

(27) "[pé(/bi)-ret(/rit)] of his head is faltering" *means* SÍG-hair of his head is faltering.

***Sa-gig 3: 32b/c (TDPT 3: 23b/c) ?**
The commentator explained that the "plucked" appearance of hair results from its "weak" attachment to the scalp, so that it comes off easily when the patient pulls on it.

(28) "[The hair of] his [head] is plucked, he will die."

(28) SI (*means*) to pluck.
(28) SI (*means*) to become weak.

(28) He tore out the hair of his head.

***Sa-gig 3: 33 (TDPT 3: 24)—K[I.NÁ NU ÍL] ?**

(29) ... *means* bed.

***Sa-gig 3**

(30) ...

***Sa-gig 3: 35 (TDPT 3: 26)—"his head staggers about"**
ṭamû "to stagger (about)" occurs very commonly in the Diagnostic Handbook, but not in therapeutic texts.

(31) "[It staggers about]" *means* it wanders about.

***Sa-gig 3: 35 (TDPT 3: 26)—"he makes contorted his right foot"**
kanānu "to contort" is more common in the Diagnostic Handbook than in therapeutic texts.

(32) "[He makes contorted]" *means* he rolls up.

***Sa-gig 3**

(Line 33) ...

***Sa-gig 3**

(34) ...

***Sa-gig 3**

(35) … [*means*] he keeps being disturbed.

***Sa-gig 3: 41 (TDPT 3: 32)**

(36) "[His belly keeps crushing him]" *means* it breaks him down.

***Sa-gig 3: 42 (TDPT 3: 33)—**
"a-lagab and *samālu*-cup"
In the base text, the rare term a-lagab is paired with the *samālu*-cup. Though the commentator did not know what a-lagab meant, he reasoned that this object would be associated with the *samālu*-cup also in lexical lists.

(37) ["a-lagab"] *means* staff or *kāsu*-cup.

In the lexical list quoted here, therefore, the two objects before and after "*samālu*-cup" (i.e., "staff" and "*kāsu*-cup") furnish two possible identities for a-lagab.

(38–39) "Stick, whisk, staff, *samālu*-cup, *kāsu*-cup."

Sa-gig 3: 42 (TDPT 3: 33)
KI.SIKIL.BÀN.DA "adolescent girl" is differentiated as a younger person than KI.SIKIL = *ardatu* "young woman." The term *ardatu* occurs commonly in the name of KI.SIKIL.LÍL.LÁ "*ardat lilî*-demoness."

(40) "KI.SIKIL.BÀN.DA" *means* adolescent girl.

Sa-gig 3: 42 (TDPT 3: 33)
The base text euphemistically attributes the girl's sickness to "the place of destruction(?) (and) tavern," but the commentator identified her behavior in these places as involving "*kezēru*-payment" and service as a "prostitute."

(41) "[Because of] the place of destruction(?) and tavern" *refers to* *kezēru*-payment and prostitute.

Sa-gig 3: 46 (TDPT 3: 37)
urappad "he wanders about" is very common in the Diagnostic Handbook, but absent in therapeutic texts.

(42) "He wanders about" *means* he causes shudders.

***Sa-gig 3: 50 (TDPT 3: 41)—*i-na* D[U$_{11}$.DU$_{11}$-*šú it-te-né-ep-rik-ku*] ?**
naparkû "to stop" describes the patient's speech only in the Diagnostic Handbook, not in therapeutic texts. Sobs or moans are explained as what interrupt the speech.

(43) "When he speaks, (his spoken words) keep stopping" *means* when he speaks, he keeps weeping.

***Sa-gig 3: 51 (TDPT 3: 42)—[*ana ma-al-taq*(/*tak*)-*ti lu-ʾ-tu$_4$ š*]*u-kul* ?**
Instead of *luʾtu* "corruption," the more common form *luʾâti* "dirty things" (see line 46 below) in both the Diagnostic Handbook and therapeutic texts denotes harmful substances victims were made to eat or drink.

(44) "Corruption (*luʾtu*)" *refers to* sorcery.

***Sa-gig 3: 51 (TDPT 3: 42)—[*ana ma-al-taq*(/*tak*)-*ti lu-ʾ-tu$_4$ š*]*u-kul* ?**
The commentator mistakenly read the signs *ma-al-taq*(/*tak*)-*ti* as *maltakti* "testing," from the dictionary root *latāki* "to test." The correct reading is *maltaqti* "cutting-off," from the dictionary root *šatāqi* "to cut off."

(45) "For the purpose of *ma-al-taq*(/*tak*)-*ti*" *means* in order to test.

***Sa-gig 3: 52 (TDPT 3: 43)—[*lu-ʾ-a-ti šu-kul*] ?**
The meaning of *laʾāšu* is uncertain, but it resembles the form *luʾâti* "dirty things."

(46) "Dirty things (*luʾâti*)" *are related to the verb laʾāšu.*

Sa-gig 3: 62 (TDPT 3: 53)
ŠE U.MEŠ is absent in therapeutic texts. Its definition here as "distal phalanges" agrees with the head-to-foot sequence of Sa-gig Chapter 11, where ŠE U.MEŠ is preceded by "tips of fingers" and followed by "stomachs of fingers (= proximal phalanges)."

(47) "His ŠE U.MEŠ" (*refer to*) *the parts* (i.e., distal phalanges) from the frontier of the tips of his fingers until the top of the middle (phalanges of) his (fingers).

***Sa-gig 3: 67 (TDPT 3: 58)—**
ḪÁŠ-*su da-an*
ḪÁŠ = *emšu* "lower belly" occurs commonly in the Diagnostic Handbook and in physiognomic omens, but only rarely in therapeutic texts.

(48) "His ḪÁŠ is hard" *means* below the navel, the bowels are well.

***Sa-gig 3: 80 (TDPT 3: 71)—**
ŠU.2-*šú u* GÌR.2-*šú* ⌜KÚM-*ma*⌝?

(49) "His hands (and) his feet [are hot] for him" *means the opposite of* his hands (and) his feet are cold.

***Sa-gig 3**

(50) "His hands (and) his feet are stretched out for him" *means* (/ *means the opposite of*) [his hands and his feet] are slack/stiffened(?).

***Sa-gig 3**
azû "to make unnatural noises" seems to occur only here in the medical texts.

(51) "He keeps making unnatural noises" *means* he keeps emiting wailing sounds.

Sa-gig 3: 88 (TDPT 3: 79)—
"he spews out blood"
ḫaḫû "to spew out" is very common in the Diagnostic Handbook, but absent in therapeutic texts. Forms of *qâ'u* "to disgorge (out)" here may represent colloquial expressions used in non-medical contexts.

(52) He keeps spewing out blood *means* he disgorges out blood.

(53) "He spews out blood" *means* he disgorges blood.

***Sa-gig 3**
šumšû "to stay up all night" occurs several times in the Diagnostic Handbook, but is absent in therapeutic texts. The comment may allude to the wording of *Gilgamesh* XI, 232–233, which can depict a scenario in which one spends the night drifting towards sleep, but is hindered from actually falling asleep (in the patient's case, due to discomfort or pain).

(54–54b) "He stays up all night" *means* no sooner than restful sleep befalls, he cannot fall asleep (?).

***Sa-gig 3**
"His heat is evenly high" and other medical descriptions on the parity of temperatures throughout the body are common in the Diagnostic Handbook, but unattested in therapeutic texts.

(55) "His heat is evenly high" *means* the whole of his body is seized.

Notes

Intro—It is uncertain if the pericope for this commentary consisted of a single continuous block of base text that encompassed Sa-gig Tablets 1–3, or if it consisted of selected sections from Sa-gig Tablets 1, 2, and 3 (as in the case of Comm. Sa-gig 10 & 11). While the commentary topics here do not reflect a line-by-line examination of the base text as clearly as those in the Uruk commentaries of Anu-ikṣur, they nonetheless follow the general sequence of items in Sa-gig Tablet 3, and probably in Tablets 1 and 2 as well. In particular, the base texts of entries in obv. 2 and 3 can be identified as Sa-gig U1: 38b (S1: 33) and Sa-gig U1: 42b (S1: 49) respectively. Assuming that these base text entries were not too far apart from each other, we arrive at the conclusion that the base text of Sa-gig Tablet 1 employed in this Ḫuzirīna commentary likely represents the "variant version" (Sa-gig U1) from Uruk, rather than the "standard version" (Sa-gig S1) from Dūr-Šarrukēn, Nippur, and probably Babylon, as defined by George (1991: 137–168). Numerous features in this commentary tablet may be reflective of the scribe's (not necessarily the commentator's) cuneiform proficiency or of peculiar characteristics in the local scribal culture, including: (1) Apparently miswritten signs like [EN.NU]N.BAR.RA!(ṣi) (obv. 13), [EN.NU]N.ZALAG$_2$!(sig$_5$).GA (obv. 14),

GABA!(mu) (line 47), *er*!(sa)-*ri* (line 48). (II) Less common orthographic choices such as *na-*^{ma}*mari*$_{x}$(A)-*ti* (obv. 14), *in*$_{4}$(en)-*qúr* (obv. 28), *it-te-né-ep-rik-ku*$_{8}$(gu) (line 43), and fluid uses of the cuneiform sign si for other sibilants in *i-ta-na-ší*(si) (obv. 19) and *ka-ṣi*$_{x}$(si)-*a* (line 49). (III) Atypical byforms like *ṣe*$_{x}$(si)-*nu-ni-tu*$_{4}$ (obv. 20) in place of *ṣennītu*, the unexplained shift from *a-la-tú* (obv. 24) to *i-la-ʾ-ut* (< *laʾātu*; obv. 25), and the unclear relationship between what seem to be presented as cognate forms *lu-ʾ-a-ti* || *la-ʾa-šu* (line 46). (IV) Uses of the particle *ša* that defy strict parallelism in the syntaxes of topic and comment, e.g., ... KIR$_{4}$-*šu* || ... *šá* KIR$_{4}$-*šu* (obv. 20), [*ú-ru*]-*uḫ* SAG.DU-*šú* ... || *bé-ri-it-tú šá* SAG.DU-*šú* ... (obv. 23). (V) Unusual nuances of terms, such as the use of TAG.MEŠ (obv. 22) < *lapātu* ("to touch") with the sense "to cut, make a breach," and the role of *i-da-al* (obv. 31) < *dâlu* ("to wander about") in describing "staggering" movements of the head. (VI) The erroneous interpretation of *ma-al-taq*(/*tak*)-*ti* (line 45) as *maltakti* ("testing") from *latāku* ("to test"), instead of *maltaqti* < *maštaqti* ("cutting-off") from *šatāqu* "to cut off."

Obv. 2—See Note on Comm. Sa-gig 1B, rev. 17–19 for BA.AN.ZA as "stunted" (*pessû*) and "dwarf" (*kurû*), based on the analysis BA.AN (= reference to the sign bán with its logographic value MAŠ "half") + ZA ("man") in commentaries on Sa-gig Tablet 1. It is unclear that this analysis applied to Comm. Sa-gig 1–3, and so I give the dictionary translation of *ḫuzzû* = "lame, limping" (*CAD* Ḫ, 266) here. For the proposal that KÙ.ZU.MEŠ is another writing for *ḫunzû* (= *ḫuzzû*), see Stol (2007b: 236–237 n. 26).

Obv. 3—The signs *su-nu-ša-t*[*u*$_{4}$] here represent a form of the noun *sunnušu*, whose meaning is uncertain (*CAD* S, 384). Its logogram GABA.GÁL.LA in the base text Sa-gig U1: 42b (S1: 49) seems to refer to a vehicle of sorts, and has been described as a "(cart) box" (*pitnu*) drawn by a single equid in Comm. Sa-gig 1A, lines 45–46; Comm. Sa-gig 1B, rev. 29; and Comm. Sa-gig 1C, rev. 10′–11′.

Obv. 4—Associations between *zamû* ("outer corner") and *sippu* ("wall edge") occur in the lexical texts Malku III, 127, 130 (Hrůša 2010: 368); Antagal G, 71–72 (*MSL* XVII, 223).

Obv. 5—The *pisannu* gutter is described as a wooden version of *naṣṣabu* ("drain pipe") in these lexical texts: $^{pi\text{-}sa\text{-}an}$šid = *na-ṣa-bu šá* GIŠ (Antagal F, 154 in *MSL* XVII, 216); *pi-sa-an-nu* = *na-ṣa-bu šá* GIŠ (Malku IV, 142 in Hrůša 2010: 388); giš-[šid×a] = *pi-sa-an-nu* = *na-an-ṣa-bu* (Hg. B II, 102 and L II, 13 in Vedeler 2002: 58 and 103; cf. *MSL* VI, 111).

Obv. 6—Associations between the *zību*-vulture and the *ḫarruḫāya*-vulture occur in the lexical texts Hg. B IV, 242, 307 (Vedeler 2002: 74, 77; cf. *MSL* VIII/2, 166, 170); Hg. C I, 21 (Vedeler 2002: 88; cf. *MSL* VIII/2, 172).

Obv. 7—Though the *āribu*-raven and the *qārib maṣḫâti*-raven are not directly linked in lexical lists, both names are associated with the *ḫaḫḫuru*-raven in these texts: [ara$_2$-bu-mìn-na mušen] = *ur-bal-lum* = *ḫa-ḫur* AN.MEŠ = [*qa-ri-i*]*b maṣ-ḫa-a-ti* (Hg. B IV, 301 in Vedeler 2002: 77; cf. *MSL* VIII/2, 170); šir-bur mušen = [*a*]-*ri-bu* = *ḫa-aḫ-ḫur* (Hg. D III, 347 in Vedeler 2002: 96; cf. *MSL* VIII/2, 176); uga = *a-ri-bu* = *ḫa-aḫ-ḫur* (Hg. D III, 350 in Vedeler 2002: 96; cf. *MSL* VIII/2, 176); [šir-bur mušen] *a-ri-bu* : *ḫa-ḫur* = *a-ri-bu* (Hg. C I, 20 in Vedeler 2002: 88; cf. *MSL* VIII/2, 172).

Obv. 8—I translate the comment *ki-ma* ^{d}UTU ŠÚ as "when the sun is (still) set," i.e., when the sun has not yet risen in the east. In the common expression ^{d}UTU.ŠÚ.A ("sunset"), the term ŠÚ describes the sun's condition in the west. It is interesting, therefore, that the above interpretation "when the sun is (still) set" uses ŠÚ to denote the sun's position immediately below the eastern horizon, implying spatial continuity of the regions beneath western and eastern horizons. Alternatively, it is also possible that this commentary entry consists of an antonymous pair, i.e., "'Early morning' *means the opposite of* when it is sunset" (see §1.2.3.1.6). Finally, while the logogram ŠÚ in such time expressions has been understood as the verb *erēbu* ("to enter," i.e., the region below the horizon) (*MZL*, no. 869), there may be, in addition, an attempt at wordplay between *kaṣâtu* "early morning" and *kiššatu* "totality" (also expressed by the logogram ŠÚ).

Obv. 9—The *pizallūru*-gecko is described as a larger or more decorated version of the *iṣṣû*-gecko in the lexical text Uruanna III, 235–235a (*MSL* VIII/2, 62): *pi-za-lu-ur-tu* = *iṣ-ṣu-ú ra-bi-tú*, *pi-za-lu-ur-tú* = *iṣ-ṣu-ú uṣ-ṣur-tu*. See also Landsberger (1934: 41, line 46).

Obv. 10—This argument is transliterated as [*aš*]-*qu-la-lum* = *il*(or: *ru*)-ʾ-*ta* ^{d}UTU in *CAD* A II, 452, evidently positing some kind of confusion between the terms *ruʾtu* (logogram ÚḪ) "spittle" and *illātu* (logogram ÚḪ.MEŠ) "saliva." The same view was held by Heeßel (2001/2002: 43, 45) who translated the commentator's explanation as "Speichel der Sonne." I prefer to understand the writing *il-ʾa-ta* (obv. 10) as a form of *illatu* B, "exultation" (*CAD* I/J, 85). The *Hymn to Šamaš*, line 156 (Lambert 1960: 136–137) describes how "on the twentieth day, you (the sun-god) rejoice in exultation (*il-la-ta* > *alālu* B in *CAD* A I, 331–332) and jubilation."

Obv. 11—The insects here are also named in the equation NIM.UR$_4$.UR$_4$: NIM *ḫa-me-tú ne-ne-*[*gal-lum*] (*Uruanna* III, 222–222a; misunderstood as *bil-bil-*[*lu*] in *MSL* VIII/2, 61). Note also the diagnostic verdict Ì.DAB *ḫa-wi-i-tum*, "seizure of the *ḫamītu*-insect" in MS 2670 line 37′ (George 2013: 88).

Obv. 12—In the section Sa-gig 2: 63–71, the verb *ṣarāḫu* ("to flare up"; logogram SUR) describes the movement of a shooting star from one side of the patient to his other side. For the reading UL ("star") in Sa-gig 2: 63 from a collation of the tablet A 3439, see Reiner (1960: 29); Heeßel (2001/2002: 34, 39, 44). The section that immediately follows (i.e., Sa-gig 2: 72–75) employs a different noun *birṣu* ("flash, glow") that does not seem to travel from one side of the patient to his other side, even though the same verb *ṣarāḫu* ("to flare up") is used. Our commentator, however, may have understood section Sa-gig 2: 72–75 as a continuation of omens in Sa-gig 2: 63–71 that concern shooting stars. Notice that, in spite of the medical context of the Diagnostic Handbook Sa-gig, the term *birṣu* ("flash") here was not understood as the eye condition of seeing flashes (photopsia). See also Fincke (2000: 240–241); Scurlock and Andersen (2005: 187–188).

Obv. 13—Other medical texts express *barārītu* ("evening (watch)") with the more typical writing EN.NUN.AN.USAN (Sa-gig [19/20: 112′]; 26: 38′; *CAD* B, 105–106), and the unusual form EN.NUN.BAR.RA in the base text Sa-gig 2: 72 is quite clearly influenced by the syllabic values of *barārītu*. See Note on Comm. Sa-gig 4B, obv. 16 for time phases in medical texts.

Obv. 14—Collation has confirmed the writing [EN.NU]N.ZALAG$_2$!(sig$_5$).GA, and the signs zalag$_2$ () and sig$_5$(= igi.zalag$_2$) () are obviously similar enough to account for the scribal error here. Existing manuscripts of the base text Sa-gig 2: 74 have the reading EN.NUN.ZALAG(ud).GA, so it is uncertain whether this scribal error originated with the commentator or his base text copy. In addition to the base text Sa-gig 2: 74, the logogram EN.NUN.ZALAG$_{(2)}$.GA ("morning watch") also appears in Sa-gig 2: 75; [19/20: 113′]. For the term EN.NUN.UD.ZAL.LE (Sa-gig 4: 12; *BAM* 482 iv 46′; *AMT* 19/1 obv. 29′) as a variant of EN.NUN.ZALAG$_{(2)}$.GA, see Rochberg (1998: 36). See also my remarks on time phases in Comm. Sa-gig 4B, obv. 16. The comment obviously requires the Akkadian expression *maṣṣarti namārīti* ("morning watch"). While the signs *na-ma-a-ti* may represent an error (Heeßel 2001/2002: 45), it is possible that the term *namārīti* was intended by the erudite writing *na-*^{ma}*mari*$_x$(A)*-ti*, which alludes to the logographic value of A as *māru* ("son").

Obv. 15—This line is read as [*ap*(?)*-ga*]*l*(?)*-lu* = *a-ši-pu* in *CAD* A II, 431; Heeßel (2001/2002: 45). Alternatively, M. Jursa has suggested the restoration [*ka-kù-ga*]*l-lu* (mentioned in Heeßel 2001/2002: 46).

Obv. 16—Notice that the base text of Comm Sa-gig 3C = BM 54491, obv. 4 shares the orthography *ne-ʾ-a* here, in contrast to *ne-eḫ-a* in existing manuscript(s) BM 33424 // BM 46139 (obv. 3).

Obv. 17—Existing copies of the base text Sa-gig 3: 6 have the writing SAG.KI.2-*šú* KÚM la(-)aḫ-ḫa-ḫa-šá ("his temples are hot la(-)aḫ-ḫa-ḫa-šá"). There is, however, too much damage here to be confident that this was the orthrography encountered in the commentator's base text, especially since the base text for Comm. Sa-gig 3C = BM 54491, obv. 5 apparently contained the signs la(-)ḫa-aḫ-šá. In any case, the commentator here understood the topic as "non-*ḫaḫḫaš* heat," which he proceeded to explain as "non-strong heat." The specialized term *ḫaḫḫaš* (*CAD* Ḫ, 28) appears mostly in medical contexts as part of the expression KÚM (*lā*) *ḫaḫḫaš* ("(non)-*ḫaḫḫaš* heat"): Sa-gig 3: 55, 57, 59 (TDPT 3: 46, 48, 50); Sa-gig 4: 20, 54, 56, 58; 11: 54; 22: 31, 33; 33: 91; 40: 10, 101, 115; *BAM* 145: 5; 146: 31′; 174 rev. 30. The comment KÚM *dannu* ("strong heat") appears only in the therapeutic texts *BAM* 147 obv. 1, 12, 22; 148 obv. [12], 13, 22.

Obv. 18—The ambiguous phrase "between his arms" is explained more precisely as "between his shoulders," an expression that occurs in the therapeutic text *BAM* 372 iii 14′. As a matter of fact, the body part "shoulder" (MAŠ.SILA$_3$ = *naglabu*) is only rarely attested in the Diagnostic Handbook (Sa-gig 13: 116 (TDPT 13 iii 6); Sa-gig 22: 29), but it appears frequently in therapeutic texts: *BAM* 55: 3; 372 iii 14′; 560 iii 16′ (incl. *AMT* 49/5 ii 6′); *BAM* 564 ii [14′]; 574 ii 29; 575 iii 16, 30; *AMT* 22/2 obv. 3; 31/1: 3; 45/4: 2; 45/6 obv. 9′; 48/4 rev. 13′; 49/1 ii 11′; 49/2 rev. ii 7′; 49/4 obv. 1; 50/3 obv. 11; [rev. 7′]; 51/2: 7; 51/5 rev. 7′; 51/6 ii [1′], 4′; 51/8: 2′; 51/10: 4′; 51/12: 5′. Essentially the same topic (from Sa-gig 3: 9) and comment occur also in Comm. Sa-gig 3C, obv. 9.

Obv. 19—The commentary topic here involves the less common intransitive sense of the verb *našû* ("to rise, heave") in contexts involving the body part ŠÀ, "belly/heart" (*CAD* N II, 103 s.v. *našû* A §5.2′). The expression ŠÀ-*šú ittanašši* ("his belly/heart keeps rising") is cited from the base text Sa-gig 3: 13–14 (TDPT 3: 4–5), which ends with the diagnostic verdict GIM *šá ana* UGU MUNUS ŠUB -*tu* ÍL ŠÀ TUKU-*ši* ŠU KI.[SIKI]L.LÍL.LÁ.EN.NA ("like one who lies down upon a woman, he gets arousal (ÍL ŠÀ = *nīš libbi*), Hand of the *ardat lilî*-demoness"). Given how the terms of *nīš libbi* ("arousal," lit. "rising of the heart") are cognate with the expression ŠÀ-*šú ittanašši* ("his belly/heart keeps rising/heaving"), the latter should probably be understood as the rousing of sexual desire. In the ŠÀ.ZI.GA corpus of incantations and rituals against sexual impotence, the elements ŠÀ ("heart") and *našû* ("to rise, be aroused") also appear together in expressions other than *nīš libbi*. Note the following: ŠÀ-*šú* ÍL-*šú-ma* ... ŠÀ-*šú* N[U ÍL-*šú*] (Sm 818: 6′); *a-na* MUNUS-*šú* ŠÀ-*šú* NU ÍL (*AMT* 65/7: 3′); [ŠÀ-*šú* N]U ÍL-*ma* (*STT* 280 i 1); [ŠÀ-*šú*] NU ÍL-*šú* (*STT* 280 i 10) in Biggs (1967: 50 no. 34; 51, 66); ŠÀ-*šú-nu* ÍL-*šú-nu-ti* (*SpTU* I, 9: 14′). The commentator here, however, interpreted ŠÀ-*šú ittanašši* in light of several other expressions that describe the patient's belly as "rising," "coming up," or "proceeding" to vomit: ŠÀ-*šú ana a-re-e i-ta-na-šá-a* (Sa-gig 22: 26); ŠÀ-*šú ina pi-qi ana* BURU$_8$-*e* DÙ.DÙ-*uš*

(*BAM* 49: 11′; [50 obv. 13]); ŠÀ-*šu ana pa-re-e e-ta-né-pa-áš* (*BAM* 575 ii 17); ŠÀ-*šú ana* $BURU_8$ *i-te-né-él-la-a* (Sa-gig 3: 53 (TDPT 3: 44)); ŠÀ-*šú ana pa-re-e e-te-né-la-a* (*BAM* 578 i 27); ŠÀ-*šú ana pa-re-e i-te-né-*⌊*el-la*⌋ (*BAM* 578 i 47). In other words, the commentator understood ŠÀ-*šú ittanašši* in isolation from its original context of sexual arousal (Sa-gig 3: 13–14 (TDPT 3: 4–5)) and conflated its meaning with other similar descriptions on vomiting in the medical literature. See Note on Comm. Sa-gig 7A, rev. 5–6 for other instances where the expression "his belly keeps rising to vomit" appears as topic, in order (I) to explain the less common intransitive meaning ("to rise") of the verb *našû*, and (II) to forestall confusion between inflected forms of *našû* and *âšu* ("to retch"). See also yet another iteration of the same topic in Comm. Sa-gig 3B, rev. 5–6.

Obv. 20—The rare term *ḫeḫēn* ("mucus" according to *CAD* Ḫ, 184 s.v. *ḫiḫīnu*) occurs in the medical literature only at Sa-gig 3: 15, 33 (TDPT 3: 6, 24) and not in therapeutic texts. It is tempting to understand the additional *ša* particle in the comment (absent from the topic) as a commentary notation (§II.2.2), so that *ṣenunītu šá* KIR_4-*šu* reads as "*ṣenunītu*, in the case of his nose." However, a similar construction occurs in obv. 23: [*ú-ru*]-*uḫ* SAG.DU-*šú bé-*[*e-er*] || *bé-ri-it-tú šá* SAG.DU-*šú mar-ṣa-at* ("'The *uruḫḫu*-hair of his head (is) *bēr*' *means* the partition of his head is sick"), which suggests the scribe employed the *ša* particle to indicate less intimate genitive relationships (*GAG*, §138c), without an overriding concern to maintain strict parallelism in the syntaxes of a commentary's topic and comment. The transcribed term *ṣenunītu* represents my reading of the signs $ṣe_x$(si)-*nu-ni*-tu_4. It seems to be a *hapax* and is likely a byform of the skin condition *ṣennītu* (*CAD* S, 295 s.v. *sinunītu*; cf. *CAD* Ṣ, 127 s.v. *ṣennītu*; Scurlock and Andersen 2005: 229, §10.114). Objections to my reading of the sign $ṣe_x$(si) may be partly assuaged by fluid uses of the cuneiform sign si as the syllabic value *ší* in the expression *i-ta-na-ší*(si) (obv. 19) and, more pertinently, as the value $ṣi_x$ in the expression *ka*-$ṣi_x$(si)-*a* (line 49). The skin condition *ṣennītu* is not usually connected to the nose in a particular way, and the only passage (*Lugale* VI, 32–33) explicitly linking the two may have actually inspired the commentator's explanation: u_4-bu-bu-ul è-a-bi nu-du_{10}-ga / áš-gig-ga kir_4 è-a-bi nu-sig_5-ga = *bu-bu-ʾ-tú šá a-ṣu-šu la ṭa-a-bu* / *ṣe-en-ni-tum šá ina ap-pi a-ṣ*[*u-š*]*u la dam-qu* (description of the Asakku-monster's presence: "*bubuʾtu*-boil whose issue is unwholesome, *ṣennītum* whose issue from the nose is unpleasant"). See van Dijk (1983: 1,85; 2,89; lines 268–269); attributed to "*Lugale* V, 33" in *CAD* Ṣ, 127.

Obv. 21—Collation confirmed that the first partially preserved sign is [*r*]*u*, though the drawing in *STT* 403 obv. 21 may suggest otherwise. I restore the topic as [*šu-r*]*u*-ʾ-⌜*šu*⌝; cf. the reading [*x*]-*x*-ʾ-⌜*šu*⌝ in *CAD* Š III, 367 s.v. *šurʾu* A. The following orthographies are attested in the Diagnostic Handbook, but not in therapeutic texts: *šu-ru*-ʾ-*šú* (Sa-gig 3: 22 (TDPT 3: 13); Sa-gig 5: 46′ (TDPT 5 E1 12)); *šu-ú-ra-šú* (Sa-gig 6: 103″ (TDPT 6 rev. 41′)); and *šu-u*ʾ-*ra-šú* (Sa-gig 10: 27; 33: 97). The *Chicago Assyrian Dictionary* makes the distinction between (I) *šuʾru* (byforms: *šuḫru, šūru*) "eyebrow" (*CAD* Š III, 366–367); and (II) *šurʾu* A (byform: *šūru*) "(a part of the face or head)" (*CAD* Š III, 366). Notice that these allegedly separate anatomical terms are easily confused, not only because of their similar syllabic forms, but also because of their location at the person's face or head. The comment *agappi* is a form of *kappu*, which supposedly denotes the "eyelid" (Fincke 2000: 253–254; Rutz 2011: 305); cf. the broader definition of "the eyebrows, the eyelids, and the eyelashes" in *CAD* K, 187–188 s.v. *kappu* A §4a–c. Here, I rather literally translate *agappi* IGI.2-*šú* as "the flaps of his eyes," to reflect the incommensurability between Mesopotamian and modern ways of dividing up the human anatomy. A similar entry occurs in Comm. Sa-gig 5, line 23: SIG$_7$ *šur-ru* ⌜*kap-pi*⌝ [I]GI ("'SIG$_7$' (*means*) eyebrow (*or*) flap of the eye."), where the orthography *šur-ru* once again differs from the forms attested above. The commentator here defined [*šu-r*]*u*-ʾ-⌜*šu*⌝ as "the flaps of his eyes," but it is not clear whether he had in mind a facial feature separate from "eyebrow," or whether he understood [*šu-r*]*u*-ʾ-⌜*šu*⌝ as another way of writing "eyebrow."

Obv. 22—The verb *paṭāru* often describes "slack" or "loose" body parts, especially the patient's limbs. Here, however, the verb means "split" and denotes a fissure in the "seam" of the patient's head. The commentator clarified that *paṭāru* has this latter meaning by equating it with another verb TAG.MEŠ (< *lapātu*, "to touch"). Although *lapātu* is not associated with *paṭāru* in lexical texts, it is sometimes described as having the nuance "to cut, make a breach" (KUD = *nakāsu*). See the following: tag = [*la-pa-tu*], kud-da = [MIN *šá na-ka-si*] (Antagal VIII, 123–124 in *MSL* XVII, 174); šu-tag-t[ag] = [MIN (= *lapātu*)], kud-d[a] = [MIN *šá na-ka-si*] (Nabnitu G$_1$, ii 2″, 4″ in *MSL* XVI, 283). The form TAG.MEŠ can indicate Gtn and D stems of the verb *lapātu* (*CAD* L, 82–83), and I understand its use here as a D Stative, perhaps describing a condition similar to the examples in *CAD* L, 91 s.v. *lapātu* §4f. To be sure, in medical texts, TAG.MEŠ usually expresses the plurality of either the body parts or maladies involved in the "touch" (Sa-gig 11: 29–31; *BAM* 3 ii 7; 240: 17′; *AMT* 97/4: 7′–8′), with the exception being IM GIM *di-ik-ši ina* ŠÀ-*šú* TAG.MEŠ-*su* "as in the case of *dikšu*, wind touches him (repeatedly/severely) in his belly" (*BAM* 54: 1; [575 iii 28]).

Obv. 23—The Stative verb *bé-e-er* is unattested in therapeutic texts, but occurs in the Diagnostic Handbook and its precursors, almost always in reference to the patient's *uruḫḫu*-hair: Sa-gig 3: 27–30 (TDPT 3: 18–21); Sa-gig 4: 126 (TDPT 4 rev. 41); Sa-gig 37: 10 (TDPT 36: 10); 2N-T 336, rev. 1 (restored as *be-*[*e-e*]*r*); with the notable exception IGI.2-*šú bé-e-r*[*a*] ("his eyes are parted"; Sa-gig 5: 94′ (TDPT 5 F3 14)) whose unusualness resulted in its choice as a topic at Comm. Sa-gig 5, lines 30–31. See also physiognomic descriptions of the head or cranium with this verb in *Alamdimmû* II, 33–39 (Böck 2000a: 74). The first word in the comment has been read as *pé-re-et-tú* / *pí-ri-it-tú* ("hair") in *CAD* P, 415; U/W, 270; Böck (2000a: 75 n. 372); and Couto-Ferreira (2009: 92, typo: "*pe-re-et-tu*"), even though such a writing for *pertu* ("hair") seems rather forced, and the plural *pirētu* ("hairs") is out of place with the singular verb *marṣat*. I prefer the reading *bé-ri-it-tú* for *berittu* = *birītu* ("in-between area" > "partition"; *CAD* B, 252–255), which the commentator may have understood as a cognate of the rare verb *bé-e-er*. Perhaps a bald spot is meant by the expression "the hair of his head is parted (*bé-e-er*)." In support of this interpretation are close associations among the verbs *bêru*, *bêšu* ("to move apart"), and *petû* ("to open") in the lexical texts Ea II, 73–74 (*MSL* XIV, 250); Aa I/6, 145–146 (*MSL* XIV, 229); Aa II/3 Section A, 1–2 (*MSL* XIV, 276); Aa II/6, i 21–22 (*MSL* XIV, 290). See also *bé-e-šú* = *pe-tu-u* in Lambert (1960: 72, Commentary to line 44), as well as the equation of all three terms written as *bé-e-šú* ^{ra} = *pe-tu-u* in the *Principal Commentary to Izbu* VI, 12 in Leichty (1970: 219, line 239); De Zorzi (2014: 504, line 9). All three verbs may also be linked together in Comm. Sa-gig 5, lines 30–31 already mentioned above.

Obv. 24–25—"*Uruḫḫu*-hair" is expressed by the logogram DILIB(šid) (𒋃) in the lexical texts Ea VII, iii 1′ (*MSL* XIV, 450); Recip. Ea Section D, 8′ (*MSL* XIV, 531); Proto-Izi I, 258b (*MSL* XIII, 26); and by the logogram DILIB$_3$(sag×šid) ([cuneiform]) in S^b I, 246 (*MSL* III, 117). It appears as DILIB$_2$(ka×šid) ([cuneiform]) only in this commentary. See also Civil (1987: 50); Couto-Ferreira (2009: 91–92). On the other hand, the verb *alātu* ("to swallow") may take the logograms DILIB$_2$(ka×šid) (Erimhuš III, 64 in *MSL* XVII, 49) or DILIB$_3$(sag×šid) (Antagal A, 142–143 in *MSL* XVII, 186). For the argument to make sense, the Infinitive form *a-la-tú* (obv. 24) needs to be identified with the verb *i-la-ʾ-ut* (obv. 25), so that the verbal roots *alātu* (*CAD* A I, 336–337) and *laʾātu* (*CAD* L, 6–7) are treated as byforms. These two roots appear also in the equation *a-l*[*it*] = *áš-šú la-ʾ-a-ti* ("'Swallowed (*alit* < *alātu*)' because of (the dictionary root) to swallow (*laʾātu*)") in *Izbu* Comm. V, line 250 (Leichty 1970: 229), which Reiner (in Reiner et al. 1994: 92) deemed an example of "fanciful" etymologizing. The statement "he does not swallow (*ilaʾʾut* = DILIB$_2$) spittle" (obv. 25) most likely describes a medical condition that the commentator wished to associate with the loss of *uruḫḫu*-hair (DILIB$_2$).

Obv. 26—The order of commentary entries suggests that the base text here is Sa-gig 3: 32a (TDPT 3: 23a), even though the feminine verb *saḫ-rat* (obv. 26) differs from the masculine verb *sa-ḫir* in existing manuscripts. Note also the masculine verb in *kal-li* SAG.DU-*šú su-uḫ-ḫur* (2N-T 336, rev. 6) in a Middle Babylonian diagnostic text prior to Sa-gig. The basic meaning of *kallu* is that of a "bowl," and *kalli* SAG.DU (lit. "bowl of the head") presumably refers to the curved part of the skull (cf. *CAD* K, 83). This body part is mentioned only in the above diagnostic texts, and it does not seem attested in therapeutic texts or anatomical lists in Ugu-mu (Couto-Ferreira 2009: 73–127) and Nabnitu (Tablet I = *MSL* XVI, 49–60). The section Sa-gig 3: 27–32 (TDPT 3: 18–23) was evidently devoted to the topic of 'hair,' though it is not entirely clear how *uruḫḫu*-hair (Sa-gig 3: 27–31 (TDPT 3: 18–22)) and *pertu*-hair (Sa-gig 3: 32b (TDPT 3: 23b)) relate to *šārtu*, the usual term for "hair." Accordingly, the "bowl of the head" (*kal-li* SAG.DU), sandwiched at Sa-gig 3: 32a (TDPT 3: 23a) within this 'hair' section, was viewed by the commentator as a metonym for the hair growing above it. This may be analogous to how the modern colloquialism "red*head*" refers to a person with auburn *hair*. In other words, what is said to be "curved" (*saḫrat*) is not the skull itself, but only the hair above it (i.e., curled hair). One wonders whether the feminine verb *saḫrat* may point to an elided feminine subject such as *(*šārat* or *peret*) *kalli* SAG.DU ("(hair of) the bowl of the head").

Obv. 27—I restore the topic here as [pé(/bi)-ret(/rit) SAG.]DU-*šú sa-mi* from the base text Sa-gig 3: 32b (TDPT 3: 23b). The Stative form *sa-mi* (obv. 27) denotes the root *samû* ("to become faltering, inept"; *CAD* S, 125; *AHw*, 1020) rather than the more common root *sâmu* ("to become red"), since we would expect the Stative *sa-am* (< *sām*) in the case of the latter. *Contra* Scurlock and Andersen (2005: 157, §7.8; 708 n. 7). "Faltering" hair is explained as hair that is "lacking" in Comm. Sa-gig 21 & 22a, obv. 1–2, and described as hair that is "spread (thin)" in Comm. Sa-gig 39, obv. 7–8. What concerned the commentator here, however, was not the verb but its subject. Perhaps because of the disagreement in gender between the masculine verb *sa-mi* ("is faltering") and what would be a feminine noun *pé-ret* ("*pertu*-hair"), the latter signs were read as the preposition *bi-rit* ("within") by Labat (1951: 20); Scurlock (2014: 14). Other occurrences of *birīt* + body parts include *bi-ri-*[*it* KIR_4] (Sa-gig 6: 38 (TDPT 6 obv. 38′)) and *bi-rit* MAŠ.$SILA_3$.MEŠ (*BAM* 372 iii 14′). However, essentially the same expression *pe-ret* SAG.DU-*šú sa-mat* ("*pertu*-hair of his head is faltering") appears in Comm. Sa-gig 39 (obv. 7), where the verb this time is feminine (*sa-mat*, "is faltering"), and where it is improbable that the syllable signs should be read *bì*(pe)-*rit*. Furthermore, it is highly unlikely that the prepositional phrase (DIŠ) *birīt* SAG.DU-*šú*

(Sa-gig 3: 32b (TDPT 3: 23b)) precedes other entries beginning with DIŠ SAG.DU-*su* (Sa-gig 3: 33–78 (TDPT 3: 24–69)), since the convention in Sa-gig Chapter II was to list entries beginning with DIŠ + {body part} before other entries beginning with DIŠ + preposition + {the same body part}. The above considerations likely motivated the commentator to affirm that the writing [pé(/bi)-ret(/rit)] stood for *pé-ret* ("*pertu*-hair") and not *bi-rit* ("within"). He did so in two ways: (I) by equating the signs pé-ret with the logogram SÍG that unambiguously refers to "hair," and (II) by using the same verb (*samû*, "to become faltering") in the comment, but changing it from the topic's masculine form *sami* to the feminine form *samât*. See Note on Comm. Sa-gig 21 & 22a, obv. 11 for discussion of cases where a syllabic topic (*pé-ret* or *nim-šú-šú*) is explained by a logographic comment (SÍG or SA.MEŠ-*šú* respectively), even at the expense of writing conventions that logographic forms precede their syllabic equivalents (§1.2.3.1.1).

Obv. 28—The base text here is not preserved, but it might possibly fit into the damaged portion of Sa-gig 3: 32b/c (TDPT 3: 23b/c). In any case, it closely resembles the medical sign SÍG SAG.DU-*šú sa-pat* ("the hair of his head is plucked") in Sa-gig 3: 114b (TDPT 3: 105b). SI as the logogram for *sepû* ("to pluck") occurs in the lexical text Aa III/4, 177 (*MSL* XIV, 342). Though the verb *enēšu* ("to become weak") more often takes the logogram SIG, it is also expressed by SI in the lexical text Antagal G, 119 (*MSL* XVII, 224). The commentator explained that the "plucked" appearance of the patient's hair results from the fact that it is only weakly attached to the scalp, and that it comes off easily when the patient pulls on it. The statements "He tore out the hair of his head" (obv. 28) and "He does not swallow spittle" (obv. 25) are similar in that they function as summary conclusions to their commentarial arguments, cannot be clearly identified as citations from other textual sources, and most likely represent the commentator's own words.

Obv. 29—The restoration K[I.NÁ NU ÍL] at Sa-gig 3: 33 (TDPT 3: 24) was proposed by Scurlock and Andersen (2005: 159, §7.18; 708 n. 20), which they understood as the base text for *suḫsi* ("bed") in this commentary (*CAD* S, 349). See also the lexical equation [...]x-la = *su-uḫ-su* (*SpTU* IV, 190 obv. 20).

Obv. 31—The verb *damû*/*ṭamû* ("to stagger (about)"; *CAD* D, 80 s.v. *damû*; *AHw*, 166 s.v. *dawûm*) does not seem attested in therapeutic texts, but appears very commonly in medical signs of the Diagnostic Handbook, either as a description of the patient himself (Sa-gig 3: 86, 92 (TDPT 3: 77, 83); Sa-gig 4: 42–43; 10: 39; 14: 250′ (TDPT 14 iv 49′); Sa-gig 15: 84′; 17: 22; 22: 39–40) or that of a body part (Sa-gig 3: 35–36 (TDPT 3: 26–27); Sa-gig 9: 64; 10 B rev. 1 (TDPT 10 rev. 1); Sa-gig 12: 8 (TDPT 12 i 8); Sa-gig 15: 10′, 29′, 66′; 22: 44; 26: 53′, 71′; 40: 71). The verbs *damû* and *dâlu* (*CAD* D, 58) are not associated in lexical texts, but the similarity of their meanings is clear. The base text Sa-gig 3: 35 (TDPT 3: 26) employs *damû* as a description of the patient's head, but the meaning of *dâlu* ("to wander about") seems better suited for other cases where *damû* describes wandering movements of the patient as a whole person.

Obv. 32—The verb *kanānu/qanānu* ("to contort, twist") appears many times in the Diagnostic Handbook at Sa-gig 3: 35–36 (TDPT 3: 26–27); Sa-gig 7 B rev. 2 (TDPT 7: 58′); Sa-gig [11: 18]; 12: 95″–97″ (TDPT 12 iii 32–34); Sa-gig 14: 219′, 257′ (TDPT 14 iv 13′, 56′); Sa-gig 15: 47′; 26: 14′; 27: 6, 8; 40: 4, 18. The logogram GÚR as a condition of the "spine" (GÚ.MURGU) at Sa-gig 15: 47′ has been understood as the verb *kanāšu* ("gebeugt ist") by Heeßel (2000: 153, 158, 402, 411). However, *kanāšu* appears nowhere else in syllabic form in medical descriptions of the Diagnostic Handbook and therapeutic texts. I prefer to read GÚR as a logogram for *kanānu/qanānu*, based on discussions of the "spine" (GÚ.MURGU) at Sa-gig 12: 95″–97″ (TDPT 12 iii 32–34), where the syllabic form *qa-nin* (Sa-gig 12: 95″ (TDPT 12 iii 32)) alternates with the logogram GÚR (Sa-gig 12: 96″–97″ (TDPT 12 iii 33–34). Therapeutic texts use *kanānu/qanānu* less commonly, and most of their attestations seem to occur in tablets from Assurbanipal's library at Nineveh: *BAM* [205: 8′]; *AMT* 54/3 rev. 8′; [68/1 obv. 14′]; 70/3 [i 3′]; ii 5′; 77/1 i [3], 5. There are no firm lexical associations between *kanānu/qanānu* and *qubburu* ("to roll up (D stem)"), though one wonders about cases where GUR (not GÚR) is associated with *qubburu* at Nabnitu XXIII (+Q), 213 (*MSL* XVI, 218); Nabnitu O, 267 (*MSL* XVI, 294).

Line 35—On the basis of [*i*]*t-ta-*[*n*]*a-ad-la-aḫ* ("he keeps being disturbed"; line 35) in this commentary, the reading *i*[*t-ta-na-ad-là*]*ḫ* has been restored to Sa-gig 3: 41 (TDPT 3: 32) by Scurlock and Andersen (2005: 432, §19.5; 751 n. 6); Scurlock (2014: 14). However, the position of [*i*]*t-ta-*[*n*]*a-ad-la-aḫ* in the right column of this commentary indicates its status as a comment, rather than a topic extracted from the base text.

Line 36—The topic of this commentary entry is unfortunately not preserved, but it likely consists of [ŠÀ-*šú* GAZ.MEŠ-*šú*] from the base text Sa-gig 3: 41 (TDPT 3: 32), where the logogram GAZ.MEŠ expresses the verb *ḫepû* ("to crush"). Though there are no lexical equations linking *ḫepû* and *abātu* ("to break down"), both verbs are associated in a commentary on Izbu XII, 34 in Leichty (1970: 231, Comm. W, 376h–376k); De Zorzi (2014: 673, K 1913, i 11′–13′): *ab-tu-ma* = *šá ḫe-pu-ú*, GUL = *a-ba-tu*$_4$, GUL = *ḫe-pu-ú*.

Lines 37–39—This entry includes what appears to be a quotation (lines 38–39) from a lexical list of objects. Of the five items cited in this list, only two (i.e., *ḫuṭāru* "staff" and GÚ.ZI "*kāsu*-cup") are mentioned in line 37, and there are two points of interest concerning these objects: (i) In the list (lines 38–39), they do not occur sequentially, but appear on either side of the object "*samālu*-cup," which happens to be mentioned in the base text Sa-gig 3: 42 (TDPT 3: 33). (ii) They are separated by a conjunction written as *ù* (𒅇) (line 37), in contrast to how the conjunction "and" in line 41 is twice written with the simpler sign *u* (𒌋). I propose that the topic to be restored is [a-lagab] (line 37) from the base text Sa-gig 3: 42 (TDPT 3: 33), and that the conjunction *ù* in line 37 should be understood as the disjunctive conjunction "or." For other cases of "spellings calculated to assist readers in decipherment" (e.g., *u* versus *ù* here), see Worthington (2012: 264–287, §5.4). The unusual term a-lagab has been read *a-rin* ("well") by Scurlock and Andersen (2005: 432, §19.5), but it is questionable that the Hurrian word *arinnu* is intended here (*CAD* A ii, 268). That being said, the pairing of a-lagab with the *samālu*-cup, as well as the possible interpretation of the A element as a logogram for "water," may suggest that a-lagab is some kind of water-carrying vessel. In any case, this entry gives us rare insight into the mind of a commentator who explicitly admitted his ignorance of a word's meaning. Because a-lagab is paired with the *samālu*-cup in Sa-gig 3: 42 (TDPT 3: 33), the commentator reasoned that a-lagab is an object that would be associated with the *samālu*-cup also in lexical lists. Given the lexical list in lines 38–39, however, the commentator could not be certain whether a-lagab referred to the object before or after the *samālu*-cup in the list. He therefore suggested that these two objects (*ḫuṭāru* "staff" and GÚ.ZI "*kāsu*-cup") were two possible but mutually exclusive identities for a-lagab. The commentator's ignorance is obvious from the fact that *ḫuṭāru*-staff and *kāsu*-cup are not even the same kind of object! Interestingly, a different interpretation of the objects a-lagab and *samālu* can be found in Comm. Sa-gig 3B, obv. 2′–4′: ... : *šá-niš* MUNUS M[U a-lagab *u sa-ma-li*] / [...] x ⸢: *ḫaṭ*(?)⸣-*ṭu* : *a-ri* : *kak-ku* : si ru ⸢ši⸣ ṭu : *a-tu-*⸢*ú šá Su-ti-i*⸣ / ⸢*sa*⸣-*ma-li la-a-ru-ú šá* ŠU.2 ᵈ*A-ḫa-la-mi-ti* : ... ("... 'Secondly, (for) a woman, because of [a-lagab and *samālu*.]' '..., stick, branch, weapon, ..., throwing stick in the case of the Sutean, *samālu*-wood, twig in the case of the Hands of the goddess Aḫalamîtu.'"). In this other commentary, the signs a-lagab were read as *a-rim* or *a-rì* ("branch"), while *samālu* was treated as a byform of *samānu* B (*CAD* S, 112–113) or *samu*/*allu* (*AHw*, 1020), a kind of tree or wood appropriate for this other list of objects.

Line 40—The terms KI.SIKIL = *ardatu* ("young woman") and KI.SIKIL. BANDA$_3$(tur) = *batultu* ("adolescent girl") are contrasted in the lexical texts Lu Excerpt ii, 36–37 (*MSL* xii, 105); *LTBA* ii, 1 iii 45–46 (Appendix to Lu); Lu iii, iv 1 f and g; Igituh short version 285f. (*CAD* B, 173). Note also the equation [KI.SIKI]L.BÀN.DA : *ba-tul-ti* in Comm. Sa-gig 3B, obv. 5′. In medical texts, KI.SIKIL = *ardatu* occurs very commonly in the name of the *ardat lilî*-demoness (logogram KI.SIKIL.LÍL.LÁ), who is identified as the agent of certain sicknesses.

Line 41—The cuneiform wedges depicted as ḫar (𒄯) in the hand copy of *STT* 403 line 41 have been collated and verified as two separate signs *u áš* (𒌋 𒀾) (cf. *CAD* A II, 473 §a). Note the absence of a conjunction in the base text MU *ki-gul-lim áš-tam-mi* (Sa-gig 3: 42 (TDPT 3: 33)), in contrast to the reading [MU *k*]*i-gul-lim u áš-tam-me* here. The meaning of *kigullim* ("the place of destruction(?)"; *CAD* K, 350) is not entirely clear. Collation suggests the signs depicted as *ku*(𒆪)*-ze-ru* in *STT* 403 line 41 (cf. *kuzīru* B in *CAD* K, 616) are probably *ke*(𒆠)*-ze-ru*, referring to the *kezēru*-payment required of certain women (*CAD* K, 315–316). This interpretation is supported by Comm. Sa-gig 3B, obv. 5′–6′: ... *ki-gul-*⸢*lim*⸣ : *ke-ze-ri* : NÍG.TUKU / [*áš-tam*]*-mi* : *ḫa-ri-im-ti* ("'The place of destruction(?)' *refers to kezēru*-payment, *which refers to* wealth. 'The tavern' *refers to* the prostitute."). Silver (2006: 655–656) remarked that "it is tempting to view the *kezretu*'s as a distinctive 'guild' of prostitutes and the *kezērum*/*kezertum*-silver as derived from their earnings in the profession," payments from which were made to supervisors and cult administrators for the upkeep of the cultic institution. Similarly, Stol (2016: 422–427) thought that the *kezertu* were most likely engaged in temple prostitution, earnings from which may have benefitted the temple, perhaps in lieu of a promised vow. In short, whereas the Sa-gig base text frames its diagnosis in euphemistic terms when it attributes the adolescent girl's sickness to "the place of destruction(?) (and) tavern," the commentator dispensed with the euphemism and made it explicit that her illness resulted from some fault involving "*kezēru*-payment" and service as a "prostitute."

Line 42—The topic here appears also in Comm. Sa-gig 3B, obv. 8′: *ú-rap-*[*pad*]. No lexical texts associate the verbs *rapādu* ("to wander about") and *parādu* ("(D stem) to cause shudders"), which we might expect for such verbs with evidently unrelated meanings. While there is clearly metathesis of the radicals /r/ and /p/ from *urappad* to *uparrad*, it is uncertain what argument the commentator intended to make based on such phonological affinities. The topic *rapādu* occurs very commonly in medical descriptions of the Diagnostic Handbook, but it is surprisingly absent in therapeutic texts (see Note on Comm. Sa-gig 7A, rev. 8–9). On the other hand, the comment *parādu*—at least in its G stem ("to shudder")—is well attested in both diagnostic and therapeutic texts.

Line 43—The base text citation *ina* DU_{11}.DU_{11}-*šú it-te-né-ep-rik-*ku_8 (line 43) is essentially identical to the one in Comm. Sa-gig 3B, rev. 1 (*ina* DU_{11}.DU_{11}-*šú* *da-*⸢*ba*⸣*-bi-*$šu_2$ *it-te-né-e*[*p-rik-ku*]) but without the gloss in small script. It is, of course, possible to connect both commentary citations in an imprecise way to the reading *ina* KA-*šú át-mu-šú it-te-né-ep-r*[*ik-ku*] (Sa-gig 3: 51 (TDPT 3: 42)). But a better option may be to restore the immediately preceding Sa-gig entry as the base text *i-na* D[U_{11}.DU_{11}-*šú it-te-né-ep-rik-ku*] (Sa-gig 3: 50 (TDPT 3: 41)), contrary to the restoration of this expression as *i-na* ⸢KA⸣-[*šú it-te-ne-eṭ-pu*] ("[(the words) tumble over one another (?)] in [his] ⸢mouth⸣") by Scurlock and Andersen (2005: 337, §13.263); Scurlock (2014: 15). There are no lexical associations between *naparkû* ("to stop") and *bakû* ("to weep"), but perhaps assonance between the verbs is suggestive. The commentator explained that the patient's words keep stopping, because sobs or moans interrupt his speech. Descriptions of the patient's speech that employ the verb *naparkû* ("to stop") occur only in the Diagnostic Handbook at Sa-gig 3: 51, 54 (TDPT 3: 42, 45); Sa-gig 8: 14; 22: 5, 51, 53, and not in therapeutic texts. The same commentary topic is given a more straightforward definition in Comm. Sa-gig 3B, rev. 2: [*šu-par-ku-ú* :] *ba-ṭa-lu* ("[To put a stop to *means*] to halt.").

Lines 44–45—Anticipating *ma-al-taq-ti* to be the correct understanding of the signs (see following Note on line 45), I tentatively restore the base text Sa-gig 3: 51 (TDPT 3: 42) as [NA BI *ana ma-al-taq-ti lu-ʾ-tu*$_4$ *š*]*u-kul* ("[That man is] fed [*luʾtu* for *maltaqtu*]"), following the syntax at Sa-gig 7 B obv. 7′ ([NA] BI *ana maš-taq-ti ru-ʾ-a-t*[*i šu-kul*]) and especially Sa-gig 22: 5 (NA BI *ana maš-taq-ti kiš-pu šu-kul*); *contra* the order of words in Scurlock and Andersen (2005: 298, §13.85; 734 n. 36); Scurlock (2014: 15). Along with the restoration [… *lu-ʾ-a-ti šu-kul*] at the end of Sa-gig 3: 52 (see Note on Comm. Sa-gig 3B, rev. 4–5) and sign traces of […*š*]*u-kul* at Sa-gig 3: 54, it seems that at least Sa-gig 3: 51–54 (TDPT 3: 42–45) constitutes a section focused on the consumption of harmful substances. Both *luʾtu* (line 44; *CAD* L, 256–257) and *luʾâti* (line 46; *CAD* L, 258; Stol 1998: 348–349) share the same verbal root *luʾû* ("to defile, desecrate, dirty"; *CAD* L, 258–259), and both are mentioned in connection with malicious acts of sorcery. As a matter of fact, the comment "sorcery" (*kišpū*) in line 44 may have been easily deduced by comparing the base text [*ana ma-al-taq-ti lu-ʾ-tu*$_4$ *š*]*u-kul* (Sa-gig 3: 51 (TDPT 3: 42)) with the close parallel *ana maš-taq-ti kiš-pu šu-kul* (Sa-gig 22: 5) noted above. The commentator, moreover, was likely motivated to clarify the term *luʾtu* ("corruption") here, because it was *luʾâtu* ("dirty things") that stereotypically appeared in both diagnostic and therapeutic texts for the corruptant that the victim is made to eat or drink. For *luʾâtu šūkul* ("he is fed dirty things"), see Sa-gig [3: 51, 54] (TDPT [3: 42, 45]); Sa-gig [11: 28] (*SpTU* I, 34: 27); Sa-gig 15: 16′; *StBoT* XXXVI/23 rev. 11′; and perhaps *AMT* [48/2: 14]. For *luʾâtu šaqi* ("he is given dirty things to drink"), see *BAM* [90: 5′]; *AMT* [48/2:

14]; [50/3 obv. 6–7]. Note also ŠU.MEŠ *lu'âtu* TAG (Sa-gig 37: 16 (TDPT 36: 16)) and *lu'âtu* DAB-*su* (Sa-gig 22: 24).

Line 45—The comment *a-na la-ta-ki* ("in order to test") has been confirmed by collation and acknowledged in *CAD* M I, 393 (*la-ta-ki*) and *AHw*, 596 (*la!-ta-ki*), despite the confused way it is rendered in the hand copy of *STT* 403, line 45. This means that the commentator interpreted the signs *ma-al-taq(/tak)-ti* as the term *maltakti* "testing." This interpretation has led to the dubious view by Heeßel (2000: 263) and Scurlock and Andersen (2005: 298, §13.85); Scurlock (2014: 21, 26–27 n. 60) that the sick person is only a "test subject" for the sorcerer. However, there are strong indications that the commentator was actually mistaken, and that the correct reading is *maltaqti* ("cutting-off") from the verbal root *šatāqu* "to cut off." The error is acknowledged in *CAD* M I, 393 where the correct term is identified as *maštaqtu* (a physical deficiency, lit. "cutting off") and said to be "erroneously commented on by *ana ma-al-tak-ti = a-na la-ta-ki STT* 403: 45"; *contra* the entry *maltaktu* ("Erprobung") in *AHw*, 596. See also discussion and bibliography in von Soden (1938a: 43 n. 2) and (1966: 564). The reading *maltaqtu* (< *maštaqtu* "cutting-off" < *šatāqu* "to split, fissure, cut off") is clearly indicated by syllabic writing of the same term as *maš-taq-ti* in Sa-gig 7 B obv. 7′ (TDPT 7: 46′); Sa-gig 22: 5 MS D (and perhaps MS A); *BAM* 156: 3; 167: 2′, 4′, 8′; *AMT* 22/2: 10. Furthermore, the directionality of sound shifts tends to be *št* > *lt* > *ss* (*GAG*, §30g–h, §34d), so it is more likely that *ma-al-taq(/tak)-ti* here derives from *šatāqu* ("to cut off"), than that *maš-taq-ti* elsewhere derives from *latāku* ("to test"). For the partial assimilation *št* > *lt* as possibly a Babylonianism in Neo-Assyrian texts, see Deller (1959: 225–227, §43c–f); Hämeen-Anttila (2000: 21–22, §2.2.3.2c); Luukko (2004: 80–81, §4.2.4). The meaning "cutting-off" (*maltaqtu*) also makes more sense than "testing" (*maltaktu*) in the wordplay of Comm. Sa-gig 40A (obv. 8–9), whereby the baby's "living quarters" (AMA_5 = *maštaku*), nested within the bosom of his "mother" (AMA), are transformed into the site for "cutting-off" (*maltaqtu* < *maštaqtu*) by the machinations of the sorceress.

Line 46—The root of *lu'âti* ("dirty things") is *lu'û* ("to defile, desecrate, dirty"; *CAD* L, 258–259), not *la'āšu* (*CAD* L, 6) whose meaning is uncertain. It is also possible that, though the orthography *la-'a-šu* suggests a glottal stop (perhaps to emphasize its similarity to *lu-'-a-ti*), the verb in view is *lâšu* ("to knead"; *CAD* L, 110–111). This verb *lâšu* appears very frequently in therapeutic instructions on the preparation of medicaments and seems cogent to descriptions of *lu'âti* as a substance the sick person consumed. If this interpretation is correct, it illustrates how, to an unknowing observer, the beneficent preparation of medicaments can easily resemble malign acts of creating sorcerous substances. Abusch (2007: 154), for instance, has observed that "the activities of feeding, giving drink, washing, and salving," which are attributed to the witch, "are also activities of a healer."

Line 47—Because this entry has a short topic (ŠE U.MEŠ-*šú*) and a very long comment, the comment extends across both left and right columns of the tablet. The body part ŠE U.MEŠ (read as 40 U.MEŠ by Scurlock and Andersen 2005: 325, §13.219) is attested in the Diagnostic Handbook at Sa-gig 3: 62 (TDPT 3: 53); Sa-gig 4: 94 (TDPT 4 rev. 8); Sa-gig 11 rev. 54a–54b, but not in therapeutic texts. One wonders if the signs restored as *ap-pa-at* ⸢*uz*⸣-⟨*ni*⟩-*šu* ("the tips of his ears(!)"; George 2013: 88) from an Old Babylonian diagnostic tablet MS 2670 (obv. 22′) may perhaps be *ap-pa-at* ⸢ŠE U.ME (!)⸣-*šu*. ŠE in the context of fingers functions as a logogram for the term *kittabru*, as confirmed by the syllabic writing *kit-tab-ri* ŠU.⸢SI(?)⸣ in the Middle Babylonian diagnostic tablet CBS 12580, obv. 10 (Rutz 2011: 304–305), as well as *kit-tab-ri ú-ba-na-t*[*u-šú*] in Comm. Sa-gig 4C, rev. 6′. Note the lexical equations še, [umb]in-še = *ki-it-ta-ab-ru* (Nabnitu E, 51–52 in *MSL* XVI, 106), which are followed by other entries dealing with the "hollow of hand" (*upnu*; Nabnitu E, 53–62), the "arm / side" (*aḫu*; Nabnitu E, 63–78ff.), and the "forearm / cubit" (*ammatu*; Nabnitu E, 105–108). See also ^še-e^ ŠE = *kit-tab-rum* (Aa VII/4, 39 in *MSL* XIV, 467). In physiognomic omens, however, the term ŠE (= *kittabru*) seems to denote different parts from the human head to the feet. See Böck (2000a: 212–233). In medical contexts, ŠE U designates a part of the human finger, as is evident from its position in the head-to-foot arrangement of Sa-gig Chapter 11, whereby the segment on "fingers" as a whole (Sa-gig 11 rev. 32–52) is followed by fleshy parts of the fingers, i.e., the "tips of fingers" (*ap-pat* U.MEŠ; Sa-gig 11 rev. 53), the ŠE U.MEŠ (Sa-gig 11 rev. 54), and the "stomachs of fingers" (*kar-ši* U.MEŠ; Sa-gig 11 rev. 55–59), before finally moving on to the "(finger)-nail" (UMBIN; Sa-gig 11 rev. 60). Adamson (1981: 128) suggested that ŠE U.MEŠ refers to the "terminal interphalangeal joint," while Rutz (2011: 305) wondered if "*appāt* / *kittabri* / *karši ubānāti* simply refer to the distal, medial, and proximal phalanges themselves?" There are two obscure terms in this commentary entry: GABA!(mu) and *ṣurru*. Scurlock (2014: 27 n. 68) interpreted the former as "line" (MU) and translated the comment as "'from the line represented by the tips of his fingers to the beginning of his core' or, in other words, the underside of the finger." In my understanding, there is confusion between the cuneiform sign mu (𒈬) and the logogram GABA (𒃮). GABA typically refers to the "chest," but may indicate the "frontier" to a border, which is the meaning I ascribe to it here. The term *ṣurru* can refer to the "insides (of the human body)," the "heart," or the "center (of an object)" (*CAD* Ṣ, 259–260). While the terms may be conceived in a variety of ways, I understand this commentary entry as follows: "'His ŠE U.MEŠ' (*refer to*) *the parts* (i.e., distal phalanges) from the frontier of the tips of his fingers until the top of the middle (phalanges of) his (fingers)." The comment is nicely structured, with prepositions (TA "from"; EN "until") followed by locations (GABA! "frontier"; SAG "top"), followed again by parts of the fingers (*appāt* ŠU.SI.MEŠ "tips of fingers"; *ṣurru* "middle (phalanges)"). In summary, ŠE U.MEŠ ("distal phalanges") encompass the "tips of fingers," while *ṣurru* ("middle") indicates the middle or intermediate phalanges. I am also inclined to interpret *karši* U.MEŠ ("stomachs of fingers") as the proximal phalanges.

Line 48—The topic ḪÁŠ-*su* KAL-*an* is written slightly differently in our preserved copy of the base text Sa-gig 3: 67 (TDPT 3: 58): ḪÁŠ-*su da-an*. This line has been read as ḪÁŠ-*su* KAL-*an* = KI.TA LI.DUR-*sa re-di* (*CAD* R, 237 s.v. *redû* A §4b). Though collation has confirmed this reading, it is unclear why there is a shift from a masculine suffix (-*su*) to a feminine one (-*sa*), and what the Stative form *redi* might mean in this context. Instead, I understand the comment as KI.TA LI.DUR *er*!(sa)-*ri* SILIM ("below the navel, the bowels are well"). The logogram ḪÁŠ (*emšu* = "lower belly") occurs rarely in therapeutic texts (*BAM* 237 i 23′), but appears in the Diagnostic Handbook at Sa-gig 3: 67 (TDPT 3: 58); Sa-gig 13: 22–23, 25–26, 31 (TDPT 13 i 23′–24′, 26′–27′, 32′), almost always in the medical description "his lower belly is hard," with the exception of Sa-gig 13: 25 (TDPT 13 i 26′). This body part is not the same as ḪÁŠ.GAL = *šapūlu* ("inguinal region") at Sa-gig 15: 57′–58′, and possibly ḪÁŠ.MEŠ at Sa-gig 17: 28. The syllabic form *emšu* ("lower belly"), likewise, appears predominantly in the Diagnostic Handbook at Sa-gig 13: 34, 162–165 (TDPT 13 i 35′; iv 11′–14′); Sa-gig 36: 59–65, 74 (TDPT 35: 59–65, 74); and also in the therapeutic text *BAM* 240: 17′. Bodily features involving the "lower belly" seem to be of significance also in physiognomic omens (*CAD* E, 154 §b).

Line 49—The base text here is tentatively identified as ŠU.2-*šú u* GÌR.2-*šú* ⸢KÚM-*ma*⸣ ("his hands and his feet are hot") in Sa-gig 3: 80 (TDPT 3: 71), though the conjunction -*ma* is replaced with the pronominal suffix -*šu* ("… (are hot) for him") in the commentary tablet. The argument here relies on antonymy (§1.2.3.1.6): "'His hands (and) his feet [are hot] for him' *means the opposite of* his hands (and) his feet are cold." This requires us to interpret the signs ka-si-a, not as *ka-si-a* (< *kasû*, "to bind, put in fetters"), but as *ka-ṣi*$_{x}$(si)-*a* (< *kaṣû*, "to become cold"). See Note on obv. 20 above for the fluid uses of the cuneiform sign si in this commentary, as evident in the orthographies *i-ta-na-ší*(si) (obv. 19) and *ṣe*$_{x}$(si)-*nu-ni-tu*$_{4}$ (obv. 20; a byform of the skin condition *ṣennītu*).

Line 50—Collation has shown the restoration ⌞*šag-ga*⌟ to be plausible. Although the verb *šagāgu* is defined as "to stiffen" in *CAD* Š I, 62, it is translated with the opposite meaning "erschlaffen" in *AHw*, 1125. There is, moreover, ambiguity concerning what is meant by the topic "His hands (and) his feet are stretched out (< *tarāṣu*) for him." Elsewhere, the patient is sometimes depicted as "unable to stretch out" (*tarāṣa* NU ZU-*e*) his limbs that are "rigid" (*amāšu*; "cataleptic(?)" in *CAD* A II, 28), which is a condition also described as "stiff" (*wašāṭu*, not *šagāgu*). See Sa-gig 11: 20; 14: 217′ (TDPT 14 iv 11′); Sa-gig 15: 18′–19′, 64′; as well as examples in *CAD* A II, 28. We are left uncertain whether the commentary entry here relies on synonymy (i.e., "'His hands (and) his feet are stretched out for him' *means* [his hands and his feet] are slack") or represents an argument based on antonymy (i.e., "'His hands (and) his feet are stretched out for him' *means the opposite of* [his hands and his feet] are stiffened"). For what it is worth, the verbs *tarāṣu* ("to stretch out") and *šagāgu* do not appear to be associated as synonyms in lexical lists.

Line 51—Sa-gig 3: 72 (TDPT 3: 63) has been identified as the base text here and restored as NUND[UN.MEŠ-*šú i-ta-na-zu*] by Scurlock and Andersen (2005: 50, §3.110; 690 n. 121); Scurlock (2014: 16). If so, however, it would break with the practice of addressing commentarial topics in the order in which they appear in the base text. Here, the topic is the Gtn stem of the verb *azû* ("to make unnatural noises"; *CAD* A II, 528), and it seems unattested elsewhere in medical descriptions of diagnostic and therapeutic texts.

Lines 52–53—It is straightforward enough to translate these two lines, but more difficult to elucidate the commentator's logic. The topic MÚD *i-ḫa-ḫu* ("he spews out blood"; line 53) comes from the base text Sa-gig 3: 88 (TDPT 3: 79), but it does not receive first mention in its commentary entry, contrary to the practice elsewhere on the same tablet. I interpret the rhetoric here as an A′:B:A:B′ argument involving four elements: (A′) the Gtn stem of (*ḫ*)*aḫû* ("he keeps spewing out"); (B) the D stem of *qâ'u* ("he disgorges out"); (A) the G stem of (*ḫ*)*aḫû* ("he spews out"); and (B′) the G stem of *qâ'u* ("he disgorges"). Of these four elements, only the topic (A), the G stem of (*ḫ*)*aḫû*, is attested in medical texts, where its frequent occurrences are confined to the Diagnostic Handbook: Sa-gig 3: 88 (TDPT 3: 79); Sa-gig 9: 74; 13: 40, 42, 79, 85 (TDPT 13 i 41′, 43′; ii 21, 27); Sa-gig 14: 189′ (TDPT 14 iii 56′); Sa-gig 15: 5′; 17: 27, 28; 22: 39; 27: 30; 40: 48, 123. It is therefore curious that the explanation of a common Sa-gig form (A) should require the invocation of an atypical form of the same verb (*ḫ*)*aḫû* (A′). Furthermore, one wonders why the comments (B) and (B′) involve the verb *qâ'u* / *gâ'u* ("to disgorge") that appears rarely in medical texts (*BAM* 90: 16′; *AMT* 81/4: 3′), especially since the medical literature furnishes several other common verbs like *nadû* ("to throw up"), *arû* ("to puke"), *parû* ("to vomit"), and *gešû* ("to belch") that can serve as synonyms of *(ḫ)aḫû*. Possibly, the elements A′ and B were colloquial expressions in the Syrian contexts of Ḫuzirīna, since the verb *qâʾu*, in fact, corresponds to other Semitic cognates like Hebrew *qê* and Arabic *qāʾa* (*CAD* G, 59; *CAD* K, 309). Since elements A′ and A were cognates from the same dictionary root, with the latter (G stem) representing the more basic or *Grundstamm* version of the former (Gtn stem), the commentator may have reasoned that topic A (G stem) could be equated in meaning with comment B′ (G stem), which was likewise perceived as a more basic version of comment B (D stem).

Lines 54–54b—The verb *šumšû* ("to stay up all night") does not seem attested in therapeutic texts, but appears several times in the Diagnostic Handbook at Sa-gig 4: 12; 9: 54, 74; 10: 53; 17: 78; 37: 20 (TDPT 36: 20); Sa-gig 40: 8. The comment is very damaged and difficult to understand, and my reading is only tentative: *an-ni-*⸢*mi*(?)⸣*-šu* Ù *né-*⸢*eḫ*⸣*-ḫu* ŠUB ⸢*la*⸣ *i-*⸢*na-al*(?)⸣ ("no sooner than restful sleep befalls, he cannot fall asleep."). The expression *annimmiš* ("as soon as"; *CAD* A II, 133) is quite rare, and one wonders if the commentator alluded to its other attestation in the Standard Babylonian *Epic of Gilgamesh* XI, 232–233: *an-ni-miš šit-tum ir-ḫu-ú e-li-ia* / *ḫa-an-ṭiš tal-tap-tan-ni-ma ta-ad-de-kan-ni at-ta* ("No sooner than sleep spilled over me, forthwith you touched me and roused me!"). See George (2003: 718–719). Strictly speaking, these lines relate the subjective experience of Gilgamesh, who had actually fallen asleep for a week, but felt that almost no time had passed before Uta-napishti roused him out of sleep. The commentator may have taken the wording in *Gilgamesh* out of its original context, so that it depicted the objective reality of how the patient spends the night drifting towards sleep, but is always roused by his discomfort or pain, and prevented from actually falling asleep.

Line 55—See discussion on "even fever [i.e., heat]" in Stol (2007a: 8–9). Apart from the base text here, the topic KÚM *mitḫār* ("the heat is evenly high") appears at Sa-gig 4: 33; 12: 100″ (TDPT 12 iii 37); Sa-gig 13: 71, 105, 125–126 (TDPT 13 ii 13, 48; iii 14–15); Sa-gig 14: 196′ (TDPT 14 iii 63′); Sa-gig 19/20: 45′, [49′]; 27: 27. The opposite of this condition KÚM NU *mitḫār* ("the heat is unevenly high") occurs at Sa-gig 4: 34; 12: 101″ (TDPT 12 iii 38); Sa-gig 13: 115 (TDPT 13 iii 5); Sa-gig 14: 197′–198′ (TDPT 14 iii 64′–65′). Finally, the verb *emēmu* ("to become hot") is qualified by the adverb *mitḫāriš* at Sa-gig 4: 59; 40: 31, where *mitḫāriš* describes the parity of temperature levels in different locations of the patient's body. None of the above expressions are attested in therapeutic texts.

Commentary Sa-gig 3A

Provenance:	Uruk (Warka), Area U18, Level v; Same findspot and consignment (W 22307) as Comm. Sa-gig 1C, 5, 7A, 7B, and 19 suggests library of Anu-ikṣur
Period:	Late Achaemenid
Names:	Not preserved
Script:	Neo-/Late Babylonian
Field/Museum No.:	W 22307/71 (National Museum of Iraq)
Photo:	Plate 7b (reverse)
Printed Edition/Hand Copy:	*SpTU* 1, 29 (= Hunger 1976: 37–38); Wee (2012: 562–565)
Digital Resources:	CDLI P348450; GKAB P348450 (edition digitized by Clancier 2009); CCP 4.1.3.A (printed hand copy and edition digitized by Jiménez 2016, with contributions by Clancier)
Discussion:	*SpTU* 1, 29 (= Hunger 1976: 37–38); Heeßel (2000: 133, 141 (3. Tafel MS b)); Scurlock and Andersen (2005: 373 n. 23, 556 n. 8); Clancier (2009: 388); Geller (2010a: 146); Genty (2010a: 371) and (2010b: 11, 27); Frahm (2011a: 29 n. 96, 224, 291); Wee (2012: 562–565) and (2015a: 260–261); Fincke (2013: 23 n. 35); Scurlock (2014: 28 nn. 93, 102, and 104); Gabbay (2016: 254 n. 233); Jiménez and Schmidtchen (2017: 217)
Pericope:	At least Sa-gig 3: 89–123 (TDPT 3: 80–113)

Transliteration

Reverse

1′) ⸢x *ri*(?)⸣ *šá* L[Ú(?) ...]

2′) DINGIR *šag-ga-ši* : DINGIR[...]

3′) *ina* ^giš^MÁ iš-riq(/šim) DINGIR *k*[*a-a-ri* DAB-*su*]

4′) *mim-ma šá* ^giš^MÁ *il-te-ri-*[*iq* ...]

5′) ITI GIG : *ár-ḫu* GIG-*u*[*ṣ* : ITI : *ár-ḫu*]

6′) ITI : *a-ṣu-ú* : BAD.MEŠ x[...]

7′) 2 DAL.MEŠ GAR.MEŠ-*ma* : DAL[: *tal-lu* ...]

 | DOI:10.1163/9789004417564_007

8′) *ina* EDIN TAG-*it* : *ina* UG[U SÌG-*iṣ* ...]
9′) *na-ʾi-id* : *na-kud* : x[...]
10′) *ú-maš-šad* : *ú-maš-*[*šá-aʾ* ...]

11′) IM.GÌ.DA ᵐx[...]
12′) DUMU *šá* ᵐ·ᵈ[...]

Translation

(Rev. 1′) ...

Sa-gig 3: 89 (TDPT 3: 80)
Diagnostic verdicts usually describe a "ghost" (GIDIM$_7$) as "murderous," rather than a "god" (DINGIR).

(2′) "Murderous god" *refers to* the god ...

Sa-gig 3: 96 (TDPT 3: 87)
The syllable signs are not to be read *iš-šim* "it is decreed (by a boat)," but as *iš-riq* "he stole (from a boat)."

(3′–4′) "iš-riq(/šim) from a boat, the god of the quay [seized him]," (*means*) he has stolen something of the boat. ...

Sa-gig 3: 98 (TDPT 3: 89)
Literal translation of ITI "(for a) month" + GIG "he is sick."

(5′) "ITI GIG" *means* he is sick for a month. ...

Since medical descriptions in Sa-gig 3: 98 and Sa-gig 3: 99 are opposites of each other, the commentator reasoned that their diagnoses are opposite as well. Because the verdict in Sa-gig 3: 99 is *e-reb* GIG "the entering of sickness," the verdict ITI GIG in Sa-gig 3: 98 must mean "the exiting of sickness."

(5′) [ITI *means* month.]
(6′) ITI *means* to exit.

***Sa-gig 3**

(6′) "BAD.MEŠ" ...

Sa-gig 3: 107 (TDPT 3: 98)
DAL ("transversal line") describes intersecting bodily strands in the Diagnostic Handbook, but is unattested in therapeutic texts.

(7′) "They are set as 2 DAL.MEŠ."
(7′) "DAL" [*means* transversal line.] ...

Sa-gig 3: 109 (TDPT 3: 100)
The prepositional phrases *ina ṣēr* and *ina muḫḫi* can share the idiomatic meaning "upon, on top of." The commentator argued that the nouns *ṣēru* "steppe" and *muḫḫu* "above / cranium" could be equated as well.

(8′) "He is touched in the steppe" *means* he is [struck] above / in the cranium. …

Sa-gig 3: 109 (TDPT 3: 100)
The less frequent expression *na'id* "he deserves concern" is explained by the common one *nakud* "he is worrisome."

(9′) "He deserves concern" *means* he is worrisome. …

Sa-gig 3: 123 (TDPT 3: 113)
The commentator explained the medical sign of "rubbing" performed by the patient, by comparing it to common therapeutic descriptions of the healer "messaging" his patient with liniments.

(10′) "He rubs" *means* he massages. …

(Colophon)

(11′–12′) *Imgida*-tablet of …, son of …

Notes

Rev. 2′—The signs […] / DINGIR *šag-ga-ši* (rev. 1′–2′) refer to a topic from the base text Sa-gig 3: 89 (TDPT 3: 80): ŠU DINGIR *šag-gaš-ši.* Terms such as *šaggašû* ("murderous") and *šaggašti* ("murder") in diagnostic verdicts typically describe the agency of a "ghost" (GIDIM$_7$), as in Sa-gig 12: 98″ (TDPT 12 iii 35); Sa-gig 13: 138 (TDPT 13 iii 27); Sa-gig 15: 46′; 26: 13′, 21′, 52′, 75′–76′; CBS 3831, obv. 4. See also discussion in Fincke (2013: 17–24). The writing ŠU DINGIR *šaggašî* or ŠU ^{d}*šaggašî* (Sa-gig 26: 10′ MS B = BM 47753) occurs as an independent variant of ŠU *šaggašî* (Sa-gig 26: 10′ MS A = *STT* 91+287), and both belong to a tablet (Sa-gig 26) that focuses on conditions ascribed to demons and ghosts. In medical texts, references to "ghosts" (GIDIM$_7$) do not typically take a determinative, and forms like ŠU *šaggašî* (Sa-gig 23: 4; 26: 10′ MS A) altogether avoid the divine determinative (^{d}) or any qualification of the agent as "god" (DINGIR). The topic of a "murderous god"

(DINGIR *šag-ga-ši*) was therefore unusual enough to have warranted the commentator's attention.

Rev. 3′–4′—The topic here corresponds to *ina* ^{giš}MÁ iš-riq(/šim) from the base text Sa-gig 3: 96 (TDPT 3: 87). The commentator's motivation is not very clear. He may have been concerned that the signs could be misread as *iš-šim* ("it is decreed" = N Preterite of *šiāmu*; cf. *CAD* Š 1, 364 s.v. *šâmu* B §4), which would result in the statement *ina* ^{giš}MÁ *iš-šim* DINGIR *ka-a-ri* DAB-*su* ("it is decreed by a boat, the god of the quay seized him"), i.e., the boat is somehow an omen of the god of the quay's agency in the sickness. Instead, the commentator argued for the reading *iš-riq* ("he stole" = G Preterite of *šarāqu*), so that the statement would be understood as *ina* ^{giš}MÁ *iš-riq* DINGIR *ka-a-ri* DAB-*su* ("he stole from a boat, the god of the quay seized him"), i.e., the man's sickness is retribution for his act of theft from a boat.

Rev. 6′—Hunger (*SpTU* 1, 29) remarked that "dieses Logogramm (ITI) kann ich sonst nicht nachweisen." This commentary entry vividly illustrates the extent to which the meaning of terms could be influenced by their textual context, revealing the importance of organizational principles by which individual Sa-gig entries were positioned and grouped together in larger sections, tablets, or chapters. The medical description in Sa-gig 3: 98 (TDPT 3: 89) (i.e., sick from head to waist, healthy from waist to feet) is diametrically opposite to that of Sa-gig 3: 99 (TDPT 3: 90) (i.e., healthy from head to waist, sick from waist to feet), and the commentator reasoned that the diagnostic verdicts should be opposite to each other as well. Since Sa-gig 3: 99 (TDPT 3: 90) concludes with the verdict *e-reb* GIG ("the entering (*erēb*) of sickness (GIG)"), the verdict ITI GIG in Sa-gig 3: 98 (TDPT 3: 89) should accordingly be understood as "the exiting (ITI) of sickness (GIG)." The sign ITI or ITU, however, almost always serves as the logogram for "month," and no lexical texts indicate that "to exit" is a possible meaning for this sign. Furthermore, the diagnosis "he is sick for one month" is elsewhere written as ITI.1.KÁM GIG (Sa-gig 31: 12′, 53′) and 1.ITI GIG (*BAM* 66 obv. 10), where the number 1 or the numerical complement KÁM indicates that an enumerated "month" is intended. Finally, the idiomatic way to express the lessening influence of sickness is not "exiting of sickness," but perhaps "slackening of sickness" (*paṭār murṣi*): DU_8(-*ár*) GIG (Sa-gig 14: 224′ (TDPT 14 iv 18′); Sa-gig 16:[40′], 44′; 17: 62; 22: 33); GIG-*su* DU_8(-*ár*) (Sa-gig 16: 46′, 51′, 66′, 83′); GIG.BI DU_8-*ár* (Sa-gig 17: 72); TU.BI DU_8-*ár* (Sa-gig 17: 71); *pa-ṭá-a-ar mu-ur-ṣí* (*StBoT* XXXVI, Tablet A, [obv. 2–3]; rev. 14′; [Fragment D2, rev.(?) 14]). In short, the commentator took a lot of liberty interpreting the sign ITI, in order to conform its meaning to his opinion of the context in Sa-gig 3: 98–99 (TDPT 3: 89–90). One wonders whether the argument was aided by perceived assonance between ITU (logogram for "month") and *aṣû* ("to exit").

Rev. 7′—The juxtaposition of DAL.MEŠ (Sa-gig 4: 120 (TDPT 4 rev. 35)) and *tal-lu* (Sa-gig 4: 122 (TDPT 4 rev. 37)) in nearby Sa-gig entries likely reflects the ancient editor's view that these entries address similar body features and therefore should be grouped together. The expression *tallu lā iprik*, "a transversal line does not lie across" (Sa-gig 4: 122 (TDPT 4 rev. 37)), in particular, resembles statements like *kīma talli iprik*, "lies across like a transversal line" (Koch-Westenholz 2000: 147, no. 19 line 114) in extispicy contexts. See also Nougayrol (1950: 4 n. 3); references to *tallu* in Koch (2005: 617). The equation of DAL and *tallu* is attested in the lexical texts S[a] Voc. F, 5′ (*MSL* III, 57); Arnaud (1987: 13, no. 537, line 90); *MSL* XIV, 94: 132: 1 (Proto-Aa); cf. DAL for the verb *talālu* in Goetze (1957: 99). The few occurrences of *tallu* ("transversal line") in the Diagnostic Handbook (Sa-gig 3: 107 (TDPT 3: 98); Sa-gig 4: 120, 122 (TDPT 4 rev. 35, 37)) seem to refer to intersecting "strands" in the sick man's head, temples, or hands, perhaps describing an excessively net-like appearance of superficial blood vessels near to the skin's surface. Elsewhere, a commentator affirmed that "[DAL] *means* (*šer'ānu*)-strand. Secondly, [*nimšu*-strand]" (Comm. Sa-gig 4C, rev. 13′). Similar uses of the term *tallu* are not attested in therapeutic texts.

Rev. 8′—Exactly the same equation [*ina*] EDIN TAG-*it* : *ina* UGU *ma-ḫi-iṣ* ("'He is touched [in] the steppe' *means* he is struck above") appears in Comm. Sa-gig 14, obv. 26. Commentators' names are not preserved here (Comm. Sa-gig 3A) and in Comm. Sa-gig 14, but the findspot and museum consignment of both commentaries suggest they come from the Uruk library of Anu-ikṣur, and perhaps were composed by the same author. The prepositional phrases *ina ṣēr* and *ina muḫḫi* have overlapping semantic domains and can both mean "upon, on top of." The commentator(s) extended the logic to the nouns themselves, equating the two seemingly disparate terms EDIN (= *ṣēru*, "steppe, open country") and UGU (= *muḫḫu*, "above / cranium"). Because the cranium is almost always written in medical texts with a pronominal suffix (i.e., UGU-*šú*, "*his* cranium"), the absence of the suffix here (i.e., UGU) suggests the translation "above" may be preferable to "cranium." Note, moreover, the suffixless term *muḫḫi* employed in a context involving the forehead: SAG.KI-*su* [...] / *šá* UZU *ina muḫ-ḫi ia-a-nu* ("'His forehead ...' (*refers to*) the case where there is no flesh above / on the cranium") in Comm. Sa-gig 21 & 22a, obv. 2–3.

Rev. 9′—Assonantal links between *na'id* ("he deserves concern") and *nakid* ("he is worrisome") are quite obvious. In the Diagnostic Handbook, the term *na'id* (Sa-gig 3: 109, 113, 115 (TDPT 3: 100, 104, 106); Sa-gig 37: 3–4 (TDPT 36:

3–4)) occurs much less frequently and in narrower contexts than the term *nakud* or *nakid* (Sa-gig 3: 89 (TDPT 3: 80); Sa-gig 5: 109′ (TDPT 5 G 10); Sa-gig 8: 2, 5; 10: 51; 12: 122″ (TDPT 12 iv 14); Sa-gig 13: 16, 177 (TDPT 13 i 17′; iv 26′); Sa-gig 15: 92′; 19/20: 116′; 26: 8′; 28: 36–37). It was fitting, therefore, that the commentator proceeded to explain the former by the latter. Note the observation by Stol (2009a: 44) that "the stative *nakud* ... has a meaning so similar to *naḫid* and *na'id* that people saw no difference."

Rev. 10′—The reading *ú-maš-šad* : *ú-maš-*[*šá-a'*] here is restored in view of a similar equation in Uruk Therapeutic Comm. 1 = *SpTU* 1, 47 obv. 10: *muš-šu-da* : *muš-šu-'u*. The alternative * *ú-maš-šad* : *ú-maš-*[*šá-ad*] is less probable, since *ú-maš-šad* is the most plausible way of reading these signs, and audiences were unlikely to mistake the writing for another verb. The base text for this entry consists of the partially preserved description "he rubs the hair of his head and [... his] garment" (Sa-gig 3: 123 (TDPT 3: 113)). The G stem of the verb *mašādu* commonly describes the action of the malady on the patient, as in Sa-gig 27: 1 (= Sa-gig 26: 91′); Sa-gig 27: 2, 4–5, 8; *BAM* 32: 5′; 417 obv. 4; *AMT* 77/1 i 1–2, [5]. Some examples discussed in Salin (2015: 329–330). In contrast, the D stem *muššudu* describes the patient's action of "rubbing" his face and other body parts, as in Sa-gig 3: 123 (TDPT 3: 113); Sa-gig 9: 75; 26: 42′; *AMT* [79/4: 3′]. The verb *muššu'u* ("to massage") does not occur as a description of the patient's behavior, but appears very frequently in therapeutic texts to denote the healer's action of applying liniments onto his patient (*CAD* M II, 282). In short, the commentator explained the medical sign of "rubbing" performed by the patient, by comparing the act to common therapeutic instructions for the healer to "massage" his patient with liniments.

Commentary Sa-gig 3B

Provenance:	Babylon
Period:	?
Names:	Colophon not preserved
Script:	Neo-/Late Babylonian
Field/Museum No.:	BM 43854 + 43938 = 81-7-1,1615 + 81-7-1,1699 ("Babylon Collection" at British Museum)
Photos:	Plate 8a (obverse), Plate 8b (obverse to bottom edge), Plate 9a (bottom edge to reverse), and Plate 9b (reverse)
Digital Resources:	CDLI P461216; CCP 4.1.3.C (printed hand copy, photos, and edition digitized by Geller and Schmidtchen 2016, with contributions by Jiménez)
Discussion:	Frahm (2011a: 224, categorized as Comm. Sa-gig 3b); Wee (2015a: 266 n. 65); Jiménez and Schmidtchen (2017: 217–218)
Pericope:	At least Sa-gig 3: 42–53 (TDPT 3: 33–44)

Transliteration

Obverse

1′) [...] UŠ.ME-⸢*šú*⸣ : x [...]

2′) [...] x x x x : *šá-niš* MUNUS M[U a-lagab *u sa-ma-li*]

3′) [...] x ⸢: *ḫaṭ*(?)⸣-*ṭu* : *a-ri* : *kak-ku* : si ru ⸢ši⸣ ṭu : *a-tu-*⸢*ú šá Su-ti-i*⸣

4′) ⸢*sa*⸣-*ma-li la-a-ru-ú šá* ŠU.2 ^{d}*A-ḫa-la-mi-ti* :

5′) [KI.SIK]IL.BÀN.DA : *ba-tul-ti* : *ki-gul-*⸢*lim*⸣ : *ke-ze-ri* : NÍG.TUKU

6′) [*áš-tam*]-*mi* : *ḫa-ri-im-ti* : KÚM TÉŠ.BI TUKUR$_2$-*su* : TUKUR$_2$-⸢*su*⸣

7′) [*i-ka-s*]*a*-⸢*su* :⸣ (?) *šum-ma* U$_4$-*ma* NÍG.LAL-*šú* : NÍG.NIGIN : *ta-a-a-r*[*u*]

8′) [...]-*ú* : NÍG.LAL : *ḫa-a-a-at-ti* : *ú-ra*[*p-pad* : ...]

9′) [UMUŠ-*šú* KÚR-*šum-m*]*a* : *šá-né-e ṭè-me* : ŠU.DAG : *ra-*[*pa-du* : ŠU.DAG]

10′) [*i-ta-gu-šu* (?) : ŠU.DA]G (?) : *ḫa-la-qa* : KA-*šú* DAB-*ba-at* [...]

Reverse

1) [*ana a-ma-ti* : *ana da-b*]*a-bi* : *ina* DU$_{11}$.DU$_{11}$-*šú* *da-*⸢*ba*⸣*-bi-šu*$_2$ *it-te-né-e*[*p-rik-ku*]

2) [*šu-par-ku-ú* :] *ba-ṭa-lu* : ŠU.2-*šú u* GÌR.2-*šú i-ra-ʾ-bu* :

3) [*ra-ʾ-bu*] : *sa-la-*⸤*ḫu*⸥ : KA-*šú ana at-me-e il-la-ti ú-ka*[*l*]

 | DOI:10.1163/9789004417564_008

4) [*at-me-e*] : *da-ba-bi* : *il-la-ti* : *ru-ʾ-tú* : *lu-ʾ-a-ti* ⌊*šu-kul*⌋
5) [*lu-ʾ-a-t*]*i* : *kiš-pi* : ŠÀ-*šú ana* $BURU_8$-*e* *a-re-e* : *i-te-né-el-la-*⌊*a*⌋-[*ma*]
6) [$BURU_8$: *a-ru*]-⌊*ú* : $BURU_8$: *pa*⌋*-ru-ú* : šu rat x x [...]
7) [...] x [...]

Translation

Sa-gig 3: 42 (TDPT 3: 33)—"Ištar keeps pursuing him (UŠ.ME-*šú*) because of (the game of) 'Room Four'"

(Obv. 1′–2′) ... "UŠ.ME-*šú*" *means* ...

Sa-gig 3: 42 (TDPT 3: 33)

(2′) "Secondly, (for) a woman, because of [a-lagab and *samālu*.]"

The lexical list cited here involves branches and stick-like objects, including "branch" (*a-ri*) and *samālu*- (i.e., *samānu*- or *samullu*-) wood. This implies the signs a-lagab in the base text should be read syllabically as *a-rim* ("branch").

(3′–4′) "..., stick, branch, weapon, ..., throwing stick in the case of the Sutean, *samālu*-wood, twig in the case of the Hands of the goddess Aḫalamîtu."

Sa-gig 3: 42 (TDPT 3: 33)

(5′) "KI.SIKIL.BÀN.DA" *means* adolescent girl.

Sa-gig 3: 42 (TDPT 3: 33)
The girl's sickness due to "the place of destruction(?)" may be said to arise from negligence of "*kezēru*-payment."

(5′) "The place of destruction(?)" *refers to kezēru*-payment, *which refers to* wealth.

Sa-gig 3: 42 (TDPT 3: 33)
The commentator states explicitly that "tavern" in the base text is a euphemistic reference to "prostitution."

(6′) "The tavern" *refers to* the prostitute.

Sa-gig 3: 45 (TDPT 3: 36)—KÚM TÉŠ.BI $TUKUR_2$-*su* ?

(6′) "Heat (performs the action of) $TUKUR_2$ to him all over."

(6′–7′) "(Heat performs the action of) $TUKUR_2$ to him" (*means*) [(heat) gnaws him (?)].

***Sa-gig 3: 45 (TDPT 3: 36)—*šu*[*m-ma* U_4-*ma*]⌜LAL⌝-*šú* ?**

(7′) "If at the time of its NÍG.LAL."

Since the base text describes sickness that leaves but later seizes again the patient, the commentator argued that NÍG.NIGIN referred to the sickness's departure and NÍG.LAL to its recurrence. Though "fright" (*ḫayyattu*) is usually expressed as IGI.LAL.(ŠÚ), the form NÍG.LAL was thought similar enough to indicate fearful anticipation of the sickness's approach.

(7′) NÍG.NIGIN *means* turning back.

(8′) … NÍG.LAL *means* fright.

Sa-gig 3: 46 (TDPT 3: 37)
The topic *urappad* ("he wanders about") is cited here out of its order in the base text, and is correctly resumed again as part of the next topic "His UMUŠ changes for him."

(8′) "*urappad*" *means* …

***Sa-gig 3: 46 (TDPT 3: 37)**
The sick man whose intelligence is altered "wanders about" unawares, and is said to be in danger of losing his way and "disappearing."

(9′) ["His UMUŠ changes for him"] *refers to* an alteration of intelligence.

(9′) ŠU.DAG *means* to wander about.
(9′–10′) [ŠU.DAG (*means*) to rove about. (?)]
(10′) [ŠU.DAG (?)] *means* to disappear.

***Sa-gig 3**
The unusual writing DAB-*ba-at* may express *iṣṣabbat*, "(his mouth) becomes seized."

(10′) "His mouth DAB-*ba-at*" …

Sa-gig 3: 50 (TDPT 3: 41)—
"his mouth is difficult for words"
The base text phrase "difficult for words" is replaced with an expression more idiomatic in other medical descriptions: "difficult {to do something}."

(Rev. 1) ["For words" *means*] to speak.

***Sa-gig 3: 50 (TDPT 3: 41)—*i-na* D[U$_{11}$.DU$_{11}$-*šú it-te-né-ep-rik-ku*] ?**

(1–2) "When he speaks, (his words) keep stopping."

(2) [To put a stop to *means*] to halt.

Sa-gig 3: 52 (TDPT 3: 43)
As is true elsewhere, *salāḫu* "to tremble" is often used as explanation in medical commentary.

(2–3) "His hands and his feet shiver."

(3) [To shiver] *means* to tremble.

Sa-gig 3: 52 (TDPT 3: 43)

(3–4) "His mouth holds saliva for (its) manner of speech."

(4) ["Manner of speech"] *refers to* speaking.
(4) "Saliva" *refers to* spittle.

***Sa-gig 3: 52 (TDPT 3: 53)—**
[*lu-ʾ-a-ti šu-kul*] ?

(4–5) "He is fed dirty things."

(5) ["Dirty things"] *refers to* sorcery.

Sa-gig 3: 53 (TDPT 3: 44)

(5) "His belly keeps coming up in order to BURU$_8$ (subscript: (in order) to puke)."

(6) [BURU$_8$ *means* to puke.]
(6) BURU$_8$ *means* to vomit.

***Sa-gig 3** (6–7) …

Notes

Obv. 1′–2′—Since nothing intervenes between the topics […] UŠ.ME-⸢*šú*⸣ (obv. 1′) and *šá-niš* MUNUS M[U a-lagab *u sa-ma-li*] (obv. 2′) in the base text Sa-gig 3: 42 (TDPT 3: 33), one may assume that the cuneiform traces between these two topics (obv. 1′–2′) constitute some comment on the former. For discussion on the base text's mention of "(the game of) Room Four," i.e., the "Royal Game of Ur" or the "Game of Twenty Squares," see Wee (2018: 865–867).

Obv. 2′–4′—These lines represent an attempt to identify the items "a-lagab and *samālu*" in the base text Sa-gig 3: 42 (TDPT 3: 33). The commentator seems to have cited from a lexical list (obv. 3′–4′) involving tree branches and stick-like implements. For obv. 3′–4′, Geller and Schmidtchen (CCP 4.1.3.C) have proposed ⸢$^{\text{giš(!)}}$⸣RU *u*! *me*!*-ṭu* : *a-tu-*⸢*x x* (*x*)*-zi*⸣*-i* / ⸢*x*⸣ *ma-li-la a-ru-ú šá* ŠU.2 ^{d}⸢*A*⸣*-ḫa-la-mi-ti* : ("bow and mace, … (*as in*) … the flute, the twig (*aru*) of the hands of the goddess Aḫalamītu"), but I prefer to read si ru ⸢ši⸣ ṭu : *a-tu-*⸢*ú šá Su-ti-i*⸣ / ⸢*sa*⸣*-ma-li la-a-ru-ú šá* ŠU.2 ^{d}*A-ḫa-la-mi-ti* : ("…, throwing stick in the case of the Sutean, *samālu*-wood, twig (*larû*) in the case of the Hands of the goddess Aḫalamîtu"). Although the top half of several of the signs *a-tu-*⸢*ú šá Su-ti-i*⸣ (obv. 3′) needs to be restored, the preserved portions agree considerably with this reading, which is reflected in the lexical equations giš-ru $^{\text{il-lu-lu}}$ -me-te = *a-tu-ú šá Su-ti-i* (Hh. VII A, 70 in *MSL* VI, 89); [giš-ru-me-te] = [*a-tu-ú*] *šá Su-ti-i* = *qa-*[*šat*] *kad-*[*re-e*] (Comm. Hh. VII A, 67 in *MSL* VI, 109). One wonders if the problematic signs si ru ⸢ši⸣ ṭu (obv. 3′) could be read as giš(!)-ru-me(!)-ṭu, as a garbled version of giš-ru-me-te. For discussion on giš-ru and its possible identification as the 'boomerang,' 'throw-stick,' or composite or non-composite 'bow,' see Tammuz (2017: 91–101). Moving on, I understand *la-a-ru-ú* (obv. 4′) as the term *larû* ("twig, branch, fork"; *CAD* L, 103–104), even though the first syllable is not typically written with an extra vowel sign *-a-*, taking note of the fact that *a-ri* ("branch") was already mentioned earlier in obv. 3′. For the goddess Aḫalamîtu or Aḫalamayītu, see Beaulieu (2003: 309). Whereas *samāli* was regarded as a cup of sorts that could be associated with the *kāsu*-cup (GÚ.ZI) in Comm. Sa-gig 1–3, line 39, the commentator of Comm. Sa-gig 3B seems to have interpreted *samāli* as a byform of *samānu* B (*CAD* S, 112–113) or *samu/allu* (*AHw*, 1020), which is a kind of tree or wood appropriate for the list here. This commentator evidently wanted to cite a lexical list demonstrating that *a-ri* ("branch") and *samāli* were closely related objects, therefore proving that the signs a-lagab in the base text should be read syllabically as *a-rim* or *a-rì* ("branch"). This also explains why only the terms *a-ri* (obv. 3′) and ⸢*sa*⸣-*ma-li* (obv. 4′) are written with explicitly genitive case endings, just as they appear in the base text Sa-gig 3: 42 (TDPT 3: 33), in contrast to the other items in this lexical list: ⸢*ḫaṭ*(?)⸣-*ṭu* (obv. 3′), *kak-ku* (obv. 3′), si ru ⸢ši(?)⸣ ṭu (obv. 3′), *a-tu*-⸢*ú*⸣ (obv. 3′), *la-a-ru-ú* (obv. 4′).

Obv. 5′—See Note on Comm. Sa-gig 1–3, line 40 where KI.SIKIL.BÀN.DA is likewise defined as *batultu* ("adolescent girl").

Obv. 5′—See Note on Comm. Sa-gig 1–3, line 41 where the equation of "*kezēru*" and "wealth" in Comm. Sa-gig 3B, obv. 5′ lends support to the interpretation of *kezēru* in both commentaries as the *kezēru*-payment required of certain women (*CAD* K, 315–316).

Obv. 6′—See Note on Comm. Sa-gig 1–3, line 41 where "tavern" (*aštamme*) similarly stands as a euphemism for activities of the "prostitute" (*ḫarīmtu*).

Obv. 6′–7′—The base text Sa-gig 3: 45 (TDPT 3: 36) was collated as KÚM TÉŠ.BI UNU-*su* ("heat (has) its seat equally all over") by Scurlock and Andersen (2005: 32, §3.25; 686 n. 25 and 38); Scurlock (2014: 15), who based their interpretation of UNU = *šubtu* ("seat") on lexical equations in *CAD* Š III, 172. As correctly recognized by Geller (personal communication), however, the writing in this commentary bears closer resemblance to TUKUR$_2$(ka×še) (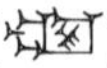) rather than UNU(ab×eš) (). The *Chicago Assyrian Dictionary* seems to assign TUKUR$_2$ exclusively to *kasāsu* A ("to gnaw, chew up"; *CAD* K, 242), as distinct from *kasāsu* B (or *kazāzu*; "to hurt, sting," esp. as action performed by sick body parts, disease, or fire; *CAD* K, 242–243), but we find both meanings and the logogram TUKUR$_2$ subsumed under a single entry *kasāsu* (or *kaṣāṣu*; "kauen, nagen") in *AHw*, 453. Indeed, the translation of the base text KÚM TÉŠ.BI TUKUR$_2$-*su* ("heat gnaws him all over") agrees with the commentarial argument in Comm. Sa-gig 14 (obv. 6–7), where the description of "gnawing" or "consuming" (*kāsistu*) fire in a fire incantation was employed to shed light on the medical condition *kiṣṣat ṣēti* ("*kiṣṣatu* of *ṣētu*-heat"; cf. "*kissatu* of fire" in Comm. Sa-gig 18, rev. 7′). While a substantial part of this commentary entry is unfortunately damaged, it can plausibly be restored as TUKUR$_2$-⸢*su*⸣ / [*i-ka-s*]*a*-⸢*su*⸣ (?), "'TUKUR$_2$-*su*' (*means*) [(heat) gnaws him (?)]" (obv. 6′–7′).

Obv. 7′–8′—The topic *šum-ma* U$_4$-*ma* NÍG.LAL-*šú* ("If at the time of his NÍG.LAL") seems to correspond to the base text reading *šu*[*m-ma* KI] ⸢LAL⸣-*šú* (Sa-gig 3: 45 (TDPT 3: 36)) collated by Scurlock and Andersen (2005: 484, §19.227; 756 n. 170–171, 174); Scurlock (2014: 15). While the compressed writing of U$_4$-*ma* (𒌓𒈠) is admittedly visually similar to the sign KI (𒆠), the reading U$_4$ is clearly preferred based on analogous expressions in Sa-gig 16: 12, 14, 81′; 17: 34–35; 19/20: 16′; 31: 35′; in addition to many entries in Sa-gig 26. It is also unclear whether or not the commentator consulted a base text that varied from manuscript copies preserved for us, but, in any case, he seems to have seriously considered the reading available to him in the context of its Sa-gig description: "(the patient's) head keeps seizing him, heat gnaws him all over, (then) his sickness leaves him, and he has NÍG.NIGIN" (TDPT 3: 36). This term NÍG.NIGIN was understood as the logogram for *ṣīdānu* ("vertigo" or "dizziness") by Labat (1951: 22–23); Scurlock and Andersen (2005: 484, §19.227); Scurlock (2014: 20), in line with the many lexical equations connecting NIGIN / NIGIN$_2$ with *ṣīdānu* in *CAD* Ṣ, 171. Here, however, the commentator apparently treated NÍG.LAL and NÍG.NIGIN as opposite concepts, with the former indicating the onset of sickness and the latter referring to its departure. The assertion that "NÍG.NIGIN *means* turning back" (obv. 7′; cf. *CAD* T, 60–61 s.v. *tayyāru* A) seems to be grounded in lexical readings such as $^{\text{ni-gin}_3}$ lagab = *ta-a-rum* (Aa I/2, 57 in *MSL* XIV, 209); $^{\text{(ni-gi-in)}}$ lagab = *ta-a-ru*, *ta-a-a-ru*; $^{\text{(ni-gi-in)}}$ lagab-lagab = *ta-a-ru*, *ta-a-a-ru* (Ea I MA Recension, 320–p, 47r–s in *MSL* XIV, 196, 197). The claim that "NÍG.LAL *means* fright" is rather curious, since the logographic form of *ḫayyattu* ("fright") is typically IGI.LAL.(ŠÚ), as expressed by the commentary equation IGI.LAL.ŠÚ : *ḫa-a-a-at-tú* (Comm. Sa-gig 13+, obv. 9). The basic meaning of LAL as *ḫâṭu* ("to overwhelm"; cf. Stol 1993: 44–46), nonetheless, appears also elsewhere as LAL : *ḫa-a-ṭu* (Comm. Sa-gig 10 & 11, obv. 5), and the commentator here evidently thought that NÍG.LAL—parallel in form to NÍG.NIGIN—could likewise indicate the patient's sensation of "fright" at the sickness's approach.

Obv. 8′–10′—If the commentator's base text is accurately reflected in manuscripts of Sa-gig 3: 46 (TDPT 3: 37) available today, it should read: UMUŠ-*šú* KÚR-*šum-ma ina* NU ZU-*ú ú-rap-pad* ("his intelligence changes for him, and he wanders about without knowing (it)"). Since the order of commentary entries typically adheres to the order their topics appear in the base text, one might expect the topic *ú-rap-*[*pad*] (obv. 8′) to be treated only after the topic [UMUŠ-*šú* KÚR-*šum-m*]*a* (obv. 9′), contrary to what we find here. As a matter of fact, the commentator returned to the idea of "wandering about" after the latter topic, without again citing the base text form *ú-rap-pad*. In Comm. Sa-gig 1–3, line 42, metathesis is employed in the argument ⸢*ú*⸣*-rap-pad* || *ú-par-rad* ("'He wanders about' *means* he causes shudders"). Here, the commentator seems to have relied on shared semantic connections with ŠU.DAG to link the verbs *rapādu* ("to wander about"), *ḫalāqu* ("to disappear"), and perhaps *itaggušu* ("to rove about"; Gtn of *nagāšu*). Note the lexical equations: šu-dag = *ra-pa-a-*du-um,* šu-dag-dag = *i-ta-gu-šum* (Nigga Bil. B 198–199 in *MSL* XIII, 120); šu-dag = *ru-up-pu-du,* šu-dag-dag = *ra-pa-du* (Erimhuš II, 232–233 in *MSL* XVII, 39); [šu]- $^{da-ag}$ dag = *ra-pa-du,* [šu]- $^{pa-ar_2}$ dag = *na-pal-ṭu-ú* (Antagal E, 11′–12′ in *MSL* XVII, 209); dag-dag = *na-ga-šu šá* LÚ (Antagal VIII, 193 in *MSL* XVII, 176); as well as the close proximity of *ḫalāqu* and *rapādu* in Malku VIII, 41–42 (Hrůša 2010: 423). While the argument [UMUŠ-*šú* KÚR-*šum-m*]*a* : *šá-né-e ṭè-me,* "['His UMUŠ changes for him'] *refers to* an alteration of intelligence" (obv. 9′) is admittedly heavily restored, the restored topic is the only option at this point in the base text that answers to the preserved comment. Stol (2009b: 1–12) attempted to distinguish nuances of *šanû* ("to alter") versus *nakāru* ("to change"; logogram KÚR) in relation to the patient's "intelligence" (*ṭēmu*), but the commentator here showed little reservation in equating the two terms.

Obv. 10′—Only what seems to be the topic KA-*šú* DAB-*ba-at* ("his mouth DAB-*ba-at*") is preserved, which supposedly corresponds to a base text entry between Sa-gig 3: 46 (TDPT 3: 37) and Sa-gig 3: 50 (TDPT 3: 41).

Rev. 1—The base text Sa-gig 3: 50 (TDPT 3: 41) consists of an idiom "his mouth is difficult for words (*ana amâti da-a-an*)" (i.e., it is too difficult for his mouth to speak) that appears also in Sa-gig 17: 57 (*ana awâti da-an*), and which is employed as explanations in other commentaries: GÌR.2-*šú* DU[GUD : *šá ana da-k*]*e-e* / *dan-na-áš-šú,* "'His/her feet are heavy' [*refers to* the case where] they are (too) difficult for him/her [to rouse]" (Comm. Sa-gig 36, rev. 4′–5′); ÚR-*šú ta-a-ka* / *šá ana da-ke-e u šá-ka-nu dan-na-niš-šú,* "'His thigh(s) *ta-a-ka*' (*refers to*) the case where they are (too) difficult for him to rouse or to set in position" (Comm. Sa-gig 39, obv. 9–10). Based on the parallels in Commentaries Sa-gig 36 and 39, the forms *da-a-an* (Sa-gig 3: 50 (TDPT 3: 41)) or *da-an* (Sa-gig 17: 57) should probably be understood as Stative verbs, and the commentator's substitution of the phrase "for words" (*ana amâti*) with the Akkadian Infinitive "to speak" (*ana dabābi*) agrees with the syntax of forms like *ana dakê* ("to rouse") and (*ana*) *šakāni* ("to set in position").

Rev. 1–2—The gloss $_{da\text{-}\ulcorner ba\urcorner\text{-}bi\text{-}šu_2}$ is written in smaller cuneiform script immediately beneath the signs DU_{11}.DU_{11}-*šú* (rev. 1). See Note on Comm. Sa-gig 1–3, line 43 where essentially the same citation occurs, as well as my preference to identify the base text of both commentary entries as Sa-gig 3: 50 (TDPT 3: 41) instead of Sa-gig 3: 51 (TDPT 3: 42). Here, I restore [*šu-par-ku-ú* :] *ba-ṭa-lu,* "[To put a stop to *means*] to halt" (rev. 2), following a similar lexical equation in Malku IV, 125 (Hrůša 2010: 386), even though the Š dictionary root *šuparkû* ("to put a stop to") of the commentator's argument does not correspond precisely to the Ntn inflected verb *it-te-né-e[p-rik-ku]* of the base text (Sa-gig 3: 50 (TDPT 3: 41)). But notice how, in similar fashion, the Ntn dictionary root *itanṣulu* ("to keep becoming sluggish") differs from the N inflected verb *inneṣil* ("(his right hip) becomes sluggish") of the base text (Sa-gig 14: 25) in Comm. Sa-gig 14, obv. 5.

Rev. 2–3—Although there is damage at the very end of rev. 2, the lengthened writing of the *bu* cuneiform sign in *i-ra-ʾ-bu* : (rev. 2), as well as the allowance for at most one cuneiform sign in the damaged portion, suggest that there are in fact no more signs to be restored at the end of the line. The restored [*ra-ʾ-bu*] (rev. 3) represents the dictionary root of the topic *i-ra-ʾ-bu* (rev. 2), which has a cognate *raʾību* that appears also as the topic in Comm. Sa-gig 40B, rev. 7′. Although the commentary equation *raʾābu* : *salāḫu* ("To shiver *means* to tremble") has no parallel in existing lexical texts, the two terms are obviously similar in meaning. As a matter of fact, Sa-gig commentators favored the verb *salāḫu* ("to tremble") as explanation for other verbs of quaking or shivering: *ra-a-du* : *sa-la-ḫa*, "To shake *means* to tremble" (Comm. Sa-gig 4A, obv. 9); [*it*]*-ta-na-as-la-ʾ-ma* : *sa-la-a*$_4$: *na-ka-da*, "'*ittanaslaʾ-ma*' *derives from the dictionary root salāʾa* (understood not as *salāʾu* 'to become ill,' but as a byform of *salāḫu* 'to tremble'), *which means* to quiver" (Comm. Sa-gig 40A, obv. 7); and probably [...]x : *sa-la-ḫu* : *šá* [...], "... *means* to tremble in the case of ..." (Comm. Sa-gig 4B, obv. 18). Whereas other verbs were often employed in more restrictive contexts, the verb *salāḫu* ("to tremble") was used broadly to describe the patient's head (Sa-gig 3: 112 (TDPT 3: 103)), his ears (Sa-gig 8: 16), and the patient as a whole (Sa-gig 40: 70), among other features (Sa-gig [18: 43′–44′]), and its preference by commentators may reflect tendencies towards a unified understanding of behaviors by different parts of the patient's body.

Rev. 3–4—The individual terms of KA-*šú ana at-me-e il-la-ti ú-ka*[*l*] ("His mouth holds saliva for (its) manner of speech"; rev. 3) cited from the base text Sa-gig 3: 52 (TDPT 3: 43) are lucid enough, but the idiom as a whole is not common in medical texts. The base text is mistakenly restored as KA-*šú ana at-me-e il-la-a* U$_4$[...] ("he raises his mouth to the words, [(and) he has been sick for ...] days") in Scurlock (2014: 15, 21). The argument [*at-me-e*] : *da-ba-bi* ("['Manner of speech'] *refers to* speaking"; rev. 4) in this commentary appears also as *at-mu-ú* : *da-ba-ba* in another commentary (Scheil 1916: 137–138, obv. 12′). The equation of *illāti* ("saliva"; logogram ÚḪ.MEŠ) and *ruʾtu* ("spittle"; logogram ÚḪ) in rev. 4 needs little comment.

Rev. 4–5—As is typical for Sa-gig commentaries in this volume and other commentaries elsewhere, topics are cited at their first occurrence in the base text pericope and roughly according to the order in which they appear in the base text. Since the topic here ("He is fed dirty things"; rev. 4) is sandwiched between other topics from Sa-gig 3: 52 (base text of rev. 2–4) and Sa-gig 3: 53 (base text of rev. 5), we might posit the existence of *lu'âti šūkul* ("He is fed dirty things") among these Sa-gig entries, and there is in fact a lacuna at the end of Sa-gig 3: 52 (TDPT 3: 43) where the statement might possibly fit. See Note on Comm. Sa-gig 1–3, line 44 for my restoration of the section Sa-gig 3: 51–54 (TDPT 3: 42–45) focused on the consumption of harmful substances, as well as attestations of *lu'âtu* as the corruptant that the victim is made to eat or drink.

Rev. 5–6—The gloss $_{\textit{a-re-e}}$ is written in smaller cuneiform script immediately beneath the signs $BURU_8$-*e* (rev. 5). In several other Sa-gig commentaries, the terms *arû* ("to puke") and *parû* ("to vomit") are related to each other and to the logogram $BURU_8$. Note: [pi-pi-ru : *i*]⌜-*ʾá*-⌝*a-ru* : *i-par-ru* : *a-ru-u* : *pa-ru-u*, "['The cuneiform signs pi-pi-ru (read as ia_8/i_{16}-*à-ru*)' *mean*] he pukes, *which means* he vomits. To puke *means* to vomit." (Comm. Sa-gig 4B, obv. 15); $BURU_8$: *ia-ár-ru*, "'$BURU_8$' *means* he pukes." (Comm. Sa-gig 7A, rev. 6); [ŠÀ-*šú ana*] $BURU_8$ *i-ta-na-áš-šá-a* : *lìb-ba-šú a-na pa-re-e* / [*i-ša*]*q-qa-a*, "'[His belly] *i-ta-na-áš-šá-a* [to] vomit ($BURU_8$)' *means* his belly ascends to vomit." (Comm. Sa-gig 7B, rev. 2′–3′).

Commentary Sa-gig 3C

Provenance:	Babylon
Period:	Hellenistic (266/265 BCE)
Names:	"Babylon, Arahsamna (VIII), Day 9, Year 46 (of the Seleucid Era, i.e., 266/265 BCE), Kings Antiochus (I) the Great King and Antiochus (II) his son"
Script:	Neo-/Late Babylonian
Field/Museum No.:	BM 55491 = 82-7-4,65 ("Sippar Collection" at British Museum)
Printed Edition/Hand Copy:	Lambert Folio 9238; Jiménez and Schmidtchen (2017: 217–225)
Digital Resources:	CDLI P461263; CCP 4.1.3.B (note that a different tablet BM 43854+43938 is labeled as Comm. Sa-gig 3b in Frahm 2011a: 224; printed hand copy, photos, and edition digitized by Jiménez 2016, with contributions by Schmidtchen)
Discussion:	Leichty (1986: 177); Frahm (2011a: 261, 311) and (2018: 18 n. 28); Gabbay (2016: 75 n. 323, 227 n. 111); Jiménez (2016b: 232 n. 24); Jiménez and Schmidtchen (2017: 217–225); Schmidtchen (2018: 322); Geller (2018: 303)
Pericope:	At least Sa-gig 3: 1–9

Transliteration

Obverse

1) ⸢*ana* GIG *ina* TE⸣-*ka* EN É[N *ana* SU]-⸢*ka*⸣ ŠUB-*ú ana* GIG NU TE-[*ḫi*]
2) én ĝá-e lú ⟨d⟩Namma-me-en ĝá lú ⟨d⟩Nan[še-me-en *šá*]-*niš* én ĝá ^{lu_2}kíĝ-gi$_4$-a diĝir gal-g[al-e-ne]
3) SU : *zu-ú-ru* : SU : *ra-ma-nu* : ⸢*i*⸣-[*nar-r*]*u-uṭ* : *i-sal-liḫ* : *na-ra-ṭ*[*u* : SÌG]
4) *se-le-eḫ* : *ne-ʾ-a* : *nu-uḫ-ḫa* ⸢:⸣ T[U.L]U : *né-ʾ-ú* : TU.LU : *ra-*[*mu-ú*]
5) la(-)ḫa-aḫ-šá : *i-su*(!) SAG.2-*šú em-mu* : *šá-niš la* Ú[Ḫ : *la ḫa*]-*ḫa-šú* : *la ṣar-ḫa-áš* : ⸢ÚḪ⸣ [: *ṣa-ra-ḫu*]
6) *lìb-bu-ú* níĝ-izi-ba-zu-ta sug-ge úḫ-ba šu ḫa-⸢an⸣-[ta]g-ga-e ḫu-uz x[…]

 | DOI:10.1163/9789004417564_009

7) *šá* GI.NU.TAG.GA-*u qa-bi* : šag$_4$ íb-ba-dab$_5$-e-ne ⸢ĝe⸣ [...]
8) *ina ug-ga-tu$_4$ lìb-bi-šú-nu ú-šá-aṣ-ṣú*(!)*-ú ṣi-*⸤*ri*⸥-[*iḫ-ta* ...]
9) *bir-ta* Á-*šú* : *bi-rit nag-la-*⸤*ba-šú*(?)⸥ x[...]
10) ... [...]

Reverse
1′) *la ú-šel-liš šá* GUR$_{17}$-*šú a-*⸢*na*⸣ [U$_4$-*šú* (?)]
2′) *ana* EN-*šú* GUR-*šú* ⸢E^{ki}⸣ ^{iti}APIN ⸢U$_4$.9⸣.K[AM]
3′) MU.46.KAM ^{m}*An-ti-ʾ-u*[*k-s*]*u* LUGAL G[AL]
4′) ⸢*u* ^{m}⸣*An-ti-ʾ-uk-su* ⸢A⸣-*šú* LUGAL.[MEŠ]

Translation

Incipit-title of Sa-gig 3

(Obv. 1) "As you approach the sick man, until you cast an incantation [on] your [body (SU)], do not approach the sick man" (*refers to*)

Incipit-title of the incantation *Utukkū Lemnūtu* III, 124–145

(2) (the incantation titled) "Incantation: I am the man of the goddess Nammu, I [am] the man of the goddess Nanše."

Incipit-title of the incantation VAT 8803

(2) Secondly, (the incantation titled) "Incantation: I am the emissary of the great gods."

Incipit-title of Sa-gig 3
The commentator was concerned to specify that the "body" receiving the incantation is the healer's, not the patient's.

(3) SU *means* body.
(3) SU *means* oneself.

Sa-gig 3: 3
narāṭu "to quake" is not attested elsewhere as a medical description, and the commentator explained it by using a more general synonym *salāḫu* "to tremble."

(3) "(His epigastrium) quakes" *means* it trembles.

(3–4) To quake [*means* SÌG, (*which means*)] to tremble.

***Sa-gig 3: 5—**
"his temples are *ne-eḫ-a*"
The commentator understood *ne-ʾ-a* in his base text as a byform of *nêḫu* "(G stem) to become calm," which he explained by the same verb's D stem *nuḫḫu* of similar meaning "to calm down."

(4) "(His temples) are *ne-ʾ-a*" *means* they are calmed down.

"Calm" temples are related to a state of "limpness," a description more common in therapeutic texts than the Diagnostic Handbook.

(4) TU.LU *means* to become calm.
(4) TU.LU *means* to go limp.

Sa-gig 3: 6—"his temples are hot la(-)ḫa-aḫ-šá"
The cuneiform signs la(-)ḫa-aḫ-šá may be read as *la-ḫa-ʾá*(aḫ)*-šá* "its jaw," which the commentator explained using the synonym *isu* "jaw, cheekbone."

(5) "The cuneiform signs la(-)ḫa-aḫ-šá" *mean* the cheekbones (on both sides) of his head are hot.

The cuneiform signs may also be read *lā ḫa-aḫ-šá* for "non-*ḫaḫḫaš* (heat)," an expression more common in the Diagnostic Handbook than in therapeutic texts. By taking advantage of similarities between the labels KÚM *ḫaḫḫaš* ("*ḫaḫḫaš* heat") and KÚM ÚḪ ("flaring-up heat"), the commentator explained the difficult expression *ḫaḫḫaš* using the more lucid verb *ṣarāḫu* "to flare up."

(5) Secondly, ("the cuneiform signs la(-)ḫa-aḫ-šá" refer to) non-ÚḪ (heat), *or* non-*ḫaḫḫaš* (heat) *refers to* non-flaring-up (heat).

(5) ÚḪ [*means* to flare up].

The Sumerian quote from Gi-nu-tag-ga may read, "Let the shrine lay claim on a burnt (úḫ) portion from your burnt offerings, ... a roasted ...," thus supporting the argument that ÚḪ describes a heat condition.

(6–7) As in, "níĝ-izi-ba-zu-ta sug-ge úḫ-ba šu ḫa-an-tag-ga-e ḫu-uz ...," it is said in the case of (the composition) Gi-nu-tag-ga.

This other bilingual quote presumably includes the Sumerian term úḫ (not preserved in the commentary tablet), which corresponds to the Akkadian term *ṣiriḫtu* "flare," confirming the commentator's assertion that non-ÚḪ heat can refer to non-flaring-up (< *ṣarāḫu*) heat.

(7–8) "šag$_4$ íb-ba-dab$_5$-e-ne ĝe … *means* (When) I expel the flare from the wrath of their heart."

Sa-gig 3: 9
"Between his arms" is explained more precisely as "between his shoulders." The "shoulder" occurs rarely in the Diagnostic Handbook, but is common in therapeutic texts.

(9) "Between his arms" *means* between his shoulders.

(10) …

(Colophon)

(Rev. o′–1′) … he must not bring it (i.e., this commentary tablet) out …

(1′–2′) He who lifts it out must return it by its [(appointed) day (?)] to its owner.

(2′–4′) Babylon, Arahsamna (VIII), Day 9, Year 46 (of the Seleucid Era, i.e., 266/265 BCE), Kings Antiochus (I) the Great King and Antiochus (II) his son.

Notes

Obv. 1–3—Two prophylactic incantations are recommended for the healer's recitation, before he exposes himself to potential harm by approaching the afflicted patient (Jiménez and Schmidtchen 2017: 218–219). The first incantation (*Utukkū Lemnūtu* III, 124–145 in Geller 2016: 114–120; cf. Geller 2007a: 106–107, 200–201), in fact, includes the expression "as I approach the sick man" (lú-tu-ra-šè te-ge$_{26}$-e-dè-mu-[…] // *ana marṣa ina ṭeḫêya*; III, 129), which almost exactly repeats the incipit-title of Sa-gig 3, and designates the healer by the titles maš-maš and *mašmaš* (III, 126), ka-pirig (III, 127), and *āšipu* (III, 125 and 127). The second incantation (VAT 8803 = *KAR* 31 in Geller 2016: 38–40; cf. Stol 1993: 24 n. 5; Heeßel 2000: 71 n. 12), likewise, prescribes its ritual at the time "when you approach the sick man" (*enūma ana* ^{lu_2}GIG *teṭeḫḫû*; line 31) and addresses the healer by the title MAŠ.MAŠ. It is unlikely that the logogram SU (obv. 3) in this context would have been confused for something other than "body." Instead, the commentator seems to have been concerned to clarify that this "body" belonged to the healer (i.e., "oneself") and not to the patient, since one could mistakenly assume that the latter's sick body was the object of a healing incantation here.

Obv. 3–4—The base text topic ⸢*i*⸣-[*nar- r*]*u-uṭ* (obv. 3) cited here indicates that Scurlock (2014: 13) is wrong to restore *i-nar-*⸢*ru*⸣-[*bu*] for Sa-gig 3: 3. This verb *narāṭu* ("to quake") seems not to occur elsewhere in medical texts. For commentators' tendency to use the general verb *salāḫu* ("to tremble") as explanation for other verbs of quaking or shivering (as in the case here), see Note on Comm. Sa-gig 3B, rev. 2–3. See also the equation *na-ra-ṭu* : *sa-la-ḫu* (*SpTU* I, 72, rev. 3) in a cultic commentary on the behavior of a sacrificial lamb. I restore the argument as *na-ra-ṭ*[*u* : SÌG] / *se-le-eḫ* (obv. 3–4), in view of lexical relationships connecting both verbs to the logogram SÌG in S^{a} Voc. N, 15′ (*MSL* III, 66) and Erimhuš II, 184 (*MSL* XVII, 36); cf. SÌG.GA = *sa-la-ḫu* in the commentary BM 34989, rev. 12 (courtesy I. L. Finkel in *CAD* S, 88). This restoration, however, results in the unusual situation, whereby a syllabic topic (*na-ra-ṭu*) precedes its logographic comment (SÌG). For a similar situation elsewhere, see Note on Comm. Sa-gig 21 & 22a, obv. 11 where the syllabic topic *nimšū* is explained by the logographic comment SA.MEŠ, as well as further discussion in § 1.2.3.1.1. Another possible restoration **na-ra-ṭ*[*u* : *nu-*(*ur*)*-ru-ṭu*] / *se-le-eḫ* (obv. 3–4) is less likely, because of the transitive meaning of the D stem *nurruṭu* ("to make something quake").

Obv. 4—Our commentator interpreted the writing *ne-ʾ-a* in his base text as a byform of *nêḫu* "(G stem) to become calm" (*contra CAD* N II, 198 s.v. *nêʾu*, lexical section; *AHw*, 783–784), and the orthography *ne-eḫ-a* in existing manuscript(s) of Sa-gig 3: 5 (e.g., Scurlock 2014: 13, 705 MS A (BM 33424) and MS B (BM 46139)) suggests that this interpretation was not unique to our commentator. The base text of Comm Sa-gig 1–3, obv. 16 likely also has the orthography [*ne*]-*ʾ-a*. This reference to the patient's "temples" (Sa-gig 3: 5) as "calm" is elsewhere clarified to be a condition of the "strands of the temple," which are also described as "set in position" (*šakānu*) (Sa-gig 4C, rev. 5′). Whereas the logographic forms TU.LU and TU.UL commonly represent the verb *ramû* ("to go limp") in both lexical and bilingual texts (*CAD* R, 128), they do not seem attested for *nâḫu* ("to become calm"). The commentator chose to explain the condition of "calm" temples by describing them as having "gone limp" (*ramû*), a verb that is used in the Diagnostic Handbook at Sa-gig 4: 122 (TDPT 4 rev. 37); Sa-gig 13: 129 (TDPT 13 iii 18); Sa-gig 17: 29; 22: 38; but more commonly in therapeutic texts at *BAM* 49 obv. 10′; 50 obv. 12; 90: 9′; [434 iii 11]; 574 i 27; 575 iv 48; *AMT* 85/1 vi 17′; in addition to numerous therapeutic references to the malady *rimûtu* ("limpness").

Obv. 5—Existing copies of the base text Sa-gig 3: 6 have the writing SAG.KI.2-*šú* KÚM la(-)aḫ-ḫa-ḫa-šá ("his temples are hot la(-)aḫ-ḫa-ḫa-šá"), but the commentator evidently used a manuscript with the signs la(-)ḫa-aḫ-šá. The latter was interpreted in two ways: First, the signs were read as *la-ḫa-ʾá*(aḫ)*-šá* ("its (i.e., each temple's) jaw"), from the noun *laḫû* ("jaw"; *CAD* L, 44–45). Using the synonym *isu* ("jaw, cheekbone") in his explanation, the commentator seems to have envisioned heat in the upper cheekbones on both sides of the patient's head, an area close enough to the temples to be named in association with them. Secondly, the signs were read as *lā ḫa-aḫ-šá* and thought to refer to "non-*ḫaḫḫaš* (heat)." This was also the interpretation assumed in Comm. Sa-gig 1–3, obv. 17. For the prevalence of this expression in the Diagnostic Handbook rather than in therapeutic texts, see Note on Comm. Sa-gig 1–3, obv. 17. Our commentator then drew attention to the parallel syntax of the labels KÚM *ḫaḫḫaš* ("*ḫaḫḫaš*-heat") and KÚM ÚḪ, which he went on to explain as KÚM *ṣarḫu* ("flaring-up heat"). See discussion of this latter term in Heeßel (2000: 162–163); Stol (2007a: 7–8). Among its various orthographies, KÚM ÚḪ appears in Sa-gig 14: 106 (TDPT 14 ii 34); Sa-gig 16: 19; [18: 5]; 37: 8 (TDPT 36: 8); KÚM *ṣarḫu* in Sa-gig 16: 31; 22: 14; 31: 6, 36′; and *ummašu ṣaruḫ* in *MDP* LVII/11 iii 4. In therapeutic texts, KÚM *ṣarḫa* may be found at *BAM* 66 obv. 21; 201: 23′. Here, the written form *la ṣar-ḫa-áš* (obv. 5) seems to include a terminative (-*š*) suffix, which may reflect the commentator's understanding of what was thought to be the parallel form *ḫaḫḫaš*. In the base text (Sa-gig 3: 6), depending on whether one reads (I) *laḫâša* or (II) *lā ḫaḫša*, one arrives at the following sentence: "his temples (have) (I) heat of (each temple)'s cheekbone / (II) non-*ḫaḫḫaš* (heat)."

Obv. 6–8—These lines furnish proof that the logogram ÚḪ could indeed be interpreted as the verb *ṣarāḫu* ("to flare up"). The first quotation (obv. 6–7) is explicitly attributed to the obscure composition Gi-nu-tag-ga (see Jiménez and Schmidtchen 2017: 219), of which little is known other than its status as one of the arts of the magician in the *Exorcist's Manual* (*KAR* 44, line 3 in Jean 2006: 64, 76). Geller (2000: 252) suggested that the title could be sandhi writing for *ginû* (*ū*)*taqqû* ("they watch for the regular offerings"). Due to the unavailability of the original source text, I only tentatively suggest a translation of the quoted Sumerian: "níĝ-izi-ba-zu-ta sug-ge úḫ-ba šu ḫa-an-tag-ga-e ḫu-uz ...” (“Let the shrine lay claim on a burnt (úḫ) portion from your burnt offerings, ... a roasted ...”). Here, the context is what defines the term úḫ in relation to heat and burning. The next quotation (obv. 7–8) from an unknown bilingual source is unfortunately damaged, but there is good reason to suspect that it contains the Sumerian term úḫ (not preserved in this commentary), which in turn corresponds to the Akkadian term *ṣiriḫtu* (“flare”): “šag$_4$ íb-ba-dab$_5$-e-ne ĝe ... *means* (When) I expel the flare from the wrath of their heart.” If this interpretation is correct, the quotation supplied a direct lexical connection between úḫ and the verb *ṣarāḫu* (“to flare up”).

Obv. 9—See Note on Comm. Sa-gig 1–3, obv. 18 where essentially the same topic (from Sa-gig 3: 9) and comment appear.

Rev. 1′–2′—The sign GUR$_{17}$ (here, written indistinguishably from the sign giš) indicates the root *našû*, “to lift (out)” (*MZL*, no. 470) or *tabālu*, “to carry off” (Lambert in Maul 2005: 30); see Jiménez (2016b: 230 n. 6); Mirelman (2017: 161 note on colophon). For an alternative view of GIŠ as the root *šaṭāru* (“to write”), see *MZL*, no. 469; Schmidtchen (2018: 154). My restoration *a*-⌜*na*⌝ [U$_4$-*šú* (?)] (“by [its (appointed) day (?)])” at the end of rev. 1′ is based on other similar injunctions in colophons: *a-na šanî* U$_4$-*mu* (“by the next day”; no. 96 line 4) and *ina ūmī*(!)-*šú* (“by its (appointed) day(!)”; no. 91 line 6; no. 97 line 2) in Hunger (1968: 40–42); with the latter expression also conceivably read “by its (appointed) star” and written *ina* MÚL-*š*[*ú*] (*SpTU* I, 139 line 4′) or *ina* ÁB-*šú* (VAT 7825, rev. 14′ in Rochberg 1988: 227). See Wee (2016a: 155 n. 187). Alternatively, the reading here could be *a*-⌜*na*⌝ [ITI-*šú*] (“by [the same month]”), following *ina* ITI-*šú ana* UMUN-*šú* GUR-[*šú*] (“May he return [it] in the same month to its owner!”) in Comm. Sa-gig 36, rev. 15′.

Rev. 2′–4′—This commentary tablet is datable with remarkable precision to Year 46 (of the Seleucid Era) = –265/–264 = 266/265 BCE. As noted by Sachs and Hunger (1989: 7) in reference to royal titulature in the astronomical diaries, “two kings named Antiochus, of whom the older one is called ‘great king’, are attested only for years 46 to 51 of the Seleucid era.” The two kings in view are Antiochus I (281–261 BCE) and his son Antiochus II (261–246 BCE). While Antiochus III (223–187 BCE) also achieved the title “Great King” according to the Greek tradition, Boiy (2002: 250) has disputed whether cuneiform sources in fact record this title for him. The convention of postponing the cuneiform writing LUGAL.[MEŠ] (“Kings”; rev. 4′) until after both kings’ names occurs alongside Greek parallels, which instead preface each name with βασιλεύς (“King”). See Berson (2014: 118).

Commentary Sa-gig 4A

Provenance:	Uruk (Warka), Area U18, Level v; Same findspot and consignment (W 22307) as Comm. Sa-gig 1C, 5, 7A, 7B, and 19 suggests library of Anu-ikṣur
Period:	Late Achaemenid
Names:	Not preserved
Script:	Neo-/Late Babylonian
Typology:	Perhaps *ṣâtu* 6b in Frahm (2011a: 53)
Field/Museum No.:	W 22307/60+79+80 (+) 75 (National Museum of Iraq)
Photos:	Plate 10 (W 22307/60+79+80 obverse), Plate 11a (W 22307/60+79+80 reverse), Plate 11b (W 22307 /60+79+80 right edge), Plate 12a (W 22307/75 obverse), and Plate 12b (W 22307/75 reverse)
Printed Edition/Hand Copy:	*SpTU* 1, 30 (= Hunger 1976: 38–39); Wee (2012: 567–578)
Digital Resources:	CDLI P348451; GKAB P348451 (edition digitized by Clancier 2009); CCP 4.1.4.A (printed hand copies digitized by Frahm, Frazer, and Jiménez 2013)
Discussion:	*SpTU* 1, 30 (= Hunger 1976: 38–39); Fincke (2000: 140 n. 1063); Heeßel (2000: 141 (4. Tafel MS a)) and (2010c: 183); Scurlock and Andersen (2005: 803, see references to *SpTU* 1.30); Clancier (2009: 388); Geller (2010a: 146–147, 196 n. 200); Genty (2010a: 373) and (2010b: 12, 19, 20, 22–28); Frahm (2011a: 53 n. 231, 105, 224, 291); Wee (2012: 567–578), (2015a: 259–260), and (2016b: 150); Jiménez (2013: 196, 332); Scurlock (2014: 41–42 (various notes), 44 n. 101); Gabbay (2016: 93–95, 146 n. 87, 226 n. 108); Jiménez and Schmidtchen (2017: 225–227, 232 n. 31, 234, 236); Steinert (2018: 268)
Pericope:	At least Sa-gig 4: 1–26

 | DOI:10.1163/9789004417564_010

Transliteration

Obverse

1) [DIŠ SAG.KI *ḫe-si-ma* KÚM-*im* : S]ED ŠU ^{d}*Kù-bu*
2) [... ŠÀ.MEŠ-*š*]*ú* al-du : ŠÀ.MEŠ-*šú* [*i*]*l-la-ku*
3) [... D]U : *a-la-ku* : *e-bé-ṭu* : *na-pa-ḫi*
4) [...] SAG.KI DAB-*su-ma* : *ti-bi* SAG.KI TUKU-*ma*
5) [...] ⌜SA SAG.KI (?)⌝-*šú* : *kal* : *nap-ḫa-ri* : pi-pi-ru : *ia-ár-ru*
6) [*ina* ma-rak(/šal)] U$_4$-*mi* : *ina* [*a-r*]*a-ku* U$_4$-*mu* : ŠU LÍL.[L]Á.EN.NA
7) [*la-ʾ*]*i-bi* : *šá li-lu-ú i-zi-*[*b*]*u-uš*
8) [*la-ʾ*]*i-bi* : *le-e-bu* : *zi-i-pi* : ne-ʾ-*et* : *né-ḫe-et*
9) [*i-ra*]*d-ma* : *ra-a-du* : *sa-la-ḫa* : KI.UŠ SAG.TUK KI.UŠ-*us*
10) [*ki-b*]*i-is ra-bi-ṣi ik-bu-*[*u*]*s* : KI.UŠ : ⌞*kib*⌟-*si*
11) [SA]G.TUK : *ra-bi-ṣi* : SA[G].KI-*šú šá* 15 G[U$_7$-*š*]*ú* ŠU ^{d}UTU TIN
12) [SAG.KI-*šú šá* 1]50 GU$_7$-*šú* ŠU ⌞^{d}⌟15 TIN : ⌜IGI⌝ 15 : ^{d}15 : IGI 150 : ^{d}UTU
13) [SAG.KI.2-*šú* (?) : ^{d}]UTU *u* ^{d}15 1-*ma* : DÙ : *ib-nu* : DÙ : *ba-nu-u*
14) [D]É-*qí* : *i-n*[*a-q*]*í* : DÉ-*qí* : *na-qu-u áš-šú* DAM LÚ
15) [*lìb-bu*]-*u* : SAG : [*a*]-*me-lu* : K[I :] KI-*tim* : KI : *sin-niš-ti*
16) [^{d}*Anu*] LUGAL DIN[GIR.M]EŠ KI-*tim ir-ḫe-e-ma* IMIN DINGIR.MEŠ
17) [*uldaššum-m*]*a* $^{[\text{din}]\text{gir}}$IMIN.BI *it-ta-bi* ⌞*zi-kìr*⌟-[*šu-un*]
18) [...]x DUG$_4$.GA x[...]
19) [...] x [...]

(Gap of a few lines)

x+1′) [...] x x x É(?) x
x+2′) [...]x ^{d}*Ereš-ki-gal*
x+3′) [... IM *i-ma-a*]*l-li u i-ra-qa*
x+4′) [... *nu-uṭ* (?)]-*ṭu-ú* : *nu-ʾu-ú-sú*
x+5′) [...] x : *ia-ár-ru*
x+6′) [... ^{d}*E*]*reš-ki-gal*

Reverse

1) [...] ^{d}ME.ME
2) [...]x *ḫa-a-ma*
3) [...] ti x
4) [...] 15 : ^{lu_2}GIG.B[I]
5) [...] x x [*m*]*ur-ṣa* DAB-*su*
6) [...] x : *ne-ʾ-i*
7) [...] x [x x x] x

(Gap of a few lines)

y+1′) [...] x [...]
y+2′) [... *ta*]-*ra-ka*
y+3′) [...] x x *šú*
y+4′) [... *a*]-*la-ku*
y+5′) [...] x x
y+6′) [...] x *šú* x
y+7′) [...] x x *ud*
y+8′) [... *it-ta*]-*nab-lak-kat*
y+9′) [...] x *zu*(?)
y+10′) [...] *ma at*

---

y+11′) [... *šá* K]A UM.ME.A
y+12′) [...] x LÚ x [x x] x
y+13′) [...] x x

Translation

Incipit-title of Sa-gig 4

(Obv. 1) "[If he (feels) covered up in the temple, and he/it becomes hot :] cold; Hand of the Stillborn Child."

Sa-gig 4: 2

The signs al-du are treated as a fossilized form AL.DU that is indistinguishable from the usual meaning of DU "to move" in medical texts, without taking into account the original stative sense of the Sumerian prefix al-.

(2) ... "[His innards] al-du" *means* his innards move.

(3) ... DU *means* to move.

Sa-gig 4: 3—*it-te-nin-bi-ṭu* "(his innards) keep having cramps"

(3) To have cramps *means* to inflame.

Sa-gig 4: 7

"Seized temple," "pulsating of the temple," "seizure of ghost," and "Hand-of-ghost" are closely related maladies often found together on the same therapeutic tablet.

(4) ... "The temple is seized for him" *means* he has pulsating of the temple.

***Sa-gig 4: 8**

Elsewhere, commentators make the title of the Diagnostic Handbook SA.GIG conform to its definition in *Esagil-kīn-apli's Manifesto* as "a bundling together (SA) of sickness (GIG)," i.e., a compilation on "all (SA) sickness (GIG)." Here, actual "strands" (SA) of the sick man's temple are interpreted as depicting the "whole" or "all" of his temple.

(5) … "Strands (SA) of his temple (?)" *means* whole, *which means* all.

Sa-gig 4: 11—"pi-pi-ru"

The cuneiform signs pi-pi-ru (𒉿 𒉿 𒊒) may be read with the unusual syllabic values *ia*$_8$/*i*$_{16}$-*à-ru* (𒉿 𒉿 𒊒) = *i'arru* "he pukes."

(5) "The cuneiform signs pi-pi-ru" *mean* he pukes.

Sa-gig 4: 21—*ma-rak*(/*šal*)

One is tempted to read these syllable signs as *ma-šal* "half," because *mašil* "middle" occurs in other time expressions. Instead, the commentator argued these signs should be read as *ma-rak* "length, extent."

(6) "[In the ma-rak(/šal)] of days" *means* when days become long.

***Sa-gig 4: 21—**
ŠU KI.SIKIL.LÍL.LÁ.EN.NA
"Hand of the *ardat lilî*-demoness"

The base text mentions only the *ardat lilî*-demoness, but the commentator's following arguments apply more broadly to the entire class of "*lilû* (type)" demons, which includes individual male *lilû*-demons, female *lilītu*-demonesses, and *ardat lilî*-demonesses.

(6) Hand of the *lilû* (type) demon.

Sa-gig 4: 21
li'bu may have been read as a contraction of "*lilû* (type) demon" + *īzibu* "which it left behind."

(7) "Suffering from *li'bu*-sickness" *refers to* what the *lilû* (type) demon left behind for him.

Besides the possible word play here between *īzibu* "which it left behind" and "*zi'pu*-sickness," the sicknesses *li'bu*, *zi'pu*, and *šību* are closely associated in lexical entries.

(8) "Suffering from *li'bu*-sickness" *refers to li'bu*-sickness, *which is related to zi'pu*-sickness.

***Sa-gig 4: 22—"His right temple is cold, the left one ne-*e-et*"**
One may be tempted to read the signs ne-ʾ-*et* as KÚM-ʾ-*et* "(the left temple) is hot," in contrast to the cold right temple in Sa-gig 4: 22. Instead, the commentator read the signs as *ne-ʾ-et* < *nēḫet* "(the left temple) is at rest," in contrast to the shaking right temple in the next base text entry Sa-gig 4: 23 (see below).

(8) "ne-ʾ-*et*" *means* (his left temple) is at rest.

Sa-gig 4: 23—"his right temple shakes, the left one ne-*e-et*"

(9) "(His right temple) shakes."

râdu "to shake" occurs rarely and only in descriptions of the patient's temple. The commentator explained it by using a more general synonym *salāḫu* "to tremble."

(9) To shake *means* to tremble.

Sa-gig 4: 23
The *rābiṣu*-demon is typically designated in medical texts as MAŠKIM, and the writing SAG. TUK is unusual. The base text Sa-gig 4: 23 has a parallel in the Middle Babylonian Nippur tablet Ni. 470 (obv. 8), which also otherwise refers to the *rābiṣu*-demon as MAŠKIM.

(9–10) "KI.UŠ SAG.TUK KI.UŠ-*us*" (*means*) he trod on the tracks of a *rābiṣu*-demon.

(10) "KI.UŠ" *means* tracks.
(11) "SAG.TUK" *means* *rābiṣu*-demon.

Sa-gig 4: 25

(11) "His right temple hurts him; Hand of the god Šamaš, he will live."

Sa-gig 4: 26

(12) "His left [temple] hurts him; Hand of the goddess Ištar, he will live."

The writing for "Ištar" (^{d}15) resembles the writing for "right" (15).

(12) Complement to the right *is* the goddess Ištar.

The name "Šamaš" displays assonance with the word for "left" (*šumēl*).

(12) Complement to the left *is* the god Šamaš.

The deity who is complement to a side harms the opposite side, rather than his or her own side.

(13) ["Both his temples (hurt him)" (?) *means*] Šamaš and Ištar at the same time.

Sa-gig 4: 27—"(His right eye) DÙ a shadow"
DÙ means *banû* "to form," instead of *retû*/*reṭû* "to fix in place" that describes the eyes in several therapeutic texts. This expression "formed a shadow" is unique to Sa-gig Chapter 11, and therapeutic texts use several other verbs to describe the eye's shadow.

(13) "DÙ" *means* it formed.
(13) "DÙ" *derives from the dictionary root* to form.

Sa-gig 4: 31—
"(His right eye) DÉ-*qí* tears"
DÉ occurs only in Sa-gig 4: 31–32. Medical texts use several more idiomatic expressions to describe tears in the eyes.

(14) "DÉ-*qí*" *means* it pours out.
(14) "DÉ-*qí*" *derives from the dictionary root* to pour out.

***Sa-gig 4: 38—⌜MU DAM LÚ⌝?**

(14) "Because of (another) man's wife."

This argument shows that medical problems of the "temple" (SAG.KI) result from illicit relations between a "man" (SAG) and "female" (KI).

(15) [As in], SAG *means* man.
(15) KI *means* earth.
(15) KI *means* female.

This quotation from *Erra Epic* I, 28–29, describes the impregnation of the "earth" (KI), thus proving that KI is "female."

(16–18) "[Anu,] King of the gods, impregnated the earth. Seven gods [did she bear him], and he called their name The Seven." ... it is said.

(18–19ff.) ...

***Sa-gig 4: 44—["Hand of Ereškigal"]**
The medical condition described in Sa-gig 4: 44 is identical to Sa-gig 13: 38 (TDPT 13 i 39′), where the diagnosis is "Hand of Ereškigal."

(x+1′) ...
(x+2′) ... Ereškigal

***Sa-gig 4**

(x+3′) ... "He [fills up with wind] and empties out"

***Sa-gig 4**

(x+4′) ... ["*nuṭṭû*" (?)] *means* to chew.

***Sa-gig 4: 65—**
***ú-gaš-⟨ši⟩* "he belches" ?**

(x+5′) ... *means* he pukes.

(x+6′) ... Ereškigal

(Rev. 1) ... Gula
(2–3) ...
(4) ... 15 : that sick man
(5) ... sickness seized him
(6) ... to turn back.
(7) ...
(Gap of a few lines)

(y+1′) ...
(y+2′) ... to throb
(y+3′) ...
(y+4′) ... to move.

(y+5′–7′) ...
(y+8′) ... it keeps shifting.
(y+9′–10′) ...

(Colophon) (y+11′–13′) ... [from the] mouth of the *ummânu*-scholar ...

Notes

Obv. 1—Note the difference in syntax between SAG.KI *ḫesi* ("he (feels) covered up in the temple") in Sa-gig 4: 1–4 and the more typical construction SAG.KI-*šú ḫesât* ("his temple (feels) covered up") in Sa-gig 13: 40 (TDPT 13 i 41′); Sa-gig 14: 174′ (TDPT 14 iii 41′); Sa-gig 15: 55′; [19/20: 63′]. The commentator, however, did not feel the need to explain this disparity here. See Note on Comm. Sa-gig 4B, obv. 8 for textual variants of the reading [KÚM-*im* : S]ED ("[he/it becomes hot :] cold"; as restored here in Comm. Sa-gig 4A, obv. 1) and what this expression might mean.

Obv. 2–3—Logographic writings of verbs in Mesopotamian medical texts typically do not include Sumerian grammatical features such as the verbal prefix al-, which is treated as a fossilized feature (i.e., AL.DU as a fixed form) by this commentator. In descriptions of the patient's behavior, the verb *alāku* "to move" is usually written as DU-(*ak/ku/ka*) or DU.ME(Š), but the form DU.DU does appear in Sa-gig [4: 91, 93]; 17: 61; 33: 49(!); *AMT* 54/3 rev. 6′; 68/1 rev. 9. For other attestations of the al- prefix, see al-dab (*BAM* 380: 46′) and al-šub (*AMT* 96/4: 9′; 99/3 obv. 4′). An interesting bilingual collection of diagnostic entries appears in *SpTU* III, 86. Sumerian grammatical forms were chosen as topics as well in Comm. Sa-gig 19, obv. 6–8. Whereas the form al-du (Sa-gig 4: 2) is translated by the Durative verb [*i*]*l-la-ku* ("they move") in this commentary, the same signs were read as *al-ṭù* ("they are stiff") and explained by the synonym *dan-nu* "they are hard" in Comm. Sa-gig 4B, obv. 9; Comm. Sa-gig 4C, obv. 4′. In these other commentaries, the stative sense of the Sumerian prefix al- (Edzard 2003: 111, §12.10) was evidently considered incompatible with movement.

Obv. 3—The equation of the verbs *ebēṭu* ("to have cramps") and *napāḫu* ("to inflame") occurs as well in Uruk Therapeutic Comm. 1 = *SpTU* I, 47 obv. 1; a commentary on Uruanna (BM 76487:[17] in *CT* 41, 45); and possibly in the damaged portion of Comm. Sa-gig 40A, obv. 15–16: [... *na-pa-ḫi* :] *e-me-ri* : *na-pa-ḫi* / [*e-bé-ṭi* (?)]. For concerns about commensurability between the intransitive G stem of *ebēṭu* and the transitive-intransitive G stem of *napāḫu*, see Note on Comm. Sa-gig 4B, obv. 9–10.

Obv. 4—The maladies "seized temple" (SAG.KI.DAB.BA), "pulsating of the temple" (ZI SAG.KI), "seizure of ghost" (DAB-*it* GIDIM), "Hand-of-ghost" (ŠU.GIDIM.MA), and similar expressions are closely related and frequently found together on the same therapeutic tablet. See especially the tablets *BAM* 3; 9; 11; 228; 229; 323; 471; 482; *AMT* 14/5; 19/1+20/1; 97/4; 102/1+103/1+104/1.

Obv. 5—I tentatively restore the topic at the beginning of this line as [...] ⸢SA SAG.KI (?)⸣-*šú* ("strands of his temple (?)") from the base text Sa-gig 4: 8. Here, the commentator seems to have reinterpreted SA ("strands") as the term for "whole" or "all." More specifically, the term "strands" (SA) came to include the idea of "bundling together" (i.e., "strand-ing," behaving as strands do), as well as the meaning "all," since items were bundled together as a comprehensive group. The logic of this argument was often utilized by commentators in order to make the title of the Diagnostic Handbook SA.GIG conform to its definition in *Esagil-kīn-apli's Manifesto* as a "bundling together (SA) of sickness (GIG)," i.e., a comprehensive compilation that included "all (SA) sickness (GIG)." See Note on Comm. Sa-gig 1A, line 47, as well as how *riksū* ("bonds") as a body part is identified with "strands" in Comm. Sa-gig 13+, obv. 7. The application of the meaning SA = "all" to actual body parts occurs also in another commentary on astronomical and physiognomic omens that, like Comm. Sa-gig 4A, should also be assigned to the Uruk library of the magician Anu-ikṣur (Clancier 2009: 390; Frahm 2011a: 258–259): SA GÌR-*šú* : *nap-ḫar* GÌR.ME-*šú* : S[A] : *nap-ḫar* ("'Strands (SA) of his foot' *refers to* all of his feet. SA *means* all.") (*SpTU* 1, 84 obv. 19).

Obv. 5—The cuneiform signs pi-pi-ru (𒉿 𒉿 𒊒) are explained here and in Comm. Sa-gig 4B, obv. 15, as *i'arru* ("he pukes"), presumably by ascribing to these signs the highly unusual syllabic values *ia*$_8$/*i*$_{16}$-*à-ru* (𒉿 𒉿 𒊒). The verb *arû* ("to puke") is otherwise expressed by the logogram BURU$_8$ or by more perspicuous syllabic writings, though the orthography *i-'a*$_4$(ḫa)-*rù*(aš) in *BAM* 221 ii 2′ and *AMT* [81/7: 5] is admittedly also not the most lucid.

Obv. 6—The writing *ina* ma-rak(/šal) U$_4$-*mi* (Sa-gig 4: 21) in the base text bears close resemblance to other time expressions such as *ina* U$_4$.SA$_9$.ÀM (*ūm mašil*) "at midday" (Sa-gig 3: 78 (TDPT 3: 69)) and *ina* GE$_6$ *ma-šil* "at midnight" (Sa-gig 17: 91), both of which are affiliated with the verbal root *mašālu* ("to become halved"). The commentator's choice to read *ma-rak* ("length, extent"), rather than *ma-šal* ("half"), seems to go against conventional time expressions elsewhere and reflects his understanding of the specific medical condition described. Note that *mi-šil* ("half") is supplied as the comment to *ba-mat* ("half") in Comm. Sa-gig 18, rev. 6′. Here, the writing [*a-r*]*a-ku* instead of **a-ra-ak* for the construct Infinitive *arāk* (i.e., *ina arāk* *ūmī* = "when days become long") may reflect the use of syllable signs for their consonantal values, particularly in cases involving the elucidation of syllabic readings (see §1.2.3.1.2 and Note on Comm. Sa-gig 39, obv. 7).

Obv. 6—The base text of Sa-gig 4: 21 mentions only the "Hand of the *ardat lilî*-demoness" (ŠU KI.SIKIL.LÍL.LÁ.EN.NA), but the commentator chose to expand the subject to the entire class of "*lilû* (type)" (ŠU LÍL.[L]Á.EN.NA) demons, which includes individual male *lilû*-demons, female *lilītu*-demonesses, and *ardat lilî*-demonesses. Genty (2010b: 25) did not recognize this attempt at generalization, and he thought that the writing ŠU LÍL.[L]Á.EN.NA stands for "main de l'Ardat-Lilî." This class of demons focuses its attacks on humans of the opposite sex, as clarified by statements such as Sa-gig 26: 46′–47′: ŠU KI.SIKIL.LÍL.LÁ.EN.NA GÍD-*ma* GAM : *ana* MUNUS LÍL.LÁ.EN.NA *ana* NITA MUNUS.LÍL.LÁ.EN.NA ("Hand of the *ardat lilî*-demoness ... *or*, for a woman, (it is) the *lilû*-demon; for a male, (it is) the *lilītu*-demoness"). The verdict DAB-*it* LÍL.LÁ.EN.NA ("seizure of *lilû*-demon") at Sa-gig 37: 12–14 (TDPT 36: 12–14) should probably be understood narrowly as a reference to the "(male) *lilû*-demon" instead of a "*lilû* (type) demon," since it occurs in the context of female sickness.

Obv. 7–8—These arguments may rely, in part, on the view that *li'bu*-sickness represents a contraction of *li̲lû īzi̲b̲u̲* ("what the *lilû* (type) demon left behind"), as well as assonantal links between *īzibu* ("which it left behind") and *zi'pu*-sickness.

Obv. 8—As in this commentary, Comm. Sa-gig 19, obv. 9–10 equates *le-e-bu* with [*zi*]-*i-pu*. For both commentaries, I understand the writing *le-e-bu* to denote the noun *lēbu* ("*li'bu*-sickness") rather than the verb *le'ēbu* ("to infect, said of *li'bu*-sickness"), because the term equated with *le-e-bu* is the noun "*zi'pu*-sickness." The same writing *le-e-bu* also appears in Comm. Sa-gig 1A, obv. 14: su-ul šáḫ : *le-e-bu* : BA.ÚŠ ("The cuneiform sign šáḫ as the logogram SUL *means li'bu*-sickness, *which means* he will die."). *Zi'pu*-sickness appears to be, in essence, a skin condition (*AHw*, 1530 s.v. *zi'pu, zīpu* III §4). The maladies *li'bu, zi'pu,* and *šību* are closely associated in lexical entries such as *li-ʾ-bu, ši-i-bu* = *zi-i-pi* (*CT* 18, 31 rev. 15–16 // *STT* 394: 161–162) and *li-ʾ-bu, ši-i-bu* = *zi*-[*ir-qu*] (Malku VIII, 161–162 in Hrůša 2010: 427; *CAD* Š II, 399). For discussion on the term *li'bu*, see Stol (2007a: 11–12).

Obv. 8–9—The two commentary entries in obv. 8–9 obviously refer to Sa-gig 4: 22 and 23, but the exact form of the base text utilized by the commentator may be questioned. In MS B (= AO 6682), the entry Sa-gig 4: 22 contains the signs ne-*e-et*, while the next entry Sa-gig 4: 23 contains only the sign ne, which very probably was understood as the logogram KÚM ("is hot"). On the other hand, a diagnostic tablet from Middle Babylonian Nippur (Ni. 470) includes a parallel (obv. 8) to the later entry Sa-gig 4: 23, but contains no corresponding parallel to entry Sa-gig 4: 22. This Nippur tablet has the reading ne-*e-et* (Ni. 470, obv. 8), which leads to the suspicion that the sign ne in MS B of Sa-gig 4: 23 represents an interpretive simplification of the writing ne-*e-et* (i.e., interpreted as KÚM-*e-et* and simplified as KÚM). The opposite scenario, whereby KÚM (= the ne sign) or KÚM-*et* becomes mistakenly written as KÚM-*e-et*, seems to be much more improbable. In this commentary, the topic ne-*ʾ-et* (obv. 8) likely represents an unpreserved base text variant of the form ne-*e-et* in available manuscripts of Sa-gig 4: 22, and the same writing (ne-*ʾ-et*) probably occurred in the next base text entry Sa-gig 4: 23 as well. One may be tempted to interpret the signs ne-*ʾ-et* as KÚM-*ʾ-et* "(the left temple) is hot," which presents an appropriate contrast to the description "his right temple is cold" in Sa-gig 4: 22. Instead, the commentator argued that ne-*ʾ-et* was the writing for *nēḫet* ("(the left temple) is at rest"), which contrasts with the description "his right temple shakes" (Sa-gig 4: 23). To make this argument clear, the commentator's explanation replaced the sign ne (𒉈), which has the logographic value KÚM, with the sign ni (𒉌), which has the syllabic value *né* but not the logographic value KÚM. He also seems to have conflated the signs *eʾ* (𒀪) and *eḫ* (𒄴), so that ne-*ʾ-et* could represent the term *nēḫet*, which could then be written syllabically as *né-ḫe-et*. In summary, because the commentator was convinced that his base text presented a contrast between a "shaking" right temple versus a left temple "at rest" in Sa-gig 4: 23, he was willing to forgo the neat dichotomy of a "cold" right temple versus a "hot" left temple in the preceding base text entry Sa-gig 4: 22.

Obv. 9—The verb *râdu* ("to shake") appears only in Sa-gig 4: 23, 66; 9: 61 and seems confined to medical descriptions of the temple (SAG.KI). For commentators' tendency to use the general verb *salāḫu* ("to tremble") as explanation for other verbs of quaking or shivering (as in the case here), see Note on Comm. Sa-gig 3B, rev. 2–3.

Obv. 9–11—Medical texts typically denote the *rābiṣu*-demon by the writing MAŠKIM, but the logogram SAG.TUK for *rābiṣu* does appear in bilingual literary compositions: sag-tuk dingir-ug$_5$-ga-àm // *rābiṣ dingiruggê* (W 18828, obv. 9) in Lenzen et al. (1959: 36); sag-tuk-zu // *rābiṣka* (Tablet IV.B, 49–50) in Hruška (1969: 489). The diagnostic entry Sa-gig 4: 23 has an earlier parallel in the Middle Babylonian Nippur tablet Ni. 470 (obv. 8), which is devoted to the theme of the *rābiṣu*-demon. Although this particular line where the demon is named (Ni. 470, obv. 8) is damaged, the demon is designated elsewhere on this Nippur tablet by the logogram MAŠKIM, which is the conventional way of referring to this demon in later medical texts.

Obv. 12—For the commentary notation IGI = *pān*(*i*) ("complement to"), see §II.2.5. The correspondence between the "right" side (expressed by the numeral 15) and the goddess Ištar (^{d}15) is obvious. See also Comm. Sa-gig 1B, rev. 26 where the goddess Ištar (^{d}15) is associated with a measure of 15 *qû*. The connection between the "left" side (expressed by the numeral 150) and the god Šamaš (^{d}UTU) may have been determined by default or by assonance between the name *Šamaš* and *šumēlu* ("left"). According to one way of thinking, the deity who is complement to a particular side harms the opposite side (*pars hostilis*), rather than his or her own side (*pars familiaris*). This rule, however, was not always followed. For example, in a Middle Assyrian diagnostic tablet from Assur (VAT 11122) that seems to focus on conditions attributable to the goddess Ištar, there are several descriptions involving ailments on the "right" (ZAG)—but not "left"—side of the patient's body (obv. 2–4, 10). For more on such correlations, see Jeyes (1991/1992); Stol (1993: 36 n. 122–127).

Obv. 13—The logogram DÙ describing the eye here is explained as *banû* ("to form") instead of *retû*/*reṭû* ("to fix in place"). The verb *retû*/*reṭû* describes the eye at Sa-gig 4: 109 (TDPT 4 rev. 23); cf. *SpTU* III, 86 obv. 1–2; but appears mostly in therapeutic texts in the expression *ur-ra u mu-ša ur-ta-na-at-tú la it-ta-na-a-a-al* ("day and night, he keeps fixing his eyes and does not sleep"). See *AMT* [35/6: 6′]; [76/5: 11′–12′]; 79/4: 2′; *SpTU* I, 46: 17(!). Note also Comm. Sa-gig 21 & 22a, obv. 9 where *retû*/*reṭû* ("to fix in place") is the base text topic explained. Only three diagnostic entries in Sa-gig Chapter II (i.e., Sa-gig 4: 27–30) speak of the eye "forming shadows" (GISSU DÙ), which may perhaps refer to the initial stages of the condition GISSU SA$_5$ ("(the eye) is full of shadows") mentioned in the therapeutic texts *BAM* 20: 13′; 159 iv 3′; 515 ii 49; *AMT* 18/6: 4′. In addition, therapeutic texts describe the eye's shadow (GISSU) by using the verbs *kullu* (VAT 13732: 16; see *CAD* Ṣ, 190), *arāmu* (*BAM* 3 iv 46), *nukkupu* (*BAM* [510 ii 17′]; 514 ii 28′), GAR (*BAM* 22: 16′), NU DU$_8$ GUR.GUR (*BAM* 22: 12′–13′), and ZI (*BAM* 382: 6). For a proposed interpretation of the term GISSU, see Veldhuis (*NABU* 1991/106) and (*NABU* 1992/32). The combination GISSU DÙ does not seem attested in therapeutic texts, and its rarity likely prompted the commentator's explanation.

Obv. 14—Hunger's reading DÉ ^{de} (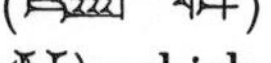) in *SpTU* I, 30 should be understood instead as DÉ-*qí* (), which is the form in preserved manuscripts of the base text Sa-gig 4: 31. I restore *i-n*[*a-q*]*í* here, but *i-n*[*a-q*]*a* is also possible. The logogram DÉ (= *naqû*, "to pour out") describes the shedding of tears only at Sa-gig 4: 31, 32, and therapeutic texts express the same verb (*naqû*) by means of another logogram BAL (*BAM* 482 ii 62′; iii 1; *AMT* [18/3: 6–7]; K 2611 ii 8′; iii 1 (in *CT* 23, 43 and 44)). Logograms aside, there were several more idiomatic ways to describe tears in the eyes, including uses of the verbs *kullu* "to hold" (*BAM* 3 iii 20, 24, 26; 6: 2, 8; 9: 14, 16, [18]; [35 iv 1′, 4′–5′]; 159 iv 28′; 482 ii 20, 22, 24; *AMT* 14/5: 8); ŠUB or *nadû* "to cast" (Sa-gig 5: 67′ (TDPT 5 D2 7); MS 2670 obv. 19′ (George 2013: 88); *BAM* 3 i 3; 22: 23′; 159 iv 12′, 16′; v 3; 480 i 3; [521: 10′]); DU "to flow" (Sa-gig 13: 21 (TDPT 13 i 22′); Sa-gig 15: 34′; 40: 61′; *BAM* 515 ii 49; *AMT* 18/6: 4′); SA$_5$ "to become full" (*BAM* 14: 5; [18: 14]; *AMT* 14/5: 7); and È "to go out" (*BAM* [510 ii 16′]; 514 ii 27′). Both the uncommon use of *naqû* ("to pour out") and its atypical logogram DÉ would have warranted the commentator's attention.

Obv. 14–15—I tentatively identify the base text here as Sa-gig 4: 38, which has been transliterated as ŠU ^{d}EN.x NIN.x (𒋗 𒀭 𒂗 x 𒎏 x) ("'hand' of Enlil(?) (and) Ninlil(?), he will get well") by Scurlock (2014: 30, 35), but which I understand to be ŠU ^{d}EN ⸢MU DAM LÚ⸣ (𒋗 𒀭 𒂗 𒈬 𒁮 𒇽) ("Hand of Bēl (?), because of (another) man's wife"). Expressions like "because of (another) man's wife" occur at Sa-gig 4: 117 (TDPT 4 rev. 32); Sa-gig 6: 16; 13: 37 (TDPT 13 i 38′); Sa-gig 17: 32, [79]; 18: 16. They represent one among several illicit heterosexual relations that can result in the patient's sickness, in addition to relations with "a (forbidden) woman" (Sa-gig 3: 100–104 (TDPT 3: 91–95); Sa-gig 18: 21–23), "his mother" (Sa-gig 6: 88″ (TDPT 6 rev. 25′)), "his sister" (Sa-gig 12: 125″ (TDPT 12 iv 17)), or even one named "the *ēntu*-priestess of his god" (Sa-gig 7 A obv. 20 (TDPT 7: 20); Sa-gig 13: 23 (TDPT 13 i 24′); Sa-gig 14: 134, 137–139 (TDPT 14 ii 62, 65–67)) who has been interpreted as the patient's mother by Scurlock and Andersen (2005: 745 n. 29). The illicit relationships mentioned are probably heterosexual, instead of homosexual (cf. Bullough 1971: 188–202), in view of their complementary distribution with the analogous statement "the son of her god has approached her" (DUMU DINGIR-*šú* TE-*ši*) in Sa-gig Tablet 36 that addresses the female patient. Such expressions are already attested earlier in the 2nd millennium BCE. The entry Sa-gig 3: 100 (TDPT 3: 91) appears also in the Middle Assyrian Assur tablet VAT 10235, while a diagnostic text from 13th century BCE Ḫattuša includes the statement *itti sinnilt*[*i*] *ina mayyāli k*[*ašid*] (*StBoT* XXXVI, p. 40, Tablet C obv. 10′). I restore the notation [*líb-bu*]-*u* ("as in"; §11.2.4) to the damaged beginning of obv. 15, though [*šá* E]-*u* ("which it said"; §11.2.3) may be another possibility. The commentator's intention here is clear: to show how illicit relations between a "man" (SAG) and a "female" (KI) can result in medical conditions of the "temple" (SAG.KI). The equation of SAG with *amēlu* is well attested in the lexical texts Lu I, 11 (*MSL* XII, 93); Idu I, 111 (*CAD* A II, 48); S^{b} I, 244 (*MSL* III, 116); Berlin Vocab., iii 38 (Reisner 1894: 163); Ai. VII, iv 14 (*MSL* I, 103); Nabnitu I, 161–163 (*MSL* XVI, 55). Notice that, in this particular context, *amēlu* ("man") is implied to be "male." The equation of KI with "female" is the objective of the following lines in the commentary.

Obv. 16–18—These lines are cited from *Erra Epic* I, 28–29 in Cagni (1969: 60–61). Geller (2010a: 146–147) thought this quotation "is intended to explain the disease name 'Hand of the Sibitti' [reading ^{d}IMIN.BI (𒀭 𒅓 𒁉) in place of ^{d}*Kù-bi* (𒀭 𒆬 𒁉) in Sa-gig 4: 37]" and "suggests that sex can sometimes have negative results, as was the case with Anu having spawned the feared Sibitti demons." As I argued in the Note on obv. 14–15 above, however, the expression "because of (another) man's wife" is one of several stereotypical ways to denote illicit relations in the Diagnostic Handbook, and I posit its existence in Sa-gig 4: 38. In other words, the *Erra Epic* quotation merely serves to validate the equations "KI *means* earth, *and* KI *means* female." The impregnation of the "earth" (KI) described in the *Erra Epic*, as well as its subsequent birthing of the Seven, demonstrates its "female" (KI) status. The signs DUG_4.GA in broken context (obv. 18) may represent the statement "it is said" in anaphoric reference to the *Erra Epic* citation, even though this expression is written with the logogram E (= *qabi*) in Comm. Sa-gig 19, obv. 17; Comm. Sa-gig 14, obv. 23 (see §11.2.3.5).

Obv. x+2′—The medical signs in Sa-gig 4: 44 (i.e., "he is struck in his temple, his epigastrium, and his rib") appear in a slightly different order in Sa-gig 13: 38 (TDPT 13 i 39′), where the diagnosis is "Hand of the goddess Ereškigal." See Scurlock and Andersen (2005: 472, §19.173; 755 n. 135). Although such a diagnosis has not been preserved in the base text of Sa-gig 4: 44, it was probably present as well, constituting the topic of the commentator's argument here. Apart from Sa-gig 13: 38 (TDPT 13 i 39′), the goddess Ereškigal is so far clearly attested in medical texts only at NA.BI *ka-šip* NU.MEŠ-*šú* DÙ.MEŠ-*ma ina* KI.GUL.MEŠ *ana* ^{d}*Ereš-ki-gal pa-aq-du* (*BAM* 214 i 7–9). Besides the obscure references to this goddess in obv. x+2′ and x+6′ of this commentary, Ereškigal is also mentioned twice in Comm. Sa-gig 18 (rev. 8′, 13′), where she may be associated with the goddess Išḫara.

Obv. x+3′—For parallels to the expression IM SA_5 *u i-ra-aq* ("he fills up with wind and empties out"), see *AMT* [1/5: 4′]; 87/6: 4′. This description of filling up and emptying out may explain the iterative action of the Ntn verb in ŠÀ.MEŠ-*šú it-te-*[*nin-bi-ṭu* (?)] ("his innards keep cramping up (?)") at Sa-gig 4: 45. However, the Ntn form of *ebēṭu* ("to have cramps") in Sa-gig 4: 3 has already received comment in obv. 3 of this commentary, and perhaps the repetition of the same topic here would be inappropriate. Instead, the base text to the commentary entry here may not be preserved in existing manuscripts.

Obv. x+4′—I tentatively make the restoration [... *nu-uṭ* (?)]-*ṭu-ú* : *nu-ʾu-ú-sú*. The verb *naṭû* ("(G stem) to hit, beat"; *CAD* N II, 132–133) occurs as a medical sign in its transitive D stem *nuṭṭû*, always with the tongue as its object (Sa-gig 7 A obv. 9; 11: 36; 13: 91 (TDPT 13 ii 33)). The commentator may have equated this action (*nuṭṭû*) with the behavior of "chewing on" (*nuʾʾusu* < *naʾāsu*; *CAD* N I, 8) the tongue, thereby bringing the meaning of *nuṭṭû* in line with the idiom EME-*šú nuššuku* ("to gnaw the tongue") at Sa-gig 7 A obv. 16; *BAM* [445: 11] (incl. *AMT* [64/2: 11′]). Note also the G Stative in EME-*šú* ... *našik* ("his tongue ... is gnawed") at Sa-gig 7 A obv. 17. On the other hand, expressions such as EME-*šú* LÀL.KUR.RA *ú-na-aṭ-ṭa* (*SpTU* I, 44: 3, 6; *AMT* 54/1 [rev. 6]) may portray the tongue not as the object of chewing or gnawing, but as the instrument for lapping up edible substances, i.e., "he laps (?) mountain honey with his tongue." See also *CAD* N II, 133 s.v. *nâṭu* §2.

Obv. x+5′—The form *ú-gaš* at Sa-gig 4: 65 has been translated as "he vomits" in Scurlock and Andersen (2005: 122, §6.30); Scurlock (2014: 37), where it is interpreted as a form of *gâšu* II, "sich erbrechen" (*AHw*, 283; not recognized as such in *CAD*). Alternatively, the form could represent a defective writing of the verb *ú-gaš-*⟨*ši*⟩ (< D stem of *gešû* "to belch"), even though more typical orthographies are *ú-ga-aš-ši* (Sa-gig 7 B rev. 11 (TDPT 7: 67′); *BAM* 564 ii 18′; *AMT* 27/2 obv. 16′; [81/7: 8]), *ú-ga-áš-ši* (*BAM* 146: 37′; 221 ii 5′), and *ú-ga-áš-šá* (Sa-gig 15: 37′). In any case, if this term indeed meant something along the lines of "to vomit, throw up," its unusual form likely prompted the commentator's explanation.

Obv. x+6′—See Note on obv. x+2′ above concerning the goddess Ereškigal in medical texts.

Rev. y+2′ff.—Though I tentatively restore the readings [*ta*]-*ra-ka* "to throb" (line y+2′), [*a*]-*la-ku* "to move" (line y+4′), and [*it-ta*]-*nab-lak-kat* "it keeps shifting" (y+8′), the absence of a sure context for the reverse side of this commentary means that we cannot be certain whether these terms represent topics (i.e., quotations from the base text) or the commentator's remarks.

Commentary Sa-gig 4B

Provenance:	Same consignment (82-9-18) as Comm. Sa-gig 18
Period:	?
Names:	Colophon not preserved
Script:	Neo-/Late Babylonian
Field/Museum No.:	BM 66965 + 76508 = 82-9-18,6959 + 83-1-18,1878 ("Sippar Collection" at British Museum)
Photo:	Plate 13 (obverse)
Transliteration:	Lambert Folio 9882
Printed Hand Copy:	*CT* 51, 136
Printed Edition:	Wee (2012: 579–591)
Digital Resources:	CDLI P285998; CCP 4.1.4.B (printed hand copy, photos, and edition digitized by Jiménez 2016, with contributions by Schmidtchen)
Discussion:	Lambert (1984: 9); Stol (2000: 31 n. 28); Heeßel (2000: 141 (4. Tafel MS b)); Scurlock and Andersen (2005: 516 n. 287, 349 n. 16); Goodnick Westenholz (2006: 2 n. 7); Genty (2010a: 503) and (2010b: 12, 23, 24, 28–31); Frahm (2010a: 172 n. 459) and (2011a: 61, 64, 67–68, 105–106, 224, 287, 401); Wee (2012: 579–591), (2015a: 279–280), and (in press: discussion on obv. 8); Jiménez (2013: 332); Scurlock (2014: 41 n. 16); Gabbay (2016: 75 n. 323, 81 n. 354, 135 n. 30); Jiménez and Schmidtchen (2017: 225–227, 232 n. 31, 233–236)
Pericope:	At least Sa-gig 4: 1–12

Transliteration

Obverse

1) [DIŠ SAG.KI *ḫe-si* : G]AZ : *ḫe-su-u* : GAZ : *ṭe-bu-ú* : DAB : *ḫe-su-ú* : DAB : *ka-ba-šu* [...]

2) [...]x : ^{d}30 : SAG.KI : *ana na-ka$_4$-pu* : *qar-ra-du šá ki-ma* ^{d}30 *qar-nu* DÙ-*ú* : [...]

3) [...] : ^{d}*Kù-bi* : ^{d}⸤U.GUR : MIN : ^{d}⸥*A-nun-na-ki* : *i-la-at* ^{d}*A-nun-na-ki ina* ŠU.N[IGIN$_2$-*šu-nu* (?)]

4) [...] ⸢SAG.GÁ (?)⸣.⸢GÁ⸣ : ^{d}*Kù-bi* : SAG : *qaq-qa-du* : ⸢SAG.UŠ : *kul*⸣-*lu šá re-e-šú* : SAG.GÁ.GÁ : *ṣi-bit n*[*ak-kap-ti* ... (?)]

 | DOI:10.1163/9789004417564_011

5) [...]x : ^{d}*Kù-bu* : $^{d.ku_3}$*Ku*$_{10}$*-bu* : KU$_{10}$: *e-ṭu-tu* : B[U : *n*]*u-ú-ri* : *ki-ma* ^{d}*Kù-bu ul-tu* Š[À ...]
6) [...]x x *la na-ma-ri ta-re-ed-di* : ⸤*šá*⸥*-niš* KU$_{10}$ [: *e*]*k-let* : BU : *na-mar* : ⸤GI⸥. IZI.LÁ : ^{d}30 : ^{din}[^{ger}*Kù-bu* ...]
7) [... *k*]*ù* ⸢KI-*tim* : BA(?) *ana*(?)⸣ *na-ṣa-ri* : *šá šap-la-*⸢*a-tú*⸣ *ma-al-ku* ^{d}*Kù-bi* ^{d}*A-nun-na-ki ta-paq-qid* : SAG.K[I ...]
8) [...] ^{d}PA.BIL.SAG ŠUB-*su* KÚM-*im u* SED : *ina* ITI.GAN ^{d}UTU *ina* ^{mul_2}PA.BIL.SAG GUB-*ma* EN.TE.[NA ...]
9) [ŠÀ.MEŠ-*šú*] ⸢al⸣-du^{tu} : *dan-nu* : *ana na-pa-ḫu šá* ŠÀ : *it-te-nen-bi-ṭu* : *e-bé-ṭu* : *na-pa-ḫu* : *ub-bu-*[*ṭu* ...]
10) [... *na*]*p-paḫ-tú* (?) : ⸢*ub-bu-uṭ* (?)⸣ ⸢: MÚ⸣ : *e-bé-ṭu* : [M]Ú : *na-pa-ḫu* : ŠU DINGIR-*šú* : ^{d}UK.URU : DINGIR *a-lu* : ^{d}[UK : *ú-mu*]
11) [... U]RU : *a-lu* ⸢: UGU-*šú*⸣ *um-mu-da-at* : UŠ : *e-me-du šá qa-tu*$_4$: UŠ : *ka-a-nu* : ŠUB-*ut* : [*mu-uq-qut* (?)]
12) [*ana šá-pa-lu* :] ⸢a⸣-ši-a : *e-šu-ú* ⸤*da*⸥*-la-ḫu* : *šá-niš* a-ši-a *ba-ka-a* : *šá dim-tú ina* ŠÀ.BI DU-*ku* x[...]
13) [... UG]U SAG.DU-*šú* : *ši-bit* SAG.DU-*šú* : ḫa-biš : *ḫa-bi-iš* : ŠÀ ŠÀ GÙ.GÙ-*s*[*i* ...]
14) [ŠU GIDIM$_7$] *šá-né-e* ^{d}15 GAM ŠÀ : ^{d}15 : *is-suk mul-mul iḫ-te-pi ka-r*[*as-sa* ...]
15) [pi-pi-ru : *i*]⸢*-ʾá-*⸣*a-ru* : *i-par-ru* : *a-ru-u* : *pa-ru-u* : KI.NÁ : KI ⸢:⸣ *ši-i-*[...]
16) [... TA ^{d}UTU.ŠÚ].⸤A EN⸥ EN.NUN.UD.ZAL.⸤LE :⸥ TA *še-e-ri* EN *ki-iṣ* U$_4$ x[...]
17) [...] x x [...] *da-mu* : *ina ra-a-*x[...]
18) [...]x : *sa-la-ḫu* : *šá* [...]

Translation

Incipit-title of Sa-gig 4 = Sa-gig 4: 1
ḫesû, defined here as "to cover up," is common in the Diagnostic Handbook, but rare in therapeutic texts.

(Obv. 1) ["If he (feels) covered up in the temple."]

(*1*) *Definition of the verb ḫesû :*
The meaning of *ḫesû* as "to cover up" is illustrated by the use of synonyms.

(1) GAZ *means* to cover up.
(1) GAZ *means* to submerge.

Like a "*kubšu*-cap/headdress," the similar-sounding ^{d}*Kūbu* "Stillborn Child" is the one who "covers up" the

(1) DAB *means* to cover up.
(1) DAB *means* to put on a *kubšu*-cap. ...

temple, as affirmed by the base text Sa-gig 4: 1.

(*II*) *The moon-god is associated with the temples of the head:*
ḫesû describes the sick man's "covered up" temples here and the "covered up" horns of the moon-crescent in astronomical texts.

(2) ... the moon-god Sîn.

nakkaptu "temple" and *nakāpu* "butting (with horns)" are presented as cognates.

(2) "The temple" (points) to butting (with horns).

This quotation from *Lugale* IV, 8 shows that horns belong to the moon-god, concluding the argument that "covered up" temples are a sign of the moon-god's involvement.

(2) "The hero who has grown horns like the moon-god Sîn." ...

The Stillborn Child is linked to Nergal, and ultimately to the Anunnaki, perhaps alluding to the composition i-nam-giš-ḫur-an-ki-a, where the total number of Anunnaki (i.e., 600 written 𒁹𒌋) becomes Nergal's number 11 (𒌋𒁹) when written back-to-front.

(3) ... "The Stillborn Child" *refers to* the god Nergal.
(3) Ditto (i.e., Nergal) *refers to* the Anunnaki gods.
(3–4) The Anunnaki gods in [their totality (?)] ...

(*III*) *The Stillborn Child is associated with the temples of the head:*

(4) ... SAG.GÁ.GÁ (?) *refers to* the Stillborn Child.

This seems to be a list of logographic forms compounded with the element SAG ("head"). SAG.GÁ.GÁ connects the "Stillborn Child" with "seizure of [the temple]," thus validating the diagnostic verdict (Sa-gig 4: 1) that

(4) SAG *means* head.
(4) SAG.UŠ *means* to hold, in the case of the head.
(4) SAG.GÁ.GÁ *means* a seizure of [the temple (?)] ...

this Stillborn Child is responsible for the sick man "(feeling) covered up in the temple."

(IV) *The name "Stillborn Child" (Kūbu) implies a connection with the moon-god:*
The "Stillborn Child" (*Kù-bu*) may be expressed by the homophonic signs *Ku*$_{10}$*-bu*, whose component signs (ku$_{10}$ and bu) are then analyzed as follows:

(5) ... "The Stillborn Child (*Kūbu*)" *may be expressed as Ku*$_{10}$*-bu.*

Analysis #1:
The "Stillborn Child" (*Ku*$_{10}$*-bu*) is conveyed from "darkness" (KU$_{10}$) to "light" (BU).

(5) KU$_{10}$ *means* darkness.
(5) BU [*means*] light.

This quotation may describe the conveyance of the Stillborn Child from the darkness of its mother's belly (i.e., womb).

(5–6) "Like the Stillborn Child from the belly ... you convey ... without brightness."

Analysis #2:
The "Stillborn Child" (*Ku*$_{10}$*-bu*) "becomes bright" (BU) out from the "gloom" (KU$_{10}$).

(6) Secondly, KU$_{10}$ [*means*] gloom.
(6) BU *means* to become bright.

The analyses imply that the Stillborn Child shines forth from darkness like a "torch" (GI.IZI.LÁ), which is also a fitting description of the moon-god.

(6) A torch *refers to* the moon-god Sîn *or* the [Stillborn Child]. ...

The argument comes full circle, showing why the "Stillborn Child" is diagnosed for temple problems (Sa-gig 4: 1), which one expects to be associated with the moon-god.

(v) *Another connection between the Stillborn Child and the moon-god*
The "Stillborn Child" (*Kūba*) seems to be depicted here as one "guarding" (BA?) the "earth" (KU$_{11}$). This yet again links the Stillborn Child to the moon-god, whose name ^{d}ŠEŠ.KI may be similarly analyzed as "to guard" (šeš) + "earth" (KI).

(7) ... [/*ku*/] (*refers to*) the earth,
(7) BA (points) to (?) guarding,

This quotation from the *Hymn to Šamaš*, line 31 supports the claim that the Stillborn Child is assigned to guard the "lower regions."

(7) *which refers to* the case where "You (the sun-god Šamaš) assign the *malkū*-demons, the Stillborn Child, (and) the Anunnaki gods to the lower regions."

(vi) *Sun's position in the zodiacal sign Pa-bil-sag explains the medical condition :*
Perhaps SAG.KI "temple" is analyzed as KI ("place of / with") + SAG (abbreviation for the constellation or zodiacal sign Pa-bil-*sag*).

(7–8) The temple ...
(8) ^{d}Pa-bil-sag befalls him.

Medical condition in **Sa-gig 4: 1**

(8) "It becomes hot and cold."

Allusion to Mul-apin (ii, Gap A 7) or quotation of a similar astronomical statement. The hot sun stands in the zodiacal sign ^{mul_2}Pa-bil-sag (Sagittarius) during the cold winter month Kislīmu (Nov/Dec). Also, ^{mul_2}Pa-***bil-sag*** alludes to a "hot temple" because of its component signs bil ("hot") + SAG ("head"). In this way, the commentator explained why a sick man seems to experience cold (e.g., chills and shivering), even when his temple feels hot.

(8) "In the month Kislīmu (ix), the sun stands in the zodiacal sign ^{mul_2}Pa-bil-sag, and (it is) winter." ...

Sa-gig 4: 2
The signs al-du are not treated as a fossilized form AL.DU indistinguishable from DU "to move." Instead, because the stative sense of the Sumerian prefix al- seemed incompatible with movement, the commentator understood them as the syllable signs *al-ṭù* "they are stiff," which describe innards that "are hard."

(9) "[His innards] al-du," (read as the syllable signs) *al-ṭù, means* they are hard,

Since "hard" does not usually describe the patient's innards or belly, a more typical term "inflaming" is used to clarify.

(9) *which* (points) to inflaming, in the case of the belly.

Sa-gig 4: 3

(9) *"ittenenbiṭū" derives from the dictionary root* to have cramps.

The commentator showed that *napāḫu* "to inflame" can have meanings that are transitive ("to cause cramps") and intransitive ("to have cramps"). The semantic link between *ebēṭu* "to have cramps" and *napāḫu* "to inflame" is implied by their shared logogram MÚ.

(9) To inflame *means* to cause cramps. ...

(10) ... MÚ *means* to have cramps. MÚ *means* to inflame.

Sa-gig 4: 4
Quotation from the god-list AN = *Anu* (VI, 113), where the god $^{d}U_{4}$.UK.URU is explained as a "storm(-deity) of the city." Here, the sick man's personal god may be defined as the god of the city he identifies with.

(10) "Hand of his god" *refers to* the god ^{d}UK.URU, *which refers to* the god of the city.
(10) [^{d}UK *refers to* a storm-deity.]
(11) ... URU *means* city.

Sa-gig 4: 4
UŠ expresses *emēdu* "to lean on," but not *kânu* "to become constant." However, since SAG.UŠ means *kayyānu* "constant," the commentator reasoned that the Hand of the god "imposed" (D stem of *emēdu*) on the sick man is "constantly" on him.

(11) "(The Hand of his god) is imposed on him."
(11) UŠ *means* to lean on, in the case of the Hand (of his god).
(11) UŠ *means* to become constant.

Sa-gig 4: 5
The D Stative form *muqqut* "is collapsed" appears primarily in formulaic sequences of Sa-gig Chapter 11.

(11–12) "ŠUB-*ut*" *means* [it is collapsed (?), (*which* points) to being low].

Sa-gig 4: 6—"his eyes a-ši-a"
The cuneiform signs a-ši-a may be read as the syllables *a-ši-a*, which derive from the verb *ešû*/*ašû* "to blur" common in therapeutic texts.

(12) "The cuneiform signs a-ši-a" *derive from the dictionary root* to blur, (*which means*) to obscure.

The cuneiform signs a-ši-a may also be read as ÉR-*a*, where ÉR is the logogram for the verb *bakû* "to weep tears" common in the Diagnostic Handbook.

(12) Secondly, "the cuneiform signs a-ši-a" (*mean*) they are tearful, *which refers to* the case where tears flow in their midst …

The orthographies and context of *a-ši-a* and ÉR-*a*, however, are unusual for therapeutic texts and the Diagnostic Handbook.

***Sa-gig 4**

(12–13) …

Sa-gig 4: 8—
"cranium of his head is split"
Only here does "cranium" occur with the verb *paṭāru* "to split," whereas "seam of his head" is regularly described as "split."

(13) "The cranium of his head" *refers to* the seam of his head.

Sa-gig 4: 9
The cuneiform signs ḫa-biš are to be read as *ḫabiš* "it is swollen." This verb is rarely attested in medical and physiognomic texts.

(13) "The cuneiform signs ḫa-biš" *mean* it is swollen.

Sa-gig 4: 10

(13) "He cries out '(my) inside, (my) inside!'" ...

(14) "[Hand of a ghost]; (in) a second (version), the goddess Ištar; he will die."
(14) "Inside" *refers to* the goddess Ištar.

This quotation from *Enūma eliš* IV, 101, shows why the goddess Ištar (here identified with the mother goddess Tiamat) is associated with problems involving the patient's "inside."

(14) "He (Marduk) shot off the arrow, it broke open [her (Tiamat's)] stomach." ...

***Sa-gig 4: 11—"pi-pi-ru"**
The cuneiform signs pi-pi-ru (𒉿 𒉿 𒊒) may be read with the unusual syllabic values ia_8/i_{16}-*à-ru* (𒉿 𒉿 𒊒) = *i'arru* "he pukes."

(15) ["The cuneiform signs pi-pi-ru" *mean*] he pukes, *which means* he vomits.
(15) To puke *means* to vomit.

Sa-gig 4: 11
Here, the components of KI.NÁ "bed" may be analyzed as KI + NÁ.

(15) "KI.NÁ"
(15–16) KI [*means*] ...

Sa-gig 4: 12
The topic literally reads "from sunset until the morning watch," which denotes the half of the day opposite to what is described in the comment.

(16) "[TA] ^{d}UTU.ŠÚ.A EN EN.NUN.UD.ZAL.LE" *means the opposite of* from morning until the cool of day. ...

***Sa-gig 4: 14—"blood flows" ?**

(17) ... blood (?) ...

***Sa-gig 4: 23—"his right temple shakes" ?**	(18) ... *means* to tremble in the case of ...

Notes

Intro—Commentary Sa-gig 4B (with its pericope of at least Sa-gig 4: 1–12) appears to have its topics and comments duplicated at least on the obverse of Comm. Sa-gig 4C. What is preserved on the reverse of Comm. Sa-gig 4C, however, represents quite a significant advancement in the base text (with its pericope of at least Sa-gig 4: 85–127), and it is uncertain that this has a counterpart in the damaged portion of Comm. Sa-gig 4B. Commentaries Sa-gig 4C and 4B respectively belong to the so-called "Babylon" and "Sippar" collections at the British Museum—with the latter including tablets not only from Sippar, but also from Babylon and Borsippa—so one wonders if duplication between the two commentaries could possibly have resulted from actual overlaps in their textual histories.

Obv. 1—The verb *ḫesû* appears commonly in the Diagnostic Handbook, but not particularly in therapeutic texts (cf. *BAM* 111 ii 16′, 22′; 159 i 16). Its meaning is difficult to ascertain, and the *Chicago Assyrian Dictionary* identifies 7 separate homophones whose Infinitive root is *ḫesû* (*CAD* Ḫ, 176–178; cf. *AHw*, 342). See also discussion of *ḫesû* in Stol (1998: 344–347). Whatever may have been the original intent of the base text Sa-gig 4: 1, the commentator understood *ḫesû* to mean "to cover (up)" (*AHw*, 342; *CAD* Ḫ, 176–177 s.v. *ḫesû* A), probably referring to the sensation of pressure that the patient felt around his temples during a headache. This is evident from the arguments that follow. The logograms GAZ and DAB, which typically express the verbs *ḫepû* ("to break, split") and *ṣabātu* ("to seize") respectively, form equations here that are not attested elsewhere. If one may be allowed to speculate, GAZ alludes to the "obliteration" of presence that comes from "covering up" one's being, while DAB alludes to the act of "seizing" another object as a "cover." Setting aside these logograms, however, connections implied by the syllabically written verbs make good sense. For example, the lexical text Erimhuš v (*MSL* XVII, 76) groups together the terms *na'butu* "runaway, fugitive" (line 212), *marqītu* "refuge, hiding place" (line 214), and *ḫesû* "to cover (up)" (line 213), along with *ṭebû* "to sink, submerge (perhaps with the nuance 'to lie low')" (line 211). *Contra* the reading GAZ : *ṭe-pu-ú* in Genty (2010b: 30); Frahm (2011a: 64); Jiménez (CCP 4.1.4.B). I understand *ka-ba-šu* (obv. 1) not as a byform of the well-known verb *kabāsu* ("to tread, trample"; cf. Frahm 2011a: 64), but as the less common verb *kabāšu* ("to put on a *kubšu*-cap/headdress"; *CAD* K, 11; *AHw*, 416). Similar meanings, in fact, seem to be attested in Comm. Sa-gig 10 & 11, rev. 7′: ⌜*te-eḫ*⌝-*si-ma* : *ana ka-ba-su*

[…] ("You cover up (the sick nail)" (points) "to putting on a *kubšu*-cap …"), referring to some kind of a protective or therapeutic covering over a sick and sensitive nail. The commentarial equations here, therefore, elaborate on the topic of "covering up," whether in the case of being "submerged" or in the case of putting on a "head-cover." In accordance with the diagnostic verdict in Sa-gig 4:1 that identifies ^{d}*Kūbu* as the agent of sickness, this "Stillborn Child" (^{d}*Kūbu*) is assonantally comparable to a "*kubšu*-cap/headdress" that covers up the patient's temple.

Obv. 2—The beginning of obv. 2 is damaged, but the argument clearly presents "covering up" the temple as analogous to "covering up" the horns of the moon-crescent, a phenomenon recorded in astronomical texts. Interest in the "covered up" horns of the moon, for example, motivated the following commentary (K 4336, i 14–15): DIŠ SI.MEŠ-*šú ḫe-sa-a* LAL : *he-sú-ú* LAL : *ma-lu-u* LAL : *ša-pa-la* ("'If (the moon's) horns are covered up.' LAL *means* to cover up. LAL *means* to become full. LAL *means* to become low."). Weidner (1941–1944) pl. VII; cf. bibliography on the joints K 4166 + K 4336 + K 9652 at Frahm (2011a: 135). The argument in obv. 2 takes place in two steps: (I) To show that *nakkaptu* ("temple") and *nakāpu* ("butting (with horns)") are cognates, and that the "temple" is therefore semantically related to "horns" (cf. the inclusion of *nakāpu* in Nabnitu I, 86–98 = *MSL* XVI, 53 in a listing of parts of the head). (II) To show by a quotation from *Lugale* IV, 8, that these horns pertain to the moon: [ur-sa]g ^{d}en.zu-na-gim si mú-mú = [*qarrādu ša kīma* ^{d}*Si*]*n qar-ni ba-nu-u* (van Dijk 1983: 1,70; 2,68–69; line 143). The identification of *Lugale* here is new (Wee in Frahm 2011a: 106 n. 551). In existing manuscripts of bilingual *Lugale*, the Sumerian term mú (instead of the logographic value DÙ in this commentary) is used for the verb *banû* ("to grow"). The moon is associated with "butting" horns also in Comm. Sa-gig 40A, obv. 12: [… *ni-ki*]*p-ti* : *a-na bu-um-bu-lu ma-šil* NU DÙ ("'Butting' is equivalent to the day of the New Moon"). This statement refers either to the fact that the New Moon crescent resembles "butting" horns, or perhaps to the seven "butting" storm-demons that darken the moon-god in the *Lunar Eclipse Myth* (*Utukkū Lemnūtu* XVI, 1 in Geller 2016: 501; cf. Geller 2007a: 178).

Obv. 3—Jiménez (CCP 4.1.4.B) restored ^{d}*Kù-bi* : ^{d}U*.GUR* :* MIN* : ^{d}*A-nun-na-ki* : *i-la-at* ^{d}*A-nun-na-ki ina šu-*⸢*bat*(?)⸣ [^{d}*Kù-bi* (?)], "Kūbu means 'Nergal,' alternatively, it means 'Anunnaki' (as in) 'the goddess (*ilat*) of the Anunnaki in the *dwelling* [*of Kūbu* (?)]'" (obv. 3), with the later part representing a quotation from an unknown literary text. I interpret this later part as *i-la-at* ^{d}*A-nun-na-ki ina* ŠU.N[IGIN$_{2}$-*šu-nu* (?)], "the group (*illat*) of the Anunnaki gods in [their totality (?)]" (obv. 3); cf. Genty (2010b: 30). In my understanding, this could allude to the composition i-nam-giš-ḫur-an-ki-a or a similar kind of argument elsewhere: [*ina*(?) *ki*(?)-]*ip*(?)*-pa-at* AN.KI DINGIR : AN.TA KI.TA SAR.E.DÈ EN DIŠ+U | 11 | ^{d}U+GUR ^{d}ŠAKKAN$_2$, "The god(s) [in the] circumference(?) of heaven (and) earth : To write upside down, (he is) lord of the 600 (i.e., Anunnaki gods) | the number 11 | the god Nergal (or) Šakkan" (K 170 + Rm 520, rev. 4); cf. Livingstone (1986: 32–33); Pearce (1982: 87). According to the logic here, the total number of the Anunnaki gods, i.e., 600 (𒁹𒌋), becomes the number 11 (𒌋𒁹) when written "upside down" or, more precisely, back-to-front. This number 11 was deemed to signify the god Nergal, perhaps because the number 600—*nēru* in Akkadian—recalls the name "*Ner*gal." The mention of Anunnaki deities in obv. 3, moreover, anticipates or even inspired the commentator's quotation from the *Hymn to Šamaš* later in obv. 7, which depicts the Stillborn Child and the Anunnaki as guardians of the Netherworld.

Obv. 4—This line is rather badly damaged, but seems to list several logographic forms compounded with the element SAG ("head"). The equation ⸢SAG.UŠ : *kul*⸣*-lu šá re-e-šú* is attested also in the lexical text Antagal A, 43 (*MSL* XVII, 183). For sag gá-gá as a Sumerian compound verb meaning "to oppose, confront, advance," see Karahashi (2000: 135–136). If my restoration is correct, the commentator appears to have connected both the "Stillborn Child" and "a seizure of [the temple]" with the form SAG.GÁ.GÁ, presumably to validate the diagnostic verdict in Sa-gig 4: 1 that the Stillborn Child is responsible for the sick man's "covered up" temple. The descriptions in this line recall the name of another demon *mukīl-rēš-lemutti*, lit. "the evil one holding the head" (cf. Farber 1975: 87–95), and one wonders if the logographic form of this demon's name (i.e., SAG.ḪUL.ḪA.ZA) might also have been included in a damaged part of this list.

Obv. 5–6—The signs are $^{\text{d.ku}_3}$*Ku*$_{10}$*-bu*, not $^{\text{d.ku}_3}$*Ku*$_{10}$*-bi* (obv. 5), as rendered by the typo in Jiménez and Schmidtchen (2017: 233). Although the commentator's argument involves the singly written KU$_{10}$ (as the first component of *Ku*$_{10}$*-bu*), lexical equations imply that the double KU$_{10}$.KU$_{10}$ was the usual way to express *eṭûtu* ("darkness"): KU$_{10}$ $^{\text{ku-uk-ku}}$ KU$_{10}$ = *e-ṭù-tum* (Erimhuš VI, 171 in *MSL* XVII, 85); $^{\text{ku-uk-ku}}$KU$_{10}$.KU$_{10}$ = *eṭûtu, ikletu* (Diri I, 253–254 in *MSL* XV, 112); KU$_{10}$ ⸢$^{\text{ku-ku}}$⸣ KU$_{10}$ = *e-*⸢*ṭú*⸣-[*tu*], *ek-le-t*[*u*] (Izi H Appendix, 1 in *MSL* XIII, 209). BU as the logogram for *namāru* ("to become bright") occurs in the lexical texts S^{b} I, 120 (*MSL* III, 105); *MSL* II, 143 i 22 (Proto-Ea); Aa VI/1, 185, 197 (*MSL* XIV, 438, 439). The disjunction sign before *ta-re-ed-di* (obv. 6) indicated in the hand copy of *CT* 51, 136 and Genty (2010b: 31) is actually absent in the tablet, and the expression *la na-ma-ri*, "without brightness" (obv. 6) occurs also in *balāṭa ša lā namāri*, "life without brightness" (Alster 2005: 303–304, 316 = Syr. 19 and SS 19) and *ekletu lā namāri*, "gloom without brightness" (Lauinger 2012: 103, lines 485–486). The statement "Like the Stillborn Child from the belly ... you convey ... without brightness" appears to be a quotation, but is unfortunately not sufficiently preserved. The argument likely alludes to the birth process, whereby the Stillborn Child is conveyed from its mother's womb, a place of gloom without brightness.

Obv. 6—The equation of KU$_{10}$.KU$_{10}$ with *ekletu* ("gloom") occurs in many of the same lexical texts listed above: $^{\text{ku-uk-ku}}$ KU$_{10}$.KU$_{10}$ = *ikletu* (Diri I, 254 in *MSL* XV, 112; Diri Nippur, 43 in *MSL* XV, 12); KU$_{10}$ ⸢$^{\text{ku-ku}}$⸣ KU$_{10}$ = *e*-⸢*ṭú*⸣-[*tu*], *ek-le-t*[*u*] (Izi H Appendix, 1 in *MSL* XIII, 209). Also, see references above for BU as the logogram of *namāru* ("to become bright, shine"). Here, the commentator implied that the Stillborn Child shines forth from the gloom like a "torch" (GI.IZI.LÁ) and therefore shares the same characteristic of luminosity as the moon-god Sîn. Note that the tantalizing translation "Kubu, the high priest of Enlil, swung censer and torch (gi-izi-lá)" (BA 5 649 = K 1279 rev. 3–4 in *CAD* G, 113 s.v. *gizillû*, lexical section) is better interpreted as a reference to the god [^{d}]kù-sù. See Conti (2000: 129–130, rev. 3) with bibliography. In any case, the argument from the beginning of this commentary has come full circle: Whereas one might expect the patient's temple to be associated with the moon-god, the diagnosis "Hand of the Stillborn Child" in Sa-gig 4: 1 is acceptable, because of the connection between these two divine beings.

Obv. 7—The beginning of obv. 7 may be restored based on Comm. Sa-gig 4C, obv. 2′: [...]x : *kù* : KI-*ti*[*m* ...] ("... /*ku*/ *refers to* the earth ..."). The reading /*ku*/ (written as kù  here) represents the value of the logogram KU$_{11}$ (), which can stand for "earth" (*erṣetum*) according to the lexical equation: $^{\text{ku-u}_2}$ KU$_{11}$(ki) = MIN (= *er-ṣe-tum*) (Ea IV, 96 in *MSL* XIV, 359). Aligned with recurring commentarial practice, we would expect the name of the Stillborn Child (*Kūbu*) to be analyzed here into its components. So, whereas the name was earlier written ^{d}*Kù-bi* (obv. 3–4), it was later expressed with a different case vowel as ^{d}*Kù-bu* or ^{d}*Ku*$_{10}$-*bu* (obv. 5–6), in order to facilitate the analysis KU$_{10}$ ("darkness, gloom") + BU ("light, to become bright"). Here, I tentatively assume the analysis of ^{d}*Kù-ba* into KU$_{11}$ ("earth") + BA(?) ("guarding"), as a way to make sense of the difficult writing: ⸢BA(?) *ana*(?)⸣ *na-ṣa-ri*, "BA (points) to (?) guarding" (obv. 7)—mirroring patterns like *ana na-ka*$_4$-*pu* (obv. 2), *ana na-pa-ḫu* (obv. 9), and perhaps [*ana šá-pa-lu*] (obv. 12) elsewhere on the same tablet. Given the way this notation *ana* ("(points) to") is often used to posit superficial or even pseudo- etymologies (see §II.2.6), I wonder if the logogram BA, by denoting *nušurrû* ("diminution, decrease"), is alleged to be related to the different verb *naṣāru* ("guarding"). Jiménez and Schmidtchen (2017: 233) read the signs differently as ⸢SU⸣ : *na-ṣa-ri* ("SU (means) 'to guard'"), supposedly alluding to the reading ^{d}*Kù-su*$_{13}$(bu) that is assumed for manuscripts of the *Hymn to Šamaš* (line 31 in Lambert 1960: 126–127; *contra* the more natural reading ^{d}*Kù-bu* in *CAD* K, 487 s.v. *kūbu* §2a), while conceding that "an equation of SU with *naṣāru* is not attested, but SA is equated with *naṣāru* in the *Götteradressbuch* (*KAV* 42 = *BTT* 180 l. 175)." In any case, the quotation from the *Hymn to Šamaš*—"you (i.e., the sun-god Šamaš) assign the *malkū*-demons, the Stillborn Child, and the Anunnaki to the lower regions (i.e., the Netherworld)" (line 31 in Lambert 1960: 126–127)—served to confirm the Stillborn Child's role in guarding the "earth" or Netherworld. The particle *ša* ("the case of / where") is not part of the quote, but a commentary notation (§11.2.2). Also, perhaps because what follows *ša* is a quotation, the cited form *ta-paq-qid* was not modified to include a subordination marker, in contrast to other instances involving this commentary notation, such as *šá la il-la-ku-ú-nu*, "the case where they do not move" (Comm. Sa-gig 14, obv. 16). For associations among these Netherworld beings in divinatory, prayer, or ritual contexts, see Ebeling (1931: 58, K 7856, lines 19–22); Aro (1961: 604). For Anunnaki deities described as deciding verdicts for "people of the lower regions" (*nišī šaplâti*), see Ebeling (1931: 130, VAT 13657, col. 3, lines 12–13), Farber (1977: 148–149, line 135); listed as *Prayers to the Anunnaki* in Mayer (1976: 379). Finally, it remains to be explained why the commentator portrayed the Stillborn Child as one guarding the "earth" or Netherworld. This is most likely an extension of the argument in preceding lines that attempts to connect this Stillborn Child to the moon-god, whose name ^{d}ŠEŠ.KI can be similarly analyzed as "to guard" (šeš as the logogram URU$_{3}$) + "earth" (logogram KI).

Obv. 7–8—I cannot confidently restore the beginning of this commentary entry, but it is likely an analysis of the components of SAG.KI ("temple"), with SAG being an abbreviation for the constellation / zodiacal sign ^{d}Pa-bil-sag, and KI meaning "with" or "place." In abbreviated writing typical of astronomical texts, it can be difficult to differentiate the expressions "with (a celestial body)" and "(in the) place of (a celestial body/region)." For KI in astronomical contexts, see, for example, Rochberg (1998: 83 (Text 10, obv. 7, 9; rev. 10); 86 (Text 11, obv. 10); 93 (Text 14, obv. 9)). For this commentary, Genty (2010b: 31) has read the signs ^{d}PA.BIL.SAG.⌜GÁ⌝.ŠÈ (obv. 8), evidently reflecting how the signs are drawn in the hand copy of *CT* 51, 136. The reading ^{d}PA.BIL.SAG ŠUB-*su*, "^{d}Pabilsag befalls him" (obv. 8), however, is confirmed by the restoration [^{d}PA.BIL.SA]G⌝ ŠUB-*su* in Comm. Sa-gig 4C, obv. 3′. For the identification of Pa-bil-sag as Sagittarius (and part of Ophiuchus), see Gössmann (1950: 178–180 nos. 356–358); Reiner and Pingree (1981: 14); Hunger and Pingree (1999: 274); Kolev (2013: 270). In astronomical diaries, horoscopes, and other astronomical texts, the abbreviation for Pa-bil-sag is usually PA (Gössmann 1950: 178–179 no. 356; cf. Sachs and Hunger 1988: 18; Rochberg 1998: 29) and occasionally PA.BIL (Gössmann 1950: 179 no. 357), so the abbreviation SAG here must be considered a contrivance on the part of the commentator in order to associate Pa-bil-sag (abbreviated SAG) with the "temple" (SAG.KI). In obv. 8, the switch in determinatives from ^{d}PA.BIL.SAG to ^{mul_2}PA.BIL.SAG is intriguing, but the argument is not clear enough for us to be certain whether this was a deliberate attempt to distinguish the constellation Pa-bil-sag from the zodiacal sign of the same name.

Obv. 8—Although the hand copy of *CT* 51, 136 and Genty (2010b: 31) depict the signs as KÚM-*im-šú* SED (obv. 8), the commentary tablet more likely contains the writing KÚM-*im u* SED, where the wedge of the *u* sign is significantly larger than wedges used for disjunction signs elsewhere on the same tablet. The same reading KÚM-*im u* ⸢SED⸣ appears also in Comm. Sa-gig 4C, obv. 3′. In the place of these *u* signs, however, several manuscripts of the base text Sa-gig 4: 1 seem to have a disjunction sign, which then serves to separate the semantically opposite (§ EV.6) embedded variants KÚM-*im* : SED ("he/it becomes hot : cold"). The manuscript sources of Sa-gig Tablet 4 are listed under the abbreviation DPS 4 in Scurlock (2014: 705–706). This particular type of discrepancy is found also among manuscript copies of Sa-gig 26: 29′, which include either the disjunction sign (MS B = BM 47753, line 25′) or the conjunction *u* (MS A = *STT* 91+287, line 27′) at the same position in the text. In this commentary, the reading KÚM-*im u* SED closely resembles other medical statements that describe the sick person (Sa-gig 3: 59 (TDPT 3: 50); [Sa-gig 7 B rev. 6 (TDPT 7: 63′?)]; Sa-gig 13: 23, 28, 31 (TDPT 13 i 24′, 29′, 32′)), his temple (Sa-gig 4: 17), the head of his nose (Sa-gig 6: 22–23), and his belly (Sa-gig 13: 69–70 (TDPT 13 ii 11–12)) as KÚM *u* SED ("hot and cold" or perhaps "hot-cold"). The commentator was probably concerned to explain this contradiction of terms, and what follows is either an allusion to or paraphrase of Mul-apin, or the quotation of a similar astronomical statement. Existing manuscripts of the possible Mul-apin (II, Gap A 7) allusion read: [DIŠ TA U_4.1.K]AM *šá* ITI.GAN EN U_4.30.KAM *šá* ITI.ZÍZ ^{d}UTU *ina* KASKAL *šu-ut* ^{d}*É-a* GUB-*ma* EN.TE.NA, "[If, from Day 1] of Month Kislīmu (IX) until Day 30 of Month Šabaṭu (XI), the sun stands in the path of those (stars) of the god Ea, (it is) winter" (Hunger and Steele 2019: 85; cf. Hunger and Pingree 1989: 89). The hot sun's position in the zodiacal sign ^{mul_2}Pa-bil-sag (Sagittarius) corresponds to the cold winter month Kislīmu. As noted previously, the sick person's "temple" (SAG.KI) could be identified as "place of / with" (KI) ^{d}Pa-bil-***sag*** (abbreviated as SAG), i.e., the zodiacal sign ^{mul_2}Pa-bil-sag. Furthermore, since BIL and KÚM are values of the same cuneiform sign, the name Pa-***bil-sag*** would naturally suggest the idea of a "head" (SAG) that is "hot" (KÚM). What results is a complex of ideas associating { hot ^{mul_2}Pa-bil-sag : cold winter } with { hot temple : cold sensation }. The commentator likely alluded to the phenomenon that, though the sick man's temple feels hot at the healer's touch, the sick man himself exhibits behavior (i.e., shivering and chills) that suggests he experiences cold. When sickness and inflammation result in the elevation of the body's thermostatic set point, the patient feels colder relative to the same environmental temperature, while physiological processes simultaneously increase his body temperature to meet the new set point. This phenomenon is readily attested today and was probably recognized by ancient healers, even if they could not explain the mechanics behind it.

Obv. 9—The restoration [ŠÀ.MEŠ-*šú*] ⸢al⸣-du $^{\textit{ṭu}}$: *dan-nu*, "'[His innards] al-du,' (read as the syllable signs) *al-ṭù, means* they are hard" is supported by a similar statement in Comm. Sa-gig 4C, obv. 4′ (Jiménez and Schmidtchen 2017: 231, 234), and refers to the base text Sa-gig 4: 2. See Note on Comm. Sa-gig 4A, obv. 2 for Sumerian grammatical features (e.g., the verbal prefix al- here) in Akkadian medical texts. The commentator of Comm. Sa-gig 4A treated the signs al-du as a fossilized form AL.DU that is indistinguishable in meaning from the common logogram DU "to move." The commentator here, however, felt that the stative sense of the Sumerian prefix al- (Edzard 2003: 111, §12.10) was incompatible with movement, and therefore opted to read the cuneiform signs al-du as the syllables *al-ṭù* from the root *wašāṭu* ("to become stiff"). Since the synonym *danānu* ("to become hard") is not the usual way of describing the patient's belly or innards, further elaboration is provided by the use of another term typical for such cases: *napāḫu* ("inflaming").

Obv. 9–10—In addition to this commentary entry, the verbs *ebēṭu* ("to have cramps") and *napāḫu* ("to inflame") are also equated in Comm. Sa-gig 4A, obv. 3; Uruk Therapeutic Comm. 1 = *SpTU* 1, 47 obv. 1; a commentary on Uruanna (BM 76487:[17] in *CT* 41, 45); and possibly in the damaged portion of Comm. Sa-gig 40A, obv. 15–16: [... *na-pa-ḫi* :] *e-me-ri* : *na-pa-ḫi* / [*e-bé-ṭi* (?)]. Whereas all the above commentaries simply equate the G stems of both verbs, the commentator here first equated the D stem of *ebēṭu* with the G stem of *napāḫu* (obv. 9) and, only after some intervening argument (unfortunately damaged), the G stems of both verbs (obv. 10). Like its English translation "to inflame," the G stem of *napāḫu* can have both transitive and intransitive meanings, but its intransitive meaning is particularly used for the perceived self-ignition of celestial bodies (*CAD* N I, 265–268 s.v. *napāḫu* §4). Since *napāḫu* frequently occurs in the Stative in medical descriptions, its transitivity may not always be an obvious issue. Here, however, the commentator was careful to connect the transitive-intransitive G stem of *napāḫu* ("to inflame") with both the transitive D stem of *ebēṭu* ("to cause cramps") and the intransitive G stem of *ebēṭu* ("to have cramps"). As was the case with the Sumerian al- prefix earlier in obv. 9, the commentator of Comm. Sa-gig 4B seems to have had a fine eye for grammatical detail. The tentative restoration [*na*]*p-paḫ-tú* (?) : ⌜*ub-bu-uṭ* (?)⌝ (obv. 10), suggested by Jiménez and Schmidtchen (2017: 234), is left untranslated.

Obv. 10–11—Jiménez and Schmidtchen (2017: 235) identified the quotation here from the god-list AN = *Anu* VI, 113 (in Litke 1998: 208): ᵈU_4.UK.URU = MIN (i.e., *ú-mu*) *āli*, which I understand to describe a "storm(-deity) of the city." For UK or ÚK(pirig) as logographic expressions of the "storm (a mythical being or demon)," see *CAD* U/W, 139 s.v. *ūmu*, lexical section. This commentary entry may be significant for our understanding of imagined communities in ancient Mesopotamia, because it presents the view—not necessarily accepted by all—that the patient's personal god is also the god of the city he identifies with. Livingstone (2013: 259), for example, observed that "all personal gods identifiable are full, regular members of the pantheon and not a different category of minor god, as has sometimes been believed, nor do they belong to the muster of nameless minor deities."

Obv. 11—The comment "to lean on, in the case of the Hand (of his god)" does not refer to the generic action of someone's hand leaning (*emēdu*) on something, but specifically to the situation described in the base text: "the Hand of his god is imposed (D stem of *emēdu*) on him" (Sa-gig 4: 4). While the verb *kânu* ("to become firm in place") is not expressed by the logogram UŠ in lexical texts (*CAD* K, 159–160), the commentator likely alluded to its cognate adjective *kayyānu* ("permanent, constant"), which has the logogram SAG.UŠ. The Hand of the god "imposed" on the sick man is therefore characterized by its "constant" effect on him.

Obv. 11–12—Restored on the basis of Comm. Sa-gig 4C, obv. 5′–6′: [ŠUB-*ut*] / [*mu-uq*]-⌜*qut* (?) : *ana*⌝ *šá-pa-lu* x[...] ("['ŠUB-*ut*' *means* it is collapsed (?)], *which* (points) to being low"). A similar explanation occurs in Comm. Sa-gig 14, obv. 4: *muq-qú-ut* : *šá-pil* ("'It is collapsed' *means* it is low"). For the syllabic writing of the D Stative form *muqqut* ("it is collapsed") as primarily a feature of certain formulaic sequences in Sa-gig Chapter 11, see Note on Comm. Sa-gig 14, obv. 2. This may therefore have justified the need for syllabic comment here, which eliminates the possibility of interpreting ŠUB-*ut* (obv. 5′) as G stem forms such as *imqut* or *imaqqut*.

Obv. 12—The cuneiform signs a-ši-a may be interpreted as the syllables *a-ši-a* (𒀀 𒅆 𒀀) for the verb *ešû*/*ašû* "to blur," or they may be read as the logogram ÉR (𒀀𒅆) "to weep tears" with a phonetic complement -*a* (𒀀). In any case, the commentator seems to have understood the writing as a Stative verb—either *ašâ* "they are blur" or *bakâ*(ÉR-*a*) "they are tearful"—which takes the "eyes" (IGI.2) as its subject in Sa-gig 4: 6, [40]; 5: 64′, 65′ (TDPT 5 D2 4, 5). Elsewhere, however, it is the sick man or infant who functions as the subject of the non-Stative verb *bakû* ("to weep tears"), which is written either syllabically or as the logogram ÉR.(MEŠ): Sa-gig 7 B rev. 9 (TDPT 7: 65′); Sa-gig 10: 38; 13: 118 (TDPT 13 iii 8); Sa-gig 16: 4–5, 64′, 87′–88′; 17: 86–87, 89; 40: 17, 20, 24, 28, 30, 46, 55, 64, 102, 106–108. As the references show, such descriptions are largely confined to the Diagnostic Handbook. On the other hand, the verb *ešû* is used to describe the eyes in therapeutic texts, even if its orthography is typically not *a-ši-a*, but *a-šá-a* (*BAM* 159 iv 16′, v 7; 510 iv 11; 515 i 17; 518: 9′; 521: 10′) or perhaps *a-ša-a* (*BAM* [159 iv 12′]). In other words, the orthographies and context of both *a-ši-a* ("they are blur") and ÉR-*a* ("they are tearful") would have appeared unusual to scribes familiar with conventional descriptions elsewhere in the medical literature. Moreover, it is telling that the commentator's first proposal is the verb *ešû* "to blur" (typical for therapeutic texts), and his second proposal is the verb *bakû* "to weep tears" (typical for the Diagnostic Handbook). For the significance of the order of comments in commentaries, see discussion in §11.2.7. The hand copy of *CT* 51, 136 depicts a conjunction *u* after *ba-ka-a* (obv. 12), but close study of the tablet reveals this to be a disjunction sign.

Obv. 13—The expression UGU SAG.DU-*šú* DU_8 ("the cranium of his head is split") at the base text Sa-gig 4: 8 is unusual for a couple of reasons. First, the body part UGU ("cranium") does not typically require the qualification "of the head" in both the Diagnostic Handbook and therapeutic texts. Secondly, the "cranium" is nowhere else described with the verb *paṭāru* ("to loosen, split"; logogram DU_8). The commentator's strategy was to substitute the term "cranium of his head" with another body part "seam of his head" (*šibīt* SAG.DU-*šú*), which regularly takes the verb *paṭāru*. See Sa-gig 3: 24–25 (TDPT 3: 15–16); Sa-gig 40: 44–45. In similar fashion, Comm. Sa-gig 39, obv. 2, 6–7 explains "the seam of his head" by means of a common expression referring to the antagonist in *šigû*-lamentations and other incantations, i.e., *māḫiṣ muḫḫi* ("the one who strikes the top"), implying that "seam of the head" and "cranium" (*muḫḫu*) are comparable anatomical features.

Obv. 13—Although the hand copy depicts the signs *ḫa-ḫa* (𒄩 𒄩) (*CT* 51, 136, obv. 13), the tablet itself quite clearly has the signs *ḫa-biš* (𒄩 [illegible]). Existing manuscripts of the base text Sa-gig 4: 9 also read *ḫa-biš*. Two homophones of *ḫabāšu* ("hart werden, anschwellen (*ḫabāšu* I)" and "zerkleinern (*ḫabāšu* II)") are listed in *AHw*, 303, but only the latter meaning ("to break into pieces, chop up") seems to be acknowledged in *CAD* Ḫ, 9. Apart from this commentary entry and its base text, the verb *ḫabāšu* I ("to become swollen") does not seem to occur in medical texts elsewhere. It however appears once in a physiognomic description of the "cranium": DIŠ *mu-úḫ-ḫa-šu ḫa-bi-iš* (*Alamdimmû* II, 21 in Böck 2000a: 74).

Obv. 14—This quotation is from the *Babylonian Creation Myth* (*Enūma eliš* IV, 101 in Lambert 2013: 92–93). For other instances where the goddess Ištar is identified with Tiamat, see *KAR* 307, obv. 19 in Livingstone (1989: 99, no. 39); cf. Da Riva and Frahm (1999/2000: 174); Frahm (2011a: 105 n. 544). The analogy here is, of course, not precise. Whereas the goddess is portrayed as the agent of sickness in the base text Sa-gig 4: 10, she takes on the role of sufferer in the narrative of *Enūma eliš*. Such semantic shifts were not unusual in Mesopotamian efforts to attribute meaning to signs. Another example may be found in the claim of Comm. Sa-gig 40A, obv. 12 that "'Butting' is equivalent to the day of the New Moon." Although the malady name *nikipti* ^{d}30 ("Butting of the moon-god Sîn") at the base text Sa-gig 40: 42 seems to envision the moon-god as the one performing the action of "butting" (*nakāpu*), the commentary explanation may allude to the *Lunar Eclipse Myth*, where the moon-god is instead the one who suffers from being darkened due to the seven "butting storm-demons" (UD.MEŠ *muttakpūtu* < *nakāpu*). See *Utukkū Lemnūtu* XVI, 1 in Geller (2016: 501); cf. Geller (2007a: 178).

Obv. 15—In place of my reading [pi-pi-ru : *i*]⸢-*ʾá*-⸣*a-ru* : *i-par-ru* (obv. 15), the signs are read as [(x)] ⸢*i*$_{16}$(pi)-*à*(pi)⸣-*a-ru* : *i-par-ru* by Jiménez and Schmidtchen (2017: 235). See Note on Comm. Sa-gig 4A, obv. 5 for the reading of signs pi-pi-ru (𒉿 𒉿 𒊒) with the unusual syllabic values *ia*$_8$/*i*$_{16}$-*à*-*ru* (𒉿 𒉿 𒊒) meaning "he pukes" (*iʾarru*).

Obv. 16—The following time phases are attested in medical texts: [...] ^{d}UTU.È ("... sunrise") at *BAM* 460: 6′; TA ^{d}UTU.È EN ^{d}UTU.ŠÚ.A ("from sunrise until sunset") at Sa-gig 4: 13; *BAM* 482 iii 7; *AMT* 14/5: 11; TA ^{d}UTU.È EN EN.NUN.UD.ZAL.LE ("from sunrise until the morning watch") at *BAM* 482 iv 46′; TA/*kīma* ^{d}UTU *šaqê* ("from/when the sun ascends") at Sa-gig 19/20: 110′; TA ^{d}UTU.ŠÚ.A EN EN.NUN.UD.ZAL.LE ("from sunset until the morning watch") at Sa-gig 4: 12; *AMT* 19/1 obv. 29′; TA *tašrīt*/SAG GE$_6$ EN [...] ("from the beginning of/early night until ...") at Sa-gig 13: 125–126 (TDPT 13 iii 14–15); TA *tašrīt* GE$_6$ EN SA$_9$ EN.NUN ("from the beginning of the night until the middle of the watch") at Sa-gig 27: 28; TA *tašrīti* EN SAG GE$_6$ ("from the beginning until the early night") at Sa-gig 13: 71 (TDPT 13 ii 13–14); *ina* AN.USAN/*šimītān* ("at evening") at Sa-gig 17: 82–83, 86–87; 19/20:

111′; 26: 5′, 31′–37′; 29: 60′; 33: 34; 37: 13 (TDPT 36: 13); *ina* EN.NUN.AN.USAN ("at the evening watch") at Sa-gig [19/20: 112′]; TA EN.NUN.AN.USAN EN EN.NUN.MURUB$_4$.BA ("from the evening watch until the middle (night) watch") at Sa-gig 26: 38′; *ina* EN.NUN.BAR.RA ("at the evening watch") at Sa-gig 2: 72–73; EN/*ina* EN.NUN.MURUB$_4$.BA ("until/at the middle (night) watch") at Sa-gig 17: 32; 19/20: 112′; 26: 33′, 45′; *ina* EN.NUN.ZALAG$_{(2)}$.GA ("at the morning watch") at Sa-gig 2: 74–75; [19/20: 113′]. As can be seen, the majority of such expressions appear in the Diagnostic Handbook, rather than in therapeutic texts. For the term EN.NUN.UD.ZAL.LE as a variant of EN.NUN.ZALAG$_{(2)}$.GA, see Rochberg (1998: 36). The commentary equation here appears to involve definition by antonymy (§1.2.3.1.6): "[TA] dUTU.ŠÚ.A EN EN.NUN.UD.ZAL.LE (lit. 'from sunset until the morning watch') *means the opposite of* 'from morning until the cool of day.' …" One might object that the impression of antonymy arises out of a misunderstanding of the damaged end of obv. 16, so that the topic and comment of this commentary entry may actually be synonymous, e.g., "(it becomes prolonged) from sunset until the morning watch *means* *[it ceases] from morning until the cool of day." However, such a maneuver would require a verb such as *"[it ceases]" in the comment where there is unmistakenly no verb written in the topic, resulting in a needless breach of symmetry in the A:B commentary equation.

Obv. 17—The hand copy depicts the signs *ša-mu* (𒊭 𒈬) (*CT* 51, 136, obv. 17), but it is conceivable that the reading is actually *da-mu* (𒁕 𒈬) in reference to "blood" (MÚD = *dāmu*) in the base text Sa-gig 4: 14.

Obv. 18—Although the hand copy depicts the signs sa si ḫu (*CT* 51, 136, obv. 18), the signs on the tablet seem to be *sa-la-ḫu* ("to tremble"). For commentators' tendency to use the general verb *salāḫu* ("to tremble") as explanation for other verbs of quaking or shivering (as in the case here), see Note on Comm. Sa-gig 3B, rev. 2–3. A possible candidate for the base text here is Sa-gig 4: 23 (SAG.KI-*šú šá* 15 *i-rad-ma*, "his right temple shakes"), though this would require a considerable move away from the base texts (i.e., Sa-gig 4: 12 and perhaps 14) of the immediately preceding commentary entries.

Commentary Sa-gig 4C

Provenance:	Babylon
Period:	?
Names:	Colophon not preserved
Script:	Neo-/Late Babylonian
Field/Museum No.:	BM 40837 + 41252 = 81-4-28,384 + 81-4-28,800 ("Babylon Collection" at British Museum)
Printed Edition/Hand Copy:	Jiménez and Schmidtchen (2017: 225–239)
Digital Resources:	CDLI P461193 + P461199; CCP 4.1.4.C (photos digitized by Jiménez 2016) + 4.1.4.C.b (photos and edition digitized by Jiménez 2014, with contributions by Schmidtchen)
Discussion:	Gabbay (2016: 75 n. 323, with BM 41252 previously categorized as CCP 7.2.u46); Jiménez and Schmidtchen (2017: 225–239)
Pericope:	At least Sa-gig 4: 1–12 (TDPT 4 obv. 1–12) and Sa-gig 4: 85–127 (TDPT 4 rev. 1–42)

Transliteration

Obverse

1′) [...] ⸢TA *ek-let*⸣ x[...]

2′) [...]x : *kù* : KI-*ti*[*m* ...]

3′) [... ^{d}PA.BIL.SA]G ŠUB-*su* KÚM-*im u* S[ED ...]

4′) [ŠÀ.MEŠ-*šú* al-du] ⸢:⸣ *áš-ṭu* : *dan-*⸢*ni*⸣ : *ana n*[*a-pa-ḫu šá* ŠÀ ...]

5′) [MÚ : *e-bé-ṭ*]*u* ⸢:⸣ MÚ : *na-*⸢*pa*⸣-[*ḫu* ... ŠUB-*ut*]

6′) [*mu-uq*]-⸢*qut* (?) : *ana*⸣ *šá-pa-lu* x[...]

7′) [... G]Ù.GÙ-⸢*si*(?)⸣ [...]

8′) [... ŠU] ⸢GIDIM$_7$⸣ *šá-né-e* [^{d}15 GAM ...]

9′) [... :] ⸢*i*⸣-*par-ri* [...]

10′) [... TA *še-e-ri* (?)] ⸢EN *ki-iṣ* (?)⸣ [U$_4$ ...]

Reverse

1′) [...] x x [...]

2′) [... 1 :] ⸢^{d}*A*⸣-*nim* : 2 : $^{d+}$*En-líl* : 3 : ⸢$^{d+}$*En*⸣-[*ki* ...]

3′) [...]x x lu : *tar-ku* : GE$_6$ $^{ge-e}$: *ta-r*[*a-ku*]

4′) [GE$_6$] : *ṣa-la-mu* : *ta-ḫ*[*i-iz* GIG ...]x *tar-ku* : *ta-ra-ku* : *ṣa-la-mu* : ta x[...]

 | DOI:10.1163/9789004417564_012

5′) [... DU : *a-la-ku*] : DU : *re-du-*⸢*u*⸣ [: GAR-*nu* : GAR : *šá*]*-ka-nu* : GAR : *na-a-ḫi* : GABA.RI SÌG-*iṣ* : x[...]

6′) [... ŠE U.M]EŠ-*šú kit-tab-ri ú-ba-na-t*[*u-šú* : U (?) : *u-b*]*a-nu* (?) : Á *ana* Á *šá* ŠU.SI : *ip-te-ru-ni*[*m* ...]

7′) [...]x ⸢*šá-niš*⸣ *šá bi-rit a-ḫa-meš* x[...]x : *šu-taq-ru-ub* : *a-lak-šú-nu qé-ru-*[*ub* ...]

8′) [... : Š]Ú : *a-ra-pu* : ŠÚ : *ka-ta-*⸢*mu* :⸣ x x x ⸤*ina* DU⸥*-ki im-taḫ-ru* [...]

9′) [...] x *i-na-ap-*⸤*pa*⸥*-*[*ḫ*]*u* (?) : *šá* ⸢*ḫa-an-ṭu*⸣ (?) x x x x[...]

10′) [... IGI.2-*šú u-rat-ta*] ⸢: DÙ :⸣ [*re-tu-u* : DÙ : *za-q*]*a-pu* : DÙ : GUB-*zu šá-niš* ⸢DUL⸣.D[UL ...]

11′) [...] *ú* : MAŠ.MAŠ-*su* ⸢*a*⸣*-ši-pu-u*[*s-su* ...]

12′) [...] la mu : IGI.BAR-*su it-ta-n*[*ap*(?)*-la-su* (?) ...]

13′) [... DA]L $^{[d]a\text{-}al}$: *šér-a-ni* ⸢*šá-niš n*[*im-šú* ...]

14′) [... t]um : SAG ⸢ŠÀ⸣-*šú* ⸤*i-ru-ur*⸥ [...]

Translation

***Sa-gig 4: 1**
The "Stillborn Child" (*Ku*$_{10}$*-bu*) "becomes bright" (BU) out from the "gloom" (KU$_{10}$).

(Obv. 1′) ... from the gloom ...

The "Stillborn Child" (*Kūba*) seems to be depicted here as one guarding the "earth" (KU$_{11}$), in an analysis that recalls the moon-god's name ^{d}ŠEŠ.KI = "to guard" (šeš) + "earth" (KI).

(2′) ... /*ku*/ *refers to* the earth ...

***Sa-gig 4: 1**
The patient's "temple" (SAG.KI) is perhaps analyzed as KI ("place of / with") + SAG (abbreviation for the constellation or zodiacal sign Pa-bil-*sag*).

(3′) ... [^{d}Pa-bil-sag] befalls him.

Medical condition in **Sa-gig 4: 1**

(3′) "It becomes hot and cold." ...

***Sa-gig 4: 2**
The signs al-du are not treated as a fossilized form AL.DU indistinguishable from DU "to move."

(4′) ["His innards al-du"] *means* they are stiff, *which means* they are hard,

Instead, because the stative sense of the Sumerian prefix al- seemed incompatible with movement, the commentator understood them as the syllable signs *al-ṭù* "they are stiff," which describe innards that "are hard."

Since "hard" does not usually describe the patient's innards or belly, a more typical term "inflaming" is used to clarify.

(4′) *which* (points) to [inflaming, in the case of the belly] …

***Sa-gig 4: 3**
The semantic link between *ebēṭu* "to have cramps" and *napāḫu* "to inflame" is implied by their shared logogram MÚ.

(4′) …
(5′) [MÚ *means* to have] cramps. MÚ *means* to inflame. …

***Sa-gig 4: 5**
The D Stative form *muqqut* "is collapsed" appears primarily in formulaic sequences of Sa-gig Chapter 11.

(5′–6′) ["ŠUB-*ut*" *means* it is collapsed (?)],
(6′) *which* (points) to being low. …

Sa-gig 4: 7

(7′) … "GÙ.GÙ-*si*" …

Sa-gig 4: 10

(8′) … "[Hand] of a ghost; (in) a second (version), [the goddess Ištar; he will die]." …

***Sa-gig 4: 11—"pi-pi-ru"**
The cuneiform signs pi-pi-ru (𒉿 𒉿 𒊒) may be read with the unusual syllabic values *ia*$_8$/*i*$_{16}$-*à-ru* (𒉿 𒉿 𒊒) = *i'arru* "he pukes."

(9′) … [*means*] he vomits …

***Sa-gig 4: 12**
The topic literally reads "from sunset until the morning watch," which

(10′) … [*means the opposite of* from morning (?)] until the cool (?) [of day]. …

denotes the half of the day opposite to what is described in the comment.

(Rev. 1′) ...

These gods' numbers are likely replicated in a metrological recombination text (W 23273) from Late Achaemenid Uruk.

(2′) ... 1 *refers to* the god Anu.
(2′) 2 *refers to* the god Enlil.
(2′) 3 *refers to* the god Enki. ...
(3′) ...

Sa-gig 4: 85—"strands of his temple on the right are dark"

(3′) "They are dark."
(3′) GE_6 *means* to become dark.
(4′) [GE_6] *means* to become black.

Sa-gig 4: 85—"Grip (*tāḫīz*) of sickness"

(4′) "Grip [of sickness]" ...
(4′) ... are dark.
(4′) To become dark *means* to become black. ...

***Sa-gig 4: 91 (TDPT 4 rev. 5)—"[strands of] his [temple] on [the right DU.D]U"**

(5′) ... [DU *means* to move].
(5′) DU *means* to move along.

***Sa-gig 4: 91 (TDPT 4 rev. 5)—"[strands of] his [temple] on the left GAR-*nu*"**

(5′) ["GAR-*nu*."]
(5′) [GAR *means*] to set in position.
(5′) GAR *means* to become calm.

Sa-gig 4: 91 or 90 (TDPT 4 rev. 5 or 4)

(5′) "He is struck in front" *means* ...
(6′) ...

***Sa-gig 4: 94 (TDPT 4 rev. 8)**
ŠE U.MEŠ is absent in therapeutic texts, and they are elsewhere defined as the distal phalanges of the fingers.

(6′) "His [ŠE U].MEŠ" (*refer to*) the *kittabrū* of his fingers.

Among other metrological functions, the ŠE represents the unit of length immediately smaller than the "finger-width" (ŠU.SI).

(6′) [U *means* (?)] finger (?), *which refers to* the side-to-side of a finger (i.e., a finger-width).

Sa-gig 4: 95 (TDPT 4 rev. 9) The topic *ipterrûnim* "(strands) cut into each other" derives from the root *parā'u* "to sever," not the more common *parû* "to vomit."	(6′) "*ipterrûnim*" ...
This is likely a description of strands intertwined with one another.	(7′) ... secondly, the case where ... between one another.
***Sa-gig 4** Perhaps clarifying what "has approached closely" does so temporally, rather than spatially	(7′) "It has approached closely" *means* they are imminent (lit. their movement is near). ...
***Sa-gig 4: 100 (TDPT 4 rev. 14)—"his eyes [...]" ?** The description of eyes as "clouded over" is much more common in the Diagnostic Handbook than in therapeutic texts.	(8′) ... ŠÚ *means* to become clouded over. (8′) ŠÚ *means* to cover. ...
Sa-gig 4: 106 (TDPT 4 rev. 21)—"[strands of] his temple on the right and left correspond in movement" Only in the Diagnostic Handbook are strands said to "correspond in movement," which is explained elsewhere as moving "in accordance with one another at the same time."	(8′) "They correspond in movement" ...
***Sa-gig 4**	(9′) ... they inflame (?), in the case of one who is feverish (?) ...
***Sa-gig 4: 109 (TDPT 4 rev. 23)** The uncommon description of eyes "fixed in place" is connected by the shared logogram DÙ to the condition of "protruding" eyes, which is recognized elsewhere as a medical sign.	(10′) ... ["He fixes in place his eyes."] (10′) DÙ *means* [to fix in place]. (10′) [DÙ *means*] to protrude. (10′) DÙ *means* to stand (still).

Sa-gig 4: 111 (TDPT 4 rev. 25)—"DUL.DUL"
A "second" base text is incorporated into the argument above. Though eyes are not explicitly mentioned here, DUL.DUL is said to indicate the "closing, lit. covering" of the eyes, rather than the "inundation" of the patient described elsewhere.

(10′) Secondly, "DUL.DUL" ...

Sa-gig 4: 112 (TDPT 4 rev. 27)—"You shall perform the magician arts for him"
Perhaps, as elsewhere, this comment clarifies that the magician arts are performed by the healer addressed ("you") in the Diagnostic Handbook, implying that this healer is a member of the magician profession.

(11′) ... "MAŠ.MAŠ-*su*" (*means*) (you shall perform) the magician arts for him (i.e., the patient) ...

***Sa-gig 4: 117 (TDPT 4 rev. 32)—"IGI.BAR.MEŠ his body"**
Existing Sa-gig manuscripts read: "He will keep gazing at (IGI.BAR.MEŠ) his (own) body." But the commentator's base text may read: "They keep gazing at (IGI.BAR-*su*) his body (i.e., the patient's corpse)."

(12′) ... IGI.BAR-*su* (*means*) [they will keep gazing at (?)] ...

***Sa-gig 4: 120 (TDPT 4 rev. 35)—"They are set as DAL.MEŠ"**
DAL ("transversal line") describes intersecting bodily strands in the Diagnostic Handbook, but is unattested in therapeutic texts.

(13′) ... [DAL] *means* (*šerʾānu*)-strand.
(13′) Secondly, [*nimšu*-strand] ...

Sa-gig 4: 127 (TDPT 4 rev. 42)

(14′) ... "His epigastrium *i-ru-ur*" ...

Notes

Intro—A recent edition of this commentary tablet was provided by Jiménez and Schmidtchen (2017: 231–239), though many of these authors' labels of the Sa-gig base texts had to be amended, in order to bring them in line with the numbering system used by Heeßel (2000, 2001/2002, and 2010) and Scurlock (2005 and 2014), which I adopt for my two volumes. See *Medical Text Labels and Abbreviations* in the front matter. Surprisingly little is entirely new—which speaks to shared hermeneutical concerns and methods of argumentation among scholars, perhaps even from different cities in ancient Babylonia. Judging from what is preserved on the obverse of Comm. Sa-gig 4C (§11.1.11), it seems almost identical to Comm. Sa-gig 4B (§11.1.10) in its choices of topics and methods of argumentation, with the two commentary tablets belonging respectively to the closely related "Babylon Collection" and "Sippar Collection" at the British Museum. The reverse of Comm. Sa-gig 4C also addresses many issues in the medical lexicography that I already explained elsewhere. In particular, sequences of entries in Comm. Sa-gig 4C (rev. 8′–13′) correspond remarkably with those in Comm. Sa-gig 21 & 22a (obv. 8–11), which had links to Nippur and Uruk (Frahm 2011a: 227, 298–300). These resemblances imply not that the commentaries themselves were directly related, but that the heavily damaged base text of Sa-gig 21 likely included a section similar to the base text of Sa-gig 4: 106–117+ (TDPT 4 rev. 21–32+). My Notes below, therefore, mostly direct the reader to the corresponding Note under Comm. Sa-gig 4B, Comm. Sa-gig 21 & 22a, and various other Sa-gig commentaries, where I had earlier on explored many of the same topics.

Obv. 1′—See Note on Comm. Sa-gig 4B, obv. 5–6 for what appears to be a badly preserved quotation "Like the Stillborn Child from the belly ... you convey ... without brightness," which likely alludes to the Stillborn Child's origin from the womb, a place of gloom without brightness.

Obv. 2′—See Note on Comm. Sa-gig 4B, obv. 7 for the portrayal of the Stillborn Child (*Kūba*) as one "guarding" (BA?) the "earth" (KU_{11}), a role that connects it to the moon-god, whose name ^{d}ŠEŠ.KI can be similarly analyzed as "to guard" (šeš as the logogram URU_3) + "earth" (logogram KI).

Obv. 3′—See Note on Comm. Sa-gig 4B, obv. 7–8 for how the name Pa-***bil-sag*** (Sagittarius) became descriptive of a "head" (SAG) that is "hot" (KÚM, same sign as bil), so that the complex of ideas associating { hot ^{mul_2}Pa-bil-sag : cold winter } with { hot temple : cold sensation } helped explain the patient's condition of being "hot and cold."

Obv. 4′—See Note on Comm. Sa-gig 4B, obv. 9 for the interpretation of the cuneiform signs al-du either as a fossilized form AL.DU that is indistinguishable in meaning from the common logogram DU ("to move"), or as the syllable signs *al-ṭù* from the root *wašāṭu* ("to become stiff").

Obv. 4′–5′—See Note on Comm. Sa-gig 4A, obv. 2–3 and Comm. Sa-gig 4B, obv. 9–10 where the commentator affirms the G stem of *napāḫu* ("to inflame") can have meanings that are transitive (e.g., "to cause cramps," D stem of *ebēṭu*) as well as intransitive (e.g., "to have cramps," G stem of *ebēṭu*).

Obv. 5′–6′—See Note on Comm. Sa-gig 4B, obv. 11–12 on the interpretation of ŠUB-*ut* as the D Stative form *muqqut* ("it is collapsed"), which otherwise occurs primarily in certain formulaic sequences of Sa-gig Chapter 11 and therefore justified the need for comment here.

Obv. 7′—I read the signs as [... G]Ù.GÙ-⌜*si*(?)⌝ [...] (obv. 7′), rather than as [...] ⌜DAB/*lu*⌝ : *ma*(?)-⌜*ḫa*⌝-[...] in Jiménez and Schmidtchen (2017: 231). A commentary entry on the topic "GÙ.GÙ-*si*" (Sa-gig 4: 7) is perhaps to be restored in the damaged portion of Comm. Sa-gig 4B, at the end of obv. 12 and the beginning of obv. 13. This is not contradicted by the topic "ŠÀ ŠÀ GÙ.GÙ-*si*" cited a little later in the tablet (Comm. Sa-gig 4B, obv. 13), since the point of the later topic has to do with the patient's "inside" (ŠÀ) rather than his act of "crying out" (GÙ.GÙ-*si*). Note also the topic "*ittanasla*ʾ" (obv. 7) and, a little later, the logographic form of the same term "[LÍL.LÍL-*a*ʾ]" (= *ittanasla*ʾ; obv. 10) occuring in the same tablet (Comm. Sa-gig 40A).

Obv. 8′—See Note on Comm. Sa-gig 4B, obv. 14 where the patient's hurting "inside" is ascribed to the goddess Ištar, as suggested by a quotation from the *Babylonian Creation Myth* (*Enūma eliš* IV, 101).

Obv. 9′—See Note on Comm. Sa-gig 4B, obv. 15 for the reading of the cuneiform signs pi-pi-ru (𒉿 𒉿 𒊒) with the unusual syllabic values *ia*$_8$/*i*$_{16}$-*à-ru* (𒉿 𒉿 𒊒), meaning "he pukes" (*iʾarru*).

Obv. 10′—See Note on Comm. Sa-gig 4B, obv. 16 for my view that the commentary entry here involves definition by antonymy (§1.2.3.1.6).

Rev. 2′—The gods' numbers here may be plausibly restored to a table (§1) at the beginning of a metrological recombination text (*SpTU* IV, 127 = W 23273; see Friberg and Al-Rawi 2016: 26, 109), which was owned by Rīmūt-Anu, the brother of Anu-ikṣur and a member of the Šangû-Ninurta magician family in Late Achaemenid Uruk. In addition to numbers in cuneiform cryptography (Pearce 1982) that reflect a divine order—namely, the number 60 for Anu, 50 for Enlil, 40 for Enki/Ea, 30 for Sîn, 20 for Šamaš, and 10 for Bēl or Marduk—Rīmūt-Anu's table is remarkable in also expressing a similar order by means of smaller numerals in reverse sequence: 1 for Anu, 2 for Enlil, 3 for Enki/Ea, etc. The scheme found coherence in the fact that numbers ascribed to Anu (1 and 60) were both written in sexagesimal place value notation using the same cuneiform sign (𒁹).

Rev. 3′–4′—The association of the roots "to become dark" (*tarāku*) and "to become black" (*ṣalāmu*) on the basis of their shared logogram GE_6 occurs also in the *Principal Commentary to Izbu* IV, 6 (Leichty 1970: 216, lines 126–127; De Zorzi 2014: 439, lines 1–2) and in an astronomical omen commentary (1904-10-9, 20, rev. 3 in Weidner 1941–1944: Tafel XIV; Verderame 2002: 93–94 and 104–106).

Rev. 5′—See Note on Comm. Sa-gig 3C, obv. 4 where (the strands of) a patient's temple is similarly described as "calmed down" (D stem of *nêḫu*) and implied to be in a state of "limpness" (*ramû*).

Rev. 6′—See Note on Comm. Sa-gig 1–3, line 47 for my proposal that ŠE U.MEŠ, *ṣurru* ("middle"), and *karši* U.MEŠ ("stomachs of fingers") refer respectively to the distal, intermediate, and proximal phalanges of the fingers. In this commentary entry, the mention of Á (*idu*, "side") recalls the lexical equation *kit-tab-ru* = *i-di* (*LTBA* II, 1: xiii 90); cf. *CAD* K, 468 s.v. *kittabru* with meanings "1. arm, side; 2. (a mole)." In my understanding, the commentator here was not defining the term ŠE as "the side-to-side of a finger (i.e., a finger-width)." Rather, the anatomical feature ŠE belongs to and is a part of the finger (U), just as the metrological unit ŠE—among other functions—represents the unit of length immediately smaller than the "finger-width" (e.g., *CAD* U/W, 356–357 s.v. *uṭṭatu* §3b). As a measuring unit, the "finger-(width)" is usually written as ŠU.SI or SI (rather than U), and this could account for the change in orthography from U.MEŠ of the base text (Sa-gig 4: 94) to ŠU.SI (later in rev. 6′) in the commentary.

Rev. 6′–7′—See Note on Comm. Sa-gig 14, obv. 16 for commentators' motivations for distinguishing the root *parā'u* ("to cut, sever") from the root *parû* ("to vomit, to void") that is much more common in the medical literature. Here, strands that "cut into each other" may be described in ways similar to Comm. Sa-gig 1A (obv. 25–26), where the verb is also unfortunately not preserved: *ik-tap-pi-lu* : *šá a-*⌜*ḫa-meš*⌝ x[...], "'... they are intertwined' *refers to* the case where ... one another."

Rev. 7′—The translation "their course is close" (*a-lak/lík-šú-nu qer*[*ub*]) was suggested by Jiménez and Schmidtchen (2017: 232, 238). However, the idiom {*alāk* + personal suffix + Stative of *qerēbu*} has to do with temporal imminency rather than spatial nearness (*CAD* Q, 229 s.v. *qerēbu* §1c), and a desire to clarify the specific nuance in the base text may have motivated the commentator here. The topic "it has approached closely" (*šutaqrub*; *CAD* Q, 240 s.v. *qerēbu* §17) is not common, and appears elsewhere as a description of how the sickness as a whole behaves: "AN.TA.ŠUB.BA-epilepsy will approach him closely (*uš-ta-qar-rab-šú*) at midday" (Sa-gig 26: 8′); "If what seizes him has approached closely (*šu-te-eq-ru-ub*)" (Sa-gig 26: 43′).

Rev. 8′—The base text here is tentatively identified as IGI.2-*šú* [...] (Sa-gig 4: 100 (TDPT 4 rev. 14)), with probably some syllabic form of the root *arāpu* ("to cloud over") to be restored in the damaged portion, so that preserved parts of this commentary line involve a B:A′:B:C argument. The topic of "clouded over" eyes occurs much more frequently in the Diagnostic Handbook at Sa-gig 3: 84 (TDPT 3: 75); Sa-gig 9: 55; 12: 129″–130″ (TDPT 12 iv 21–22); Sa-gig 19/20: 15′–16′; 26: 34′; and in therapeutic texts only at *BAM* 174 obv. 36′; 175: 1. The comment "to cover" seems to be less specific to medical contexts, but also appears as a description of the eyes in the Diagnostic Handbook at Sa-gig 10: 1; 16: 64′; 26: 11′, 64′, 66′; and in the therapeutic texts *BAM* 510 i 32′; 513 i 6′; 514 i 39′.

Rev. 8′—See Note on Comm. Sa-gig 21 & 22a, obv. 8 where the same topic on bodily strands that "correspond in movement" was explained as "the case where they [move] in accordance with one another at the same time" (interpretation mine).

Rev. 9′—The reading in this highly damaged line comes from Jiménez and Schmidtchen (2017: 231–232), and is uncertain because the base text cannot be plausibly identified around the vicinity of the Diagnostic Handbook consulted at this point.

Rev. 10′—See Note on Comm. Sa-gig 21 & 22a, obv. 9 where essentially the same topic and comment occur in reference to the patient's eyes. Elsewhere, I also restore a similar argument for a different body part: *ir-te-né-*⌜*et*⌝*-ti* : ⌜*it*⌝-[*ta-na-az-qap* (?) : DÙ : *re-tu-ú*] / DÙ : *za-qap*, "He keeps fixing in place (his tongue) *means* [it keeps protruding out (?)]. [DÙ *means* to fix in place.] DÙ *means* to protrude." (Comm. Sa-gig 7Ca, obv. 3′–4′).

Rev. 10′—Jiménez and Schmidtchen (2017: 231, 239) read the sign ⌜DU_6⌝ (rev. 10′) and thought it continued commentary on the base text Sa-gig 4: 109 (TDPT 4 rev. 23), by introducing "a second (*šanîš*) interpretation of DÙ based on the sign's homophony." On the contrary, the sign in question—which I read as DUL based on the traces—incorporates a "second" *topic* from a different Sa-gig base text (Sa-gig 4: 111 (TDPT 4 rev. 25)). Crucially, both base texts begin in exactly the same way ("If the strands of his temples on the right and left move ...") up to a point of divergence, where one continues with the statement "he fixes in place his eyes" (Sa-gig 4: 109), while the other describes the patient as DUL.DUL *u* BAL.BAL (Sa-gig 4: 111), before both base texts finally agree again on the same prognosis that the patient "will die." The commentator here evidently considered both Sa-gig entries to be synonymous, and the expression DUL.DUL *u* BAL.BAL (Sa-gig 4: 111) to be a descriptor of the patient's eyes as in Sa-gig 4: 109, even though the "eyes" are not mentioned explicitly in Sa-gig 4: 111. In fact, both logographic forms appear together elsewhere as IGI.2-*šú* DUL-*ma* / BAL-*ma* (Sa-gig 10: 1–2), and are the subject of another commentary: ... : DUL-*ma* ⌊*ú*⌋-*ka-at-tam-ma* : BAL.MEŠ : *n*[*a-bal-ku-ta*] / [BAL : *na-bal-ku-tu*] : BAL : *pa-la-su* : ..., "'DUL' (*means*) he closes (his eyes). 'BAL.MEŠ' *means* [(his eyes) are rolled.] [BAL *means* to roll (eyes).] BAL *means the opposite of* to look at." (Comm. Sa-gig 10 & 11, obv. 2–3). The commentator, nonetheless, correctly recognized that DUL.DUL could not be taken for granted as referring to the eyes, and that he needed to clearly affirm so. For an alternative explanation by ancient interpreters, see Note on Comm. Sa-gig 18, rev. 13′ for the prognosis that the patient himself—not his eyes—"will keep becoming inundated" (DUL.DUL = Ntn of *katāmu*). For an analogous use of the notation "secondly" (*šanîš*) to incorporate a second base text topic into an existing argument, see Comm. Sa-gig 1B, obv. 16′–17′: [*ki-i* lu₂GI]G munusKALA.GA IGI TIN *ki-i* munusKA[LA.G]A NU IGI BA.ÚŠ *šá-niš ki-i* / [GIG *na-qu-d*]*u a-na* 3 U_4-*mu* ⌜*ki-i*⌝ *la na-*[*a*]*q-du ana* ITI 3 ÚŠ : ..., "[**If**] **the sick man sees hardship, he will become healthy** (base text Sa-gig U1: 10 = S1: 7). If he does not see hardship, he will die. Secondly (*šanîš*), '**if** [**the sick man**] **is critically sick, he will die in three days. If he is not critically sick, in three months** (base text Sa-gig U1: 11 = S1 : 8).'"

Rev. 11′—The base text (Sa-gig 4: 112 (TDPT 4 rev. 27)) represents a shorter variation on the statement "You shall perform the magician arts for him and wipe him down." See Note on Comm. Sa-gig 21 & 22a, obv. 10 where the logographically written verb (ŠU.ÙR.ÙR) is clarified to be in the 2nd person singular (*tukappar*, "*you* shall wipe him down"), implying that the addressee is one who wipes the patient and performs the magician arts, and that the healer using the Diagnostic Handbook is therefore imagined to be a member of the magician profession. This may be significant, because several other statements in Sa-gig portray the magician in the 3rd (rather than 2nd) person. One of these, in fact, appears in the base text's vicinity—i.e., "the magician shall perform (his arts)" (lu₂MAŠ.MAŠ DÙ-*uš*) in Sa-gig 4: 107 (TDPT 4 rev. 21)—without having triggered any explanation from the commentator of Comm. Sa-gig 4C.

Rev. 12′—The base text entry (Sa-gig 4: 116–117 (TDPT 4 rev. 31–32)) concerns a patient who is suffering as retribution for an illicit sexual affair—lit. "because of (another) man's wife" (MU DAM LÚ)—and the topic in question straddles the boundary between the description of his medical signs and the diagnostic/prognostic verdict. This topic appears as AD_6-*šú* IGI.BAR.MEŠ in existing Sa-gig manuscripts, and has been understood as a continuation of the medical signs, e.g., "he continually gazes at his body" (Scurlock 2014:

39), with the plural marker .MEŠ presumably expressing iterations of the action rather than a plural subject. In Comm. Sa-gig 4C, the writing IGI.BAR-*su* (rev. 12′) most likely represents a faithful quotation from the base text used by the commentator, which differs in its reading from available Sa-gig manuscripts. It is, in fact, easy to see how the plural marker .MEŠ could have been confusedly rendered as the phonetic complement -*su* to a verb (*ittanaplasū*) with a supposed plural subject. *Contra* the proposal that "-*su* should be regarded as a phonetic complement indicating the final consonant of *ittanaplas*" (Jiménez and Schmidtchen 2017: 239). In my interpretation, the base text would have read: "they (impersonal subject) will keep gazing at his body (i.e., the patient's corpse)," as a prognosis of death that is otherwise not included elsewhere in the Sa-gig entry.

Rev. 13′—See Note on Comm. Sa-gig 3A, rev. 7′ for essentially the same topic in a different base text: "they are set as 2 transversal lines" (2 RI.MEŠ GAR.MEŠ in Sa-gig 3: 107 (TDPT 3: 98)). In Comm. Sa-gig 4C, the commentator clarified that the description refers to the appearance of intersecting bodily strands, i.e., in what is described earlier in the base text as "the strands of his temples and his hands" (Sa-gig 4: 120 (TDPT 4 rev. 35)). See also Note on Comm. Sa-gig 21 & 22a, obv. 11 for discussion on *šer'ānu* (the general term for "strand" as a human bodily feature in the Diagnostic Handbook) and *nimšu* (a narrower term that is often translated "sinews" and occurs in descriptions of sheep anatomy).

Rev. 14′—See Note on Comm. Sa-gig 10 & 11, obv. 3 where I discuss the verb (*ḫ*)*arāru* that commonly describes the behavior of a sick man's "bowels" (suggestively, *errū*) and likely also his epigastrium (as in the base text here: Sa-gig 4: 127 (TDPT 4 rev. 42)).

PART ONE ✧ SECTION TWELVE

Commentary Sa-gig 5

Provenance:	Uruk (Warka), Area U18, Level v; Library of Anu-ikṣur
Period:	Late Achaemenid
Names:	"Readings of Anu-ikṣur, descendant of Šangû-Ninurta"
Script:	Neo-/Late Babylonian
Typology:	*ṣâtu* 6b in Frahm (2011a: 53)

Field/Museum No.:	W 22307/16 (National Museum of Iraq)
Photos:	Plate 14 (obverse) and Plate 15 (reverse)
Printed Edition/Hand Copy:	*SpTU* 1, 31 (= Hunger 1976: 39–40); Wee (2012: 592–602)
Digital Resources:	CDLI P348452; GKAB P348452 (edition digitized by Clancier 2009); CCP 4.1.5 (printed hand copies digitized by Frahm, Frazer, and Jiménez 2013)
Discussion:	*SpTU* 1, 31 (= Hunger 1976: 39–40); Schramm (1979: 123); Lambert (1987: 154); Heeßel (2000: 95–96 n. 103; 133, 142 (5. Tafel MS a)); Fincke (2000: 73, 77, 107, 121, 145, 147, 149, 158, 170, 221) and (2009: 83); Scurlock and Andersen (2005: 803, see references to *SpTU* 1.31); Clancier (2009: 50, 52, 55, 71, 265, 388); Geller (2010a: 148–150, 196 n. 205); Genty (2010a: 374) and (2010b: 12, 20–25, 28, 30); Frahm (2011a: 53 n. 230–231, 67, 224, 291); Wee (2012: 592–602); Scurlock (2014: 50 nn. 2, 6, 8 and 15; 56 n. 1); Gabbay (2016: 105 n. 115, 119–120, 128–130, 145); Schmidtchen (2018: 322, 327 n. 40)
Pericope:	Indeterminate due to damaged state of available Sa-gig manuscripts

Transliteration

Obverse

1) DIŠ GI[G] IGI 1[5]-⸢*šú*⸣ GU$_{7}$-*šú* [ŠU DINGIR AD]-*šú* x x [GI]G-*ma* TIN

2) ŠU DINGIR AD-*šú* ⸢: *šá* $^{d(?)}$AD⸣ : ⸢^{d}⸣30

 | DOI:10.1163/9789004417564_013

3) *e-sír-ta lìb-bu-ú* [...] ⌜*e*(?)-*si*⌝-*ir* : *e* x *ḫi* x(?)
4) IGI 15-*šú tar*-⌞*kat*⌟ : *šá ṣu-lum* ⌞IGI(?)⌟ DIŠ LÚ x [...]
5) [q]u bu x x x x x [...] tar [...]
6) *bal-ṭa-at* x [...]
7) LÚG NU TUKU : *ḫ*[*i-ṭ*]*u* [*u*]*l i-ši* [...]
8) ME.ZÉ-⌞*šú*⌟ *n*[*u-u*]*š-šú* : *kan-zu-u*[*s-su* ...]
9) ÍL IGI.2-*šú pa-rid lìb-b*[*u-ú* ...]
10) *i-la-wi* : *i*-[*la*]*m-mu* x[...]
11) *ul* x x x x [...]
12) *na-pal-ku-ú r*[*a*]-*p*[*a*]-⌞*šú*⌟ [...]
13) šu mu k[a (?)] x [...]
14) DAB : *ṣa-b*[*a-t*]*u* x [...]
15) ka[r (?)] x la x [...]
16) [...] x tuk ku [...]
17) x ra : lá [...]
18) [Š]À-⌜*šú*⌝ x x [...]
19) [i]d [...]
20) IGI.2-⌜*šú*⌝ [...] x [...]
21) u an x : [...]

Reverse

22) ^{d}LUGAL.URU.BAR.RA : ^{d}*Nin-ur*[*ta* ...] x ši x [...]
23) *ka-šu-ú* : *ma-lu-ú* : SIG$_7$ *šur-ru* ⌜*kap-pi*⌝ [I]GI *ul* [...]
24) EME-*šú i-tál-lal* : LAL : *ta-la-lu* : LAL : *šá*-[*qa-lu*]
25) NÍG.GU$_7$: *ú-kul-tú* : *mu-sa-ri* : *ú-šá*-[*ri*]
26) *su-qat-su* : *kan-zu-us-su* : *kab-ta i-šá* x [x]
27) *ina* U$_4$ BI.IZ AN-*e áš-šú ku-ṣu* : BI.IZ : *na-ta-k*[*a*]
28) [Š]ID : *mi-na-a-tú* : ḪAŠ-*ir* : *še-bi-ir* : IGI.2-[*šú* ...]
29) *lìb-bu-ú* IGI.2-*šú taq-na* : IGI.2-*šú ú-am-ma-aṣ* : [...]
30) ḪUM : *a-ma-šú* : ḪUM : *ḫa-ma-šú* : *bé-e-ra* : *b*[*é-e-šu*]
31) *bé-e-ra* : *pe-tu-ú* : ÚḪ-*su* ḪAR.MEŠ x[...]
32) *lìb-bu-ú i-sa-ʾ-ul u* ÚḪ-*su i*-[*šal-lu*]
33) L[Ú.N]A.ME : *mam-ma* : SA.GIG : *nap-ḫar mur-ṣ*[*u*]
34) [SA :] *ri-ik-su* : GÌR.2-*šú ana* ŠÀ-*šú tu*[*r-ra*]
35) *kin-ṣa*-⌜*a*⌝-⌞*šú*⌟ *ana* ŠÀ-*šú* [*tu*]*r-ra* : *eʾ-i-l*[*u* ...]
36) *u*[*š*]-*šu*-ʾ-⌜*ri*⌝ (?) [...] x : SÌG-*iṣ* [...]
37) *il-te-ḫi-i*[*ṭ* ...]
38) GIM *ḫi-in-qí* GÁL-*ma lìb*-⌜*bu-ú*⌝ [...]

---

39) DIŠ GIG KIR$_4$-*šú* SA$_5$ ⌜TIN⌝

40) *ṣa-a-tú ù šu-ut* KA *šá* KA UM.ME.A *šá* DIŠ GI[G] IGI 15-*šú* GU$_7$-*šú*
41) *mál-su-ut* $^{m.d}$*A-nu-ik-ṣur* DUMU ^{lu_2}SANGA-^{d}[*N*]*in-urta* ^{lu_2}MAŠ.MAŠ

Translation

Incipit-title of Sa-gig 5
The diagnosis "Hand of his father's god" is not very common and does not occur in therapeutic texts.

(Obv. 1) "If the sick man's right eye hurts him; [Hand of] his [father's god]; he will be sick …, and he will become healthy."

***Sa-gig 5: 1**
The signs DINGIR AD "(his) father's god" are reinterpreted as ^{d}AD "the divine father," who is then identified as the moon-god Sîn, well known as father of the sun-god Šamaš and the goddess Ištar in the Mesopotamian pantheon.

(2) "Hand of his father's god" *refers to* the case of the divine (?) father, *which refers to* the moon-god Sîn.

***Sa-gig 5**
The context for esirtu "enclosed thing" is uncertain, but its dictionary root seems to be identified here as *esēru* "to enclose."

(3) "*esirta.*" As in, … is enclosed (?) …

Sa-gig 5: 12′ (TDPT 5 B1 12)

(4) "His right eye is dark" *refers to* the case of the black of the eye(?) …

***Sa-gig 5**

(4–5) …
(6) it is healthy …

***Sa-gig 5**
The prognosis "he will incur no harm" is idiomatic in the Diagnostic Handbook, but not in therapeutic texts.

(7) "LÚG NU TUKU" *means* he will incur no harm. …

***Sa-gig 5**
The "jaw" (ME.ZÉ) is part of the "larger" (GAL) area of the "chin region" (ME.ZÉ.GAL). The "jaw" is very seldom mentioned in medical signs.

(8) "His ME.ZÉ is shaky" *means* his chin region [is shaky] ...

***Sa-gig 5**
parādu "to shudder" elsewhere describes the person as a whole or his "belly/heart" and "innards," but rarely his eyes.

(9) "The raising of his eyes is shuddery."
(9) As in, ...

***Sa-gig [5: 36′] (TDPT [5 E1 2]) ?**
Elsewhere, *lawû* / *lamû* "to go round" is not written syllabically, but as the logogram NIGIN.

(10) "(His right eye) *i-la-wi*" *means* it goes round.
(11) ...

***Sa-gig 5**
napalkû "to extend wide open" describes only the eyes in medical texts and occurs primarily in the Diagnostic Handbook. It is explained here by a more general synonym *rapāšu* "to become wide."

(11–12) ... *napalkû* (*means*) to become wide.

***Sa-gig 5**

(13) ...

(14) DAB *means* to seize ...
(15) ... (16) ... (17) ...
(18) His belly ... (19) ...
(20) His eyes ... (21) ...

***Sa-gig 5**
The deities ^{d}LUGAL.ÙR.RA and ^{d}LUGAL.GÌR.RA are more common in medical texts.

(Line 22) "^{d}LUGAL.URU.BAR.RA" *refers to* the god Ninurta.

***Sa-gig 5—"eyebrow is copious" ?**
Hair that is "copious" (*kašû*) is hair that is "full" (*malû*). The base text possibly describes "eyebrow" hair, which is also the topic of the next commentary entry.

(22–23) ... To become copious *means* to become full.

***Sa-gig 5 (same base text entry as above?)**
SIG_7 very commonly means "to become yellow / green," and its unusual meaning here required comment. *šuʾru* "eyebrow" and *kappi īni* "flap of the eye" appear mostly in the Diagnostic Handbook and seldom in therapeutic texts.

(23) "SIG_7" (*means*) eyebrow (*or*) flap of the eye.

(Scribal Comment)

(23) [I did] not [see / hear] (?).

***Sa-gig 5**
talālu "to draw out" occurs rarely in medical descriptions.

(24) "He draws out his tongue."
(24) LAL *means* to draw out.
(24) LAL *means* to [suspend].

***Sa-gig 5**
NÍG.GU_7 "devouring" occurs rarely as a diagnostic verdict, and these logographic signs are not to be misread as NINDA GU_7 "he eats food."

(25) "NÍG.GU_7" *means* devouring.

***Sa-gig 5**
The writing *mu-sa-ri* should be understood as a byform of *mušari* "penis," instead of *musarî* "sick rectum."

(25) "*mu-sa-ri*" *means* penis.

***Sa-gig 5**
suqtu "chin" occurs rarely in medical texts.

(26) "His *suqtu*" *means* his chin region.

***Sa-gig 5**

(26) “They are heavy” …

***Sa-gig 5**
“On the day of the sky’s BI.IZ” occurs rarely in medical prognoses.

(27) “On the day of the sky’s BI.IZ, because of the coldness.”
(27) “BI.IZ” *means* dripping.

***Sa-gig 5: 89′ (TDPT 5 F3 9) ?**
minâtu “limbs” is written elsewhere as the logogram UB.NIGIN or syllabically, but not as the logogram ŠID.

(28) “ŠID” *means* limbs.

***Sa-gig 5**
šebēru “to break” and *šebirtu* “break” do not occur often in medical texts.

(28) “ḪAŠ-*ir*” *means* it is broken.

***Sa-gig 5**

(28) “[His] eyes …”
(29) As in, his eyes are placid.

Sa-gig 5: 92′ (TDPT 5 F3 12)—
ú-am-ma-aṣ < *amāṣu* (meaning unknown)

(29) “He (performs the action of) *uammaṣ* to his eyes” *means* …

The commentator understood the obscure verb *amāṣu* as a byform of the more common verb *amāšu*, which describes the patient’s hands and feet, but not his eyes.

(30) ḪUM *means* to become rigid (*amāšu*).

Ambiguity about the meaning of *amāšu* in the context of “eyes” may have motivated this comparison to the verb *ḫamāšu*, which shares the same logogram ḪUM. Unfortunately, all these verbs cannot be defined with precision.

(30) ḪUM *means* to become anomalous(?) (*ḫamāšu*).

Sa-gig 5: 94′ (TDPT 5 F3 14)
bêra typically describes "hair" and refers to the "eyes" only here. The verbs *bêra*, *bêšu* "to move apart," and *petû* "to open" are often linked in lexical texts.

(30) "*bêra*" *means* [moved apart.]
(31) "*bêra*" *means* opened.

***Sa-gig 5**
The commentator may be arguing that "spittle" or phlegm originates from the lungs instead of another part of the inner anatomy.

(31) "His spittle ... lungs ..."
(32) As in, he coughs and [expels] his spittle.

***Sa-gig 5**
The logographic form LÚ.NA.ME does not typically occur in medical texts.

(33) "LÚ.NA.ME" *means* somebody.

***Sa-gig 5**
An effort to make the title of the Diagnostic Handbook SA.GIG conform to its definition in *Esagil-kīn-apli's Manifesto* as "a bundling together (SA) of sickness (GIG)," i.e., a compilation on "all (SA) sickness (GIG)."

(33) SA.GIG *refers to* all sickness.
(34) [SA *means*] bundling together.

***Sa-gig 5**
Here, the commentator did not so much clarify rare or atypical medical vocabulary, as describe a bodily behavior or technical procedure.

(34–35) "To turn his feet inwards (lit. to his belly)" (*means*) to turn his lower legs inwards.

***Sa-gig 5 (same base text entry as above?)**
The demon *eʾēlu* "binder" may be the one responsible for the patient's inability "to turn his feet inwards."

(35) "The *eʾēlu*-demon" ...

***Sa-gig 5**	(36) "Strike of ..." ...
***Sa-gig 5**	(37) "it jumped" ...
***Sa-gig 5**	(37–38) ... "it occurs like *ḫinqu*-sickness." As in, ...
(Colophon)	
Incipit-title of Sa-gig 6	(39) "If the sick man's nose is red, he will live."
Incipit-title of Sa-gig 5	(40) Glossary including oral lore from the mouth of the *ummânu*-scholar on "If the sick man's right eye hurts him."
	(41) Readings of Anu-ikṣur, descendant of Šangû-Ninurta the magician.

Notes

Obv. 1–2—The diagnosis "Hand of his father's god" is not particularly common and occurs elsewhere only at Sa-gig 9: 55; 16: 1; 19/20: 114′; [23: 1] (= Sa-gig 22: 79). It does not seem attested in therapeutic texts. The commentator apparently reinterpreted the writing DINGIR AD ("(his) father's god") as ᵈAD ("divine father"), whom he then identified as the moon-god Sîn. In the Mesopotamian pantheon, the moon-god is often given the epithet "Father," especially with regards to his status as father to important deities like the sun-god Šamaš and the goddess Ištar. See Hall (1985: 625–626, 736–745).

Obv. 4—Hunger's transliteration *tar-kàt* (*SpTU* 1, 31) follows that of Sa-gig 5: 12′ (TDPT 5 B1 12). However, the cuneiform of the commentary probably reads *tar-*⌊*kat*⌋ instead. I tentatively restore *ṣu-lum* ⌊IGI(?)⌋ ("the black of the eye," i.e., the iris), but the traces of ⌊IGI(?)⌋ are admittedly very damaged.

Obv. 7—The prognosis LÚG NU TUKU "he will incur no harm" occurs elsewhere at Sa-gig 6: 26, 28; 12: 40′; Sa-gig 12: 69″, 78″, 121″ (TDPT 12 iii 6, 15; iv 13); Sa-gig 13: 100 (TDPT 13 ii 42); Sa-gig 14: 3, [34] (TDPT 14 i 3, [34]); Sa-gig 16: 51′, 52′, 84′. While the expression also "appears not infrequently in Neo-Assyrian and Neo-Babylonian letters" (Scurlock and Andersen 2005: 725 n. 173), it does not seem to be idiomatic in therapeutic texts.

Obv. 8—See Note on obv. 10 for difficulties in identifying the base text here. The topic ("His ME.ZÉ is shaky") resembles the reading *i-su-šú nu-*⸢*šá-át*⸣ ("his jaw is shaky") at Sa-gig 5: 37′ (TDPT 5 E1 3), collated by Scurlock and Andersen (2005: 556, §Ap.21; 764 n. 9); Scurlock (2014: 45). Due to the fragmentary condition of existing manuscripts, however, we cannot tell whether the commentator employed a version of Sa-gig 5: 37′ with "jaw" written logographically (ME.ZÉ) instead of syllabically (*i-su*), or whether the logogram ME.ZÉ belonged to another base text entry altogether. Note, for example, the writing [M]E.ZÉ-*šú nu-uš-šá* in Sa-gig 26: 12′ MS $A_{10'}$. As a body part, the "jaw" (ME.ZÉ / *isu*) does not receive much mention in medical descriptions, and the term seems firmly attested only at Sa-gig 5: 37′–39′ (TDPT 5 E1 3–5); Sa-gig 8: 22; [33: 97]; *STT* 89 iv 208.

Obv. 9—See Note on obv. 10 for difficulties in identifying the base text here. A similar statement IGI.2-*šú pár-da* ("his eyes are shuddery") occurs in Sa-gig 12: 112″ (TDPT 12 iv 4). Elsewhere in the medical literature, the verb *parādu* ("to shudder") describes the behavior of the sick person as a whole or occasionally the "belly" (ŠÀ) (Sa-gig 10 B rev. 8; 12: 3 (TDPT 12 i 3); Sa-gig 13: 73 (TDPT 13 ii 15); *BAM* 397: 36; *AMT* [31/1: 4]) and "innards" (ŠÀ.MEŠ) (Sa-gig 40: 42), but not the "eyes."

Obv. 10—The following restorations were proposed by Scurlock (2014: 45): [DIŠ IGI-*šú šá* 15 *i*]-*la-wi u i-su-šú nu-*⸢*šá-át* DIN⸣ (Sa-gig 5: 37′ (TDPT 5 E1 3)) and [DIŠ NA IGI-*šú šá* 150 *u i-su-šú* K]I.MIN GIG-*su* DUGUD-*ma* DIN (Sa-gig 5: 38′ (TDPT 5 E1 4)). However, given that Sa-gig entries from the beginning of tablet 5 appear in groups of threes (each addressing the "right eye," "left eye," and then "both eyes"), and given that the 18 fragmentary lines of Sa-gig 5: 18′–35′ must consist of 6 (= 18 ÷ 3) such complete groups, I prefer to number the Sa-gig entries as follows: [DIŠ IGI-*šú šá* 15 *i-la-wi u i-su-šú nu-šá-át* ... (whole line fragmentary)] (Sa-gig 5: 36′ (TDPT 5 E1 2)); [DIŠ IGI-*šú šá* 150 *i*]-*la-wi u i-su-šú nu-*⸢*šá-át* DIN⸣ (Sa-gig 5: 37′ (TDPT 5 E1 3)); and [DIŠ IGI.2-*šú i-la-wa u i-su-šú* K]I.MIN GIG-*su* DUGUD-*ma* DIN (Sa-gig 5: 38′ (TDPT 5 E1 4)). According to my interpretation, the base text for *i-la-wi* (obv. 10) would be its first mention at Sa-gig [5: 36′] (TDPT [5 E1 2]). While it is tempting to identify this same entry as the base text for obv. 8 (assuming that the commentator's manuscript copy had the logogram ME.ZÉ instead of the syllable signs *i-su*), the same cannot be said for the topic in obv. 9 ("the raising of his eyes is shuddery"), and perhaps it is better to suppose that the base text entries for obv. 8–9 belong to the fragmentary lines preceding Sa-gig [5: 36′] (TDPT [5 E1 2]). Frahm (2011a: 67) remarked that this entry "[deals] with the change in intervocalic *w* to *m* that occurred in Akkadian after the Old Babylonian period." Also pertinent is the fact that, in other preserved medical texts, the verb *lawû* or *lamû* ("to go round") is not written syllabically but as the logogram NIGIN. Note that the writing *i-lem-mu* in *BAM* 156: 1 derives from a different verb *lêmu* ("to consume, eat and drink").

Obv. 12—The verb *napalkû* "to extend wide open" is used primarily in the Diagnostic Handbook to describe the eyes. See Sa-gig [5: 72′, 73′] (TDPT [5 E2 6, 7]); Sa-gig 10: 4; 27: 16; but also the therapeutic text *CTN* 4.72 i 3. It is uncertain whether the commentator's topic here was derived from Sa-gig [5: 72′] (TDPT [5 E2 6]) or from an earlier but damaged medical entry.

Line 22—For ^{d}LUGAL.URU.BAR.RA as the god Ninurta, see *SpTU* I, 60 rev. 22′, as well as the god list An = *Anum* I, 221 (Litke 1998: 46); cf. An = *Anum* VI, 53 (Litke 1998: 204). See also discussion in Lambert (1987: 154). The deities denoted as ^{d}LUGAL.ÙR.RA (Sa-gig 28: 17, 19–20; 29: 1, 21; *BAM* 311: 23′, 77′; *AMT* 96/3: 2) and ^{d}LUGAL.GÌR.RA (Sa-gig 9: 58, 65; [11: 24]) are more common in medical texts. For a discussion of ^{d}LUGAL.ÙR.RA in Sa-gig 29: 1–7 with regards to infantile and childhood convulsions, see Kinnier Wilson (2007: 62–66).

Lines 22–23—The damaged end of line 22 probably constitutes a citation from the base text that includes an inflected form of the verb *kašû*, which is then followed by the dictionary roots *kašû* : *malû* in the following line 23. While the base text cannot be reconstructed with certainty, I tentatively identify the meaning of *kašû* as "to yield profit, to become copious (said of hair growth)" (*CAD* K, 294 s.v. *kašû* B §3b). The commentary argument here, therefore, defines "copious" (< *kašû*) hair as hair that is "full" (< *malû*). The following commentary entry that explains "SIG$_7$ (*means*) 'eyebrow'" (line 23) possibly refers to the same base text entry, which would then be a description of "copious eyebrows" that are full of hair.

Line 23—The sign SIG$_7$ occurs very commonly in medical texts as the logogram for *warāqu* ("to become yellow/green"), and its unusual meaning as "eyebrow" here apparently prompted the commentator's remark. While traces of *šu-ru-ʾ-šú* (Sa-gig 5: 46′ (TDPT 5 E1 12)) are suggestive, too much of the context is broken to identify this as the base text. More importantly, it is much easier to imagine the potentially confusing term SIG$_7$ as a topic cited from the base text, than as the commentator's own contribution. For SIG$_7$.IGI as the logogram for *šūr īni* "eyebrow," and SIG$_7$ alone as *šu-uḫ-ru* (< *šuʾru*), see *CAD* Š III, 366. The orthography *šur-ru* (line 23) is not ideal, since one would expect *šu-ʾ-ru* (as is the case elsewhere in the Diagnostic Handbook) or even *šu-uḫ-ru* (as it appears in some lexical texts). The term *kappi īni* supposedly denotes the "eyelid" (Fincke 2000: 253–254; Rutz 2011:

305); cf. the broader definition of "the eyebrows, the eyelids, and the eyelashes" in *CAD* K, 187–188 s.v. *kappu* A §4a–c. Here, I rather literally translate *kappi īni* as "flap of the eye," to reflect the incommensurability between Mesopotamian and modern ways of dividing up the human anatomy. Also, though I tentatively consider *kappi* IGI as part of the commentary entry beginning with SIG_7, it is possible that *kappi* IGI begins a new entry whose end is damaged. Both *šu'ru* and *kappi* (+ IGI) are more typical of descriptions in the Diagnostic Handbook than in therapeutic texts. For *šu'ru*, see Sa-gig 6: 103″ (TDPT 6 rev. 41′); Sa-gig 10: 27; 33: 97. For *kappi* or its logogram PA, see Sa-gig 3: 62, 107 (TDPT 3: 53, 98); Sa-gig 4: 120 (TDPT 4 rev. 35); Sa-gig 5: 123′–124′ (TDPT 5 G 24–25); TDPT 5 H 3–8; Sa-gig 13: 110 (TDPT 13 ii 52; understood instead as *pa*-IGI^{II} ⌜ŠÀ⌝, "umbilical area," by Scurlock 2014: 107, 114); Sa-gig 17: 70–72; the Old Babylonian diagnostic tablet MS 2670 obv. 18′ (George 2013: 88); and *BAM* 515 ii 25. Note also the translation of *kappu* (without *īni*) in Sa-gig 17: 70–72 as "Handfläche" by Heeßel (2000: 210).

Line 23—There is not much space after *ul* [...] at the end of line 23, and the following line 24 begins with a new topic. The sign *ul* [...], therefore, is possibly part of a short scribal comment such as *ul āmur* ("I did not see"), *ul ašme* ("I did not hear"), or *ul īdi* ("I do not know"). See Note on Comm. Sa-gig 7A, rev. 4; cf. Comm. Sa-gig 40A, obv. 12–13.

Line 24—In addition to the damaged base text here, the verb *talālu* ("to draw out") is attested only at Sa-gig 7 A obv. 21, 22, also in reference to the tongue. This commentary entry was restored differently in *CAD* T, 91 s.v. *talālu*, lexical section: "LAL *means* to draw out. LAL *means* to [ascend]" (LAL : *ta-la-lu* : LAL : *šá*-[*qu-ú*]), likely on the basis of the lexical associations $^{tu\text{-}u_2}$ TÙM = *ta-la-lu* : *šá-qu-ú* : *ta-la-lu* : *ma-a*[*ḫ-ru-u*] (Aa VIII/3 Comm., 14 in *MSL* XIV, 506); cf. *CAD* Š II, 19 s.v. *šaqû* A "to ascend", lexical section. In this commentary, my choice of *šaqālu* ("to suspend") over *šaqû* ("to ascend") gives priority to *šaqālu*'s well-known connection to the logogram LAL.

Line 25—Apart from its attestation here, NÍG.GU_7 appears only in the diagnostic verdict NÍG.GU_7 ^{d}DÌM.ME.LAGAB ("devouring of *aḫḫāzu*-sickness/demon") at Sa-gig 16: 12. The commentator probably felt the need to distinguish NÍG.GU_7 ("devouring") from the very common description NINDA(níg) GU_7 ("he eats food").

Line 25—The commentator understood *mu-sa-ri* in the base text as a byform of *mušaru* "penis" (*CAD* U/W, 298) instead of the rectal sickness *musarû* = DÚR.GIG (*CAD* M II, 234 s.v. *musarû* C). In the medical literature, these two terms are not usually confused, because they are written logographically: GÌŠ instead of *mušaru* ("penis"), and DÚR.GIG instead of *musarû* ("sick rectum"). Note, however, the syllabic writing *mu-šar-ri-šú* and *mu-šar-šú* at Sa-gig 14: 109–110 (TDPT 14 ii 37–38), in the context of penis sicknesses.

Line 26—Other than in the damaged base text here, the term *suqtu* ("chin") is attested only in Sa-gig 9: 38, 56; 27: 14. As a body part, the "chin" is seldom mentioned in medical descriptions. Note the lexical equation: uzu *su-uq-t*[*ú*] = (blank) = [*k*]*an-zu-zu* (Hg. B IV, 2 in Vedeler 2002: 67; cf. *MSL* IX, 34). The use of *kanzūzu* ("chin region") here and in obv. 8 is surprising, since *kanzūzu* is more typical of descriptions in physiognomic and terrestrial omens rather than medical texts (*CAD* K, 172), but perhaps the limited number of synonyms for "chin" accounted for this choice.

Line 26—*kab-ta* ("they are heavy") may refer to a base text description similar to Sa-gig 5: 95′ (TDPT 5 F3 15): IGI.2-*šú* DUGUD-*ma* ("his eyes are heavy"). Though the verb *kabātu* is written logographically as DUGUD most of the time, syllabic writings appear in Sa-gig 8: 14; 19/20: 86′; [27: 8]; 33: 4, 40, [89]; 40: 97; *BAM* 393 rev. 3; *AMT* 53/11: 3′; 77/1 i 5.

Line 27—The rare expression *ina* U_4-*um* BI.IZ AN-*e* also occurs in the prognosis of Sa-gig 13: 20 (TDPT 13 i 21′), but without the qualifier "because of the coldness." This qualifier has been ascribed to the commentator by Genty (2010b: 25), but one should not discount the possibility that it is an explanatory phrase original to the base text. For meanings of *aššu* ("concerning, because") in commentaries, see Gabbay (2016: 144–166). The equation BI.IZ : *na-ta-ka* also appears in Uruk Therapeutic Comm. 7 = *SpTU* I, 54: 16′. The logogram BI.IZ is equated with the verb *natāku* in the lexical texts Ea V, 39 (*MSL* XIV, 398); Aa V/1, 162 (*MSL* XIV, 411); S^a Voc. F, [13a] (*MSL* III, 57); as well as the related noun *tīku* in the lexical text Aa V/1, 169 (*MSL* XIV, 412).

Line 28—In the Diagnostic Handbook, *minâtu* ("limbs") is typically written with the logogram UB.NIGIN$_{(2)}$.NA at Sa-gig 5: 89′ (TDPT 5 F3 9); Sa-gig 9: 60, 64; 17: 5, 15, 16; 22: 44–45; 26: 19′–20′, 22′, 71′–73′, 75′–76′; 27: 21, 29; but syllabic writings appear at Sa-gig 17: 103; 26: 53′. Therapeutic texts, on the other hand, record only syllabic writings of *minâtu* at *BAM* 52: 39; 96 ii 1; 97: 9′; 231 i 2, 12; 234: 7; 438 obv. 6; 449 iii 24′; [453: 8′]; 516 ii 25′ (incl. *AMT* 18/2: 3′); *BAM* 579 iv 44 (incl. *AMT* 41/1 iv 44); *AMT* 31/1: 1; 40/5 iii 14′; [43/6: 1]; 90/1 iii 24′; *STT* [89: 24?]. The logogram ŠID for *minâtu* ("limbs") does not occur in the preserved manuscripts and is therefore worthy of comment. Since commentary entries in lines 29–31 seem to refer to the base text Sa-gig 5: 92′, 94′ (TDPT 5 F3 12, 14), one may be tempted to assign this commentary entry (line 28) to the base text Sa-gig 5: 89′ (TDPT 5 F3 9), even though existing manuscripts bear the reading UB.NIGIN$_2$.NA (*AMT* 105/2: 9′) instead of ŠID. It is possible that the commentator's manuscript copy had the reading ŠID, or that ŠID appears in a damaged portion of available manuscripts.

Line 28—The verb *šebēru* ("to break") may occur at Sa-gig [40: 73], and the noun *šebirtu* ("break," i.e., fracture) appears at *BAM* 124 iii 57; 125: 28; [413 obv. 1′–2′]; BM 30918: 32. In addition to the rarity of these terms as bodily descriptions, available attestations do not employ the logogram ḪAŠ.

Lines 28–29—The statement "his eyes are placid" may be a comment on the medical description in the base text Sa-gig 5: 91′ (TDPT 5 F3 11), which has been restored and translated as IGI.2-*šú iz-za-naq*!-*qa*!-*p*[*a*! ...] ("his eyes are continually constricted") by Scurlock and Andersen (2005: 71, §3.216); Scurlock (2014: 47). If this reading is correct, however, it would be the only instance whereby the Gtn stem of *zaqāpu* describes the patient's eyes. In the context of "eyes," the verb *zaqāpu* is attested in the G stem (Sa-gig 27: 20), D stem (Sa-gig 26: 80′–81′; *AMT* [19/1 obv. 9]), Dtn stem (Sa-gig 40: 56), and Ntn stem (Sa-gig [11 rev. 51]).

Line 29—It is suggested that the obscure verb *ú-am-ma-aṣ* (Sa-gig 5: 92′ (TDPT 5 F3 12)) < *amāṣu* is a byform of *ḫamāṣu*, because, like the latter, it seems to be used in the base text to describe an eye condition. See *CAD* A II, 27 s.v. *amāṣu*; *CAD* Ḫ, 60 s.v. *ḫamāṣu* A. Note also the lexical entry OB Lu B, iv 49 (*MSL* XII, 183): lú igi-dub-dub = *ša i-na-šu ḫu-mu-ṣa*. The commentator, however, argued that *ú-am-ma-aṣ* derives from the verb *amāšu* ("to become rigid"; cf. "to become cataleptic(?)" in *CAD* A II, 28) and is related to the verb *ḫamāšu* ("to become anomalous(?)"; *CAD* Ḫ, 60–61), both of which may be expressed by the logogram ḪUM. Unfortunately, the meanings of all these verbs cannot be determined with precision. While *amāṣu* and *ḫamāṣu* are not attested elsewhere in medical texts, the verb *amāšu* does occur commonly in the Diagnostic Handbook to describe the patient's hands and feet (Sa-gig 10: 1; 11: 20, [49]; 13: 36 (TDPT 13 i 37′); Sa-gig 14: 217′ (TDPT 14 iv 11′); Sa-gig 15: 18′–20′, 64′; 16: 59′; 26: 53′; 40: 110–111), and *ḫamāšu* appears in *BAM* 66 rev. 16′. In other words, the commentator interpreted an obscure verb (*amāṣu*) as a byform of a more common one (*amāšu*), even though the verb *amāšu* is not known elsewhere to describe the eyes. Moreover, *amāšu* is not typically used in therapeutic texts, and it may constitute the topic of an entry in Comm. Sa-gig 10 & 11, obv. 1–2.

Lines 30–31—See Note on Comm. Sa-gig 1–3, obv. 23 for attestations of the verb *bêru* almost always describing *uruḫḫu*-hair, as well as the close lexical associations among the verbs *bêru*, *bêšu* ("to move apart"), and *petû* ("to open"). Given the way entries in this commentary all begin by citing the base text topic, the writing *bé-e-ra* would depict the Stative *bērā* ("(his eyes) are parted") at Sa-gig 5: 94′ (TDPT 5 F3 14). Although the comment *b*[*é-e-šu*] (line 30) admittedly needs to be restored and the comment *pe-tu-u* (line 31) does not show the 3fp verb ending, I tentatively understand them as the commensurable Stative 3fp forms *bēšā* ("(his eyes) are moved apart") and *petâ* ("(his eyes) are opened").

Line 31—The base text here is unfortunately uncertain. The commentator, however, seems to have demonstrated knowledge that coughed out "spittle" or phlegm originates from the lungs instead of another part of the patient's inner anatomy.

Line 32—I restore this line as *i-sa-ʾ-ul u* ÚḪ-*su i*-[*šal-lu*] ("he coughs and [expels] his spittle"), following a similar expression in Sa-gig 22: 30: *ú-sa-al ú-na-ḫaṭ u* ÚḪ-*su i-šal-lu* ("he coughs out, wheezes(?), and expels his spittle").

Line 33—In medical texts, the syllabic form *mamma* ("somebody") occurs at Sa-gig 17: 84, but the logographic form LÚ.NA.ME seems attested only in the base text here.

Lines 33–34—See Note on Comm. Sa-gig 1A, line 47 for how commentators made the title of the Diagnostic Handbook SA.GIG conform to its definition in *Esagil-kīn-apli's Manifesto* as a "bundling together (SA) of sickness (GIG)," i.e., a comprehensive compilation that included "all (SA) sickness (GIG)."

Line 34—A similar statement GÌR.2-*šú tur-ra* NU ZU-*ú* ("he is unable to turn his feet") appears at Sa-gig 14: 216′ (TDPT 14 iv 10′), but without the expression *ana* ŠÀ-*šú* ("inwards," lit. "to his belly"). Although the physical movement envisioned here is not entirely clear, the comment was evidently motivated not so much by lexical concerns (i.e., because of rare or atypical medical vocabulary), as for pragmatic reasons (i.e., to clarify a bodily behavior or technical procedure).

Line 35—In addition to the damaged base text here, the diagnosis ŠU *eʾ-e-li* ("Hand of the *eʾēlu*-demon") occurs at Sa-gig 26: 44′, and *eʾ-e-lu* appears in a list of sicknesses in K 8487: 7 (*CAD* E, 40). The term *eʾēlu* literally means "binder," and one wonders whether this demon was responsible for the condition described in the previous commentary entry: "he is unable to turn his feet / lower legs inwards." In Sa-gig 26: 44′, for example, the *eʾēlu*-demon is responsible for the condition that the patient "stretches out his feet" (GÌR.2-*šú* LAL-*aṣ*). In the *Babylonian Almanac* and *Offering Bread Hemerology*, the *eʾēlu*-demon was of special concern on the 20th day of the month Du'uzu (IV). Livingstone (2013: 31, line 20; 129, line 50).

Line 41—The syllable signs here are *mál*(dir)-*su-ut*, not *mal*(gá)-*su-ut* (line 41) as rendered by the typo in the printed edition *SpTU* I, 31.

Commentary Sa-gig 7A

Provenance:	Uruk (Warka), Area U18, Level v; Library of Anu-ikṣur
Period:	Late Achaemenid
Names:	"Readings of Anu-ikṣur, son of Šamaš-iddin, descendant of Šangû-Ninurta"
Script:	Neo-/Late Babylonian
Typology:	*ṣâtu* 6a in Frahm (2011a: 53)
Field/Museum No.:	W 22307/2 (National Museum of Iraq)
Photos:	Plate 16a (obverse) and Plate 16b (reverse)
Printed Edition/Hand Copy:	*SpTU* 1, 32 (= Hunger 1976: 40–41); Wee (2012: 603–610)
Digital Resources:	CDLI P348453; GKAB P348453 (edition digitized by Clancier 2009); CCP 4.1.7.A (printed hand copies digitized by Frahm, Frazer, and Jiménez 2013)
Discussion:	*SpTU* 1, 32 (= Hunger 1976: 40–41); George (1991: 157); Wilhelm (1994: 28, 58); Heeßel (2000: 133, 142 (7. Tafel MS a)); Scurlock and Andersen (2005: 351, §14.36; 425, §18.39); Clancier (2009: 50, 52, 55, 71, 265); Geller (2010a: 148); Genty (2010a: 375) and (2010b: 12, 20, 23, 24, 30); Frahm (2011a: 40 n. 148, 53, 224–225, 291) and (2014: 325); Wee (2012: 603–610), (2015a: 263 n. 54), and (2016b: 180–181 n. 118); Böck (2013: 70); Scurlock (2014: 62 nn. 1 and 4; 63 nn. 35 and 50); Gabbay (2016: 66 n. 273, 97–98, 201, 206 n. 22); Wiggermann (2018: 360 n. 17)
Pericope:	At least Sa-gig 7 B obv. 3′–rev. 8 (TDPT 7: 42′–64′)

Transliteration

Obverse

1) [...] / 2) x [...]

3) *um* [...]

4) ka [...]

5) kúr k[a ...]
6) *ba* x [...]
7) GE_6 ⌜*ṣal*⌝-[*mu* ...]
8) *ra* x [...]
9) *qu-ur*-⌜*ru*⌝-[*šu* ...]
10) NÍG.ZI.⌜IR⌝(?) [...]
11) NÍG.ZI.[IR(?) ...]
12) *šá mu* x x [...]
13) x *el* x [...]
14) *ra bi* x [...]
15) *ana* šá x x [...]
16) tab x [...]
17) KA-*šú* x[...]
18) na x x[...]
19) ŠÀ x [...]
20) ÚḪ-⌜*su*⌝ [...]
21) ki me [x x x] *ri* x [...]
22) *it-te*(?)*-ne-ri* x [...]
23) pi ⌜x x x x x⌝ [...]
24) *i*-⌜x x x x⌝ [...]

Reverse
1) [DIN]GIR-*šú* KI-*šú sa-bu-us* : DINGIR-*šú* K[I-*šú ze-ni*]
2) [G]Ú.ŠUB.BA : *ze-nu-ú* : GÚ.ŠUB.[BA : *sa-ba-su*]
3) [*an-n*]*a ma-gal la ip-pal* : *an-na* : x[...]
4) [... k]a [: (?)] *qí-bi-tú* : ka *a-mat ina* IM NU IGI : [giš]GID[RU *šá* DINGIR-*šú*]
5) [*ḫaṭ-ṭ*]*u šá* DINGIR-*šú* ⌞:⌟ *i*(!)-*ta*(!)-*na-šá-a* : ÍL : *na*-⌜*šú*⌝-[*u*]
6) [Í]L : *šá-qu-u* : $BURU_8$: *ia-ár-ru* : *iš-te-na* [x (?)]
7) [*ut-t*]*a-nab-ba-ak* : ka-*šú* KÚR.KÚR : *il-ta-na-an*-[*ni*]
8) [ka :] *ri-gim* : *ra-pa-du su-ud-dur*-[*šú*]
9) [*šá*(?)-*n*]*e*(?)*-e ṭè-e-me sa-dir-šú* : *a-šu-uš*-[*tu*]
10) [*a*]-*šá*!(a)-*šá* (?) : $UD.DUG_4$.GA : *a-dan-nu* : *ḫa-a-a-át*-[*tu*]
11) [*g*]*i-lit-tú* : DIŠ GÙ GIG *taš*-⌜*mi*⌝-*ma* GIM GÙ AN[ŠE ...]
12) [*ana* (?)] U_4.1.KAM GAM *šá* E-*ú mu-ú-tu pa-ni* [d]IM.DU[GUD.MUŠEN]
13) *an-zu-u* : *an-šu-ú* : *i-me*-[*ru*]

---

14) *ṣa u* MIN *šá* DIŠ GIG EME-*šú* SA_5-*át* TIN *šá* KA U[M.ME.A]
15) *mál-sut*$_x$(BÁN) [m.d]*A-nu-ik-ṣur* DUMU *šá* [m.d]UTU-MU DUMU [lú2]SAN[GA-[d]*Nin-urta*]
16) DIŠ GIG GEŠTUG.2 15-*šú*

Translation

***Sa-gig 7**
The expression "his god is offended with him" occurs in several therapeutic texts, and here it explains the atypical description *sabus* "is angry."

(Rev. 1) "His god is angry with him" *means* his god [is offended] with [him].

(2) GÚ.ŠUB.BA *means* to become offended.
(2) GÚ.ŠUB.BA [*means* to become angry.]

Sa-gig 7 B obv. 3′ (TDPT 7: 42′)

(3) "He does not frequently answer 'yes.'"
(3) "Yes" *means* ...

***Sa-gig 7 B obv. 6′ (TDPT 7: 45′) ?**
The sign ka here indicates logograms such as DU$_{11}$ "speech" or INIM "words," rather than body parts such as KA "mouth" or KIR$_{4}$ "nose."

(4) ... "The cuneiform sign ka" [*means* (?)] speech.
(4) "The cuneiform sign ka" (*means*) words.

(Scribal comment)

(4) I did not see (/ it is not seen) in the tablet.

Sa-gig 7 B obv. 15′ (TDPT 7: 54′)
^{giš}GIDRU is common in the Diagnostic Handbook but much less frequent in therapeutic texts.

(4–5) "^{giš}GIDRU [of his god]" (*means*) [stick] of his god.

***Sa-gig 7**

(5) "*i-ta-na-šá-a.*"

The writing *i-ta-na-šá-a* "(his belly) keeps rising" derives from the verb *našû* "to rise," not *âšu* "to retch" despite the context of "puking." Also, though the verb *našû* is usually transitive ("to raise"), it should be understood with an intransitive meaning ("to rise" = "to ascend") here.

(5–6) ÍL *means* to rise.
(6) ÍL *means* to ascend.

(6) "BURU$_{8}$" *means* he pukes.

***Sa-gig 7**

(6–7) "He urinated (?)" (*means*) he keeps pouring out.

Sa-gig 7 B rev. 3 (TDPT 7: 59′)
KÚR.KÚR commonly describes the patient's voice in the Diagnostic Handbook, but not in therapeutic texts.

(7) "His ka (performs the action of) KÚR.KÚR" *means* it keeps altering.

The sign ka here indicates the logogram GÙ "voice." This clarifies that the medical condition concerns the quality of sound, not the contents of speech.

(8) ["The cuneiform sign ka" *means*] voice.

Sa-gig 7 B rev. 4 (TDPT 7: 60′)
rapādu "to wander about" occurs commonly in the Diagnostic Handbook, but not in therapeutic texts.

(8–9) "He intermittently wanders about" (*means*) he intermittently (has) alteration(?) of intelligence.

Sa-gig 7 B rev. 8 (TDPT 7: 64′)
In medical texts, *ašāša* "to become distressed" is much more common than its cognate noun *ašuštu* "distress."

(9–10) "*ašuštu*" (*derives from the dictionary root*) to become distressed (?).

Sa-gig 7 B rev. 8 (TDPT 7: 64′)
The syllabic writing *adannu* "fixed time" is more typical for medical texts than its logogram U_4.DUG_4.GA.

(10) "U_4.DUG_4.GA" *means* the fixed time.

***Sa-gig 7**
The syllabic writing *hayyattu* "fright" here is typical of therapeutic texts, in contrast to its logogram (IGI).LAL in the Diagnostic Handbook.

(10–11) "*ḫayyattu*" (*means*) jitters.

***Sa-gig 7**
The commentator sought to prove the logic in the base text quotation that "donkey" ↔ "death."

(11–12) "If you listen to the sick man's voice, and [it sounds] like the voice of a donkey, he will die [on] the first day," which it said.

p ("death") ↔ *q* ("*Anzû*-bird")

(12) Death is complement to ^{d}IM.DUGUD.MUŠEN,

This refers to the "death" of the *Anzû*-bird at the hands of the god Ninurta in the *Myth of Anzû*, or the "deadliness" of the *Anzû*-bird itself.

q ("*Anzû*-bird") ↔ *r* ("donkey")

(13) (*which means*) *Anzû*-bird, *which sounds like anšû* (𒀲), *which is the sign name for* donkey (ANŠE).

Therefore, *r* ("donkey") ↔ *p* ("death")

(Colophon)

Incipit-title of Sa-gig 7

(14) "*Ṣâ-* et cetera" (abbreviated writing of *Ṣâtu u šūt pî*, "Glossary including oral lore") on "If the sick man's tongue is red, he will become healthy," from the mouth of the *ummânu*-scholar.
(15) Readings of Anu-ikṣur, son of Šamaš-iddin, descendant of Šangû-Ninurta.

Incipit-title of Sa-gig 8

(16) "If the sick man's right ear."

Notes

Obv.—The obverse of this commentary tablet is very badly damaged, but here are some suggested readings and the base text topics they address: GE$_6$ ⸢*ṣal*⸣-[*mu*] (obv. 7) // UD.A GE$_6$.MEŠ (Sa-gig 7 A obv. 10 (TDPT 7: 10)); *qu-ur-*⸢*ru*⸣-[*šu*] (obv. 9) // *ú-qar-ra-aš* (Sa-gig 7 A obv. 15 (TDPT 7: 15)); NÍG.ZI.⸢IR⸣(?) (obv. 10) & NÍG.ZI.[IR(?)] (obv. 11) // ⸢NÍG.GIG(?)⸣ (Sa-gig 7 A obv. 15 (TDPT 7: 15); collated in Scurlock and Andersen 2005: 556, §Ap.27;

764 n. 12; Scurlock 2014: 57); ÚḪ-⸢*su*⸣ (obv. 20) // ÚḪ-⸢*su*⸣ [...] (Sa-gig 7 A obv. 25 (TDPT 7: 25)); *it-te*(?)-*ne-ri* x [...] (obv. 22) // [DIŠ KA-*šú* ...]-*ne-ri* x[...] (Sa-gig 7 A obv. 32 (TDPT 7: 32)).

Rev. 2—The verbs *zenû* ("to become offended") and *šabāsu* ("to become angry") are associated in the lexical text Erimḫuš II, 197–198 (*MSL* XVII, 37), as well as in the commentarial equations GÚ.ŠUB.BA = *z*[*e*]-*nu-u*, GÚ.ŠUB.BA = ⸢*ša*⸣-*ba-su* (*Principal Commentary to Izbu* II, 54′ in Leichty 1970: 215, lines 105–106; De Zorzi 2014: 392, lines 29–30); [... GÚ].ŠUB.BA = *sa-ba-su* (*ACh* Ištar 7: 51 (comm.)); cf. *CAD* Š I, 4. The expressions DINGIR-*šú* KI-*šú ze-ni* ("his god is offended with him") and DINGIR-*šú u* ^{d}15-*šú* (/ *Ištar-šú*) KI-*šú ze-nu* ("his god and his goddess are offended with him") appear in several therapeutic texts: *BAM* 234: 10; 316 iii 9′, 14′; 376 i 18′; 447: 4′; 480 iii 48. The verbal root *sabāsu*/*šabāsu*, on the other hand, appears less commonly and typically in the form *šibsāt* (*BAM* 234: 9; *AMT* 15/5: 6′). Here, the commentator explained an unusual form (*sabus* < *sabāsu*/*šabāsu*) by means of an idiomatic therapeutic statement. Notice that the appeal to the shared logogram GÚ.ŠUB.BA in this B:C:B:A′ argument only served to confirm a conclusion reached beforehand based on therapeutic conventions.

Rev. 4—The cuneiform sign ka has several common logographical values in medical texts. For the base text here, the commentator clarified that it indicates logograms such as DU_{11} for *qibītu* ("speech") and INIM for *amâtu* ("words"), in contrast to its role as the logogram GÙ for *rigmu* ("voice") in rev. 8 of this commentary. The base text of this entry may be Sa-gig 7 B obv. 6′ (TDPT 7: 45′): [*ina* k]a-*šú atmû ittenetpû*, where the sign ka was interpreted as "speech" or "words" in the context of the term *atmû* ("manner of speech"). Note also the equation [*at-me-e*] : *da-ba-bi*, "['Manner of speech'] *refers to* speaking" in Comm. Sa-gig 3B, rev. 4, which appears as *at-mu-ú* : *da-ba-ba* in Scheil (1916: 137–138, obv. 12′).

Rev. 4—One might be tempted to emend the scribal comment *ina* IM NU IGI (𒀸 𒅎 𒉡 𒅆) ("I did not see (/ it is not seen) in the tablet") to the similar signs *ina* IM NU SILIM (𒀸 𒅎 𒉡 𒁲) ("it is not intact in the tablet"), in view of similar comments such as *ina* IM NU SILIM(*šalim*) (*SpTU* I, 83 rev. 4, 10), *ina ṭup-pi ul šá-lim* (*CT* 41, 29, obv. 3), and [*ina* I]M NU GI(*šalim*) (*SpTU* I, 50 rev. 30). On the other hand, note the syllabic writing [...] *ul a-mur* ("I did not see ...") in *SpTU* V, 272 rev. 31′–32′; [... *ul á*]*š*(?)-*me-e-ma* ("I did not hear ...") in *SpTU* V, 272 rev. 6′; cf. Leichty (1973: 79–82, obv. 5, 17); and *ul i-di* ("I do not know") in Comm. *Ālu* 17–20 = K 2895, rev. 6′ (*CT* 41, 25); Comm. *Ālu* 94 = K 118, obv. [2–3], rev. 3, 10–11, 14 (*CT* 41, 33); Comm. *Ālu* 103–104(+) = K 103, lines 2′, 4′, 12′, 14′–15′, 21′ (*CT* 41, 34). See discussion in Frahm (2011a: 40 n. 148). With regards to the similar statement *gaba-ru-u la-bi-ru ul* *a-mur* ("I did not see the ancient copy"; CBS 1516 = *PBS* 1/2 no. 106, rev. 30), Laessøe remarked that "oral tradition was only reluctantly relied upon, and in this particular case only because for some reason or other an original written document was not available." Laessøe (1953: 212–213); cf. Clancier (2014: 58–59). Such expressions may also be related to the scribal comment NU DÙ ("it is not done") in Comm. Sa-gig 40A, obv. 12, 13. See also Gabbay (2012: 284–285).

Rev. 4–5—Most attestations of the term ^{giš}GIDRU ("stick") occur in the Diagnostic Handbook, where it is associated with the agency of various Mesopotamian gods. See the diagnoses ^{giš}GIDRU ŠU ^{d}UTU GAR-*su* (Sa-gig 17: 39); [^{giš}GID]RU *šá* ^{d}UTU GAR-*su* (Sa-gig 18: 31); ^{giš}GIDRU ^{d}30 *u* ^{d}15 (Sa-gig 40: 56); ^{giš}GIDRU DUMU *šipri šá* ^{d}30 (Sa-gig 40: 57); ^{giš}GIDRU *šá* DINGIR-*šú* (Sa-gig 13: 28 (TDPT 13 i 29′); Sa-gig [19/20: 52′]); ^{giš}GIDRU DUMU *šipri šá* DINGIR-*šú* (Sa-gig 19/20: 47′); ^{giš}GIDRU *šá* ^{d}x (Sa-gig 7 B obv. 15′ (TDPT 7: 54′)). This malady is also mentioned as the first medical sign in Sa-gig 13: 39–43; 82–90 (TDPT 13 i 40′–44′; ii 24–33). By contrast, references in therapeutic texts are much fewer. See GIM ^{giš}GIDRU *šá* ^{d}EN.ZU GAR-*šum* (*BAM* 385 i 15′; 471 ii 21′), as well as *lū ina* ^{giš}GIDRU as one among other medical conditions (*AMT* 88/3: 1).

Rev. 5–6—I understand the signs here as *i*(!)-*ta*(!)-*na-šá-a*, which constitute the Gtn Durative of the verb *našû* (intransitive), "to rise, heave." This commentary entry shares two features with Comm. Sa-gig 7B, rev. 2′, which has the same designation "Readings of Anu-ikṣur." In both these Anu-ikṣur commentaries, the verb *našû* (intransitive) is explained by the verb *šaqû* ("to ascend"). Secondly, the belly's action of "rising" or "heaving" occurs for the purpose of "vomiting" or "puking." Though the base texts for both commentaries are not preserved, the original expression was probably similar to the one in Sa-gig 22: 26: ŠÀ-*šú ana a-re-e i-ta-na-šá-a* ("his belly rises to puke"). It is curious that a very frequently used verb like *našû* should require explanation by the verb *šaqû*, which, though common enough in prosaic use, appears in medical texts only at Sa-gig 4: 117 (TDPT 4 rev. 32); Sa-gig 19: 110′; 27: 6; *AMT* 16/5 ii 4; 77/1 i 3. Note also that the verb at Sa-gig 4: 97 (TDPT 4 rev. 11) may be *šaqû* ("to ascend"), instead of *šaqû* ("to water") as suggested by Scurlock and Andersen (2005: 350, §14.31); or *leqû* ("to take (away)") in Scurlock (2014: 38). There are two possible explanations for the commentator's interest here. First, the syllabic writing for the Gtn Durative of *našû* ("to rise") appears as *i*(!)-*ta*(!)-*na-šá-a* here, as *i-ta-na-áš-šá-a* in Comm. Sa-gig 7B, rev. 2′, and as *i-ta-na-šá-a* in Sa-gig 22: 26. Such orthographies were easily confused with the form *i-ta-na-áš* (Sa-gig 22: 25, 28), which derives from a different verb *âšu* ("to retch"). The confusion was all the more likely, since both commentary expressions (*i*(!)-*ta*(!)-*na-šá-a* and *i-ta-na-áš-šá-a*) appear in the context of "vomiting" and "puking." The commentator likely felt the need to prevent this confusion between *našû* ("to rise") and *âšu* ("to retch"). Secondly, while the verb *našû* is more commonly used in a transitive sense ("to raise"), it has an intransitive meaning ("to rise, i.e., heave") here and elsewhere in contexts of the belly (*CAD* N II, 103 s.v. *našû* A §5.2′). Anu-ikṣur's interest in the transitivity of *našû* ("to raise" vs. "to rise") mirrors concerns for the transitivity of *napāḫu* ("to inflame") by the commentator of Comm. Sa-gig 4B, obv. 9–10.

Rev. 6—This commentary entry may relate to the base text Sa-gig 7 B rev. 5 (TDPT 7: 61′). Although the available Sa-gig manuscript has *i-ár-ru*, it is possible that the commentator worked with a base text copy that had the logogram $BURU_8$. If this was in fact the case, rev. 6 of this commentary would represent a disruption of the progressive order in which the commentator selected topics from the base text, because rev. 7–9 comment on the base text Sa-gig 7 B rev. 3–4 (TDPT 7: 59′–60′).

Rev. 6—I tentatively understand the signs *iš-te-na* as the G Preterite of *šatānu* ("to urinate"), with its comment [*ut-t*]*a-nab-ba-ak* as the Dtn Durative of *tabāku* ("to pour out"). In fact, the verb *tabāku* has been linked with urination or urine in other commentaries: [SUR : *ša-ta-nu*] | SUR : *ta-ba-ku* (*Principal Commentary to Izbu* XXII, 136 in Leichty 1970: 227, line 531; De Zorzi 2014: 857, line 9); A *it-bu-uk* : *ás-sú ši-na-a-te* (Comm. *Ālu* 49 = DT 37, rev. 9c in Freedman 2017: 75). In the Diagnostic Handbook, *tabāku* describes the "pouring out" of urine at Sa-gig 9: 70; 13: 131 (TDPT 13 iii 20); while therapeutic texts use the same verb to describe the "pouring out" of blood or green/yellow matter from the penis at *BAM* [112 ii 17′]; 159 i 9; 182 obv. 6′; 396 iv 3′; 578 i 29. The orthography *iš-te-na* is admittedly unusual, and one may expect a form closer to *iš-tin* (Sa-gig 16: 7; *BAM* [115 obv. 14′; rev. 4′]; *AMT* 63/5 iii 17′, [21′, 23′], 25′; 65/4: 8′), *i-šá-ti-nu* (*AMT* 58/6: 2′), or possibly *iš-tan* (Sa-gig 22: 33; cf. translation in Heeßel 2000: 260).

Rev. 7–8—In the Diagnostic Handbook, the verb *nakāru* ("to change"; logogram KÚR.KÚR) often describes the patient's "voice" (GÙ) or "speech" (DU_{11}), both of which may be expressed logographically with the cuneiform sign ka. See the medical entries in Sa-gig 7 B rev. 3–17 (TDPT 7: 59′–85′), as well as Sa-gig 22: 49′, 56′. By contrast, the only attestation of such a kind in therapeutic texts seems to be *BAM* 202 obv. 2 // *STT* 286 ii 15: *a-ma-tu-šú* KÚR.KÚR-*ru*/*ra* ("his words keep changing"). The commentator not only felt it necessary to explain the term KÚR.KÚR, he did so not with its usual equivalent *nakāru* ("to change"), but with a synonymous verb *šanû* ("to alter") that never describes the patient's "voice" or "speech" in the Diagnostic

Handbook. The verb *šanû* ("to alter"), however, does appear in the therapeutic description *at-mu-šú i-šá-an-ni* ("his manner of speech alters") at *BAM* 316 vi 4′ // *STT* 95 ii 84. In short, the commentator explained a form (KÚR.KÚR) less typical of therapeutic texts, by means of an idiom (*šanû*) attested in therapeutic texts but not the Diagnostic Handbook. Comparison with the following lines suggests there is room for the restoration *il-ta-na-an-*[*ni*] (rev. 7), and there is no need to posit that "*il-ta-na-an* … is probably a mistake for *iltani*" (Böck 2013: 70). As noted above, the cuneiform sign ka has several common logographical values in medical texts. The commentator clarified that, here, it serves as the logogram GÙ for *rigmu* ("voice"), even though the same sign functioned as the logogram DU$_{11}$ for *qibītu* ("speech") in rev. 4 of this commentary. The base text here, therefore, is concerned with the quality of sound/voice produced by the patient and not the contents of his speech. However normative the commentator may have believed his interpretation to be, we should not conclude that all occurrences of the cuneiform sign ka with the verb *nakāru* necessarily refer to the "voice." Note, for example, the syllabic writing in Sa-gig 19/20: 14′: *da-bab-šú* KÚR.KÚR-*ir* ("his speaking keeps changing").

Rev. 8–9—The quotation *ra-pa-du su-ud-dur*( )-[*šú*] is from the base text Sa-gig 7 B rev. 4 (TDPT 7: 60′), which has been erroneously transliterated as *ra-pa-du su-ud kišâdi*(GÚ:)-*šú* in Labat (1951: 64). The verb *rapādu* ("to wander about") is very commonly used in the Diagnostic Handbook, occasionally to describe the patient's "mouth" (Sa-gig 15: 21′) or "tongue" (Sa-gig 22: 48), but mostly to describe his behavior as a whole: Sa-gig 3: 46 (TDPT 3: 37); Sa-gig 6: 15; 7 B rev. 6 (TDPT 7: 62′); Sa-gig [11: 27]; 11 rev. 36; 12: 4, 84″, 86″–87″, 127″ (TDPT 12 i 4; iii 21, 23–24; iv 19); Sa-gig 14: 66, 177′, 179′ (TDPT 14 i 66; iii 44′, 46′); Sa-gig 15: 26′, 30′, 32′, 39′, 44′–45′, 52′–53′, 57′; 22: 57; 27: 19. In stark contrast, this verb is not used to depict the patient's behavior in therapeutic texts. For the description of the patient's "intelligence" (*ṭēmu* = UMUŠ) with the verb "to alter" (*šanû* = MAN), see Sa-gig 22: 47–49; *BAM* [202 obv. 1]; *STT* [286 ii 14]. See also Comm. Sa-gig 3B, obv. 9′: [UMUŠ-*šú* KÚR-*šum-m*]*a* : *šá-né-e ṭè-me* ("['His UMUŠ changes for him'] *refers to* an alteration of intelligence"), which comments on the base text Sa-gig 3: 46 (TDPT 3: 37). Notice that, whereas the topic cited from the base text has the D Stative form *suddur*, the comment uses the G Stative form *sadir*. The forms *suddur* and *sadir* have considerable overlap in their meanings (*CAD* S, 11–17), and the commentator's choice to use the latter in explanation may have reflected current or local idioms of language.

Rev. 9–10—The restoration [*a*]-*šá*!(a)-*šá* (?) (rev. 10) is not certain, and tentatively follows the interpretation by Hunger (*SpTU* 1, 32) who restored the signs slightly differently as [*a-šá*(?)]-*a-šá*. In medical texts, verbal forms of *ašāšu* are much more common than the noun form *ašuštu*. For the verb *ašāšu* (logogram ZI.IR.(MEŠ)), see Sa-gig 3: 73 (TDPT 3: 64); Sa-gig 3: 76; 13: 62–63, 65, 77 (TDPT 13 ii 4–5, 7, 19); Sa-gig 15: 36′, 43′; 17: 12, 29; [18: 9]; 19/20: 51′, [55′]; 22: 68; 36: 105 (TDPT 35: 105); Sa-gig 37: 24 (TDPT 36: 24); *BAM* 145: 7; [146: 32′, 44′]; 174 obv. 25′; 216: 56′; 231 i 9; [574 ii 29]; 575 iii 16; *AMT* 48/3: 6′. For the noun *ašuštu* (logogram (NÍG).ZI.IR), see Sa-gig 7 B rev. 8 (TDPT 7: 64′); Sa-gig 22: 8, 35; 26: 17′; 27: 29; *BAM* 174 obv. 25′; 231 i 2; 584 ii 23′; *AMT* 45/6 rev. 7′; 48/3: 6′. Note also the possible restoration NÍG.ZI.⸢IR⸣ (?) (obv. 10) and NÍG.ZI.[IR(?)] (obv. 11) in this commentary tablet.

Rev. 10—The logographic form U_4.DUG_4.GA occurs only at Sa-gig 7 B rev. 8–9, 14 (TDPT 7: 64′–65′, 70′). The syllabic form *adannu* appears at Sa-gig 17: 97; 33: 11; *AMT* 74/1 ii 25′; *STT* 89: 117; *KAR* 202 iii 7 (*CAD* A I, 101 s.v. *adannu* §2′).

Rev. 10–11—The base text is unfortunately not preserved, but the syllabic form of the cited topic *ḫa-a-a-át-*[*tu*] ("fright") is unusual in the Diagnostic Handbook, where this word is typically written with the logogram (IGI). LAL: Sa-gig 3: 45 (TDPT [3: 36]; collated in Scurlock and Andersen 2005: 484, §19.227; 756 n. 171); Sa-gig 13: 136 (TDPT 13 iii 25); Sa-gig 16: 14, 82′; 17: 34–35; 18: 3; 26: 15′–16′. By contrast, the syllabic form is the norm in therapeutic texts, where it occurs in *BAM* 174 rev. 30; 183: 33; 323: 66; 338 rev. 8′; 344: 2; 367: 16; 376 ii 26′; [385 i 23′]; 469 rev. 35; 471 ii 26′. Note, however, the exception LAL-*ti ṣe-ti* in *BAM* 177: 12. The noun *gilittu* ("jitters") also seems more typical of therapeutic texts than the Diagnostic Handbook, appearing in *BAM* 344: 13, 15–16; 379 iii 12; 423 i 34′. While both Comm. Sa-gig 7A and Comm. Sa-gig 7B are attributed to Anu-ikṣur, notice that the same topic *ḫayyattu* was explained as *gilittu* ("jitters") in the former, but as *puluḫtu* ("fear") in the latter.

Rev. 11–13—Though the base text for this commentary entry is damaged, it probably belongs to the section Sa-gig 7 A rev. 12′–17′ (TDPT 7: 87′–92′) whose diagnostic entries each begin with the expression DIŠ *ri-gim* GIG *taš-me-ma* ("If you listen to the sick man's voice, …"). In this same section is part of a diagnostic entry cited in Comm. Sa-gig 7B, rev. 6′: "like the voice of a ghost." The extended A:B:C argument (§1.2.3.2.3) in rev. 11–13 seems to include the following steps of logic: $p \leftrightarrow q$, $q \leftrightarrow r$, therefore $r \leftrightarrow p$. As I discuss also in §1.1.4.2 and §1.2.3.2, this argument supplies a striking illustration of how logical relationships such as A:B in commentaries do not express unidirectional predication, whereby one element (A) is interpreted as the *subject* about which some identity or quality (B) is *predicated*. Instead, we may visualize the A:B relationship as a Venn diagram depicting a significant degree of overlap between elements A and B, regardless of the sequence in which they appear. Here, the premises that *p* ("death") ↔ *q* ("*Anzû*-bird") and *q* ("*Anzû*-bird") ↔ *r* ("donkey") lead to the conclusion that *r* ("donkey") ↔ *p* ("death"), hence validating the diagnosis that a patient who sounds like a donkey will die. It is not entirely clear whether rev. 12 refers to the "death" of the *Anzû*-bird when slayed by the god Ninurta in the *Myth of Anzû*, or to the "deadliness" of the *Anzû*-bird itself. The logogram for "donkey" is typically given the value ANŠE, but the writing *an-šu-ú* with a long final vowel could indicate the sign name anšu (𒀲). See also [an-šu] [ANŠE] = ⸢*i*⸣-*mi-ru* = (Hitt.) ANŠE-aš in the lexical text Sª Voc. L, 14′ (*MSL* III, 64; cf. *CAD* I/J, 110). The donkey and equids in general are also associated with the *Anzû*-bird elsewhere. Note the relief of the *Anzu*-bird and two stags from the temple of Ninhursag at Tell al-Ubaid (British Museum, W.A.1144308). In the narrative of *Lugalbanda and the Anzû-bird*, equids appear as prey to the bird (Vanstiphout 2003: 138–139, lines 63–66). For discussion on the *Anzû*-bird in the form of a horse, see Weidner (1959/1960: 108); Livingstone (1986: 147). Finally, note the connection between the *surinnakku*-bat with the *Anzû*-bird in these lexical equations: su-din-mìn mušen = *še-u-ri-in-nak-ku* = [*pa-an*] *an-zi-i* (Hg. B IV, 258 in Vedeler 2002: 75; cf. *MSL* VIII/2, 168); su-din-mìn mušen = *su-ri-nak-ku* = *pa-an an-ze-e* (Hg. D III, 330 in Vedeler 2002: 95; cf. *MSL* VIII/2, 176). The use of the notation *pān* ("complement to"; see §11.2.5) here suggests that the *surinnakku*-bat is not precisely identified as the *Anzû*-bird, but only in some way comparable to the *Anzû*-bird.

Rev. 14—I translate the signs *ṣa u* MIN as "*ṣa*- et cetera" (lit. "*ṣa*- and *ditto*"). The notation MIN ("*ditto*") signals the repetition of a previous word, phrase, or sentence, which is usually located in the same tablet on the line or section immediately preceding, and which typically occurs in a text of similar formal structure. In rev. 14, however, because context demands the stereotypical and predictable expression *ṣâtu u šūt pî* ("Glossary including oral lore"), the anaphoric properties of MIN applied, not to an expression previously mentioned in the tablet, but to an expression anticipated due to precedents in tablet format. Alternatively, note the suggestion by Frahm (2011a: 53) that "the writing min for *šūt pî* might be based on the well attested rendering of *ša*/*kīma iqbû* 'what/as it/he says' with *šá*/gim min."

Rev. 15—The writing *mál-sut*$_x$(BÁN) ("Readings (of Anu-ikṣur ...)") is a play on the fact that logogram BÁN expresses *sūtu*, a unit of measurement (*CAD* S, 420–426 s.v. *sūtu* A).

Commentary Sa-gig 7B

Provenance:	Uruk (Warka), Area U18, Level v; Library of Anu-ikṣur
Period:	Late Achaemenid
Names:	"Readings of Anu-ikṣur, son of Šamaš-iddin, descendant of Šangû-Ninurta"
Script:	Neo-/Late Babylonian
Typology:	*ṣâtu* 6b in Frahm (2011a: 53)

Field/Museum No.:	W 22307/10 (National Museum of Iraq)
Photo:	Plate 17 (reverse)
Printed Edition/Hand Copy:	*SpTU* 1, 33 (= Hunger 1976: 41–42); Wee (2012: 611–615)
Digital Resources:	CDLI P348454; GKAB P348454 (edition digitized by Clancier 2009); CCP 4.1.7.A (printed hand copy digitized by Frahm, Frazer, and Jiménez 2013)
Discussion:	*SpTU* 1, 33 (= Hunger 1976: 41–42); Farber (1987b: 37 n. 43) and (1989a: 239); Heeßel (2000: 133, 142 (7. Tafel MS b)); Kouwenberg (2005: 91 n. 34); Clancier (2009: 50, 52, 55, 71, 227, 265, 388); Berlejung (2009: 77 n. 29); Genty (2010a: 376) and (2010b: 13, 21, 23, 24, 30); Abusch and Schwemer (2011: 359 nn. 8–9); Frahm (2011a: 53 n. 231, 66, 225, 291, 337 n. 1606); Wee (2012: 611–615) and (2015a: 262–263); Scurlock (2014: 63 n. 50; 66 n. 1); Gabbay (2016: 74 n. 323); Jiménez (2016b: 228 n. 2)
Pericope:	Indeterminate due to damaged state of available Sa-gig manuscripts

Transliteration

Reverse

1′) [...]x : *ku-ṣu* : *ḫa-a-a-át-t*[*ú*] : *pu-luḫ-ti*

2′) [ŠÀ-*šú ana*] BURU$_8$ *i-ta-na-áš-šá-a* : *lìb-ba-šú a-na pa-re-e*

3′) [*i-ša*]*q-qa-a* : *ig-da-nar-ru-ur* : *i-gàr-ru-ur*

 | DOI:10.1163/9789004417564_015

4′) *šá-ni-iš i-šá-as-si* : *i-za-mur* : *i-za-am-mu-ur*
5′) DÚR-*šú ḫa-niq* : *šu-uḫ-ḫa-šú ḫa-di-iq*
6′) GIM GÙ GIDIM : *ki-ma ri-gim e-ṭém-mu*

7′) DIŠ GIG GEŠTUG 15-*šú tar-kát* GIG-*su* DUGUD-*it*
8′) *ṣa-a-tú ù šu-ut* KA *šá* KA UM.ME.[A]
9′) *šá* DIŠ GIG EME-*šú* SA$_5$-*át mál-su-ut* $^{m.d}$*A-nu-ik-*⸢*ṣur*⸣
10′) DUMU *šá* $^{m.d}$UTU-SUM.NA ŠÀ.BAL.BAL ^{lú_2}É.MAŠ-^{d}*Nin-urta*
11′) ^{lú_2}MAŠ.MAŠ BÀN.DA LÚ *qaq-qar-*^{d}*A-nu*^{ki}*-u*
12′) *pa-liḫ* ^{d}*A-nu ù An-tu*$_4$ *là i*$_{11}$*-ta-áb-bà-alla*

Translation

***Sa-gig 7**

(Rev. 1′) … *means* coldness.

***Sa-gig 7**
The syllabic writing *hayyattu* "fright" is typical of therapeutic texts, while its logogram (IGI).LAL is more commonly used in the Diagnostic Handbook.

(1′) "*ḫayyattu*" *means* fear.

***Sa-gig 7**
The writing *i-ta-na-šá-a* "(his belly) keeps rising" derives from the verb *našû* "to rise," not *âšu* "to retch" despite the context of "vomiting." Also, though the verb *našû* is usually transitive ("to raise"), it should be understood with an intransitive meaning ("to rise" = "to ascend") here.

(2′–3′) "[His belly] *i-ta-na-áš-šá-a* [to] vomit" *means* his belly ascends to vomit.

***Sa-gig 7**
The base text may read ŠÀ-*šú igdanarrur* "his belly keeps writhing." This comment clarifies that a writhing belly is detected by the "noise" it makes.

(3′) "*igdanarrur*" *means* it writhes.

(4′) Secondly, it makes noise.

***Sa-gig 7**
The syllable signs are to be read as *i-za-mur* "he sings," and not as *i-sà-ḫur* "it turns around," which is a common verb in medical descriptions.

(4′) "*i-za-mur*" *means* he sings.

***Sa-gig 7**
The "constricted rectum," which appears in therapeutic texts, may be explained more precisely as a "squeezed (anal) sphincter."

(5′) "His rectum is constricted" *means* his (anal) sphincter is squeezed.

***Sa-gig 7**

(6′) "GIM GÙ GIDIM" *means* like the voice of a ghost.

(Colophon)

Incipit-title of Sa-gig 8

(7′) "If the sick man's right ear is dark, his sickness is severe."

Incipit-title of Sa-gig 7

(8′–9′) Glossary including oral lore from the mouth of the *ummânu*-scholar on "If the sick man's tongue is red."

(9′–11′) Readings of Anu-ikṣur, son of Šamaš-iddin, descendant of Šangû-Ninurta, junior magician, man of the Territory of the god Anu (i.e., Uruk).

(12′) He who fears Anu and Antu must not carry off (this tablet).

Notes

Rev. 1′—One possible restoration is [*ḫur-ba-š*]*ú* : *ku-ṣu*, which mirrors a similar argument at Comm. Sa-gig 19, obv. 19: [SE]D : *ku-uṣ* : SED *ḫur-ba-šú*. Other possibilities for the damaged portion include [SE]D and [EN.TE.N]A, but sign traces at the edge of the damage resemble [-*š*]*ú* more than [SE]D or [.N]A. The order *ḫurbāšu* : *kuṣṣu*, however, implies that *ḫurbāšu* is the topic quoted from the base text, and *kuṣṣu* is its comment. This is surprising, because *ḫurbāšu* appears more frequently in medical texts than *kuṣṣu*. For syllabic writings of *ḫurbāšu*, see Sa-gig 16: 65′; 17: 77; *BAM* 66 rev. 10′; 232 i 13′; [314 obv. 4′]; 315 iii 39; 338 rev. 7′; 438 obv. 10; 445: 14 (incl. *AMT* 64/2: 14′); *AMT* [14/7: 7]; 27/3 obv. 2. For syllabic writings of *kuṣṣu*, see Sa-gig 19: 53′, 103′; 22: 72; 26: 43′; *BAM* 66 rev. 10′; *AMT* 14/7: 7. For the logogram SED as a noun instead of a verb, see Sa-gig 10 B rev. 5; 13: 55 (TDPT 13 i 56′); Sa-gig 17: 7. More logical is the order in Comm. Sa-gig 19 (obv. 19), where the unusual noun form SED is first translated into Akkadian as *kuṣṣu*, then explained by the synonym *ḫurbāšu* more common in medical texts.

Rev. 1′—The signs *ḫa-a-a-át-t*[*ú*] were evidently cited from the base text, but the exact form of the base text is uncertain. This syllabic writing is unusual in the Diagnostic Handbook, where the word *ḫayyattu* typically appears as the logogram (IGI).LAL: Sa-gig 3: 45 (TDPT [3: 36]; collated in Scurlock and Andersen 2005: 484, §19.227; 756 n. 171); Sa-gig 13: 136 (TDPT 13 iii 25); Sa-gig 16: 14, 82′; 17: 34–35; 18: 3; 26: 15′–16′. By contrast, the syllabic form is the norm in therapeutic texts, where it occurs in *BAM* 174 rev. 30; 183: 33; 323: 66; 338 rev. 8′; 344: 2; 367: 16; 376 ii 26′; [385 i 23′]; 469 rev. 35; 471 ii 26′. But note the exception LAL-*ti ṣe-ti* in *BAM* 177: 12. The term *puluḫti* ("fear") occurs commonly in non-medical contexts, but is not typically used in medical descriptions (*CAD* P, 505–509). Medical entries with *pu-luḫ-tú* (*BAM* 316 iii 13′; *STT* 95 iv 145) may appear elsewhere as the variant [*p*]*i-rit-tú* (compare *BAM* 317 rev. 16 with *BAM* 317 rev. 25; the word is unfortunately not preserved in *BAM* [447: 4′]). The term *pirittu*, in fact, appears as a legitimate diagnostic verdict in Sa-gig 16: 80′. While both Comm. Sa-gig 7A and Comm. Sa-gig 7B are attributed to Anu-ikṣur, notice that the same topic *ḫayyattu* was explained as *gilittu* ("jitters") in the former, but as *puluḫtu* ("fear") in the latter.

Rev. 2′–3′—The signs *i-ta-na-áš-šá-a* constitute the Gtn Durative of the verb *našû* (intransitive), "to heave, rise." One is tempted to restore the comment [*iš-ta-na*]*q-qa-a* (rev. 3′) as a Gtn verb commensurable with *i-ta-na-áš-šá-a* (rev. 2′) of the topic, but cuneiform traces on the tablet favor the reading [*i-ša*]*q-qa-a* (rev. 3′). See Note on Comm. Sa-gig 7A, rev. 5–6 for discussion on features shared by the two commentary entries (i.e., Comm. Sa-gig 7A, rev. 5–6 and Comm. Sa-gig 7B, rev. 2′–3′), as well as the commentator Anu-ikṣur's motivations for providing explanations in both cases.

Rev. 3′–4′—It is tempting to interpret *i-za-mur* ("it sings") as a comment to *i-šá-as-si* ("it makes noise"), as understood by Hunger (*SpTU* 1, 33) in his remarks on this text; cf. Genty (2010b: 30); *CAD* Š 11, 149. Two points, however, argue against such an interpretation. First, the item that immediately follows the expression *šanîš* ("secondly")—i.e., *i-šá-as-si* (rev. 4′)—usually functions as an alternative explanation to a previous topic, and not a new topic in itself. See Comm. Sa-gig 1A, obv. 10–12, 14, 18, 20; rev. 29–30, 36, 41, 45, 47; Comm. Sa-gig 1B, obv. 12′, 16′, 21′; rev. 9, 11, 15, 21, [23, 26, 28]; Comm. Sa-gig 1C, rev. 1′, [11′]; Comm. Sa-gig 1D, rev. 3′, [5′], 10′; Comm. Sa-gig 4B, obv. 6, 12; Comm. Sa-gig 10 & 11, obv. 1; Comm. Sa-gig 21 & 22a, obv. 2, 18; rev. 16′; Comm. Sa-gig 39, obv. 4; and Comm. Sa-gig 40A, obv. [4]; but note the exceptions in Comm. Sa-gig 1B, obv. 16′–17′ and Comm. Sa-gig 4C, rev. 10′, where "secondly" (*šanîš*) indicates the incorporation of a second base text topic into the existing argument. Moreover, it makes better sense to understand *i-za-mur* as a quotation from the base text whose reading the commentator clarified as *i-za-am-mu-ur*, rather than to view *i-za-mur* as the commentator's own contribution. Although the base text for rev. 3′–4′ is not preserved, it probably resembles the statement ŠÀ-*šú igdanarrur* ("his belly keeps writhing") in the therapeutic texts *BAM* 145: 9; 146: 33′. Elsewhere in the Diagnostic Handbook, this verb does not occur in the Gtn form *igdanarrur*, but only in the Ntn form *ittanagrar* (Sa-gig 4: 65, 67; 15: 42′; 26: 29′). The comment here clarifies that a writhing belly is detected by the "noise" it makes.

Rev. 4′—The verb *zamāru* ("to sing") does not usually occur in medical texts, and, in the absence of a preserved base text, it is difficult to imagine the context in which "singing" happens. A less likely alternative would be to read the signs here as *i-ṣa-mur* from the verb *ṣemēru* (= *ṣamāru*), which describes the distension and swollenness of body parts, since this verb is only attested in Stative forms elsewhere (*CAD* Ṣ, 126–127). The ambiguous reading of the signs *i-za-mur*, as well as the atypical occurrences of *zamāru* in medical texts, may have prompted the commentator to clarify the sign values as *i-za-am-mu-ur*. In any case, this comment eliminates the possibility of the reading *i-sà-ḫur*, which derives from a common verb in medical descriptions: *saḫāru* ("to turn around").

Rev. 5′—The "constricted rectum" is attested mainly in therapeutic texts *BAM* 95: 14 (= *BAM* VII/21); *BAM* 114: 10 (= *BAM* VII/5); *AMT* 22/2 obv. 7 (= *BAM* VII/50); *AMT* 40/5 iii [9′], 16′ (= *BAM* VII/23); *AMT* 56/1 obv. 3 (= *BAM* VII/32). Also, Geller's restoration of *n*[*ik*]⟨*-kim*⟩*-ti* DÚR GIG for *BAM* 95: 23 (= *BAM* VII/21) could be read instead as [*ḫi*]*-n*[*iq*]*-ti* DÚR GIG. Apart from the damaged base text here, the only attestation of a "constricted rectum" in the Diagnostic Handbook may be DÚR-*šú ḫa-niq* at Sa-gig 40: 95. The signs here were read as *ḫa di ik* by Hunger (*SpTU* I, 33) and as *ḫa-di-iq* in *CAD* Š III, 206 s.v. *šuḫḫu* A; even though no Akkadian verb *ḫadāku* or *ḫadāqu* is attested elsewhere. The *CDA* has an entry on *ḫadāqu*, which seems derived solely from this commentary: "*ḫadāqu* 'to press together' jB G comm., stat. of part of body; < Aram." The Aramaic cognate of the root *hdq* has the meanings "to plug, fit snugly, make tight" (D); "(knot) to become tight" (Dt) in DJBA, 363a; "to squeeze" (D) in Jastrow Dict. 334, which certainly correspond well to the Akkadian verb *ḫaniq* "is constricted" (< *ḫanāqu* "to constrict") here. In a ritual text, the same root *ḫadāqu* describes how "a bronze ring and another wooden item are used to constrict the [ritual] figurines' waist" (Abusch and Schwemer 2011: 359 nn. 8–9). In this commentary, we may have a case where the commentator explained an Akkadian medical description by means of a later expression or idiom influenced by Aramaic. See Frahm (2011a: 337 n. 1606). The usual Akkadian translation for the logogram DÚR is *šuburru* ("rectum"), but the term *šuḫḫu* can also mean "buttocks," "(a part of the intestine)," or "(a stand or base)." See *CAD* Š III, 206–207 s.v. *šuḫḫu* A; Geller (2004: 1); discussion in Couto-Ferreira (2009: 236–237, 270). Here, I translate *šuḫḫu* as "(anal) sphincter" (i.e., bottom part of rectum); cf. Genty (2010b: 24). Note also the possible restoration ⸢*šu-uḫ*(?)-*ḫi*⸣ -*at*-⸢*ti* ŠÀ⸣-*šú* ("*šuḫḫiātti* of his belly") at *BAM* VII/49 i 28′, which I understand to be the base text for Comm. Sa-gig 14, obv. 15: *šu-ḫa-at-ti er-ru-šú* : *šu-uḫ-ḫi-iṭ-ṭa-a-ti* ("'*šuḫḫâtti* of his bowels' *refers to šuḫḫiṭṭāti*"). It is possible that *šuḫḫâtti* (< *šuḫḫiātti*) and *šuḫḫiṭṭāti* are terms etymologically related to *šuḫḫu*.

Rev. 6′—The syllable signs here are *e-ṭém*(gim)-*mu*, not *e-ṭem*(dim)-*mu* (rev. 6′) as rendered by the typo in the printed edition *SpTU* I, 33. Though the base text for this commentary entry is damaged, it probably belongs to the section Sa-gig 7 A rev. 12′–17′ (TDPT 7: 87′–92′) whose diagnostic entries each begin with the expression DIŠ *ri-gim* GIG *taš-me-ma* ("If you listen to the sick man's voice, …"). In fact, one of these entries is cited in Comm. Sa-gig 7A, rev. 11–12: "If you listen to the sick man's voice, and [it sounds] like the voice of a donkey…, he will die [on] the first day." The base text for the commentary entry here (rev. 6′), therefore, may be something along the lines of *"If you listen to the sick man's voice, and it sounds like the voice of a ghost, …"

Rev. 9′—The syllable signs here are *mál*(dir)-*su-ut*, not *mal*(gá)-*su-ut* (rev. 9′) as rendered by the typo in the printed edition *SpTU* I, 33.

Rev. 10′—The signs here are ^{lú_2}É.MAŠ-^{d}*Nin-urta*, not ^{lú_2}SANGA-^{d}*Nin-urta* (rev. 10′) as rendered by the typo in the printed edition *SpTU* I, 33.

Rev. 11′—Note the parallel expressions LÚ *qaq-qar-*^{d}*A-nu*^{ki}*-ú* in *SpTU* I, 45 rev. 25 and LÚ KI.60^{ki}-*u* in *SpTU* I, 48 rev. 9′. For *qaqqar Anu* as a reference to Uruk, see the lexical equation *qaq-qa-ra* AN = MIN (= *Uruk*) in Malku I, 218 (Hrůša 2010: 317); cf. *qaq-qa-ra* AN ki = ŠU (Hh. XXI, Section 3, 20a in *MSL* XI, 13); *CAD* Q, 113, 117 s.v. *qaqqaru* A §3c. See also Berlejung (2009: 77 n. 29).

Rev. 12′—One wonders whether the atypical writing i_{11}*-ta-áb-bà*(30)*-alla* alludes to a well known trope in medical incantations on the "cow" (ÁB) of the "moon-god Sîn" (^{d}30). See Lambert (1969: 33–35).

Commentary Sa-gig 7Ca

Provenance:	Same consignment (81-11-3) as Comm. Sa-gig 7Cb and 7Cc
Period:	?
Names:	Colophon not preserved
Script:	Neo-/Late Babylonian
Field/Museum No.:	BM 48727 + 48741 = 81-11-3,1438 + 81-11-3,1452 ("Babylon Collection" at British Museum)
Digital Resources:	CDLI P461244; CCP 4.1.7.C.a (photos and edition digitized by Jiménez 2016, with contributions by Finkel and Heeßel)
Discussion:	Jiménez and Schmidtchen (2017: 238 n. 43)
Pericope:	At least Sa-gig 7 A obv. 1–16 (TDPT 7: 1–16)

Transliteration

Obverse

1′) [DIŠ GIG EME]-⸢*šú* SA$_5$⸣-*át* TIN : [...]

2′) ⸢EME⸣-*šú* ⸢*e-bi*⸣ : *e-bu-ú* : EM[E-*š*]*ú* ⸢*ir-te*⸣-[*ṭi* ...]

3′) *ana* UGU *ba-ta-qu* : *ir-te-né-*⸢*et*⸣*-ti* : ⸢*it*⸣-[*ta-na-az-qap* (?) : DÙ : *re-tu-ú*]

4′) DÙ : *za-qap* : NA.BI AMA-*šú i-nik* : GÌ[Š : *ni-a-ku* : GÌŠ : *na-qa-bu* (?)]

5′) ⸢x⸣ ti iš gàr ⸢x ni (?)⸣ : *uš-te-*⸢*eḫ*⸣*-ḫ*[*u* ... *lìb-bu-ú*]

6′) [*ana* A]MA-*šú* TE-*ḫi* : EME : ^{d}*Uraš* : ^{d}*Uraš* : ⸢*ḫa*⸣-*a*[*r-bu* (?) ...]

7′) *na-gu-ú* : *ḫa-du-ú* : *tas-lim-ti* : *ta-*[*as-li-im-ti* : ...]

8′) [K]A.⸤É.GAL⸥ : *šil-la-tu$_4$* : DIŠ EME-*šú* ⸢*ú-na*⸣-[*aš-šak* ...]

9′) [...] a x[...] ⸢...⸣ [...]

Translation

Incipit-title of Sa-gig 7

(Obv. 1′) "[If the sick man]'s [tongue] is red, he will become healthy." ...

***Sa-gig 7**

The description of body parts or urine as *ebû* "thick" is uncommon both in the Diagnostic Handbook and therapeutic texts.

(2′) "His tongue is *ebi*" *derives from the dictionary root* to become thick.

 | DOI:10.1163/9789004417564_016

Sa-gig 7 A obv. 7 (TDPT 7: 7)—
"EME-*šú* *ir-te-ṭ*[*i*]"
The tongue is described as "fixed in place" only here in the medical texts. The immobility of the patient's tongue may be said to be the cause of his stammering or stuttering.

(2′–3′) "He has fixed in place his tongue" ... concerns the breaking up (of speech?)

Perhaps alluding to how eyes "fixed in place" are explained as "protruding" eyes, the commentator described how the patient's inability to properly move his tongue resulted in the tongue repeatedly protruding out from the mouth.

(3′) He keeps fixing in place (his tongue) *means* [it keeps protruding out (?)].

(3′) [DÙ *means* to fix in place.]
(4′) DÙ *means* to protrude.

***Sa-gig 7**

(4′) "That man fornicated with his mother."

These lexical relationships are restored from *MSL* 11, 144 ii 13–14 (Proto-Ea).

(4′) GÌŠ [*means* to fornicate].
(4′) [GÌŠ *means* to penetrate sexually (?)].

(5′) ... they are engaged in illicit sex ...

For illicit sexual relations, this is a more idiomatic expression than the topic "He fornicated with his mother."

(5′–6′) [As in], "he approached his mother (for sex)."

***Sa-gig 7**
The unpreserved base text probably identified a deity of agriculture, "Uraš," as the agent responsible for the "tongue" ailment. The commentator here may be attempting to demonstrate the connection between "tongue" and "Uraš."

(6′) "Tongue" *refers to* "the deity Uraš."
(6′) The deity Uraš *refers to* the [(tongued)-plow ... (?)]

***Sa-gig 7**
The quoted topic (not preserved here) involves an inflected form of *nagû* "to sing joyously," a description that appears only here in medical texts.

(6′–7′) "…"
(7′) To sing joyously *means* to rejoice.

***Sa-gig 7**
The syllable signs *tas-lim-ti* are to be read as *taslimti* "insult."

(7′) "*tas-lim-ti*" *means* [insult …].
(8′) KA.É.GAL *means* blasphemy.

Sa-gig 7 A obv. 16 (TDPT 7: 16)

(8′) "He keeps biting on his tongue." …

(9′) …

Notes

Obv. 1′—The form of the incipit-title of Sa-gig 7 restored here is fully preserved at Comm. Sa-gig 7A, rev. 14; Comm. Sa-gig 7B, rev. 9′.

Obv. 2′—The base text here is not preserved among existing Sa-gig manuscripts, but probably corresponds to an entry in Sa-gig 7 A obv. 2–4 (TDPT 7: 2–4). The verb *ebû* ("to become thick") is uncommon in medical texts and describes a baby's "belly" (Sa-gig 40: 1) and the patient's "urine" (*BAM* 114: 7; *AMT* 58/4: 3′; and possibly […]x GÌŠ-*šú ib-bi* in *AMT* 39/9: 6′).

Obv. 2′–4′—Given how the expression (DIŠ) EME-*šú* ("his tongue") seems to be quoted where appropriate for each new commentary entry at obv. 2′ (×2) and 8′, I am not inclined to view *ir-te-né-*⸢*et*⸣*-ti* (obv. 3′) as the beginning of a new entry devoted to the discussion of the verb *retû*/*reṭû* ("to fix in place") (obv. 3′–4′). Instead, the true beginning of this entry is probably in obv. 2′: EM[E-*š*]*ú* ⸢*ir-te*⸣-[*ṭi* …] ("He has fixed in place his tongue"), whose base text Sa-gig 7 A obv. 7 (TDPT 7: 7) has been misunderstood as EME-*šú ir-te-d*[*i*] ("he sticks out (?) his tongue") by Scurlock (2014: 57, 60). Accordingly, the verb *batāqu* ("to break up") may refer to the breaking up of speech in some kind of a stammer or stutter. The verb *retû*/*reṭû* is not particularly common as a bodily description in medical texts, being applied to the tongue only here and more frequently to the eyes (Sa-gig 4: 109 (TDPT 4 rev. 23); *AMT* [35/6: 6′]; [76/5: 11′–12′]; 79/4: 2′; *SpTU* 1, 46: 17(!)). Similar lexical arguments connecting *retû*/*reṭû* with *zaqāpu* ("to erect, protrude (of eyes)") occur in Comm. Sa-gig 21 & 22a, obv. 9; Comm. Sa-gig 4C, rev. 10′; as well as the *Šumma izbu* commentary *SpTU* 1, 72 rev. 1. Although the body part "fixed in place" (*retû*/*reṭû*) in this commentary is the tongue, one cannot help but suspect that the choice of *zaqāpu* as an explanation was influenced by both verbs' affinity with the eyes, since *zaqāpu* is not otherwise known to designate the tongue (*CAD* Z, 53 s.v. *zaqāpu* A §1e2′).

Obv. 4′–6′—The mention of the patient's "mother" (AMA) in obv. 4′ and 6′ suggests that these lines encompass a single commentary entry. The cited topic "That man fornicated with his mother" comes from an incompletely preserved base text entry, which is similar to the diagnosis NIN.DINGIR DINGIR-*šú iš-šiq* ("he kissed the *ēntu*-priestess of his god"; Sa-gig 7 A obv. 20 (TDPT 7: 20)) in a nearby medical entry. The suggested emendation to a prognosis ⟨*ana*⟩ AMA-*šú i-*⟨*sa*⟩*-niq* ("he approaches his mother") by Finkel (CCP 4.1.7.C.a) is unpersuasive, and contrary to many similar statements in the Diagnostic Handbook that identify as their diagnostic verdict the culpability of the patient (cf. Figure 9 in §1.3.1.2.1) in engaging with various illicit heterosexual relations (see Note on Comm. Sa-gig 4A, obv. 14–15). Apart from the base text here, such taboos involving the patient's "mother" are mentioned only at Sa-gig 6: 88″ (TDPT 6 rev. 25′), unless one were to agree with Scurlock and Andersen (2005: 745 n. 29) that prohibited relations with a so-called "*ēntu*-priestess of his god" (Sa-gig 7 A obv. 20 (TDPT 7: 20); Sa-gig 13: 23 (TDPT 13 i 24′); Sa-gig 14: 134, 137–139 (TDPT 14 ii 62, 65–67)) should also be interpreted as references to the patient's mother. In addition to the base text here, the verb *niāku* ("to fornicate") occurs in Sa-gig 13: 37 (TDPT 13 i 38′): DAM LÚ *it-ta-na-a-a-ak* ("he keeps engaging in fornication with (another) man's wife"). My restoration GÌ[Š : *ni-a-ku* : GÌŠ : *na-qa-bu* (?)] (obv. 4′) is based on the lexical entries ^{giš} GÌŠ = *ne-a-kum, na-qá-bu-um* (*MSL* II, 144 ii 13–14 (Proto-Ea); with corrections in *MSL* III, 223). At the beginning of obv. 5′, Jiménez (CCP 4.1.7.C.a) suggested the reading ⌜*it*(?)⌝*-ti iš-tik-ku-ni* for *ištikkūni* < *irtikkūni*, an otherwise unattested Gtn form of *râku* ("to pour out"). Instead of *uš-te-*⌜*pu-ú*⌝ (obv. 5′) by Finkel (CCP 4.1.7.C.a), I read *uš-te-*⌜*eḫ*⌝*-ḫ*[*u*] ("they are engaged in illicit sex"), though other attestations of this Dt stem of *šuḫḫû* A (*CAD* Š, 207) admittedly appear with /a/ instead of /e/ vowels. This last verb is associated with *niāku* as well as *reḫû* in an astronomical omen commentary: *uš-taḫ-ḫa-a* : *aš-šum re-ḫu-ú* / *na-a-ku*, "*uštaḫḫâ*, on account of pouring out (i.e., semen), (*or*) fornicating" (*TCL* VI, 17 = AO 6464, rev. 32). In short, the commentator reworded the topic ("He fornicated with his mother") into an expression more idiomatic in the Diagnostic Handbook, i.e., "He approached his mother (for sex)." In Comm. Sa-gig 1B, rev. 9; Comm. Sa-gig 1C, rev. 2′, the topic "Hand of (another) man's wife" (Sa-gig U1: 25 (S1: 23)) is reformulated as a similar idiom: "He approached (another) man's wife (for sex)" (cf. Sa-gig 17: 32). It is easy to see the connection between such diagnoses and this Sa-gig section concerning ailments of the "tongue," since illicit kissing and other oral sexual acts were thought to be responsible for the patient's suffering.

Obv. 6′—The base text entry here is not preserved, but presumably discusses an ailment of the "tongue" in its protasis, and identifies "the deity Uraš" (cf. Krebernik 2015: 401–406) as the agent responsible for the sickness in the apodosis. The commentator endeavored to demonstrate this connection between "tongue" and "Uraš," but the argument is broken and cannot be confidently restored. I tentatively suggest the commentator had in view the relationship between Uraš and agriculture, as exemplified by the description ^{d}Uraš = ^{d}MAŠ *ša alli* ("Uraš = the god Ninurta as pertaining to the hoe") in the god list An = *Anu ša amēli* 71 (Litke 1998: 233), as well as the association between ^{d}Ninurta, ^{d}Uraš, and ^{d}"ENGAR in An = *Anum* I, 227–229 (Litke 1998: 47). My restoration ^{d}*Uraš* : ⸢*ḫa*⸣-*a*[*r-bu* (?) ...] ("The deity Uraš *refers to* the [(tongued)-plow ... (?)]") is reminiscent of lexical equations such as eme-apin-šu-«uš»-kin = EME *ḫarbi* ("tongue of plow"), eme-apin = *lišānu* ("tongue") in Gantzert (2011: I 109 and II 61, nos. 4111–4112); ^{giš}eme-apin = *emû* ("plowshare"), *lišānu* ("tongue") in Hh. V, 137–138 (*MSL* VI, 17); and ^{giš}eme-apin = *lišānu ša marri* ("tongue of shovel") in Hh. VII B, 30 (*MSL* VI, 117); where the anatomical feature "tongue" is used metaphorically for the blade of an agricultural implement. If this interpretation is correct, Uraš's affinity with such implements explains the deity's involvement in ailments of the human tongue.

Obv. 6′–7′—The Infinitive verb forms *na-gu-ú* : *ḫa-du-ú* ("To sing joyously *means* to rejoice"; obv. 7′) represent dictionary roots that are a part of the commentator's explanation. The topic cited from the base text, which presumably contains an inflected form of *nagû* (possibly as an action by the tongue), is not preserved in the damaged end of obv. 6′. This verb *nagû* ("to sing joyously") appears only here in medical texts.

Obv. 7′–8′—The base text is not preserved, but probably involves behavior by the patient (or his tongue) in sprouting "insults" (*taslimtu*), similar to the description at Sa-gig 19/20: 42′. The commentator was concerned to clarify the reading of the syllable signs *tas-lim-ti*. The term *taslimtu* ("insult") is expressed by the logogram KA.É.GAL also in the lexical texts Sag Bil. B 280 (*CAD* T, 282); Erimhuš Bogh. A, iv 20 (*da-aš-li-im-du* in *MSL* XVII, 114); OB Lu, A line 123 (*ta-aš-ši-tim* in *MSL* XII, 161). The equation KA.É.GAL = *šillatu* ("KA.É.GAL *means* blasphemy"; obv. 8′) appears in the lexical lists Erimhuš I, 282 (*MSL* XVII, 20); Igituh I, 203 (*CAD* Š II, 445); as well as in a commentary to *Šumma ālu* XXV (Funck 2 rev. 8 in *AfO* 21, pl. X) privately owned by Pastor Adolphe Funck, Roubaix (present whereabouts unknown).

See Weidner (1966: 46); Frahm (2011a: 197 n. 927). The logographic form KA.É.GAL (interpreted as INIM.É.GAL in *CAD* Š II, 445–447; *CAD* T, 282–283) may be etymologized as "word/speech of the palace," which could be some kind of a euphemism. See Note on Comm. Sa-gig 19, obv. 15–16 where the plural form *taslimāti* ("insults") is analyzed positively as *taslimā* ("you made peace") + TI ("(you) will become healthy").

Commentary Sa-gig 7Cb

Provenance: Same consignment (81-11-3) as Comm. Sa-gig 7Ca and 7Cc
Period: ?
Names: Colophon not preserved
Script: Neo-/Late Babylonian

Field/Museum No.: BM 48729 = 81-11-3,1440 ("Babylon Collection" at British Museum)
Digital Resources: CDLI P481113; CCP 4.1.7.C.b (photos and edition digitized by Jiménez 2015, with contributions by Finkel and Schmidtchen)
Pericope: At least Sa-gig 7 A obv. 16–18 (TDPT 7: 16–18)

Transliteration

1′) [...] ⌜...⌝ [...]
2′) [... *ú-na-aš-šak* :] ⌜*ú-ga*⌝-*ra*-⌜*aṣ*⌝ *šá-niš* ⌜*ú*⌝-[...]
3′) [...]x ⌜EME⌝-*šú ik-ka*-⌜*ṣir*⌝ [...]
4′) [...] ⌜x x : EME-*šú* (?) *i-tal-lal* (?)⌝ : x[...]
5′) [... : ŠU : *qa*]-⌜tu_4⌝ : ⌜*la* :⌝ *la-a* : KÙ : ⌜*el*⌝-[*lu* ...]
6′) [...]x *qa-ti* ^{d}UTU x[...]
7′) [...]x x ⌜...⌝ x ru [...]
8′) [...] x x [...]

Translation

(1′–2′) ...

Sa-gig 7 A obv. 16 (TDPT 7: 16)
Perhaps the commentator was clarifying that the patient had not bitten off his tongue, but was taking little nips at it.

(2′) ["He bites (his tongue)" *means*] he nips (his tongue).

(2′–3′) Secondly, he ...

Sa-gig 7 A obv: 18 (TDPT 7: 18)
The tongue is described as "tied up" (*kaṣāru*) only in the Diagnostic Handbook.

(3′) "His tongue is tied up" [*means*] ...

 | DOI:10.1163/9789004417564_017

Sa-gig 7 A obv. 21 (TDPT 7: 21)—"his tongue hangs out (*i-tál-lal*)"	(4′) "His tongue (?) hangs out (?)" *means* ...
***Sa-gig 7** The name of the lavatory demon "Šulak" is analyzed into components that described "hand(s)" (ŠU) that are "not" (*lā*) "clean" (KÙ), thus linking the demon to sickness resulting from unsanitary practices in the lavatory.	(4′–5′) ... (5′) [ŠU, *which means*] hand, (5′) *lā*, *which means* not, (and) (5′) KÙ, *which means* clean. ...
***Sa-gig 7**	(6′) ... the sun-god Šamaš ...
	(7′–8′) ...

Notes

Line 2′—Jiménez (CCP 4.1.7.C.b) thought the base text here is *ú-qar-ra-aš* ("he kneads (his tongue)") in Sa-gig 7 A obv. 15 (TDPT 7: 15). This verb seems indeed to be attested only here in the medical literature and is certainly worthy of comment. However, the cited topic in this line may be better restored as [*ú-na-aš-šak*] from the base text Sa-gig 7 A obv. 16 (TDPT 7: 16), in view of a similar equation in the *Principal Commentary to Izbu* XXIV in Leichty (1970: 229, line 561); De Zorzi (2014: 914, line 6): *na-šá-ku* = *ka-ra-ṣu* ("To bite *means* to nip"). The verb *našāku* ("to bite") is common enough, and the commentator may have wanted to clarify that the patient had not bitten off his tongue but was taking little nips at it, perhaps in response to experienced irritation or pain.

Line 3′—The tongue is described as "tied up" (*kaṣāru*) only in the Diagnostic Handbook and not in therapeutic texts, with the passive N stem of the verb in Sa-gig 7 A obv. 18–19 (TDPT 7: 18–19), and its G Stative form in Sa-gig [10: 55–56] (TDPT [10 obv. 55–56]); Sa-gig 15: 9′.

Line 4′—This line is very severely damaged, and the restoration [...] ⸢x x : EME-*šú* (?) *i-tal-lal* (?)⸣ : x[...] hesitantly follows the reading by Schmidtchen and Finkel (CCP 4.1.7.C.b). Note that this orthography would differ from *i-tál*(pi)-*lal* in the existing manuscript of the base text (Sa-gig 7 A obv. 21 (TDPT 7: 21)).

Line 5′—The argument here is better preserved in Uruk Therapeutic Comm. 1 = *SpTU* 1, 47 obv. 2–5 (cf. Reiner in Reiner et al. 1994: 92): ... MAŠKIM *mu-sa-a-ti* : ᵈ*Šu-lak* / *a-na* É *mu-sa-a-tú là* TU-*ub* : ᵈ*Šu-lak* SÌG-*su* / ᵈ*Šu-lak šá* E-*ú* : ŠU : *qa-tu*₄ : *la* : *la-a* : KÙ : *el-lu* / *ana* É *mu-sa-a-tú* TU-*ub* ŠU.2-*šú là* KÙ *ana* UGU *qa-bi* ("'The *rābiṣu*-demon of the lavatory' *refers to* the demon Šulak. 'He must not enter the lavatory, the demon Šulak will strike him.' 'The demon Šulak,' which it said, *refers to* ŠU, *which means* hand; *lā*, *which means* not; (and) KÙ, *which means* clean. It is said concerning (the situation whereby) he enters the lavatory, (and) his hands become unclean."). According to the logic here, the demon's name "Šulak" can be analyzed into the components ŠU + *lā* + KÙ, whose individual meanings explain the connection between this demon and the lavatory, i.e., the demon's agency in sickness results from improper sanitary practices in the lavatory as evinced by "hand(s)" (ŠU) that are "not" (*lā*) "clean" (KÙ). The Sa-gig base text that names Šulak as the agent of sickness is, unfortunately, not preserved. The base text to the therapeutic commentary entry (DIŠ NA EME-*šú eb-ṭe-et-ma*, "If a man's tongue is cramped"; *SpTU* 1, 47 obv. 1), interestingly, shares the concern of Sa-gig 7 for ailments of the tongue, but the description of "cramped" tongue otherwise seems to be confined to therapeutic texts: *BAM* [28 obv. 2]; [438 obv. 6–7]; 445: 11 (incl. *AMT* [64/2: 11′]); *BAM* [543 i 49′]. George (2005: 86–91) discusses the demon Šulak, sicknesses associated with it, and the employment of lion centaurs as guards against it.

Commentary Sa-gig 7Cc (?)

Provenance:	Same consignment (81-11-3) as Comm. Sa-gig 7Ca and 7Cb
Period:	?
Names:	Colophon not preserved
Script:	Neo-/Late Babylonian
Field/Museum No.:	BM 49044 = 81-11-3,1755 (“Babylon Collection” at British Museum)
Digital Resources:	CDLI P470057; CCP 4.1.7.C.c (photos and edition digitized by Jiménez 2016, with contributions by Schmidtchen)
Pericope:	Indeterminate due to damaged state of available Sa-gig manuscripts

Transliteration

Obverse

1′) ⸢...⸣ [...]
2′) ⸢...⸣ [...]
3′) ⸢...⸣ [...]
4′) ⸢...⸣ [...]
5′) ši x ⸢...⸣ x[...]
6′) *šá-a-qu* : *la* [...]
7′) *saḫ-ḫa* (?) bi : x [...]
8′) *ka-as-*lu_4 : ⸢GÚ⸣.[MURGU ...]
9′) ÚR : *še-e-pi* : x[...]
10′) U_4.31.KAM ŠU ⸢^{d}⸣[30 ...]
11′) ITI : ^{d}30 [...]
12′) ⸢*šá-ḫu*(?)⸣*-ra* GÌ[R.2 ...]

Translation

***Sa-gig**

(Obv. 1′–7′) ...

***Sa-gig**

(8′) “*kaslu*” *refers to* the spine ...

The body part *kaslu* “transverse process(es) of the vertebra” is rarely applied to humans and only in the Diagnostic Handbook.

 | DOI:10.1163/9789004417564_018

***Sa-gig**
ÚR typically designates the "thigh" (*sūnu*) instead of the "foot" (*šēpu*).

(9′) "ÚR" *means* foot …

***Sa-gig**
"Day 31" from the beginning of a 30-day "month" (ITI) represents the first day of the next month, roughly corresponding to the synodic period (~29.5 days) of the moon.

(10′) "Day 31, Hand of the [moon-god Sîn]" …

(11′) ITI *refers to* the moon-god Sîn …

***Sa-gig**
The part of the foot known as *šaḫūru* (possibly the Achilles' Tendon) is attested in other medical texts in a confusing variety of byforms—*suḫru*, *zuḫru*, *tuḫru*, etc.

(12′) "The *šaḫūrā* (?) of the feet" [*refer to*] …

Notes

Intro—This commentary tablet is tentatively labeled here as "Comm. Sa-gig 7Cc (?)," following the suggestion of Jiménez (CCP 4.1.7.C.c) who, in spite of the indeterminate base text, made this classification in view of the tablet's shared museum consignment and alleged epigraphical similarities with Commentaries Sa-gig 7Ca and 7Cb.

Obv. 6′—For the many homophones of *šâqu* or *šêqu*, many of which have uncertain meaning, see *CAD* Š II, 32–33 and 308.

Obv. 8′—Rather than the reading GÙ $^{gu\text{-}za}$.⌜LUM(?)⌝ (obv. 8′) by Jiménez (CCP 4.1.7.C.c), the signs are more likely to be *ka-as-*lu_4 ("transverse process(es) of the vertebra"; byform of *kislu* in *CAD* K, 425), which appears as a human body part elsewhere only at Sa-gig 40: 41: *kàs-lu-šu* DU$_8$ ("his (the baby's) transverse processes are loose").

Obv. 9′—With the base text indeterminate, we cannot identify for certain the medical scenario wherein the descriptor "ÚR," which typically designates the "thigh" (*sūnu*), should be understood instead as the "foot" (*šēpu*). As a possibility, the part of the foot in view may be the *šaḫūru* or *šuḫāru* (*CAD* Š I, 109 s.v. *šaḫūru* B), which is expressed in logographic writing as ÚR.GÌR, where the element ÚR denotes a feature of the "foot" rather than of the "thigh." Note the lexical equation ÚR.GÌR = [*šu*]-*ḫar* GÌR (Nabnitu IX (= X), 224 in *MSL* XVI, 121), as well as the physiognomic commentary entry ÚR.GÌR = [*š*]*u*-⌜*ḫar*⌝ *še-e-pi* (BM 38788, rev. 3 = line 18). Mirelman (*NABU*

2008/65) suggested that the "Achilles' tendon" is meant by the term. The *šaḫūru* seems also to be mentioned later in the same tablet as ⸢*šá-ḫu*(?)⸣*-ra* GÌ[R.2 ...] (obv. 12′).

Obv. 10′–11′—The time reference U$_4$.31.KÁM ("Day 31") occurs only in the Diagnostic Handbook in connection with ŠU ^{d}20, "Hand of the sun-god Šamaš" (Sa-gig 13: 67 (TDPT 13 ii 9)); ŠU ^{d}U.GUR, "Hand of the god Nergal" (Sa-gig 13: 79 (TDPT 13 ii 21)); ŠU ^{d}*Iš-ḫa-ra*, "Hand of the goddess Išḫara" (Sa-gig [13: 108] (TDPT [13 ii 50]); Sa-gig 18: 38′); among other agents or factors (Sa-gig 13: 130 (TDPT 13 iii 19); Sa-gig 19/20: 47′). It is suggestive that most of these references come from Sa-gig tablet 13, in entries that make first mention of ailments concerning the "belly" (ŠÀ) or "innards" (ŠÀ.MEŠ). If my restoration ŠU ⸢^{d}⸣[30], "Hand of the [moon-god Sîn]" (obv. 10′) is correct, the commentator could be attempting to show the relationship between "Day 31" and the moon-god Sîn, in that the 31st day from the beginning of a 30-day "month" (ITI) represents the first day of the next month. The ideal month was deemed to be 30 days in duration, while the moon's average synodic period of around 29.5 days resulted in individual lunar months consisting of 29 or 30 days.

Obv. 12′—It is easy to see why the commentator felt the need to discuss "the *šaḫūrā* (?) of the feet," which is attested in other medical texts as potentially confusing byforms: *su-ḫar* GÌR.2 (Sa-gig 14: 253′ (TDPT 14 iv 52); Sa-gig 17: 65; 19/20: 26′); *zu-ḫar* GÌR.2 (Sa-gig 11: 46, 50); *tu-ḫar eqbi* (*BAM* 124 i 50; ii 2). The reading KIN *mi-šit-ti šá tuḫ-ri* TAG (*AMT* 77/5: 16′–17′) was proposed in *AHw*, 1133 s.v. *šaḫurrum* II; but with the signs *tuḫ-ri* read as *qab-ri* (for *qabli*) in *CAD* Š I, 109 s.v. *šaḫūru* B. Note also what seems to be a similar expression KIN *mi-šit-ti šá* EGIR TAG (*BAM* [132: 3′]; *AMT* 77/1 i 11). See Note above on obv. 9′ for the possibility that this part of the foot is mentioned also earlier, and its identification as the "Achilles' Tendon" by Mirelman (*NABU* 2008/65).

Commentary Sa-gig 10 & 11

Provenance:	Perhaps Babylon
Period:	End of 2nd century BCE
Names:	"[*Imgida*-tablet (?) of] Nabû-balāssu-iqbi, son of Marduk-zēra-ibni, descendant of [Egibatila]. [By the hands of] Marduk-zēra-ibni, his son."
Script:	Neo-/Late Babylonian
Typology:	*ṣâtu* 3b or 6a in Frahm (2011a: 51–52, 53)

Field/Museum No.:	DT 87 ("Daily Telegraph" Collection at British Museum)
Photos:	Plate 18 (obverse) and Plate 19 (reverse)
Printed Hand Copy:	Geers copy, notebook N 39
Printed Edition:	Wee (2012: 616–623)
Digital Resources:	CDLI P461113; CCP 4.1.10 (printed hand copy, photos, and edition digitized by Jiménez 2014)
Discussion:	Bezold (1896: 4,1549); Leichty (1973: 83); Borger (1975: 132); Stol (1993: 7 n. 21); Heeßel (2000: 134, 143 (10.–11. Tafel MS a)); Finkel (2005: 283); Frahm (*NABU* 2005/43) and (2011a: 51 n. 214, 225, 308); Genty (2010a: 377–378) and (2010b: 3, 13); Wee (2012: 616–623); Gabbay (2016: 75 n. 232, 135 n. 30)
Pericope:	At least a collection of medical entries that correspond to Sa-gig 10: 1–26 and Sa-gig 11 rev. 51–60

Transliteration

Obverse

1) [DIŠ GIG GÚ-*s*]*u ana* 15 NIGIN.ME *il-ta-nam-ma šá-niš suḫ*$_4$*-ḫ*[*ur* …]
2) […]x-*še-e* : DUL-*ma* ⌞*ú*⌟-*ka-at-tam-ma* : BAL.MEŠ : *n*[*a-bal-ku-ta*]
3) [BAL : *na-bal-ku-tu*] : BAL : *pa-la-su* : *i*-ḫar-*ru-ur* : *i-gar-r*[*u-ur*]
4) [*na-pal-ku-u* : *r*]*a-pa-šú* : MIN : *pe-tu-ú* : *ina* ⌞*taq*⌟*-ti-i*[*t* …]
5) [*iḫ-ta-niṭ-ṭa-áš*]-*šú* : LAL : *ḫa-a-ṭu* : LAL : *na-ḫa-su* : *i*-x[…]
6) [… SA].DUGUD : *šá-áš-šá-ṭu* : *pi-qam*^{qa} MUD-*ud* […]
7) [… *ut-ta-nar* :] ⌞GUR : *ta-a*⌟*-ri* : GUR : *sa-ḫa-ri* […]
8) [… *a*]*t*(?) : ^{na_4}NUNUZ : *e-rim-m*[*a-tu* …]
9) [… K]AR : *e-ke-mu* : *du-u*[*s-su* …]
10) [… PA.AN.BI : *n*]*a-pi-*⌞*is-su*⌟ : DIŠ *pur-q*[*í-dam* ŠUB …]
11) […]x x x x x […]

 | DOI:10.1163/9789004417564_019

Reverse

1′–3′) (Too damaged to read)

4′) [...] ⸢IGI.2-*šú it-ta-na-az-qa*⸣-*p*[*u* ...] (?)

5′) [... U.M]EŠ-*šú* ⸤*i-lam*⸥-*ma-am* : *la-ma-m*[*a* ...]

6′) [...]x x x : ⸢*sa*⸣-*am-ta* ⸤: *da*⸥-*mu* : x [...]

7′) [...]x x : ⸢*te-eḫ*⸣-*si-ma* : *ana ka-ba-su* [...]

8′) [*ṣa-a-tú ù šu-u*]*t* KA *šá* DIŠ GIG *rit-ta-šú šá* 15 GU$_{7}$-*šú* [...]

9′) [IM.GÍD.DA (?) ^{d}A]G-TIN-*su*-E A *šá* $^{m.d}$AMAR.UTU-NUMUN-DÙ A $^{m.d}$[*Egibatila*]

10′) [ŠU.2 $^{m.d}$AM]AR.UTU-NUMUN-DÙ A-*šú pa-liḫ* [... NU TÙM]

Top edge

11′) [GIM SUMUN-*šú* SAR-*ma* IGI.TAB *u*] IGI.K[ÁR]

Translation

Incipit-title of Sa-gig 10

NIGIN most often describes the face, where it means "to spin" (*ṣâdu*). Only a few times in the Diagnostic Handbook does NIGIN describe a neck that tends to "circle back" (*lawû*) towards the right, or that is "turned" (*suḫḫuru*) immobile to the right side.

(Obv. 1) "[If the sick man]'s [neck] NIGIN.ME to the right" (*means*) it keeps circling back.

(1) Secondly, it is turned away.

Sa-gig 10: 1—*am-šá

The topic here is likely the verb *amāšu* "to become rigid," which occurs commonly in the Diagnostic Handbook, but not in therapeutic texts.

(1–2) ...

Sa-gig 10: 1

Another common medical description of closed eyes is IGI.2-*šú* NU BAD "his eyes do not open."

(2) "DUL" (*means*) he closes (his eyes).

Sa-gig 10: 1–2—
"his eyes BAL.MEŠ"
BAL describes "rolled" eyes only in the Diagnostic Handbook, not in therapeutic texts.

(2) "BAL.MEŠ" *means* [(his eyes) are rolled.]

The opposite of "rolled" eyes are eyes that are focused on "looking."

(3) [BAL *means* to roll (eyes).]
(3) BAL *means the opposite of* to look at.

Sa-gig 10: 2
i-ḫar-*ru-ur* in the base text may have been interpreted as the similar signs *i-gàr-ru-ur*, whose reading the commentator clarified using the more lucid writing *i-gar-ru-ur* "(spittle) dribbles."

(3) "*i*-ḫar-*ru-ur*" *means* it dribbles.

***Sa-gig 10: 4—"his eyes (are) *napalkâ*"**
napalkû "to become wide open" occurs as a medical description of the eyes only in the Diagnostic Handbook, not in therapeutic texts.

(4) [*napalkû means*] to become wide.
(4) *Ditto* (i.e., *napalkû*) *means* to open.

Sa-gig 10: 5
ḫâṭu "to overwhelm" occurs frequently in the Diagnostic Handbook, but rarely in therapeutic texts.

(4–5) "At the end of [... it overwhelms] him."

(5) LAL *means* to overwhelm.

The commentator's proposal that LAL means "to recede" seems to contradict its usual meaning "to overwhelm" in the Diagnostic Handbook, but reflects the common use of LAL in therapeutic texts as a logogram for *maṭû* "to become diminished (esp. in appetite)."

(5) LAL *means* to recede.

***Sa-gig 10**

(5–6) …

Sa-gig 10: 10
The logogram SA.DUGUD occurs mainly in the Diagnostic Handbook and lexical texts, while the syllabic form of the comment *šaššaṭu* is typical of therapeutic texts.

(6) "SA.DUGUD" *means* *šaššaṭu*-sickness.

Sa-gig 10: 11

(6) "He sometimes shudders" [*means*] …

***Sa-gig 10: 14a**

(7) ["He keeps turning back (his neck)."]
(7) GUR *means* to turn back.
(7) GUR *means* to turn round. …

Sa-gig 10: 17
erimmātu-beads are mentioned only a few times in the Diagnostic Handbook, as propitiatory gifts to the goddess Ištar.

(8) "^{na_4}NUNUZ" *refers to* the *erimmatu*-bead.

Sa-gig 10: 18
The medical description "his virility is taken away" occurs only a few times in the Diagnostic Handbook. Therapeutic texts prefer another idiom: "he is diminished (in his appetite) to go to a woman."

(9) … KAR *means* to take away.

(9–10) "[His] virility" [*refers to*] …

***Sa-gig 10: 24**
The logogram PA.AN(.BI) occurs in only diagnostic texts, while the syllabic form of the comment *napīssu* "his breathing" is typical of therapeutic texts.

(10) ["PA.AN.BI" *means*] his breathing.

Sa-gig 10: 26
purqidam "on the back" is not especially common in medical texts, though it appears repeatedly in descriptions of sex positions.

(10–11) "If [he falls] *purqidam*" [*means*] ...

(Rev. 1′–3′) ...

Sa-gig 11 rev. 51

(4′–5′) "His eyes keep protruding" (?). ...

Sa-gig 11 rev. 52
lamāmu "to chew" commonly denotes "chewing" by animals, and it occurs only here to describe the patient's behavior.

(5′) "He (performs the action of) *ilammam* to his [fingers]" *derives from the dictionary root* to chew.

***Sa-gig 11**

(5′–6′) ...

Sa-gig 11 rev. 58
sāmtu "redness" and other nominals expressed by the logogram SA_5 (i.e., "red substance") are more characteristic of the Diagnostic Handbook than therapeutic texts.

(6′) "Redness" *refers to* blood.

***Sa-gig 11**

(6′–7′) ...

Sa-gig 11 rev. 60—DIŠ UMBIN GIG *te-eḫ-*[*si-ma*] "If the nail is sick, (and) you cover (it) up"

(7′) "You cover up (the sick nail)" (points) to putting on a *kubšu*-cap ...

(Colophon)

Incipit-title of Sa-gig 11

(8′) [Glossary including] oral [lore] on "If the sick man's right wrist hurts him" ...

(9′) [*Imgida*-tablet (?) of] Nabû-balāssu-iqbi, son of Marduk-zēra-ibni, descendant of [Egibatila].
(10′) [By the hands of] Marduk-zēra-ibni, his son.

(10′) He who fears ... [must not carry off (this tablet).]
(11′) [Written, checked, and] examined [against its original].

Notes

Intro—The pericope of this commentary tablet consists of two separate blocks of base text from Sa-gig Tablets 10 and 11: The obverse of the commentary tablet (at least obv. 1–11) is concerned with at least Sa-gig 10: 1–26, while the reverse of the commentary tablet (at least rev. 4′–7′) deals with at least Sa-gig 11 rev. 51–60. These two blocks of base text (Sa-gig 10 obv. 1–26 and Sa-gig 11 rev. 51–60) are too far separated to imagine that they represent the ends of a single continuous pericope (i.e., Sa-gig 10: 1 to Sa-gig 11 rev. 60). I therefore label this commentary "Comm. Sa-gig 10 & 11" instead of "Comm. Sa-gig 10–11." The final colophon (rev. 8′) mentions the incipit-title of only Sa-gig Tablet 11, and the incipit-title of Sa-gig Tablet 10 (not preserved) was likely recorded on the damaged portion of the tablet's obverse. This arrangement of separate sections (each ending with the incipit-title of its base text) may also be found in Comm. Sa-gig 21 & 22a, where its first section (obv. 1–14) provides comments on Sa-gig Tablet 21 and ends with the incipit-title of Tablet 21 (obv. 14), while its following section (obv. 15–rev. 19′) explains Sa-gig Tablet 22a and ends with the incipit-title of Tablet 22a (rev. 19′). Because the base text of Comm. Sa-gig 21 & 22a is not preserved well enough, however, we are uncertain if its pericope consists of one continuous block of base text that encompassed Sa-gig Tablets 21–22a, or if it consists of separate sections from Sa-gig Tablets 21 and 22a (as in the case of Comm. Sa-gig 10 & 11). For Comm. Sa-gig 13+, separate topics are at times so far apart from each other in the base text, it becomes less helpful to imagine them as part of a continuous pericope.

Obv. 1—In both the Diagnostic Handbook and therapeutic texts, the body part most often described with the logogram NIGIN is the "face" (IGI.MEŠ), where NIGIN(.MEŠ-*du*) expresses the Akkadian verb *ṣâdu* ("to spin"). See Sa-gig 4: 18; the medical entries in Sa-gig 9: 53–54; 26: 20′, 71′–72′; *BAM* 40 obv. 14; 52: 101; [60: 7′]; [106 obv. 1]; [108 rev. 2′]; 145: 2; [146: 29′–30′]; 159 i 29; 214 i 1; 216: 55′; 231 i 1; 312: 9, 13; 317 rev. 24; 376 ii 15′; 578 i 38; *AMT* 22/2 obv. 1; [39/4 rev. 3′]; [54/3 rev. 5′]; BM 42298: 23. This logogram is applied to the neck (GÚ) only in the Diagnostic Handbook at Sa-gig 10: 1, 4; 13: 54 (TDPT 13 i 55′); Sa-gig 33: 28. I understand the comments as follows: 1) "it keeps circling back" (the Gtn iterative verb *iltanamma* < *lawû*), referring to a neck that is still mobile but with a tendency to drift towards the right side; and 2) "it is turned away" (the D Stative verb *suḫḫur*), referring to a neck that is fixed in position towards the right side. The orthography *suḫ*$_4$*-ḫur* also occurs at Sa-gig 10: 15b.

Obv. 1–2—Although the commentary entry [...] / [...]x-*še-e* (obv. 1–2) is too damaged to restore with certainty, the topics of NIGIN.ME and DUL (both from the base text Sa-gig 10: 1) that immediately precede and follow this entry strongly suggest that the topic here is *am-šá* (Sa-gig 10: 1). This verb *amāšu* ("to become rigid"; cf. "to become cataleptic(?)" in *CAD* A II, 28) occurs commonly in the Diagnostic Handbook to describe the patient's hands and feet (Sa-gig 10: 1; 11: 20, [49]; 13: 36 (TDPT 13 i 37′); Sa-gig 14: 217′ (TDPT 14 iv 11′); Sa-gig 15: 18′–20′, 64′; 16: 59′; 26: 53′; 40: 110–111), but seems unattested in therapeutic texts. Lexical texts suggest the following associations: $^{\text{ḫu-um}}$ḪUM = *ḫa-ma-šu, za-ma-šu, a-ma-*⸢*šu*⸣ (Aa V/1, 18-20 in *MSL* XIV, 407–408); ḫum $^{\text{ḫu-um}}$-ma = *ḫa-ma-šum*, dim$_4$-ma = *a-ma-šum* (Erimhuš V, 221–222 in *MSL* XVII, 76). However, traces of the comment [...]x-*še-e* (obv. 2), however, do not lend themselves easily to forms of *ḫa-ma-šu* or *za-ma-šu*. The verb *amāšu* also appears as part of the argument on a similar-sounding verb *amāṣu* in Comm. Sa-gig 5, lines 29–30.

Obv. 2—The verb *katāmu* ("to cover, close (eyes)") occurs as the logogram DUL in medical signs of the eyes at Sa-gig 10: 1; 16: 64′; 26: 11′, 64′, 66′; *BAM* 510 i 32′; 513 i 6′; 514 i 39′. Almost equally attested is the expression IGI(.2)-*šú* NU BAD ("his eyes do not open") at Sa-gig 5: 17′ (TDPT 5 B1 17); Sa-gig 16: 64′; *BAM* 159 iv 2′; 510 i 18′; 513 i 8′ (incl. *AMT* 8/1 obv. 8′); *BAM* 515 ii 45.

Obv. 2–3—My restoration *n*[*a-bal-ku-ta*] (obv. 2) agrees with the (admittedly scarce) sign traces, the plural subject required by BAL.MEŠ (obv. 2) quoted from the commentator's base text manuscript, as well as the few syllabic renderings of this verb in the N Stative in the Diagnostic Handbook: IGI.2-*šú* ... *na-bal-ku-ta*$_5$ (Sa-gig 23: 6); IGI.2-*šú na-bal-*[*ku-ta*] (Sa-gig 5: 72′, 73′ (TDPT 5 E2 6, 7), which is restored instead as *na-pa*[*l-ka-a*] by Scurlock 2014: 46, 50 n. 2 on the uncertain assumption that this is the base text for Comm. Sa-gig 5, obv. 12); also, *contra* the Durative 3cs form ⸢*ib*⸣-[*ba-lak-kàt*] by Jiménez (CCP 4.1.10). Although the verb *nabalkutu* occurs not uncommonly in medical texts, the base text Sa-gig 10: 1–2 employs this verb in a specific technical sense pertaining to the patient's eyes. For the meaning of *nabalkutu* as "to roll (eyes)," see *CAD* N I, 17–18 s.v. *nabalkutu* §3d; especially the description: [BAD G]U$_4$ IGI.2-*šú* BAL-*ma* BABBAR *ú-kal-lam* "if an ox rolls its eyes and shows the whites (of its eyes)" (*CT* 40, 32 rev. 17). The Diagnostic Handbook also includes several medical signs involving rolling "the whites of the eyes" (Sa-gig 5: 102′–105′ (TDPT 5 G 3–6); Sa-gig 26: 30′) and the "blacks of the eyes" (Sa-gig 5: 106′–107′ (TDPT 5 G 7–8)). Other references simply describe rolled eyes, without specifying the manner of rolling: Sa-gig 5: 72′–73′ (TDPT 5 E2 6–7); Sa-gig 10: 1; 23: 6; 36: 89 (TDPT 35: 89). This meaning of *nabalkutu* does not seem attested in therapeutic texts, where the verb is not used to describe the eyes. The equation BAL : *pa-la-su* does not appear in lexical texts, and the meaning of *palāsu* ("to look at") seems contradictory to the notion of "rolling" the eyes. It is likely that BAL : *pa-la-su* (obv. 3) represents an antonymous pair, i.e., "BAL *means the opposite of* to look at" (see §1.2.3.1.6). As an alternative to antonymy, Uri Gabbay (personal communication) suggested that the phonological similarities between BAL and *palāsu* accounted for their pairing.

Obv. 3—The commentator evidently understood his base text topic *i*-ḫar-*ru-ur* as a byform of the verb *garāru*, which fits well with the base text description here of how liquid spittle "flows" or "dribbles" from the sick person's mouth. This must have appeared to be a plausible solution to an otherwise confusable term *iḫarrur*: There exists a verb (*ḫ*)*arāru*, which commonly describes the behavior of a sick man's "bowels" (suggestively, *errū*), and which appears as *i-ḫar-ru-ur* in the Diagnostic Handbook (Sa-gig 13: 172–175 (TDPT 13 iv 21′–24′)), *i-ḫa-ar-ru-ru* in a Middle Babylonian diagnostic work (CBS 3424(A), line 5), and as various orthographies of *iarrur*(*ū*) in therapeutic texts: *i-ár-ru-ru* (*BAM* 52: 101; [106 obv. 1]; 159 v 48; *AMT* 22/2 obv. 4), *i-ár-ru-ur* (*AMT* 43/5: 8), and *ia-ru-ru* (*AMT* 21/2: 6). Descriptions of the epigastrium such as SAG ŠÀ-*šú i-ru-ur* (Sa-gig 4: 127 (TDPT 4 rev. 42)) and SAG ŠÀ-*šú* DU$_8$-*ma i-ár-ra-ár* (Sa-gig 13: 27 (TDPT 13 i 28′)) may also involve the same verb, though the *a* theme vowel of the Durative form *iarrar* is admittedly problematic. On the other hand, the writing *i-ḫar-ru-ur* also occurs in descriptions of the sick man's larynx (Sa-gig 10: 29, 34), where we cannot be sure whether the same verb or a homophone was intended. Our commentator may have had in mind the idea expressed elsewhere in the Diagnostic Handbook by the variants ÚḪ NU TUKU : *it-ta-nag-ra-ár*, "he has no spittle : (spittle) keeps dribbling" (Sa-gig 26: 29′ MS B). In place of spittle, we find comparable descriptions of how "his sweat keeps dribbling" (IR-*su it-ta-nag-ra-ár*; Sa-gig 4: 65, 67 // *SpTU* III, 88 ii 10′–11′), or of "dribbling sweat" (*zu*!(su)-*tum i-tág-ru-ur-rum* in the lexical list Kagal; Veldhuis 2009: 45–46, obv. 17′–19′, 24′). To be sure, the interpretation of *i*-ḫar-*ru-ur* as *i-gar-ru-ur* stands on shaky philological ground: The cuneiform sign ḫar does not typically express the syllable /gar/ (*MZL*, no. 644), and there is disputable evidence that (*ḫ*)*arāru* readily serves as a byform of *garāru*, particularly in the G stem: The byform "**ḫarāru* in *naḫarruru, qarāru*" is noted in *CAD* G, 47 s.v. *garāru* A; but not in *AHw*, 902–903 s.v. *q/garāru*. On the other hand, Neo-/Late Babylonian versions of the cuneiform signs ḫar and gàr are very similar, and it is not improbable that the commentator interpreted the signs in his base text as *i-gàr-ru-ur*, which he then proceeded to explain using more lucid writing: *i-gar-ru-ur* ("(spittle) dribbles").

Obv. 4—At the damaged beginning of obv. 4, I restore the dictionary root [*na-pal-ku-u*], which derives from the inflected form *na-pal-ka-a* in the base text Sa-gig 10: 4. Associations between *napalkû* and *rapāšu* ("to become wide") occur in the lexical text Aa I/6, 248–249 (*MSL* XIV, 232; read as [*r*]*a*-⌈*pa*⌉-*šu* in *CAD* N I, 270), as well as in the commentarial equations *na-pal-ku-ú* // *ra-pa-ša* (*SpTU* I, 83 rev. 16); *ne-pel-ku-ú* // *ra-pa-šú* (*SpTU* I, 72 rev. 8). The verb *napalkû* appears as a medical description of the eyes only in the Diagnostic Handbook (Sa-gig 5: 72′–73′ (TDPT 5 E2 6–7); Sa-gig 10: 4; 27: 16), not in therapeutic texts.

Obv. 4–5—Scurlock and Andersen (2005: 319, §13.194) gave the translation "at the beginning when ⌈his⌉ [confusional state] comes over him" (*ina taq-ti-it* [LÁ-*š*]*ú iḫ-ta-niṭ-ṭa-áš-šú*; Sa-gig 10: 5), but *taqtītu* means the "end, termination of a time period" (*CAD* T, 202), and should not be confused with the common time reference *tašrītu* "beginning" (*CAD* T, 297). The topic here, therefore, is the form *iḫ-ta-niṭ-ṭa-áš-šú*, which the commentator identified as the verbal root *ḫâṭu* ("to overwhelm"; cf. Stol 1993: 44–46), and which he compared with another verb *naḫāsu* that shares the same logogram LAL. The verb *naḫāsu* ("to recede") may not be explicitly equated with LAL in lexical texts, but LAL is used as its logogram in various contexts (*AHw*, 713; *CAD* N I, 128–132; *MZL*, no. 750). Occurrences of the logogram LAL as the noun *hayyattu* ("fright") or as the verb *ḫâṭu* ("to overwhelm") are common in the Diagnostic Handbook. By contrast, apart from the malady name LAL-*ti ṣe-ti* at *BAM* 177: 12, therapeutic texts almost uniformly prefer the syllabic form *ḫayyattu*: *BAM* 174 rev. 30; 183: 33; 323: 66; 338 rev. 8′; 344: 2; 367: 16; 376 ii 26′; [385 i 24′]; 469 rev. 35; 471 ii 26′. Furthermore, the verb *ḫâṭu* is largely absent from therapeutic texts, appearing in syllabic writing only at *BAM* 161 ii 19′; 436 vi 13′. The writing SAG.DU-*su gi-na-a* LAL [...] (*BAM* 575 iii 16) may denote the verb *tarāṣu* ("to stretch") or *šaqālu* ("to suspend, hang") instead. In therapeutic texts, the logogram LAL most commonly expresses the verb *maṭû* ("to become diminished (esp. in appetite)"): *BAM* 87: 14; [106 rev. 1′]; 112 i 18′, 35′; 190: 23; [221 ii 2′]; [231 i 14]; 232 i 17′; 434 i 14′; 445: 14 (incl. *AMT* 64/2: 14′); *BAM* 575 ii 38, 43; iii 7; 578 i 29; *AMT* 32/1 rev. 11; 40/5 iii 9′; 48/2: 2; [81/7: 5]; *STT* 102: 8. In other words, by proposing that LAL means "to recede," the commentator set aside a common meaning of LAL in the Diagnostic Handbook (i.e., "to overwhelm"), in favor of the typical sense of LAL in therapeutic texts (i.e., "to become diminished").

Obv. 6—In the Diagnostic Handbook, the logogram SA.DUGUD appears at Sa-gig 3: 40 (TDPT 3: 31); Sa-gig 10: 10–11, 27; and its syllabic form *šaššaṭu* occurs at Sa-gig 33: 94–97. In therapeutic texts, however, the syllabic form *šaššaṭu* is predominant: *BAM* 1 iii 22–23; 68: 2; 69: 2′; 129 iv 3′, [6′], 14′, 19′; [131 obv. 1]; 168: 18; 171: 14′; 422 ii 10′; *AMT* 31/2 rev. 5′. The ailment *šaššaṭu* is equated with both sa-ad-dugud and sa-ad-gal in the *List of Diseases* (SB Recension, lines 79 (259), 81 (261) in *MSL* IX, 94), whereas, in various medical texts, *šaššaṭu* is denoted by SA.DUGUD and *sagallu* by SA.GAL. The close relationship between *šaššaṭu* and *sagallu* is also illustrated by the inclusion of both in the same therapeutic tablet *BAM* 129.

Obv. 7—The restored base text topic [... *ut-ta-nar* :] ("[... He keeps turning back (his neck).]") at the beginning of this commentary entry comes from Sa-gig 10: 14a. GUR as the logogram for the N stem of *saḫāru* ("to return, turn away from, turn about") occurs in the lexical texts Nabnitu IX (=X), [231] (*MSL* XVI, 122); Erimhuš VI, 12 (*MSL* XVII, 81); Antagal III, 56 (*MSL* XVII, 152).

Obv. 8—The item "*erimmātu*-beads" (^{na_4}NUNUZ.MEŠ) is attested in the base text Sa-gig 10: 17, as well as in another medical entry Sa-gig 10 B rev. 5, both following after the diagnosis "Hand of the goddess Ištar." In the myth of *Descent of Ištar*, a necklace of such beads is removed from the goddess as she descends into the Netherworld (*CT* 15 45: 49), and the mention of "*erimmātu*-beads" at Sa-gig 10: 17; 10 B rev. 5 likely refers to propitiatory gifts to the goddess responsible of the sickness (*CAD* E, 294).

Obv. 9—Apart from the base text Sa-gig 10: 18, the expression *dūssu* KAR-*et* ("his virility is taken away") appears as a medical description only in the Diagnostic Handbook at Sa-gig 13: 164, 169 (TDPT 13 iv 13′, 18′). Therapeutic texts have other more idiomatic ways of expressing this idea, including *ana* MUNUS *alāka muṭṭu* ("he is diminished (in his appetite) to go to a woman") at *BAM* 112 i 18′, 35′; 232 i 17′; [438 obv. 9]; 445: 14 (incl. *AMT* 64/2: 14′); *BAM* [467 ii 8′] (// K 2351+:7′–8′); *AMT* 88/3: 2′; and *ana* MUNUS *alāka lā ile*ʾʾ*i* ("he is unable to go to a woman") at *BAM* 140: 8′.

Obv. 10—The logogram PA.AN(.BI) seems to be attested only in the base text Sa-gig 10: 24 and possibly in the Middle Babylonian diagnostic tablet CBS 12580, obv. 12: *i*-[*na*] ⸢KA-*šú*(?) PA(?)⸣.[AN...]. The syllabic form *na-pi-is-su* appears in the Diagnostic Handbook at Sa-gig 3: 63 (TDPT 3: 54).

By contrast, the writing *na-piš* KIR_4-*šú* ("the breathing of his nose") occurs several times in therapeutic texts, where the pregenitive *napīšu* is always written syllabically: *BAM* [28 obv. 2]; [533: 2]; 566 i 6′ (incl. *AMT* 55/5 i 6′); *AMT* 45/6 obv. 5′; [51/2: 8′].

Obv. 10—The adverb *purqidam* ("on the back"; *CAD* P, 521) is not especially common in medical texts, occuring in the base text Sa-gig 10: 26, as well as *CT* 37, 46: 8, 13; [49b:3] (+K 14843: 3). Of particular note is the tablet *AMT* 65/3, where *purqidam* occurs repeatedly (lines 3′, 5′, 7′, 10′) to describe various positions adopted during sexual intercourse. The signs *pur-qí-dam* were earlier interpreted as "*bur-ki-tam* [*sic*]" ("on his knees") by Campbell Thompson (1934: 145–146).

Rev. 4′—See Note on Comm. Sa-gig 21 & 22a, obv. 9 for the explanation of eyes "fixed in place" (< *retû*/*reṭû*) as "protruding" (< *zaqāpu*) eyes.

Rev. 5′—The verb *lamāmu* ("to chew") appears only in the base text Sa-gig 11 rev. 52 to describe the patient's behavior, but some therapeutic instructions do involve the "chewing" of medicaments on the part of the healer (*AMT* 25/6 ii [3′], 6′; cf. the verb *lummu* as possibly a variant of *lamāmu* at *AMT* 16/5 ii 7). Otherwise, *lamāmu* denotes the "chewing" activity of animals (*CAD* L, 59).

Rev. 6′—The syllabic form *sāmtu* ("redness") is attested only at Sa-gig 11 rev. 58–59, and nominals expressed by the logogram SA_5 (i.e., "red substance") seem likewise characteristic of the Diagnostic Handbook: Sa-gig 9: 10; 13: 157 (TDPT 13 iii 45); Sa-gig 16: 86′; 40: 32. Atypical labels like *samtu* ("redness") may reflect uncertainties in the identification of phenomena encountered in medical practice. Here, the commentator evidently interpreted "redness" as "blood," illustrating the tendency to conflate atypical medical descriptions with the usual medical phenomena.

Rev. 7′—This commentary entry derives from the base text Sa-gig 11 rev. 60 and helps to restore it: DIŠ UMBIN GIG *te-eḫ*-[*si-ma* ...] ("If the nail is sick, (and) you cover (it) up ..."). Statements like this are not particularly common in Sa-gig Chapters II and III, where the healer's actions (in the 2nd person: "you") are included in descriptions of the patient's medical signs, sometimes as a diagnostic test (cf. Sa-gig 11 rev. 50; 15: 27′; as well as Comm. Sa-gig 21 & 22a, obv. 10). The pairing of *ḫesû* "to cover (up)" and *kabāsu*, apparently a byform of *kabāšu* ("to put on a *kubšu*-cap/headdress"; *CAD* K, 11; *AHw*, 416), occurs also in Comm. Sa-gig 4B, obv. 1: DAB : *ḫe-su-ú* : DAB : *ka-ba-šu* ("DAB *means* to cover up. DAB *means* to put on a *kubšu*-cap."). There, the common sense of *kubšu* as some kind of a headdress is directly applicable to the base text situation, in which the patient "(feels) covered up in the temple" (SAG.KI *ḫe-si*), probably referring to a sensation of pressure around the temples. Here, the *kubšu*-cap may refer to some kind of a protective or therapeutic covering over a sick nail that is sensitive to touch.

Rev. 9′–10′—The colophon has been restored according to the suggestion by Finkel (2005: 283). The tablet was written by Marduk-zēra-ibni of the Egibatila family in Babylon, who was the son of Nabû-balāssu-iqbi, and who shared the same name (i.e., Marduk-zēra-ibni) as an ancestor of Nabû-balāssu-iqbi. Both Nabû-balāssu-iqbi and Marduk-zēra-ibni date towards the end of the second century BCE. See Frahm (2011a: 225). The restoration "He who fears ... [must not carry off (this tablet)]" (rev. 10′) is based on similar statements elsewhere: "He who fears Anu and Antu must not carry off (this tablet)" (Comm. Sa-gig 7B, rev. 12′); "He who fears the gods Enlil, Šamaš, and Marduk must not carry off (this tablet)" (Comm. Sa-gig 21 & 22a, rev 23′); and "He who fears Anu and Ištar must not carry off (this tablet)" (Comm. Sa-gig 36, rev. 15′).

Commentary Sa-gig 13+

Provenance:	Probably Uruk (Warka)
Period:	Late Babylonian–Hellenistic
Names:	None
Script:	Neo-/Late Babylonian
Typology:	*ṣâtu* 3b in Frahm (2011a: 51–52)

Field/Museum No.:	GCBC 766 (Yale Babylonian Collection, USA)
Photos:	Plate 20a (obverse), Plate 20b (right edge), Plate 21a (bottom edge), and Plate 21b (reverse)
Printed Hand Copy:	*GCCI* II, 406
Printed Edition:	Wee (2012: 624–632)
Digital Resources:	CDLI P294665; CCP 4.1.13.B (printed hand copy, photos, and edition digitized by Jiménez 2015, with contributions by Gabbay)
Discussion:	Meissner (1937: 65); Labat (1951: 124 n. 219, 130); Reiner (1958: 55); Lambert (1960: 321 n. 115) and (2013: 60, 137); Von Soden (1961: 72); Landsberger (1964: 49 n. 13); Leichty (1973: 83); Köcher (1978: 36); Heeßel (2000: 134, 144 (13. Tafel MS a)); Wiggermann (2003: 363–364); Scurlock and Andersen (2005: 337 n. 209); Geller (2010a: 151–152) and (2010b: 7); Genty (2010a: 379) and (2010b: 13, 18, 22–24, 26); Frahm (2011a: 51 n. 214, 225–226, 302); Wee (2012: 624–632) and (in press: §B5); Böck (2013: 50 n. 21); Scurlock (2014: 117 n. 4; 119 nn. 77, 82, and 91 with typo "GCCI 4"); Nurullin (2014: 214 n. 203); Frahm and Jiménez (2015: 317 n. 37); Gabbay (2016: 108 n. 131); Jiménez (2017: 270 n. 684); Steinert (2018: 259); Schmidtchen (2018: 327 n. 41);
Pericope:	Indeterminate due to uncertainty of the base text form

Transliteration

Obverse

1) *ḫe-em-ret* : *še-eb-ret*

2) ŠU KI.NE : ŠU ᵈNUSKA

3) *id-dá*^(*da*)*-lip* : *ik-tu-uš*

 | DOI:10.1163/9789004417564_020

4) *pa-šit-tú im-tú* : *pa-šit-tú šá mar-tú ú-kal-lu*
5) šu gá-gá : *na-še-e bi-il-tú*
6) šu gá-gá : *na-še-e še-er-ti*
7) *rík*(zum)*-su-šú ir-mu-ú* : *ri-ik-su-šú* : *šér-a-nu-šú*
8) *gi-lid-su* : *giš-šá-a-šú*
9) IGI.LAL.ŠÚ : *ḫa-a-a-at-tú*

Bottom edge
10) ḫu-uṣ-ṣa : *še-mu-ú šá ka-ba-bu*
11) *ṣa-a-tú u š*[*u*]*-ut* KA *šá* DIŠ GIG KIŠIB
12) KIR$_4$ ŠU GÁL : *la-ba-ni ap-pi*

Reverse
13) KI.GUB-*su* : *man-zal-ta-šú*
14) [$^{\mathrm{na}_4}$*e-t*]*an-de-e-ti* : *pu-ra-ṭa-a-tú*
15) ⌜*šá-niš* (?)⌝ *a-na ik-rib qa-bé-e i-bal-luṭ*
16) *šit-ti* : *zu-ú*
17) SA.GIG : *ki-is-sa-tu*$_4$

Translation

Sa-gig 13: 2
ḫemēru "to pucker" is a rare description of the tongue in the Diagnostic Handbook, and seems unattested in therapeutic texts.

(Obv. 1) "It is puckered" *means* it is broken up.

Sa-gig 13: 5 (TDPT 13 i 6′)
Though the writing KI.NE likely originated from manuscript corruption or scribal uncertainty, the commentator understood it as the logogram for "brazier," thus identifying the fire-god Nusku as the agent of sickness.

(2) "Hand of KI.NE" *refers to* Hand of the god Nusku.

Sa-gig 13: 72 (TDPT 13 ii 14)
dalāpu "to linger" occurs only rarely in the Diagnostic Handbook and not in therapeutic texts.

(3) "It has lingered" *means* it has tarried on.

***Sa-gig 13 ?**
imtu "poison" is atypical for medical texts unlike the common term "gall," which is also already associated with *pāšittu*-sickness.

(4) "*pāšittu*-sickness (and) poison" *refers to pāšittu*-sickness that contains gall.

***Sa-gig 13 ?**
The statement here mirrors the lexical entry: "gú-un-šu-gá-gá = to carry, in the case of a load" (Nabnitu K). Though the Sa-gig base text is uncertain, the commentator likely implied that the medical condition here results from the patient's guilt.

(5) šu gá-gá *means* to carry a load.
(6) šu gá-gá *means* to carry guilt.

Sa-gig 13: 129 (TDPT 13 iii 18)
The signs *rík-su* refer to the uncommon term *riksu* "bonds," which the commentator identified with the common body part "strands."

(7) "His *rík-su* became slack" *refers to* his bonds, *which refer to* his strands.

Sa-gig 13: 135 (TDPT 13 iii 24)
The signs *gi-lid-su* refer to the "hip" (*gilšu*) and not the "skin" (*gildu*) or "jitters" (*gilittu*). It was especially easy to read *gilittu* "jitters" by mistake, due to synonymy with IGI. LAL.ŠÚ "fright" in the base text entry immediately following.

(8) "*gi-lid-su*" *means* his hip.

Sa-gig 13: 136 (TDPT 13 iii 25)
IGI.LAL.ŠÚ occurs only here, and it is explained by a syllabic form *ḫayyattu* "fright" that is typical of therapeutic texts.

(9) "IGI.LAL.ŠÚ" *means* fright.

Sa-gig 13: 154 (TDPT 13 iii 43)
The intangible sensation of *ḫuṣṣa* pain is explained here by an erudite argument, whereby the signs ḪU.UZ.ZA serve as the logogram for the verb "to roast."

(Line 10) "ḫu-uṣ-ṣa" *means* to roast, in the case of charring.

(Colophon)
Incipit-title of Sa-gig 11 ?

(11) Glossary including oral lore on "If the sick man('s) wrist."

Sa-gig 12: 5 (TDPT 12 i 5) ?
This common expression for contrite prayer occurs as a medical sign only here.

(12) "KIR$_4$ ŠU GÁL" *means* touching the nose.

Sa-gig 12: 98″ (TDPT 12 iii 35)
KI.GUB occurs only rarely in the Diagnostic Handbook. It originally meant *manzāzu* "position," but was confused or associated by the rebus principle with the similar-sounding term *manzaltu* "flow of excrement."

(Line 13) "Its KI.GUB" *means* its flow of excrement.

Sa-gig 12: 108″ (TDPT 12 iii 45)
This identification of the stones is found in Hg. B IV, 105.

(14) "^{na_4}*etandētu* stones" *refers to puraṭātu* stones.

To show that the *puraṭātu* stones' efficacy in healing was intrinsic to their nature, the commentator analyzed their name ^{na_4}*etandēti* as "for" (NA$_4$) + "vow/prayer" (e-tan as syllables *ík-rib*) + "he said" (di / e) + "he will become healthy (TI).

(15) [Secondly (?)], for a vow/prayer that he said, he will become healthy.

Sa-gig 12: 109″ (TDPT 12 iv 1)
The commentator explained the rare word *šittu* by the common medical term *zû* "excrement."

(16) "*šittu*" *means* excrement.

Sa-gig 12: 126″ (TDPT 12 iv 18)
SA.GIG is analyzed as "strand, i.e., muscle" (SA) + "sickness" (GIG).

(17) "SA.GIG" *refers to* (the muscle sickness) *kiṣṣatu.*

Notes

Intro—Available manuscripts of Sa-gig Tablet 13 suggest that large portions of base text exist between the topics cited in this commentary. For example, more than sixty lines of diagnostic entries separate Sa-gig 13: 5 (TDPT 13 i 6′) (= base text for the commentary entry in obv. 2) and Sa-gig 13: 72 (TDPT 13 ii 14) (= base text for the commentary entry in obv. 3), which may rather implausibly imply that the many lines between these two base text entries contain no items that required comment. Such 'skips' over large portions of the base text present a marked contrast to the method displayed in many other commentaries (especially those of Anu-ikṣur), whereby the commentator moved systematically line-by-line through the minutiae of his base text. One possibility is to regard this tablet as a text produced by a student in the course of an examination. While the student may have been expected to possess a line-by-line understanding of the base text, topics chosen for the examination need not have tested the student on every point of his knowledge, and only a few selected topics could have been chosen from a large section of the text examined. Another option is to question whether the base text used by the commentator, in fact, resembled manuscripts of Sa-gig tablet 13 available to us. The colophon in line 11 apparently cites the incipit-title of Sa-gig 11 instead of Sa-gig 13, for example, which may suggest that the base text here deviates from standardized forms of Sa-gig. While Frahm (2011a: 225) ascribed this commentary to "Sa-gig 13 and 12/14(?)," Jiménez (CCP 4.1.13.B) clarified that the final entries can be satisfactorily explained as having Sa-gig 12 (not Sa-gig 14) as their base text. Here, I adopt the label "Comm. Sa-gig 13+," while allowing the possibility that the base text does not exactly follow the standardized arrangement and contents of Sa-gig tablets.

Obv. 1—The verb *ḫemēru* ("to pucker") appears in the Diagnostic Handbook only at Sa-gig 13: 2, 11 (TDPT 13 i 12′); Sa-gig 15: 33′, always as a description of the patient's tongue. It does not seem attested in therapeutic texts, but it does occur in a physiognomic omen (*CAD* Ḫ, 169). Although the verb *šebēru* ("to break") is not particularly common as a medical sign, its non-medical attestations are plentiful, and its basic meaning is transparent enough. There are distinct differences here in the sign forms of *ret* (obv. 1, and perhaps KIŠIB in line 11) and *šit* (obv. 4; line 16), which resemble each other more closely in Neo-Assyrian lapidary script. Based on this entry, Lambert

(2013: 60, 137) made the following restoration to a commentary on *Enūma eliš* I, 121: [*ḫe-me-r*]*u še-bé-ru*.

Obv. 2—The base text Sa-gig 13: 5 (TDPT 13 i 6′) contains a pair of alternative diagnoses and prognoses: ŠU KI TIN : ŠU KI.NE GAM ("Hand of KI, he will become healthy, *or* (*alternatively*) Hand of KI.NE, he will die"). I am inclined to understand these as a pair of epigraphical variants (§EV.7 in §1.1.3), whereby cuneiform writing at the position of TIN was somehow confused as NE GAM in another manuscript tradition, perhaps due to tablet damage. Possibly, the position of TIN was occupied originally by another prognosis *ne-kud* (𒉈 𒋻) ("he is worrisome"), which would have been more easily confused as NE GAM (𒉈 𒄣) due to the visual similarities. The verdict ŠU KI also occurs in an Akkadian diagnostic text from Ḫattuša (*StBoT* XXXVI, p. 21; Tablet A obv. 8), and its translation as "Hand of the Netherworld (lit. earth)" is confirmed by the syllabic reading ŠU *er-ṣe-ti* at Sa-gig 40: 30. On the other hand, ŠU KI.NE is unattested elsewhere, which would be understandable, if it indeed represents the product of manuscript corruption or scribal uncertainty. The commentator here, however, read KI.NE as the logogram for *kinūnu* ("brazier"), in line with the many lexical equations linking the two (CAD K, 393). He accordingly attributed divine agency to Nusku, who was a fire god similar to and associated with the god Girra. Note, for example, the related roles of Nusku and Girra in *maqlû* rituals (Abusch 1974: 258–259; Daxelmüller and Thomsen 1982: 51).

Obv. 3—The topic cited (*id-dá* ^{da}*-lip*) differs from the orthography *id-da-lip* in the preserved manuscript entry (MS B) of Sa-gig 13: 72 (TDPT 13 ii 14; mistakenly transliterated as *id-dal-lip* by Labat 1951: 118); cf. *CAD* K, 295. The verb *dalāpu* ("to linger") is attested only in the Diagnostic Handbook at Sa-gig 13: 72 (TDPT 13 ii 14); Sa-gig 26: 33′, 38′; always describing the action of the malady. It does not seem to appear in therapeutic texts. Commensurable with the G Perfect form of the comment *ik-tu-uš*, the writing *id-dá* ^{da}*-lip* should be interpreted likewise as a G Perfect form, rather than an N stem verb. A similar equation may perhaps be found in another commentary on the *Šumma ālu* series: *id-*[*x-x*]*-ma* = *i-ka-áš-ma* (*CT* 41, 33 rev. 8).

Obv. 4—One is tempted to understand this line as an A:B:A:C commentary argument: "'*pāšittu*-sickness' (*refers to*) poison. '*pāšittu*-sickness' *refers to* the case where it contains gall." While A:B:A:C patterns are well attested elsewhere (§1.2.3.2.1), this particular tablet almost always presents a single two-member argument per line regardless of the length of the argument, with topic and comment consistently separated by a disjunction sign. Moreover, the interpretation of *imtu* ("poison") as topic and *martu* ("gall") as comment is supported by the lexical equation *im-tum* = *mar-tum* (Malku

VIII, 124 in Hrůša 2010: 426). The topic requiring comment is therefore the grouped items "*pāšittu*-sickness (and / with) poison" and not *pāšittu*-sickness alone, which seems to be named more commonly in therapeutic texts than in the Diagnostic Handbook: *BAM* 183: 39; 578 ii 9, 13–14, 18, 20, [39]. Despite its meaning and appearance in certain lists of plants and sicknesses (e.g., Uruanna II, 391; *CT* 19 3 ii 4), the topic *imtu* ("poison") is not really part of the usual terminology in diagnostic and therapeutic texts. The comment, on the other hand, employs a far more prevalent medical term *martu* ("gall"), which was already known to be associated with *pāšittu*-sickness; cf. von Soden (1961: 72, notes on line 10). Note also the incantation beginning with "Gall, gall, gall, *pāšittu*" at *BAM* 578 ii 39–44. The commentary entry here has influenced my translation of KI.MIN | MIN *pa-šit-t*[u_4] ^{munus}*mar-*tu_4 (*SpTU* I, 43 obv. 11) as "Ditto (i.e., from the mouth and/of stomach) | Ditto (i.e., mouth and tooth) of *pāšittu* sickness (with) gall" (Wee in press: §B5).

Obv. 5–6—The expressions šu gá-gá and šu gar are equated with the Akkadian verb *gamālu* ("to become obliging; to spare, save") (*CAD* G, 21), but we are unable to identify the base text with this verb in Sa-gig tablet 13. The following lexical equations, however, seem to underlie the commentarial argument here: gú-un-íl-la, gú-un-šu-gá-gá = *na-š*[*u-u š*]*á bil-tim* (Nabnitu K, 187–188 in *MSL* XVI, 147). The logogram GÚ(.UN), which expresses the term *biltu* ("load") in these equations, most commonly denotes the "neck" in medical texts. One therefore wonders if these lexical entries were cited in order to comment on a condition involving "raising" (ÍL) the "neck" (GÚ). Unfortunately, no such description is preserved in the entries of Sa-gig 13. In any case, the commentator probably implied that the patient's condition here carries with it implications of "guilt." This interpretation is also expressed in Lambert (1960: 321 n. 115). The term gá-gá occurs elsewhere in commentary arguments like gá-gá : *za-ba-lu šá mur-ṣu* (Comm. Sa-gig 1B, obv. 11′; Comm. Sa-gig 1C, obv. 7) and ⸢gá-gá : *kul*⸣*-lu šá re-e-šú* (Comm. Sa-gig 4B, obv. 4).

Obv. 7—The term *rík-su* ("bonds") is quoted from the base text Sa-gig 13: 129 (TDPT 13 iii 18) and does not seem attested elsewhere in the Diagnostic Handbook and therapeutic texts, despite its common use in non-medical contexts. Though ancient readers would likely have understood *rík*(zum)*-su* as syllable signs, a quick survey of orthographies in *CAD* R, 347–355 s.v. *riksu* suggests that the signs here were unusual enough to benefit from explicit clarification as *ri-ik-su* (= *riksū*, "bonds"), which in turn was identified with the common body part "strands" (*šer'ānū*, logogram SA). See also Note on Comm. Sa-gig 1A, line 47 for how commentators made the title of the Diagnostic Handbook SA.GIG conform to its definition in *Esagil-kīn-apli's*

Manifesto as a "bundling together (SA = *riksu*) of sickness (GIG)," i.e., a comprehensive compilation that included "all (SA) sickness (GIG)." The status of *riksu* itself as a body part here and in lexical texts (Couto-Ferreira 2009: 341–342), as well as the emphasis on the "head-to-foot" arrangement of the Diagnostic Handbook, suggests even deeper meaning to the expression "bundling together of sickness": The Diagnostic Handbook was a counterpart to the human body in its structure, integrity, and completeness, representing in the most literal sense a textual *corpus*.

Obv. 8—In the "hip" (*gilšu*) segment of the head-to-foot sequence in Sa-gig Chapter II (Sa-gig 14: 1–31 (TDPT 14 i 1–31)), preserved manuscripts represent this body part as the logogram TUGUL or as the syllabic construct form *gi-liš*. In the expression "from his hip to his ankle/toes," the form *giššu* ("hip") is used instead, both in the Diagnostic Handbook and in therapeutic texts: Sa-gig [14: 170′] (TDPT [14 iii 37′]); Sa-gig 33: 99, 101–102; *AMT* 52/8: 6′; [69/9: 2′]. Other medical attestations outside the Diagnostic Handbook also seem to prefer the form *giššu*: BE 17 74: 11 (Middle Babylonian medical report); *CT* 23 9: 12; 11: 38. Here at the base text Sa-gig 13: 135 (TDPT 13 iii 24), the term *gilissu* ("his hip") is written with the signs *gi-lid-su*, which could potentially be confused with the terms *gildu* ("skin") and *gilittu* ("jitters"). It was, in fact, especially easy to read *gilittu* by mistake, because the next diagnostic entry Sa-gig 13: 136 (TDPT 13 iii 25) includes the close synonym IGI. LÁ.ŠÚ (= *ḫayyattu*, "fright"). Note the equation *ḫa-a-a-át-*[*tu*] / [*g*]*i-lit-tú* ("'*ḫayyattu*' (*means*) jitters") in Comm. Sa-gig 7A, rev. 10–11. The commentator here clarified the reading "hip" for an audience possibly uncertain of its orthography in Sa-gig Chapter II (*gilšu*), by using an alternative form (*giššu*) common outside the Diagnostic Handbook.

Obv. 9—The absence of a pronominal suffix in the comment suggests that the commentator understood all the signs in the topic as the logogram IGI.LAL. ŠÚ ("fright"), instead of IGI.LAL-*šú* ("his fright"). The logogram IGI.LAL(. ŠÚ) is only attested at the base text Sa-gig 13: 136 (TDPT 13 iii 25), though the noun LAL appears elsewhere in the Diagnostic Handbook at Sa-gig [3: 45] (TDPT [3: 36]; collated by Scurlock and Andersen 2005: 484, §19.227; 756 n. 171); Sa-gig 16: 14, 82′; 17: 34–35; 18: 3; 26: 15′–16′. Its syllabic form *ḫayyattu* does not seem to occur in the Diagnostic Handbook. By contrast, apart from the malady name LAL-*ti ṣe-ti* at *BAM* 177: 12, therapeutic texts almost uniformly prefer the syllabic form *ḫayyattu*: *BAM* 174 rev. 30; 183: 33; 323: 66; 338 rev. 8′; 344: 2; 367: 16; 376 ii 26′; [385 i 24′]; 469 rev. 35; 471 ii 26′. The equation NÍG.LAL : *ḫa-a-a-at-ti* appears in Comm. Sa-gig 3B, obv. 8′.

Line 10—The malady *ḫuṣṣa*/*ḫūṣ* GAZ ŠÀ appears only at Sa-gig 13: 154 (TDPT 13 iii 43) in the Diagnostic Handbook, but occurs in a variety of therapeutic texts: *BAM* 159 iii 29; 232 i 14′; 311: 22′; 316 iii 23′; 317 rev. 10, 24; [438 obv. 6]; 444 rev. 14′; 445: 1, 10; *AMT* [64/2: 10′]. The form GAZ ŠÀ (unpreceded by *ḫuṣṣa*/*ḫūṣ*) is attested almost as frequently in therapeutic texts at *BAM* 234: 4; 316 iii 13′; 317 rev. 16, [22]; 370 i a4′; 372 i 2; 375 i 11; [379 i 21′]; 388 i 6–7, 11; 480 iv 38. The appearance of *ḫuṣṣa* as a topic here is therefore surprising, because the Sa-gig commentaries tend to select topics that are atypical for therapeutic texts. As part of an erudite argument, the commentator interpreted the signs ḫu-uṣ-ṣa as the logogram ḪU.UZ.ZA, which represents the Akkadian verb *šamû*/*šemû* ("to roast"). What seems to be a related form šu-ḫu-uz appears in these lexical equations: šu-ḫu-uz = MIN (= *šá-mu-u*) *šá šá-ba-a-b*[*i*] (Antagal III, 181 in *MSL* XVII, 156); šu-ḫu-uz = *šu-um-mu*-⌜*ú*⌝ (Antagal VII, 230 in *MSL* XVII, 166); izi šu-ḫu-uz = izi *šu-um-mu*-[*u*] (Izi I, 77 in *MSL* XIII, 157). Note also the equivalence of mi-ni-íb-hu-u[z] = *i-ša-a-me* in the bilingual text of *Lugale* III, 5 (van Dijk 1983: 1,64; 2,58; line 94). Moreover, lest the form *šemû* ("to roast") should be confused with the common verb *šemû* ("to hear"), the commentator attached the qualifier *šá ka-ba-bu* ("in the case of charring"). By designating the commentary equation here merely as "akkadien : akkadien" (instead of also "sumérogramme : akkadien"), Genty (2010b: 18) understates the complex ways that the commentator understood the writing "ḫu-uṣ-ṣa." Note also the misunderstanding that "(this commentary) does not understand the word: *ḫu-uz-za* …" expressed in *CAD* Ḫ, 260 s.v. *ḫūṣu*. Rather than "not understand the word," the commentator sought to describe the intangible sensation of *ḫuṣṣa* pain by appealing to the logographic possibilities (ḪU.UZ.ZA) of the signs ḫu-uṣ-ṣa.

Line 11—The reading KIŠIB in the colophon has also been collated by Frahm (2011a: 225), though he allows for the possibility of scribal error. If he is correct that KIŠIB here stands for *rittu* ("wrist"), it would constitute one of the few instances whereby this body part is not written out syllabically (see also *BAM* 212: 20; 213: 13′). The title "If the sick man('s) wrist" presumably represents the incipit-title of Sa-gig tablet 11, though the Sa-gig catalog provides slightly different wording: DIŠ *rit-ta-šú šá* 15 GU_7-⌜*šú*⌝ ("If his right wrist hurts him"). See Finkel (1988: 146, obv. A 14); Heeßel (2000: 14, line 14). Based on the topics in the preceding lines of this commentary, we would have expected the incipit-title of Sa-gig 13 instead of Sa-gig 11. As I remarked earlier, it is possible that the base text for this commentary did not conform to the standardized version of Sa-gig Tablet 13.

Line 12—The expression KIR_4 ŠU GÁL ("touching the nose") appears as a medical sign only at Sa-gig 12: 5 (TDPT 12 i 5), though it represents a common description of contrite prayer in non-medical contexts. See the lexical equations at Nabnitu E, 173–176 (*MSL* XVI, 110); Igituh I, 121 and Igituh short version 92 (*CAD* L, 10); Antagal III, 291 (*MSL* XVII, 161), as well as the entry in an *Enūma eliš* commentary: KIR$_4$.ŠU.GÁL *la-ba-ṣu* KIR$_4$.ŠU.GÁL *la-ban ap-pi* (*CT* 13, 32 rev. 11).

Line 13—The same equation between KI.GUB and the Akkadian word *manzaltu* ("flow of excrement") appears in Comm. Sa-gig 14 (obv. 10), where KI.GUB is, however, mistakenly written as GU.DU. The logogram KI.GUB occurs only in the Diagnostic Handbook at Sa-gig 12: 98″ (TDPT 12 iii 35); Sa-gig 14: 60 (TDPT 14 i 60); Sa-gig 15: 46′, 51′. It originally meant *manzāzu* "position" (< *izuzzu* "to stand"), as evident from the etymology of its components KI ("place") and GUB ("to stand"). Here and elsewhere, however, the term was confused or associated by the rebus principle with the similar-sounding Akkadian word *manzaltu* "flow of excrement" (< *nazālu* "to pour out"). For example, KI.GUB MAŠKIM$_2$ in the therapeutic text *AMT* 69/2: 3′ has a parallel in *man-za-a*[*z* MAŠKIM$_2$] at *BAM* 152 iv 2. In any case, medical texts have other more idiomatic ways of expressing problems in defecating. The term ŠE$_{10}$ "excrement, stools," for example, has a designated segment (Sa-gig 14: 88–93 (TDPT 14 ii 15–21)) in the head-to-foot arrangement of Sa-gig Chapter 11, and the expressions *errū* / ŠÀ / ŠÀ.MEŠ + *ešēru* are common ways in diagnostic and therapeutic texts to denote bowel movement (*CAD* E, 356 s.v. *ešēru* §3).

Lines 14–15—The topic ^{na_4}*e-tan-de-e-ti* in the base text Sa-gig 12: 108″ (TDPT 12 iii 45) is erroneously rendered as *ter-de-e-ti* ("sequellae") in Scurlock (2014: 96, 100). The stones here are equated also in Hg. B IV, 105 (in Vedeler 2002: 70; cf. *MSL* X, 33): ^{na_4}*e-tan-de-e-tum* = MIN (i.e., *ṣip-re-e-tum*) = *pur-ṭa-a-tum*. The term *etandētu* may refer to stones that are "collected" or "joined" together (*CAD* I/J, 298 s.v. *itmudu*; cf. *CAD* E, 380 s.v. *etamdu*), and recall the *erimmātu*-beads (^{na_4}NUNUZ.MEŠ in Sa-gig 10: 17; 10 B rev. 5) offered as propitiatory gifts to the goddess Ištar. See Note on Comm. Sa-gig 10 & 11, obv. 8. The status of line 15 as a learned exegesis on the stone's name was first proposed by Wee (2012: 631), along with the meanings E ("saying") + TI ("he will live / become healthy"). Building on this, Jiménez (CCP 4.1.13.B) suggested the line begins with ⸢*šá-niš* (?)⸣ ("secondly (?)"), the cuneiform signs e-tan (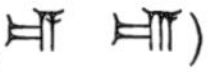) could be read *ík-rib* ("vow/prayer") and, perhaps less securely, "NA$_4$ = *ana* (elsewhere unattested, but *nam* and *ia* = *ana* is common)." The only element left to be explained is /de/ or /di/, which I now interpret—along with e ("to say")—as forms of the same Sumerian verb "to say" (see Attinger 1993). Note also various later attestations of di ("to say") in the lexical and bilingual tradition, listed at *CAD* Q, 22–23 s.v. *qabû*, lexical section. In short then, the stone's name ^{na_4}*etandētu* can be analyzed as "for (NA$_4$)

a vow/prayer (e-tan = *ík-rib*) that he said (di / e), he will become healthy (TI)." This statement closely resembles the expression *ana* ŠÙD /*ik-rib qí-bit* KA-*šú* TIN at Sa-gig 10: 7; 11: 1. The commentator in effect explained that the efficacy of the *puraṭātu* stones in healing was intrinsic to their name and nature.

Line 16—Apart from the base text here (Sa-gig 12: 109″ (TDPT 12 iv 1)), it is unclear whether *šitti* ("feces") ever appears in medical texts, and the writing *šit-ta-šu* at *AMT* 47/1 obv. 1, [5] refers instead to the homophone "sleep." The commentator explained *šitti* by the term *zû* (logogram $ŠE_{10}$), which is the typical way to denote human "excrement" in medical texts.

Line 17—The topic SA.GIG appears as the diagnostic verdict in the base text Sa-gig 12: 126″ (TDPT 12 iv 18). The orthography *ki-is-sa-*tu_4 indicates the muscle condition *kiṣṣatu* (*CAD* K, 428–429 s.v. *kissatu* B), whereby the individual components of SA.GIG bear the meanings "strand, i.e., muscle" (SA) + "sickness" (GIG). Other lexical and commentarial texts, however, seem to equate SA.GIG with another muscle condition *maškadu* instead of *kiṣṣatu*: sa-gig = *maš-ka-du* (*List of Diseases* SB Recension, 76 (256) in *MSL* IX, 94); sa-gig // *maš-*ka_{15}(kak)-*du* (VAT 14258, ii 11).

Commentary Sa-gig 14

Provenance:	Uruk (Warka), Area U18, Level v; Same findspot and consignment (W 22307) as Comm. Sa-gig 1C, 5, 7A, 7B, and 19 suggests library of Anu-ikṣur
Period:	Late Achaemenid
Names:	Not preserved
Script:	Neo-/Late Babylonian
Typology:	Perhaps a *ṣâtu* commentary (Frahm 2011a: 226)
Field/Museum No.:	W 22307/20 (National Museum of Iraq)
Photos:	Plate 22 (obverse) and Plate 23 (reverse)
Printed Edition/Hand Copy:	*SpTU* 1, 36 (= Hunger 1976: 44–45); Wee (2012: 633–651)
Digital Resources:	CDLI P348457; GKAB P348457 (edition digitized by Clancier 2009); CCP 4.1.14 (printed hand copies digitized by Frahm, Frazer, and Jiménez 2013)
Discussion:	Hunger (1975: 63–64) and *SpTU* 1, 36 (= Hunger 1976: 44–45); Schramm (1979: 123); Kouwenberg (1997: 416); Heeßel (2000: 134, 145 (14. Tafel MS a)); Scurlock and Andersen (2005: 803, see references to *SpTU* 1.36); Clancier (2009: 388); Genty (2010a: 380) and (2010b: 13, 21, 25, 27); Frahm (2011a: 29 n. 96, 61, 98, 101, 226, 291); Wee (2012: 633–651), (2015a: 263–265), and (2015b: 230 n. 47); Scurlock (2014: 28 n. 104; 136–137 (various notes)); Gabbay (2016: 88 n. 17, 107–109, 115 n. 158, 129 n. 6, 131 n. 19); Steinert (2017: 337)
Pericope:	At least Sa-gig 14: 1–70 (TDPT 14 i 1–70) and Sa-gig 14: 94–135 (TDPT 14 ii 22–63)

Transliteration

Obverse

1) [DIŠ] GIG *gi-liš* 15-*šú* SA$_5$ TIN : GIG-*su ú-zab-bal* ⸢*i*⸣-[*ka-áš*]

2) *du-ʾ-um i-da-mu* : MUD : *da-a-mu* : *šá a-na* x x [...]

3) *il-la-ku* : ADAMA *a-da-ma-tu*$_4$ MÚD : *da-mu* : GE$_6$: *ṣa-a*[*l-mu*]

 | DOI:10.1163/9789004417564_021

4) *muq-qú-ut* : *šá-pil* : DU$_{8}$-*ir* : *šá pi-tíš-šú in-né*-ne-[x(?)]
5) *in-né-ṣil* : *i-ta-an-ṣu-lu* : *ra-ba-ba* : DIŠ TUGUL.MEŠ-*šú šal*-[*ma* TIN]
6) *šá* TUGUL.MEŠ-*šú* GIG *u* KALA-*tu ina* ŠÀ *la i-šu-ú* : *ki-iṣ-ṣat* U[D.DA]
7) *ḫi-miṭ* UD.DA *lìb-bu-ú i-šat mu-ú-tú i-šat šib-ṭu* KI.MIN : GU.[DU]
8) *qin-na-tu*$_{4}$: GÙ.DÉ : *šá-su-ú* : GU.DU 15-*šú šu-uḫ-ḫu-ṭ*[*a-at*]
9) *šá maš-ku ina* UGU *iš-šá-a*[*ḫ*]-*ṭu* : GU.DU.MEŠ-*šú šal-ma šá pi-ṭir* x[...]
10) *la ib-šu-ú* : GU.DU-*s*[*u*] NU.È.A *šá man-zal-tu*$_{4}$ *la ú-še*-[*ṣu*]
11) A.GA SÌG!(kád)-*iṣ ár*!(bi)-*kát ma-ḫi-iṣ* A.GA *ár-kát* A.GA ^{giš}TUKUL *ár-kát ka*[*k-ki*]
12) ig(?) lu(?) *šér-a-nu šá* AN.TA-*nu a-si-du šá-pu-lu bi*-⸤*rit*⸥ PAP.[ḪAL]
13) UMUŠ LÍL-*šú* KÚR *ṭè-eme si-li-ti-šú* KÚR-*ir* : GUB-*az* : *man-za*-[*az*]
14) DÚR-*šú iz-zi-iz* : *šá* DÚR-*šú ir-rak-su* : DIŠ DÚR-*šú* BÙR-*liš* : *šá* DÚR-*šú ir-pi*-[*šu*]
15) *šu-ḫa-at-ti er-ru-šú* : *šu-uḫ-ḫi-iṭ-ṭa-a-ti* : *zu-ú-šú* GUB-x
16) *šá la il-la-ku-ú-nu* : *zu-ú-šú pur-ru-šú* : *pur-ru-s*[*u-šú*]
17) *zu-ú-šú dak-ku šá la raq-qa* : x x a bal ⸢ŠÀ *di-ki* (?)⸣ [...]
18) *di-i-ki šá mim-ma ul-tu du-ur-ri-šú la uṣ-ṣa-a* [: ḪAR GIG]
19) *ḫa-šu-u ma-ru-uṣ* : *i-ṣal-lal-ma* : *it-tal-«li»-ma* : GÌŠ [...]
20) *šá ma-gal ma*-⸢*ṭu*$_{5}$(!)⸣-*ú* (?) : ŠÀ.MEŠ-*šú ma-ḫu* : ŠÀ-*šú šu-ṣi-iš* : ⸢È⸣ [: *ma-ḫu*]
21) È : *a-ṣu-ú* : ka x x mu ne : i-gi-in-zu [...]
22) mu-un-è-dè : *ina* ḪUL [ŠÀ]-*ia tu-šá-ma-a a-na* ŠÀ-*i*[*a* (x?) : *ina* GÌŠ-*šú* (?)]
23) *ina mu-šar-šu* : ki nu gi E *it-ti sin-niš-ti la-a*[*m-du*]
24) KI *it-ti* nu *sin-niš-tu*$_{4}$ gi *la-ma-du šá zi-kìr u* MUNUS : [...]
25) GA GEŠTIN *ni-iš* DINGIR-*šú* : *lìb-bu-ú niš* ŠU.2 : A.RI.A [: *ri-ḫu-tu*]
26) [*ina*] EDIN TAG-*it* : *ina* UGU *ma-ḫi-iṣ* : *ṣe-e-r*[*i*] UGU [...]
27) [x x] x : *muḫ-ḫi* : EME-⸤*šú*⸥ *i-te-néq-qí-iq* : x [...]
28) [...] G[I]G *šá* x *di*(?) x x [...]
29) [...] x x x [...]
30) [...] x [...]

Reverse

1′) [...] *ta* x x [...]
2′) x *šú* : x x [...]
3′) [x x] *ru ma* x [...]
4′) [x] x *a nam*(?) [...]
5′) *šá-ga-mu* [...]

6′) DIŠ U$_{4}$.1.KAM G[I]G-*ma* x x[...]

7′) *ul*(?) x [x] x x x [...]
8′) *lu*(?) [...] x x [...]
9′) *a-na* [...] x x [...]
10′) x *u* [...]
11′) [x] x x [...] *ḫa* [...]
12′) [x x] *na* [...]
13′) [x x] $^{m.d}$[...]

Translation

Incipit-title of Sa-gig 14

(Obv. 1) "[If] the sick man's right hip is red, he will live."

Sa-gig 14: 2 (TDPT 14 i 2)
The basic meaning of *zubbulu* is "to carry, deliver," and the commentator felt the need to clarify its derived nuance "to carry on," i.e., "to tarry on" in the context of sickness.

(1) "His sickness will carry on" (*means*) [it will tarry on].

***Sa-gig 14: 13 (TDPT 14 i 13)—"[his right hip is darkened]"**
du''um "is darkened" appears primarily in formulaic sequences of Sa-gig Chapter 11. It is explained by the similar-sounding but more common verb *idammu* "it convulses."

(2) "*du''um*" (*means*) it convulses.

MUD and *da'āmu* both mean "to become dark," but they are explained here as forms of the more common verb *damû* "to convulse," i.e., "that which moves ..."

(2–3) MUD *means da'āmu, which refers to* that which moves to ...

***Sa-gig 14**
ADAMA "black blood" consists of the components MÚD "blood" + GE_6 "black."

(3) "ADAMA" (*means*) black blood.
(3) MÚD *means* blood.
(3) GE_6 *means* black.

***Sa-gig 14: 19 (TDPT 14 i 19)— "[his right hip is collapsed]"**
The D Stative form *muqqut* "is collapsed" appears primarily in formulaic sequences of Sa-gig Chapter 11. The comment *šapil* "is low" occurs in several therapeutic texts.

(4) "It is collapsed" *means* it is low.

***Sa-gig 14: 22 (TDPT 14 i 22)— "[his right hip DU$_8$-*ir* ?]"**
The G Stative form *paṭir* (written DU$_8$-*ir*) "it is slack" supposedly appears in the base text, though one expects the D Stative *puṭṭur* in such formulaic sequences.

(4) "It is slack" *refers to the case* where its sturdiness ...

***Sa-gig 14: 25 (TDPT 14 i 25)— "[his right hip becomes sluggish]"**
The N form *in-né-ṣil* "it becomes sluggish" is unusual in medical texts. Notice that the commentator did not directly explain the N form, but the much more common Ntn form "to keep becoming sluggish."

(5) "It becomes sluggish."

(5) To keep becoming sluggish *means* to become weak.

Sa-gig 14: 29 (TDPT 14 i 29)
Such statements on the "wellness" of body parts occur only in the Diagnostic Handbook, but not in therapeutic texts.

(5–6) "If his hips are well, [he will become healthy]" (*means the opposite of*) the case where his hips are sick and have no strength within.

Sa-gig 14: 31 (TDPT 14 i 31)
"*kiṣṣatu* of *ṣētu*-heat" appears only in a few diagnostic texts and is explained here by the more common term "burning of *ṣētu*-heat."

(6–7) "*kiṣṣatu* of [*ṣētu*-heat" (*means*)] burning of *ṣētu*-heat.

išātu kāsistu "consuming fire" appears in the original text of the fire incantation quoted, but has been replaced here by the term *kiṣṣatu*. This implies that *kiṣṣatu* is another way of expressing "burning."

(7) As in, "Fire of death, fire of plague, *ditto* (i.e., *kiṣṣatu*)."

Sa-gig 14: 32 (TDPT 14 i 32)
Perhaps a clarification to avoid confusing expressions with similar logographic values: GU.DU "buttock" versus GÙ.DÉ "to cry out".

(7–8) "GU.DU" (*means*) buttock. GÙ.DÉ *means* to cry out.

Sa-gig 14: 53 (TDPT 14 i 53)
šuḫḫuṭat derives from the verb *šaḫāṭu* "to tear off," not the homophone *šaḫāṭu* "to jerk." Both these terms occur only in the Diagnostic Handbook.

(8–9) "His right buttock is *šuḫḫuṭat*" (*refers to*) the case where the skin above is torn off.

Sa-gig 14: 59 (TDPT 14 i 59)
Such statements on the "wellness" of body parts occur only in the Diagnostic Handbook, not in therapeutic texts.

(9–10) "His buttocks are well" (*refers to*) the case where there is no fissure of ...

Sa-gig 14: 60 (TDPT 14 i 60)—GU.DU.MEŠ-*šú* ... KI.GUB-*su* NU È-*a*
KI.GUB occurs only rarely in the Diagnostic Handbook, and the scribe here seems to have mistakenly written GU.DU instead. KI.GUB originally meant *manzāzu* "position," but was confused or associated by the rebus principle with the similar-sounding term *manzaltu* "flow of excrement."

(10) "He does not put out his GU.DU (mistake for KI.GUB)" (*refers to*) the case where he does not put out the flow of excrement.

Sa-gig 14: 60 (TDPT 14 i 60)
The diagnosis "he is struck (at the) back" occurs only in the Diagnostic Handbook, where "back" is typically written EGIR, not A.GA.

(11) "He is struck A.GA" (*means*) he is struck (at the) back.

(11) "A.GA" (*means*) (at the) back.

Quotation from lexical text similar to Hh. VII A, 31.

(11) "A.GA of the weapon (*means*) the back of the weapon."

***Sa-gig 14**

(12) … strands that are above the heel.

Sa-gig 14: 61 or 63 (TDPT 14 i 61 or 63)
šapūlu "inguinal region" occurs mainly in specialized contexts of medicine, divination, and physiognomy. Here, it is explained by means of a more general idiom.

(12) "*šapūlu*" (*refers to* the area) between the legs.

Sa-gig 14: 64 (TDPT 14 i 64)
UMUŠ typically denotes the patient's "intelligence" in the Diagnostic Handbook, not the "disposition" of the illness.

(13) "UMUŠ LÍL-*šú* KÚR" (*means*) the disposition of his illness changes.

***BAM* VII/49 i 18′**

(13) "GUB-*az*" *means* position.

***Sa-gig 14: 70 (TDPT 14 i 70)**
"His rectum stands" is a unique expression. This comment clarifies that the rectum is "bound," and its excretory functions are at a standstill.

(14) "His rectum stands" *refers to* the case where his rectum is bound.

***Sa-gig 14**
BÙR "is breached" describes body parts in a variety of contexts, but not usually in the language of medical signs.

(14) "If his rectum is breached" *refers to* the case where his rectum widened.

***Sa-gig 14: 80 (*BAM* VII/49 i 28′)?**
šuḫḫâtti and *šuḫḫiṭṭāti* do not seem attested elsewhere, though *šuḫḫu* may refer to the "(anal) sphincter."

(15) "*šuḫḫâtti* of his bowels" *refers to šuḫḫiṭṭāti.*

***Sa-gig 14**
"His stoods stand" is a unique expression, and this comment clarifies that the stools are at a standstill and "do not move" through the rectum.

(15–16) "His stools stand" (*refers to*) the case where they do not move.

***Sa-gig 14**
The writing *pur-ru* does not refer to the common root *parû* "to vomit, to void" (which can refer to bowel evacuations), but to another root *parāʾu* "to sever."

(16) "His stools are *pur-ru* for him" (*means*) they are cut up [for him].

***Sa-gig 14: 93 (TDPT 14 ii 21)?**
"His stools are crushed" is a unique expression, and this comment clarifies that the stools do not appear in elongated forms.

(17) "His stools are crushed" (*refers to*) the case where they are not thin.

***Sa-gig 14: 94 (TDPT 14 ii 22)**

(17) "… ŠÀ *di-ki* (?) …" [*means*] (18) *di-i-ki, which refers to* the case where nothing comes out from his anus.

Sa-gig 14: 94 (TDPT 14 ii 22)
The base text comes from the "stools" segment in the head-to-foot order of Sa-gig Chapter II. The diagnosis of "sick lung" instead of rectal sicknesses is unexpected and needed to be confirmed by the commentator.

(18–19) ["ḪAR GIG" (*means*)] the lung is sick.

***Sa-gig 14**

(19) "It sleeps" *means* it lies down.

***Sa-gig 14**

(19–20) "[His] penis ..." (*refers to*) the case where it is much diminished (?).

***Sa-gig 14: 106 (TDPT 14 ii 34)—ŠÀ-*šú ma-ḫu* "his belly is raving"**

(20) "His innards are raving" *means* (in order) to bring out his belly (ŠÀ).

The semantic link between *maḫû* "to rave" and *aṣû* "to go out" is implied by their shared logogram È.

(20–21) È [*means* to rave.] È *means* to go out. ...

In this bilingual quote, the expressions "heart" (ŠÀ) and "mu-un-è-dè" probably constitute a comment on the medical condition that "innards" (ŠÀ.MEŠ) are "raving" (È).

(21–22) "i-gi-in-zu ... mu-un-è-dè *means*
(22) In my distress,
as if to my heart (ŠÀ) (... ?)"

Sa-gig 14: 109 (TDPT 14 ii 37)—*ina mu-šar-ri-šú
Mušaru "penis" may represent an atypical syllabic form in the base text, which differs from the usual logographic writing GÌŠ "penis." Following the custom that logograms precede their syllabic equivalents, the commentator may have stated his comment (GÌŠ) before its topic (*mušaru*) here.

(22–23) [In his GÌŠ-penis (*means*) (?)] "in his *mušaru*."

Sa-gig 14: 109 (TDPT 14 ii 37)
"ki nu gi" is a unique expression, which the commentator interpreted as a variant of the common statement KI MUNUS *ina* KI.NÁ KUR "he is encountered with a female in bed."

(23) "ki nu gi," it is said, (*means*) he is acquainted with a female.

The following argument attempts to find possible readings for ki, nu, and gi, whose collective meaning has been predetermined:

Common lexical equation

(24) KI (*means*) with.

The term nu in the Emesal dialect means "female."

(24) nu (*means*) female.

Whereas zu denotes acquaintance with facts, gi denotes sexual acquaintance in the lexical texts Nabnitu A, etc.

(24) gi (*means*) to become acquainted, in the case of male-and-female (relations).

Thus, "ki nu gi" depicts the cause of the patient's sickness: "he is (illicitly) in sexual acquaintance (gi) with (KI) a female (nu)."

***Sa-gig 14**

(24–25) … milk, wine.

Sa-gig 14: 111 (TDPT 14 ii 39)
"Hand of (the oath on) his god's life" is a rare diagnosis, unlike the similar but common diagnosis "Hand of his god."

(25) "(Oath on) his god's life."

Metathesis occurs between ŠU *nīš* "Hand of (the oath on) the life" and *nīš* ŠU.2 "raising of hands." This may imply that the cause or solution of the malady pertained to the patient's offering of Šu-íl-lá (lit. "raised hand") prayers to the offended deity.

(25) As in, the raising of hands.

Sa-gig 14: 117 (TDPT 14 ii 45)
The logogram A.RI.A is more typical of the Diagnostic Handbook than therapeutic texts, and it only here refers to the patient's own "semen," not that of an offending agent.

(25) "A.RI.A" [*means* semen.]

Sa-gig 14: 124 (TDPT 14 ii 52)
The prepositional phrases *ina ṣēr* and *ina muḫḫi* can share the idiomatic meaning "upon, on top of." The commentator argued that the nouns *ṣēru* "steppe" and *muḫḫu* "above / cranium" could be equated as well.

(26) "He is touched [in] the steppe" *means* he is struck above / in the cranium.

(26) "Steppe" (*refers to*) above / cranium ...
(27) ... above / cranium.

Sa-gig 14: 135 (TDPT 14 ii 63)
The syllable signs here are not to be misunderstood as *i-te-nék-ki-ik* from the common verb *ekēku* "to scratch." Instead, they are to be read *i-te-néq-qí-iq* from the rare verb *eqēqu* "to become (tongue)-tied."

(27) "His tongue *i-te-néq-qí-iq*" *means* ...

(28–30) ...
(Rev. 1′–4′) ...
(5′) to roar ...

Incipit-title of Sa-gig 15

(6′) "If he is sick for one day, and ..."
(7′–13′) ...

Notes

Obv. 1—See Note on Comm. Sa-gig 1B, obv. 10′–11′ for *zubbulu* ("to carry on (said of a sick person or sickness)") as derivative of the basic meaning "to carry, deliver" and its attestations in medical texts, as well as *kâšu* ("to tarry on") as the preferred explanation in several commentaries. The latter accounts for my restored comment ⸢*i*⸣-[*ka-áš*] ("[it will tarry on]") at the end of obv. 1. Another possible restoration might be ⸢*i*⸣-[*kab-bi-it*] ("[it will become severe]"). Though one might expect a disjunction sign immediately after *ú-zab-bal* (obv. 1), the traces do not resemble those of disjunction signs elsewhere on the commentary tablet.

Obv. 2—The D Stative *du''um* ("it is darkened") derives from the verb *da'āmu* ("to become dark"), and it appears as part of a formulaic list of possible conditions of the "breast" (Sa-gig 12: 21–23 (TDPT 12 i 15–16)), "kidney" (Sa-gig 12: 61″–63″ (TDPT 12 ii 56′–58′)), "spine" (Sa-gig 12: 92″ (TDPT 12 iii 29)), "coccyx" (Sa-gig 12: 119″ (TDPT 12 iv 11)), "innards" (Sa-gig 13: 99 (TDPT 13 ii 41)), "hip" (Sa-gig 14: 13–15 (TDPT 14 i 13–15)), "buttock" (Sa-gig 14: 44–46 (TDPT 14 i 44–46)), "excrement, stools" (Sa-gig 14: 91 (TDPT 14 ii 19)), "penis" (Sa-gig 14: 99 (TDPT 14 ii 27)), "testicles" (Sa-gig 14: 130 (TDPT 14 ii 58)), and "thigh" (Sa-gig 14: 156–158 (TDPT 14 iii 11–13)). Such formulaic sequences were briefly discussed by Heeßel (2000: 37–38); Böck (2009b: 393–394); and I would also observe that they share several characteristics: (I) They occur only in Chapter II of the Diagnostic Handbook Sa-gig. (II) They are concerned with only parts of the body below the head in the head-to-foot sequence of Chapter II. (III) They largely consist of medical entries each with only a single medical sign. (IV) The verbs expressing the medical signs occur in a predictable sequence that includes SA_5 ("to become red"), SIG_7 ("to become green/yellow"), GE_6 ("to become black"), *tarāku* ("to throb, become dark (Stative meaning)"), *du''umu* ("to darken"), *napāḫu* ("to inflame"), *muqqutu* ("to collapse"), *šuḫḫuṭu* ("to tear off"), *ḫesû* ("to (feel) covered up"), *paṭāru*/*puṭṭuru* ("to become slack, loosen, split"), GU_7 ("to hurt"), and *šalāmu* ("to become well"). (V) Where the body parts consist of paired members, the medical entries systematically describe the right member, then the left member, then both members. Thus, although the verb *du''um* appears frequently as part of this formulaic list, it very seldomly occurs elsewhere (Sa-gig 6: 2; 9: 25, 26). Here, the commentator explained the form *du''um* by means of another verb *damû*/*ṭamû* ("to convulse, stagger"), which phonologically resembles *da'āmu* ("to become dark"), but which is attested in a much wider variety of contexts in the Diagnostic Handbook, either as a description of the patient himself (Sa-gig 3: 86, 92 (TDPT 3: 77, 83); Sa-gig 4: 42–43; 10: 39; 14: 250′ (TDPT 14 iv 49′); Sa-gig 15: 84′; 17: 22; 22: 39–40) or that of a body part (Sa-gig 3: 35–36 (TDPT 3: 26–27); Sa-gig 9: 64; 10 B rev. 1 (TDPT 10 rev. 1); Sa-gig 12: 8 (TDPT 12 i 8); Sa-gig 15: 10′, 29′, 66′; 22: 44; 26: 53′, 71′; 40: 71).

Obv. 3—The same equation [... ADAM]A : *a-da-ma-tu*$_4$ ("['ADAMA'] *means* black blood") may be restored in Comm. Sa-gig 18, rev. 2′.

Obv. 4—The signs should be read *muq-qú-ut* in agreement with the 3ms Stative *šá-pil*, not *muq-qú-tú*(ut) by Hunger (*SpTU* I, 36). The syllabic writing of the D Stative form *muqqut* ("it is collapsed") is a feature of the formulaic sequences in Sa-gig Chapter 11 discussed above (see Note on obv. 2). The only other clear attestation of the syllabic form is in the broken context of Sa-gig 19/20: 37′: [x].2-*šú muq-qú-ta*$_5$. In contrast, the comment *šapil* ("it is low") appears in the Diagnostic Handbook only at Sa-gig 9: 12 in relation to the eyes, and in several therapeutic texts describing the patient's "belly" (ŠÀ): *BAM* 231 i 3; 232 i 10′; [438 obv. 5]; *AMT* [76/1: 7].

Obv. 4—Although the Stative verb DU$_8$-*ir* ("it is slack") is not preserved in the base text, we know from formulaic sequences elsewhere that this verb appears after the verbs *muqqut* ("it is collapsed") and *šuḫḫuṭ* ("it is torn off") in descriptions of the "coccyx" (Sa-gig 12: 123″ (TDPT 12 iv 15)) and the "buttock(s)" (Sa-gig 14: 56–58 (TDPT 14 i 56–58)). In the base text, the verb DU$_8$-*ir* ("it is slack") likely appears in the medical entries of Sa-gig [14: 22–24] (TDPT [14 i 22–24]), rather than the verb *šuḫḫuṭ* ("it is torn off") restored by Labat (1951: 130). In addition, the fact that this commentary deals with *šuḫḫuṭ* ("it is torn off") later in obv. 8–9 in the context of another body part (i.e., "buttock") suggests that this verb is absent from the formulaic sequence for the "hip" in Sa-gig 14: 1–29 (TDPT 14 i 1–29), since commentators usually did not repeat their explanation of the same term in a single commentary tablet. The form DU$_8$-*ir* is the G Stative *paṭir*, though one has reason to expect the D Stative *puṭṭur*, because of the syllabic writing *pu-uṭ-ṭu-rat* in Sa-gig 12: 123″ (TDPT 12 iv 15), and because of the predominance of D stem forms like *du*ʾʾ*um* ("it is darkened"), *muqqut* ("it is collapsed"), and *šuḫḫuṭ* ("it is torn off") in such formulaic sequences of Sa-gig Chapter 11. Perhaps this dissonance motivated the commentator's explanation of an otherwise very common verb (*paṭāru*) in medical texts. The reading *pi-lik-šú* ("Gebiet," "district") has been proposed by Hunger (*SpTU* 1, 36); *CAD* P, 373 s.v. *pilku* A; and an appropriate restoration might be *šá pi-lik-šú in-né-pel-*[*ku*] ("the case where its area widens"), though only the Stative of the N stem is attested for *napalkû*/*nepelkû* so far (*CAD* N I, 270). Here, I suggest another possible reading *pi-tíš-šú* ("its sturdiness"), from the substantivized adjective *pitnu* ("strong, sturdy"). In both cases, it is difficult to be sure of the intended verb *in-né*-ne-[x(?)].

Obv. 5—The verb *in-né-ṣil* likely appears in the medical entries of Sa-gig [14: 25–28] (TDPT [14 i 25–28]), judging by the traces of signs preserved. The form *in-né-ṣil* represents the N stem of the verb *eṣēlu* ("to become sluggish"), which occurs in medical texts only at Sa-gig 10 B rev. 9; 14: [25–26], 27–28 (TDPT [14 i [25–26], 27–28); *BAM* 397: 34. Much more common is the Ntn form of the same verb, which appears at Sa-gig 11: 18, [55]; rev. 35, 45; 13: 130 (TDPT 13 iii 19); Sa-gig 14: [28], 219′ (TDPT 14 [i 28]; iv 13′); Sa-gig 18: 5; 33: 102; 36: 84 (TDPT 35: 84); Sa-gig 40: 48; *BAM* 152 iv 7; *AMT* 40/5 iii 9′;

70/5 ii 8′, 16′. The form *i-ta-an-ṣu-lu* is the Ntn Infinitive *itaṣṣulu* (< *eṣēlu*), which is commensurable with the following G Infinitive *ra-ba-ba*. The Ntn Infinitive forms of I-*e* verbs are not well attested, and von Soden thought that "jB *itaṣṣulu*/*itanṣulu* (*LTBA* II 1 XII 84) 'immer wieder gelähmt werden' ist wohl ein Assyriasmus" (*GAG* Paradigm 17 n. 33). The comment *rabāba* ("to become weak, grow soft") is lucid enough, though atypical as a medical description. The commentator's purpose was probably not to explain the very common Ntn stem of *eṣēlu*, but to connect it with the unusual N stem of *eṣēlu* in the base text. While this association between an N stem inflected verb (from the base text) and its Ntn dictionary root (in commentarial argument) may appear incongruous, a similar maneuver occurs in Sa-gig 3B, rev. 2 ([*šu-par-ku-ú* :] *ba-ṭa-lu*, "[To put a stop to *means*] to halt"), where the Š stem dictionary root *šuparkû* (in commentarial argument) corresponds to the Ntn stem inflected verb *it-te-né-e*[*p-rik-ku*] from the base text (Sa-gig 3: 50 (TDPT 3: 41)).

Obv. 5–6—A diagnostic statement like "If his hips are well," whose sole medical sign specifies the wellness (*šalāmu*) of a body part, is absent in therapeutic texts and attested only in the Diagnostic Handbook at Sa-gig 3: 26, 31a (TDPT 3: 17, 22); Sa-gig 4: 5, 140 (TDPT 4 rev. 55); Sa-gig 9: 39; 12: 94″ (TDPT 12 iii 31); Sa-gig 14: [29], 59, [103, 133] (TDPT 14 i [29], 59; [ii 31, 61]). Instead of *šal-mat* at Sa-gig 4: 140 (TDPT 4 rev. 55), the mistaken reading *rak-sat* appears in Labat (1951: 44–45). For other medical entries with the verb *šalāmu*, see Sa-gig 9: 40; 10: 51; 16: 41′, 61′; 18:[10], 12; 19/20: 125′; 40: 85. Though Hunger (*SpTU* I, 36) read *líp-tu* ("(falls richtig gelesen hier unklar)") for obv. 6, I treat the sign líp(kala) logographically: "'If his hips are well, [he will become healthy]' (*means the opposite of*) the case where his hips are sick and have no strength (KALA-*tu* = *dannūtu*) within." The absence of a pronominal suffix -*šú* in the phrase *ina* ŠÀ suggests it should be understood as "within (i.e., the sick hips)" instead of "in (his) belly (i.e., a body part separate from the hips)." In my preferred interpretation, this entry represents an example of definition by antonymy (§1.2.3.1.6). To be sure, though, the logogram KALA in medical texts more typically expresses the meaning *dannatu* ("hardship"), so that the entry could read: "'If his hips are well, [he will become healthy]' (*refers to*) the case where his hips are sick but have no hardship (KALA-*tu* = *dannatu*) within." In this view, "wellness" (*šalāmu*) and "sickness" (*marāṣu*) are not mutually exclusive conditions, but a "sick" body part may still be considered "well," if it is not ailed to the extent that the patient experiences "hardship." Such an explanation, however, strikes me as somewhat strained, and my preference is still to understand KALA-*tu* as "strength" (*dannūtu*).

Obv. 6–7—There are traces of a sign at the end of obv. 6, and Hunger (*SpTU* I, 36) has restored the reading *ki-is-sat* I[ZI(?)] / *ḫi-miṭ* UD.DA. I prefer the reading *ki-iṣ-ṣat* U[D.DA] ("*kiṣṣatu* of *ṣētu*-heat"), which refers to *ki-iṣ-ṣat* [UD.DA] in the base text Sa-gig 14: 31 (TDPT 14 i 31), and which is paralleled by [*k*]*i*(?)-*iṣ*(?)-*ṣat* UD.D[A] at Sa-gig 33: 102 and *ki-iṣ-ṣa-at ṣe-e-ti* at *StBoT* XXXVI, D2 13′ in Wilhelm (1994: 48). The term *kiṣṣatu* can occur alone without the mention of *ṣētu*-heat, where it may refer to at least two distinct kinds of sicknesses. The *Chicago Assyrian Dictionary* lists the two sicknesses separately as (I) *kissatu* B (*kiṣṣatu*, or *kizzatu*) at *CAD* K, 428–429, and (II) *kiṣṣatu* (*giṣṣatu*) at *CAD* K, 443. The first is translated as "gnawing" and identified as "muscle pain (myalgia)," while the second is simply transliterated as *kiṣṣatu* and glossed as "hairless" in Scurlock and Andersen (2005: 54–55, §3.129; 213–214, 635 n. 29, 638 n. 78′–79′); see also Heeßel (2000: 189 n. 29). The designation "*kiṣṣatu* of *ṣētu*-heat" appears only in a few diagnostic texts, and the commentator identifies it with another much more common expression in both the Diagnostic Handbook and therapeutic texts: "burning of *ṣētu*-heat."

Obv. 7—Here, the commentator quoted from a fire incantation, which begins by addressing its subject as *išātum-ma išātum* [*i*]*šāt meḫû išāt qabli* [*iš*]*āt mūtu išāt šibṭu išātu kāsistu* ("Fire, fire, fire of storm, fire of battle, fire of death, fire of plague, consuming fire"). See Lambert (1970: 40, lines 5–7). The incantation section where the commentary quotation appears is attested in tablet copies from Assurbanipal's library at Nineveh, from late Assur, and from late Nippur, and this quotation suggests that the incantation was also known in late Uruk. For the reading *šibṭu* ("plague") instead of *šipṭu* ("judgment"), see *CAD* Š II, 387 s.v. *šibṭu* A §a. Although *išātu* ("fire") is not necessarily a medical term, it readily lends itself as a description of bodily heat at least in popular speech. Besides the medical conditions mentioned in Lambert's article, note the comparison of "heat" (KÚM) with fire that "consumes the vast forest" in an etiological narrative in Madi-Dagan's therapeutic tablet (Tsukimoto 1999: 192–193, lines 27–35), as well as how "fires" (*išātātu*) and "heat" (*ummu*) seem to be used interchangeably in a group of Middle Babylonian letters from Nippur (Stol 2007a: 2–3). Most pertinently, the commentator here was likely encouraged by the expression "*kissatu* of fire" that appears in the context of magic incantations (*CAD* K, 429 s.v. *kissatu* B §a; cf. Comm. Sa-gig 18, rev. 7′). The adjective *kāsistu* ("consuming") from the fire incantation derives from a verb classified in *CAD* as *kasāsu* B "to hurt, to sting, to consume(?)," which may be etymologically related to the term *kiṣṣatu* or *kissatu* here (see *CAD* K, 242, 243, 429). In the place of *išātu kāsistu*, however, the commentator wrote KI.MIN ("*ditto*"), which refers to the signs *ki-iṣ-ṣat* directly above KI.MIN in the commentary tablet. Earlier, he had argued that "*kiṣṣatu* of [*ṣētu*-heat]" *means* "burning of *ṣētu*-heat," and, by this modified quotation, he showed that *kiṣṣatu* was another way of expressing "burning."

Obv. 7–8—The syllable signs here are *šá*(níg)-*su-ú*, not *ša-su-ú* (obv. 8) as rendered by the typo in the printed edition *SpTU* I, 36. The argument here is unclear, but these lines may represent a clarification to avoid confusion between expressions with similar logographic values: GU.DU ("buttock") versus GÙ.DÉ ("to cry out").

Obv. 8–9—The syllable signs in obv. 9 are *iš-šá*(níg)-*aḫ-ṭu*, not *iš-ša-aḫ-ṭu* (obv. 9) as rendered by the typo in the printed edition *SpTU* I, 36. The Infinitive form *šaḫāṭu* can refer to at least two homophonic verbs: (I) "to jerk, (D) to attack" (*CAD* Š I, 88–92 s.v. *šaḫāṭu* A) and (II) "to tear off" (*CAD* Š I, 92–95 s.v. *šaḫāṭu* B). Both these verbs appear in medical signs of the Diagnostic Handbook, but not those of therapeutic texts. In manuscripts preserved for us, the two verbs are usually distinguished by their orthography. The verb *šaḫāṭu* ("to jerk") is mostly written as the logogram GU_4.UD at Sa-gig 4: 94 (TDPT 4 rev. 8); Sa-gig 10: 30–31; 13: 73 (TDPT 13 ii 15); Sa-gig [26: 58′], though the syllabic form *i-šaḫ-ḫi-iṭ* is attested at Sa-gig 40: 25. The verb *šaḫāṭu* ("to tear off") appears syllabically as the D Stative form *šuḫḫuṭ-* at Sa-gig 16: 76′; 22: 36, but mainly in the formulaic sequences of Sa-gig Chapter II: Sa-gig 10: 49–52; 12: 93″, 122″ (TDPT 12 iii 30; iv 14); Sa-gig 14: 53–55, 102, 132, 165–[167] (TDPT 14 i 53–55; ii 30, 60; iii 20–[22]). Here, the commentator clarified that the meaning of *šuḫḫuṭ-* in formulaic sequences is "torn off" by describing it as a condition of the patient's "skin."

Obv. 9–10—As with obv. 5–6 above, the commentator here sought to clarify the general term *šalāmu* "to become well" by specifying the presence or absence of precise features. The value of "wellness" as a medical sign is unique to the Diagnostic Handbook and absent in therapeutic texts. The restoration *šá pi-ṭir-*[*šú*(?)] / *la ib-šu-ú* (obv. 9–10) by Genty (2010b: 25) is probably inadequate, because traces of the damaged sign do not resemble *šú*, and there is space for one or two additional signs at the end of obv. 9: *pi-ṭir* x[x x].

Obv. 10—Available manuscripts of the base text Sa-gig 14: 60 (TDPT 14 i 60) read GU.DU.MEŠ-*šú* GE_6.MEŠ-*ma* KI.GUB-*su* NU È-*a* ("his buttocks are black, and he does not put out his KI.GUB"). The quotation GU.DU-*s*[*u*] NU.È.A ("he does not put out his GU.DU") in obv. 10 may be due to confusion between the logograms GU.DU and KI.GUB, since both terms occur in the context of defecation, and since DU and GUB are alternative values of the same cuneiform sign. It is unclear whether this scribal mistake originated with the scribe of the commentary or with the copy of the base text employed. For attestations of the logogram KI.GUB (*manzāzu* "position" < *izuzzu* "to stand") and its confusion or association by the rebus principle with *manzaltu* "flow of excrement" (< *nazālu* "to pour out"), see Note on Comm. Sa-gig 13+, line 13.

Obv. 11—The signs A.GA SÌG-*iṣ* appear in the base text Sa-gig 14: 60 (TDPT 14 i 60), though a parallel medical entry in Sa-gig 15: 51′ has the orthography EGIR-*ta*$_5$ SÌG-*iṣ*. This latter way of writing *arkata* ("back") is, in fact, the more common one, with EGIR-*ta*$_5$ SÌG attested at Sa-gig 10 B rev. 3; 14: 60 (TDPT 14 i 60); Sa-gig 15: 51′; 22: 38, and *ina* EGIR-*šú* SÌG-*iṣ* at Sa-gig 15: 9′. Note the lexical equation giš-a-ga-tukul (var. giš-egir $^{\text{e-gir}_2}$-tukul) = *ár-kát kak-ki* (Hh. VII A, 31 in *MSL* VI, 86). The commentator employed this known equation to support his argument that A.GA means *arkat* ("back"), but it is not entirely necessary that "the 'striking' in question was done with a weapon" as posited by Scurlock and Andersen (2005: 699 n. 56). We would notice from the medical entries cited above that such diagnoses are characteristic of the Diagnostic Handbook, but not therapeutic texts.

Obv. 12—I am unable to make sense of the signs ig(?) lu(?) at the beginning of this line, which have been transliterated as such by Hunger (*SpTU* I, 36); *CAD* Š II, 309.

Obv. 12—It is uncertain whether the term *šapūlu* ("inguinal region") first appears in the base text of Sa-gig Tablet 14 at Sa-gig 14: [61] (TDPT 14 i [61]) or Sa-gig 14: [63] (TDPT 14 i [63]). The body part *šapūlu*/ḪÁŠ.GAL ("inguinal region") appears in syllabic and logographic forms in medical signs of the Diagnostic Handbook: Sa-gig 4: 21; [14: 63–69] (TDPT [14 i 63–69]); Sa-gig 15:⟨57′⟩, 58′; 33: 94. In therapeutic texts, only syllabic forms are attested so far: *BAM* 231 i 6; *AMT* [21/2: 5]; 54/3 rev. 7′; 70/3 i 3′. The expression *birīt purīdi* ("between the legs") seems to be an idiom not limited to medical contexts (*CAD* P, 518 s.v. *purīdu* A §1b; Couto-Ferreira 2009: 304–305) and does not typically occur in medical signs, though it can appear in therapeutic instructions (*BAM* 141: 10′) and medical incantations (*STT* 136 i 45). For its derived meaning as a "stride" (i.e., the distance covered between legs outstretched when walking), see George (2003: 784 note 57). The equation *šá-pu-lu bi-*⌊*rit*⌋ PAP.[ḪAL] here occurs also in the lexical text Hg. B IV, 21 (Vedeler 2002: 68; cf. *MSL* IX, 34), as well as in a non-medical commentary to *Šumma ālu* XXVIII: ⌈*šá*⌉*-pu-ul* = *bi-rit pi-ri-du* (*CT* 41, 26 obv. 14). Whereas *šapūlu* ("inguinal region") tends to be restricted to specialized contexts of medicine, divination, and physiognomy, the commentator here explained it in terms of a more general idiom.

Obv. 13—The term UMUŠ very frequently describes the patient's "intelligence" in the Diagnostic Handbook, and only a few times in therapeutic texts (*BAM*

316 vi 5′; 449 iii 25′ (incl. *AMT* 90/1 iii 25′)). The use of UMUŠ to denote the "disposition" of an illness is unique to the base text Sa-gig [14: 64] (TDPT [14 i 64]), and this may explain the commentator's motive for discussing the term. For the syllabic writing, see *ṭè*-⸢*eme*⸣-⸤*šú*⸥ (Comm. Sa-gig 19, obv. 8).

Obv. 13—The disjunction sign is omitted in the transliteration of GUB-*az* : *man-za*-[*az*] (obv. 13) in the printed edition *SpTU* I, 36. The commentary explanation "'GUB-*az*' *means* position" seems to contradict the translation "if he stands up" for AŠ GUB-*az* in *BAM* VII/49 i 18′.

Obv. 14—The syllabic writing *iz-zi-iz* reflects the orthography of the base text version of Sa-gig 14: 70 (TDPT 14 i 70) employed by the commentator, whereas other copies available to us have the reading GUB-*iz* (e.g., *BAM* VII/49 i 23′). The description DÚR-*šú iz-zi-iz* ("his rectum stands") is attested in only two medical entries at Sa-gig 14: 70–71. The comment "his rectum is bound" clarifies that the problem lies with the rectum "standing *still*" or remaining stationary and not performing its function.

Obv. 14—I agree with the suggested reading "*šumma* DÚR-*šú pališ* // *šá* DÚR-*šú irpišu SpTU* I, 36: 14f. ... ibid. p. 112" in *CAD* Š III, 190 s.v. *šuburru*; which understands the signs as BÙR-*liš* (𒌋 𒇺) ("it is breached"). Another possibility would be to interpret the writing as BÙR GAM (𒌋 𒃵) "(If his rectum) is breached, he will die." The base text for this commentary entry is, unfortunately, not preserved, though it functions well as the converse of the situation in Sa-gig 14: 72 (*BAM* VII/49 i 24′): DIŠ DÚR-*šú* BAD.BAD-*ir* ... ("If his rectum is stopped up, ..."). For more examples of "breaches" (BÙR/*palāšu*) in body parts, see *CAD* P, 60–61 s.v. *palāšu* §1c, 2c. These examples, however, are not typical for medical signs in the Diagnostic Handbook or therapeutic texts, and the commentator may therefore have felt the need to explain the medical condition here. The verb *irpiš* ("widened") also does not usually describe the rectum in medical texts, but is general enough of a term to function as the comment.

Obv. 15—Geller has restored the medical sign of Sa-gig 14: 80 (*BAM* VII/49 i 28′) as DIŠ *ina* DÚR-*šú* ALAN ad ti(?) di(?)-*šú* ŠUB.ŠUB-*a* (𒁹 𒀸 𒆪 𒋙 𒀩 𒀜 𒋾(?) 𒁲(?) 𒋙 𒋛 𒋛 𒀀) ("If he excretes a figurine of his ... from his anus"). Instead of this reading, Scurlock (2014: 122, 130) suggests DIŠ *ina* DÚR-*šú* [*d*]*a-ku-ti* ŠÀ-*šú* ŠUB.ŠUB-*a* ("If he continually produces material recovered from his insides(?) from his anus"). From Geller's hand copy (*BAM* VII/49 pl. 31, obv. i 28′), however, it is possible to reinterpret the sign traces as DIŠ *ina* DÚR-*šú* ⸢*šu-uḫ*(?)-*ḫi*⸣-*at*-⸢*ti* ŠÀ⸣-*šú* ŠUB.ŠUB-*a* (𒁹 𒀸 𒆪 𒋙 𒋗 𒌮(?) 𒄭 𒀜 𒋾 𒊮 𒋙 𒋛 𒋛 𒀀) ("If he excretes *šuḫḫiātti* of his belly from his rectum"), and I tentatively identify this statement as the base text to the commentary entry *šu-ḫa-at-ti er-ru-šú* : *šu-uḫ-ḫi-iṭ-ṭa-a-ti* ("'*šuḫḫâtti* of his bowels' *refers to šuḫḫiṭṭāti*"). Unfortunately, the curious terms *šuḫḫâtti* (< *šuḫḫiātti*) and *šuḫḫiṭṭāti* do not seem attested elsewhere, though I interpret a similar term *šuḫḫu*—a part of the intestines—as "(anal) sphincter" in Comm. Sa-gig 7B, rev. 5′. See *CAD* Š III, 206–207 s.v. *šuḫḫu* A §2; Couto-Ferreira 2009: 236–237, 270.

Obv. 15–16—Apart from its occurrence in the damaged base text, the description "his stools stand" does not seem attested elsewhere. The comment "they do not move" clarifies that the problem lies with the stools "standing *still*" or not "moving" through the rectum. For *-ūnu* instead of *-ūni* as the Assyrian subordination marker in *il-la-ku-ú-nu* (line 16), see Deller (1959: 115, §24c–d); Hecker (1968: 135, §79e); Hämeen-Anttila (2000: 92, §3.12.4); Luukko (2004: 92, §4.5). The use of *-ūnu* here is surprising, because the subordination marker elsewhere on this same tablet simply takes the form *-u*. See *il-la-ku* (obv. 3), *iš-šá-a*[*ḫ*]*-ṭu* (obv. 9), *ir-rak-su* (obv 14), and perhaps *ú-še-*[*ṣu*] (obv. 10) and *ir-pi-*[*šu*] (obv. 14). The form *il-la-ku-ú-nu* (obv. 16) may reveal its derivation from an alternative source. Note, for example, the writing *zu-ú-šú* in obv. 15–17 of this commentary, in contrast to ŠE$_{10}$-*ú-šú* in manuscripts of the base text available to us. In any case, *il-la-ku-ú-nu* here presents a particularly clear use of the subordination marker after the commentary notation *ša*, in contrast to the case in Comm. Sa-gig 4B (obv. 7), where a line from the *Hymn to Šamaš* is quoted after the notation *ša* in its original form without any inclusion of a subordination marker (see discussion in §II.2.2).

Obv. 16—It is tempting to relate the verb *pur-ru-šú* to the noun *paršu* ("excrement, gore") (*CAD* P, 205–206), though there are no other attestations of a verbal derivative of *paršu*. However, the choice of the sign *-šú* instead of *-šu* in the orthography of *pur-ru-šú* may indicate its role as a pronominal suffix, not as part of the verbal root. Note the use of the *šu* sign as part of the verbal root in *i-šu-ú* (obv. 6), *šu-uḫ-ḫu-ṭ*[*a-at*] (obv. 8), *ib-šu-ú* (obv. 10), *šu-ṣi* (obv. 20). For similar cases where the choice of the sign *ša* versus *šá* helps clarify ambiguities in writing, see Worthington (2012: 269–280). In other words, the form *pur-ru-šú* consists of the D Stative 3mp verb *purrû* ("are severed" < *parā'u* "to sever") with the 3ms dative suffix *-šu*(*m*). While Hunger (*SpTU* 1, 36) has restored the end of this line as *pur-ru-š*[*u*], another possibility would be *pur-ru-s*[*u-šú*] ("are cut up [for him]"), which fits well with the meaning of *purrû* ("are severed"). The D stem *purrû* (root: *parā'u*, "to sever") occurs only here, while the reciprocal Gt stem *ipterrûnim* ("(strands) cut into each other") appears at Sa-gig 4: 95 (TDPT 4 rev. 9); *contra* the translation "[blood vessel(s)] of his [temples] vomit forth" in Scurlock (2014: 38). The commentator here, therefore, had good cause to distinguish this root from the much more common *parû* ("to vomit, to void") in the medical signs of Sa-gig 9: 20; 15: 5′; 17: 60; 19/20: 108′; 23: 1, [2, 3, 5]; 36: 81 (TDPT 35: 81); *BAM* 49: 11′; [50 obv. 13]; 75: 6; 389: 5′, 7′, 10′; 558 i 18′ (incl. *AMT* 55/1 obv. 10′); *BAM* 574 i 27; 575 ii 17; iii 44, 56, 66; iv 43; 578 i 27, 29, 47; *AMT* 50/3 obv. 6, 11; [84/7: 3]. This distinction was especially needful, because *parû* ("to vomit, to void") can also refer to "evacuation from the bowels" (see *BAM* 96 i 16′; 159 iii 13 in *CAD* P, 208), which would seem fitting for the context of "stools" here. For similar reasons, the commentator of Comm. Sa-gig 4C, rev. 6′–7′ felt the need to comment on *ipterrûnim* (Sa-gig 4: 95 (TDPT 4 rev. 9); see above).

Obv. 17—The form *dak-ku* is difficult, and I tentatively understand it as the Stative verb *dakāku* ("to crush"), which is related to the verb *duqququ* of the same meaning (*CAD* D, 34 s.v. *dakāku* B). Apart from its occurrence in the damaged base text here, the statement "his stools are crushed" is not attested elsewhere. This base text is likely Sa-gig 14: 93 (TDPT 14 ii 21), which should be restored as DIŠ ŠE_{10}-(*ú*)-*šú da*[*k-ku*], rather than DIŠ ŠE_{10}-(*ú*)-*šú* ŠÀ[...] by Labat (1951: 134); Scurlock (2014: 122).

Obv. 17–18—Though Geller (followed by Scurlock 2014: 122) has transliterated the signs of Sa-gig 14: 94 (TDPT 14 ii 22 = *BAM* VII/49 ii 4′) as *i*[*t-te-n*]*ek-ki-ik* in agreement with Labat (1951: 134), his hand copy (pl. 32) suggests that the signs are x[...] ŠÀ *di-ik* instead. This disparity becomes more evident when comparison is made with the sign-forms of ŠÀ (*BAM* VII/49 ii 10′), KI (*BAM* VII/49 ii 12′) and *i-te-ník-ki-ik* (*BAM* VII/49 ii 28′) later on the same tablet (pl. 32). While obv. 17–18 of this commentary are admittedly difficult to interpret, the writing ⌜ŠÀ *di-ki* (?)⌝ [...] (end of obv. 17) and *di-i-ki* (beginning of obv. 18) appear to point to ŠÀ *di-ik* in Sa-gig 14: 94 (*BAM* VII/49 ii 4′) as their base text. The photo of this commentary tablet does not reveal a disjunction sign between the signs bal and ŠÀ (as indicated by the transliteration of obv. 17 in *SpTU* I, 36), and so it is possible that the signs immediately before ŠÀ represent a quotation from the base text as well. While it is tempting to see *di-ki* and *di-i-ki* as a continuation of the topic *zu-ú-šú dak-ku* (beginning of obv. 17), the intervening explanation *šá la raq-qa*, as well as what appears to be a fresh citation from the base text Sa-gig 14: 94, discourages this interpretation. Damage in both the base text and the commentary entry, unfortunately, hinder a fuller understanding here. As Hunger (*SpTU* I, 36) pointed out, the term *durrīšu* (obv. 18) represents a loanword from the Sumerian dúr (= *šuburru*). See *CAD* Ṭ, 166 s.v. *ṭurru* D.

Obv. 18–19—Whereas one would anticipate diagnoses of rectal sicknesses in this base text segment on the patient's "stools," the verdict ḪAR GIG ("the lung is sick") is unexpected and begs confirmation. This explains the commentator's concern to explain ḪAR GIG, even though the terms for "lung" and "sick" are common enough in medical texts.

Obv. 19—The syllable signs here are *i-ṣal-lal-ma*, not *i-ṣal-la-ma* as rendered by the typo in *CAD* U, 344 s.v. *utūlu*. The equation between the verbs *ṣalālu* ("to sleep") and *niālu* or *i/utūlu* (both meaning "to lie down") is a natural one. See brief discussion in *CAD* U/W, 345–346 for the complicated relationship between the verbs *nâlu* and *i/utūlu*, with some scholars regarding them as separate dictionary roots, while others consider *i/utūlu* to be the Gt form of *nâlu*. Note also the observation: "the relationship between *ṣalālu*, 'to become asleep, to lie asleep,' and *nâlu*, 'to go to bed,' is illustrated by the contrast of the former with *êru*, 'to become awake'" (*CAD* Ṣ, 70 s.v. *ṣalālu*). I understand the signs in this line as *it-tal-«li»-ma* for *ittāl-ma*. The following commentary entry may address a penis diminished in function, and one wonders if a penis that "sleeps" or "lies down" due to erectile dysfunction could be the topic here.

Obv. 20—Where Hunger (*SpTU* 1, 36) has transliterated ma x ú, I tentatively restore *ma-*⸢*$ṭu_5$*(!)⸣*-ú* (?), though the syllabic value of the sign gab as $ṭu_5$ is far from satisfactory in this context. In medical texts, *maṭû* ("to diminish") frequently describes the *functions* of body parts or the person as a whole, instead of their *physical size*. Note, for example, uses of *maṭû* (logogram LAL) in reference to the patient's appetite for food and drink (Sa-gig 18: 8; 22: 71; 33: 30; *BAM* 87: 14; [106 rev. 1′]; 190: 23; [193 ii 3′]; [221 ii 2′–3′]; [231 i 14]; 232 i 17′; 234: 9; 409 obv. 28′; 434 i 14′; 438 obv. 5; 575 ii 38, 43; iii 7, 12; 578 i 29; *AMT* 40/5 iii 9′; 48/2: 2; [81/7: 5]), his appetite for sex (*BAM* 112 i 18′, 35′; 232 i 17′; [438 obv. 9]; 445: 14 (incl. *AMT* 64/2: 14′); *AMT* 88/3: 2′), as well as his faculty of sight (Sa-gig 33: 5; *BAM* 159 iv 17′; 516 ii 8′ (incl. *AMT* 17/4 ii 8′); *BAM* 575 iii 49; AO 11447: 81).

Obv. 20–21—Hunger (*SpTU* 1, 36) has read *ba-ḫu* (obv. 20), perhaps in part due to the slant of the horizontal wedges of the sign identified as *ba*. However, the writing of *ra-ba-ba* (obv. 5) may suggest little effort by this tablet's scribe at distinguishing the syllable signs *ba* and *ma*. The verb in question describes the patient's "belly" (ŠÀ) in Sa-gig 14: 106 (TDPT 14 ii 34) and Sa-gig 22: 14, where it has been transliterated *ma-ḫu* (the G Stative 3ms of *maḫû*) and translated as "rasen" by Heeßel (2000: 252, 413); "goes crazy" by Scurlock and Andersen (2005: 19, §2.18; 97, §4.34; 525, §19.378); Scurlock (2014: 131, 189); "are spasmodic" by Geller (2005: 251); and "are in spasm" by *CAD* M I, 116 s.v. *maḫû*. Whereas the base text Sa-gig 14: 106 (TDPT 14 ii 34) presents *ma-ḫu* as a 3ms Stative verb to a singular noun subject ŠÀ ("belly"), both the verb (*ma-ḫu*) and its subject (ŠÀ.MEŠ "innards") are plural in this commentary entry. It is uncertain whether the plural forms were original to the commentator's copy of the base text or to the commentator himself. Interestingly, the commentary entry reverts back to the singular ŠÀ ("belly") in its comment. In view of the consonantal values in *šu-ṣi-iš* and the following argument on the logogram È (obv. 20–21), *šu-ṣi-iš* likely represents a form of the verb *aṣû* ("to go out"). I am grateful to Marten Stol (personal communication) for the suggested reading *šūṣîš* ("(in order) to bring out" > "(in order) to reveal") = Š Infinitive of *aṣû* + terminative ending *-iš*. Whereas the most common meaning of È is *aṣû* ("to go out"), note these lexical and commentarial equations for the verb *maḫû*: [e] ud-du = *maḫû* (Diri I, 158 in *MSL* XV, 110); [e] ud-du = [*ma-ḫu*]-*u* (Aa III/3, 154 in *MSL* XIV, 337; restored in *CAD* M I, 115); [e] du_6-du = *ma-ḫu-ú* (Diri Sippar, 6: 10 in *MSL* XV, 57; cf. Diri I, 208 in *MSL* XV, 112); È : *ma-ḫu-ú* (*CT* 41, 28 rev. 6; Alu Comm.). In addition, the writing lú-al-è-dè can denote an "ecstatic" (*maḫḫû*), whose raving mannerisms were linked to certain cultic activities and rituals (*CAD* M I, 90).

Obv. 21–22—I follow the reading *ina* ḪUL [ŠÀ]-*ia* (obv. 22) by Hunger (*SpTU* I, 36), though *ina* ḪUL-[*ti*]-*ia* is also possible. The cuneiform signs that I transliterate as ka x x mu ne are hardly legible on the tablet, and I am not persuaded by the reading *ka-ra*(?)-*ra* MU.NE ("*karara* (is) its name") by Hunger (*SpTU* I, 36). The source of the quotation here is uncertain, partly due to the damaged condition of the text. It may derive, however, from a bilingual prayer of the Ér-šà-ḫun-gá (lit. "cry that pacifies the heart") genre, which would have been considered appropriate for a commentary entry on the "belly" (ŠÀ). In fact, the unusual long final vowel in the writing *tu-šá-ma-a* (obv. 22) has an exact parallel in an Ér-šà-ḫun-gá prayer (Ešḫ n125, line 7′). See Maul (1988: 382). I am grateful to Uri Gabbay for this observation, though it is unclear if Ešḫ n125 is the specific textual source quoted here. In any case, the expressions "heart" (ŠÀ) and "mu-un-è-dè" seem intended as a comment on the medical condition described earlier in this tablet (obv. 20), i.e., that the sick man's "innards" (ŠÀ.MEŠ) are "raving" (È). Notice that the term ŠÀ in the original prayer probably referred to the person's "heart" (i.e., his seat of emotion), but the commentator invested this term with its technical meaning in medical texts as the anatomical feature known as "belly" or "innards." For a similar case where *muḫḫu* in literary contexts is treated as the technical term for the body part "cranium," see Comm. Sa-gig 39, obv. 6–7.

Obv. 22–23—There are several unusual features in this short commentary entry. The base text here is most likely a syllabic expression similar to *ina mu-šar-ri-šú* (= *ina mušarīšu*, "from his penis") in Sa-gig 14: 109 (TDPT 14 ii 37). It is curious that the "penis" would be chosen as a topic, since conditions of the penis are very common in medical texts, and one might be expected to take the term for granted. This body part was also mentioned earlier in Sa-gig 14: 95 (TDPT 14 ii 23), where it did not elicit any explanation from the commentator. Furthermore, though *ina mu-šar-šu* (obv. 23) seems to resemble the expression *ina mu-šar-ri-šú* in available copies of the base text, it is not followed by any written comment in the commentary. Finally, the orthography *ina mu-šar-šu* is odd, because *mu-šar-šu* is not the correct form of the genitive (*mušarīšu*), and because the use of the sign *šu* instead of *šú* for the pronominal suffix seems atypical for this commentary tablet and its base text. Notice, however, what seems to be the suffix -*šu* in one manuscript version of the base text (*BAM* VII/49 ii 12′–13′). One solution is to restore the commentary entry as [*ina mu-šar-ri-šú/šu*] / *ina mu-šar-šu* (obv. 22–23), whereby the commentator expresses his concern for the false doubling of /r/ in the base text writing *mu-šar-ri-šú* (= *mušarīšu*), so that the comment should be understood as *ina mu-šari*$_x$(šar)-*šu*. It is doubtful, however, that there is enough space at the end of obv. 22 for the signs [*ina mu-šar-ri-šú/šu*]. Another solution, which I tentatively adopt here, is to understand the entry as [*ina* GÌŠ-*šú*] / *ina mu-šar-šu* (obv. 22–23). In medical texts, the "penis" is almost uniformly denoted by the logogram GÌŠ, and syllabic writings such as *ina mu-šar-ri-šú* or *ina mu-šar-šu* are very rare. The commentator may have intended to equate the form *ina mu-šar-šu* in his base text copy with its more common orthography *ina* GÌŠ-*šú*. In keeping to the custom that logographic forms precede their syllabic translations, however, the commentator ended up stating his comment ([*ina* GÌŠ-*šú*] at the end of obv. 22) before his topic (*ina mu-šar-šu* at the beginning of obv. 23). A different strategy was adopted in Comm. Sa-gig 1–3 (obv. 27) and Comm. Sa-gig 21 & 22a (obv. 11), where the topic-comment sequence is preserved by stating the syllabically written term ([*pé-ret*], *nim-šú-šú*) before its logographically written explanation (SÍG, SA.MEŠ-*šú*). See further discussion in §1.2.3.1.1.

Obv. 23–24—The signs mu ki nu gi are unique to the base text Sa-gig 14: 109 (TDPT 14 ii 37), and they have been translated by Geller as "because of the Netherworld," presumably due to their resemblance to KUR.NU.GI$_{(4)}$ ("Land of no return"). See *CAD* K, 564 s.v. *kurnugi*. Whatever their original meaning, the commentator conflated this unusual writing with a roughly similar expression that occurs much more frequently: MU KI MUNUS *ina* KI.NÁ KUR ("because he is encountered with a female in bed") at Sa-gig 3: 100–104 (TDPT 3: 91–95); Sa-gig 18: 21–23. Instead of the term MUNUS ("female, woman"), other parallel statements indict the patient of illicit heterosexual relations with "(another) man's wife" (Sa-gig 4: 117 (TDPT 4 rev. 32); Sa-gig

6: 16; 13: 37 (TDPT 13 i 38′); Sa-gig 17: 32, [79]; 18: 16), "his mother" (Sa-gig 6: 88″ (TDPT 6 rev. 25′)), "his sister" (Sa-gig 12: 125″ (TDPT 12 iv 17)), or even one named "the *ēntu*-priestess of his god" (Sa-gig 7 A obv. 20 (TDPT 7: 20); Sa-gig 13: 23 (TDPT 13 i 24′); Sa-gig 14: 134, 137–139 (TDPT 14 ii 62, 65–67)). See also Note on Comm. Sa-gig 4A, obv. 14–15 where I discuss other similar statements in the Diagnostic Handbook that ascribe sickness to a variety of illicit heterosexual relations. In obv. 23–24 of this commentary, the sign nu is unfortunately not written very clearly, and Hunger (*SpTU* I, 36) and Genty (2010b: 27) have proposed the reading MÍ (the usual logogram for *sinništu*) in place of nu. For lack of more decisive evidence, however, I have gone with the base text reading ki nu gi (preserved at SBH 148, ii 11′ and less clearly in TDPT II, pl. XXXV, ii 37), which would require the commentator to explain the nu sign. For nu in association with *sinništu*, see the lexical equations: nu-nus = MU[NUS] = [*sin-niš-tu*] (Emesal Voc. II, 68 in *MSL* IV, 16); nu$^{\text{nu-nu-nu-us}_2}$ nu-nus, nu-nus = *si-*[*in-niš-tu*] (Lu III, i 18′–19′ in *MSL* XII, 123). In the commentator's understanding, writings like nu-nus might have seemed like a duplication of the element nu, and nu-nu-nus like its triplication, so that nu itself appeared to account for the Emesal meaning "female." The following lexical texts make the distinction that zu denotes acquaintance with facts, while gi denotes sexual acquaintance: [(x)]-zu = *la-ma-du šá a-wa-a-ti*, [(x)]-gi$_4$ = MIN *šá* NITA *u* MUNUS (Nabnitu A, 274–275 in *MSL* XVI, 67); GI = *la-ma-du ša* NITA *u*(!) MUNUS(!) (*CT* 12, 29 rev. 5). The syllable signs in obv. 24 are *zi-kìr*(lagab), not *zi-kir* (obv. 24) as rendered by the typo in the printed edition *SpTU* I, 36. In summary, therefore, the signs (mu) ki nu gi were made to depict the transgression that resulted in the patient's sickness: "(because (MU)) he is acquainted sexually (gi) with (KI) a female (nu)."

Obv. 24–25—One is tempted to relate the terms GA GEŠTIN ("milk, wine") in obv. 25 to the base text Sa-gig 14: 121–122 (TDPT 14 ii 49–50), which compares the patient's urine to these fluids. Such an interpretation, however, would disrupt the progressive order in which the commentator selected topics from the base text, because the next two commentary entries respectively refer to the base texts ŠU MU DINGIR-*šú* at Sa-gig 14: 111 (TDPT 14 ii 39) and A.RI.A at Sa-gig 14: 117 (TDPT 14 ii 45).

Obv. 25—The expression ŠU MU DINGIR-*šú* ("Hand of (the oath on) his god's life") appears only in the base text Sa-gig 14: 111 (TDPT 14 ii 39), as well as at Sa-gig 22: 58. Interestingly, the full expression is found only in MS A of the base text (Sa-gig 14: 111), whereas the more common version ŠU DINGIR-*šú* ("Hand of his god") is found in MS C (*BAM* VII/49 ii 14′). Such variants between copies of the same base text suggest that ancient scribes tended to harmonize unusual medical expressions with more conventional terminology. They also give us insight into the commentator's motivation for taking note of atypical expressions. There seems to be a disjunction sign before *lìb-bu-ú* (obv. 25), which is not reflected in the transliteration by Hunger (*SpTU* I, 36). The comment here not only employs the homophones *nīš* ("(oath on) the life") and *nīš* ("raising"), it also plays on the metathesis between ŠU *nīš* ("Hand of (the oath on) the life") and *nīš* ŠU.2 ("raising of hands"). The reversal implied by metathesis may allude to the solution to (or cause of) the diagnosed malady, which involves the patient's performance (or lack of performance) of Šu-íl-lá (lit. "raised hand") prayers to the offended deity.

Obv. 25—The term A.RI.A in the base text Sa-gig 14: 117 (TDPT 14 ii 45) refers to the patient's "semen." In the Diagnostic Handbook, the logographic writing A.RI.A most often denotes the "semen" of an offending agent such as ᵈ*Šulpaea*, ᵈLUGAL.ÙR.RA, or another human being (Sa-gig 28: 11, 19–20; 29: 22, 83′), and only rarely that of the patient himself (Sa-gig 14: 117 (TDPT 14 ii 45)). In therapeutic texts, the syllabic writing *riḫûtu* is predominant, mostly in reference to the patient's own "semen" (*BAM* 112 i 17′, 34′; 205: 20′, 40′; 396 iv 6′; *AMT* 32/1 rev. 11; [58/6: 2′]; 61/1: 5′, 9′). The "semen" of another human responsible for the patient's condition is sometimes written syllabically (*BAM* 417 obv. 11) and sometimes with the logogram A.RI.A (*BAM* 470 obv. 23′; *AMT* 97/4: 7′). In other words, A.RI.A in the base text to this commentary entry is not only more typical of the Diagnostic Handbook than of therapeutic texts, it also represents a less common use of the logographic form to describe the patient's own "semen."

Obv. 26—See Note on Comm. Sa-gig 3A, rev. 8′ where exactly the same commentary equation occurs.

Obv. 27—The syllable signs here are EME-⌊*šú*⌋ *i-te-néq*(níg)-*qí-iq*, not EME *i-te-neq*(nig)-*qí-iq* (obv. 27) as rendered by the typo in the printed edition *SpTU* I, 36. Although the comment is not preserved, we may surmise why the commentator chose to remark on this base text Sa-gig 14: 135 (TDPT 14 ii 63). In addition to its prosaic uses, the verb *ekēku* ("to scratch") is attested several times in both the Diagnostic Handbook and therapeutic texts, always with syllabic writing: Sa-gig 15: 68′; 27: 34; [31: 32′]; 33: 2, 8, 22; *BAM* 120 iii 8; *AMT* [39/6: 7′] 58/1:[1], 8; 74/1 ii 32, 34; 95/3 i 18. For the reading x[...] ŠÀ *di-ik* instead of *i*[*t-te-n*]*ek-ki-ik* at Sa-gig 14: 94 (TDPT 14 ii 22 = *BAM* VII/49 ii 4′), see Note on obv. 17–18 of this commentary. It is therefore very natural to read the signs in this line as *i-te-nék-ki-ik* ("he keeps scratching (his tongue)") from the common verb *ekēku* ("to scratch"). This was indeed the interpretation adopted by Geller: "he continually scrapes the tongue" (*BAM* VII/49 ii 28′). Given how common the verb *ekēku* is, however, one might question whether it even required comment. In fact, the commentator may have been trying to avoid the easy interpretation above, choosing instead to read the signs as *i-te-néq-qí-iq* ("(his tongue) keeps becoming (tongue)-tied") from the rare verb *eqēqu* "to become (tongue)-tied." This verb *eqēqu* is attested only here at Sa-gig 14: 94 in medical texts, and its logograms EME.DAB (lit. "seized tongue") and INIM.GI_4 ("repeating words") show that *eqēqu* is not merely a byform of *ekēku* (*CAD* E, 249).

Rev. 5′—Hunger (*SpTU* 1, 36) identified *i-šag-gum* in Sa-gig 14: 266′ (TDPT 14 iv 65′) as the base text for *šagāmu* ("to roar") here. However, it is questionable that the commentator moved so far ahead in his base text so quickly. We should not discount the possibility that *šagāmu* here constitutes the comment, rather than a topic quoted from the base text.

Rev. 6′—This line represents the incipit-title of Tablet 15 in the Diagnostic Handbook. Unfortunately, existing manuscripts of Tablet 15 do not preserve its incipit, and Hunger (*SpTU* 1, 36) has restored it as DIŠ U_4.1.KAM GIG-*ma ina* SA[G.DU *maḫiṣ*] ("If he is sick for one day, and he is struck on the head"). The Sa-gig catalog, however, records this incipit-title as [DIŠ $U]_4$.1.KÁM GIG-*ma* GAR TAG-*t*[*i*] ("If he is sick for one day, and the nature of the touch …"). See Finkel (1988: 146, obv. A 20); Heeßel (2000: 14, line 20). The tablet is too damaged here for me to come to a decision about the signs.

Rev. 7′—Frahm (2011a: 226) remarks that "if the beginning of line rev. 7′ really reads ul, then this line might identify the tablet as a *ṣâtu*-commentary." The commentary designation *ṣâtu* ("glossary") may be expressed using the rebus-writing UL.LA, which more properly expresses the homophone *ṣâtu* ("distant time"). See discussion in §1.2.1.1.

Commentary Sa-gig 18

Provenance:	Same consignment (82-9-18) as Comm. Sa-gig 4B
Period:	?
Names:	Probably none
Script:	Neo-/Late Babylonian
Typology:	Perhaps *ṣâtu* 3b in Frahm (2011a: 51–52)

Field/Museum No.:	BM 66873 = 82-9-18,6867 ("Sippar Collection" at British Museum)
Photos:	Plate 24 (reverse), Plate 25a (top edge), and Plate 25b (right edge)
Transliteration:	Lambert Folio 9840
Digital Resources:	CDLI P461278; CCP 4.1.18 (photos and edition digitized by Jiménez 2015, with contributions by Finkel, Frahm, and Gabbay)
Discussion:	Leichty and Grayson (1987: 189); Heeßel (2000: 135 n. 32); Scurlock (2004: 256); Frahm (2011a: 226, 287); Gabbay (2016: 107 n. 124, 111 n. 138, 130 n. 14, 138 n. 49, 144 n. 79)
Pericope:	At least Sa-gig 18: 38′

Transliteration

Reverse

1′) [...]x-⸢*mu*⸣-tu_4
2′) [... ADAM]A : *a-da-ma*-tu_4
3′) [...]x-*šú a-na* UGU *ra-bi-ti-šú*
4′) [...]x-*i-šu* : GAL : *ra-bu-ú*
5′) [GÍD.GÍD : *im-ta-na*]*g-ga-ag* : GÍD.GÍD : *ú-te-il-lu*
6′) [...] : *ba-mat* : *mi-šil* : 1-*át* : *eš-ta-at*
7′) [...]x ⸢*lìb*⸣-*bu-ú ki-is-sat i-šá-tú*
8′) [... ^{din}]^{gir}*Ereš-ki-gal* kur IGI-*šú* ⸢*kúr-ru*⸣
9′) [... *i-n*]*ak-kud* : *ri-mu-tú šá i*-⸢*ram*(?)⸣-*mu-ú*
10′) [...]-*tú áš-šú ki-iš-pi* : ⸢DAB-*it* (?) *šá* (?)⸣ *ka-mu-ú*
11′) [... ŠUR]UN-*su* : *zu-ú-šú* : *lìb-bu-ú šit-ta-šú*
12′) [...]x-*šu-ma* : GIM U.MEŠ-*šú* : *re*-⸢*šet*(?)⸣ *ú-ba-na-tu*-[*šú*]

 | DOI:10.1163/9789004417564_022

13′) [^{d}*Iš-ḫa-ra* (?) : ^{d}*Ere*]*š-ki-gal* : DUL.DUL-*ma* : *it-ta-*⌞*nak-tam-ma*⌟
14′) [...]x *šá pi-i-šú*

15′) [*ṣa-a-tú u šu-ut* K]A *šá* DIŠ GIG SU-*šú* KÚM-*im* S[ED]

Translation

***Sa-gig 18**

(Rev. 1′–2′) ...

***Sa-gig 18**

(2′) [ADAMA] *means* black blood.

***Sa-gig 18**

Perhaps an abstruse argument associating the terms *rebītu* "pubic region" and *rabītu* "bigness."

(3′–4′) "His ..." concerns his bigness (?) ...
(4′) GAL *means* big.

***Sa-gig 18**

Perhaps a depiction of "stiff" body part(s) as "bound up."

(5′) [GÍD.GÍD *means*] it keeps becoming stiff.
(5′) GÍD.GÍD *means* they are bound up.

***Sa-gig 18**

This is perhaps a graphic argument involving the elements *bam-* (interpreted as bán, 𒑏) and 1 (𒁹), where the horizontal wedge of the sign bán ("half") appears as a line bisecting the sign 1 ("one") into two halves.

(6′) ... "*bamat*" *means* half.
(6′) 1-*át means* one.

***Sa-gig 18**

The comment "*kissatu* / *kiṣṣatu* of fire" occurs in magic incantations, and elsewhere helped to define "*kiṣṣatu* of *ṣētu*-heat," a sickness described in only a few diagnostic texts.

(7′) ... as in *kissatu* of fire.

***Sa-gig 18**

(8′) ... the goddess Ereškigal

***Sa-gig 18**
The cuneiform sign kur (𒆳) has many syllabic values, but is to be interpreted here as *kūr* "daze."

(8′) "kur of his eye" (*refers to*) (its) daze.

***Sa-gig 18**

(9′) … it quivers.

***Sa-gig 18**

(9′) "*Rimûtu*" (*refers to*) the case where it goes limp.

***Sa-gig 18**

(10′) … because of sorcery.

***Sa-gig 18**

(10′) "Seizure (?)" (*refers to*) the case of (?) capturing.

***Sa-gig 18**
ŠURUN typically refers to animal "dung," while human "excrement" in medical texts is usually expressed as *zû* (logogram ŠE$_{10}$).

(11′) … "His ŠURUN" *means* his excrement, as in his feces.

***Sa-gig 18**
GIM U.MEŠ does not designate parts of the fingers elsewhere in medical texts.

(12′) … "His GIM U.MEŠ" *refer to* the heads (?) of [his] fingers.

***Sa-gig 18: 38′—**
"Hand of the goddess Išḫara"
This connection with the Netherworld goddess Ereškigal may reflect Išḫara's association with the Netherworld in Hurrian / Hittite contexts.

(13′) … ["The goddess Išḫara" *refers to* (?)] the goddess Ereškigal.

Sa-gig 18: 38′
This prognosis of the patient becoming inundated seems unattested elsewhere.

(13′) … "DUL.DUL" *means* he will keep becoming inundated.

***Sa-gig 18: 44′—**
"His mouth [palate (?)] is parched"?
The commentator may be clarifying the term *liq pî* "mouth palate" or *šābul* "is parched," either of which is more common in the Diagnostic Handbook than therapeutic texts.

(14′) ... in the case of his mouth (?).

(Colophon)

Incipit-title of Sa-gig 18

(15′) [Glossary including] oral [lore] on "If the sick man's body becomes hot (and) cold."

Notes

Obv.—Only a few traces of signs are visible on the very damaged obverse side.

Rev. 1′—Finkel (CCP 4.1.18) suggested the reading [... MÚD(?)] ⸢*ṣal*⸣-*mu-tu*$_4$ ("[...] black [blood]").

Rev. 2′—Essentially the same equation ADAMA *a-da-ma-tu*$_4$ ("'ADAMA' (*means*) black blood") occurs in Comm. Sa-gig 14, obv. 3.

Rev. 3′–4′—It is unclear what topic elicited the comment *ra-bi-ti-šú* ("his bigness (?)"), and one wonders if the commentator wanted to explain the body part *rebītu* ("pubic region"; *CAD* R, 321), a term that appears rarely in therapeutic texts (*BAM* 157, obv. 10′; *AMT* 6/6: 6′) but commonly in the Diagnostic Handbook: Sa-gig 13: 79 (TDPT 13 ii 21); Sa-gig 14: [175′–177′, 179′, 181′], 183′–188′, 190′ (TDPT 14 iii [42′–44′, 46′, 48′], 50′–55′, 57′); Sa-gig 15: 52′–53′; 19/20: 18′–19′; 33: 32. For the notation *ana muḫḫi*(UGU) with the meaning "concerning, concerns," see, for instance, DIŠ AN.GE$_6$: *ina* U$_4$.7.KAM U$_4$.14.KAM U$_4$.21.KAM / : *ana* UGU IGI-*šú u* TIL-*tú*, "'If (the moon-god brings about) an eclipse on the seventh, fourteenth, (or) twenty-first day' concerns its (first) sighting and termination" (*EAE* XX §XII commentary, rev. 14′–15′ in Al-Rawi and George 2006: 48); *gi-iṣ-ṣa-tú* : *ana* UGU *ga-za-az šá* SÍG ÙZ, "*giṣṣatu*-sickness concerns shearing, as pertaining to she-goat fleece" (*SpTU* I, 51, rev. 3); GE 10-*ḫi šá bir-bir-ru-šú u*[*b-ba-tu* BÀD *ab-ni* :] *ana* UGU $^{\text{mul}_2}$LÚ.⸢ḪUN⸣.GÁ, "'I am Asalluhi, whose luminosity [destroys a stone wall]' concerns the Hired Man" (BM 47529 + 47685, rev. 4 in Wee 2016a: 136–137, 151, §10a–b).

Rev. 5′—Finkel (CCP 4.1.18) suggested the reading [... GÍD.GÍD : *im-ta-na*]-⸢*ag*⸣-*ga-ag* : GÍD.GÍD : *ú-te-du-lu* ("[... GÍD.GÍD means] 'it is continually stiff,' GÍD.GÍD also means 'it is shut'"). Because the base text is uncertain, we cannot be sure whether the logographic or syllabic writing represents the quoted topic. The syllabic Gtn stem of *magāgu* ("to keep becoming stiff, taut") occurs predominantly in the Diagnostic Handbook: Sa-gig 13: 6 (TDPT 13 i 7′); Sa-gig 22: 10, 67; 40: 4, 107. By contrast, attestations of this verb in therapeutic texts occur in the Gtn stem only at *BAM* 232 i 18′, but in the G stem at *BAM* 449 iii 24′ (incl. *AMT* 90/1 iii 24′), in the D stem at *BAM* 397: 34; [*AMT* 16/5 ii 9], and perhaps in the Ntn stem at [*BAM* 49: 3′; 50 obv. 2]. It is further possible that the dictionary root of this verb was obscured by writings such as *in-da-na-ag-ga-ag* (< *imtanaggag*). Concerning the logogram GÍD.GÍD, note the lexical equations: gú-gíd-i = *ma-ga-gu*, gú-gíd-gíd-i = *mi-tan-gu-gu* (Nabnitu IX (= X), 137–138 in *MSL* XVI, 121) gú-gíd = *ma-qa-qu*, gú-gíd-gíd = *mi-tan-gu-gu* (Antagal D, 169–170 in *MSL* XVII, 206). *Contra* Finkel's reading, the later signs appear to me as *ú-te-il-lu* (rev. 5′), which perhaps make the most sense in this context as *ūteʾʾilū* (< *eʾēlu*), "they are bound up," though a good case can be made as well for *ūtellû* (< *elû*), "they are being raised." Admittedly, though, neither *eʾēlu* nor *elû*—nor even *edēlu* ("to shut") in Finkel's reading—is associated in the lexical tradition with gíd-gíd. Perhaps relevant, however, is the fact that a demon known as *eʾēlu* ("binder") afflicts the patient who "stretches out his feet" (GÌR.2-*šú* LAL-*aṣ*) in Sa-gig 26: 44′, while the same demon may also be diagnosed for a condition in which the patient "is unable to turn his feet / lower legs inwards" (see Note on Comm. Sa-gig 5, line 35).

Rev. 6′—The juxtaposition of *bamat* (< *bamtu*, "half") and 1-*át* (< *ištât*, "one") as visually commensurable forms seems calculated, perhaps in order to make a graphic argument involving the elements *bam-* (interpreted as bán, 𒑐) and 1 (𒁹), where the horizontal wedge of the sign bán ("half") appears as a line bisecting the sign 1 ("one") into two halves. See also Note on Comm. Sa-gig 1A, lines 38–40 where BA.AN is said to depict the sign bán ("half"), so that the person designated as ^{lu_2}BA.AN.ZU is a "stunted" man whose stature is "half" (bán) that of a normal "man" (ZA), or a "half-witted" man who has only "half" (bán) his "wits" (ZU).

Rev. 7′—As an explanatory comment, the commentator employed the phrase "*kissatu* of fire" that does not occur in the Diagnostic Handbook, but that appears in the context of magic incantations (*CAD* K, 429 s.v. *kissatu* B §a). In Comm. Sa-gig 14, obv. 6–7, this same expression was likely behind the argument that, based on the alleged reading "*kiṣṣatu* of fire" in a fire incantation, the uncommon description "*kiṣṣatu* of *ṣētu*-heat" could be treated as a synonym for the well-attested condition "burning of *ṣētu*-heat."

Rev. 8′—The goddess Ereškigal is not often attested in medical texts, appearing only as ŠU ^{d}*Ereš-ki-gal* (Sa-gig 13: 38 (TDPT 13 i 39′)), NA.BI *ka-šip* NU.MEŠ-*šú* DÙ.MEŠ-*ma ina* KI.GUL.MEŠ *ana* ^{d}*Ereš-ki-gal pa-aq-du* (*BAM*

214 i 7–9). Note also the obscure references to Ereškigal in the broken contexts of Comm. Sa-gig 4A, obv. x+2′, x+6′. The base text *Sa-gig 4: 44 of the commentary entry in Comm. Sa-gig 4A, obv. x+2′ is probably similar to the entry Sa-gig 13: 38 (TDPT 13 i 39′).

Rev. 8′—This line was understood as [...] ^{d}EREŠ.KI.GAL *kur* IGI-*šú* ⸢KÚR⸣^{ru}, "[...] Ereškigal shall alter his *weak-sightedness*" by Jiménez (CCP no. 4.1.18). This interpretation does not satisfactorily account for the existence and form of the gloss in ⸢KÚR⸣^{ru}, or requires some plural subject in the damaged portion before "Ereškigal" that corresponds to the plural verb form ⸢KÚR-*ru*⸣. A better solution may be to interpret the name "Ereškigal" as comment to an unpreserved topic earlier in rev. 8′, and kur IGI-*šú* as a separate commentary topic. For *kūr ēnēšu* meaning "seine Schwachsichtigkeit" and ascribed to the dictionary root *kâru* II ("benommen sein"; *CAD* K, 240 s.v. *kâru* B, "to become in a depression, in a stupor"), see *AHw*, 452, 512; cf. Held (1961: 16–17). I understand this commentary entry as kur IGI-*šú* ⸢*kúr-ru*⸣ ("'kur of his eye' (*refers to*) (its) daze"), whereby the choice of the homophonic sign *kúr* (𒉽) was employed so that the cuneiform sign kur (𒆳) might not be mistaken for its other syllabic values. To be sure, there is no clear disjunction sign after IGI-*šú* (rev. 8′), and the dictionaries do not explicitly list *kurru* as a byform of *kūru* ("daze, depression, stupor"). See *CAD* K, 570–571; *AHw*, 512. Note, however, the existence of the obscure verb *karāru* II that tantalizingly describes an eye condition of sorts (*AHw*, 447; *CAD* K, 209).

Rev. 9′—This line was restored [... *it-ta-na-as-la-ʾ* : *i*]-*nak-kud*, "['*He is ill*' means 'he] is worried'" by Jiménez (CCP no. 4.1.18), on the basis of another commentary equation [LÍL.LÍL-*aʾ* : *i*]*t-ta-na-as-la-ʾ* : *i-nak-kud* (Comm. Sa-gig 40A, obv. 10). See Note on the latter equation, where I suggest that the basic meaning of *nakādu* is "to throb, palpitate, quiver" (*CAD* N I, 153), and derivative meanings such as "to worry, fear, be anxious" reflect emotional states involving a "throbbing" heart. The sickness *rimûtu* is attested elsewhere in the Diagnostic Handbook only at Sa-gig 4: 125 (TDPT 4 rev. 40), where it is found in a group with ZI SAG.KI ("pulsating of the temple") and *šimmatu* ("paralysis"), and it is possible that the unpreserved base text here resembles Sa-gig 4: 125 (TDPT 4 rev. 40). As a matter of fact, these conditions, along with SAG.KI.DAB.BA ("seized temple") tend to appear together also in the therapeutic texts *BAM* 11: 30, 32, 34; [68: 1]; 69:[1′]–2′; 168: 18; 194 iv 5–6; 228: 23–26; 229 obv. 17′–20′; 323: 89–91; 482 i 54′; *AMT* 20/1: 36′, 38′; 52/5 obv. 4′. The reading *i-*⸢*ram*(?)⸣*-mu-ú* (rev. 9′) was suggested by Frahm (CCP no. 4.1.18), and perhaps the entire argument could be restored as [ZI-(*ib*) SAG.KI *šá i-n*]*ak-kud* : *ri-mu-tú šá i-*⸢*ram*(?)⸣*-mu-ú*, "['ZI-(*ib*) SAG.KI" (i.e., pulsating of the temple) (*refers to*) the case where] it quivers; "*Rimûtu*" (*refers to*) "the case where it goes limp" (rev. 9′). For the inconsistent use of the subordination marker after the notation *ša* ("the case of / where"), see §11.2.2.

Rev. 10′—The unpreserved base text perhaps describes the "seizure of" (DAB-*it* = *ṣibit*) a sickness, or the Hand of a deity, demon, or ghost. For equations connecting DAB (or DIB) with *kamû* ("to capture"), see *CAD* K, 128 s.v. *kamû* A, lexical section. The interpretation "'Prisoner' (*ṣabtu*) (is said) of a captive" by Jiménez (CCP no. 4.1.18) seems less likely.

Rev. 11′—The term *zu-ú-šú* ("his excrement") is very common in medical texts, and it more likely functions as a comment to what precedes it, rather than as a topic needing explication. Jiménez (CCP no. 4.1.18) read the signs preserved at the beginning of this line as [...]-⌈*sis*⌉-*su* (rev. 11′). I suggest the restoration [ŠUR]UN-*su* in view of sign traces on the tablet, the fact that ŠURUN ("(animal) dung") can serve as a synonym of "excrement," and because the word (/*kabūt* + *šu*/ >) *kabūssu* = ŠURUN-*su* explains why the suffix is -*su* rather than -*šú*. While the logogram ŠURUN can express either *kabû* / *kabūtu* (*CAD* K, 28–29) or *rubṣu* (*CAD* R, 395), the basic meaning of *rubṣu* is probably "litter" with derived meanings "bedding place / lair" (where litter serves as bedding material), "womb" (the bedding place of the unborn child), and "dung" (where the litter consists of waste matter). While the original context for ŠURUN is not preserved, the commentator's explanation provides a far more typical word for human "excrement" in medical texts: *zû* (logogram $ŠE_{10}$). For the association between *zû* ("excrement") and *šittu* ("feces"), see also *šit-ti* : *zu-ú* in Comm. Sa-gig 13+, line 16.

Rev. 12′—The writing GIM U.MEŠ does not seem to be attested elsewhere. Instead of *ri-kis*(?) *ú-ba-na-tu* ("band (?) of the fingers") by Jiménez (CCP no. 4.1.18), I read *re*-⌈*šet*(?)⌉ *ú-ba-na-tu*-[*šú*] ("the heads (?) of [his] fingers"), perhaps referring to the same body part as SAG ŠU.SI.MEŠ (< *rēš ubāni*, "Fingerspitze, Fingerkuppe") that appears in the physiognomic series *Šumma sinništu qaqqada rabât*, line 133 (Böck 2000: 53, 158). Despite Böck's translation, it is not entirely certain that *rēš ubāni* ("head of finger") is synonymous with *appi ubāni* ("tip of finger"). One also wonders if GIM U.MEŠ could have been understood as *kim* U.MEŠ, which represents a byform or an abbreviation of *kimkimmi* U.MEŠ (translated "Fingergrundgelenk" in Böck 2000: 53).

Rev. 13′—"Hand of the goddess Išḫara" is the diagnostic verdict in Sa-gig 18: 38′, which can be identified also as the base text for the very next commentary entry. In Babylonian contexts, the goddess Išḫara may be identified with Ištar and venerated as a mother goddess or a goddess of love, war, or extispicy (Lambert 1977a: 176–177). In the Hurrian / Hittite pantheon, however, the name Išḫara can designate a goddess of the Netherworld (Frantz-Szabo 1977: 177–178). I tentatively restore [^{d}*Iš-ḫa-ra* (?) : ^{d}*Ere*]*š-ki-gal* (rev. 13′), which suggests such an association of Išḫara with the Mesopotamian Netherworld goddess Ereškigal. See Note on rev. 8′ above for attestations of Ereškigal in medical texts.

Rev. 13′—The base text for DUL.DUL-*ma* here is likely Sa-gig 18: 38′ (transliterated DU_6.DU_6-*ma* in Heeßel 2000: 219; Scurlock 2014: 174). This expression that the patient "will keep becoming inundated" (Ntn of *katāmu*) is not attested in prognoses elsewhere. See Note on Comm. Sa-gig 4C, rev. 10′ where the commentator felt the need to explain DUL.DUL (Sa-gig 4: 111 (TDPT 4 rev. 25)) as "closing, lit. covering" (*katāmu*) the eyes, perhaps because of the possibility of interpreting DUL.DUL as the inundation of the patient himself as in Sa-gig 18: 38′.

Rev. 14′—The base text here may be Sa-gig 18: 44′: [... *liq*(?) K]A-*šú šá-bul* ("his mouth palate(?) is parched"). Heeßel (2000: 219) does not restore the term [*liq*(?)] ("palate"), but I have done so on the basis of similar expressions in Sa-gig 7 B obv. 15′–17′ (TDPT 7: 54′–56′); Sa-gig 40: 69; *BAM* 484 obv. 4; *AMT* 76/1: 4. Other references to the "mouth palate" (*liq pî*) may be found at Sa-gig 6: 82″–84″ (TDPT 6 rev. 19′–21′); Sa-gig 7 A obv. 13 (TDPT 7: 13); Sa-gig 7 B obv. 14′; rev. 2 (TDPT 7: 53′, 58′). As these references show, the rarity of this body part in therapeutic texts (*BAM* 484 obv. 4; *AMT* 76/1: 4) may account for the commentator's interest in the term. See also the equation *la-aq* KA-*šú* : *ša-me-e pi-šú* in a commentary on Izbu XII, 82 in Leichty (1970: 231, Comm. W, 377b); De Zorzi (2014: 673, K 1913, ii 21′). Alternatively, the commentator may have been concerned to explain the Š Stative form *šābul* ("is parched"), which occurs as a description of the mouth (palate) only in the Diagnostic Handbook: Sa-gig 7 B obv. 15′ (TDPT 7: 54′); Sa-gig [12: 133″] (TDPT [12 iv 26]); Sa-gig 18: 44′. Note that the verb in UZU.SA ZAG *u* GÙB *uš-tab-ba-lu*$_4$ (*AMT* 44/4: 1) may not be *abālu* B "(Š) to parch, cause to dry up" (*CAD* A I, 29–31), but the homophone *abālu* A, "(G) to bring, transport; (Št) to move(?)" (*CAD* A I, 10–29).

Commentary Sa-gig 19

Provenance:	Uruk (Warka), Area U18, Level v; Library of Anu-ikṣur
Period:	Late Achaemenid
Names:	"[Readings of] Anu-ikṣur, junior magician"
Script:	Neo-/Late Babylonian
Typology:	*ṣâtu* 6b in Frahm (2011a: 53)
Field/Museum No.:	W 22307/32 (National Museum of Iraq)
Printed Edition/Hand Copy:	*SpTU* 1, 38 (= Hunger 1976: 47–48); Heeßel (2000: 234–235, 240–245); Wee (2012: 653–663)
Digital Resources:	CDLI P348459; GKAB P348459 (edition digitized by Clancier 2009); CCP 4.1.19 (printed hand copies digitized by Frahm, Frazer, and Jiménez 2013)
Discussion:	Hunger (1975: 65) and *SpTU* 1, 38 (= Hunger 1976: 47–48); Heeßel (2000: 135, 226 (19./20. Tafel MS a), 234–235, 240–245); Scurlock and Andersen (2005: 803, see references to *SpTU* 1.38); Stol (2007a: 9 n. 15); Clancier (2009: 50, 52, 55, 227, 265, 388); Geller (2010a: 151); Genty (2010a: 381) and (2010b: 14, 20, 21, 22, 24, 26, 28); Frahm (2011a: 53 n. 231, 89 n. 446, 226, 291); Wee (2012: 653–663); Scurlock (2014: 182 n. 1; 193 n. 9); Gabbay (2016: 64 n. 264, 226 n. 107)
Pericope:	Indeterminate due to damaged state of available Sa-gig manuscripts

Transliteration

Obverse

1) DIŠ G[I]G ⌊KÚM⌋-*i*[*m u* SED ...]
2) [Š]U ^{d}⌈30⌉ *šá* x[...]
3) [...]x-*uṣ* : ^{d}3[0 ...]
4) $^{\text{[din]ger. [d]a-pa-ri}}$ gud : x [...]
5) [K]ÚM-*ma* ad bi ⌈úḫ⌉ GAM : [a]d b[i ...]
6) [a]l-zu-[b]i na[m-ba-zu-zu]

 | DOI:10.1163/9789004417564_023

7) [*m*]*u-da-a-šú la ú*-[*ád-da*]
8) [umu]š-bi nam-ba-ḫa-za : *ṭè*-⌜*eme*⌝-⌞*šú*⌟ [NU DAB]
9) [di-i]ḫ DIḪ : *le-e-bu* : x[...]
10) [*zi*]-*i-pu* : *le-e-bu* : *di-ḫu* [...]
11) [*ig-d*]*a-nar-ru-ru* : *ip-ta-na-a*[*l-l*]*a*-[*ḫu*]
12) [mu-u]m-mu MU$_7$.MU$_7$-*um* : *i-ra-am*-[*m*]*u-um*
13) [MU$_7$].MU$_7$: *ra-ma-ma* : MU$_7$.MU$_7$: ⌜*ri-gim*⌝
14) [...] LUL.AŠ : *ma-a-di-iš*
15) [*tas-l*]*i-ma-a-ti* DU$_{11}$.DU$_{11}$-*ub*
16) [*lìb-b*]*u-ú ta-as-li-ma-a* : TI
17) [...]-*ti* : *nu-ul-lat ina ṣa-a-tú* E
18) [*qer-b*]*é-nu-uš-šú* : *qer-bé-nu* : *lìb-bi*
19) [SE]D : *ku-uṣ* : SED *ḫur-ba-šú*
20) [*mu-k*]*il* SAG : *um-mu* šal šú x (*ḫe-pi*$_2$ *eš-šu*$_2$)
21) [*e-di*]-*il-ma* : *e-te*-[*é*]*l*(il)-*ma* : *e-te-el-lu-ú*
22) [*e-lu*]-*u* : *ana a-te-e* GAR-*šú*

Reverse
23) [... *a-t*]*u-ú* : *a-ma-ri*
24) [... b]i(?) *lìb-bi*
25) [...]-*ku-lu*
26) [... *i*]*k-k*[*a*]-*lu-uš*
27) [...] x tuk ra
28) [...] *ma*-⌜*a*⌝-*du*
29) [... È].A : *ṣi*-⌜*i*⌝-*tu*$_4$
30) [*ina*(?) EN].NUN.AN.USAN
31) [*ina*(?) *ba-ra-ri*]-*ti*
32) [... *b*]*a-la-ṭu*
33) [...]-*re-eš*

---

34) [*ṣa-a-tú ù šu-ut p*]*i-i šá* KA UM.ME.A
35) [*šá* DIŠ GIG KÚM-*im*] *u* SED
36) [*mál-su-ut* m.d*A-nu*]-*ik-ṣur* lu$_2$MAŠ.MAŠ BÀ[N.DA]
37) [...] x [...]

Translation

Incipit-title of Sa-gig 19 (Obv. 1) "If the sick man becomes hot [and cold]" ...

***Sa-gig 19/20** (2) "Hand of the moon-god Sîn" ...

(3) … "the moon-god Sîn" …

The cuneiform sign gud (𒄞) represents the god DAPAR, and is not to be confused with GIDIM$_7$ "ghost" that is often the agent responsible for sickness.

(4) The god Dapar …

Sa-gig 19/20: 20′
"ad bi úḫ" appears only here in medical texts.

(5) "He becomes hot and ad bi úḫ, he will die."
(5) ad bi […]

Sa-gig 19/20: 21′
Sumerian grammatical forms here are atypical for Akkadian medical texts. The expression "he does not recognize his acquaintance" occurs only in the Diagnostic Handbook, but not in therapeutic texts.

(6–7) "al-zu-bi nam-ba-zu-zu" (*means*) he does not recognize his acquaintance.

Sa-gig 19/20: 22′
The expression "he is not in possession of his intelligence" is common in the Diagnostic Handbook, but absent in therapeutic texts.

(8) "umuš-bi nam-ba-ḫa-za" *means* [he is not in possession of] his intelligence.

***Sa-gig 19/20**
The sicknesses *li'bu*, *zi'pu*, and *šību* are closely associated in lexical entries. Not only are the logographic value DIḪ ("*li'bu*-sickness") and the syllables *di-ḫu* ("*di'u*-sickness") assonantally linked, the sicknesses are both associated with heat and *ṣētu*-heat.

(9) "DIḪ" *means li'bu*-sickness …

(10) *zi'pu*-sickness *is related to li'bu*-sickness, *which is related to di'u*-sickness …

***Sa-gig 19/20**
igdanarrurū "they keep becoming scared" derives from the verb *garāru* "to become scared," not the homophone *garāru* "to roll, dribble, writhe" that is more common in medical texts.

(11) "*igdanarrurū*" *means* they keep becoming frightened.

***Sa-gig 19/20**
The sign MU_7 is not to be read as TU_6 "incantation," which it often denotes in therapeutic texts. The verb *ramāmu* "to groan" appears only here as the logogram $MU_7.MU_7$.

(12) "$MU_7.MU_7$-*um*" *means* he groans.

The meaning of $MU_7.MU_7$ as "to groan" is supported by its alternative reading "voice."

(13) $MU_7.MU_7$ *means* to groan.
(13) $MU_7.MU_7$ *means* voice.

Sa-gig 19/20: 39′
mādiš "very much" appears as the logogram LUL.AŠ only here.

(14) ... "LUL.AŠ" *means* very much.

Sa-gig 19/20: 42′
taslimāti is analyzed here as *taslimā* "you made peace" + TI "(you) will live." Speaking *taslimāti*, therefore, was viewed as a sign that the patient would recover.

(15) "He keeps speaking *taslimāti*."
(16) [As in], you made peace, you will live.

(17) ... *refers to* foolish talk, it is said in a *ṣâtu* composition.

***Sa-gig 19/20 (cf. Sa-gig 19/20: 57′)**
qerbēnu "interior" is associated with the rectum or womb in therapeutic texts, but should be understood here as "inside," perhaps of a bodily feature.

(18) "In his/its interior" *refers to* the interior, *which means* the inside.

Sa-gig 19/20: 53′—*kuṣṣi* "coldness"
The semantic link between *kuṣṣu* "coldness" and *ḫurbāšu* "chill" is implied by their shared logogram SED. The comment *ḫurbāšu* "chill" is a term more confined to therapeutic texts.

(19) SED *means* coldness.
(19) SED (*means*) chill.

Sa-gig 19/20: 53′
mukīl SAG "that which holds the head" is a less common form of the malady name SAG.ḪUL.ḪA.ZA (*mukīl-rēš-lemutti*) "the evil one holding the head."

(20) "That which holds the head" *refers to* heat … ***new break***

Sa-gig 19/20: 72′
Signs *e-di-il-ma* (𒂊 𒁲 𒅋 𒈠) are to be read as *e-te*$_{10}$*-él-ma* (𒂊 𒁲 𒅋 𒈠) or /*etel-ma*/, which awkwardly stands for *etellū-ma* "it keeps going up."

(21) "*e-di-il-ma*" *is to be read* /*etel-ma*/,
(21–22) *which is related to the dictionary root* to keep going up,
(*which derives from the dictionary root*) [to go up.]

Sa-gig 19/20: 97′
The base text belongs to a section of the Diagnostic Handbook more akin to hemerological texts, with certain terms that are atypical for medical texts.

(22) "It is destined for him to find out."
(Line 23) …

Common lexical equation

(23) To find out *means* to perceive.

***Sa-gig 19/20**

(24–28) …

***Sa-gig 19/20: 110′—**
[*ina* ᵈUTU.È.A]
The usual writing is ᵈUTU.È, not ᵈUTU.È.A.

(29) "… È.A" *means* (sun)rise.

Sa-gig 19/20: 112′
This time reference occurs rarely in medical texts.

(30–31) "[At (?)] EN.NUN. AN.USAN" (*means*) [at (?)] the evening watch.

(32–33) …

(Colophon)

Incipit-title of Sa-gig 19

(34–35) [Glossary including] oral [lore] from the mouth of the *ummânu*-scholar [on "If the sick man becomes hot] and cold."

(36) [Readings of] Anu-ikṣur, junior magician, …

Notes

Obv. 1—The incipit-title of Tablet 19 of the Diagnostic Handbook Sa-gig is not preserved in existing manuscripts, but the Sa-gig catalog lists it as DIŠ *i-mim u* SED ("If he becomes hot and cold"). See Finkel (1988: 146, obv. A 24); Heeßel (2000: 14, line 24).

Obv. 3—The beginning of obv. 3 is unfortunately damaged, though one possible restoration may be [*k*]*u-uṣ* ("coldness"), in line with *ku-uṣ* of obv. 19. In any case, it is uncertain whether […]x-*uṣ* in obv. 3 introduces a commentary topic, or whether it represents the comment to a topic at the damaged end of obv. 2. It should be noted that, judging from Hunger's hand copy of the tablet (*SpTU* I, 38), quite a substantial amount of text is missing at the ends of obv. 1–4.

Obv. 4—Note the following lexical readings: di-pa-ar = gud = $^{\text{d. di-par}}$gud, da-par = gud = $^{\text{d. da-par}}$gud (Ea IV, 140, 141 in *MSL* XIV, 360, 361); cf. An = *Anum* VI, 203, 204 (Litke 1998: 215). In medical contexts, it was perhaps needful to clarify the reading of gud with glosses like $^{\text{[d]a-pa-ri}}$ (obv. 4), because the cuneiform sign gud (𒄞) more commonly adopts the logographic value GIDIM$_7$ ("ghost") in diagnoses that attribute the patient's condition to the agency of a ghost. In a therapeutic commentary, however, we do find a different gloss for the same writing: $^{\text{ni-ra-aḫ. d}}$gud : *ni-ra-ḫu* (11N-T3, line 25 in Civil 1974: 332). For a good survey with bibliography on the various vocalizations and proposed identities of the deity ^{d}gud, see Peterson (2009: 68–69).

Obv. 5—The base text Sa-gig 19/20: 20′ has been restored as [DIŠ KÚM-*ma*] AD.BI ÚḪ [KUD] and translated literally ("[Wenn er heiß ist und] sein Vater(?) den Speichel(fluß) [stoppt(?)]") by Heeßel (2000: 227, 235). In the only manuscript attestation of this entry (MS B = K 6422, line 10′ in TDPT II, pl. XXIX), there is considerable blank space after the sign úḫ and the very next sign may be the final sign of this medical entry in the damaged right edge of the tablet. This consideration, as well as traces of the sign in Hunger's hand copy (*SpTU* I, 38), have led me to understand the final sign as the prognosis GAM ("he will die") instead of KUD (Heeßel: "stoppt(?)"). It is less clear what the remaining signs of "ad bi úḫ" mean, but they bear some similarity to the form KÚM ÚḪ. For the definition of this latter term as KÚM *ṣarḫu* ("flaring-up heat"), see Note on Comm. Sa-gig 3C, obv. 5. The only attestation of ÚḪ without the accompanying term KÚM, however, may be in Sa-gig 11 rev. 30: U.MEŠ-*šú* ÚḪ(!).MEŠ, translated "his fingers feel burning hot" by Scurlock and Andersen (2005: 554, §Ap.9); Scurlock (2014: 90). If the sign úḫ in Sa-gig 19/20: 20′ indeed refers to the verb *ṣarāḫu* ("to flare up"), it fits well with the first medical sign that the patient "becomes hot" (KÚM).

Obv. 6–7—The use of Sumerian grammatical features (not only logographic values) is atypical for Akkadian medical texts (see Note on Comm. Sa-gig 4A, obv. 2), but these appear in Sa-gig 19/20: 21′ and 22′ as the base texts for obv. 6–7 and 8 respectively of this commentary. Understandably, such unusual features prompted the commentator's remarks. The form al-du was also chosen as a topic in Comm. Sa-gig 4A (obv. 2), where the commentator considered it to be a fossilized form AL.DU indistinguishable from the logogram DU ("to move"), without taking into account the original stative sense of the Sumerian verbal prefix al- (Edzard 2003: 111, §12.10). The expression "he does not recognize his acquaintance" appears as a medical sign only in the Diagnostic Handbook: ZU-*šú* NU *ú-ád-da* (Sa-gig 16: 11; 17: 73), al-zu-bi nam-ba-zu-zu (Sa-gig 19/20: 21′), al-zu-zu n[am-ba-zu-bi] (Sa-gig 22: 56 MS A), and al-zu-bi nam-ba-zu-bi (Sa-gig 22: 56 MS E). My restoration *ú*-[*ád-da*] in this commentary follows the forms in Sa-gig 16: 11; 17: 73.

Obv. 8—The expression "he is not in possession of his intelligence" does not seem to appear in the medical signs of therapeutic texts, but is very common in the Diagnostic Handbook: Sa-gig 6: 74′(?) (TDPT 6 rev. 11′); Sa-gig 7 A obv. 22; 9: 38; 10: 34; [11: 20, 28]; 12: 84″–85″, 97″ (TDPT 12 iii 21–22, 34); Sa-gig 14: 66 (TDPT 14 i 66); Sa-gig 15: 8′, 18′–19′, 24′, 39′–40′, 57′, [64′], 86′; 22: 47. The orthography here—*ṭè*-⸢*eme*⸣-⸤*šú*⸥—occurs also as *ṭè-eme* in Comm. Sa-gig 14, obv. 13.

Obv. 9–10—Comm. Sa-gig 4A, obv. 8 equates *le-e-bu* with *zi-i-pu* as well. In both Comm. Sa-gig 4A and Comm. Sa-gig 19, I understand the writing *le-e-bu* to denote the noun *lēbu* ("*li'bu*-sickness") rather than the verb *le'ēbu* ("to infect, said of *li'bu*-sickness"), because the term equated with *le-e-bu* is the noun "*zi'pu*-sickness." The same writing *le-e-bu* also appears in Comm. Sa-gig 1A, line 14: su-ul šáḫ : *le-e-bu* : BA.ÚŠ ("The cuneiform sign šáḫ as the logogram SUL *means li'bu*-sickness, *which means* he will die"). *Zi'pu*-sickness appears to be, in essence, a skin condition (*zi'pu, zīpu* III, §4 in *AHw*, 1530). The maladies *li'bu, zi'pu*, and *šību* are closely associated in lexical entries such as *li-'-bu, ši-i-bu* = *zi-i-pi* (*CT* 18, 31 rev. 15–16 // *STT* 394: 161–162) and *li-'-bu, ši-i-bu* = *zi-*[*ir-qu*] (Malku VIII, 161–162 in Hrůša 2010: 427; *CAD* Š II, 399). DIḪ as the logogram of *lēbu* ("*li'bu*-sickness") occurs in the lexical texts Aa III/5, 13 (*MSL* XIV, 343); *MSL* II, 136 line k (Proto-Ea). In this commentary, it was particularly important to clarify the reading of the logogram DIḪ by the preceding signs [di-i]ḫ, in order to demonstrate the assonantal link between the logographic value DIḪ ("*li'bu*-sickness") and the syllables *di-ḫu* ("*di'u*-sickness") in obv. 10. For the interpretation of *di'u* as "malaria," see Stol (2007a: 15–18). See also [din]ger [d]a-pa-ri gud (obv. 4) and [mu-u]m-mu MU$_7$.MU$_7$-*um* (obv. 12) in this commentary as other examples of explicating logographic values through glosses. The sicknesses [*zi*]-*i-pu* : *le-e-bu* : *di-ḫu* in obv. 10 of this commentary are connected not only by means of erudite readings, but also by actual nosological relations. *Li'bu*-sickness and *di'u*-sickness, for example, are both known to be associated with heat and *ṣētu*-heat. See Scurlock and Andersen (2005: 29–32, 59–61); Kinnier Wilson and Finkel (2007: 20–22); Stol (2007a: 11–12).

Obv. 11—The topic [*ig-d*]*a-nar-ru-ru* is the Gtn Durative of the verb *garāru*, though the base text is too damaged to discern. The Infinitive form *garāru* can refer to at least two homophonic verbs: (I) "to roll, dribble, writhe" (*garāru* A in *CAD* G, 47–48) and (II) "to shy away, become scared" (*garāru* B in *CAD* G, 49). In the Diagnostic Handbook, the Ntn stem of *garāru* A describes the "dribbling" of sweat or spittle at Sa-gig 4: 65, 67; 26: 29′ (interpreted as semantically opposite variants in MS B: "he has no spittle : (spittle) keeps dribbling"), as well as the "writhing" of the patient at Sa-gig 15: 42′; 26: 29′ (not interpreted as variants in MS A: "he has no [spittle] and he keeps writhing"). The term *i-*ḫar-*ru-ur* in the base text manuscript of Comm. Sa-gig 10 & 11, obv. 3 (cf. Sa-gig 10: 2, 5) may also have been interpreted by the commentator as the similar signs *i-gàr-ru-ur* "(spittle) dribbles." In the therapeutic texts *BAM* 145: 9; [146: 33′], the description ŠÀ-*šú ig-da-na-ru-ur* should be understood as "his belly keeps writhing," not "his heart is constantly in panic" as translated in *CAD* G, 49 s.v. *garāru* B §1b. The context involves an upset belly, "flowing" of the bowels, defecation, and the diagnosis "flaring up heat of the belly," and therefore suggests that ŠÀ refers to the "belly," rather than to the "heart" or seat of the emotions. See also Comm. Sa-gig 7B, rev. 3′–4′: *ig-da-nar-ru-ur* : *i-gàr-ru-ur* / *šá-ni-iš i-šá-as-si* ("*igdanarrur*" *means* "it writhes." Secondly, "it makes noise."), which likely describes a writhing belly as one that makes noise (i.e., a rumbling belly). In other words, the equation [*ig-d*]*a-nar-ru-ru* : *ip-ta-na-a*[*l-l*]*a-*[*ḫu*] ("*igdanarrurū*" *means* "they keep becoming frightened") represents the commentator's effort to identify the verb as *garāru* B ("to become scared"), instead of the more common *garāru* A ("to roll, dribble, writhe"). A similar argument occurs also in Comm. Sa-gig 34, obv. 3: [*i-gar-r*]*u-ur* : *ga-ra-ra* : *pa-la-ḫu* ("['*igarrur*'] *derives from the dictionary root* to become scared, *which means* to become frightened"). Though there are no equations of *garāru* B with *palāḫu* in lexical texts, note the pairing of these two verbs as *ú-pa-liḫ-a-ni ú-šag-ri-ra-a-ni* (Thureau-Dangin 1921: 197, fig. 2, line 2), as well as the fact that both verbs are associated with the logogram UR_4 (*CAD* G, 49; *CAD* P, 38).

Obv. 12–13—The beginning of obv. 12 marks the start of a new commentary entry, and I tentatively restore the signs as $^{\text{[mu-u]m-mu}}$ MU_7.MU_7-*um*. Perhaps there was a need to clarify the logographic value of MU_7, because the same cuneiform sign appears very frequently in therapeutic texts with the value TU_6 = *šiptu* ("incantation"). See also $^{\text{[din]ger [d]a-pa-ri}}$ gud (obv. 4) and $[^{\text{di-i}}]^{\text{ḫ}}$ DIḪ (obv. 9) in this commentary as other examples of explicating the value of a logogram. MU_7 as the logogram of *ramāmu* ("to groan") and *rigmu* ("voice, noise") occurs in the lexical texts Diri Nippur, 30, 33 (*MSL* XV, 12); Diri Oxford, 31–32 (*MSL* XV, 40); Diri Ugarit I, 51, 53–54 (*MSL* XV, 69); Diri I, 56–60 (*MSL* XV, 106, 108); Lanu A, 107f. (*CAD* R, 116). The verb *ramāmu* appears only a few times in the Diagnostic Handbook and therapeutic texts, always in its syllabic form: Sa-gig 7 B rev. 15 (TDPT 7: 71′; collated by Lambert and mentioned in Scurlock and Andersen (2005: 375, §16.41; 745 n. 30); Sa-gig 27: 36; *BAM* 202 rev. 6′; [311: 51′]; 385 i 16′.

Obv. 14—LUL.AŠ as the logogram for *mādiš* occurs in the lexical text Diri Oxford, 508 (*MSL* XV, 48), as well as in a commentary of the Assyrian scholar Nabû-zuqup-kēnu: LUL.AŠ = *ma-ᵓ-diš* // *dan-niš*, MAḪ.BI = *ma-ᵓ-diš* (K 4387 = 2R 47, v 54ff.; *CAD* M I, 17). See discussion and bibliography on *mādiš* in Stol (1998: 349). In descriptions of medical signs, the term *mādiš* ("very much") appears syllabically at Sa-gig 9: 22; 40: 62; *BAM* 575 iii 40, and as the logogram LUL.AŠ only in the base text Sa-gig 19/20: 39′ here. Unfortunately, the damaged state of the base text does not allow us to determine the direct object of the statement KI.MIN *ba-de* LUL.AŠ *i-ši* (Sa-gig 19/20: 39′). Note, however, the use of an alternative and more common adverb *magal* (logogram UL_4.GAL) with the verb TUKU = *išû* ("to have") at Sa-gig 19/20: 56′; 40: 29, 59; *BAM* 66 obv. 24; 174 rev. 29; 416 obv. 4′, 8′. One wonders if the choice of either *magal* or *mādiš* reflected different nuances in expressing, for example, frequency in time versus quantity of substance.

Obv. 15–16—The term [*tas-l*]*i-ma-a-ti* (singular: *taslimtu*) derives from the base text Sa-gig 19/20: 42′, though its meaning is questionable. Translators of medical texts have generally preferred a positive meaning such as "Freundlichkeiten" (Hunger in *SpTU* I, 38), "freundlich (spricht)" (Heeßel 2000: 236, line 42′), "greetings" (Scurlock and Andersen 2005: 646, line 42′), and "(re)conciliation" (*CDA* s.v. *taslimtu*(*m*)), presumably reflecting the etymology of the word from the verb *salāmu* ("to become reconciled, to make peace"). The *Chicago Assyrian Dictionary* is noncommittal about the meaning "malicious talk(?), insult(?)" based, among other things, on associations of *taslimtu* with *šillatu* "blasphemy, insult" (Erimḫuš I, 282 in *MSL* XVII, 20) and *nullâtu* "improper matters, malicious/foolish talk" (Lambert 1960: 32–33, lines 57–58; *SpTU* I, 38 obv. 15–17), its inclusion in a lexical list of the "unspeakable" (i.e., *nullâtu, magrītu, taslimtum* = *lā qabī*[*tu*] (*CT* 18, 6 rev. 43–45)), as well as its derogatory Hittite translation "those who always speak twice" (*CAD* T, 282–283). The term *taslimtu* is also attested logographically as INIM.É.GAL and less often as KÙR.DUG_4.GA, though it is uncertain to what extent the literal meanings of these logograms reflect current usage. To complicate matters further, even if the literal meaning of *taslimtu* is a positive one, the custom may have been to employ the term as a euphemism or in a sarcastic way. In this commentary, the beginning of obv. 16 is unfortunately damaged, but I restore [*lìb-b*]*u-ú* ("as in"). The signs *ta-as-li-ma-a* : TI (obv. 16), however, are clearly distinct in Hunger's hand copy of the commentary tablet, though he ignores the disjunction sign in his transliteration *ta-as-li-ma-a-ti* (*SpTU* I, 38); followed by Heeßel (2000: 234). Whatever the original etymology of the word *taslimāti*, the commentator seems to have made an erudite argument here by analyzing the form as *taslimā* (< *salāmu* "to make peace") + the logogram TI ("will become healthy"). Although the end of the base text entry Sa-gig 19/20: 42′ is not preserved, it likely contains the prognosis "he will become healthy" (logogram TIN or TI). Another diagnostic entry Sa-gig 26: 78′–80′, for example, mentions features of the patient's speech and clothing just like Sa-gig 19/20: 42′, before ending with the prognosis "he will live." The commentator's motivation, therefore, was to demonstrate why the speaking of *taslimāti* constituted a sign that the patient would eventually recover. The term *taslimti* ("insult") is the topic of an entry also at Comm. Sa-gig 7Ca, obv. 7′–8′: "'*tas-lim-ti*' *means* [insult, *which means* KA.É.GAL]. KA.É.GAL *means* blasphemy."

Obv. 17—Hunger (*SpTU* I, 38) transliterated [x x x] *ti* for obv. 17, even though his hand copy seems to allow, at most, a single cuneiform sign before *ti*. If there is indeed sufficient space for restoration, the following are possible candidates for equation with *nullât* (obv. 17): [*šil-la*]-*ti* (cf. *CT* 18, 6 [rev. 40]), [*la qa-bi*]-*ti* (cf. *CT* 18, 6 [rev. 43]; *LTBA* II, 2: 408, and dupl. 3 vi 4; Šurpu p. 51: 44), [*la ki-it*]-*ti* (cf. Lambert 1960: 88, comm. to line 284), or even [*tas-li-ma*]-*ti* (cf. *CT* 18, 6 rev. 45; this is also the preference of Frahm 2011a: 89 n. 446, 226).

Obv. 18—The form [*qer-b*]*é-nu-uš-šú* consists of the term *qerbēnu* ("interior"), the *-um* locative, and the 3ms suffix *-šú*. Though [*q*]*er-bé-nu-uš*⌉-*šú* may be detected at Sa-gig 19/20: 57′, it is uncertain whether this entry indeed represents the base text here, because the following commentary lines 19–20 refer to two different topics from the base text Sa-gig 19/20: 53′, which precedes Sa-gig 19/20: 57′. As a whole, however, our available manuscripts of Diagnostic Tablet 19/20 yield so fragmentary a picture that it is often difficult to track the commentator's progress through the base text. In any case, therapeutic texts refer several times to the body part *qereb* DÚR "middle of rectum" (*BAM* 95: 27 (= *BAM* VII/21); 99: 17 (= *BAM* VII/35)), as well as the conditions *qereb* DÚR GIG "sick middle of rectum" (*BAM* 89: 9 (= *BAM* VII/54); *AMT* 53/1 iv 6′) and *qerbēni* DÚR GIG "sick interior of rectum" (*BAM* 94 rev. 7′; 95: 29 (= *BAM* VII/21); *AMT* 101/3 i 21′ (= *BAM* VII/38)). In the same context as the above expressions are references to *qerbēnu* GIG "sick interior" (*BAM* 96 iii 10′ (= *BAM* VII/26); *BAM* 99: 1, 30 (= *BAM* VII/35); *BAM* 104: 42 (= *BAM* VII/28); *BAM* 152 iii 11; 575 iv 54; 578 i 1). Thus, although the term *qerbēnu* GIG "sick interior" does not explicitly mention the patient's rectum, its occurrences in therapeutic tablets dealing with rectal sicknesses leave little doubt of its affinity with *qerbēni* DÚR GIG "sick interior of rectum." Another similar term is the female body part *qerbītu* ("womb"), which appears in medical descriptions where it receives human semen (*BAM* 240:[67′], 69′–70′). In other words, there was a high likelihood that *qerbēnuššu* would have been understood as a reference to the rectum or perhaps the womb. The commentator made it clear, however, that *qerbēnu* in this context denotes "the inside" (perhaps of a bodily feature), and not necessarily the rectum or the womb.

Obv. 19—That the base text here is Sa-gig 19/20: 53′ is confirmed not only by the occurrence of *ku-uṣ-ṣi*(?) (MS D), but also *mu-kil* SAG (MS C) that supplies the topic for the comment in line 20. The noun *kuṣṣu* ("coldness") is attested syllabically at Sa-gig 19/20: 53′, 103′; 22: 72; 26: 43′; *BAM* 66 rev. 10′; *AMT* 14/7: 7, and as the logogram EN.TE.NA at Sa-gig 22: 70; *BAM* [124 iii 8, 11]; 131 rev. 3′; 161 vii 19; 431 v 36′; 571 ii 16′. In addition, though the logogram SED in medical texts very commonly denotes the verb *kaṣû* ("to become cold"), there are times in the Diagnostic Handbook when it seems to indicate a noun (Sa-gig 10 B rev. 5; 13: 56 (TDPT 13 i 57′); Sa-gig 17: 7). On the other hand, the noun *ḫurbāšu* ("chill") appears very rarely in the Diagnostic Handbook, written syllabically at Sa-gig 16: 65′; 17: 77, and as the logogram MIR.SES at Sa-gig 3: 91 (TDPT 3: 82). Occurrences of *ḫurbāšu* in therapeutic texts are much more common, where the term is written syllabically: *BAM* 66 rev. 10′; 232 i 13′; 314 obv. 4′; 315 iii 39; 338 rev. 7′; 438 obv. 10; 445: 14 (incl. *AMT* 64/2: 14′); *AMT* 14/7: 7; 27/3 obv. 2; *STT* 89: 100. In other words, the commentator explained the term *kuṣṣu* ("coldness") by means of the synonym *ḫurbāšu* ("chill"), whose attestations are more confined to therapeutic texts. The term *ḫurbāšu* also appears in Comm. Sa-gig 21 & 22a, rev. 9′, though the context there is too damaged to ascertain whether it serves as topic or comment. In Comm. Sa-gig 34, obv. 1–2, both *ḫurbāšu* and *kuṣṣu* are associated with the term [*šuruppû*] ("frost").

Obv. 20—I restore the topic [*mu-k*]*il* SAG ("that which holds the head"), which comes from the base text Sa-gig 19/20: 53′. Other versions of this expression include DAB SAG.ḪA.ZA (*BAM* 323: 2) and *mukīl* SAG-*šú* with the pronominal suffix (Sa-gig 27:[3], 4). Much more common, however, is the malady name SAG.ḪUL.ḪA.ZA (*mukīl-rēš-lemutti*, "the evil one holding the head"), which appears in Sa-gig 3: 47; 22: 62–64; 27: 4; 28: 4, 21; *BAM* 185 v 51′; 204: 2′, [6′–7′]; 338 rev. 8′, 22′; 344: 15; 520 ii [2′], 8′, (9′) (incl. *AMT* 83/2 ii [2′], 8′, (9′)); *AMT* 14/2: 4′; 14/3: 11′; 34/6: 4; 48/7: 9′; 76/1: 1; 96/3: 2; 96/9: 3′. For the proposal that *mukīl-rēš-lemutti* referred to "a generalized headache," see Scurlock and Andersen (2005: 311). The commentator's motivation here may have been to explain a term (*mukīl* SAG) that deviated from the usual form SAG.ḪUL.ḪA.ZA (= *mukīl-rēš-lemutti*). The comment itself is interrupted by a "new break" in the base text manuscript employed, and the most natural reading of the preserved signs yields the obscure phrase *um-mu šal-šú* ("third heat"). While it is possible to understand *šal-šú* adverbially (i.e., "thirdly") as introducing a alternative comment, there is no indication that such a "third" comment exists in this position, and the form *šal-šiš* is preferred elsewhere: See Comm. Sa-gig 1A, obv. 13; Comm. Sa-gig 1B, rev. 15, 22; Comm. Sa-gig 39, obv. 5; and Comm. Sa-gig 40A, obv. 5. Other possible readings include *um-mu rak-šú* (< *ummu raksu*, "bound heat") and *um-mu mim-šú* ("any heat," with *mim* as a short form of *mimma* in *CAD* M II, 79 s.v. *mimma* §e). Finally, we should be aware that medical texts do not indicate a consistent correlation between the malady SAG.ḪUL.ḪA.ZA and heat.

Obv. 21–22—The -*ma* conjuction in [*e-di*]-*il-ma* implies that the form is a direct quotation from the highly damaged base text [...] *e-di-il*(?)-*ma*⌉ DAB-[*su* ...]

at Sa-gig 19/20: 72′, rather than *e-tel-liš* at Sa-gig 19/20: 101′, 102′. It is most natural to interpret the writing *e-di-il-ma* (= *edil-ma*) as the G Stative 3ms of *edēlu* ("to shut off"), even though this verb is not attested elsewhere in medical descriptions. Another option would be to read the signs as *e-te*$_{10}$(di)-*él*(il)-*ma* (= *etēl-ma*) as the Gt Stative 3ms of *e'ēlu* ("to bind"). Related to the latter would be the sickness *e'-e-lu* (K 8487: 7 = list of sicknesses similar to those in Goetze 1955: 8–18; *CAD* E, 40), as well as the *e'ēlu*-demon that is named at Sa-gig 26: 44′ and that appears as the topic of Comm. Sa-gig 5, line 35. Note also the lexical equation *e-'-lu* = MIN (= *mur-ṣu*) in Malku IV, 61 (Hrůša 2010: 382). The commentator, however, seems to have chosen yet another alternative. I restore these lines as [*e-di*]-*il-ma* : *e-te*-[*é*]*l*(il)-*ma* : *e-te-el-lu-ú* / [*e-lu*]-*u* (obv. 21–22). The identification of the signs as *e-te*-[*i*]*l-ma* (obv. 21) has also been adopted by Hunger (*SpTU* I, 38) and Heeßel (2000: 234). The form *e-te-el-lu-ú* (= *etellû*, "to keep going up") in obv. 21 represents the Gtn Infinitive of *elû* ("to go up"). What follows [*e-lu*]-*u* (obv. 22) is the topic for a new commentary entry, so this term undoubtedly belongs to the preceding commentary argument. Although [*e-lu*]-*u* (obv. 22) needs to be extensively restored, the syllable sign -*u* indicates a verb with a long final vowel like *elû* ("to go up"), rather than *edēlu* ("to shut off") or *e'ēlu* ("to bind"). In short then, the signs [*e-di*]-*il-ma* (𒂊 𒁲 𒅋 𒈠) (obv. 21) are said to be read as *e-te*$_{10}$-*él-ma* (𒂊 𒁲 𒅋 𒈠) or /*etel-ma*/, which awkwardly stands for *etellū-ma* ("it keeps going up"; Gtn Stative 3ms of *elû*). The connection from /*etel-ma*/ *to etellū-ma* is admittedly weak, but reflects the commentator's constraints in working with available alternatives of syllabic values of the base text signs *e-di-il-ma* (= *e-te*$_{10}$-*él-ma*).

Lines 22–23—The base text here seems to be *ana a-te-e* ⌈GAR⌉-⌈*šú*⌉ at Sa-gig 19/20: 97′. The first legible line on the commentary's reverse (i.e., line 23) represents an immediate continuation of obv. 22. This is confirmed by frequent lexical equations linking the verbs *atû* ("to find out") and *amāru* ("to perceive"): $^{\text{pa-ad}}$PÀD = [*a*]-*ma-ru*, [*a*]-*tu-u* (Idu I, 54f. in *CAD* A II, 518); *a-tu-ú*, *ḫi-a-rum*, *ḫi-a-šu* = *a-ma-rum* (*CT* 18, 6 obv. 19–21); *a-tu-ú* = *a-ma*-[*ru*], *da-ga*-[*lu*], *nap-lu*-[*su*] (K 4587, ii 8–10 in *CT* 18, 18). The verdict *ana a-te-e* ⌈GAR⌉-⌈*šú*⌉ (Sa-gig 19/20: 97′) is unusual for medical texts and, in fact, the entire section Sa-gig 19/20: 88′–99′ appears more akin to hemerological texts whose verdicts are correlated with activities on particular months and days.

Line 29—The section Sa-gig 19/20: 110′–113′ in the Diagnostic Handbook describes the agency of the *lamaštu*-demoness in "seizing" (DAB) the patient at different times of the day, from sunrise to the last night watch. Although the beginning of the diagnostic entry at Sa-gig 19/20: 110′ is damaged, it likely contains the expression [^{d}UTU.È.A] ("at sunrise"), which represents the base text for the commentary here. Elsewhere in medical texts, this time reference is not particularly frequent, and it appears typically in the form dUTU.È without the final sign A: Sa-gig 4: 13; 12: 132″ (TDPT 12 iv 25); Sa-gig 15: 50′; *BAM* 460: 6′; 482 iii 7; iv 46′; *AMT* 14/5: 11.

Lines 30–31—I restore line 31 as [*ina*(?) *ba-ra-ri*]-*ti*, and considerable blank space between the signs [*ri*] and *ti* suggests that this comment to EN.NUN. AN.USAN (end of line 30) occupies the entire line 31. See also Heeßel (2000: 235). The logogram EN.NUN.AN.USAN is attested elsewhere in medical texts only at Sa-gig [19/20: 112′]; 26: 38′, though other expressions for *barārītu* include BAR.EN.NUN, PA.EN.NUN, or simply EN.NUN (variant manuscript readings at Sa-gig 17: 97).

Line 36—The full restoration is not merely lu₂MAŠ.MAŠ TU[R] as suggested by Hunger (*SpTU* I, 38); Heeßel (2000: 235); but lu₂MAŠ.MAŠ BÀ[N.DA], based on the parallel in Comm. Sa-gig 7B, rev. 11′: lu₂MAŠ.MAŠ BÀN.DA ("junior magician").

Commentary Sa-gig 21 & 22a

Provenance:	Written by Nippur scribe, but probably found in Uruk (Warka); see Frahm (2011a: 227, 298–300)
Period:	?
Names:	"*Imgida*-tablet of [Enlil-šumu-iddin (?)] son of Sîn-nādin-ahhē, whose god is [Nusku (and) whose goddess] is Dumuzi-abzu, servant of [Ninurta (?), descendant (?) of] Ur-Me-me, suppliant of the Three Lords ..."
Script:	Neo-/Late Babylonian
Typology:	*ṣâtu* 7c in Frahm (2011a: 54–55)
Field/Museum No.:	Not numbered in John Frederick Lewis Collection (Free Library of Philadelphia, USA)
Photos:	Plate 26 (obverse) and Plate 27 (reverse)
Printed Edition:	Leichty (1973: 82–86, fig. 3); Heeßel (2000: 247–249, edition and notes of only obv. 1–14); Wee (2012: 664–682)
Digital Resources:	CDLI P461062; CCP 4.1.21 (printed hand copy digitized by Frahm, Frazer, and Jiménez 2013, photos by Frazer)
Discussion:	Leichty (1973: 82–86, fig. 3); Heeßel (2000: 135–136, 246 (21. Tafel MS a), 247–249); Genty (2010a: 382) and (2010b: 14, 19 with obv. 9 erroneously described as "commentaire à TDP 4, 40 :r. 23"; 21, 23–26, 29–30); Frahm (2011a: 54 n. 242, 99, 226–227, 255, 298–299; referenced as commentary on "Sa-gig 21 & 21a"); Fincke (2011b: 473–474); Wee (2012: 664–682); Scurlock (2014: 185 nn. 1, 3, 5, 7, and 13); Gabbay (2016: 74 n. 323, 109 n. 134, 128 n. 5, 230, 245 n. 190, 350); Jiménez and Schmidtchen (2017: 238–239); Gabbay and Jiménez (2019: 73–74)
Pericope:	Indeterminate due to damaged state of available Sa-gig manuscripts

Transliteration

Obverse

1) DIŠ GIG NIGIN SA.ME-*šú* SILIM-*ma* : sa_5-*át* : SI : *sa-mu-ú* : SI : [*ma-ku-ú*]

2) *šá* SÍG SAG.DU-*šú ma-ku-*tu_4 *tal-lu*!(ib) *šá-niš šá sa-ma-at* : SAG.KI-*su* [...]

 | DOI:10.1163/9789004417564_024

3) *šá* UZU *ina muḫ-ḫi ia-a-nu* : *ka-ra-an* IGI.2-*šú šad-du* [...]
4) *šá kak-kul-tu*$_4$ IGI.2-*šú a-na bi-ta-nu i-ru-b*[*u* : *š*]*i-qá* ŠUB-*a* [: *ši-qá*]
5) *ru-ṭib-tu*$_4$: UD.A GE$_6$.MEŠ : *ra-mi-ṭu ṣal-mu-tu*$_4$: *ut-tu-*[*qu* ...]
6) *ṣu-ub-bu-tu*$_4$ *lìb-bu-ú šip-ri* DUG$_4$.GA : *e-de-qu* : du$_8$ [...]
7) *la-ab-ka* : *iš-ta-na-ad-da-ad* : *šá* LU$^{\textit{ma-du}}$ *it-*[...]
8) *ina* DU-*ku im-taḫ-ru* : *šá a-na tar-ṣi a-ḫa-meš iš-te-*[*niš il-la-ku*]
9) IGI.2-*šú ú-rat-tu*$_4$: DÙ : *re-tu-ú* : DÙ : *za-qa-pu* : DÙ [: *ú-zu-uz-zu*]
10) ŠU.ÙR.ÙR-*šú-ma* : *tu-kap-par-šu-ma* : ŠU.ÙR.ÙR [: *kup-pu-ru*]
11) *nim-šú-šú* : SA.MEŠ-*šú* : SA : *ni-im-šú* : SA : *šé*[*r-a-nu* ...]
12) MAN-*ma* GIG : *šá-ni-im-ma i-mar-ru-*[*uṣ* ...]

---

13) *ṣa-a-tú šu-ut* KA *u maš-ʾa-a*[*l-tú* ...]
14) *šá lìb-bi* DIŠ GIG NIGIN SA.[MEŠ-*šú* SILIM-*ma* ...]

---

15) DIŠ GIG GIM ŠUB-*ú* : *ki-ma in-na-du-*⸢*ú*⸣ [...]
16) *ḫa-sis-su* : *a-ṣi-it-su* : tab nim ma [... TAB]
17) *šur-ru-ú* : TAB : *ḫa-ma-ṭu* : MU.1.KAM NU S[I.SÁ ...]
18) ÚŠ ^{giš}TUKUL : *mu-ut kak-ku šá-niš* ^{giš}TUKUL SÌG-*iṣ* x[...]
19) *lìb-bu-ú* MUNUS ^{giš}TUKUL SÌG-*at šá ki bul-ṭu* D[UG$_4$.GA-*ú*]
20) *šá-da-du* : *ú-tu-lu* : TAG-*su-m*[*a* ...]
21) TAG : *ma-ḫa-ṣi* : KIN.KIN x[... *ši-te-ʾu-u*]
22) *bu-ʾu-ú* : MÁŠ IGI *lìb-b*[*u-ú* ... *i-lam-ma-am*]
23) *ik-kal* : *la-ma-ma* : *a-k*[*a-lu* ...]
24) *i-lam-ma-am šá it-*x[...]
25) ^{d}DUMU.ZI : a bu x [...]
26) *šá-su-u* : *a-ri* : du x[...]
27) x x x [...]

Reverse

5′) x [...]
6′) x [...]
7′) x [...]
8′) *lìb-*[*bu-ú* ...]
9′) *ḫur-ba-šú* x[...]
10′) *mu-de-e ṭè-mi-šú šá* x[...]
11′) *ku-tál* NA ŠUB-*ut mu-k*[*il ku-tál-li* NA ÚŠ ... (?)]
12′) *šur-ru-u* : LUGUD *ip-piq* [...]
13′) *šur-ru-u šá mur-ṣi* : *ana* KU[R ...]
14′) KUR : ^{d}50 : pag : *mu-ú-d*[*u* ...]

15′) *šá* EME-*šú ú-šaq-qu-ú* : EM[E ... TUR]
16′) *ṣa-ha-ra* : TUR : *e-mu-qu šá-ni*[*š* ...]
17′) *i-te-lip* : *šá* EME-*šú ú-x*[...]

18′) *ṣa-a-tú šu-ut* KA *u maš-ʾa-*[*al-tú šá* KA UM.ME.A *šá* (*lìb-bi*)]
19′) DIŠ GIG GIM ŠUB-*ú* IM.GÍD.DA [$^{m.d}$*En-líl*-MU-SUM (?)]
20′) DUMU $^{m.d}$30-*na-din*-ŠEŠ.MEŠ LÚ DINGIR.BI ^{din}[^{gir}NUSKA.KE$_4$ AMA.$^{d+}$INNIN.BI]
21′) ^{d}DUMU.ZI.ABZU.KE$_4$ AMA.A.TU ^{din}[^{gir}ZÚ.LUM.MA ...]
22′) Ur-Me-me *mu-sa$_7$-ap-pú-u* EN EN EN x[...]
23′) *pa-liḫ* ^{d}ŠID ^{d}UTU *u* ^{d}AMAR.UTU NU TÙM [...]

Translation

Incipit-title of Sa-gig 21

(Obv. 1) "If all of the sick man's strands are well."

***Sa-gig 21—**
"the hair of his head is sa$_5$-*át*"?
The sign sa$_5$ (𒋛𒀀) should not be understood as the logogram (SA$_5$) for "red," but as the combination si (𒋛) + a (𒀀). The component si represents the verb, whose meaning is further discussed. The component a (𒀀) was perhaps viewed as a grammatical marker irrelevant to the verb's root meaning.

(1) "(The hair of his head is) sa$_5$-*át*."

The commentator explored the semantic range of the logogram SI, by considering two of its possible Akkadian meanings.

(1) SI *means* to become faltering.

(1–2) SI *means* [to become lacking], in the case of the hair of his head.

In an aside, the commentator clarified that *makû* "to become lacking" should not be confused with the near homophone *makūtu* "pole."

(2) /*makutu*/ (*means*) a pole.

The commentator thought the base text does not describe "red" (SA_5) hair, but hair that is "lacking" or "faltering" (SI), elsewhere described as hair "spread (thinly)."

(2) Secondly, (*it means*) that which is faltering.

***Sa-gig 21**

(2–3) "His forehead ..." (*refers to*) the case where there is no flesh above / on the cranium.

Sa-gig 21: 3′
This refers to the irises' movement towards each other (i.e., esotropia) or inward to each eye's center (i.e., pupil constriction).

(3–4) "The grapes of his eyes are pulled" ... (*refers to*) the case where the iris goes inwards.

***Sa-gig 21**
šīqu and *ruṭibtu* denote medical conditions, but their association here seems to be based on the non-medical meanings "irrigation" (*šīqu*) and "flooded ground" (*ruṭibtu*).

(4) "They are overlaid with *šīqu*."

(4–5) ["*šīqu*"] (*refers to*) *ruṭibtu*.

***Sa-gig 21**
"*ramīṭu*-marks" do not occur in therapeutic texts, but appear several times as the logogram UD.A in the Diagnostic Handbook.

(5) "UD.A GE_6.MEŠ" *means* black *ramīṭu*-marks.

Sa-gig 21: 17′—"his hands and his feet are *ut-tu-*[*qu*]"

(5–6) "They are bent crooked" (*means*) ... they are incapacitated. As in, (their) activities, it is said.

This argument probably defines hands and feet "bent (crooked)" as ones that are "flexible."

(6) To bend *means* ...
(6–7) ... (*means*) they are flexible.

Sa-gig 21: 21′—
"his sickness keeps pulling [him]"
One of the rare instances in the Diagnostic Handbook whereby the malady, not a body part, is described with the verb "to pull."

(7) "It keeps pulling" *refers to* the case where it ... much.

***Sa-gig 21—"[the strands of his ... on the right and left] correspond in movement"?**
The description of bodily strands "corresponding in movement" is attested only in the Diagnostic Handbook.

(8) "They correspond in movement" *refers to* the case where they [move] in accordance with one another at the same time.

***Sa-gig 21**
The uncommon description of eyes "fixed in place" is connected by the shared logogram DÙ to the condition of "protruding" eyes, which is recognized elsewhere as a medical sign.

(9) "He fixes in place his eyes."

(9) DÙ *means* to fix in place.
(9) DÙ *means* to protrude.
(9) DÙ [*means* to stand (still).]

***Sa-gig 21—"[You shall perform the magician arts for him and wipe him down]"?**
The comment clarifies that the action of wiping the patient—and, by implication, performing magician arts—are undertaken by the healer addressed ("you") in the Diagnostic Handbook, who is imagined to be a member of the magician profession.

(10) "One (performs the action of) ŠU.ÙR.ÙR to him" *means* you shall wipe him down.

(10) ŠU.ÙR.ÙR [*means* to wipe down.]

***Sa-gig 21**
nimšū frequently appears as a feature of sheep anatomy. The commentator compared *nimšū* to human "strands" that are commonly mentioned in medical texts.

(11) "His *nimšū*" *refer to* his SA-strands.

(11) SA *means nimšu.*
(11) SA *means* strand. ...

***Sa-gig 21**
MAN-*ma* GIG "he is altered and becomes sick" is a noteworthy variation on the stereotypical prognosis GIG-*su* MAN-*ni* "his sickness becomes altered."

(12) "MAN-*ma* GIG" *means* he is altered and becomes sick. ...

Incipit-title of Sa-gig 21

(13–14) Glossary (including) oral lore and questionings ... on the contents of "If all of the sick man's strands [are well]" ...

***Incipit-title of Sa-gig 22a**

(15) "If the sick man GIM ŠUB-*ú*" *means* when he is being laid down. ...

***Sa-gig 22a**
The commentator reasoned that *ḫa-sis-su* was a byform of *āṣīssu* "his exit / issue," rather than *ḫasīssu* "his ear," since medical texts consistently denote "ear" as GEŠTUG.

(16) "*ḫa-sis-su*" *means* his exit / issue.

***Sa-gig 22a**
Perhaps the commentator explained the less common verb "to begin," by referring to the more usual meaning of its logogram TAB in medical texts: "to burn."

(16–17) ... [TAB] (*means*) to begin.
(17) TAB *means* to burn.

***Sa-gig 22a**
The prognosis NU SI.SÁ "it will not go well" is typical of the Diagnostic Handbook, in contrast to therapeutic texts where the patient is consistently said to "become healthy."

(17) "For one year, NU [SI.SÁ" *means*] ...

***Sa-gig 22a**
ÚŠ ^{giš}TUKUL is only attested here, and the commentator interpreted it by paraphrasing a similar idiom for menstruation in therapeutic texts: GIM MUNUS ^{giš}TUKUL *maḫiṣ* "he is struck with a weapon, as in the case of a woman."

(18) "ÚŠ ^{giš}TUKUL" *means* death by weapon.

(18) Secondly, he is struck with a weapon. ...
(19) As in, "a woman is struck with a weapon," which [it said] according to therapeutic prescriptions.

***Sa-gig 22a**
The base text may describe the "stretching out" of limbs or the whole body, as it does elsewhere in the Diagnostic Handbook.

(19–20) To stretch out *means* to lie down.

***Sa-gig 22a**
TAG "to touch" is a common verb in medical texts, but the atypical translation "to strike" may reflect the specific context here.

(20) "It (performs the action of) TAG to him" [*means*] ...

(21) TAG *means* to strike.

***Sa-gig 22a**
KIN.KIN "to seek out" and "to search for" are often equated in lexical texts, but are atypical of medical signs. This comment may imply that medical signs, like omens, need to be reasoned out inductively.

(21) "KIN.KIN" ...

(21–22) [To seek out (*means*)] to search for, *which means* to observe omens. As in, ...

***Sa-gig 22a**
The verb *lamāmu* "to chew" occurs very rarely in medical texts and warrants explanation here.

(22–23) ["He chews" (*means*)] he eats.
(23) To chew *means* to eat. ...
(24) "He chews" (*refers to*) the case where he ...

***Sa-gig 22a**
Dumuzi does not appear elsewhere in medical texts as a divine agent of sickness.

(24–25) ... the god Dumuzi ...

***Sa-gig 22a**

(25–26) ... to call out ...

(27) ...
(Rev. 5′–7′) ...
(8′) As in, ...
(8′–9′) ... chill ...

***Sa-gig 22a**
The patient's "intelligence" is mentioned frequently in the Diagnostic Handbook, but only a few times in therapeutic texts.

(9′–10′) ... "one who knows his intelligence" (*refers to*) the case where ...

***Sa-gig 22a**
The sick body part is identified as the patient's "back." Its negative prognosis is possibly supported by a quotation from *Šumma ālu* XXII, 73: "If a snake falls on to a man's shoulders, one who backs the man will die."

(10′–11′) ... the man's back falls.
(11′) "One who [backs the man will die (?)]." ...

***Sa-gig 22a**
Perhaps solidifying pus is said to characterize the "beginning" of some process.

(11′) ...
(12′) To begin (*šurrû*) *means* the pus becomes solid.
(12′–13′) ... to begin (*šurrû*), in the case of sickness.

***Sa-gig 22a**
Enlil is addressed as "the great Mountain."

(13′–14′) ... "Mountain" *refers to* the god Enlil.

Sumerian pag-dù is equivalent to Akkadian *mūdû* "one who knows" in the bilingual text of *Lugale* XI, 46.

(14′) pag *refers to* one who knows ...

***Sa-gig 22a**

(14′–15′) ... (*refers to*) the case where he raises his tongue.

***Sa-gig 22a**

(15′) "His tongue ..."

***Sa-gig 22a** Common lexical equation	(15′–16′) … [TUR (*means*)] to become small.
Does this argument associate DUMU (another reading of the TUR sign) and *dunnu* "might"?	(16′) TUR *means* strength. (16′) Secondly, …
***Sa-gig 22a** The verb "to become entangled" is atypical of medical descriptions.	(17′) "It is entangled" *refers to* the case where his tongue …
(Colophon)	
Incipit-title of Sa-gig 22a	(18′–19′) Glossary (including) oral lore and questionings [from the mouth of the *ummânu*-scholar on (the contents of)] "If, when the sick man was laid down."
	(19′–22′) *Imgida*-tablet of [Enlil-šumu-iddin (?)] son of Sîn-nādin-ahhē, whose god is [Nusku (and) whose goddess] is Dumuzi-abzu, servant of [Ninurta (?), descendant (?) of] Ur-Me-me, suppliant of the Three Lords …
	(23′) He who fears the gods Enlil, Šamaš, and Marduk must not carry off (this tablet) …

Notes

Intro—This commentary has been ascribed to "Sa-gig 21 and 21a" by Frahm (2011a: 226), but appears in this book under the label "Comm. Sa-gig 21 & 22a." For my rationale, see Note on rev. 19′ below. In this commentary, the first section (obv. 1–14) provides comments on Sa-gig Tablet 21 and ends with the incipit-title of Tablet 21 (obv. 14), while the following section (obv. 15–rev. 19′) explains Sa-gig Tablet 22a and ends with the incipit-title of Tablet 22a (rev. 19′). This arrangement of separate sections (each ending with the incipit-title of its base text) probably also occurs in Comm. Sa-gig

10 & 11. Because the base text for Comm. Sa-gig 21 & 22a is not preserved well enough, however, we cannot be sure if its pericope consists of one continuous block of base text that encompassed Sa-gig Tablets 21–22a, or if it consists of separate sections from Sa-gig Tablets 21 and 22a (as in the case of Comm. Sa-gig 10 & 11). Remarkably, sequences of entries in Comm. Sa-gig 21 & 22a (obv. 8–11) correspond well with those in Comm. Sa-gig 4C (rev. 8′–13′). This is not likely due to any direct copying between the commentaries themselves, but the use of comparable methods of argumentation for the heavily damaged base text of Sa-gig 21, which probably included a section similar to the base text of Sa-gig 4: 106–117+ (TDPT 4 rev. 21–32+).

Obv. 1—Though existing manuscripts of Sa-gig Tablet 21 do not preserve the tablet's incipit, the incipit-title is listed in the colophon of Sa-gig Tablet 20 as [DIŠ GIG NIGI]N SA.MEŠ-*šú šal-mu-ma* SÍG S[AG.DU-*šú in*]*a* GEŠTUG-*šú zaq-pat* GAM ("[If all of the sick man's] strands are well and the hair of [his head at] his ear stands on end; he will die"; Sa-gig 19/20: 125′), as well as in the Sa-gig catalog as DIŠ NIGIN SA.MEŠ-*šú* SILIM.MEŠ-*ma* ("If all of his strands are well"; Finkel 1988: 146, obv. A 26; Heeßel 2000: 14, line 26). Leichty (1973: 84) suggests that the commentator understood SILIM as SÁ, which he then explained as SA$_5$. This suggestion, however, is unnecessary, since the incipit-title of the base text tablet is often listed at the beginning of a commentary without any intent to comment on it. See Comm. Sa-gig 4A, obv. 1; Comm. Sa-gig 14, obv. 1; Comm. Sa-gig 19, obv. 1; Comm. Sa-gig 23, obv. 1; and Comm. Sa-gig 39, obv. 1.

Obv. 1–2—Although the base text to this commentary entry is not preserved, the comment "in the case of the hair of his head" (obv. 2) suggests that the base text topic was similar to the expression SÍG SAG.DU-*šú* sa$_5$ ("the hair of his head becomes sa$_5$") at Sa-gig 3: 122 (TDPT 3: 112) and 2N-T 336 rev. 2′, 3′. Though modern scholars have typically understood the sign sa$_5$ (𒋛𒀀) in such contexts as the logogram SA$_5$ for the verb *sâmu* ("to become red"), the commentator argued that sa$_5$ (𒋛𒀀) instead consists of the sign combination si (𒋛) + a (𒀀). His subsequent arguments are concerned with the meaning of only the component si, and perhaps the component a (𒀀) was interpreted as a phonetic complement (-*a*) or a grammatical marker (-a) for the Sumerian participle (Edzard 2003: 132, §12.14.2), which could be ignored in discussions on the semantics of the verbal root. First, the commentator explored the semantic range of the logogram SI, by considering two of its possible Akkadian verb meanings: *samû* ("to become faltering, inept"; *CAD* S, 125; *AHw*, 1020) and *makû* ("to become lacking"). The equation SI = *samû* is not attested elsewhere, but SI as the logogram for *makû* occurs in the lexical text Aa III/4, 176 (*MSL* XIV, 342). Next, in an aside to his main argument, the commentator clarified that *makû* ("to become lacking") should not be confused with the near homophone *makūtu* ("pole"). I understand the signs in obv. 2 as *tal-lu*!(ib) ("crossbeam, pole, transversal line"), instead of the suggestion *tal-ib* by Leichty (1973: 83–84); Heeßel (2000: 247); or *ri-ib* by *CAD* M I, 143. The commentator's refusal to interpret the base text writing sa$_5$ (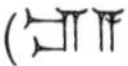) as "red" mirrors the practice in Comm. Sa-gig 39 (obv. 7–8), where hair described syllabically as *sa-mat* is likewise not understood as *sāmat* ("red" < *sâmu*) but as *samât* ("faltering" < *samû*). "Faltering" hair is mentioned elsewhere at Sa-gig 3: 32b (TDPT 3: 23b) and discussed in Comm. Sa-gig 1–3, obv. 27.

Obv. 3–4—Fincke (2000: 19, Abb. 2) identified *karān īni* ("grape of the eye") as the iris edge bordering the pupil, and *šer'ān kakkulti īni* ("strands of the *kakkultu* of the eye") as muscles of the iris. Despite the translation of *kakkultu* as "eyeball" in *CAD* K, 59–60, the examples in §b of "lapis lazuli inlays shaped as to be part of the representation of a human or animal eye on a statue" do not seem to refer to the eyeball as a whole, but the dark portion of the eye consisting of both the iris and pupil. The distinction between iris and pupil in Mesopotamian statuary is often obscured, and both can be represented by a single circular piece of lapis lazuli inlay, which resembles the two-dimensional view of a "grape" (*karānu*). For well known examples, see the statue of "Ebih-Il, the Superintendent of Mari" at the Louvre (AO 17551), the "Lyre with Bearded Bull's Head" from Ur Royal Tomb PG789, and the "Ram in a Thicket" at the British Museum (ME 122200). I follow Fincke in understanding *kakkultu* as the iris, especially since references to "strand(s)" of the *kakkultu* in Sa-gig 5: 113′–120′ (TDPT 5 G 14–21) seem to refer to the radial striations visible in the iris. The clause *ka-ra-an* IGI.2-*šú šad-du* appears also in Comm. Sa-gig 39, obv. 8, with the explanation that "the iris goes out." Here, the verb *šaddū* seems to describe the opposite case whereby "the iris enters within." The exact meaning of "going out" and "entering within" is not certain, though one possibility concerns the deviation of the irises (and the eyeball as a whole) away from each other (i.e., exotropia) or towards each other (i.e., esotropia, a cross-eyed condition), as suggested by Frahm (2011a: 227–229). Another possibility concerns the dilation or constriction of the pupil, which may have been perceived in terms of iris movement outwards from or inwards to the center of each eye. For the proposal that both descriptions refer to the condition of "*Seclusio pupillae*," see Fincke (2000: 163–164). The verb *šadādu* ("to pull") as a description of the eye or its parts is also attested in the therapeutic texts *BAM* 516 ii 27′; *AMT* 13/1: 3′.

Obv. 4–5—In contrast to the reading [*ši*]-*ga-ru a* (line 4) by Leichty (1973: 83–84); Heeßel (2000: 247), I understand the signs as [*š*]*i-qá* ŠUB-*a*, possibly from a base text similar to NUNDUN.MEŠ-*šú ši-qá* ŠUB-*a* ("his lips are overlaid with *šīqu*") in Sa-gig 13: 89 (TDPT 13 ii 31). The term *ru-ṭib-tu*$_4$ at the beginning of obv. 5 represents the comment to a topic in the damaged end of obv. 4 and, from my estimation of tablet spacing, I restore this commentary entry as [*š*]*i-qá* ŠUB-*a* [: *ši-qá*] / *ru-ṭib-tu*$_4$ (obv. 4–5). The sickness *ruṭibtu* and the medical condition *šīqu* do not seem particularly related to each other in medical texts. For *ruṭibtu*, see Sa-gig 33: 18, 19, 22; *AMT* 74/1 ii 11, 32, 34; [86/1 ii 6]; *SpTU* IV, 153 obv. 4. For the medical condition *šīqu* (*CAD* Š III, 101–102 s.v. *šīqu* B), see Sa-gig 13: 89, 92 (TDPT 13 ii 31, 34); *BAM* 1 ii 37–40; 379 iv 6; 421 i 38′; 423 i 2′; *STT* 92 ii 15–19; 93: 28; BM 78963: 50, 52, 55. Perhaps the commentator's logic was based on the non-medical meaning of *ruṭibtu* as "flooded ground" (*CAD* R, 437) and the meaning of the form *šīqu* as "irrigation" (*CAD* Š III, 101 s.v. *šīqu* A). While the *Chicago Assyrian Dictionary* differentiates between the homophones *šīqu* A ("irrigation") and *šīqu* B (the medical condition), one wonders whether the argument here is an erudite one conceived by the commentator, or whether it reflects some folk etymology concerning the medical condition *šīqu*.

Obv. 5—The term UD.A ("*ramīṭu*-marks") does not seem to appear in therapeutic texts, but occurs several times in the Diagnostic Handbook at Sa-gig 6: [8–10], 26–30; 7 A obv. 10; 9: 43–46, 77–78, always in logographic form. The expression UD.A GE$_6$.MEŠ (Sa-gig 7 A obv. 10) may represent the base text for GE$_6$ ⸢*ṣal*⸣-[*mu*] in Comm. Sa-gig 7A, obv. 7.

Obv. 5–6—Note the lexical equation lú dùg-dab = *ṣú-ub-bu-tum* (OB Lu Frag. I, 13 in *MSL* XII, 201), in the context of various defective conditions such as *ḫummurum* ("crippled," lines 9–11) and *tubbukum* ("crookkneed(?)," line 12). I therefore restore *ut-tu-*[*qu* ...] / *ṣu-ub-bu-tu*$_4$ ("'They are bent' (*means*) ... they are incapacitated"). See also *ut-tu-*[*qu*(?)] in *CAD* Š III, 79 s.v. *šipru* §3c. The verb *etēqu* ("(G) to become bent; (D) to become bent crooked") is not particularly common, but is recognized in von Soden (1955: 379); *AHw*, 86 s.v. *atāku*; *CAD* E, 395 s.v. *etēqu* B; and *CAD* A II, 481 s.v. ***atāku*. The base text is likely ŠU.2-*šú u* GÌR.2-*šú ut-tu-*[*qu*] (Sa-gig 21: 17′). The verb written *it-ta-ku*(qú) describes the same body parts (i.e., hands and feet) at Sa-gig 4: 114 (TDPT 4 rev. 29), but has been regarded as an error for *it-ta-*[*na*]-⸢*lak*⸣-*ku* (DPS IV A$_2$ rev. 29 + A$_5$ rev. 13 // B rev. 9) by Scurlock and Andersen (2005: 176, §8.55); Scurlock (2014: 32). The commentarial argument here is not easy to understand. The interpretations "*ṣubbutum*/*ṣupputum* means work, it is said" (Leichty 1973: 84) and "*uttu*[*qu*(?)] is *ṣubbutum*, it is said on account of work" (*CAD* Š III, 79) both treat the signs DUG$_4$.GA as the commentarial notation *qabi* ("it is said"). I tentatively follow these suggestions, though, elsewhere in our commentaries, the notation *ša iqbû* ("which it said") is typically expressed by the logogram E, not DUG$_4$. See examples in §11.2.3. The term *šiprī* may refer to the "activities" of the limbs or body parts earlier described as "incapacitated."

Obv. 6–7—Leichty (1973: 83–84) understood the signs as *e-de-qu* (obv. 6) and *la-ab-ka* (obv. 7), though he was uncertain how to connect these to other terms in the context. I understand *edēqu* here as a byform of *etēqu* ("to become bent"), which is the G stem of the D stem topic *uttuqū* ("they are bent crooked"; obv. 5), though this byform is not acknowledged in the modern dictionaries. The argument probably involves some definition of limbs "bent (crooked)" as ones that "are flexible" (*labkā*); cf. the adjective *labku* as a description of flexible bows in *CAD* L, 33. The D Stative 3mp form of the comment *ṣubbutū* (obv. 6) was likely inflected to mirror the form of the topic *uttuqū* (obv. 5) in the base text, but the commentator lapsed into the G Stative 3fp form *labkā* here, as an appropriate verb form for the dual subjects "hands and feet."

Obv. 7—The base text here is GIG-*su iš-ta-na-*[*ad-da-as-su*] ("his sickness keeps pulling him") at Sa-gig 21: 21′, which represents a rare instance whereby the malady, not a body part, is described as the subject of the verb *šadādu* ("to pull"). A similar expression may be found at Sa-gig 19/20: 117′: DAB(?)-⌜*su*⌝ *ir-te-né-eḫ-ḫi-šu u iš-ta-na-da-as-su* ("his seizure keeps dousing him and pulling him"). The term *iš-ta-na-ad-da-ad* here, therefore, represents the topic to a new commentary entry, not the comment to *la-ab-ka* (line 7) as suggested by Leichty (1973: 84). For my reading LU *ma-du*, note the following lexical equations: [lu-u] LU = *ma-a-dum* = (Hitt.) me-ik-ki, [MIN] [L]U = *ma-du-tum* = (Hitt.) me-iq-qa-e-eš (S^{a} Voc. H, 16′–17′ in *MSL* III, 60). It is admittedly strange, however, that a logogram requiring such explication should be part of the comment instead of a quoted topic, and possibly this comment itself represents a citation from a lexical or other source text.

Obv. 8—The topic *ina* DU-*ku im-taḫ-ru* here very likely derives from a base text similar to [SA SA]G.KI.2-*šú šá* 15 *u* 150 *ina* DU-*ki im-taḫ-ru* ("[the strands of] his temples on the right and left correspond in movement") at Sa-gig 4: 106 (TDPT 4 rev. 21), which itself provided the topic for another commentary (Comm. Sa-gig 4C, rev. 8′). The expression is rare and not attested so far in therapeutic texts. The syllable signs of the preposition are *a-na*, not *ana* as rendered by the typo in Heeßel (2000: 247). For the comment, my restoration *iš-te-*[*niš il-la-ku*] ("they move at the same time") is influenced by the Infinitive DU-*ku* ("to move") in the topic. This verb choice is confirmed by the fact that, in the Diagnostic Handbook, "strands" acting "at the same time" are described most often with the verb *alāku* ("to move"; Sa-gig 4: 112–113 (TDPT 4 rev. 26, 28); Sa-gig 11 rev. 22–28) and slightly less frequently with *tebû* ("to pulsate"; Sa-gig 3: 61, 64, [66], 90 (TDPT 3: 52, 55, [57], 81) and *akālu* ("to hurt"; Sa-gig [14: 172′] (TDPT [14 iii 39′]); Sa-gig 17: 39; 33: 98). An alternative restoration *iš-te-*[*mu*(?)] ("they made an agreement with each other," cf. *CAD* Š II, 285b) has been suggested by Genty (2010b: 24), though the damaged end of the line seems to allow for several more signs—judging from the ends of obv. 1 and 2—and a new topic only begins at the start of the next line (i.e., obv. 9). In any case, the crux of the comment is the meaning of the phrase *ana tarṣi aḫāmeš*, which I loosely translate as "in accordance with one another" (*CAD* T, 244 s.v. *tarṣu* §c), whatever such "movement" may have meant to the healer.

Obv. 9—The topic here probably derives from a base text similar to IGI.2-*šú ú-rat-ta* ("he fixes in place his eyes") at Sa-gig 4: 109 (TDPT 4 rev. 23); cf. *SpTU* III, 86 obv. 1–2. It is not fortuitous that the commentary entries in obv. 8 and 9 here correspond to unpreserved base texts in Diagnostic Tablet 21, which in turn resemble diagnostic entries in Sa-gig 4: 106, 109 (TDPT 4 rev. 21, 23). Single entries or even small groups of entries may be repeated in more than one chapter of the Diagnostic Handbook, but arranged in different ways appropriate to the different functions of individual chapters. The condition of eyes "fixed in place" is not particularly common, but is attested elsewhere in the expression *ur-ra u mu-ša ur-ta-na-at-tú la it-ta-na-a-a-al* ("day and night, he keeps fixing in place his eyes and does not sleep") at *AMT* [35/6: 6′]; [76/5: 11′–12′]; 79/4: 2′; *SpTU* I, 46: 17(!). The commentator elaborated on the meaning of *retû*/*reṭû* ("to fix in place") by exploring other verbs that share its logogram DÙ. The suggested synonym *zaqāpu* ("to erect, protrude (of eyes)") is, in fact, recognized elsewhere as a description of the eyes: Sa-gig 5: 91′ (TDPT 5 F3 11); Sa-gig [11 rev. 51]; 26: 80′–81′; 27: 20; 40: 56. The appeal to an abstract lexical argument involving the logogram DÙ may, therefore, serve as a front for pragmatic considerations of how the eyes are described in actual medical practice. Although the final verb of obv. 9 is not preserved, my restoration *uzuzzu* ("to stand (still)") is supported by the reading [DÙ] : *re-tu-u* : *ú-zu-uz-zu* : DÙ : *za-qa-pa* in another commentary on the *Šumma izbu* omen series (*SpTU* I, 72 rev. 1); as well as DÙ : GUB-*zu* in Comm. Sa-gig 4C, rev. 10′.

Obv. 10—The base text here is very likely a version of the statement "You shall perform the magician arts for him and wipe him down (root: *kapāru*)," with the latter verb written variously as ŠU.GUR.GUR-*šu-ma* (Sa-gig 9: 2) and ŠU.⌈ÙR⌉-*šú-ma* (Sa-gig 13: 64 (TDPT 13 ii 6); with typo ŠU.⌈ÚR⌉-*šú-ma* in Scurlock 2014: 105). Both ŠU.GUR.GUR and ŠU.ÙR are, in fact, the forms acknowledged in *CAD* K, 178 (s.v. *kapāru* A, lexical section), rather than

ŠU.ÙR.ÙR in the commentary topic. The verb "to wipe" (*kapāru*) is associated with the "sick man" (GIG) and his "body" (SU) in these lexical entries: [ŠU.ÙR.Ù]R = *kup-pu-ru šá* GIG (Antagal III, 60 in *MSL* XVII, 152); u₂-r[u ÙR] = *kup-pu-ru šá* SU (Aa IV/4, 125 in *MSL* XIV, 386). Note also the commentarial equation: *ma-ša-šú* = *ka-pa-ru* in Lambert (1960: 54, K 3291 (G) Reverse, line j). Leichty (1973: 84) has reasonably suggested that the end of obv. 10 should be restored with either *pašāṭu* or *muššudu*. Given the available space, I make my restoration simply as ŠU.ÙR.ÙR [: *kup-pu-ru*], though ŠU.ÙR.ÙR [: *ka-pa-ru*] is conceivable as well. In a shorter variation on the base text here, the "magician arts" are mentioned but not "wiping down" (Sa-gig 4: 112 (TDPT 4 rev. 27); [11 rev. 21]; 28: 33–35). Significantly, the syllabic comment (*tu-kap-par*) clarifies that the logographic topic (ŠU.ÙR.ÙR) is in the 2nd person singular ("you"), implying that the addressee is one who wipes the patient and performs the magician arts, and that the healer using the Diagnostic Handbook is therefore imagined to be a member of the magician profession. That a magician is directly addressed may have been brought into question by other statements in Sa-gig, such as "the magician shall perform (his arts)" (lu₂MAŠ.MAŠ DÙ-*uš* in Sa-gig 4: 107 (TDPT 4 rev. 21)), "the magician shall not establish a verdict for his (the patient's) healing" ((lu₂)MAŠ.MAŠ *ana* TIN-*šú* ME.A NU GAR-*an* in Sa-gig 16: 74′; 22: 3; 27: 13; cf. *AMT* [77/1 i 10]), "in the presence of the magician" (*ina* IGI MAŠ.MAŠ in Sa-gig 3: 23 (TDPT 3: 14)), and "inform the physician, the magician, the diviner, the dream-interpreter" (lu₂A.ZU lu₂MAŠ.⟨MAŠ⟩ lu₂ḪAL lu₂EN.SI *šu-ud-di* in Sa-gig 18: 14)—all of which portray the magician in the 3rd (rather than 2nd) person. See §1.1.2.2 for my discussion of magician interest in the healing arts, as well as how the scholar Esagil-kīn-apli, who created the Diagnostic Handbook, came to be regarded as a scribal ancestor to the magician profession.

Obv. 11—The term *nimšū* has been translated as "sinews" and often occurs in anatomical descriptions of sheep (*AHw*, 790; *CAD* N II, 235). Apart from the unpreserved base text here, other syllabic writings of *nimšū* as a human body part appear in a diagnostic fragment from Ḫattuša: *nimšūšu šalmū-ma* ("his *nimšū* are well"; KBo VII, 13 rev. 2′–3′, [6′, 8′]; identified by R. Biggs and mentioned in Leichty 1973: 84). Fincke (2011b: 472–476) argued that the expression "his *nimšū* are well" also underlies the logographic writing SA.ME-*šú* SILIM-*ma* in the incipit-title of Sa-gig Tablet 21, which is not preserved in exisiting manuscipts of the tablet itself, but attested in this commentary (obv. 1) and in the Sa-gig catalog (Finkel 1988: 146, A 26; Heeßel 2000: 14, line 26). The comment SA.MEŠ ("SA-strands") is a very common feature of the human anatomy in medical texts, designating a variety of strand-like structures such as blood vessels, muscles, tendons, ligaments, and nerves. Just because the same word could be used for different structures, however, does not imply that the ancient healer was uncertain what the term "strand" meant in particular contexts. Unfortunately, the base text here is not preserved, and we cannot be certain why the term *nimšū* was employed instead of the usual term "strands." Perhaps *nimšū* (i.e., "sinews") with its more precise meaning was used to specify the kind of "strands" referred to in ambiguous contexts. Another commentary also has the equation *nim-šu-šu* // SA.ME-*šú* (*SpTU* 1, 72 rev. 9). Because the less familar term in the topic (*nim-šú-šú*) is syllabically written and the more familiar term in the comment (SA.MEŠ-*šú*) takes the form of a logogram, the result is a breach in the writing convention that logographic forms precede syllabic ones. For similar reasons, the syllabic form [*pé-ret*] is explained by means of the logogram SÍG in Comm. Sa-gig 1–3, obv. 27. A different strategy may have been adopted in Comm. Sa-gig 14 (obv. 22–23), whereby the convention is preserved by stating the logographically written comment [*ina* GÌŠ-*šú*] before its syllabically written topic *ina mu-šar-šu*.

Obv. 12—The syllable signs here are *šá*(níg)-*ni-im-ma*, not *ša-ni-im-ma* as rendered by the typo in Leichty (1973: 83); Heeßel (2000: 247). Also, the logogram MAN suggests that *šá-ni-im-ma* does not indicate *šanim-ma* (< *šanin-ma*, from the verb *šanānu* "to equal, rival"), but *šanī-ma* (from the verb *šanû* "to become changed, altered"). The logogram MAN is common in prognoses of the Diagnostic Handbook and other diagnostic texts, but not in therapeutic texts where the patient's outcome after treatment is almost consistently described as "he will become healthy." The statement GIG-*su* MAN-*ni* ("his sickness will become altered") appears at Sa-gig 9: 6; 10: 43; 12: 12, 18, 22, 24, [62″], [64″], 116″, 119″ (TDPT 12 i 10, 13, 15–16; [ii 57′]; [iii 1]; iv 8, 11); Sa-gig 13: 47 (TDPT 13 i 48′); Sa-gig 14: 4, 10, 14, 16, 18, 20, 35, 45, 47, 49, 53, 56, 63 (similarly numbered entries in TDPT 14 i); Sa-gig 14: 153 (TDPT 14 iii 8); Sa-gig 14: 230′; 18: 28; 22: 42 (variant $E_{22'}$), at least twice with an explicitly negative outcome (Sa-gig 9: 6; 22: 42 (variant $E_{22'}$)) and never with a positive outcome. On the other hand, the rare occurrences of KÚR ("to change") in the prognoses of Sa-gig 11: 45; 16: 93′–95′ seem to be linked with the patient's recovery. See especially the diagnostic entries Sa-gig 14: 63–64 (TDPT 14 i 63–64) for the contrast between MAN and KÚR. While the base text here MAN-*ma* GIG ("he is altered and becomes sick") is aligned with the deterioration of the patient's condition implied by MAN, it nonetheless differs from the stereotypical expression GIG-*su* MAN-*ni* ("his sickness will become altered"). This may explain why the commentator chose to remark on what are otherwise common verbs (MAN and GIG) in medical texts.

Obv. 15—For DIŠ GIG GIM ŠUB-*ú* as the incipit-title of what I have designated Sa-gig Tablet 22a, see Note on rev. 19′ below. The signs read as *i-na-du-*⸢*ú*⸣ by Leichty (1973: 83); Heeßel (2000: 136) are actually *in-na-du-*⸢*ú*⸣. Compare how the *i* sign is written elsewhere on this tablet (see obv. 4, 12, 24; rev. 17′), and notice how the syntax seems to fit better with the passive sense of the N stem. The terms GIM and ŠUB are very common in medical texts and it is not entirely clear why they warranted comment here. One possibility could be to clarify the aspect of the verb ŠUB-*ú*, not as the Stative *nadû* ("(when) he is laid down"), but as the processual *innaddû* ("(when) he is being laid down"). Another possibility might be to avoid confusion with the common use of GIM ("like, as in the case of") that compares the patient's condition with other known maladies. See, for example, Sa-gig 26: 11: [DIŠ GI]M ŠUB-*ti* ŠUB.ŠUB-*su* ("If, as in the case of a Fall, it befalls him").

Obv. 16—The term *ḫasīsu* can denote the "ear" or its faculty of "hearing," and, apart from the base text here, it occurs only at Sa-gig 3: 89 (TDPT 3: 80): Collated as *ḫa-si-si-šú* ⸢*kùd*(?)*-du*(?)⸣*-ta-at* GEŠTUG.2? ... ("his hearing is low (and) his ears ...") in Scurlock and Andersen (2005: 203, §9.94; 715 n. 120); but reinterpreted as *ḫa-si-si-šú ṣa-bit* TA KÚM *lam* GUR-*ma* DIB-*bat* ... ("his hearing is affected (and) after the heat, before it returns and afflicts him ...") in Scurlock (2014: 17, 23). The commentator may have reasoned that *ḫa-sis-su* could not refer to the "ear," since GEŠTUG (= *uznu*) is by far the more common writing for the human "ear" in the Diagnostic Handbook and therapeutic texts. The writing *ḫa-sis-su*, therefore, was thought not to represent *ḫasīssu* (< *ḫasīs* "ear" + *šu* "his"), but a byform of *āṣīssu* (< *āṣīt* + *šu* "his"). The word *āṣīt*(*u*) derives from the root *aṣû* ("to go out") and has a range of related meanings that includes "export duty," "drainage canal," "exit," and presumably protuding parts of buildings and apparatuses (*CAD* A II, 355–356). Because the base text here is not available to us, we cannot be certain how such an interpretation of *āṣīt*(*u*) might fit into a bodily context, and I tentatively translate the term as "exit / issue."

Obv. 16–17—One is tempted to relate the group of signs tab nim ma (obv. 16) to discussions of the logogram TAB that begin at the end of obv. 16, though about half a tablet line's spacing (broken) separate the two. The verbs *šurrû* ("to begin") and *ḫamāṭu* ("to burn") are both commonly equated with the logogram TAB in lexical texts (*CAD* Š III, 358 s.v. *šurrû* A; *CAD* Ḫ, 64 s.v. *ḫamāṭu* B). In medical texts, however, TAB predominantly denotes *ḫamāṭu* ("to burn"), especially in the expressions UD.DA TAB.BA ("he is burned by *ṣētu*-heat") and TAB UD.DA ("burning of *ṣētu*-heat"). The commentator may have tried to explain the less common verb *šurrû* ("to begin") by referring to the more usual meaning of its logogram TAB.

Obv. 17—The prognosis NU SI.SÁ ("it will not go well") is typical of the Diagnostic Handbook, in contrast to therapeutic texts where the patient's outcome after treatment is almost consistently described as "he will become healthy." For NU SI.SÁ, see Sa-gig 9: 73; 36: 26, 30, 34, 39, 54–55, 102 (similarly numbered entries in TDPT 35); Sa-gig 40: 23; for the positive prognosis SI.SÁ ("it will go well"), see Sa-gig 36: 27, 33, 56 (TDPT 35: 27, 33, 56).

Obv. 18–19—ÚŠ ^{giš}TUKUL ("death by weapon") seems unattested elsewhere in the medical texts. The comment here represents the paraphrase of an expression that appears in several therapeutic texts: GIM MUNUS ^{giš}TUKUL *maḫiṣ* ("as in the case of a woman, he is struck with a weapon") at *BAM* 99: 27 (= *BAM* VII/35); *BAM* 152 iii 8; 159 i 9; *BAM* VII/10: 4; as well as the variant reading GIM DAM ^{giš}TUKUL *maḫiṣ* at *BAM* 396 iv 3 (= *BAM* VII/1). In these medical entries, a prominent medical sign is the dripping of blood from the patient's penis or rectum. The comparison, therefore, most likely pertains to the dripping of menstrual blood in the case of a woman, and "weapon" is intended, not literally, but metaphorically in reference to the cause of blood loss. Leichty (1973: 83, 85) understood the signs as *šá ki bul-ṭu k*[*a-aš-da-at*], "who when she recuperates [...]" (obv. 19), but I largely follow the restoration by Gabbay (2016: 230): *šá* KI *bul-ṭu* D[U$_{11}$.GA-*ú*], "which it sa[id] with the medical texts." Attestations of the term *bulṭū*, in fact, do seem to refer to therapeutic prescriptions and recipes, rather than diagnostic texts (*CAD* B, 312 s.v. *bulṭu*). The commentator, in other words, extended the implications of female conditions to the base text here, which otherwise does not seem concerned specifically with women patients.

Obv. 19–20—The verbs *šadādu* ("to pull, stretch") and *i*/*utūlu* ("to lie down") do not seem to be equated in the lexical texts, and their association here probably reflects the context of *šadādu* in the base text. In therapeutic texts, the verb *šadādu* describes a sensation of the head (*BAM* 3 iii 43; [480 iv 32]; 578 i 46) or movement pertaining to the eye and its parts (*BAM* 516 ii 27′; *AMT* 13/1: 3′). In the Diagnostic Handbook, *šadādu* denotes malady behavior (Sa-gig 19/20: 117′; 21: 21′), movement of the patient's strands (Sa-gig 13: 96, 104–105 (TDPT 13 ii 38, 46–47); Sa-gig 15: 37′), and the "stretching out" of limbs or the whole person (Sa-gig 11: 32; 40: 84). This last meaning corresponds well with the verb *i*/*utūlu* ("to lie down"), which occurs commonly in the Diagnostic Handbook and therapeutic texts.

Obv. 21—TAG as the logogram for *maḫāṣu* ("to strike") occurs in the lexical texts Ea V, 61 (*MSL* XIV, 398); Aa V/1, 224, 244 (*MSL* XIV, 413, 414); Idu II,

349 (*CAD* M I, 72). Such "striking," however, seems to occur in the context of "clothing" (*šá* TÚG in Ea V, 61; A V/1, 244) perhaps as part of the cleaning process, or with reference to some inanimate object (*šá mim-ma* in Idu II, 349). In contrast, "striking" in the case of a human (*šá* LÚ) is expressed by the logogram RA (*CT* 12, 29 (no. 38266) rev. 29). In medical texts, as might be expected, *maḫāṣu* ("to strike") is usually expressed by the logograms SÌG or RA, not TAG.

Obv. 21–22—kin-kin = *šite*''*û* (Gtn stem of *še'û* "to seek") and *bu*''*û* (D stem verb "to search for") are associated in the lexical text Antagal VIII, 53–54 (*MSL* XVII, 171). See also KIN.KIN : *ši-te-ʾ-ú* : *bu-ʾ-ú* in Comm. *Ālu* 22–23 = BM 129092, obv. 16′ (Freedman 2006: 11 n. 21). The G stems of both verbs occur together at *CT* 18, 6 obv. 27; *LTBA* II, 1 v 38–40; 2: 246–248. Both verbs are atypical in medical descriptions. While the base text here is uncertain, the patient suffering from love sickness in Sa-gig 22: 6–7 is described as *iš-ta-na-ʾ-i*, an expression that has been translated as "unruhig umherläuft / sich andauernd räuspert" (Heeßel 2000: 258) and "continually flutters about" (Scurlock and Andersen 2005: 372, §16.23; presumably from the verb *šâ'u* "to fly about, flutter" (*CAD* Š II, 243), though it can also refer to the verb *šite*''*û*, "to seek out, yearn for"). No known lexical equations link the verbs *šite*''*û* and *bu*''*û* to MÁŠ IGI, and the logic behind this connection is unfortunately lost in the damaged text after the notation *lìb-b*[*u-ú*] ("as in"). Leichty (1973: 86), however, has correctly noted that "the nuance of *bu'û* 'to examine exta' given by *CAD* B 363a would seem to fit the general nature of MÁŠ IGI." If the base text here is similar to Sa-gig 22: 6–7, the patient may be depicted as one who seeks out ominous signs from the object of his infatuations that his affections are reciprocated. If the verb describes the action of the healer, he may be portrayed as exercising inductive reasoning in order to arrive at diagnostic and prognostic verdicts from medical signs, resembling the process by which diviners derive meaning from observed omens. Note the description of the "magician" (*āšipu*) healer in Sa-gig as KA.PIRIG, because he "speaks (ka) what is bright (PIRIG)," i.e., his spoken diagnosis illumines the identity of the patient's malady (Comm. Sa-gig 1A, obv. 1–2; Comm. Sa-gig 1C, obv. [1]).

Obv. 22–24—I restore the topic at the end of line 22 as [*i-lam-ma-am*], perhaps from a base text similar to U.MEŠ-*šú i-la-am-ma-am* ("he chews his fingers"; Sa-gig 11 rev. 52). Apart from these references, the verb *lamāmu* ("to chew") does not seem to appear in medical signs of the Diagnostic Handbook or therapeutic texts. Another non-medical commentary on the *Šumma ālu* series (DT 37, rev. 10 in Freedman 2017: 75), likewise, equates *lamāmu* with the very common verb *akālu* ("to eat").

Obv. 25—The god Dumuzi does not seem attested elsewhere in medical texts as the divine agent responsible for sickness, and the broken context makes it uncertain whether the divine name represents a topic or comment here.

Obv. 25–26—Leichty (1973: 86) suggested that "the commentator explains *šasû* as *a-ri*. This must be for *âru* in the sense of 'to give an order.' Cf. *i-ʾ-ir* : *a-ri* : *a-lak CT* 41, 30: 18 [= DT 37 obv. 19b in Freedman 2017: 74]. … This explanation of *šasû* seems to be unique." I am less certain that the verb *šasû* ("to call out"), which occurs commonly in medical texts, would function as the topic, rather than the comment to a topic at the damaged end of line 25. On the other hand, there may be good reason for the form *a-ri* to serve as the topic, especially if it represents something other than the common medical verb *arû* ("to puke"). One possibility, for example, may be to interpret *a-ri* : DU.[DU(?)] as the verb classified in *CAD* A II, 313, as *arû* A ("to lead, bring"). The position of the logogram after its Akkadian translation is admittedly awkward, though not altogether foreign to the practice of this particular scribe. See *nim-šú-šú* : SA.MEŠ-*šú* (obv. 11) and *bu-ʾu-ú* : MÁŠ IGI (obv. 22).

Rev. 9′—The term *ḫurbāšu* ("chill") appears also in Comm. Sa-gig 19, obv. 19, as the comment to the topic *kūṣ* ("coldness"). Of the two terms, *ḫurbāšu* is the one more confined to therapeutic texts. Here, we cannot be certain whether *ḫurbāšu* functions as the topic or comment of this entry.

Rev. 10′—There does not seem to be another attestation of the expression "one who knows his intelligence" in the medical texts, whether written syllabically or with logograms. The patient's "intelligence," however, is mentioned very frequently in the Diagnostic Handbook and always written with the logogram UMUŠ. By contrast, the term only occurs a few times in therapeutic texts, both as the logogram UMUŠ (*BAM* 316 vi 5′; 449 iii 25′ (incl. *AMT* 90/1 iii 25′)) and in its syllabic form *ṭēmu* (*BAM* 59: 23; 202 obv. 1; 575 iii 52; *STT* 286 ii 15). It is unclear whether the reading at *BAM* 240: 29 should be DÚR-*šá maqit* or UMUŠ-*šá maqit*. The rarity of UMUŠ ("intelligence") in therapeutic texts likely prompted the commentator's explanation of the term here. We might assume the topic here refers to a self-awareness of one's own intelligence. Possibly, however, the individual designated as "one who knows his (i.e., the patient's) intelligence" can be a person other than the patient himself. The testimony of an acquaintance, for example, is mentioned at Sa-gig 9: 23–24: *mūdûšu ul* GIG-*ma iqabbi* ("one who knows him (i.e., the patient) says, 'Is he not sick?'").

Rev. 11′—Leichty (1973: 84, 86) read the signs as *ku-tál* NA ŠUB-*ut* (rev. 11′), perhaps to be translated "the man's back falls." The term *kutallu* ("back") is attested elsewhere in the expression "his arms turn towards his back" (Á.2-*šú ana ku-tal-li-šú* GUR) at Sa-gig [14: 169′] (TDPT [14 iii 36′]); Sa-gig

15: 56′, and it is uncertain whether it here represents a Sa-gig topic or comment. What follows may be a quotation of an apodosis from the terrestrial omen series *Šumma ālu* XXII, 73: DIŠ MUŠ *ana bu-di* NA ŠUB-*ut mu-kil ku-tal* LÚ BA.ÚŠ, "If a snake falls on to a man's shoulders, one who backs (lit. holds the back of) the man will die" (Freedman 2006: 17, 29). The logic of this terrestrial omen is clarified by another commentary, which affirms that "the shoulders *refer to* the back" (*bu-di* : *ku-tal-la* in Comm. *Ālu* 22–23 = BM 129092, obv. 24′). See Freedman 2006: 17 n. 73; Jiménez (CCP 3.5.22.A.b). If present in the Sa-gig commentary, this quotation may have been intended to support a negative prognosis in the Sa-gig base text.

Rev. 12′–13′—The base text here is not preserved for us, but I wonder if it may have taken a form similar to MÚD … *uš-tar-ru-nim-ma* DU-*ku* ("blood has begun to flow") at Sa-gig 31: 3, 9. In this expression, the finite verb *uš-tar-ru-nim* ("it has begun"; see Heeßel 2000: 348) is used in hendiadys with another finite verb DU-*ku* ("it flows"). The verb *šurrû* ("to begin"), in fact, occurs very rarely in medical texts (Sa-gig 17: 100; 31: 3, 9), and a reader who does not recognize the hendiadys may come under the impression that the two verbs describe two different actions of blood. Perhaps then, it is in this sense that "To begin (*šurrû*) *means* the pus becomes solid," i.e., solidifying pus occurs at the beginning of blood flow or some other process.

Rev. 13′–14′—Even if my restoration *ana* KU[R …] is correct, it is puzzling what the form of the base text might have been, so as to require explanation by the logograms KUR and PAG. There are several maladies that involve the term KUR ("mountain"), such as DIḪ/*liʾbu* KUR (Sa-gig 3:60 (TDPT 3: 51); *AMT* 53/7: 1; see also *CAD* L, 182 s.v. *liʾbu* A §b; Stol 2007a: 12–13), DAB(-*it*) KUR (Sa-gig 16: 27, 28), and *tašnīq* KUR.RA (Sa-gig 29: 8, 29, [41′]). Moreover, the logogram KUR may also stand for the verb *kašādu* ("to defeat"), which not uncommonly describes the action of maladies. The cuneiform sign pag can serve as the logogram MUŠEN ("bird"), which appears in the medical condition *ḫiddūr* MUŠEN ("*ḫindūru* of a bird") at *BAM* 1 ii 53; 32: 7′; 417 obv. 6; 421 i 24′; [*AMT* 51/8: 6′]; the diagnosis *muttillu*^{mušen} TAG-*ma* KI-*šú* KEŠDA ("the *muttillu*-bird has touched him and is bound with him (and) stands at his head") at Sa-gig 26: 86′–87′; as well as the medical sign GIM MUŠEN *ùʾ* GÙ.GÙ-*si* ("he keeps crying out '*u*' like a bird") at Sa-gig 15: 90′. The equation in line 14′ refers to the god Enlil's epithet as "the great mountain (KUR)." The meaning of pag-dù as "expert" or "one who knows" (*mūdû*) is attested in the bilingual text of *Lugale* XI, 46: gal-an-zu pag-dù nì-nam-ma-ke$_4$ = *eršu mūdû mimma šumšu* (suggestion by Sjöberg in Leichty 1973: 86; van Dijk 1983: 1,117; 2,138; line 508).

Rev. 14′–15′—Neither the base text nor its quotation here is preserved, though the comment resembles EME-*šú* ÍL.ME(Š)-*ši* ("he keeps lifting his tongue") at Sa-gig 17: 72.

Rev. 16′—TUR is the usual logogram for the verb *ṣahāra* ("to become small"). On the other hand, the equation TUR : *emūqu* ("strength") is nowhere else attested, though lexical texts do show a good variety of logograms that have been equated with *emūqu* (*CAD* E, 157). One possibility may be to consider the near homophony between DUMU (another reading of the TUR sign) and the Akkadian noun *dunnu* ("might"). For literary parallelism involving the word pair *emūqu* and *dunnu*, see *dunnu zikrūtu emūqān ṣīrāti* (Piepkorn 1933: 28, Edition B i 11; cf. TH. 1929-10-12, 2, iv 13–14 in Campbell Thompson 1931: 33, pl. 16); *dunni zikrūte emūqi lā šanān ušaršû gattī* (Streck 1916: 2,210 (K 2867, obv. 10), 2,254 (K 3050+2694, i 12)).

Rev. 17′—If the reading *i-te-lip* is correct, it represents a rare occurrence of the verb *elēpu* ("to become grown together, entangled") in the medical texts. One possible restoration of the comment is *šá* EME-*šú ú-b*[*u-ṭa-at*] ("the case where his tongue is cramped"), though descriptions of a "cramped" tongue elsewhere prefer the G Stative *eb-ṭe-et* (*BAM* [543 i 49′]; *SpTU* I, 44: 84; 46: 1) or the Ntn Durative *it-te-nen-bi-iṭ* (*BAM* [438 obv. 6–7]) or *it-te-nen-biṭ* (*BAM* 445: 11). The 3ms Stative *e-bíṭ* probably does not take the feminine subject EME ("tongue"), contrary to the restoration of [EM]E(?)-*šú e-bíṭ* ("his ⸢tongue⸣ is cramped"; *BAM* 28 obv. 2; 533: 2) by Scurlock and Andersen (2005: 287, §13.19).

Rev. 19′—DIŠ GIG GIM ŠUB-*ú* ("If, when the sick man is laid down") is the incipit-title to what is designated here as Sa-gig Tablet 22a, which constitutes the base text of commentary entries from obv. 15 to rev. 17′. This text is described as "a non-canonical tablet that was inserted after Sa-gig 21 in some versions of the series" by Frahm (2011a: 226); cf. Heeßel (2000: 135–136). Frahm labeled this tablet as Sa-gig "21a." The catalog list of Sa-gig Tablets preceding *Esagil-kīn-apli's Manifesto*, however, implies that this so-called Sa-gig Tablet "21a" is better regarded as a version of Tablet 22. At a position in this catalog where we would expect the incipit-title of Sa-gig Tablet 22, we find the following entry: DIŠ GIG ⸢*iṣ-búr*⸣ 1 2 *u* 3 GIG *ina* ⸢*še*⸣-*re-e-ti il-te-*⸢*né*⸣-*eb-bu* (Finkel 1988: 147, line A 27; Heeßel 2000: 14, line 27; Wiseman and Black 1996: pl. 44, obv. 27; Schmidtchen 2018: 314, pl. 14). Four out of five available manuscripts of Sa-gig Tablet 22 (MSS A–D in Heeßel 2000: 250) preserve in their first line the incipit DIŠ GIG *ina še-re-e-ti il-te-né-eb-bu* ("If the sick man keeps groaning in the morning hours"). This suggests that the catalog entry for Sa-gig Tablet 22 includes more than one incipit-title, perhaps of different versions of this tablet. Furthermore, the cuneiform writing interpreted by scholars as DIŠ GIG ⸢*iṣ-búr*⸣ (𒁹 𒍼 𒄑 𒁙) shows a suspicious resemblance to that of DIŠ GIG GIM ŠUB-*u* (𒁹 𒍼 𒁶 𒊒 𒌋), and one wonders whether DIŠ GIG GIM ŠUB-*u/ú* ("If, when the sick man is laid down") was the incipit-title of a version of Sa-gig Tablet 22 that is attested in damaged and/or corrupted condition in the catalog list. For the above reasons, I prefer to identify the base text of this commentary as Sa-gig 21 & 22a. Although it is easy to call Sa-gig Tablet 22a "non-canonical" because of its lack of attestation in available Sa-gig manuscripts, one should remember that the commentary itself makes no clear distinction between canonical vs. non-canonical base texts, and that Tablet 22a may actually be referenced in the catalog list of Sa-gig tablets.

Rev. 19′–23′—Frahm (2011a: 227) thought "the tablet seems to have been written by a Nippur scribe, but was probably found in Uruk." The names in this colophon appear also in another commentary on the astronomical omen series *Enūma Anu Enlil* at *SpTU* III, 101 rev. 18′–21′, which can be restored with the help of Comm. Sa-gig 21 & 22a as follows: … IM.GÌ.D[A m.d*En-líl*-MU-SUM (?) DUMU m.d30-*na-din*-ŠEŠ.MEŠ] / LÚ DINGIR.BI dNUSKA.KE$_4$ AMA.d+INNIN.BI DUMU.Z[I.ABZU.KE$_4$ AMA.A.TU dZÚ.LUM.MA …] / Ur-dMe-me *mu-sa$_7$-ap-pú*(!)-*ú* ZA.GÌN.NA *ka-bit* […] / EDURU(?) m.d+*En-líl*-EN-*šú-nu* lú₂NU.ÈŠ d+*En-líl* DU[MU(.UŠ?) m*Gimil*-d30], "… *Imgida*-tablet [of Enlil-šumu-iddin(?), son of Sîn-nādin-ahhē], whose god is Nusku (and) whose goddess is Dumuzi-[abzu, servant of Ninurta(?), descendant (?) of] Ur-dMe-me, suppliant of Enlil(?), Ea/Bēl(?) […] son of Enlil-bēlšunu *nêšakku*-priest of Enlil, descendant of [Gimil-Sîn]." Adapted from Frahm (2011a: 298); Gabbay and Jiménez (2019: 74–75); with suggestions by the latter that ZA.GÌN.NA for *ellu* or *elēlu* was homophonic and representative of the god Enlil, and *ka-bit* or *kabtu* was equatable with BAD (writing for the god Ea) or UMUN (writing for the god Bēl). Lambert (1995: 134) agreed with Di Vito (1993: 88–89) that "ama can mean mother (of the city)," and thought that "the term for 'goddess' written AMA.dMÙŠ [or AMA.dINNIN] in Sumerian, rendered *amālu, amalītu, amalūtu, amaluktu, maluktu* and *maruktu* in Akkadian, is etymologically ama-uru-(a)k [lit. 'mother of the city']." George (2003: 861 note 181) provided a good summary of the sources and identifications for the deity Dumuzi-abzu, while a manuscript edition of the god-list *An = Anum* I by Lambert (= Litke 1998: 51 line 260) explains Dumuzi-abzu as Sadarnuna (cf. Gabbay and Jiménez 2019: 73 n. 76). A divine determinative is absent for Ur-Me-me (rev. 22′) here, in contrast to Ur-dMe-me in *SpTU* III, 101 rev. 20′. For Ur-Meme and his family of priests and temple administrators in Nippur from around Old Akkadian times to the early Isin I period, see Hallo (1972: 87–95); Zettler (1984: 1–9).

The syllable sign in rev. 22′ is *pú*(bu_4), not *bú* as rendered by the typo in Leichty (1973: 84), and the proposal to read "*mu-sa*$_x$*-ap-pú-u*" is original to Reiner in Leichty (1973: 86). The cryptographic writing EN EN EN (rev. 22′) may stand for *bēl bēlē* ("lord of lords"), or possibly "the Three Lords" who are named as "^{d}ŠID, Šamaš, and Marduk" in the next line (rev. 23′). For the writing ^{d}ŠID (or ^{d}*Elal*$_2$) as a reference to the god Enlil, see Krebernik (2010: 451); Frahm (2011a: 198 n. 936, 298 n. 1424).

Commentary Sa-gig 23

Provenance:	?
Period:	?
Names:	Colophon absent
Script:	Neo-/Late Babylonian

Field/Museum No.:	RMC 193 (Rare Manuscript Collections at Cornell University Museum, USA)
Printed Edition:	Heeßel (2000: 273–275, based on unpublished hand copy by D. Owen); Gadotti and Sigrist (2011: 153 no. 193); Wee (2012: 683–686)
Digital Resources:	CDLI 270807; CCP 4.1.23 (printed hand copy and edition digitized by Jiménez 2015, with contributions by Frahm and Veldhuis)
Discussion:	Heeßel (2000: 136, 272 (23. Tafel MS a), 273–275); Genty (2010b: 14); Gadotti and Sigrist (2011: 153 no. 193); Frahm (2011a: 227, 312); Wee (2012: 683–686); Scurlock (2014: 195 n. 1); Gabbay (2016: 107 n. 128, 109 n. 134)
Pericope:	Indeterminate due to damaged state of available Sa-gig manuscripts

Transliteration

Obverse

1) DIŠ GIG ZÉ *ip-ru* : ÚḪ *ina* ŠUB-*šú i-ṣar-r*[*a-ár*]
2) *it-ta-na-at-tuk* : ŠUR : *ṣa-ra-ri*!(šú) : ŠUR : *na-t*[*a-ki*]
3) MÚD MUD ŠUB.ŠUB-*a* : MÚD : *da-mu* : MUD : *da-mu* : [MÚD *pe-la-a* : SÙ]
4) *pe-la-a* : igi sù : igi sù-a : sù-a : [sù-sù-a]
5) *za-ar-ri-iq* : *za-ar-riq-tú* : *p*[*e-lu-u* : *pe-li-tu*]
6) ⸢NINDA / A (?)⸣ URU$_4$-*iš* : *šá ina la ṭè-mi-š*[*ú* ...]
7) *ú-ḫab-ba-at* : *šá* aš šu eš [...]
8) *šá a-kal ina* ŠU.2-*šú* : *ú*-x[...]
9) *ina pi-i-šú ma-á*[*r* ...]
10) *šá ina la ṭ*[*è-mi-šú* ... (?)]
11) ka-x[...]
12) x [...]

 | DOI:10.1163/9789004417564_025

Translation

Incipit-title of Sa-gig 23

(Obv. 1) "If the sick man vomited gall."

***Sa-gig 23**
The verb *ṣarāru* "to flow" is less typical of therapeutic texts than the Diagnostic Handbook, where it usually occurs as the logogram ŠUR, not as the syllabic form *iṣarrar* here.

(1–2) "When he throws up spittle, it flows" (*means*) it keeps dripping.

The semantic link between *ṣarāru* "to flow" and *natāku* "to drip" is implied by their shared logogram ŠUR.

(2) ŠUR *means* to flow.
(2) ŠUR *means* to drip.

***Sa-gig 23**
MÚD MUD "dark blood" is a common expression in the Diagnostic Handbook, but seems to be absent in therapeutic texts.

(3) "He keeps throwing up MÚD MUD."
(3) "MÚD" *means* blood.
(3) "MUD" *means* dark.

***Sa-gig 23: 9**
pelû-red occurs only rarely in the Diagnostic Handbook, and medical texts more commonly describe bodily features as *sāmu*-red.

(3) ["*pelû*-red blood."]

The semantic link between *pelû*-red and *zarriq*-coloring is implied by their shared logogram SÙ.

(3–4) [SÙ (*means*)] "*pelû*-red."

Quotation from Erimhuš II, 310–313 underscores resemblances between *zarriq*-coloring and *pelû*-red, as a means of distinguishing *pelû*-red from *sāmu*-red.

(4–5) "igi sù, igi sù-a, sù-a, *and* [sù-sù-a] *mean zarriq*-coloring, *zarriqtu*-coloring, [*pelû*-red, *and pelītu*-red] *respectively*."

***Sa-gig 23**
Patient "requests" are common in the Diagnostic Handbook but rare in

(6) "He requests for [food / drink (?)]" *refers to* the case where without his intelligence …

therapeutic texts. Perhaps a diagnostically significant request is one that is made without full consciousness and reflective of deep needs.

***Sa-gig 23**
ḫabātu "to move across" occurs rarely in the Diagnostic Handbook and seems to be absent in therapeutic texts.

(7) "He moves (his hand) across(?) (his mouth)" *refers to* ...

(7–8) ... in the case of bread that (is) in his hands ...

(9) in his mouth ...

(9–10) ... (*refers to*) the case where without [his intelligence (?)] ...

(11–12) ...

Notes

Obv. 1–2—Heeßel (2000:273) read the signs as *i-ṣar-r*[*aḫ*] (obv. 1) and *ṣa-ra-ḫu*(?) (obv. 2), even though the logogram SUR/ŠUR seems to refer primarily to the verb *ṣarāḫu* C ("to flare up"; *CAD* Ṣ, 100), whose Durative form *iṣarriḫ* has an /i/ instead of /a/ theme vowel. It is much less certain that this logogram SUR/ŠUR was used for other homophonic verbs: *ṣarāḫu* B ("to sing a lamentation"; *CAD* Ṣ, 99–100, note editor's comment in lexical section: "for sur and sar see, however, *ṣarāḫu* C"), *ṣarāḫu* A ("to heat, scotch"; *CAD* Ṣ, 98–99), and *ṣarāḫu* D ("to dispatch quickly"; *CAD* Ṣ, 100), which all have the Durative form *iṣarraḫ*. Furthermore, none of the *ṣarāḫu* verbs has a (Durative) transitive meaning that really fits the context here "when (the sick man) throws up spittle." Another verb *šurruḫu* ("to drool(?), dribble(?)"; *CAD* Š III, 361) may work in this context, but neither is attested in the G stem nor has the byform *ṣurruḫu*. Gadotti and Sigrist (2011: 153 no. 193) kept the reading *i-ṣar-*⸢*raḫ*⸣ in obv. 1, but transliterated the signs as *ṣa-ra-šú* in obv. 2, even though the commentator was evidently making an argument based on the same root. Jiménez (CCP 4.1.23) read *i-ṣar-*⸢*riš*⸣ (obv. 1) and *šá-ra-šú* (presumably a typo for *ṣa-ra-šú* in obv. 2), as representatives of the very rare G stem of the root *ṣarāšu*. This is problematic. The G stem appears lexically only at [giš].

⌜a⌝-ab-ta-sal = *i-ṣu ka-pi-il* ("gnarled tree/wood") / [giš.x]-zé-àm-bar = *i-ṣu ṣa-ri-iš* ("… tree/wood") (AO 5401, i 5–6 in *MSL* SS 1, 97) and at lú zé-a-al-ra = *ṣa-ar-*[*š*]*um* (OB Lu A, 354 and C_4, 2 in *MSL* XII, 168 and 194), and the context of trees/wood seems aligned with its D stem meanings "to grow shoots, branches" (*CAD* Ṣ, 260–261 s.v. *ṣurrušu*), "(1) etwa ausstrahlen(?), (2) wachsen lassen, (3) (mit Behandlung) fortfahren" (*AHw*, 1085), all of which are unrelated to the desired meaning "to drip / dribble (i.e., spittle)" (CCP 4.1.23). Moreover, there is no evidence that ŠUR may serve as the logogram of *ṣarāšu*. I understand the signs as *i-ṣar-r*[*a-ár*] (obv. 1) and *ṣa-ra-ri*!(šú) (obv. 2), even while acknowledging that a scribal error must be posited in obv. 2, and that the Durative form *iṣarrar* (rather than *iṣarrur*) becomes attested only in Neo-/Late Babylonian times (*AHw*, 1084). The verb *ṣarāru* ("to flow") is readily paired with the verb *natāku* ("to drip") and is used in similar contexts elsewhere that describe the flow of blood (Sa-gig 3: [76] (TDPT 3: [67]); Sa-gig 10 B rev. 2; 13: 86 (TDPT 13 ii 28); Sa-gig 14: 109 (TDPT 14 ii 37); Sa-gig 15: 11′), the flow of gall (Sa-gig 3: 77 (TDPT 3: 68)), the flow of urine (Sa-gig 19/20: 107′), and the flow of pus (*BAM* 503 iii 12 (incl. *AMT* 36/1 obv. 12)). This verb *ṣarāru* appears only rarely in medical signs of therapeutic texts, and it occurs in the Diagnostic Handbook as the logogram ŠUR. Thus, the syllabic form *i-ṣar-r*[*a-ar*] in the base text represented atypical writing that called for comment. The comment *natāku* occurs in the Diagnostic Handbook at Sa-gig 17: 59, but seems to have more attestations in therapeutic texts: *BAM* 66 obv. 25; 111 ii 21′; *AMT* 62/1 ii 9′; [63/1: 14′]. Though unacknowledged in *MZL*, no. 151, ŠUR as the logogram for *natāku* occurs in the lexical text Aa III/6, 93 (*MSL* XIV, 350). See also sur-ma-s[ur] = [šur-m]a-šu-úr = *i-da-*[…] (Erimhuš Bogh. E, b8′ in *MSL* XVII, 124) that is read as šur(!)-š[ur-ra] = [šu-ú]r-šu-úr = *i-tá-*[*at-tu-ku*(?)] in *CAD* N II, 116. Note, finally, the parallelism between the verbs *ṣarāru* and *natāku* in the following lines: "*kakkaka ušumgallu ša ištu pīšu imtu la inattuku* // *damu la i-ṣar-ru-ru* 'your weapon is a dragon from whose mouth venom will not drip // blood will not flow' 4R 20 No. 3: 15ff." (*CAD* Ṣ, 106).

Obv. 3—Heeßel restored Sa-gig 23: 10 as [MÚD MUD ŠU]B.ŠUB-*a*, perhaps motivated by the desire to identify the base text for this commentary entry. If the base text for the commentary entry *pe-la-a* (obv. 4) is Sa-gig 23: 9, however, Heeßel's proposal would imply a disruption of the progressive order in which the commentator selected topics from the base text. The expression MÚD MUD ("dark blood") does not seem attested in therapeutic texts, but occurs frequently in the Diagnostic Handbook at Sa-gig 3: 87 (TDPT 3: 78); Sa-gig 13: 39–40, 78, 90 (TDPT 13 i 40′–41′; ii 20, 32); Sa-gig 14: 85, 184′ (TDPT 14 ii 13; iii 51′); Sa-gig 14: 206′; 15: 60′; 16: 10; [23: 10]. Notice that the Akkadian translations of MÚD (= *dāmu*, "blood") and MUD (= *da'mu*, "dark") have not been distinguished orthographically and are both written with the syllable signs *da-mu*. The different meanings of the two occurrences of *da-mu* must have been explained in the course of actual scribal teaching, and such cases give us insight into the importance of oral instruction that accompanied written commentarial forms.

Obv. 3–5—The form MÚD *pe-la-a* ("red blood") appears at Sa-gig 23: 9 and most likely represents the base text of what I have restored as [MÚD *pe-la-a*] in obv. 3 of this commentary. Besides this base text, the term *pelû*-red blood appears only at Sa-gig 16: 55′, 79′; 17: 43, and not in medical signs of therapeutic texts. By far the more common way of expressing the color red in the Diagnostic Handbook and therapeutic texts is the use of the verb *sâmu* and its related adjective *sāmu* (*CAD* S, 126–132; cf. Landsberger 1967a: 144, §ϑ.1). The commentator here, therefore, endeavored to clarify how the shade of *pelû*-red differed from that of *sāmu*-red. According to his argument, the terms *pelû* and *zarriqu* are semantically related, since both could be expressed by the same logogram SÙ. A lexical excerpt juxtaposing both these terms (Erimhuš II, 310–313 in *MSL* XVII, 43) is cited as further evidence of their close relationship; see Jiménez and Veldhuis (CCP 4.1.23). In lexical texts, the color *pelû* is most often expressed by the logograms SU_4 and SU_x(si-*gunû*), though the equation with SÙ appears in the following commentary to the astronomical omen series *Enūma Anu Enlil*: U_4.1.KÁM U_4.14.KÁM *ina* DUNGU *pe-li-tu*$_4$ IGI-*ma* : SÙ : *pe-lu-ú* (*TCL* VI, 17 = AO 6464, rev. 17). The term *zarriqu* is attested in lexical texts as the logogram SU_4, SU_x(si-*gunû*), and SU_9 (*CAD* Z, 69), though not with the form SÙ as it appears in this commentary. In any case, *zarriqu* seems to denote a particular coloring of the eye (IGI), as suggested by the lexical forms "igi sù" and "igi sù-a" (Erimhuš II, 310–311), and it is the resemblance of *pelû*-red to this coloring that distinguishes it from *sāmu*-red. *Pelû*-red is described as the color of a newborn's eyes in K 6288 = *CT* 28, 33, obv. 9′. Landsberger (1967a: 144, §ζ.2).

Obv. 6—I understand the beginning of this line as ⌜NINDA / A (?)⌝ URU_4-*iš* ("he requests for food / water (?)"), instead of [*m*]*ar-si-iš* as proposed by Heeßel (2000: 273); Gadotti and Sigrist (2011: 153 no. 193). Descriptions of patient requests occur frequently in a section of Diagnostic Tablet 23, which includes the medical entries Sa-gig 23: 15′–17′. Diagnostic verdicts are based on what the patient often "requests for" during his sickness. Though Sa-gig 23: 15′ is the first preserved instance of URU_4-*iš* in this tablet, we cannot with certainty identify it as the base text here, because it is likely that earlier damaged entries also contained the term [URU_4-*iš*]. Medical signs involving such "requests" do not appear often in therapeutic texts (cf. *BAM* 407: 2′, 6′), but are a common feature of the Diagnostic Handbook: Sa-gig 3: 56, 78 (TDPT 3: 47, 69); Sa-gig 7 B rev. 13–14 (TDPT 7: 69′–70′); Sa-gig 9: 19, 26; [10: 8]; 13: 69–71, 124–126 (TDPT 13 ii 11–13; iii 13–15); Sa-gig 15: 6′; 16: 15, 98′–101′; 19/20: 7′, 106′; 22: 4, 40, 42–43; 23: 15′–17′; [24: 1] (= Sa-gig 23: 19′); Sa-gig 27: 27; 40: 52–53. The comment "the case where without his intelligence ..." is, unfortunately, broken. Perhaps the commentator was describing the prerequisites for such diagnostically significant "requests," i.e., they should not be deliberated or calculated requests, but perhaps requests made instinctively or without full consciousness and reflective of the patient's deeply felt needs.

Obv. 7—Frahm (2011a: 227 n. 1058) has suggested the reading *ú-ḫab-ba-at* not only in line 7, but also in line 8: *ú-ḫ*[*ab-ba-at*]. For line 7 at least, this is a better reading than *ú-ni-ba-at* (Heeßel 2000: 273) or *ú-si-ba-at* (Gadotti and Sigrist 2011: 153 no. 193). Apart from the base text here, the verb *ḫabātu* ("to move across"; *CAD* H, 12 s.v. *ḫabātu* D) only occurs in the Diagnostic Handbook at Sa-gig 11: 28; 15: 16′, where it involves some movement of the hand in relation to the mouth. See the discussion of this verb in Heeßel (2000) 164. This verb seems to be absent in medical signs of therapeutic texts.

Obv. 7–8—I am unable to make good sense of this entry due to the damaged context of both the commentary and its base text. Instead of ILLU ("exudation, resin") suggested by Heeßel (2000: 273); Gadotti and Sigrist (2011: 153 no. 193), I opt to read *a-kal* ("bread"), which seems to fit the context of the patient's food and drink preferences at the end of Diagnostic Tablet 23. Note the writing *a-kal u* A URU$_4$-*e*[*š*] ("he requests bread and water") in VAT 10748, line 16′.

Commentary Sa-gig 29

Provenance:	Babylon or Borsippa
Period:	?
Names:	Not preserved
Script:	Neo-/Late Babylonian

Field/Museum No.:	BM 38375 = 80-11-12, 257 (British Museum)
Photos:	Plate 28a (obverse) and Plate 28b (reverse)
Printed Edition/Hand Copy:	Heeßel (2000: 323, 465); Wee (2012: 687–689)
Digital Resources:	CDLI 461169; CCP 4.1.29 (printed hand copy, photos, and edition digitized by Jiménez 2015)
Discussion:	Finkel (1988: 147 n. 29) and (1994: 87); Heeßel (2000: 136–137, 318 (29. Tafel MS a), 323, 465); Kinnier Wilson (2007: 65); Genty (2010b: 14, 20); Frahm (2011a: 227, 311); Wee (2012: 687–689)
Pericope:	At least Sa-gig 29: 1–16

Transliteration

Obverse

1) [DIŠ ^{d}LUGAL.Ù]R.RA KI.BI Ù.[TU]
2) [KI.B]I Ù.TU *it-ti-šú a-*⸢*lid*⸣
3) [$^{ša-ki}$]-⸢ri⸣. ^{u_2}ŠAKIR : *šá-ki-ru-ú*
4) [ZI : *na*]-*sa*(?)-*ḫu* : SÚD : *sa-a-ku*
5) [...] ⸢DÈ : *ṭi-ik*⸣-*me-ni*
6) [GAG.GA]G : *šá-pu-ú* : [I]M.SA$_5$
7) [*šar-š*]*ér-ú* : KUŠ ⸢ÙZ(?)⸣ : *ma-*⸢*šak*(?)⸣
8) [*en-zi* : NA]M.LÚ.U[$_{18}$.L]U TUR
9) [... *t*]*a-šar-rap*
10) [...] x x šu
11) [...] x

Reverse

1′) [...]x
2′) [...]x [...] šú
3′) [...]x [...] bad(?)
4′) [*ṣâtu u šu*]-*ut pi*-[*i* (x x)]
5′) [*šá* K]A(?) ⸤UM⸥.M[E.A (?)]

 | DOI:10.1163/9789004417564_026

Translation

Incipit-title of Sa-gig 29	(Obv. 1) "[If] ^{d}LUGAL.ÙR.RA (is) KI.BI Ù.TU."
Sa-gig 29: 1 Diagnoses that a malady "is born with him (the patient)" are not very common.	(2) "KI.BI Ù.TU" (means) (it) is born with him.
Sa-gig 29: 5	(3) "^{u_2}ŠAKIR" *means* the *šakirû* plant.
***Sa-gig 29: 5**	(4) ["ZI" *means*] to tear out.
Sa-gig 29: 5	(4) "SÚD" *means* to pound.
Sa-gig 29: 6	(5) ... "DÈ" *means* ashes.
Sa-gig 29: 12 (?)	(6) "GAG.GAG" *means* to wrap up.
Sa-gig 29: 16 (?)	(6–7) "IM.SA$_5$" (*means*) red paste.
Sa-gig 29: 14 (?)	(7–8) "KUŠ ÙZ(?)" (*means*) skin(?) of [goat].
***Sa-gig 29**	(8–9) "NAM.LÚ.U$_{18}$.LU TUR" ...
***Sa-gig 29**	(9) ... you shall burn.
***Sa-gig 29**	(10–11) ...
(Colophon)	(Rev. 1′–3′) ... (4′–5′) [Glossary including] oral lore [from] the mouth of the *ummânu*-scholar (?) ...

Notes

Obv. 1–2—Diagnoses that the patient has suffered from a malady since his birth are not particularly common, and most of them address babies who are sick. The logographic forms KI.BI Ù.TU are used at the base text Sa-gig 29: 1 and at Sa-gig 29: 22, but syllabic writing appears at Sa-gig 40: 110: ŠU.DINGIR.

RA-*ku* KI-*šú a-lid* ("Hand-of-god is born with him"). For sorcery targeting the baby since birth or infancy, note the statements "*šulḫû* of sorcery has been performed against him from his mother's womb" (Sa-gig 40: 19) and "*šulḫû* of sorcery has been performed against him in his mother's cradling arm" (Sa-gig 40: 16–17), which is also a topic in Comm. Sa-gig 40A, obv. 8.

Obv. 3—For other examples of commentarial glosses that explicate logographic values, see $^{\text{[din]ger [d]a-pa-ri}}$ GUD (obv. 4), $^{\text{[di-i]ḫ}}$ DIḪ (obv. 9), and possibly $^{\text{[mu-u]m-mu}}$ MU_7.MU_7-*um* (obv. 12) in Comm. Sa-gig 19.

Obv. 6–8—The commentary topics GAG.GAG (obv. 6), $IM.SA_5$ (obv. 6), and KUŠ ÙZ(?) (obv. 7) appear at Sa-gig 29: 12, 16, and 14 respectively in preserved copies of the base text, not in the sequential order we have come to expect from commentaries. Furthermore, there seems to be a considerable gap between the base text attestation of DÈ (obv. 5) at Sa-gig 29: 6 and GAG.GAG (obv. 6) at Sa-gig 29: 12. It is possible that some of the commentary topics in obv. 6–7 actually occurred earlier in unpreserved portions of the base text, so that their order of appearance in the commentary reflects that of their base text.

Rev. 4′—Most of the reverse of this commentary tablet is too damaged to meaningfully restore. The restoration [*ṣâtu u šu*]-*ut pi*-[*i* (x x)] is suggested by Frahm (2011a: 227).

Commentary Sa-gig 34

Provenance:	Uruk (Warka), Area U18, Level II or III; Library of Iqīšāya
Period:	Late Achaemenid–Early Hellenistic
Names:	"[Tablet of Iqīšāya, son of Ištar-šumu-ēreš], descendant of Ekur-zakir, the Urukean"
Script:	Neo-/Late Babylonian

Field/Museum No.:	W 22730/2 (National Museum of Iraq)
Printed Edition/Hand Copy:	*SpTU* II, 39 (= von Weiher 1983: 166–167)
Digital Resources:	CDLI P348644; GKAB P348644 (edition digitized by Clancier 2009); CCP 4.1.34 (printed hand copy and edition digitized by Jiménez 2015, with contributions by Clancier, Gabbay, and Schmidtchen)
Discussion:	*SpTU* II, 39 (= von Weiher 1983: 166–167); Farber (1987b: 30); Clancier (2009: 54–57, 73); Genty (2010a: 488); Frahm (2011a: 55 n. 245, 67 n. 317, 127–128 (categorized as a Šà-zi-ga commentary), 293); Gabbay (2016: 153 n. 123); Geller (2016: 175 nn. 1 and 3)
Pericope:	Indeterminate due to damaged state of available Sa-gig manuscripts

Transliteration

Obverse

1) [... : *šu-ru-up-pu*]-⸢*ú*⸣ *ḫur-ba-šú mu-na-áš-šìr nap-ḫar*
2) [*mim-ma šum-šú* : *šu-ru-up-pu*]-⸢*ú*⸣ : *ku-ṣi* : *nam-tar* DUMU *na-ra-am* ^{d}50
3) [*i-lit-ti* ^{d}*Ereš-ki-gal* : *i-gar-r*]*u-ur* : *ga-ra-ra* : *pa-la-ḫu*
4) [...] ⸢:⸣ *ki-is lìb-bi* : *ut-ta-ta-*⸢*al*(!)-*lil*⸣
5) [*ut-ta-al-lil* (?) : *um-ta-al-l*]*í* (?) *áš-šú ta-la-lu* : *ma-lu-ú* : *ú-zab-bal-ma*
6) [*i-kaš-ma* : ... : ...] ⌞ru⌟ : MÚŠ.ME-*šú* : *pa-ni-šú* : SAG :
7) [...]x : *lìb-bu-u* šà-maḫ šà-ta-ḫa-ri
8) [*e-sil-tu ṣe-me-er-tu* (?) : ...] be *ta-bal-lal* : LÙ.LÙ :
9) [*ba-la-lu* : LÙ.LÙ : *da-la-ḫu* : ...]x ⌞x x⌟ *ik-kab-ba-su* :
10) [...]x-*ba-ṭu*
11) [...]x

 | DOI:10.1163/9789004417564_027

Reverse

1′) [...] x ma

2′) [...]-⌈*ú*⌉ : *e*-x[...]-⌈*ú*⌉

3′) [...] ⌈nu⌉ : *du-ur* x x [...]-*šú*

4′) [... *ir-t*]*a-na-ḫaṣ* : *mar-ḫaṣ* : *nar*-⌈*ma*⌉-*ku*

5′) [... :] ⌈*i*⌉-*šá-as-sa-a* : *šul-bu-šú-šú*-⌈*ma*⌉

6′) [*ka-at-mu-šú-ma* : *šul-bu-šú* : *ka*]-*ta-mu* : NA.BI *ina kiš-pi du-um-ma*

7′) [... *di-im-tu* (?)] : *di-im-mat* : *da-ma-ma*

8′) [*ṣa-a-tú u šu-ut* KA *šá* KA *um-man*]-*nu šá* ŠÀ DIŠ NA *ana* MUNUS-*šú* ŠÀ-*šú* ÍL-*šú-ma*

9′) [IM ^{m}BA-*šá-a* bu_{12}-*kúr* $^{\mathrm{m.d}}$INNIN–MU–KAM ŠÀ.BAL].⌈BAL⌉ ^{m}É.KUR–*za-kir* UNUG^{ki}-*ú*

Translation

***Sa-gig 34**
This quotation is from the incantation series *Utukkū Lemnūtu* V, 1. "Frost" is defined as "coldness," which together with "chill" are attested elsewhere as medical conditions.

(Obv. 1–2) ... "[Frost] (and) chill that deplete everything whatsoever."
(2) ["Frost"] *refers to* coldness.

***Sa-gig 34**
This quotation is from the incantation series *Utukkū Lemnūtu* V, 3 and may validate or put forth Namtar or Ereškigal as the agent of sickness in the base text.

(2–3) "Namtar, beloved son of the god Enlil, [offspring of the goddess Ereškigal]."

***Sa-gig 34**
igarrur "he becomes scared" derives from the verb *garāru* "to become scared," not the homophone *garāru* "to roll, dribble, writhe" that is more common in medical texts.

(3) ["*igarrur*"] *derives from the dictionary root* to become scared, *which means* to become frightened.

***Sa-gig 34**
The sickness *kīs libbi*, lit. "trammeling of the belly," which is provided as

(4) ... *refers to kīs libbi* sickness.

comment here, seems absent so far from the Diagnostic Handbook but is common in therapeutic texts.

***Sa-gig 34**
The Dt(n) Perfect verb *uttatallil* in the base text is implied to mean "it has been filled," with *talālu* (of uncertain meaning) as its dictionary root.

(4) "*uttatallil*."
(5) [*uttallil means* it has filled (?)],
(5) because *the dictionary root talālu means* to become full.

***Sa-gig 34**
The basic meaning of *zubbulu* is "to carry, deliver," but it can mean "to carry on," i.e., "to tarry on" in the context of sickness.

(5–6) "It will carry on" (*means*) [it will tarry on.] ...

***Sa-gig 34**
Medical texts almost always refer to the "face" as IGI.MEŠ, and rarely as MÚŠ.(ME).

(6) "His MÚŠ.ME" *refers to* his face.

***Sa-gig 34**

(6–7) "SAG" *refers to* ...

***Sa-gig 34**
This quotation comes from the Standard Babylonian *List of Diseases* 66 (246)–67 (247) (*MSL* IX, 93), or from a parallel tradition (*CT* 4, 3 obv. 11).

(7–8) ... As in, "šà-maḫ (*and*) šà-ta-ḫa-ri (*refer to*) [constipation (*and*) distension *respectively*." (?)]

***Sa-gig 34**

(8) "You shall mix ..."
(8–9) LÙ.LÙ *means* [to mix].
(9) [LÙ.LÙ *means* to stir up.]

***Sa-gig 34**

(9–10) "They begin / tend to tread ..." *means* ...
(10–11) ...

***Sa-gig 34**
irtanaḫḫaṣ should be understood as "he keeps rinsing himself," from the dictionary root *raḫāṣu* "to rinse," and not from homophones meaning "to trample, destroy" or "to trust."

(Rev. 1′–4′) ...
(4′) "He (keeps performing the action of) *irtanaḫḫaṣ*" *refers to* rinsing, *which refers to* bathing.

***Sa-gig 34**

(5′) ... [*means*] they call out.

***Sa-gig 34**

(5′–6′) "They are clothed for him" *means* [they are covered for him.]
(6′) [To clothe *means*] to cover.

***Sa-gig 34**
The commentator seems to have connected verbs of different dictionary roots—*dummâ* and "to mourn" (*damāmu*), by using as intermediaries the nouns "weeping" (*dīmtu*) and "mourning" (*dimmatu*).

(6′) "That man is *dummâ* by sorcery."
(7′) ... [weeping (*dīmtu*) (?)] *refers to* mourning (*dimmatu*), *which derives from the dictionary root* to mourn (*damāmu*).

(Colophon)

Incipit-title of Sa-gig 34

(8′) [Glossary including oral lore from the mouth of the *ummânu*-scholar] on the contents of "If a man's heart is aroused for his woman."

(9′) [Tablet of Iqīšāya, son of Ištar-šumu-ēreš], descendant of Ekur-zakir, the Urukean.

Notes

Obv. 1–2—The quotations from the incantation series *Utukkū Lemnūtu* V, 1 and 3 (in obv. 1–3) were earlier recognized by von Weiher (*SpTU* II, 39) and Frahm (2011a: 128). *Utukkū Lemnūtu* V, 1 (Geller 2016: 175; cf. Geller 2007a: 118, 208) was cited perhaps to associate the terms *kūṣ* / *kuṣṣu* ("coldness") and *ḫurbāšu* ("chill"), both of which are attested elsewhere as medical signs.

Between the two, "chill" seems to be one more confined to therapeutic texts, but both appear as commentarial explanations in Comm. Sa-gig 7B, rev. 1′; Comm. Sa-gig 19, obv. 19; and perhaps Comm. Sa-gig 21 & 22a, rev. 9′. The restoration [*mim-ma šum-šú* : *šu-ru-up-pu*]-⌜*ú*⌝ (obv. 2) assumes space for around 9 or 10 cuneiform signs in the broken beginnings of obv. 1–5, an assumption that seems consistent also in other reasonably restored readings [*i-lit-ti* ᵈ*Ereš-ki-gal* : *i-gar-r*]*u-ur* (obv. 3) and [*ut-ta-al-lil* : *um-ta-al-l*]*í* (?) (obv. 5).

Obv. 2–3—This quotation from *Utukkū Lemnūtu* v, 3 (Geller 2016: 175; cf. Geller 2007a: 118, 208) lies very near to that from *Utukkū Lemnūtu* v, 1 (in obv. 1–2), and both were likely cited in reference to the same Sa-gig entry in the base text. Here, the motivation may have been to validate or put forth as agents of the ailment being described: Namtar (cf. Sa-gig 15: 4′; 22: 39b; [29: 60′]; 33: 114) or the goddess Ereškigal (cf. Sa-gig 13: 38 (TDPT 13 i 39′); *BAM* 214 i 9; and probably Sa-gig [4: 44] = base text of Comm. Sa-gig 4A, obv. x+2′).

Obv. 3—See Note on a similar argument made in Comm. Sa-gig 19, obv. 11: [*ig-d*]*a-nar-ru-ru* : *ip-ta-na-a*[*l-l*]*a-*[*ḫu*] ("'*igdanarrurū*' *means* they keep becoming frightened").

Obv. 4—The intestinal sickness *kīs libbi* (lit. "trammeling of the belly") functions as the comment to a damaged topic, since what immediately follows (i.e., *ut-ta-ta-*⌜*al*(!)*-lil*⌝) represents another topic to a separate commentary entry. The expression *kīs libbi* does not seem to be attested so far in the Diagnostic Handbook, but appears commonly in therapeutic texts at *BAM* 159 v 35; 574 i 1, 4, 11, 21, [26]; ii 28, 33, 43; *AMT* [39/5: 4′, 6′]; 58/5: 9′.

Obv. 4–5—The reading UD-*ta-ta-az*(?)-*ziq*(?) (< *nazāqu* "to worry, be upset"?) by von Weiher (*SpTU* II, 39 obv. 4) was modified to *ut-ta-ta-*⌜*aḫ*(!)*-ḫáš*(ziq) (?)⌝ ("he has been granted prosperity"; Dt Perfect of *naḫāšu*) by Jiménez (CCP 4.1.34). I understand these signs as *ut-ta-ta-*⌜*al*(!)*-lil*⌝ (obv. 4), the Dt(n) Perfect of *talālu*, which would explain the existence of the dictionary root *talālu* in the very next line (obv. 5) where it is equated with *malû* ("to become full"). The tentative restoration [*ut-ta-al-lil* (?) : *um-ta-al-l*]*í* (?) (obv. 5) compares D stem versions of the two roots, and takes into account space for around 9 or 10 cuneiform signs in the broken beginning of the line (see Note on obv. 1–2 above). To be sure, however, the Dt(n) stem of *talālu* is not clearly recognized by the dictionaries, and even the meaning of its G stem in medical contexts is not entirely certain: "1. to draw a bow, to stiffen(?). 2. (uncert. mng.)" (*CAD* T, 91–92); "hinstrecken" (*AHw*, 1309).

Obv. 5–6—See Note on Comm. Sa-gig 1B, obv. 10′–11′ for *zubbulu* ("to carry on (said of a sick person or sickness)") as derivative of the basic meaning "to carry, deliver" and its attestations in medical texts, as well as *kâšu* ("to tarry on") as the preferred explanation in several commentaries. The latter accounts for my restored comment [*i-kaš-ma*] "[it will tarry on]") at the beginning of obv. 6.

Obv. 6—In the medical literature, the "face" (*pānū*) is almost always denoted by the logogram IGI.ME(Š), and only rarely by MÚŠ.(MEŠ) in Sa-gig 14: 186′–187′ (TDPT 14 iii 53′–54′); *BAM* 578 i 29. Observe that a therapeutic entry addresses *pa-nu* (*BAM* 578 i 28) as well as MÚŠ.MEŠ (*BAM* 578 i 29) in the same description of the patient, so the two terms were not precisely synonymous.

Obv. 7–8—The main argument to this commentary entry lies in the damaged beginning of obv. 7. This is subsequently followed by a supporting quotation either from the Standard Babylonian *List of Diseases*, 66 (246)–67 (247): šà-maḫ = *e-sil-tu*, šà-ta-ḫa-ar-gig = *ṣe-me-er-tu* (*MSL* IX, 93); or from a parallel tradition such as šà-maḫ šà-ta-ḫa-ar-gi$_4$ … = [*e-sil*]-*tu ṣi-mir*-[*tu* …] (*CT* 4, 3 obv. 11 // Sm 28 in Falkenstein 1931b: 94; cf. *MSL* IX, 106). The writing šà-ta-ḫa-ri in this commentary differs slightly from forms elsewhere. Though I restore syllabic labels (obv. 8) that correspond to the logographic ones (obv. 7), it is possible that only the logographic forms were cited, and that space in the damaged beginning of obv. 8 should be assigned instead to a fresh commentary entry.

Obv. 8–9—*ta-bal-lal*, "You shall mix" (obv. 8) appears very commonly in therapeutic instructions for the preparation of *materia medica* (cf. Böck 2009a: 114). The verb is typically expressed in therapeutic texts using the logogram ḪE.ḪE, instead of LÙ.LÙ here. The choice of the latter must have been intended to link *balālu* ("to mix") with another verb *dalāḫu* ("to stir up") for reasons that are not quite transparent. As a medical sign (rather than therapeutic instruction), *balālu* occurs only a few times in the Diagnostic Handbook (Sa-gig 6: 24; 18: 20; 37: 9 (TDPT 36: 9)), while *dalāḫu* is much more broadly attested in both diagnostic and therapeutic texts (Sa-gig 40: 20, 24, 35, 46–47, 55, 83, 103; *BAM* 214 i 5; 228: 26; 229 obv. 20′; 231 i 3; 232 i 20′; 323: 91; [449 iii 13′]; [455 iii 4′]; 510 iv 10; 522: 6′ (incl. *AMT* 10/4: 5′); *AMT* 12/4: 1; 12/7: 5′). See Note on Comm. Sa-gig 1–3, line 35 for objections to the restoration *i*[*t-ta-na-ad-là*]*ḫ* (Sa-gig 3: 41 (TDPT 3: 32)) by Scurlock (2014: 14).

Obv. 9–10—The term *ik-kab-ba-su* (obv. 9) is understood to be the N stem of *kabāsu* used in the ingressive sense—i.e., "to *begin / tend to* tread" (cf. *CAD* K, 11 s.v. *kabāsu* §8). The ingressive or tendential use of *kabāsu* may be found also in Comm. Sa-gig 36, rev. 3′–4′.

Rev. 4′—While it is easy to connect the base text verb *irtanaḫḫaṣ* to the dictionary root *raḫāṣu*, the commentator needed to differentiate between the many homophones of *raḫāṣu*: "to trample, kick, destroy, devastate" (*CAD* R,

69–72); "to wash, bathe, soak" (*CAD* R, 72–74); "to trust, rely" (*CAD* R, 74–75); and "to gather(?)" (*CAD* R, 75). He did so by providing, as explanation, a cognate noun with an unconfusable meaning (i.e., *marḫaṣu*, "rinsing"), followed by its synonym *narmaku* ("bathing").

Rev. 5′–6′—Instead of the dictionary root *šul-bu-šú* ⌈x x⌉ ("to clothe"; rev. 5′) by Jiménez (CCP 4.1.34), this item evidently begins a new commentary entry and therefore represents an inflected form cited as topic, which I restore as *šul-bu-šú-šú-*⌈*ma*⌉ (rev. 5′) and translate "they are clothed for him" (Š Stative 3mp of *labāšu*, with an ethical dative *-šu*(*m*) suffix and *-ma* conjunction). Moreover, my restoration [*ka*]*-ta-mu* (rev. 6′) and the argument linking it with *šulbušu* ("to clothe") is supported by well-attested meanings of *katāmu* involving "covering with garments, etc." (*CAD* K, 299 s.v. *katāmu* §1a).

Rev. 6′–7′—The writing *du-um-ma* (rev. 6′) is probably best understood as *dummâ* = *dummu-* (D Stative verb) + *-a* (ventive). The dictionaries supply two possibilities of what this verb might be: (I) *damû*/*ṭamû* ("to stagger (about)") in *CAD* D, 80 s.v. *damû*; *AHw*, 166 s.v. *dawûm*; see also Note on Comm. Sa-gig 1–3 (obv. 31) where *damû* seems not to be attested in therapeutic texts, but appears very commonly in the G stem in the Diagnostic Handbook. (II) *dummû*, which is defined as "weinend halten" in *AHw*, 176; "to bring to tears" in *CDA*; but considered of uncertain meaning in *CAD* D, 179, which rejects any proposal to connect it to *damāmu* ("to mourn"). Here in this tablet, the commentator seems to have connected *dummâ* and "to mourn" (*damāmu*)—despite their different dictionary roots—by using as intermediaries the nouns ["weeping" (*dīmtu*)] and "mourning" (*dimmatu*). Notice that the commentator dismissed the choice of a verb (*damû*, "to stagger (about)") ubiquitous in the Diagnostic Handbook but not in therapeutic texts, in favor of an option that is attested elsewhere only in the therapeutic entry *BAM* 316 iv 3–4 and its duplicates/variants: NINDA NU GU_7 A/KAŠ NU NAG *i-dam-mu-um* ("he eats no bread (and) drinks no water/beer, (and) he mourns").

Rev. 8′—The base text title cited in this colophon led to earlier definitions of this tablet as a Šà-zi-ga commentary by von Weiher (*SpTU* II, 39); Frahm (2011a: 55 n. 245, 67 n. 314, 127–128, 293). Schmidtchen (CCP 4.1.34), however, identified it as the incipit-title to Sa-gig Tablet 34, which is so far preserved in only a single base text exemplar BM 33357.

Commentary Sa-gig 36

Provenance:	Uruk (Warka), Area U18, Level v; Same findspot and consignment (W 22307) as Comm. Sa-gig 1C, 5, 7A, 7B, and 19 suggests library of Anu-ikṣur
Period:	Late Achaemenid
Names:	"*Imgida*-tablet of Šamaš-aḫa-iddin, son of Ištar-…"
Script:	Neo-/Late Babylonian
Field/Museum No.:	W 22307/23+74 (National Museum of Iraq)
Photo:	Plate 29 (reverse)
Printed Edition/Hand Copy:	*SpTU* I, 39 (= Hunger 1976: 48); Wee (2012: 690–695)
Digital Resources:	CDLI P348460; GKAB P348460 (edition digitized by Clancier 2009); CCP 4.1.36 (printed hand copy digitized by Frahm, Frazer, and Jiménez 2013)
Discussion:	*SpTU* I, 39 (= Hunger 1976: 48); Heeßel (2000: 95–96 n. 103; 137, 146 (36. Tafel MS a)); Scurlock and Andersen (2005: 260 n. 4); Clancier (2009: 64, 388); Geller (2010a: 196 n. 204); Genty (2010a: 384) and (2010b: 14, 16, 26–27); Frahm (2011a: 228, 291, 315 n. 1500); Wee (2012: 690–695) and (2017: 240); Steinert (2018: 275); Schmidtchen (2018: 327 n. 40)
Pericope:	At least Sa-gig 36: 94–99 (TDPT 35: 94–99)

Transliteration

Reverse

1′) [… -*u*]*s*(?) : *šá* S[AG(?) …]

2′) […] *šu*(?) : *i le* x[…]

3′) *ina* ŠÀ *ma-ru-uṣ-ti-šú* : x[… ZUKU]M(?)

4′) *ik-ka-ba*!(zu)-*sa*!(ta) (?) : GÌR.2-*šú* DU[GUD : *šá ana da-k*]*e-e*

5′) *dan-na-áš-šú* : MUNUS GÌR-*šú* TUR [: *ṣe-eḫ-ra* :] *qal-la-la*

6′) *sa-gu-u* : *da-mu a*[*r-da*]-*tu*$_4$: SA [: *d*]*a-mu* : gi

7′) *ar-da-tu*$_4$: *ša na-*[*aḫ-š*]*á-a-tú* GIG-*át*

 | DOI:10.1163/9789004417564_028

8′) MUNUS *šá ina me-re-e-šú da-mu i-ta-nam-ma-ru*
9′) SA.GIG : *ri-[kis m]ur-ṣu* : *nap-ḫar mu[r-ṣ]u*
10′) gul-la : gú [: g]ú-sa-a : ki-šá-ra :
11′) *kul-lat* : *na-[ga]b* : *nap-ḫar* : *kiš-šat* : gú-sa-a
12′) gú : *nap-ḫar* : sa : [*n*]*ap-ḫa-rù*

13′) D[I]Š MUNUS.PEŠ$_4$ GIG-*ma šum-ma šá* ITI.3.KAM *ir-ṭú-pu-niš-ši*
14′) IM.GÍD.DA $^{m.d}$20-PAP-MU DUMU.A.NI $^{m.d}$KÁR.ŠUL-⸢x⸣-[...]
15′) *pa-liḫ* ^{d}60 *u* $^{d+}$INNIN NU TÙM *ina* ITI-*šú ana* UMUN-*šú* GUR-[*šú*]

Translation

(Rev. 1′–2′) ...

Sa-gig 36: 94 (TDPT 35: 94)

(3′) "In the midst of her difficulty" *means* ...

***Sa-gig 36: 94 (TDPT 35: 94)—"she tends to tread (ZUKUM-*as*) towards the right side"**

(3′–4′) ["ZUKUM" (?)] (*means*) she tends to tread (?).

Sa-gig 36: 96 (TDPT 35: 96)
"Heavy" does not refer to the objective weight of the feet, but the patient's subjective difficulty in lifting the feet.

(4′–5′) "Her feet are heavy" [*refers to* the case where] they are (too) difficult for her [to rouse].

Sa-gig 36: 99 (TDPT 35: 99)
The sign TUR ("small") is perhaps not to be confused with DUMU ("son"), despite the base text's theme of female reproduction.

(5′) "The woman's feet (lit. foot) (are) TUR" [*means* they are small, *which means*] they are little.

***Sa-gig 36: 100 (TDPT 35: 100) —šà-ku**
The signs šà-ku in available Sa-gig manuscripts were understood by the commentator as *sagû* "flow of blood (?)," which was then analyzed as SA + GI.

(6′) *sagû refers to* the blood of a young woman.

This equation is attested in lexical texts, possibly alluding to bodily "strands" (SA) as "blood" vessels.

(6′) SA [*means*] blood.

gi means "young woman" in the Emesal dialect.

(6′–7′) gi (*means*) young woman, *which refers to*

Quote from **Sa-gig 36: 108 (TDPT 35: 108)**. "Haemorrhage" refers to menstrual bleeding in this context.

(7′) one who is sick from haemorrhage,
(8′) (*or*) the woman during whose pregnancy blood keeps appearing.

***Sa-gig 36 (TDPT 35)**
The above analysis SA + GI naturally recalls the title of the Diagnostic Handbook: SA.GIG.

An effort to make the title of the Diagnostic Handbook SA.GIG conform to its definition in *Esagil-kīn-apli's Manifesto* as "a bundling together (SA) of sickness (GIG)," i.e., a compilation on "all (SA) sickness (GIG)."

(9′) SA.GIG *refers to* the bundling together of sickness, *which refers to* all sickness.

In order to prove that SA means "all," the lexical text Erimhuš v, 43–46 is quoted. Each of the eight terms cited means "all."

(10′–11′) "gul-la, gú, gú-sa-a, *and* ki-šá-ra *mean* all (*kullat*), all (*nagab*), all (*napḫar*), *and* all (*kiššat*) *respectively*."

gú-sa-a is analyzed as gú + sa.

(11′) "gú-sa-a" (*consists of*)

Since the addition of sa to gú "all" does not affect the meaning of gú-sa-a "all," the element sa must also mean "all."

(12′) gú, *which means* all, *and*

(12′) sa, *which means* all.

(Colophon)

Incipit-title of Sa-gig 37 (TDPT 36)	(13′) "If a pregnant woman is sick, and if one engages in sexual intercourse with her in (her) third month."
	(14′) *Imgida*-tablet of Šamaš-aḫa-iddin, son of Ištar-…
	(15′) He who fears Anu and Ištar must not carry off (this tablet). May he return [it] in the same month to its owner!

Notes

Intro—Our four commentaries on Sa-gig Chapter VI (i.e., Comm. Sa-gig 36, 39, 40A, and 40B) mainly employ masculine pronominal suffixes. No manuscripts of Sa-gig Tablet 39 are available to us, and the masculine suffixes in Comm. Sa-gig 40A and 40B evidently refer to the woman's newborn baby or infant. At least in Comm. Sa-gig 36, however, it is clear that the masculine suffixes correspond to feminine suffixes in preserved copies of the diagnostic tablet Sa-gig 36 (TDPT 35), which deals with bodily conditions and actions of a pregnant woman. Moreover, the phrase MUNUS GÌR-*šú* (rev. 5′) with its masculine suffix in this commentary must be understood as "the woman's feet (lit. foot)." I accordingly translate the Akkadian masculine suffixes here into English feminine pronouns: "she" and "her." It is possible, however, that the commentator's use of masculine suffixes may have been intentional, reflecting his view that (at least some) explanations were applicable to both male and female patients.

Rev. 3′—Judging by Labat's hand copy (pl. LV, line 92), there is a major typo in the signs transliterated for line Sa-gig 36: 92 (TDPT 35: 92), but Labat's French translation of this line does reflect the reading in the hand copy (pp. 208–209). The first attestation of the phrase *ina* ŠÀ *ma-ru-uš-ti-šá* is in Sa-gig 36: 94 (TDPT 35: 94). This phrase, as it applies to women, has been understood to mean "in her menstrual period" by Stol (2000: 26).

Rev. 3′–4′—There is much to be dissatisfied with about the emended reading [… ZUKU]M(?) / *ik-ka-ba*!(zu)-*sa*!(ta) (?), which is only tentatively suggested here in view of the fact that the logogram ZUKUM (Sa-gig 36: 96 (TDPT 35: 96)) is the only item between *ina* ŠÀ *maruštīša* (Sa-gig 36: 94

(TDPT 35: 94)) and GÌR-*šá* DUGUD-*at* (Sa-gig 36: 96 (TDPT 35: 96)) in the base text that actually warrants comment. According to this emendation, the comment *ikkabbasa* represents the N Durative 3cs of *kabāsu* ("to tread, trample") with the female patient as subject + the ventive marker. As in Comm. Sa-gig 34 (obv. 9), the N stem is used in the ingressive sense (i.e., "she begins to tread"), which shades into a tendential meaning (i.e., "she makes as if to tread" or "she tends to tread").

Rev. 4′–5′—My restoration [*šá ana da-k*]*e-e dan-na-áš-šú* is based on a parallel turn of phrase in Comm. Sa-gig 39, obv. 10: *šá ana da-ke-e u šá-ka-nu dan-na-niš-šú*. The form *dan-na-áš-šú* (= *dannāšu*) is the G Stative 3fp of the verb *danānu* with the 3ms dative suffix (-*šu*(*m*)), while the parallel expression *dan-na-niš-šú* (= *dannāniššu*) in Comm. Sa-gig 39 includes the ventive (-*nim*) before the suffix. A similar idea about the patient's difficulties in raising his/her thighs or feet may be expressed in *StBoT* XXXVI, p. 60 (Fragment H line 1): [GÌR.MEŠ(?)-*š*]*ú ana našê kabtā*. Note also the expression KA-*šú ana awâti da-an*, "his mouth is difficult for words (i.e., it is too difficult for his mouth to speak)" in Sa-gig 17: 57, as well as in Sa-gig 3: 50 (TDPT 3: 41) (base text for Comm. Sa-gig 3B, rev. 1) where the Stative verb is written *da-a-an*.

Rev. 5′—The logographic readings here are MUNUS (or MÍ) GÌR-*šú*, not *sinništu*(MI) *šēp*(GIR)-*šú* (rev. 5′) as rendered by the typo in the printed edition *SpTU* I, 39. The singular form of GÌR ("foot") here differs from the dual GÌR.2 ("feet") in preserved manuscripts of Sa-gig 36: 99 (TDPT 35: 99). The commentator, however, seems to have understood the subject as dual (i.e., feet), as evident from the choice of plural forms in his comment: *qallalā* ("they are little") and probably [*ṣeḫrā*] ("they are small").

Rev. 6′—While the commentator seems to have interpreted the signs šà-ku as *sagû* (*CAD* S, 27 s.v. *sagû* B "flow of blood (?)"), it is unusual that he does not first cite the original form šà-ku depicted in preserved Sa-gig manuscripts of Sa-gig 36: 100 (TDPT 35: 100). There is always the possibility that the commentator worked with a base text manuscript (unavailable to us) that read *sa-gu-u* instead of the difficult expression šà-ku. For the suggestion that šà-ku may be read šà-sur_{11} = *šassūru*? ("womb"), see Scurlock and Andersen (2005: 259, §12.2 and §12.3); Frahm (2011a: 228). Note also the lexical equation: $^{su-ur}$ku = MIN (= *tu-kul-lum*) = *šá* ŠÀ+TÙR *šá-as-su-ru* (Ea I, 148 in *MSL* XIV, 184).

Rev. 6′—SA as the logogram for *damu* occurs in the lexical text Nigga, 298 (*MSL* XIII, 104; previously reconstructed as A-Tablet, 668) and the SB Recension of the *List of Diseases*, line 156 (216) (*MSL* IX, 95). Perhaps the interpretation of the "strand" (SA) as a "blood" vessel underlies the lexical equation SA =

da-mu. For contexts in which a "strand" (SA) refers to a blood-filled vein, see Oppenheim (1962: 27–33).

Rev. 6′–8′—The sign gi or gi_4 expresses the term "young woman" (*ardatu*) in various bilingual texts (*CAD* A II, 242), while the argument "gi *means* female" (gi : *sin-niš-tim*) appears in the Nippur Therapeutic Comm. 11N-T3, line 8 (Civil 1974: 323). But note the lexical equation gi-e = K[I.SIKIL] = [*ar-da-tu*] in Emesal Voc. II, 71 (*MSL* IV, 17), where the additional element -e may represent the ergative marker. The term *naḫšātu* ("haemorrhage") in line 7′ can refer to menstrual bleeding, which disqualified a woman from participation in ritual sacrifice (*CAD* N I, 141–142 s.v. *naḫšātu* §a). The expression *ša na-*[*aḫ-š*]*á-a-tú* GIG-*át* was likely cited from the commentator's base text of Sa-gig 36: 108 (TDPT 35: 108), though available Sa-gig manuscripts seem to contain the signs *ša na-aḫ-šá-ti* G[IG] (collated in Scurlock and Andersen 2005: 267, §12.41; 731 n. 40; Scurlock 2014: 248). The term *naḫšātu* also appears in the pharmacological list *BAM* 381 iii 24 and numerous times in the therapeutic tablet *BAM* 237.

Rev. 9′—The impetus for discussing the title SA.GIG is its resemblance to the terms SA and GI, as well as *sagû*, in the preceding lines. See Note on Comm. Sa-gig 1A, line 47 for how commentators made the title of the Diagnostic Handbook SA.GIG conform to its definition in *Esagil-kīn-apli's Manifesto* as a "bundling together (SA) of sickness (GIG)," i.e., a comprehensive compilation that included "all (SA) sickness (GIG)." In the base text of this commentary, the title SA.GIG appears in the colophon at the end of Sa-gig Tablet 36 (cf. TDPT 35: 117), and it seems fitting as well that the commentator should have concluded his tablet by addressing this term. One might also wonder about the intended purpose of linking the obscure term *sagû* with the definition "all sickness." In Greco-Roman medicine, for example, theories of womb behavior exerted disproportional influence over explanations of female pathology. Is the feature designated as *sagû*, with its connection to menstrual bleeding, likewise implied to be a primary indicator of female health?

Rev. 10′–11′—The definition of SA.GIG as "all sickness" (line 9′) implies the analysis of its components as SA "all" + GIG "sickness." Lines 10′–12′ serve to demonstrate that the element SA can indeed mean "all." Hunger (*SpTU* I, 39) suggested the reading gú-[gú(?)]-sa-a (rev. 10′). However, I restore these lines differently, in recognition of the fact that they constitute a quotation from the lexical text Erimhuš V, 43–46 (*MSL* XVII, 68): gul-la = *kul-la-tum*, ^{gu}gú = *na-ag-bu*, gú-$^{di-ir}$ dir = *nap-ḫa-ri*, ki-šár-ra = *kiš-šá-tum*. There are minor differences in the lexical forms recorded in this commentary, which employs indeclinable forms of the Akkadian words (e.g., *nagab* instead of *nagbu*).

More importantly, what seems to be the original reading gú-$^{\text{di-ir}}$ dir(= si.a) (𒄘 𒁲 𒅕 𒋛𒀀) has been misconstrued, perhaps with the components ir (𒅕) + si (𒋛) corrupted as the sign sa (𒊓) and the sign di interpreted as the pronunciation gloss sá, resulting in the reading gú-$^{\text{sa}_2}$ sa-a (𒄘 𒁲 𒊓 𒀀), which became simplified as gú-sa-a. Notice that the lexical reading ^{gu} gú in Erimhuš v, 44 likewise appears without its pronunciation gloss ^{gu} in the commentary citation. If my interpretation is correct, it is ironic that the corrupted reading gú-sa-a was precisely what made this lexical section relevant to the commentator, who intended to argue that sa means "all."

Rev. 11′–12′—The form gú-sa-a is analyzed here as gú + sa. In the Erimhuš citation above, gú was already shown to have the meaning "all" (*nagab*). The commentator probably reasoned that, since the notion "all" is conceptually indivisible, and the addition of sa to gú ("all") does not affect the meaning of gú-sa-a ("all"), it goes to show that the element sa also means "all." The logic employed here is similar to the one in Comm. Sa-gig 39 (obv. 2–4), where the components of SAG.GIŠ.RA ("to smite" < "to strike with a weapon") are analyzed as sag ("weapon") + GIŠ ("weapon") + RA ("to strike"). The fact that sag and GIŠ repeat the same meaning ("weapon") was not considered deleterious to the overall sense of SAG.GIŠ.RA.

Rev. 13′—The cuneiform sign, which Hunger (*SpTU* I, 39) transliterated KÁM here, is the same one that he transliterated as KAM in *SpTU* I, 32 rev. 12 and 36 rev. 6. I prefer the transliteration KAM, in accordance with *MZL*, no. 595.

Rev. 14′—For ^{d}KÁR.ŠUL as cryptographic writing for the goddess Ištar, note the lexical equations: ^{d}Kár $^{\text{ka-la-su-ul}}$ -šul = ^{d}*in-ni-na* (Erimhuš v, 4 in MSL XVII, 67); ^{d}Kar-šul = MIN (= ^{d}*Iš-tar*) *šá qar-ra-a-di* (An = *Anu ša amēli*, 87 in Litke 1998: 234) and the discussion in Lambert (1977b: 408); Frahm (2011a: 228 n. 1061).

Commentary Sa-gig 39

Provenance:	Uruk (Warka), Area U18, Level v; Close relation to findspot and consignment (W 22307) of Comm. Sa-gig 1C, 5, 7A, 7B, and 19 suggests library of Anu-ikṣur (Clancier 2009: 388)
Period:	Late Achaemenid
Names:	Not preserved
Script:	Neo-/Late Babylonian
Field/Museum No.:	W 22311 (National Museum of Iraq)
Photo:	Plate 30 (obverse)
Printed Edition/Hand Copy:	*SpTU* 1, 40 (= Hunger 1976: 48–49); Wee (2012: 696–702)
Digital Resources:	CDLI P348461; GKAB P348461 (edition digitized by Clancier 2009); CCP 4.1.39 (printed hand copy digitized by Frahm, Frazer, and Jiménez 2013)
Discussion:	Hunger (1975: 68) and *SpTU* 1, 40 (= Hunger 1976: 48–49); Heeßel (2000: 137, 146 (39. Tafel MS a) with typo "SpTU 1/39"); Fincke (2000: 155, 159, 163, 165, 183, 232); Scurlock and Andersen (2005: 199, §9.76); Clancier (2009: 388); Geller (2010a: 145, 195 n. 192, 196 n. 202); Genty (2010a: 383) and (2010b: 14, 19, 25, 28, 29); Frahm (2011a: 66, 228–229, 291); Wee (2012: 696–702); Scurlock (2014: 185 n. 8; 257 n. 1 under DPS 39); Gabbay (2016: 68 n. 285, 74 n. 323, 77 n. 336, 107 n. 128, 109 n. 134, 229 n. 120); Panayotov (2017: 238 n. 100)
Pericope:	Part of Sa-gig Tablet 39 that is unpreserved in available manuscripts

Transliteration

Obverse

1) DIŠ MUNUS *ḫa-riš-ti i-di-ip u i-geš-šú* BA.ÚŠ
2) *ši-bit* SAG.DU-*šú nu-uḫ*$_5$-*ḫu-rat* : SAG.GIŠ.RA
3) *nu-ú-ú-ru* : sag : *kak-ku* : GIŠ : *kak-ku*
4) RA : *ma-ḫa-ṣu šá-niš* RA : *na-a-ra* : RA : *ma-ḫa-ṣu*

 | DOI:10.1163/9789004417564_029

5) *šal-šiš* GAZ : *na-a-ra* : GAZ : *ḫé-pu-u*
6) *né-ʾi-ir* SAG.DU *ma-ḫi-iṣ muḫ-ḫi* : *ki ši-gu-ú*
7) *al-si-ka* : *pe-ret* SAG.DU-*šú sa-mat* : *sa-ma-ta*
8) *sa-ap-ḫa-at* : *ka-ra-an* IGI.2-*šú šad-du*
9) *šá kak-kul-tu*$_4$ *i-ni-šú ú-ṣa-a* : ÚR-*šú ta-a-ka*
10) *šá ana da-ke-e u šá-ka-nu dan-na-niš-šú*
11) *šá ši-kin-ni* NU *iš-nu-ú* : ka-*šú ṣa-pir* ÚŠ
12) *ṣa-pa-ru* : *kub-bu-lu*$_4$: *ṣa-pa-ru* : *ṣu-un-du-ru*
13) *ṣa-pa-ru* : *la ta-ra-ṣu* : SA : *šér-a-ni*

Reverse
1′) x [...]
2′) x [...]
3′) i x [...]
4′) *šá* x [...]

5′) x [...]
(Remainder broken)

Translation

Incipit-title of Sa-gig 39

(Obv. 1) "If a woman in confinement is inflated and belches, she will die."

***Sa-gig 39**
Though *nuḫḫurat* seems to be the D stem of the obscure verb *naḫāru*, the commentator understood the form as *nuʾʾurat*, the D stem of *nêru* "to smite."

(2) "The seam of his head (is) *nuḫḫurat*."

Argument #1: Analysis of Logogram
nêru "to smite" is unattested as a medical sign, and its logogram SAG.GIŠ.RA is analyzed as sag + GIŠ + RA

(2–3) SAG.GIŠ.RA (*means*) to smite.

The common equation "SAG *means* head" would show that *nêru* "to smite" relates to the head. But the

(3) sag *means* weapon.

commentator wanted sag to do double duty: Because SAG.DU means "head" (*qaqqa-du*), the element sag may be thought to represent /*qaqqa*/, which sounds like *kakka* "weapon."

^{giš}TUKUL is the usual logogram for "weapon," but GIŠ alone performs this function in some lexical texts.

(3) GIŠ *means* weapon.

Common lexical equation

(4) RA *means* to strike.

Argument #2:
Range of Meanings for RA
RA means "to smite," as implied by its other similar meaning "to strike."

(4) Secondly, RA *means* to smite,
or
(4) RA *means* to strike.

Argument #3:
Range of Meanings for GAZ
GAZ means "to smite," as implied by its other similar meaning "to break."

(5) Thirdly, GAZ *means* to smite,
or
(5) GAZ *means* to break.

The antagonist in *šigû*-lamentations and other incantations is commonly described as "The one who strikes the top (*muḫḫu*)." This suggests that the less common term "seam of head," which is likewise the object of smiting, is part of the "cranium" (*muḫḫu*).

(6–7) The one who smites the head (*refers to*) "the one who strikes the top," according to the *šigû*-lamentation (with the incipit-title) "I invoke you."

***Sa-gig 39**
The signs *sa-mat* are not to be read instead as the common verb *sa-lat* "(the hair) is ill."

(7) "The hair of his head (is) *sa-mat*" *is to be read as samât,*

sa-mat is not the verb *sâmu* "to become red," but the less common verb *samû* "to become faltering." "Faltering" hair is explained elsewhere as hair that is "lacking" and described here as hair that is "spread (thin)."

(8) (*which means*) it is spread (thin).

***Sa-gig 39**
This refers to the irises' movement away from each other (i.e., exotropia) or outward from each eye's center (i.e., pupil dilation).

(8–9) "The grapes of his eyes are pulled" (*refers to*) the case where the iris goes outwards.

***Sa-gig 39**

(9–10) "His thigh(s) *ta-a-ka*" (*refers to*) the case where they are (too) difficult for him to rouse or to set in position,

(11) (*or*) the case where (their) disposition has not changed.

***Sa-gig 39**
Not certain whether "ka" refers to the "mouth" (logogram KA) or the "nose" (cuneiform sign ka as logogram KIR_4), the commentator considered what the verb "pressed down" might mean for each possibility:

(11) "His ka is pressed down, he will die."

"To become palsied" often describes the patient's "mouth" and lips.

(12) To press down *means* to become palsied.

"To twitch" often descibes the patient's eye, but can also refer to the "nose."

(12) To press down *means* to twitch.

The basic meaning of “to press down” involves the patient’s inability to “extend” (i.e., open) his mouth or nostrils.

(13) To press down *means* not to extend.

***Sa-gig 39 ?**

(13) SA *means* strand.

(Rev.) …

Notes

Obv. 1—Although no copies of Sa-gig Tablet 39 have been preserved, the introductory line here matches the incipit-title of Tablet 39 in the Sa-gig catalog (Finkel 1988: 147, line A 47 = B 14′; Heeßel 2000: 14, line 47). Because we are ignorant of the contents of the base text, the pericope consulted by the commentator cannot be reconstructed.

Obv. 2—In preserved manuscripts of Sa-gig Chapter VI, feminine grammatical forms clearly delineate body parts and actions belonging to the woman. The preservation of Sa-gig Tablet 36 alerts us to the fact that masculine pronouns in Comm. Sa-gig 36 designate the woman, if not exclusively then at least primarily. Unfortunately, no copies of Sa-gig Tablet 39 are available for our consultation, so it is unclear whether the masculine suffixes here refer to the woman or to her baby, whose birth would be implied if the woman’s “confinement” in this tablet is understood to be postnatal. To avoid cumbersome translations, I render the Akkadian masculine pronominal suffix (-*šú*) generically as “his” or “him” in this commentary. Finally, as I suggested also earlier, the use of masculine suffixes in such contexts could reflect the commentator’s intent to give medical explanations for terminology that he considered applicable to both male and female patients.

Obv. 2–4—The form *nuḫḫurat* seems to be the D stem Stative of the obscure verb *naḫāru*, whose meaning is uncertain in *CAD* N I, 127 s.v. *naḫāru* A, but given as “(G) verdorrt sein (?), (D) verdorren lassen (?)” in *AHw*, 713 s.v. *naḫāru(m)* I. It is not difficult, however, to conjecture a meaning such as “to split” for this verb, which would explain its use to describe “split” wood and “split (perhaps parted)” lips (see examples in *CAD* N I, 127), and which would align nicely with references elsewhere of the head’s seam being “split” (*paṭāru*; see Note on Comm. Sa-gig 4B, obv. 13). By invoking the logogram SAG.GIŠ.RA, however, the commentator revealed his understanding of the verb as *nêru* “to smite, slay” (*CAD* N II, 178–179) in its D stem form *nu*ʾʾ*urat*, with *nuḫḫurat* as a byform. It is unlikely that SAG.GIŠ.RA represents a new commentary entry, because there is no other explanation given for the quotation "the seam of her head (is) *nuḫḫurat*," and because the lengthy explanation for SAG.GIŠ.RA (note the enumerators: "secondly," "thirdly") eventually refers back to the patient's head (line 6). In lines 2–4, the fact that SAG.GIŠ.RA means "to smite" (i.e., "to strike with a weapon") is demonstrated by analyzing its components as sag ("weapon") + GIŠ ("weapon") + RA ("to strike"). The analysis of different elements (sag and GIŠ) as having the same meaning ("weapon") was considered permissible. This logic is similar to the one in Comm. Sa-gig 36 (rev. 11′–12′), where the components of gú-sa-a ("all") are analyzed as gú ("all") + sa ("all"). Conversely, notice how a single element /ru/ (from *Nēberu*) could also be ascribed with the multiple meanings "he/who" (Sumerian particle ra), "by means of" (another Sumerian particle ra), and "create" (cuneiform sign rú for logogram DÙ) in Ass. 13955fx = A 163, obv. 12′–14′; discussed in Wee (2016a: 155–156). One would be right to question, however, why the commentator did not analyze SAG.GIŠ.RA instead as "to strike (RA) the head (SAG) with a weapon (GIŠ)," since such an argument would show that *nêru* ("to smite") relates to the head and is therefore the verbal root of the form *nuḫḫurat* (obv. 2), which describes "the seam of the head." The equation "SAG *means* head" could probably have been taken for granted, and the commentator wanted the sign sag to do double duty with the additional meaning "SAG *means* weapon" (obv. 3).

Obv. 3—The statement that "sag means weapon (*kakku*)" seems to have no lexical basis, and my proposal is to understand it as a play on sounds: Since SAG.DU is the logogram for *qaqqa-du* "head," the sag element presumably corresponds to the element /*qaqqa*/, which sounds like *kakka* "weapon." Less likely, the argument may be epigraphical, playing on visual resemblances among the graphs (i.e., written symbols) of sag (𒊕), *kak-ku* (𒆕 𒆪) "weapon," and ^{giš}TUKUL (𒄑 𒆪) "weapon." According to Genty (2010b: 29), "Ce sumérogramme [GAZ] est l'inverse approximatif de « SAG », ce qui rejoint l'équivalence de SAG avec l'arme « kakku » avec, sous-entendue, une idée de traumatisme violent entraînant une brisure, une fracture," but I do not find this suggestion persuasive.

Obv. 3—GIŠ as the logogram for *kakku* occurs in the lexical texts Idu II, 181 (*CAD* K, 51); Hh. VII A, 7 (*MSL* VI, 84).

Obv. 4–5—The commentator used three arguments to show how the meaning of *nêru* "to smite" is appropriate for the medical context. The first argument (obv. 2–4) involves the analysis of this verb's logogram SAG.GIŠ.RA and the meanings of its individual components. The second (obv. 4) and third (obv. 5) arguments examine the semantic overlap between *nêru* and other verbs, based on their shared representation by the logograms RA and GAZ respectively.

Obv. 6–7—*Šigû*-lamentations frequently begin with the statement *alšīka* ("I invoke you"; cf. CAD Š II, 413 s.v. *šigû* §a), which probably appears in this commentary entry as an incipit-title. Malevolent entities are denoted as *māḫiṣ muḫḫi* ("the one who strikes the top") in several ritual incantations. See, for example, Thureau-Dangin (1921: 165, obv. 26); Meier (1939: 206, iv 9–10); *ABRT* I 29: 15. Whereas the term *muḫḫu* appears in medical texts as a technical reference to a well-delineated body part (i.e., the "cranium," in contrast to other parts like SAG "head" and SAG.KI "temple"), it is unlikely that such fine distinctions were intended by uses of the term in incantation and ritual contexts. In other words, the commentator employed an idiomatic expression *māḫiṣ muḫḫi* in order to shed light on the relatively rare technical term "seam of head," which is mentioned elsewhere only in the Diagnostic Handbook at Sa-gig 3: 24–26 (TDPT 3: 15–17); Sa-gig 40: 44, 45. Since the head is struck in its "top" (*muḫḫu*), the "seam of head" similarly described as smitten must be located in the "cranium" (*muḫḫu*). For an analogous case where ŠÀ ("heart" = seat of emotion) in literary contexts is treated as the technical term for the body part "belly," see Comm. Sa-gig 14, obv. 20–22. The fact that the *šigû*-lamentation here served merely to ratify preconceived conclusions is evident from the equation of the same terms elsewhere, without support from the *šigû*-lamentation: "'The cranium of his head' *refers to* the seam of his head" ([UG]U SAG.DU-*šú* : *ši-bit* SAG.DU-*šú*) at Comm. Sa-gig 4B, obv. 13.

Obv. 7—I read the signs here as *pe-ret* SAG.DU-*šú* ("the hair of his head"), since the orthography *bì*(pe)-*rit* SAG.DU-*šú* is less likely, and the feminine verb *sa-mat* agrees with the feminine noun *pertu*. Essentially the same expression *pé-ret* SAG.DU-*šú* appears at Sa-gig 3: 32b (TDPT 3: 23b) and receives comment in Comm. Sa-gig 1–3, obv. 27. See Note on Comm. Sa-gig 1–3 against reading *pé-ret* as the preposition *bi-rit* (suggested in Labat 1951: 20), even though there is erroneous disagreement between the feminine noun *pé-ret* and the masculine verb *sa-mi* in the base text Sa-gig 3: 32b (TDPT 3: 23b). In the sequence of signs *sa-ma-ta*, the final *ta* sign probably functions as the consonant /t/, rather than the syllable /ta/. For the consonantal use of the Late Babylonian sign *ta*, see Geller (1997–2000: 144–146); Cross and Huehnergard (2003: 228). It was necessary for *sa-ma-ta* to clarify that the syllabic values are *sa-mat* (< *samû* "to become faltering") rather than *sa-lat* (< *salā'u* "to become ill"), because *mat* and *lat* are alternative values of the same cuneiform sign kur. One wonders why the scribe did not utilize the signs *sa-ma-at* instead, since the surrounding text shows the *at* sign to be well within his repertoire. Perhaps the choice to write *sa-ma-ta* instead of *sa-ma-at*(ad) stemmed from a desire to avoid confusion with the verb *samādu* ("to grind (finely)"), which could conceivably form an equation with *sapḫat* ("it is spread/ dispersed") in line 8. On the other hand, note how syllabic ambiguity in the topic [*ina* ma-rak(/šal)] U$_4$-*mi* was resolved by the explanation *ina* [*a-r*]*a-ku* U$_4$-*mu* = *ina arāk ūmī*, "when days become long" (Comm. Sa-gig 4A, obv. 6), where we would have expected the writing **a-ra-ak* instead. Syllable signs could be used for their consonantal values, particularly in such cases involving the elucidation of syllabic readings (see §1.2.3.1.2).

Obv. 7–8—Other diagnostic entries like Sa-gig 3: 122 (TDPT 3: 112) and 2N-T 336 rev. 2′, 3′ describe hair with the sign sa$_5$ (𒋢𒀀), which can be understood as the logogram SA$_5$ for *sâmu* ("to become red"). The commentator, therefore, felt the need to explain that *sa-mat* in the base text here does not mean *sâmu* ("to become red"), but refers to a much less common verb *samû* ("to become faltering, inept"; *CAD* S, 125; *AHw*, 1020). *Contra* Frahm (2011a: 66). The meaning of the latter is clearly explained in Comm. Sa-gig 21 & 22a, obv. 1–2: SI : *sa-mu-ú* : SI : [*ma-ku-ú*] / *šá* SÍG SAG.DU-*šú* ("SI *means* to become faltering. SI *means* [to become lacking], in the case of the hair of his head"). Interestingly, the base text for this entry in Comm. Sa-gig 21 & 22a seems to involve the description of hair as sa$_5$ (𒋢𒀀), which the commentator likewise refused to interpret as the verb *sâmu* ("to become red"). In the present commentary, "faltering" hair or hair that is "lacking" is described as hair that is "spread (thin)" (obv. 8).

Obv. 8–9—Fincke (2000: 19, Abb. 2) has identified *karān īni* ("grape of the eye") as the iris edge bordering the pupil, and *šer'ān kakkulti īni* ("strands of the *kakkultu* of the eye") as muscles of the iris. For discussion on *kakkultu* as "iris" based on medical desciptions and Mesopotamian statuary, see Note on Comm. Sa-gig 21 & 22a, lines 3–4. The clause *ka-ra-an* IGI.2-*šú šad-du* appears also in Comm. Sa-gig 21 & 22a, obv. 3, with the explanation that "the iris enters within." Here, the verb *šaddū* seems to describe the opposite case whereby "the iris goes out." The exact meaning of "going out" and "entering within" is not certain, though one possibility concerns the deviation of the irises (and the eyeball as a whole) away from each other (i.e., exotropia) or towards each other (i.e., esotropia, a cross-eyed condition), as suggested by Frahm (2011a: 227–229). Another possibility concerns the dilation or constriction of the pupil, which may have been perceived in terms of iris movement outwards from or inwards to the center of each eye. For the proposal that both descriptions refer to the condition of "*Seclusio pupillae*," see Fincke (2000: 163–164). The verb *šadādu* ("to pull") as a description of the eye or its parts is also attested in the therapeutic texts *BAM* 516 ii 27′; *AMT* 13/1: 3′.

Obv. 9—There is no satisfactory candidate for the root of what appears to be the verbal form *ta-a-ka*. One possibility would be to understand *ta-a-ka* as *takkā*, the G Stative 3fp of the obscure verb *takāku*, which seems to describe some physical feature or defect (*CAD* T, 61; *CAD* U/W, 56 s.v. *ukkuku*). See Fincke (2000: 163 n. 1238); George (2013: 89, note on obv. 6′). Another possibility is the Stative verb *dakâ* (< *dekû* "to rouse, raise"), though the vowel lengths are admittedly awkward in the writing *ta-a-ka*. This root *dakû* or *dekû*, in fact, appears in the explanation *šá ana da-ke-e … dan-na-niš-šú* (line 10), which likely occurs also at Comm. Sa-gig 36, rev. 4′–5′. Either of the two interpretations above assumes a dual meaning for the form ÚR-*šú* ("his thigh(s)") that is compatible with feminine plural verbs, and this assumption may be supported in part by the 3fp Stative verb *dannāniššu* (line 10) that apparently also refers to the "thigh(s)." We are unlikely to figure out the meaning of *ta-a-ka* by looking at verbs that typically describe the "thigh," since it is the verb's difficulty that prompted the comment in the first place.

Obv. 10—The form *dan-na-niš-šú* (= *dannāniššu*) is the G Stative 3fp of the verb *danānu* with the ventive (*-nim*) and 3ms dative suffix (*-šu*(*m*)). A parallel expression *dan-na-áš-šú* appears in Comm. Sa-gig 36, rev. 5′, which could represent the non-ventive form *dannāšu*. A similar idea about the patient's difficulties in raising his/her thighs or feet may be expressed in *StBoT* XXXVI, p. 60 (Fragment H line 1): [GÌR.MEŠ(?)-*š*]*ú ana našê kabtā*. Note also the expression KA-*šú ana awâti da-an*, "his mouth is difficult for words (i.e., it is too difficult for his mouth to speak)" in Sa-gig 17: 57, as well as in Sa-gig 3: 50 (TDPT 3: 41) (base text for Comm. Sa-gig 3B, rev. 1) where the Stative verb is written *da-a-an*.

Obv. 11—The term *šikinni* can refer to a vessel for liquids or a "fishing net" (*CAD* Š II, 429 s.v. *šikinnu* A and B), though both these meanings make little sense here. A contextual reading of *šikinni*, however, suggests that it continues the meaning of its cognate verb *šakānu* "to set in position" (line 10) in the preceding line, and I accordingly translate it as "disposition" here.

Obv. 11—I transliterate the Stative form as *ṣa-pir*, instead of *ṣa-par* by Hunger (*SpTU* I, 40). Though the topic's verb *ṣapāru* ("to press down") very often describes the "eyes" at Sa-gig 9: 8, 29; 26: 62′; *AMT* [35/6: 5′?]; *SpTU* I, 46: 16; *STT* [89: 96], it does refer to the body part "ka" at Sa-gig 10: 25. Note the view that *ṣapāru* can be given "a meaning appropriate to Bell's palsy where the affected eyeball rolls upward and slightly outward when an attempt is made to close the eye." Kinnier Wilson and Reynolds (2007: 82). While

Hunger (*SpTU* 1, 40) understood the commentary's description as pertaining to "his nose" (*appa*(ka)-*šú*), it seems that the reading for this body part was not quite settled in the commentator's view. The interpretation of "ka" as the logogram KA for "mouth" is reflected in the first comment *kubbulu* ("to become palsied"), which describes conditions of the "mouth" and lips (*BAM* [174 obv. 5′]; 523 iii 3′, 9′ (incl. *AMT* 24/1: 3′, 9′)). Note also the statement *šapassu uktambil-ma īnu iṣhir-ma* ("his lip became palsied, (his) eye became small") in Piepkorn (1933: 62, Edition B v 11). On the other hand, the interpretation of "ka" as the logogram KIR_4 ("nose") is reflected in the next comment *ṣudduru* ("to twitch"), which mostly describes the eyes but is attested in Sa-gig 6: 13 in a section devoted to the "nose." See also *CAD* Ṣ, 229.

Commentary Sa-gig 40A

Provenance:	Uruk (Warka), Area U18; Ambiguous archaeological context suggests library of either Anu-ikṣur or Iqīšāya
Period:	Late Achaemenid–Early Hellenistic
Names:	Colophon not preserved
Script:	Neo-/Late Babylonian
Field/Museum No.:	W 22308a (National Museum of Iraq)
Photos:	Plate 31 (obverse) and Plate 32a (right edge)
Printed Edition/Hand Copy:	*SpTU* 1, 41 (= Hunger 1976: 49–50); Wee (2012: 703–709)
Digital Resources:	CDLI P348462; GKAB P348462 (edition digitized by Clancier 2009); CCP 4.1.40.A (printed hand copy digitized by Frahm, Frazer, and Jiménez 2013)
Discussion:	*SpTU* 1, 41 (= Hunger 1976: 49–50); Heeßel (2000: 138, 146 (40. Tafel MS a)); Scurlock and Andersen (2005: 803, see references to *SpTU* 1.41); Clancier (2009: 388); Geller (2010a: 138, 196 n. 206); Genty (2010b: 15, 18–20, 22–26, 28); Frahm (2011a: 229, 296); Wee (2012: 703–709) and (in press: §C1); Scurlock (2014: 269 nn. 1, 5, 9, and 11); Gabbay (2016: 26 n. 81, 107 n. 128, 120 n. 180, 128–130)
Pericope:	At least Sa-gig 40: 1–57

Transliteration

Obverse

1) [DIŠ LÚ.TUR *la-a*ʾ]-*ḫu ki-ma al-du ṣir-ti*
2) [*i-ni-qu* : *ṣir-ti* :] *tu-lu-ú* : *ki-ša-da-nu-uš-šú*
3) [*ki-iš/ši*]-*da-nu-uš-šú* : *ki-šid* SAḪAR *lìb-bu-ú ana* KI-*tim* ki-ši
4) [*šá-n*]*iš ki-šid* SAḪAR : *šá ina e-pe-ri na-du-ú*
5) [*ša*]*l-šiš šá ina qaq-qar na-du-ú* : BI.LU : *bu-šá-nu*
6) [*me*]-*eḫ-ra* DAB-*su* : *lìb-bu-ú* ^{d}DÌM.ME *i-ḫar-šú*
7) [*it*]-*ta-na-as-la*-ʾ-*ma* : *sa-la-*a_4 : *na-ka-da*
8) [x x] x : *ina-an-ziq* : *ina ki-rim-me* AMA-*šú* : *ina tu-le-e* AMA-*šú*

 | DOI:10.1163/9789004417564_030

9) [... *lì*]*b-bu-ú* MUNUS.UŠ$_{11}$.ZU *a-na mál-taq-tú* DÙ*-ús-su*
10) [LÍL.LÍL-*a*ʾ : *i*]*t-ta-na-as-la-*ʾ : *i-nak-kud*
11) [... : DUMU.M]UNUS ^{d}*A-nu* : *šap pu ul ti* GÚ*-šú*
12) [... *ni-ki*]*p-ti* : *a-na bu-um-bu-lu ma-šil* NU DÙ
13) [*pur-ru-du* : *pa-ra-di*] ⌞:⌟ *ga-la-ti* NU DÙ
14) [... *i-qat-t*]*i* : *qa-tu-ú*
15) [... *na-pa-ḫi* :] ⌞*e*⌟*-me-ri* : *na-pa-ḫi*
16) [... *tu-kul-ti qin-na-ti-šú* : ...]*-ri qin-na-ti-šú*
17) [...] x *lìb-bu-ú*
18) [...] x x
(Remainder broken)

Translation

Incipit-title of Sa-gig 40

(Obv. 1–2) "[If] a baby, when he is born, [sucks] the teat."

Sa-gig 40: 1
Common lexical equation

(2) ["Teat" *refers to*] breast.

Sa-gig 40: 3
kišādānuššu "by his neck" is analyzed as *kišid* "reaching" + *ana ušši* "to the foundation," thus showing the connection between the bodily region and "*kišid* SAḪAR sickness" (Sa-gig 40: 2–4).

(2) "By his neck" (*means*)

The related terms "foundation," "dust" (SAḪAR), "earth" (KI), and "ground" are used interchangeably in these arguments.

(3) Reaching-to-the-foundation, *which refers to kišid* SAḪAR sickness.

kišid sounds like ki-ši, which stands for the Sumerian expression ki-šè "towards the earth."

(3) As in the fact that: towards the earth (*is expressed by*) ki-ši.

(4) Secondly, *kišid* SAḪAR sickness *refers to* one who is cast down onto the dust.

(5) Thirdly, one who is cast down onto the ground.

***Sa-gig 40: 5**
The usual logogram for *bu'šānu*-sickness is KIR_4.ḪAB, not BI.LU.

(5) "BI.LU" *refers to* *bu'šānu*-sickness.

Sa-gig 40: 7
meḫra "incident" may be analyzed as ME + *hâra* "to espouse," where the element ME represents ^{d}DÌM.ME "*lamaštu*."

(6) "An incident seized him."
(6) As in, the *lamaštu*-demoness espouses him.

Sa-gig 40: 13
Although *ittanasla'* apparently derives from *salā'a* "to become ill," the explanation here seems to identify it as the verb *salāḫa* (byform: *salā'a*) "to tremble."

(7) "*ittanasla'-ma" derives from the dictionary root salā'a, which means* to quiver.

***Sa-gig 40**

(8) ... *means* he is vexed.

Sa-gig 40: 16
The baby's "living quarters" (AMA_5 = *maštaku*), nested within the bosom of his mother (AMA), become the site for "cutting-off" (*maltaqtu* = *maštaqtu*) by the machinations of the sorceress.

(8) "In his mother's cradling arm" *means* in his mother's breast. ...

(9) As in, a sorceress acted against him for the purpose of cutting-off.

***Sa-gig 40: 20**
As in line 7 above, *ittanasla'* seems to be identified with *salāḫa* (byform: *salā'a*) "to tremble," rather than *salā'a* "to become ill" (logogram LÍL).

(10) ["LÍL.LÍL-*a*'" *means*] *ittanasla', which means* he quivers.

Sa-gig 40: 25

(11) ... daughter of the god Anu.

Sa-gig 40: 41

(11–12) "*šap pu ul ti* of his neck" (*means*) ...

***Sa-gig 40: 42—"Butting (*nikipti*) of the Moon-god Sîn"**
Refers either to the New Moon crescent's resemblance to "butting" horns, or perhaps to the seven "butting" storm-demons that darken the moon-god Sîn in the *Lunar Eclipse Myth.*

(12) "Butting" is equivalent to the day of the New Moon.

(Scribal comment)

(12) It is not done.

***Sa-gig 40: 42**
Though *parādu* is not uncommon, the D stem occurs syllabically only here.

(13) ["(His innards) are *purrudū*" *derives from the dictionary root* to shudder], *which means* to jitter.

(Scribal comment)

(13) It is not done.

***Sa-gig 40: 42**

(14) ... "[*iqatti*]" *derives from the dictionary root* to perish.

***Sa-gig 40: 56—"his hands and his feet keep becoming inflamed"**
While *napāḫu* "to inflame" is a very common verb, syllabic writings usually depict the G or D stems, instead of the Ntn stem here.

(15) ... [... To inflame *means*] to distend.
(15–16) To inflame (*means*) ...

***Sa-gig 40: 57**

(16) ["*tukulti* of his buttocks" *refers to*] the ... of his buttocks.

(17–18) ... As in, ...

Notes

Obv. 1–2—Associations between *ṣirtu* ("teat") and *tulû* ("breast") occur in the lexical texts Aa VIII/4, 180–181 (*MSL* XIV, 513); Ea IV, 59–60 (*MSL* XIV, 357); Hg. B IV, 33 (Vedeler 2002: 68; cf. *MSL* IX, 35); S^{b} II, 247–248 (*MSL* III, 145).

The two terms are also equated in a commentary on Izbu XII, 28 in Leichty (1970: 231, Comm. W, 376g); De Zorzi (2014: 673, K 1913, i 10′): *ṣer-re-ta* = *tu-lu-ú*.

Obv. 3—I tentatively restore the beginning of obv. 3 as the Sandhi writing [*ki-iš*/*ši*]-*da-nu-uš-šú*, which represents an analysis of the form *kišādānuššu* ("by his neck") into the components *kišid* ("reaching") + *ana* ("to") + *uššu* ("the foundation"). The analysis confirms the diagnosis in Sa-gig 40: 3, by showing the link between the medical condition "by his neck" and the unusual verdict "*kišid* SAḪAR sickness" (Sa-gig 40: 2–4). The close semantic connections among *uššu* ("foundation"), SAḪAR/*e-pe-ri* ("dust"), KI-*tim* ("earth"), and *qaq-qar* ("ground") further support this interpretation.

Obv. 3—The form *ki-šid* is reminiscent of the Sumerian expression ki-ši. The term ki is the logogram for "earth," while ši (or še_{20}) represents the Sumerian terminative šè "to, towards." Thus ki-ši (representing ki-šè) means "towards the earth," a notion expressed in Akkadian by *ana erṣetim* (KI-*tim*). This implies that *kišid* alone, even without the elements "foundation" and "dust," already bears the connotation of "reaching" in a downward direction.

Obv. 5—The usual logogram for *buʾšānu*-sickness is KIR_4.ḪAB, not BI.LU. I wonder if the respiratory sickness written with the signs lu.bi (*SpTU* I, 43 rev. 1) could be a version of or error for BI.LU in this commentary. Wee (in press: §C1).

Obv. 6—The vague reference to an "incident" (*mehra*) is clarified as the "espousing" (*ḫiāru*) action of a malicious being, in line with other diagnoses in close proximity on the same tablet: MUNUS.UŠ_{11}.ZU *ḫi-rat-su* (Sa-gig 40: 15); DUMU.MUNUS ^{d}*Anim* *ḫi-rat-su* (Sa-gig 40: 25). The connection was likely encouraged by the analysis of *meḫra* "incident" as ME + *ḫâra* "to espouse," where the element ME represents ^{d}DÌM.ME "*lamaštu*." According to this analysis, ME functions not as a grammatical appendage, but as an independent lexical item. This is also the case in Comm. Sa-gig 1B (obv. 25′), where the ME element of ^{d}DÌM.ME allows for the association of the *lamaštu*-demoness with heat, based on the lexical entry [ME] = *um-mu* (Izi E, 11 in *MSL* XIII, 186).

Obv. 7—Although *salāʾa* ("to become ill") occurs commonly in medical texts, it appears mostly in the G and N stems, with one possible attestation of the Gtn stem: *is-sa-na-la-ʾ* (Sa-gig 3: 109 (TDPT 3: 100)). The Ntn form is written out syllabically only in available manuscripts of Sa-gig 40: 13, 82, and the unusual repetition LÍL.LÍL in Sa-gig 40: 20 may also denote the Ntn stem. Apparently for these reasons, the commentator felt the need to clarify the verb forms of Sa-gig 40: 13 and 20 in this commentary (obv. 7, 10). Stol (2009a:

29–32, 42–44) argued that *salā'u* A ("to become ill"; *CAD* S, 96–97) and *salāḫu* A ("to sprinkle"; *CAD* S, 85–88) are forms of a single verb, whereby an "ill" person was conceived as being metaphorically "sprinked" with illness. This verb is equated with *nakādu* ("to worry") twice in this commentary (obv. 7, 10). Stol understood the argument in obv. 10 as "[LÍL.LÍL-*a*' : *i*]*t-ta-na-as-la-*' = *i-nak-kud* 'he worries'," though he admitted that "a 'worrying' baby gives no sense" and that "clearly, 'to worry' as an explanation is a guess." Indeed, the change in grammatical person in expressions like *issalla' lā tanakkud*, "*he* becomes ill, (but) *you* must not worry" (*BAM* 159 i 36–37; 578 i 41) implies that *nakādu* ("to worry") cannot be viewed merely as a synonym for *salā'u* ("to become ill"), and that the common diagnostic verdict *nakud* ("he is worrisome") speaks of worry, not by the patient himself, but by those observing his illness. I suggest that the basic meaning of *nakādu* is "to throb, palpitate, quiver" (*CAD* N I, 153), and derivative meanings such as "to worry, fear, be anxious" reflect emotional states involving a "throbbing" heart. Whether intentionally or not, the commentator may have confused the verb *salā'u*/*salāḫu* (active: "to sprinkle"; passive/intransitive and metaphoric: "to become ill") with the verb *salāḫu* B ("to tremble"; *CAD* S, 88; *AHw*, 1013 s.v. *salāḫu* II), which in turn agrees with the meaning of *nakādu* ("to throb, quiver"). For commentators' tendency to use the general verb *salāḫu* ("to tremble") as explanation for other verbs of quaking or shivering (as in the case here), see Note on Comm. Sa-gig 3B, rev. 2–3. While it is problematic that the Ntn of *salāḫu* B is not otherwise attested, the commentator may have considered the action of "throbbing" or "trembling" appropriate to the iterative sense of the Ntn stem. Finally, the choice of signs *sa-la-*a_4(a.an) (obv. 7) instead of **sa-la-*' is curious, especially in view of [*it*]-*ta-na-as-la-*'*-ma* (obv. 7) earlier in the same line, where the aleph (') is very clearly written. I cannot confidently account for this, though I toy with the idea that the intended reading may have been *sa-la-a* AN⟨.TA(?)⟩ ("*the dictionary root salā'a*—upper"), referring to an earlier (i.e., "upper") entry on *salā'a* in a lexical list that included more than one homophone, and which organized consecutive entries vertically downward.

Obv. 8–9—See Note on Comm. Sa-gig 1–3 (line 45) on an ancient commentator's mistake in identifying the signs *ma-al-taq*(/*tak*)*-ti* with the root "to test" (*latāku*)—leading modern scholars to suggest, erroneously, that the sick person is only a "test subject" for the sorcerer—as well as my argument for why the correct reading is not *maltakti* ("testing") but *maltaqtu* / *maštaqtu* ("cutting-off" < *šatāqu* "to split, fissure, cut off"). The meaning "cutting-off" (*maltaqtu*) also makes more sense than "testing" (*maltaktu*) here in the wordplay of Comm. Sa-gig 40A, obv. 8–9, whereby the baby's "living quarters" (AMA_5 = *maštaku*), nested within the bosom of his "mother" (AMA), are transformed into the site for "cutting-off" (*maltaqtu* < *maštaqtu*) by the machinations of a sorceress.

Obv. 10—There seems to be exactly enough space in the damaged beginning of the line to restore the signs [LÍL.LÍL-*a*ʾ : *i*]*t*- ... See earlier Note on obv. 7 for how the commentator may have interpreted the Ntn verb *salāʾa* (Ntn logogram LÍL.LÍL).

Obv. 11–12—The writing "*šap pu ul ti*" appears both in this commentary and in Sa-gig 40: 41 MS B (= BM 46228). Hunger (*SpTU* I, 41) wondered, "Ist *šappulti kišādišu* mißverstanden aus ... *šappu ultu kišādišu adi eṣenṣērišu*?" It would be difficult, however, to account for the form and syntax of the term *šappu*, even with the proposed meaning "bent-over" from the Hebrew *šafouf* (Scurlock and Andersen 2005: 398, §17.70; 748 n. 67). Alternatively, the form *šappulti* could be treated as a single word with meanings similar to its root *šapālu* ("to become low"); but cf. *CAD* Š I, 480 s.v. *šappultu* (mng. unkn.). Unfortunately, the comment here is completely damaged and sheds no light on the problem. Note, moreover, while the prepositions "from" (TA = *ultu*) and "to / until" (EN = *adi*) usually come together as a pair, there are some cases where the latter preposition appears alone: GÌR.2-*šú* EN *kìn-ṣi-šú* (Sa-gig 3: 61 (TDPT 3: 52); $MURUB_4$.2-*šú giš-ši-šú* EN *ki-ṣal-li-šú* (*AMT* 52/8: 6′).

Obv. 12—The commentator may have been referring to the slender appearance of the New Moon crescent, when the crescent most resembles horns used for "butting." The association of the lunar crescent with "butting" horns is also the theme of Comm. Sa-gig 4B, obv. 2. Alternatively, this may be a reference to the *Lunar Eclipse Myth* in the Incantation Series *Utukkū Lemnūtu* (XVI, 1), which narrates how seven "butting storm-demons" (UD.MEŠ *muttakpūtu* < *nakāpu*) darken the moon-god Sîn during the lunar eclipse (Geller 2016: 501; cf. Geller 2007a: 178; see also discussion of the myth in Wee 2014b: 29–67). Although the malady's name *nikipti* ᵈ30 (Sa-gig 40: 42) seems to envision the moon-god as the one performing the action of "butting" (*nakāpu*) rather than as the victim of aggression, the incongruity is not insurmountable. For example, the quotation from *Enūma eliš* (IV, 101) in Comm. Sa-gig 4B, obv. 14, which depicts the goddess as suffering from stomach afflictions, was cited in support of why the goddess is the one responsible for problems with the patient's "inside" in the base text Sa-gig 4: 10.

Obv. 12–13—The two occurrences of NU DÙ ("it is not done") at the end of lines 12 and 13 represent a scribal comment of sorts, whose meaning is not entirely clear, but which is evidently different from *ḫepi* that denotes a "break" in the original tablet copied from. Perhaps NU DÙ is related to expressions such as *ul āmur* ("I did not see"), *ul ašme* ("I did not hear"), *ul īdi* ("I do not know"), or *ina ṭuppi ul šalim* ("it is not intact in the tablet"), discussed in Note on Comm. Sa-gig 7A, rev. 4.

Obv. 13—Syllabic forms of the verb *parādu* are mainly in the G stem, though the Gtn stem (Sa-gig 40: 16–17, 46; *BAM* 232 i 12′) and possibly the Gt stem (Sa-gig 15: 85′) are attested as well. Sa-gig 40: 42 contains the only occurrence of the D stem written syllabically. Associations between *parādu* ("to shudder") and *galātu* ("to jitter") occur in the lexical texts Aa II/6, iii A 33′–36′ (*MSL* XIV, 293); Erimhuš IV, 47–48 (*MSL* XVII, 59; note the reading *pa-ra-du* instead of *pa-ra-ru* in *CAD* G, 12).

Obv. 15–16—The preserved portion of writing *e-me-ri* : *na-pa-ḫi* gives the impression that the verb *emēru* is the topic and the verb *napāḫu* is its comment. See also *e-me-ri* : *na-pa-ḫa* in Nippur Therapeutic Comm. 2 = 11N-T4, line 26. However, there are no occurrences of the verb *emēru* in the medical entries between Sa-gig 40: 42 and Sa-gig 40: 57, whereas an inflected Ntn form of *napāḫu* appears at Sa-gig 40: 56. It is therefore more likely that the dictionary form *napāḫu* (A′) is explained twice in an A′:B:A′:C argument, first by the verb *emēru* (B), then by another verb (C) that is not preserved at the beginning of line 16. The verb *napāḫu* is also explained twice in Comm. Sa-gig 4B, obv. 9–10, first by the D stem of the verb *ebēṭu*, then by the G stem of *ebēṭu*. The equation of the verbs *ebēṭu* ("to have cramps") and *napāḫu* ("to inflame") occurs in Comm. Sa-gig 4A, obv. 3; Uruk Therapeutic Comm. 1 = *SpTU* I, 47 obv. 1; and a commentary on Uruanna (BM 76487:[17] in *CT* 41, 45). For concerns about commensurability between the intransitive G stem of *ebēṭu* and the transitive-intransitive G stem of *napāḫu*, see Note on Comm. Sa-gig 4B, obv. 9–10. In any case, the frequent pairing of *napāḫu* and *ebēṭu* suggests the possible restoration [... *na-pa-ḫi* :] *e-me-ri* : *na-pa-ḫi* / [*e-bé-ṭi* (?)] in this commentary (obv. 15–16). While the verb *napāḫu* appears very commonly in medical texts, syllabic forms are overwhelmingly in the G or D stems. Syllabic writings of the Ntn stem appear only in Sa-gig 40: 56 and *BAM* 393 rev. 26, while those of the Dt stem occur in Sa-gig 11: 35 and *BAM* 568: 1. The Ntn stem is much more commonly expressed as the logogram MÚ.MÚ.

Obv. 16—In his comment on Sa-gig 40: 57, Labat suggested that the term *tukulti qinnāti* should be equated with ZAG GU.DU (Sa-gig 19/20: 45′). See also *AHw*, 1368–1369 s.v. *tukultu* §6; *CAD* T, 463 s.v. *tukultu* §4.

Commentary Sa-gig 40B

Provenance:	Uruk (Warka), Area U18, Level v; Same findspot and consignment (W 22307) as Comm. Sa-gig 1C, 5, 7A, 7B, and 19 suggests library of Anu-ikṣur
Period:	Late Achaemenid
Names:	Not preserved
Script:	Neo-/Late Babylonian
Field/Museum No.:	W 22307/73 (National Museum of Iraq)
Photo:	Plate 32b (reverse)
Printed Edition/Hand Copy:	*SpTU* I, 42 (= Hunger 1976: 50); Wee (2012: 710–712)
Digital Resources:	CDLI P348463; GKAB P348463 (edition digitized by Clancier 2009); CCP 4.1.40.B (printed hand copy and edition digitized by Jiménez 2015, with contributions by Clancier)
Discussion:	*SpTU* I, 42 (= Hunger 1976: 50); Heeßel (2000: 138, 146 (40. Tafel MS b)); Clancier (2009: 388); Genty (2010a: 386) and (2010b: 15); Frahm (2011a: 229, 291); Wee (2012: 710–712); Gabbay (2016: 203 n. 10)
Pericope:	At least Sa-gig 40: 97–122

Transliteration

Reverse

1′) [...] x [...]

2′) [UBUR NU NAG (?) : NIN]DA *u* A.MEŠ *la* ⌜*i*⌝-[*ma-ḫar* (?) ...]

3′) [... ka-*šú ka-bit* : ...]x *na-piš* KIR$_4$-*šú k*[*a-bit* (?) ...]

4′) [...] x ti ⌜:⌝ ŠU.DINGIR.R[A-*ku* : ...]

5′) [...] tu : IGI.MEŠ-*šú maḫ-ḫa* : *š*[*á*] ⌜E-*ú*⌝ [... (?)]

6′) [...]x *šá* IGI.2 : *e-sír* : *e-se-r*[*u* ...]

7′) [... UBUR *muṭ-ṭu* (?) : ...] x [U]BUR GAL-*ta* : *ra-ʾ-i-b*[*u* ...]

8′) [...] x [...]

(Remainder broken)

 | DOI:10.1163/9789004417564_031

Translation

(Rev. 1′–2′) …

***Sa-gig 40: 93—**
“he does not drink the breast” (?)

(2′) [“He does not drink the breast” (?) *means* he does] not [accept (?)] food and drink.

***Sa-gig 40: 97**
The cuneiform sign ka is to be interpreted as KIR_4 (“nose”), and the difficulty involves the patient’s breathing.

(3′) [“His ka is difficult” *means* …] the breathing of his nose [is difficult]. …
(4′) …

Sa-gig 40: 110
ŠU.DINGIR.RA “Hand-of-god (sickness)” occurs only here in the Diagnostic Handbook, which otherwise employs different forms like ŠU DINGIR (“Hand of god”).

(4′) “Hand-of-god (sickness)” [*refers to*] …
(5′) …

***Sa-gig 40: 111—**
“his IGI.2 are suffused(?)”
maḫḫā “suffused(?)” describes the “eyes,” which are typically written in the Diagnostic Handbook as IGI.2 instead of IGI.MEŠ (the writing for “face”).

(5′–6′) “His IGI.MEŠ are suffused(?),” which it said: …, in the case of the eyes.

Sa-gig 40: 114
In the medical texts, *esēru* “to stifle (an outcry)” occurs only here.

(6′) “(His outcry) *esir*” *derives from the dictionary root* to stifle. …
(7′) …

***Sa-gig 40: 119—“he is diminished (in appetite for) the breast” (?)**
If the infant is “diminished” in reference to the breast, the breast is “big” in reference to the infant.

(7′) [“He is diminished (in appetite for) the breast” (?) *means* …] a big breast.

Sa-gig 40: 122

(7′) “*ra’ību*” …

Notes

Rev. 2′—The expression UBUR NU NAG ("he does not drink the breast") occurs only in Sa-gig 40: 93, 94. Elsewhere in both the Diagnostic Handbook and therapeutic texts, the verb NAG ("to drink") appears together with its direct object, i.e., the substance imbibed, whether it be water, beer, premium beer, milk (Sa-gig 17: 87), river water (Sa-gig 17: 65), or even wife's urine (*AMT* 63/5 iv 5′). The syntax here, where NAG appears with the vessel for the fluid imbibed (i.e., the mother's breast), may have been unusual enough to prompt an explanation.

Rev. 3′—The body part denoted by the sign ka (with possible logographic values KA "mouth" and KIR_4 "nose") is described with the verb *kabātu* ("to become difficult") in both the Diagnostic Handbook (Sa-gig [33: 89]; 40: 97) and in therapeutic texts (*BAM* 533: 2 (incl. *AMT* 28/2 obv. 2); *BAM* [543 iv 59′]; 547 iv 14′ (incl. *AMT* 25/4: 11′)). The commentator's explanation here was informed by the expression *napīš* KIR_4-*šú* DUGUD ("the breathing of his nose is difficult") in therapeutic texts: *BAM* [28 obv. 2]; 566 i 6′ (incl. *AMT* 55/5 i 6′); *AMT* 45/6 obv. 5′; [51/2: 8′]; *SpTU* 1, 44: 1, 5. A different expression e-piš ka-*šú* DUGUD appears in *BAM* 159 i 39, [43]; [578 i 50], which has been understood as *epēš pî* (*CAD* E, 215–216 s.v. *epēšu* §2c). For the difficulties of interpreting e-piš ka-*šú*, however, see Testen (*NABU* 2001/95).

Rev. 4′—Despite the frequent occurrences of the term ŠU DINGIR(-*šú*) ("Hand of (his) god") in the Diagnostic Handbook, the commentator felt the need to explain the atypical but closely related form ŠU.DINGIR.RA ("Hand-of-god (sickness)"). As observed by Heeßel (2000: 49–52) and (2007: 123), divine agency is usually depicted using forms like ŠU.DINGIR.RA, ŠU.^{d}INNIN (.NA), and ŠU.GIDIM.MA in therapeutic texts, in contrast to ŠU DINGIR, ŠU ^{d}15, and ŠU GIDIM in the Diagnostic Handbook. Along similar lines, the scribe of the therapeutic tablet *AMT* 76/1 acknowledged the oddity of the orthography ŠU GIDIM (line 24) by placing its medical entry after others with the form ŠU.GIDIM.MA (lines 1, 7, 11, 15, 17).

Rev. 5′—The single manuscript (BM 92690) that preserves the reading for Sa-gig 40: 111 has IGI.2-*šú maḫ-ḫa*. The commentator must have used a copy with the reading IGI.MEŠ-*šú maḫ-ḫa*, which he then attempted to reconcile with descriptions of the eyes such as IGI.2-*šú* DIR.MEŠ-*ḫa* (Sa-gig 4: 41) and IGI.2-*šú im-ta-na-aḫ-ḫa-aḫ* (*KAR* 211, obv. 13′). It is also likely that the eyes are referenced in the expression IGI.MEŠ-*šú* [*im*]-*maḫ-ḫa-ḫu* in the therapeutic text *BAM* 216: 12′–13′, where the distinction between IGI.2 as "eyes" and IGI.MEŠ as "face" is not as consistent as in the Diagnostic Handbook.

Rev. 6′—For *esēru* "to stifle" in relation to an outcry, see the lexical equations gar-ra = MIN (= *e-se-rum*) *šá rig-me* (Antagal B, 221 in *MSL* XVII, 194); *akkil-[x]-⌜x-x⌝ = *ik-kil-lum e-ṣir* (Nabnitu F, 15′ in *MSL* XVI, 275).

Rev. 7′—The base text may be the expression "He is diminished (in appetite for) the breast" (UBUR *muṭ-ṭu*) in Sa-gig 40: 119. In what may be an erudite argument here, if the infant is "diminished" in reference to the breast, the breast is "big" in reference to the infant. Also implied may be the notion that the breast remains undiminished in its supply of milk. In this line, it is tempting to connect the word "shivering" (*ra'ību*) to "big" (*rabītu*). In fact, precisely such wordplay involving the terms "to become big" (*rabû*) and "to shiver" (*ra'ābu*) occurs in the astrological commentary K 2310 (obv. 4–5) discussed in Wee (2016a: 143–144). However, since a base text (Sa-gig 40: 122) in the close vicinity can be readily identified as the quoted source of the word "shivering," this term should probably be considered the topic rather than the comment of an argument. Adamson (1990: 28–30) argued that *ra'ību* can be both a "disease" and a "symptom." The cognate verb *ra'ābu* appears as a commentary topic in Comm. Sa-gig 3B, rev. 2–3: "'His hands and his feet shiver.' [To shiver] *means* to tremble" (ŠU.2-*šú u* GÌR.2-*šú i-ra-'-bu* : / [*ra-'-bu*] : *sa-la-*⌊*ḫu*⌋).

PART TWO

Commentary Notations

Sa-gig commentaries employ a number of recurring notations that serve to express logical relationships and formal arguments. Although the examples here mostly come from Part One of this volume (§11.1), the notations examined also occur with the same meanings in non-medical commentaries. They therefore should be considered as features of the commentary genre, rather than of medical texts per se, representing general forms of rhetoric applicable across various fields of Mesopotamian scholarship. Readers would benefit by studying my proposals in comparison with Gabbay's handy catalog of *The Exegetical Terminology of Akkadian Commentaries* (2016).[8] The discussion here highlights my own perspectives on features that have not received similar or sufficient treatment by others.

8 Gabbay (2016) relied on portions of my dissertation (2012) that are now revised as Parts One and Two in this volume, so there is some overlap in our interpretations.

Disjunction Sign

Cuneiform commentary tablets appear in three basic formats: (I) 'tabular,' (II) 'indentation type' that is well attested in Assyria, and (III) 'cola type' that is well attested in Babylonia (§1.1.4.1).[9] Other than the tabular Comm. Sa-gig 1–3 from Ḫuzirina (Sultantepe), the remaining twenty-nine commentary tablets and fragments edited in this volume are of the cola type. One of the most distinctive signs in cola type commentaries consists of typically two oblique cuneiform wedges (𒑲), i.e., two *Winkelhaken*, which separate the topic of a commentary entry from its comment. The sign is often transliterated, as in this volume, as a colon punctuation mark (:). It has very commonly been designated a *Glossenkeil*, since what follows the sign frequently represents a "gloss" or explanation of what precedes it.[10] Such an interpretation may even feel intuitive, because of the sign's visual similarity with the colon or the equals sign in our modern writing convention.

I prefer to understand this notation, however, not as a *Glossenkeil* per se, but primarily as a disjunction sign (*Trennungszeichen*) that marks a break in the linear syntax.[11] While it is true that the form A:B indicates "A *means* B" or "A *refers to* B" most of the time, the relationship between A and B is deduced from the context of juxtaposing two syntactically independent items, not as meaning intrinsic to the disjunction sign itself. Indeed, the 'separating' function of the disjunction sign is clearly illustrated by its use in the place-notation system of numbers during later periods, where the sign makes explicit a positional value of "zero" that could otherwise be indicated only by wider-than-usual spacing between numbers.[12] In short, whereas the nuance of a *Glossenkeil* can be imputed to a disjunction sign, not every disjunction sign functions as a *Glossenkeil*. On the other hand, though the disjunction sign itself carries no *semantic* content other than that of a syntactical break, it can often be

9 See also Frahm (2011a: 33–37).

10 Krecher and Souček (1957–1971: 431–440). For discussion on this sign in Hittite contexts to denote Luvianisms and Luvian loanwords, see Melchert (1993: i–ii); Yakubovich (2008: 466–501). Note the view that "the *Glossenkeil* separating variant versions in the base text was probably rendered as *šanîš* when read aloud" by Gabbay (2016: 19).

11 *MZL*, no. 592.

12 The writing 1 : 20 clearly denotes 1,0,20 (= 3620), whereas the writing 1 20 could be mistaken for 1,20 (= 80). Neugebauer and Sachs (1945: 2); Neugebauer (1952: 20); cf. Thureau-Dangin (1938: 79–81 (§164–167), 238); Deimel (1947: 129 no. 682).

 | DOI:10.1163/9789004417564_032

translated in consistent ways (e.g., "*means*" or "*refers to*") because of its stereotypical uses in *pragmatic* contexts.[13] Consider the following points:

11.2.1.1 The Disjunction Sign Can Mark the Boundary between Unrelated Commentary Entries

Excerpt 373: Comm. Sa-gig 5, line 25 (§11.1.12)
NÍG.GU$_7$: *ú-kul-tú* : *mu-sa-ri* : *ú-šá-*[*ri*]

"NÍG.GU$_7$" *means* devouring. "*mu-sa-ri*" *means* penis.

Excerpt 374: Comm. Sa-gig 4A, obv. 3 (§11.1.9)
[... D]U : *a-la-ku* : *e-bé-ṭu* : *na-pa-ḫi*

... DU *means* to move. "To have cramps" *means* to inflame.

Observe the disjunction signs in *ú-kul-tú* : *mu-sa-ri* (Excerpt 373) and in *a-la-ku* : *e-bé-ṭu* (Excerpt 374). Although the base text for Excerpt 373 is not well preserved, it is clear that NÍG.GU$_7$ and *mu-sa-ri* constitute topics of separate commentary entries. In Excerpt 374, *a-la-ku* represents a comment on the base text Sa-gig 4: 2, whereas *e-bé-ṭu* refers to a topic from a different base text (Sa-gig 4: 3).

11.2.1.2 The Disjunction Sign Can Mark the Boundary between Different Steps of Argument in a Single Commentary Entry

Excerpt 375: Comm. Sa-gig 19, obv. 13 (§11.1.22)
[MU$_7$].MU$_7$: *ra-ma-ma* : MU$_7$.MU$_7$: ⸢*ri-gim*⸣

MU$_7$.MU$_7$ *means* to groan. MU$_7$.MU$_7$ *means* voice.

Excerpt 376: Comm. Sa-gig 7A, rev. 2 (§11.1.13)
[G]Ú.ŠUB.BA : *ze-nu-ú* : GÚ.ŠUB.[BA : *sa-ba-su*]

---

13 In §1.4, I show how this absence of semantic content allows for the use of disjunction signs in both A:B embedded variants and in cola type commentary equations, helping to underscore their affinity with each other.

GÚ.ŠUB.BA *means* to become offended. GÚ.ŠUB.BA [*means* to become angry.]

Excerpt 375 represents an A′:B:A′:C argument (§1.2.3.2.1), whose logic would be unnecessarily repetitive if the disjunction signs in A′:B:A′ were each interpreted as a *Glossenkeil*—i.e., "MU_7.MU_7 *means* to groan, *which means* MU_7.MU_7, *etc.*" Similarly, for the B:A′:B:C argument (§1.2.3.2.4) in Excerpt 376, the disjunction sign in A′:B is best understood as a separator between different steps of argument: "(Step One:) GÚ.ŠUB.BA *means* to become offended. (Step Two:) GÚ.ŠUB.BA [*means* to become angry.]"

11.2.1.3 The Disjunction Sign Is Used to Clarify Breaks in Syntax That Are Not Readily Obvious and May Be Misinterpreted

Excerpt 377: Comm. Sa-gig 1A, lines 31–32 (§11.1.1)

^{lu_2}an-na-ba-ti : lú-^{giš}kéš-da : nin-nun-gal-e-ne : *eš-⸢še⸣-bu-u* / *ri-kis* ^{d}*Na-ru-du*

"^{lu_2}an-na-ba-ti *or* lú-^{giš}kéš-da : nin-nun-gal-e-ne, *which means* shaman (*or*) (man-of)-the-knot of Narudu *respectively*."

Excerpt 378: Comm. Sa-gig 19, obv. 15–16 (§11.1.22)

[*tas-l*]*i-ma-a-ti* DU_{11}.DU_{11}-*ub* / [...]x-*ú ta-as-li-ma-a* : TI

"He keeps speaking *taslimāti*." ... You made peace, you will live.

Of interest here are the disjunction signs in lú-^{giš}kéš-da : nin-nun-gal-e-ne (Excerpt 377) and in *ta-as-li-ma-a* : TI (Excerpt 378). In Excerpt 377, the sign's position indicates that the phrase should be read segmentally as "man-of-the-knot (lú-^{giš}kéš-da) of Narudu (nin-nun-gal-e-ne)," rather than "man (lú) of the-knot-of-Narudu (^{giš}kéš-da nin-nun-gal-e-ne)." In fact, other texts suggest that "man-of-the-knot" (lú-^{giš}kéš-da) is a reference to the "ecstatic" (*maḫḫû*), which was a profession similar to that of the "shaman."[14] The disjunction sign

14 The Neo-/Late Babylonian sign in Comm. Sa-gig 1A, line 31 (§11.1.1; Excerpt 377) resembles kéš rather than sar, and the Akkadian *rikis* certainly refers to the logogram KÉŠ. On the other hand, note the equation lú sar-da = *ma-ḫu-ú-um* in lexical text OB Lu, C_3 line 14 (*MSL* XII, 194), as well as the writing munus-mú(sar)-da in Charpin (1983/1984: 107); Sommerfeld (1985: 506). It is possible that the similar signs kéš and sar—listed as separate entries nos. 271 and 541 in *MZL*—were confused at some point.

in Excerpt 378 makes explicit the commentator's analysis of the word *taslimāti* as *taslimā* ("you made peace") + TI ("(you) will live").

11.2.1.4 The Disjunction Sign Can Be Omitted Where a Line Break Suggests the Required Disjunction

Excerpt 379: Comm. Sa-gig 29, obv. 6–7 (§11.1.25)
... [I]M.SA$_5$ / [*šar-š*]*ér-ú* ...

... "IM.SA$_5$" (*means*) red paste. ...

Excerpt 380: Comm. Sa-gig 39, obv. 2–3 (§11.1.28)
... SAG.GIŠ.RA / *nu-ú-ú-ru* ...

... SAG.GIŠ.RA (*means*) to smite. ...

Excerpt 381: Comm. Sa-gig 1C, rev. 4′–5′ (§11.1.3)
... ^{tug_2}NÍG.DARA$_2$ ŠU.LÁL / *ú-la-pi lu-*⸢*ʾu*⸣*-ú* ...

... "^{tug_2}NÍG.DARA$_2$ ŠU.LÁL" (*means*) dirty rag. ...

Excerpt 382: Comm. Sa-gig 36, rev. 10′–11′ (§11.1.27)
gul-la : gú [: g]ú-sa-a : ki-šá-ra : / *kul-lat* : *na-*[*ga*]*b* : *nap-ḫar* : *kiš-šat* : ...

"gul-la, gú, gú-sa-a,[15] *and* ki-šá-ra *mean* all (*kullat*), all (*nagab*), all (*napḫar*), and all (*kiššat*) *respectively*."

Excerpt 383: Comm. Sa-gig 3B, obv. 3′–5′ (§11.1.7)
[...] x ⸢: *ḫaṭ*(?)⸣*-ṭu* : *a-ri* : *kak-ku* : si ru ⸢ši⸣ ṭu : *a-tu-*⸢*ú šá Su-ti-i*⸣ / ⸢*sa*⸣*-ma-li la-a-ru-ú šá* ŠU.2 ^{d}*A-ḫa-la-mi-ti* : / [KI.SIK]IL.BÀN.DA : *ba-tul-ti* : ...

"..., stick, branch, weapon, ..., throwing stick in the case of the Sutean, *samālu*-wood, twig in the case of the Hands of the goddess Aḫalamîtu." "KI.SIKIL.BÀN.DA" *means* adolescent girl. ...

---

15 See Note on Comm. Sa-gig 36, rev. 10′–11′ (§11.1.27) for my proposal that gú-sa-a here may represent a corruption of the writing gú-$^{di-ir}$ dir (Erimhuš v, 45 in *MSL* XVII, 68) → gú-^{di} ir+si.a → gú-^{sa_2} sa-a.

Disjunction signs are absent between topic and comment in Excerpts 379–381, where the slant line (/) indicates the position of a line break. Unfortunately, because tablets tend to become broken at their edges, the ends of lines are often not well preserved, and we cannot be certain about the regularity with which scribes omitted disjunction signs at the ends of lines. At other times, however, a disjunction sign can occur immediately before a line break to separate components of the same entry as in *ki-šá-ra* : / *kul-lat* (Excerpt 382), or to separate different entries as in ŠU.2 ^{d}*A-ḫa-la-mi-ti* : / [KI.SIK]IL.BÀN.DA (Excerpt 383).[16]

11.2.1.5 The Disjunction Sign Appears Irregularly Immediately before the Commentary Notation *ša*

Excerpt 384: Comm. Sa-gig 1C, obv. 7 (§11.1.3)
... GÁ.GÁ : *za-ba-lu šá m*[*ur-ṣ*]*u*

... GÁ.GÁ *means* to carry (on), in the case of sickness.

Excerpt 385: Comm. Sa-gig 1B, rev. 4 (§11.1.2)
... ⸢: *né-kel-mu-u*⸣ : *a-ma-ri šá ze-e-e-ri*

To glare at *means* to look, in the case of hatred.

Excerpt 386: Comm. Sa-gig 14, obv. 10 (§11.1.20)
... GU.DU-*s*[*u*] NU.È.A *šá man-zal-tu*$_{4}$ *la ú-še-*[*ṣu*]

... "He does not put out his GU.DU (mistake for KI.GUB)" (*refers to*) the case where he does not put out the flow of excrement.

Excerpt 387: Comm. Sa-gig 14, obv. 14 (§11.1.20)
... DIŠ DÚR-*šú* BÙR-*liš* : *šá* DÚR-*šú ir-pi-*[*šu*]

... "If his rectum is breached" *refers to* the case where his rectum widened.

16 See also ŠU.2-*šú u* GÌR.2-*šú i-ra-ʾ-bu* : / [*ra-ʾ-bu*] : *sa-la-*⸤*ḫu*⸥ (Comm. Sa-gig 3B, rev. 2–3 in §11.1.7); SAG : / [...]x (Comm. Sa-gig 34, obv. 6–7 in §11.1.26); and LÙ.LÙ : / [*ba-la-lu*] (Comm. Sa-gig 34, obv. 8–9 in §11.1.26).

The commentary notation *ša* ("the case of / where") begins a new phrase or clause that more narrowly defines its antecedent (see §11.2.2). While the disjunction sign is typically absent immediately before *ša* when it introduces a new phrase (Excerpts 384–385), it may be absent (Excerpt 386) or present (Excerpt 387) when *ša* begins a new clause. In the last example, the disjunction sign helps to mark off the lengthier *ša* clause as a single explanatory unit, perhaps improving the readability or clarity of the commentator's argument.

11.2.1.6 Even When It Marks a Break between Two Items (*A, B*) in Order to Juxtapose Them for Comparison, the Equation *A:B* Does Not Have a Consistent Meaning

Excerpt 388: Comm. Sa-gig 4B, obv. 16 (§11.1.10)

[TA ^{d}UTU.ŠÚ].⌞A EN⌟ EN.NUN.UD.ZAL.⌞LE :⌟ TA *še-e-ri* EN *ki-iṣ* U$_{4}$ x[...]

"[TA] ^{d}UTU.ŠÚ.A EN EN.NUN.UD.ZAL.LE" *means the opposite of* from morning until the cool of day. ...

Excerpt 389: Comm. Sa-gig 10 & 11, obv. 2–3 (§11.1.18)

... BAL.MEŠ : *n*[*a-bal-ku-ta*] / [BAL : *na-bal-ku-tu*] : BAL : *pa-la-su* ...

... "BAL.MEŠ" *means* [(his eyes) are rolled.] [BAL *means* to roll (eyes).] BAL *means the opposite of* to look at. ...

The excerpts above are discussed in §1.2.3.1.6 as examples of definition by antonymy, whereby a commentary equation (A:B) consists of topic (A) and comment (B) that are opposites of each other. In Excerpt 388, the disjunction sign served to separate the topic "[TA] ^{d}UTU.ŠÚ.A EN EN.NUN.UD.ZAL.LE" (i.e., the night hours "from sunset until the morning watch") from its comment "from morning until the cool of day." Excerpt 389 illustrates how the disjunction sign may separate synonymous logographic and syllabic writings of the same expression ("'BAL.MEŠ' *means* (his eyes) are rolled"), before easily switching its role and introducing an antonym ("BAL *means the opposite of* to look at"). That the same syntactical construction A:B could be used to express synonymy and antonymy implies that the disjunction sign between A and B functions merely as a break, and that it makes no claim about the nature of the A:B relationship.

11.2.1.7 While the Disjunction Sign Is Frequently Used to Separate Embedded Textual Variants, Cases Where the Two Variants Are Obviously Not Part of the Same Syntax May Omit the Disjunction Sign

Embedded variants are discussed in §1.1.3, and a list of these in the Diagnostic Handbook is provided in Appendix One of the first volume (§1). One example of these variants is the medical verdict (Sa-gig 37: 6): TI-*uṭ* : *ma-mit* AD-*šú* DAB-*si* ("she will become healthy : the oath-curse of (her) father has seized her"). Without the disjunction sign separating the variants, a reader might suppose these alternatives to be simultaneously true, so that the patient recovers *even with* the oath-curse of her father upon her. In other pairs of prognostic variants such as TIN GAM, however, the disjunction sign is completely omitted.[17] The logograms TIN GAM may be translated without hesitation as "he will become healthy, (*or*) he will die," since the meaning "he will become healthy (and) he will die" makes no sense. The interposition of a disjunction sign (i.e., TIN : GAM) is not absolutely necessary in such cases, since meaning is unambiguous even in the absence of the notation.

11.2.1.8 Some Commentaries Vary the Number of Winkelhaken Used for Disjunction Signs, in an Effort to Define Their Function More Precisely

Excerpt 390: *CTMMA* II, 69 obv. 1

[... ^{giš}]*a-mur-di-in* :. GIŠ.BÚR : *iṣ-ṣi piš-ri* : ^{u_2}*šal-*⸢*la-pa-ni*⸣

... bramble. "GIŠ.BÚR" *means* solving wood, *which refers to* *šallapānu*-plant.

Excerpt 391: BM 59607, obv. 13[18]

ḫar $^{ḫa\text{-}ar}$*-sa-ap-nu* :. *bur-t*[*i šam-ḫat*]

"Larva-(plant)" *refers to* caterpillar-(plant).

---

17 See Sa-gig 15: 87′; 16: 88′ (MS B).

18 Cf. Frahm (2011a: 237).

Frahm has collected a handful of examples that show variation in the forms of disjunction signs.[19] In Excerpt 390, disjunction signs of three *Winkelhaken* (𒑳) (transliterated as :.) indicate breaks between different commentary entries, while disjunction signs of two *Winkelhaken* (𒑲) (transliterated as :) separate different components of the same entry. One might be tempted to understand a three-*Winkelhaken* sign as a syntactical break, and to view a two-*Winkelhaken* sign as a *Glossenkeil* that expresses the semantic relationship between a cited topic and its commentarial gloss. However, the relative scarcity of three-*Winkelhaken* signs, as well as the use of such signs to separate topic and comment in cases like Excerpt 391, suggests a lack of consensus on the use of such strategies as scribal conventions. Furthermore, even for Excerpt 390, variations in the use of three-*Winkelhaken* versus two-*Winkelhaken* signs can be interpreted as differences in levels or degrees of disjunction, rather than the distinction between a syntactical break and a *Glossenkeil*.

19 Frahm (2011a: 37).

"The Case of / Where" (*ša*)

The particle *ša*, which has been designated a "determinative pronoun," performs two major roles in Akkadian syntax: 1) it precedes the *nomen rectum* (Y) in the genitival relationship X *ša* Y ("X of Y"); and 2) it precedes a relative clause in the construction X *ša* Y ("X who / when / where / which Y").[20] In linguistic parlance, the particle *ša* serves to introduce a "postmodifier" (Y) following after the "head" (X) that is modified. In many instances, the postmodifier restricts the semantic domain of its head. Compared to the numerous possible referents of the word "man," for example, a more limited scope is denoted by the expressions "man *of Uruk*" or "man *who is loved by the goddess Ištar*." In lexical texts, this restricting function of the particle *ša* performs the important role of showing the limits within which certain meanings or nuances are applicable. The two examples below will help clarify my point.

Excerpt 392: Antagal VIII, 109–112 (*MSL* XVII, 173)

tab gír = *ḫa-ma-ṭu* / šu-ru-uz-za = MIN *šá ka-ba-bi* / ud-dù-a = MIN *šá* UD.DA / ka ka-i-zi -izi = MIN *šá* IZI

tab gír (*means*) to burn. šu-ru-uz-za (*means*) *ditto* (i.e., to burn) **in the case of** charring. ud-dù-a (*means*) *ditto* (i.e., to burn) **in the case of** *ṣētu*-heat. ka-izi (*means*) *ditto* (i.e., to burn) **in the case of** fire.

Excerpt 393: Aa V/2, 22–26 (*MSL* XIV, 416)

ḫe-e = ḪE = *ḫe-pu-u šá* GI / [*n*]*i-e-tum šá* GIŠ / [*n*]*a-pa-lu šá* IM / [*ra*]*-a-ku šá* IM / [*ka-r*]*a-ṣu šá* ESIR

/ḫe/ (*is the reading of*) ḪE, (*which means*) to crush **in the case of** reed, to chop(?) **in the case of** wood, to dig out **in the case of** clay, [to knead(?)] **in the case of** clay, [to pinch off] **in the case of** bitumen.

20 "There appears to be no real difference in the function of *ša* before substantives and before relative clauses ... except to indicate that a dependent structure (substantive or clause) follows. ... A 'dependent particle' seems most aptly to describe its character." Sinclair (1970) 41–42. See also Huehnergard (2011: 10–11, §2.3; 185–188, §19.3); Hämeen-Anttila (2000: §3.1.4.3, §4.5.2); *GAG*, §137–138, §164; *AHw*, 1116–1118; *CAD* Š I, 1.

 | DOI:10.1163/9789004417564_033

In Excerpt 392, the choice of logogram to express the meaning "to burn" depends on the specific kind of "burning" in view. The rise in body temperature of a patient sick with *ṣētu*-heat, for instance, differs from the combustive effects of a flame, and this difference is reflected in the logograms used to describe the two events. In Excerpt 393, the same logogram ḪE is translatable into different Akkadian verbs involving the breaking or smashing of substances, depending on whether the substance under consideration is reed, wood, clay, or bitumen. In both these lexical examples, the particle *ša* introduces the circumscribed context within which the logogram or syllabic expression may be applied.

The particle performs essentially the same function in cuneiform commentaries, where it helps to define a word or expression more precisely by restricting the scope of its applicability.[21] While *ša* typically introduces a single word or short phrase in lexical texts, however, it not uncommonly precedes long clauses in the commentaries. I translate this notation as "the case of {a phrase}" or "the case where {a clause}." In the Sa-gig commentaries, Infinitives or nouns after *ša* do not always display the genitive ending (see Excerpts 394–395, 398, and 401 below), but this may reflect the inconsistent loss of case distinction in cuneiform writing of the late period.[22] Verb clauses after *ša* may contain a subordination marker (Excerpt 396), though a quotation after *ša* may also retain its original form without the inclusion of a subordination marker (Excerpt 400). Consider the following ways (non-mutually exclusive) in which the particle *ša* brings clarity through restriction.

11.2.2.1 The Particle *ša* Defines an Ambiguous Form by Restricting Its Possible Identities or Meanings

Excerpt 394: Comm. Sa-gig 13+, line 10 (§11.1.19)

ḫu-uṣ-ṣa : *še-mu-ú šá ka-ba-bu*

"*ḫu-uṣ-ṣa*" *means* to roast, **in the case of** charring.

21 In fact, exactly the same distinction in meaning ("gi (*means*) to become acquainted, in the case of male-and-female (relations)") is expressed using the *ša* notation in the commentary of Excerpt 398 as well as in the lexical texts Nabnitu A, 274–275 (*MSL* XVI, 67); *CT* 12, 29 iv 5.

22 Stein (2000: 33); Hasselbach (2013: 19–20); Beaulieu (2013: 361).

Excerpt 395: Comm. Sa-gig 1A, line 41 (§11.1.1)
DIŠ [Á] 15-*šú iz-qut-su* : *šá zi-iq-tu*$_4$: *šá-n*[*iš* Á(?)] 15-*šú ana* lú₂MAŠ.MAŠ *i-zaq-qí-*⌜*it*⌝

"If his (the healer's) right [arm] stings him" *refers to* **the case of** a stinging pain. [Secondly], (some)one's right [arm (?)] points at the magician.

In Excerpt 394, it is easy to assume that the writing *še-mu-ú* denotes the familiar verb *šemû* ("to hear"). In order to avoid this misunderstanding, the *ša* phrase ("in the case of charring") makes it clear that the less common homophone *šemû* (byform of *šamû* "to roast") is intended. In Excerpt 395, the commentary suggests that the form *zaqātu* can have two closely related meanings: 1) "to sting" and 2) "to point." Although etymology alone could not tell us to which of the two the noun *ziqtu* belongs, actual attestations of *ziqtu* that represent a "sting, barb" imply its greater affinity for the first meaning over the second.[23] In this way, the expression *ša ziqtu* ("the case of a stinging pain") serves to narrow the focus to the experience of "stinging," rather than the action of "pointing."

11.2.2.2 The Particle *ša* Specifies the Meaning of an Expression That Is Too Imprecise

Excerpt 396: Comm. Sa-gig 14, obv. 15–16 (§11.1.20)
... *zu-ú-šú* GUB-x / *šá la il-la-ku-ú-nu* ...

... "His stools stand (still)" (*refers to*) **the case where** they do not move. ...

Excerpt 397: Comm. Sa-gig 21 & 22a, obv. 8 (§11.1.23)
ina DU-*ku im-taḫ-ru* : *šá a-na tar-ṣi a-ḫa-meš iš-te-*[*niš il-la-ku*]

"They correspond in movement" *refers to* **the case where** they [move] in accordance with one another at the same time.

In Excerpt 396, the abruptly terse statement that "his stools stand" is shown to have the meaning "his stools are stationary (i.e., stand still)," since the case is one "where they do not move." In similar fashion, another commentary sheds light on the abstruse description that "(the sick man's strands) correspond in movement" (Excerpt 397). To be sure, this comment hardly clarifies the

23 *CAD* Z, 132–133 s.v. *ziqtu* A.

phenomenon for the modern reader, who is foreign to the way ancient language idioms were used in their own cultural context. This, however, does not detract from the fact that ancient student-scribes were likely helped in their comprehension by the *ša* clause, which perhaps more narrowly defined how strands "correspond" in terms of directionality or simultaneity of movement.

11.2.2.3 The Particle *ša* Restricts the Meaning of an Expression, So That It Contributes to the Commentarial Argument

Excerpt 398: Comm. Sa-gig 14, obv. 24 (§11.1.20)
... gi *la-ma-du šá zi-kìr u* MUNUS : ...

... gi (*means*) to become acquainted, **in the case of** male-and-female (relations). ...

Excerpt 398 makes the same distinction as the lexical text Nabnitu A (274–275), wherein the logogram ZU indicates "acquaintance" (*lamādu*) with facts, while gi is used in cases of sexual "acquaintance" (*lamādu*).[24] But this is not merely an instance where the commentator explains a difficult term (i.e., gi) using lexical precedence. While ZU is very frequently the logogram for the verb "to know, become acquainted," the meaning ascribed to gi here hardly appears elsewhere in medical texts, where other terms instead are employed to describe sexual intimacy. Instead, the *ša* phrase ("in the case of male-and-female (relations)") should be viewed as an attempt to portray the signs "mu ki nu gi" in the base text (Sa-gig 14: 109) as a variation on the common diagnosis MU KI MUNUS *ina* KI.NÁ KUR ("because he is encountered with a female in bed"). In order to achieve this end, the commentator needed to show that nu means "female" and gi denotes "(sexual) acquaintance."

Excerpt 399: Comm. Sa-gig 1B, obv. 20′–21′ (§11.1.2)
[*a-ga-nu-ti*]*l-la-a ma-ak-*⌜*kur* DINGIR.MEŠ⌝ *la qa-a-tu-u* : A : *me-e* / [Í]L : *ḫa-bu-ú* ⌜*šá*⌝ A.MEŠ ⌜: *šá* NÍG.GA (?)⌝ : *ma-ak-kur* ...

"*aganutillâ*-sickness" (*means*) the gods' property without completion. A *means* water. ÍL *means* /*ḫabu*/ **in the case of** water, *or* **in the case of** NÍG.GA (?), *which means* property.

24 *MSL* XVI, 67.

Similarly, in Excerpt 399, the *ša* phrases "in the case of water" and "in the case of NÍG.GA (?), *which means* property" cannot be understood as merely methods of clarifying the ambiguous form *ḫa-bu-ú*. In actuality, the pronunciation /*ḫabu*/ was intentionally ambiguous, in order to suggest a link between the verbs *ḫabû* ("to draw up, raise water") and *ḫâbu* ("to raise property in consecration to the gods"), thereby proving that the logogram A ("water") could replace NÍG ("thing") in the expression NÍG.GA ("property") when this property pertains to the gods—with the resulting form A.GA denoting "the gods' property." *Aganutillâ*-sickness could therefore signify "the gods' property (A.GA) without (NU) completion (TIL)," implying that the sickness arises from the patient's failure to complete his act or promise of consecrating to the gods.

Excerpt 400: Comm. Sa-gig 4B, obv. 7 (§11.1.10)

[... *k*]*ù* ⸢KI-*tim* : BA(?) *ana*(?)⸣ *na-ṣa-ri* : *šá šap-la-*⸢*a-tú*⸣ *ma-al-ku* ᵈ*Kù-bi* ᵈ*A-nun-na-ki ta-paq-qid* : ...

... [/*ku*/] (*refers to*) the earth, BA (points) to (?) guarding, *which refers to* **the case where** "You (the sun-god Šamaš) assign the *malkū*-demons, the Stillborn Child, (and) the Anunnaki gods to the lower regions." ...

Through an analysis of its name, Excerpt 400 portrays the "Stillborn Child" (*Kūba*) as one "guarding" (BA ?) the "earth" (KU_{11}). What follows is the particle *ša* that introduces a quotation from the *Hymn to Šamaš*, showing that the Stillborn Child is assigned by the sun-god to "the lower regions" of the Netherworld,[25] thus narrowing what may be understood by "earth" to the specific location of the realm of the dead. The argument served to associate the Stillborn Child with the moon-god, whose name ᵈŠEŠ.KI could be similarly analyzed as "to guard" (šeš) + "earth" (KI).

11.2.2.4 The Particle *ša* Restricts the Meaning of an Expression to Make It Applicable to the Base Text

Excerpt 401: Comm. Sa-gig 4B, obv. 11 (§11.1.10)

... : UŠ : *e-me-du šá* $qa\text{-}tu_4$: ...

... UŠ *means* to lean on, **in the case of** the Hand (of his god) ...

25 For the quotation from the *Hymn to Šamaš*, see Lambert (1960: 126–127, line 31).

In Excerpt 401, it is dubious that the *ša* phrase "in the case of the hand" is needed to add clarity to the action of "leaning" (*emēdu*). More likely, the "hand" mentioned refers specifically to the diagnosis in the base text that "the Hand of his god is imposed (D stem of *emēdu*) on him" (Sa-gig 4: 4). The *ša* phrase, therefore, makes it explicit that the commentator was concerned not with generic meanings of "leaning," but with the particular idiom in the base text.

Excerpt 402: Comm. Sa-gig 21 & 22a, obv. 3–4 (§11.1.23)

... : *ka-ra-an* IGI.2-*šú šad-du* [...] / *šá kak-kul-tu*$_4$ IGI.2-*šú a-na bi-ta-nu i-ru-b*[*u* :] ...

... "The grapes of his eyes are pulled" ... (*refers to*) **the case where** the iris goes inwards. ...

Excerpt 403: Comm. Sa-gig 39, obv. 8–9 (§11.1.28)

... : *ka-ra-an* IGI.2-*šú šad-du* / *šá kak-kul-tu*$_4$ *i-ni-šú ú-ṣa-a* : ...

... "The grapes of his eyes are pulled" (*refers to*) **the case where** the iris goes outwards. ...

The pertinence of the base text is evident also in Excerpts 402–403, which examine the same medical description drawn from different base texts: "the grapes of his eyes are pulled." It is surprising that the comments seem to be diametric opposites of each other, with such "pulling" explained as the inward movement of the iris in one commentary and as the outward movement of the iris in the other. Admittedly, one of the two excerpts above could represent definition by antonymy, while the other made use of synonymy.[26] Alternatively, however, it is possible the two base texts address dissimilar medical conditions, and the different *ša* clauses result from medical knowledge of what "pulled grapes of the eyes" precisely meant in each situation.

26 See discussion under Excerpts 216–217 in §1.2.3.1.7.

"Which It Said" (*ša iqbû*)

The notations *ša iqbû* and *libbû* (§11.2.4) appear often in connection with textual quotations, whether of the commentaries' base text or of source texts used to support commentarial arguments. George suggested that, like the expression *ša pî ummâni* ("of the mouth of an *ummânu*-scholar") in commentary colophons, the notation *ša iqbû* ("which *he* said") could at times indicate "a living man, the scholar who expounded the text under discussion to the writer of the commentary tablet."[27] Similarly, Koch noted the ambiguity whether the phrases *ša iqbû*, *qabi*, *iqtabi*, and *kīma iqbû* "refer to the word of a teacher, to the stream of tradition in general, or maybe even to another written source."[28] Lambert, on the other hand, was skeptical of the translation "as he said," since "the phrase does not need to have reference to oral communication of a teacher, though other commentaries do refer to such."[29] At least a few Assyrian commentaries use the 'direct speech' particle *mā* in explanations, which may suggest that they "were regarded by those who studied the relevant commentaries as quotations of sorts as well, probably to be attributed to anonymous *ummânu*-scholars."[30] In our Sa-gig commentaries, *ša iqbû* is used in reference to the base text (i.e., the Diagnostic Handbook Sa-gig), as well as Nam-$erim_2$-búr-ru-da (Incantations to Undo Oath-Curses), the terrestrial omen series *Šumma ālu*, and other lexical and narratival sources that are not explicitly named, while *qabi* ("it is said") appears in relation to the composition Gi-nu-tag-ga and lexical entries designated as *ṣâtu* or otherwise (see excerpts below).[31] In my volumes, I have translated *ša iqbû* impersonally as "which it

27 George (1991: 139).

28 Koch-Westenholz (2000: 32). Note also the view that *qabû* may be used impersonally as "an indirect reference to the community of the *ummânu*-experts" in Clancier (2014: 58).

29 Lambert (2013: 137).

30 These commentaries from Assur and Nineveh are listed in Frahm (2011a: 110 n. 571).

31 Omitted from discussion is Comm. Sa-gig 7Cb, line 5′ (§11.1.16): [... ^{d}*Šu-lak šá* E-*ú* (?) : ŠU : *qa*]-⸢tu_4⸣ : ⸢*la* :⸣ *la-a* : KÙ : ⸢*el*⸣-[*lu* ...] ("['The demon Šulak,' which it said (?), *refers to* ŠU, *which means*] hand, *la*, *which means* not, (and) KÙ, *which means* clean. ..."), for which the notation [*šá* E-*ú* (?)] is only hesitantly restored, based on its presence in what appears to be the same argument in Uruk Therapeutic Comm. 1 = *SpTU* I, 47 obv. 4. Also, damage to the syntax of *ma-ar-*tu_4 *šá* [^{d}*A-nim* x]x / *šá* DINGIR.⸢MEŠ GAL.MEŠ E⸣-*ú*, "Daughter of [the god Anu] ... of the great gods, which it said" (Comm. Sa-gig 1A, obv. 19–20 in §11.1.1) makes analysis of this entry uncertain.

 | DOI:10.1163/9789004417564_034

said," while leaving open the possibility that the sayings of an actual person were envisioned in some instances.

Frahm remarked that "[a commentary's] explanation is introduced by *ša iqbû*, while *kīma iqbû* concludes it," and that "if we regard commentarial quotations and explanations as some kind of direct speech, attributed either to texts or to anonymous scholars, we can indeed claim that *ša iqbû* and *kīma iqbû* function as cuneiform quotation marks, with the former opening and the latter closing the quotation."[32] Gabbay conceded that, in this regard, the positions of *ša iqbû* and *kî iqbû* (rather than *kīma iqbû*) mirror those of their Hebrew parallels—אשר אמר and כי הוא אשר אמר respectively—that occur "before an interpretation [and] after an interpretation in the pesharim literature and the Damascus Document."[33] However, in contrast to Frahm, Gabbay saw *ša iqbû* not as "introducing a commentary by a scholar or quotation from another text which occurs after the phrase," but as "follow[ing] a quote."[34] In other words, "the phrase *ša iqbû*, 'which he/it said,' refers to a quote before the commentary, and the phrase *kî iqbû*, 'like he/it said,' which appears after the commentary, refers to the meaning of the text in light of the commentary."[35] His recent book reaffirms this position in no uncertain terms:

> A detailed examination of all occurrences of the phrase *ša iqbû* known to me demonstrates that the object of the verb *qabû* is never the explanation that follows it; rather it is always the lemma or passage from the base text cited before the phrase, the lemma that is about to be commented on. Syntactically, the commentary on this cited lemma or passage serves as the predicate of a nominal sentence, i.e., 'x (= citation of a lemma from the base text) which it (= the text) said (*ša iqbû*) (is/means) y (– commentary).'[36]

The notation *kî iqbû* ("as if it / he said") does not unambiguously occur in our Sa-gig commentaries, while *iqtabi* ("it / he has said") and *qabi* ("it is said") are

32 Ibid., 109–110.

33 Gabbay argued that the writing GIM *iqbû* stood for *kî iqbû* and not *kīma iqbû*: "Especially revealing is CT 13, 32+, which contains the syllabic spellings *ki* and *ki-i* in line 5 and r.5'-6', but the writing GIM in r.13' (cf. Matsushima 2009, 60). This would indicate a reading of the sign GIM as *kî*, although it is possible that variation also occurred (cf. also Borger 2003, 399, ad no. 686)." Gabbay (2012: 306–308), (2014: 355 n. 97), and (2016: 246–247).

34 Gabbay (2014: 351–352) claims that his interpretation differs from those of George (1991: 139); Koch-Westenholz (2000: 32); Frahm (2011a: 108–109).

35 Gabbay (2014: 356).

36 Gabbay (2016: 203).

only scarcely attested.[37] Instances of *ša iqbû* in this commentary corpus, however, cast doubt on Gabbay's claims that the object of *qabû* is exclusively the "base text," or that *ša iqbû* always refers to a quotation preceding it (i.e., anaphoric) rather than a quotation following after it (i.e., cataphoric). Furthermore, while improvements in elucidating the meanings and syntaxes of *qabû* notations are welcome, an important issue remains largely unaddressed: Judging by the Sa-gig commentaries, entries with *qabû* and *libbû* (§11.2.4) are actually in the minority, and numerous examples involve the successful explanation of topics by means of comments without recourse to either notation, which begs the reason for their occurrences. My approach here is mainly descriptive, in hopes that the following observations on the referentiality of *ša iqbû* may contribute to future theories of the notation as an element of discourse.

11.2.3.1 The Notation *ša iqbû* Is Anaphoric and Refers to a Base Text Quotation before It

The Sa-gig commentaries include few clear examples where *ša iqbû* refers to a preceding quotation of the base text. This may not be surprising, despite importance attached to the combination ... *ša iqbû* ... *kî iqbû* by Frahm and Gabbay (discussed above). Most of our Sa-gig commentators seem to have combed through their base texts methodically in a line-by-line manner, so that the order and proximity of quoted topics adhere closely to their positions in the base texts. In a given commentary, these topics appear very frequently, and they are often quoted in the most succinct form possible—e.g., a word or phrase, instead of the entire clause or sentence. In commentaries of this nature, therefore, it was likely deemed cumbersome and excessive to mark off every single short base text quotation with *ša iqbû*.

Excerpt 404: Comm. Sa-gig 1C, obv. 9–10 (§11.1.3)

[DIŠ ŠÁ]Ḫ ⸢SA_5⸣ [IGI GIG B]I *a-na* ITI.⸢3⸣.KAM : *ana* U_4.[3.KAM ÚŠ *š*]*á* E-*ú* / [*ki*]-*i* ⸢*na*⸣-*a*[*q-du ana* 3 U_4-*mu*] ⸢*ki-i*⸣ *la na-aq-d*[*u ana*] ⸢3⸣ ITI ÚŠ

"[If he sees a] red pig, [that sick man will die] in three months : in [three] days," **which it said.** If he is critically sick, he will die [in three days]; if he is not critically sick, [in] three months.

37 *iq-ta-bi* (Comm. Sa-gig 1B, rev. 15 in §11.1.2); *šá* GI.NU.TAG.GA-*u qa-bi* (Comm. Sa-gig 3C, obv. 7 in §11.1.8).

Excerpt 405: Comm. Sa-gig 7A, rev. 11–12 (§11.1.13)

... DIŠ GÙ GIG *taš-*⌜*mi*⌝*-ma* GIM GÙ AN[ŠE ...] / [*ana* (?)] U_4.1.KAM GAM *šá* E-*ú mu-ú-tu pa-ni* dIM.DU[GUD.MUŠEN]

... "If you listen to the sick man's voice, and [it sounds] like the voice of a donkey ... he will die [on] the first day," **which it said.** Death is complement to dIM.DUGUD.MUŠEN, ...

In Excerpt 404, the notation *ša iqbû* relates to the preceding quotation from the base text Sa-gig U1: 11 (S1: 8). What follows *ša iqbû* is the commentator's own interpretation of the conditions that would lead to the sick man's death "in three months : in three days." Here, the commentator was apparently influenced by the language of subsequent entries in the base text (Sa-gig U1: 12–13 (S1: 9–10)), which describes the sick man as "critically sick."[38] In Excerpt 405, the statement "Death is complement to dIM.DUGUD.MUŠEN, ..." evidently represents the commentator's own words rather than the quotation of an external source, especially given how it makes use of the commentary notation *pāni* ("complement to"; §11.2.5) in its argument. The expression *ša iqbû*, therefore, most probably refers to the preceding base text quotation. As is immediately obvious, these quotations in Excerpts 404–405 are unusually long, and their length possibly justified the use of *ša iqbû* in these instances.

Excerpt 406: Comm. Sa-gig 1B, rev. 5 (§11.1.2)

[DIŠ GU_4 *ik-ki*]*p-šú* GIG BI *na-qud* NU TE-*šú šá iq-bu-ú ina* ŠÀ *šá* GU_4 : *al-pi* : GU_4 : *e-ṭém-mu*

"[If an ox butted] him, that sick man is critically sick, one must not approach him," **which it said.** Implicit in that "GU_4" *means* ox, (and) "GU_4" *means* ghost.

Excerpt 406 contains the expression *ša iqbû ina libbi* (*ša*), which is also attested in other commentaries from Uruk.[39] I agree with George that the verb *iqbû* marks the end of a clause, and so *ša iqbû* likely refers to the base text quotation

38 The prognosis "(that sick man) is critically sick, one must not approach him" (*na-qud* NU TE-*šú*) occurs in Sa-gig U1: 12 (S1: 9) and again in Sa-gig U1: 13 (S1: 10).

39 See Uruk Therap. Comm. 1 = *SpTU* I, 47 obv. 14; Uruk Therap. Comm. 2 = *SpTU* I, 49 rev. 27–28; Uruk Therap. Comm. 3 = *SpTU* I, 50 rev. 31, 34.

(Sa-gig U1: 21 (S1: 18)) that precedes it.[40] For such constructions, Gabbay suggested the translation "which it said, since …"[41]

11.2.3.2 The Notation *ša iqbû* Is Anaphoric and Refers to a Quoted Source Other than the Base Text

Excerpt 407: Comm. Sa-gig 1B, obv. 12′–15′ (§11.1.2)

… : DIŠ ⸢ŠÁḪ GE$_6$⸣ IGI GIG BI ÚŠ *šá-niš uš-ta-pa-šaq-ma* TIN / … / [*lìb-bu-u*] DIŠ ŠÁḪ *ana qé-re-eb* ⸢*ur-ši* KU$_4$-*ub*⸣ *a-si-ir-ti* [*ana*] É EN-*šú* ⸢KU$_4$⸣-*ub* / [*šá ina* DIŠ URU] *ina* SUKUD-*e* GAR-*in a-si-ir-ti šá* E-*ú e-sér* ^{lu_2}GIG

"If he sees a black pig, that sick man will die. Secondly, he will get into dire straits, but he will live." … [As in,] "If a pig enters into the interior of the bedroom, a female captive will enter [into] her master's house," [which (it said) in (the terrestrial omen series) *If a City*] *is Situated on a Height*. The "female captive," **which it said**, (*refers to*) the sick man's confinement.

In Excerpt 407, *ša iqbû* refers back to an earlier quotation on the "female captive" from the terrestrial omen series *Šumma ālu* (XLIX, 41′).[42] This cited terrestrial omen is not the Sa-gig base text (i.e., Sa-gig U1: 9) that is the main *topic* of the commentator's systematic study, but a source text that constitutes part of his *comment* and that lends weight to his argument.[43]

Excerpt 408: Comm. Sa-gig 1A, obv. 6–10 (§11.1.1)

… : DIŠ KI.UD.BI IGI N[AM.ERIM$_2$ DAB-*s*]*u* / *lu-u* ⸢*šá*⸣ *ana* SISKUR *mi-ḫir lu-u šá ana* ^{d}U.GUR *lu-u šá ana ḫi-s*[*u-ú-ti* GAR-*nu* (?)] / *lìb-bu-ú ina* KI.UD.BI-*šú* NIDBA.MEŠ DINGIR.MEŠ GAL.MEŠ *uq-*[*tar-ra-bu* (?)] / *šá* KI ^{d}U.GUR *kaš-kaš* DINGIR *na-ram* ^{d}*Nin-men-na šá ina* NAM.E[RIM$_2$.BÚR.RU.D]A / E-*ú* : …

---

40 "… as was said, it is implicit in …" George (1991) 149 (section 18b). If the commentator had wished to express the idea "which it said implicitly," the syntax would have been **šá ina* ŠÀ *iq-bu-ú*, in accordance with the syntax in *šá ina* NAM.E[RIM$_2$.BÚR.RU.D]A E-*ú* (obv. 9–10) and *šá ana dum-qí u lum-nu* E-*ú* (obv. 14) of Comm. Sa-gig 1A (§11.1.1).

41 Gabbay (2016: 221–223).

42 Freedman (2017: 78).

43 See discussion in §1.1.4.2.

> … "If he sees the KI.UD.BI, an oath-curse [has seized] him." Whether (the KI.UD.BI) is one that is [set up] for a sacrificial offering, that is, for the god Nergal or for [commemoration (?)]. As in, "On his KI.UD.BI, the meal-offerings of the great gods have been [brought near (?)]," which *refers to* "Nergal the almighty god, beloved of the goddess Ninmenna," **which it said** in Nam-erim$_2$-búr-ru-da (Incantations to Undo Oath-Curses). …

We encounter a similar situation in Excerpt 408, where *ša iqbû* refers to the preceding description "Nergal the almighty god, beloved of the goddess Ninmenna." Although the commentator ascribed this epithet to Nam-erim$_2$-búr-ru-da (Incantations to Undo Oath-Curses), it evidently had wider circulation and is attested also in a Šu-íl-lá prayer to Nergal.[44] In any case, the object of the verb *qabû* is not the base text (Sa-gig S1: 3), but the incantation series. Significantly, this entry was discussed by Gabbay, apparently without any sense of dissonance,[45] which suggests that Gabbay's idea of a "base text" refers to any cited text that receives explication, without taking into account my distinction of base text versus source text (§1.1.4.2) in these volumes.

This is not merely a trivial matter of labels, since a source text represents external textual authority (§1.2.2) selectively quoted by the commentator in support of his interpretations of the base text, and this source text remains *a part of the comment* (not the *topic*) even if the commentator remarks upon it. The notion that elements of the *comment* can receive explication in service to the larger aim of explaining the base text, in fact, represents a foundational principle of multiple member A:B:C, B:A′:B:C, and other patterns of arguments (§1.2.3.2.3–5). When one is willing to acknowledge the role of comments as referents of the verb *qabû*, it becomes easy to view the examples in the following section (§11.2.3.3) as instances of cataphoric reference, where *ša iqbû* actually precedes the source text it refers to.

---

44 See van Proosdij (1952: 110, no. 27, line 4); Mayer (1976: 479); Durand (1979: 158); George (1991: 154).

45 Gabbay (2016: 122–123).

11.2.3.3 The Notation *ša iqbû* Is Cataphoric and Refers to a Quoted Source after It

Excerpt 409: Comm. Sa-gig 1B, obv. 24′–28′ (§11.1.2)

… GU$_4$ GÙN IGI GIG BI / [^{d}DÌM.M]E DAB-*s*[*u* :] … / … / … : GÙN : *ba-ra-mu šá* E-[*ú*] *ki-ma nim-ri tuk-ku*(!)-*pa* / [ELLAG$_2$.MEŠ-*šá* :] …

"(If) he sees a dappled ox, [the *lamaštu*-demoness] has seized that sick man." … "GÙN" *means* to become dappled. (According to) **that which it said:** "[Her lateral parts (lit. kidneys)] are spotted like a leopard." …

Excerpt 410: Comm. Sa-gig 1B, rev. 13–17 (§11.1.2)

… : DINGIR *saḫ-ḫi-ra* : ^{d}*Gaz-ba-ba* / […] x *še-e-ḫu* bad é me : *ina* GAŠAN-*ia*$_5$(mu) ^{d}ZUEN ^{d}INNIN ⟨É.⟩AN.NA / [*u* ^{d}*Gaz-ba*]-*ba iq-ta-bi šá-niš* ^{d}*La-ta-ra*-⌜*ak*⌝-*a šal-šiš* ^{d}*Un-na-ni-ši* / [^{d}MAR.TU ^{d}]MAŠ.TAB.BA *šá* E-*ú* : ^{mul}MAŠ.TAB.BA *šá* IGI-*et* ^{mul}SIPA.ZI.AN.NA / [GUB.MEŠ-*z*]*u* ^{d}LÚ.LÀL *u* ^{d}*La-ta-ra-ak-a* : …

… "Prowling god" *refers to* Gazbaba. … "Among Bēltīya, Sîn, Bēlet-Eanna, [and Gazbaba], he spoke." Secondly, Lātarāk. Thirdly, Unnānîši, [Amurru], the Twins. (According to) **that which it said:** "The Twins who [stand] opposite Sipazianna (Orion) are Lulal and Lātarāk." …

It may not be a coincidence that Excerpts 409–410 come from the same commentary and perhaps reflect the rhetorical style of the same commentator. In each of these excerpts, *ša iqbû* comes immediately after an explanation resembling the commentator's own words, so it is difficult to imagine *ša iqbû* ("which it said") as the conclusion to a base text citation.[46] Moreover, it is striking that both instances of *ša iqbû* here immediately precede quotations from sources other than the base text. The statement "[Her lateral parts (lit. kidneys)] are spotted like a leopard" is taken from the *Lamaštu* incantations,[47] while the description of "the Twins who [stand] opposite Sipazianna (Orion)" derives from the astral compendium Mul-apin (I ii 3–4).[48] The most natural reading

46 It seems too much of a stretch to treat these comments as merely parenthetical elements, such as "'GÙN'—*meaning* to become dappled—which it said" and "'Prowling god'—referring to … the Twins—which it said," whereby the actual referents of *ša iqbû* are the terms "GÙN" (Sa-gig U1: 18) and "Prowling god" or "Twins" (Sa-gig U1: 37a) in the base text.

47 For the quotation from the *Lamaštu* Incantation Series II, 37, see Farber (2014: 168–169, 230), as well as remarks by Hunger in *SpTU* 1, 27 obv. 27′ and George (1991: 156).

48 For the quotation from Mul-apin I, ii 3–4, see Hunger and Steele (2019: 39).

of these excerpts understands *ša iqbû* ("(According to) that which it said: ...") simply as a notation introducing the quoted source text that follows after it.[49]

11.2.3.4 It Is Disputable Whether the Notation *ša iqbû* Is Anaphoric or Cataphoric

Excerpt 411: Comm. Sa-gig 1B, obv. 17′–18′ (§11.1.2)

... : DIŠ ŠÁḪ GÙN IGI *šá* E-*ú* / [šáḫ-z]é-da-s[ur-ra :] *bu-ri-ia-a-mu šá zu-mur-šú ki-ma ṭi-me uṣ-ṣu-ru*

... "If he sees a dappled pig," **which it said**, šáḫ-zé-da-sur-ra [*means*] a *burīyāmu*-pig, whose body is patterned like yarn.

In Excerpt 411, the phrase *ša iqbû* is sandwiched between the short base text quotation ("If he sees a dappled pig" in Sa-gig U1: 12) and a succinct description reminiscent of lexical entries on pigs ("šáḫ-zé-da-sur-ra [*means*] a *buriyāmu*-pig, whose body is patterned like yarn").[50] The option to view *ša iqbû* as anaphoric runs into the question why other base text citations in the vicinity—many of which are longer than the one here—are simply quoted without the explicit use of *ša iqbû* ("which it said"). And if *ša iqbû* is to be understood as cataphoric, there arises another question whether the ensuing lexical quotation extends to everything that follows, or whether the phrase "whose body is patterned like yarn" represents an interpolation by this commentator.[51] Interestingly, Excerpt 413 in the next section includes the remark "it is said in a *ṣâtu* composition," involving a term (*ṣâtu*) employed as one of the two main commentary designations—i.e., *ṣâtu* ("glossary") versus *mukallimtu* ("exposition")—as well as a label for lexical lists even up to the Late Babylonian period (§1.2.1.1). The remark suggests that entries from lexical (*ṣâtu*) source texts constituted authorities in their own right, which could be legitimately invoked by the notation *ša iqbû*.

49 The disjunction sign after *šá* E-*ú* in Excerpt 410 does not necessarily imply that *šá* E-*ú* is more closely related to what precedes it.

50 See also šáḫ-zé-da-bar-sur-ra = MIN (= *bur-ma-mu*) in Hh. XIV, 164 (*MSL* VIII/2, 20).

51 Note the shorter version in another parallel commentary: "['If he sees a dappled pig,' which it said,] šáḫ-zé-da-sur-ra *means* a *buriyāmu*-pig" (Comm. Sa-gig 1C, obv. 11 in §11.1.3).

11.2.3.5 Attestations of the Notation *qabi*

Excerpt 412: Comm. Sa-gig 3C, obv. 5–7 (§11.1.8)

la(-)ḫa-aḫ-šá : *i-su*(!) SAG.2-*šú em-mu* : *šá-niš la* Ú[Ḫ : *la ḫa*]-*ḫa-šú* : *la ṣar-ḫa-áš* : ⸢ÚḪ⸣ [: *ṣa-ra-ḫu*] / *lìb-bu-ú* níĝ-izi-ba-zu-ta sug-ge úḫ-ba šu ḫa-⸢an⸣-[ta]g-ga-e ḫu-uz x[...] / *šá* GI.NU.TAG.GA-*u qa-bi* : ...

"The cuneiform signs la(-)ḫa-aḫ-šá" *mean* the cheek-bones (on both sides) of his head are hot. Secondly, (the cuneiform signs refer to) non-ÚḪ (heat), *which refers to* non-*ḫaḫḫaš* (heat), *which refers to* non-flaring-up (heat). ÚḪ [*means* to flare up]. As in, "níĝ-izi-ba-zu-ta sug-ge úḫ-ba šu ḫa-an-tag-ga-e ḫu-uz ...," **it is said** in the case of (the composition) Gi-nu-tag-ga.

In Excerpt 412, the absence of the subordination marker -*u* that consistently appears in *ša iqbû* ("which it said") suggests that *qabi* ("it is said") occurs in a main clause, and that the particle *ša* relates to the title GI.NU.TAG.GA-*u* that immediately follows—i.e., "in the case of (the composition) Gi-nu-tag-ga"—and not to the verb *qabi*. Arguably, the translation should reflect the status of the entire Gi-nu-tag-ga quotation as the subject of the Stative verb *qabi*—i.e., "'níĝ-izi-ba-zu-ta...' is said in the case of Gi-nu-tag-ga." Given the atomistic nature of writing in commentaries, however, and in order to make such stereotypical notations obvious to English readers, I keep to the fixed expression "it is said" in these volumes.

Excerpt 413: Comm. Sa-gig 19, obv. 15–17 (§11.1.22)

[*tas-l*]*i-ma-a-ti* DU$_{11}$.DU$_{11}$-*ub* / [...]x-*ú ta-as-li-ma-a* : TI / [...]-*ti* : *nu-ul-lat ina ṣa-a-tú* E

"He keeps speaking *taslimāti*." ... You made peace, you will live. ... *refers to* foolish talk, **it is said** in a *ṣâtu* composition.

Excerpt 414: Comm. Sa-gig 14, obv. 23 (§11.1.20)

... : ki nu gi E *it-ti sin-niš-ti la-a*[*m-du*]

... "ki nu gi," **it is said**, (*means*) he is acquainted with a female.

Excerpt 415: Comm. Sa-gig 4A, obv. 16–18 (§11.1.9)

[^{d}*Anu*] LUGAL DIN[GIR.M]EŠ KI-*tim ir-ḫe-e-ma* IMIN DINGIR.MEŠ / [*uldaššum-m*]*a* $^{[din]gir}$IMIN.BI *it-ta-bi* ⸤*zi-kìr*⸥-[*šu-un*] / [...]x DUG$_4$.GA x[...]

> "[Anu,] King of the gods, impregnated the earth. Seven gods [did she bear him], and he called their name The Seven." ... **it is said.**

These other examples express *qabi* ("it is said") logographically, either as the logogram E (Excerpts 413–414)[52] or as DUG$_4$.GA (Excerpt 415). In Excerpts 413 and 415, *qabi* appears to be anaphoric, referring to preceding source text quotations from a *ṣâtu* lexical entry[53] and from the *Erra Epic* (I, 28–29) respectively. In Excerpt 414, the notation *qabi* is also anaphoric, but points to the expression "ki nu gi" earlier cited from the base text (Sa-gig 14: 109).

52 This was also how Finkel understood the lone sign E in a *Šumma izbu* commentary. Finkel (2006: 140 (obv. 21), 143 (notes on lines 19–21)).

53 The following suggest possible ways to restore [...]-*ti* : *nu-ul-lat* (Comm. Sa-gig 19, obv. 17 in §II.1.22): [*šil-la*]-*ti* (cf. *CT* 18, 6 [rev. 40]), [*la qa-bi*]-*ti* (cf. *CT* 18, 6 [rev. 43]; *LTBA* II, 2: 408, and dupl. 3 vi 4; Šurpu p. 51: 44), [*la ki-it*]-*ti* (cf. Lambert 1960: 88, comm. to line 284), or even [*tas-li-ma*]-*ti* (cf. *CT* 18, 6 rev. 45; this is also the preference of Frahm 2011a: 89 n. 446, 226).

"As in" (*libbû*)

The *Chicago Assyrian Dictionary* recognizes a specialized use of the form *libbû* in commentaries, where it may be translated "(this) means."[54] The term is usually written out syllabically (e.g., *lìb-bu-ú*), so that the long final vowel is evident.[55] Although *libbû* is clearly related to *libbu* ("inside, heart") in etymology, there has been little attempt to elucidate the grammatical form of *libbû*. Von Soden suggested that the long final vowel includes the "Lokativ-Adverbial" ending *-um*.[56] I am, however, in favor of another explanation. At least in the commentaries, the meaning of *libbû* seems aligned with that of a denominative adjective, i.e., "inner" or "implicit." This proposed relationship between *libbu* and *libbû* follows well known patterns elsewhere, in which nouns pertaining to positions or directions such as *maḫru* ("front, front side"), *elu* ("top, upper part"), and *šaplu* ("bottom, underside") tend to form denominative adjectives such as *maḫrû* ("former, earlier"), *elû* ("upper"), and *šaplû* ("lower").[57]

In the syntax of our commentaries, *libbû* ("The thing implicit (in) …") seems to be substantivized before the quotation or item it refers to, just as the noun clause *ša iqbû*—"(According to) that which is said"—can refer cataphorically to a following quotation (§11.2.3.3). Of course, the meaning of an expression is governed not only by etymology, but also by conventional usage. Though the original noun (*libbu*, "inside") and its substantivized denominative adjective (*libbû*, "the thing implicit") are nominals with similar meanings, they carry slightly different nuances or technical meanings that are exclusive to each.[58]

54 *CAD* L, 173 (s.v. *libbu*, §4a 2′ b′); "par analogie avec" in Cavigneaux (1994: 143). Outside commentaries, *libbû* is said to have the meanings "like, instead of, according to" *CAD* L, 173 (s.v. *libbu*, §4a 2′). Note also the adverbial *libbū* with the meaning "zugehörig zu" in *AHw*, 550–551.

55 One wonders how the notation *libbû* is related to another expression *ina* ŠÀ *šá* (tentatively translated: "implicit in that") in Comm. Sa-gig 1B, rev. 5 (§11.1.2), where the logographic writing ŠÀ is employed.

56 *AHw*, 550–551. See also *GAG*, §66; Huehnergard (2011: 312–313, §28.3). Note also the semantic equivalence of *libbû* (with the locative *-um*) and *ina libbi*, with the latter argued to have an instrumental meaning ("by means of") in Ossendrijver (*NABU* 2010/44).

57 Huehnergard (2011: 40–41, §6.2); Buccellati (1996: §21.4).

58 For example, *maḫru* can be a specific reference to "the past" or "bygone time," while *maḫrû* is used to express priorities in social status, age, eminence, and family relationships (*CAD* M I, 106, 109). *Šaplu* can refer to "arrears" in payment, while *šaplû* is used in grammatical texts to indicate an element that is "suffixed" (*CAD* Š I, 468, 477).

 | DOI:10.1163/9789004417564_035

In my translations, I typically render *libbû* as the simple phrase "as in." When implication is drawn—not from a single item—but from a suggested logical relationship between separate items (§11.2.4.4), I translate *libbû* with the expression "as in the fact that."

Both the notations *ša iqbû* and *libbû* can mark out quotations from external sources.[59] As illustrated by Excerpt 412 earlier, both may even appear simultaneously in reference to the same quotation.[60] There seem to be, however, two differences in the uses of *ša iqbû* and *libbû*. First, whereas *ša iqbû* can be anaphoric or cataphoric, attestations of *libbû* are invariably cataphoric. This means that the statement from which implications are drawn follows after the term *libbû* in the commentary's text. The entry below from a commentary on *Šumma izbu* (omen series on birth anomalies) will illustrate this point.

Excerpt 416: Comm. Izbu 7, obv. 10–11[61]

... *as-suk-ku* : *kur-ban-nu* : *as-suk-ku* : *ab-nu as-pi* / *lìb-bu-u i-kim-šú as-pa-šú as-suk-ka-šú ú-saḫ-ḫi-ir*

... *assukku means* lump. *assukku means* sling-stone. **As in**, "He (Marduk) deprived him (my pursuer) of his sling, he turned aside his *assukku*."

Here, the statement after *libbû* is an abridged quotation from the *Poem of the Righteous Sufferer*, in which the term *assukku* occurs in literary parallelism with the word "sling" (*aspu*).[62] The quotation represents an effort to prove the commentator's argument that "*assukku means* sling-stone." Since "*assukku means* lump" and this lump-like object is mentioned in connection with a sling, the implication is that *assukku* denotes a sling-stone.

This brings us to the second point of difference between *ša iqbû* and *libbû*. It is not easy to distinguish the logical arguments involved in *ša iqbû* citations from those of *libbû* ones, since some 'implication' relevant to the commentator's argument is always present even in quotations introduced by *ša iqbû*. To put it in another way, the logic of Excerpt 416 would not be substantially

59 Frahm (2011a: 108).

60 Other examples are less certain: The term [*lìb-bu-u*] in Excerpt 407 needs to be restored. In Excerpt 408, *libbû* and *ša iqbû* do not actually refer to the same quotation: *libbû* introduces the quote "On his KI.UD.BI, the meal-offerings of the great gods have been [brought near (?)]," while *ša iqbû* follows after the quote "Nergal the almighty god, beloved of the goddess Ninmenna.".

61 Finkel (2006: 147, Fig. 1, obv. 10–11).

62 [d]*Marduk šá mu-kaš-ši-di-ia i-kim as-*⸢*pa*⸣*-šú as-suk-ka-šú ú-saḫ-ḫír*, "Marduk deprived my pursuer of his sling and turned aside his slingstone" in Lambert (1960: 56, line r).

changed, even if we were to substitute *ša iqbû* for *libbû*. That being said, the literal meaning of *ša iqbû* ("which it said") may have exerted some restraint in confining its use to verbatim citations or close paraphrases. The more flexible meaning of *libbû* ("as in"), on the other hand, corresponds well to its use in the wider variety of situations shown below.

11.2.4.1 The Notation *libbû* Refers to the Quotation of a Written Text Composition

Excerpt 417: Comm. Sa-gig 1A, obv. 3–5 (§11.1.1)

... DIŠ *ina* SILA ŠIKA *zaq-pa* IGI GIG [BI] / *na-qud* NU TE-*šú* : ... / *l*[*ìb-b*]*u-u it-te-eḫ-pi kar-pi ḫa-aṣ-bu-um-ma* ⸢*im-tu-ut*⸣ [LÚ ...]

... "If he sees a potsherd standing upright in the street, [that] sick man is critically sick; One must not approach him." ... **As in**, "Pot has been broken into potsherd, and [Man] has died." ...

Excerpt 418: Comm. Sa-gig 14, obv. 6–7 (§11.1.20)

... *ki-iṣ-ṣat* U[D.DA] / *ḫi-miṭ* UD.DA *lìb-bu-ú i-šat mu-ú-tú i-šat šib-ṭu* KI.MIN : ...

... "*kiṣṣatu* of [*ṣētu*-heat" (*means*)] burning of *ṣētu*-heat. **As in**, "Fire of death, fire of plague, *ditto* (i.e., *kiṣṣatu*)."[63] ...

In Excerpt 417, the quotation "Pot has been broken into potsherd, and [Man] has died" comes from a compilation of bilingual proverbs.[64] Human wellbeing is compared to the integrity of a pot, in line with the Mesopotamian tradition that humankind was fashioned from clay. By implying such a link, the citation validates the omen's logic of treating an observed potsherd as a portent that the patient is "broken" and "critically sick." In Excerpt 418, though the source cited is a fire incantation with the words "fire of death, fire of plague, consuming (*kāsistu*) fire," the commentator apparently substituted the original expression *išātu* ("fire") + *kāsistu* ("consuming") for the similar-sounding term

63 In the tablet of Comm. Sa-gig 14 (§11.1.20), the signs *ki-iṣ-ṣat* (obv. 6) are directly above the term KI.MIN, "*ditto*" (obv. 7), which therefore represents the word *kiṣṣatu*.

64 Finkel (*NABU* 1993/15). This quotation was earlier mistaken to be from "a bilingual account of the early history of mankind (unpublished BM, courtesy Finkel; the Sumerian of this line is lost)." George (1991: 153).

kiṣṣatu.[65] By doing so, he implied that *kiṣṣatu* is another way to express "burning," and that "*kiṣṣatu* of *ṣetu*-heat" therefore referred to the sickness familiarly described as "burning of *ṣetu*-heat."

11.2.4.2 The Notation *libbû* Refers to an Idiomatic Expression

Excerpt 419: Comm. Sa-gig 1B, rev. 6–7 (§11.1.2)
[DIŠ SI GU_4 IG]I GIG BI ÚŠ : SI : *qar-nu* : SI : *nu-úr* : SI : *šá-ru-ru* / [*lìb-bu*]-⸢*ú*⸣ *šá-ru-ru-šú im-qu-tu* : ...

"[If he] sees [an ox's horn (SI)], that sick man will die." "SI" *means* horn. "SI" *means* light. "SI" *means* rays. **As in**, its rays diminished. ...

Excerpt 420: Comm. Sa-gig 1B, rev. 9 (§11.1.2)
... ŠU DAM NA *lìb-bu-ú a-na* DAM NA TE-*ḫe*

... "Hand of (another) man's wife." **As in**, "He approached (another) man's wife (for sex)."

Excerpt 419 begins with the omen "if he sees an ox's horn (SI)," which comes from the base text Sa-gig U1: 22a at the very end of a section on ox omens (Sa-gig U1: 15–22a). It is awkward to imagine that the statement describes the sighting of the horn attached to the rest of the ox, since such an observation must surely be assumed for the other ox omens as well. I propose instead that Excerpt 419 refers to a horn that is detached from the ox—perhaps due to an accident—which has then "fallen" onto the ground. The negative connotations of "rays" (SI) that are "diminished" (lit. "fallen"), perhaps alluding to the failing sight of a dying man, supports the prediction that a fallen "horn" (SI) portends the sick man's death. The pithy expression "its rays diminished" introduced by *libbû* does not seem to be a citation from any particular text, and more likely represents a well-known idiom.[66]

Likewise, in Excerpt 420, the statement "he approached (another) man's wife (for sex)" and other similar constructions are very common Sa-gig diagnoses that attribute the patient's sickness to prior acts of sexual impropriety.[67]

---

65 For the fire incantation quoted, see Lambert (1970: 40, lines 5–7).

66 For numerous examples of this idiom, see *CAD* Š II, 141 s.v. *šarūru* §1a, 2′.

67 This statement appears at Sa-gig 17: 32, along with similar statements such as "he approached his sister (for sex)" at Sa-gig 12: 125″ (TDPT 12 iv 17), and "he approached the

It is more likely that the commentator had the general idiom in mind, rather than a specific entry in the Diagnostic Handbook.

Excerpt 421: Comm. Sa-gig 14, obv. 25 (§11.1.20)
... *ni-iš* DINGIR-*šú* : *lìb-bu-ú niš* ŠU.2 : ...

... "(Oath on) his god's life." **As in**, the raising of hands. ...

Excerpt 421 not only employs the homophones *nīš* ("(oath on) the life") and *nīš* ("raising"), it also plays on the metathesis between ŠU *nīš* ("Hand of (the oath on) the life") in the base text Sa-gig 14: 111 and *nīš* ŠU.2 ("raising of hands"). The latter expression alludes to the well-known genre of Šu-íl-lá ("raised hand") prayers that are offered to an offended deity, and the implication here is that such prayers may alleviate the sick man's problem. Interestingly, in order to make a connection between the homophones of *nīš*, the commentator was obliged to use an expression (*nīš* ŠU.2) that deviated from the more idiomatic writing ŠU.ÍL.LA. There is little doubt, however, that "raising of hands" was transparent enough of an allusion to "raised hand" prayers.

11.2.4.3 The Notation *libbû* Refers to the Commentator's Own Words

Excerpt 422: Comm. Sa-gig 1C, rev. 8′ (§11.1.3)
⸢AD_6⸣ IGI GIG BI TI-*uṭ* : *šá-al-ma-ti lìb-bu-ú pu-ú-ḫu* IGI

"(If) he sees a corpse, that sick man will live." *Šalmāti*. **As in**, he sees a substitute.

Excerpt 422 represents an argument by *Single Member Argument* (§1.2.3.3). Because *šalmāti* can represent the plural form of both *šalamti* ("corpse") and *šalimti* ("well being"), this one-word comment supports the omen's contention that a "corpse"—when sighted—predicts the sick man's eventual recovery. Since it seemed contradictory that a corpse would be a good omen, the commentator also felt the need to explain, by means of the notation *libbû*, that the corpse served as a "substitute" for the fate the patient would otherwise have experienced. The *libbû* statement appears so specific to this particular

ēntu-priestess of his god (for sex)" at Sa-gig 13: 23 (TDPT 13 i 24′); Sa-gig 14: 134, 137–139 (TDPT 14 ii 62, 65–67).

argument that it probably represents the commentator's own words, rather than a text quotation or a well-known idiom.

Excerpt 423: Comm. Sa-gig 5, lines 28–29 (§11.1.12)
... : IGI.2-[*šú* ...] / *lìb-bu-ú* IGI.2-*šú taq-na* : ...

... "[His] eyes ..." **As in**, his eyes are placid. ...

Excerpt 424: Comm. Sa-gig 5, lines 31–32 (§11.1.12)
... : ÚḪ-*su* ḪAR.MEŠ x[...] / *lìb-bu-ú i-sa-ʾ-ul u* ÚḪ-*su i-*[*šal-lu*]

... "His spittle ... lungs ..." **As in**, he coughs and [expels] his spittle.

Excerpts 423–424 are, unfortunately, not well preserved. However, the statements "his eyes are placid" and "he coughs and [expels] his spittle" appear to be straightforward explanations of medical conditions provided by the commentator himself, rather than citations from external textual sources.[68]

11.2.4.4 The Notation *libbû* Refers to Logical Relationships in the Commentator's Argument

As we have seen, the notation *libbû* can refer to an explanation of the commentator's own creation (§11.2.4.3). This explanation can take the form of a single phrase, clause, or sentence, but it frequently also proposes logical relationships among several such items. These items may even be explicitly marked as separate by disjunction signs that come in-between them (Excerpt 425). In such cases, the implication expressed by *libbû* is drawn not from any single item, but from the logical way in which the items relate to each other. To reflect this complexity, I have rendered such cases of *libbû* with the translation "as in the fact that."

68 To be sure, an expression similar to Excerpt 424—"he coughs out, wheezes(?), and expels his spittle" (*ú-sa-al ú-na-ḫaṭ u* ÚḪ-*su i-šal-lu*)—occurs in Sa-gig 22: 30, if my restoration of this example is indeed correct. The turn of phrase used in both texts likely reflects common ways that ancient healers described specific medical signs, which, for lack of additional attestations in this case, cannot quite be ascribed the status of a formularized idiom. It is also questionable that the commentator of Excerpt 424 would have had in mind this specific entry (Sa-gig 22: 30) in the Diagnostic Handbook.

Excerpt 425: Comm. Sa-gig 1B, obv. 10′–11′ (§ii.1.2)

... [*ú*]*-za-bal-ma i-kaš-ma* : *zu-ub-bu-lu* : *ka-a-ša lìb-bu-ú* / [*i-kab-bi-i*]*t-ma* : gá-gá : *za-ba-lu šá* ⸢*mur-ṣu*⸣ : ...

... "It will carry on" (*means*) it will tarry on. To carry on *means* to tarry on. **As in the fact that** [it will become severe] *means* gá-gá, *which means* to carry (on), in the case of sickness. ...

In Excerpt 425, the dictionary root *zubbulu*, which usually means "to carry, deliver," is argued to have the derived sense "to carry on" or "to tarry on" when referring to a sick person or sickness.[69] The commentator employed an argument based on separate lexical equations, which made use of the element gá (𒂷) as an intermediary that connected the verb *kabātu* ("to become severe") to *zubbulu* ("to carry, deliver").[70] These connections imply that sickness "carries on" or "tarries on" because of its "severity." Here, the notation *libbû* designates the process of drawing implications, not merely from gá (𒂷) or the individual dictionary roots *kabātu* or *zubbulu*, but from the complex of relationships in its entirety.

Excerpt 426: Comm. Sa-gig 40A, obv. 2–5 (§ii.1.29)

... *ki-ša-da-nu-uš-šú* / [*ki-iš/ši*]*-da-nu-uš-šú* : *ki-šid* SAḪAR *lìb-bu-ú ana* KI-*tim* ki-ši / [*šá-n*]*iš ki-šid* SAḪAR : *šá ina e-pe-ri na-du-ú* / [*ša*]*l-šiš šá ina qaq-qar na-du-ú* : ...

... "By his neck" (*means*) Reaching-to-the-foundation,[71] *which refers to kišid* SAḪAR sickness. **As in the fact that:** towards the earth (*is expressed by*) ki-ši. Secondly, *kišid* SAḪAR sickness *refers to* one who is cast down onto the dust. Thirdly, one who is cast down onto the ground.

Excerpt 426 begins by citing from its base text (Sa-gig 40: 3) the unusual term *kišādānuššu*, which can be understood as "by his neck."[72] The commentator,

69 I employ the analogous English idiom ("to carry on") in my translation here.

70 [ga-a GÁ] = *ka-ba-tum* (Aa iv/4, 65 in *MSL* xiv, 385); [gá]-gá = MIN (= *zu-ub-bu-*[*lu*]) *šá* GAB[A] (Antagal D, 53 in *MSL* xvii, 203); gá-gá = *ṣu-ub-bu-lu* (Antagal iii, 140 in *MSL* xvii, 155). The pattern of argumentation here is discussed under Excerpt 271 in §i.2.3.2.5.

71 The signs [*ki-iš/ši*]*-da-nu-uš-šú* (Comm. Sa-gig 40A, obv. 3 in §ii.1.29) represent Sandhi writing of *kišid an*(*a*) *uššu* ("reaching to the foundation").

72 In this interpretation, *kišādānuššu* consists of *kišād-* ("neck") + *-ān* (particularizing suffix in Huehnergard 2011: 198, §20.2; *GAG*, §61 i) + *-um* (locative-adverbial ending in Huehnergard 2011: 312–313, §28.3; *GAG*, §66) + *-šu* (3ms suffix).

however, analyzed the syllabic form as *kišid* ("reaching") + *ana* ("to") + *uššu* ("foundation"), thus connecting this bodily region with a sickness known by the name *kišid* SAḪAR—literally, "Reaching of Dust."[73] The next step was to show that, even without mention of words like "foundation," "dust," or "ground," the term *kišid* alone bore connotations of "reaching" in a downward direction. This was achieved by evoking similarities between *kišid* and the Sumerian expression ki-ši, where ki had its typical logographic meaning "earth" and -ši stood for the Sumerian terminative suffix -šè ("towards"). In this argument, the notation *libbû* refers not to the phrase "towards the earth" or to ki-ši in isolation, but to the logical relationship that exists between them.

73 This was evidently interpreted as an objective genitive construction, with "dust" as the direct object of the action implied by the pre-genitive ("reaching"). Note also that the dictionary root (*kašādu*) for *kišid* encompasses a range of related meanings involving "reaching," "amounting to," "attaining," "acquiring," and even "conquering."

"Complement to" (IGI / *pāni*)

Whereas reciprocals in modern mathematics invariably yield the product of 1, scholars have long noticed that reciprocity in cuneiform mathematics applied to any pair of numbers whose product is any power of 60, including products such as $1/60$, 1, and 3600.[74] To the ancients in Mesopotamia, the powers of 60 were probably regarded as round numbers, and reciprocals were considered as complementary to each other, since one completes the other in such a way as to result in a round number. On cuneiform mathematical tablets, these reciprocal pairs were frequently depicted by the formula igi *n* (gál-bi) $1/n$, which has been translated idiomatically as "its *n*th part is $1/n$."[75] The expression igi 6 gál-bi 10, for instance, can refer to the fact that 6 and 10 relate to each other as reciprocals that yield a product of 60.[76] The logographic element IGI was so characteristic of these expressions that loanwords *igû* and *igibû* came to designate the two members of such a pair.[77]

Early speculation that IGI (understood as "eye") alluded to "Horus Eye Fractions" has long been discredited, and Høyrup concluded that "the literal meaning of the expression is unclear."[78] Syllabic writing in several texts, however, shows that IGI may be equated with the Akkadian term *pāni* ("face, front").[79] Friberg's description of "IGI *n*" as the "'opposite' (that is reciprocal)" of the sexagesimal number *n* is attractive, since two objects "facing" each other may also be imagined as positioned "opposite" each other.[80] It should

74 $1/60 = 60^{-1}$; $1 = 60^{0}$; $3600 = 60^{2}$. See Neugebauer and Sachs (1945: 18); Aaboe (1965: 80); Friberg (2005: 290) and (2007: 67); Robson (2008a: 108). While most tables of reciprocals are written out using cuneiform numbers, a few that spell out the names of numbers in the Sumerian language reveal that even the ancients did not always have a fixed power of 60 in mind. When Tablet S.U. 52/5 (Hulin 1963: 74–75) is read very literally, for instance, it contains the reciprocal pair "three" ($eš_5$) and "one third" (šušana) whose product is 1 (obv. 4), as well as the pair "nine" (ilimmu) and "six and two thirds" (àš šanabi) whose product is 60 (obv. 9).

75 For example, Høyrup (1990: 53–54); Robson (2002b: 339); Friberg (2007: 506).

76 *LBAT* 1637, obv. 4. Alternatively, the expression can be understood to involve 6 and 0;10 whose product is 1, among other combinations.

77 *MCT*, 130, 164–165; *CAD* I/J, 39, 45.

78 Hilprecht (1906: 22); Robson (2002a: 257); Høyrup (1990: 53).

79 Bruins (1954: 58–59, IM 31210, iii 5ff.; coll. H. Hunger in *CAD* P, 93); Al-Rawi and Roaf (1984: 180ff.).

80 Friberg (2005: 290) and (2007: 68, 506).

 | DOI:10.1163/9789004417564_036

be emphasized, however, that this spatial metaphor depicts the two objects as complements rather than antagonists to each other. While such a distinction may not be clear in the case of reciprocal numbers, it becomes important in our commentaries, especially when a pair of complements defined by IGI is set in antagonistic opposition to another such pair (Excerpts 428–430).

I have rendered IGI and *pān*(*i*) with the translation "complement of / to." Scholars were largely unaware of this term as a commentary notation, resulting in rather curious translations of the term as "face."[81] The notation seems to have been particularly suited for arguments based on extra-linguistic, symbolic correspondence (§1.2.3.1.8), in which experienced objects and events represent only one part of reality, while their less discernable counterparts and deeper meanings (indicated by IGI) were brought to light by the commentator. Elsewhere, for instance, I have shown how astrological meanings of the real moon's motion in the *Dodekatemoria* scheme were indicated by positions of a so-called "virtual moon" in the reciprocal Calendar Text scheme, so that the virtual moon became a signifier of prescriptions comprising wood, plant, and stone ingredients in medical zodiology.[82] In Excerpt 427 below, symbolism is much more localized, but no less indicative of what the ancients perceived as genuine affinities between entities connected by IGI / *pāni*.

Excerpt 427: Uruk Therapeutic Comm. 1 = *SpTU* I, 47 obv. 13–14

ina KUŠ ÙZ *šip-ki* : *šip-ki* : *ṭu-up-pu* : MAŠKIM KA LÚ *uṣ-ṣab-bi*[*t*] / MAŠKIM *pa-ni* ÙZ *ša-kin* : ...

In a goat's *šipku*-skin. *šipku refers to* applying (medicaments).[83] "The *rābiṣu*-demon has seized the man's mouth." The *rābiṣu*-demon is **complement to** (*pāni*) the goat.

---

81 See the comment "(durch den Anblick?) des Gesichtes des Anzû" in Hunger's notes to *SpTU* I, 32 rev. 12, as well as "das Gesicht einer Ziege" in the notes to *SpTU* I, 47 obv. 14. The notation is recognized in section 22*a*, but not in section 22*bc* of George (1991: 149). Frahm (2011a: 400, 403) and Salin (2016: 126 n. 43) translate "the *rābiṣu*-demon has the face of a goat" (cf. Excerpt 427 below), but concede that "elsewhere, the *rābiṣu*-demon is credited with lion-like features instead." Similarly, the expression *pa-ni* UR.MAḪ *ša-ki-in* (AO 3112, obv. 21) has been rendered "dessine une face de lion" (Nougayrol 1963: 385) or "das Gesicht eines Löwen ausschaut" (Maul 2010: 124). My proposal for the commentary notation IGI / *pāni* (Wee 2012: 495, etc.; reiterated in Wee 2016b: 147–151) has been followed by Gabbay (2016: 94 n. 54).

82 Wee (2016b: 139–229).

83 The noun *šipku* (a type of leather; *CAD* Š III, 71 §3) seems unrelated to the dictionary root *ṭuppû* ("to apply (medicaments)"; *CAD* Ṭ, 101 §2b, cf. §1c), and what is implied by the

The base text to the section of commentary above consists of therapeutic instructions for treating a man seized by the "*rābiṣu*-demon of the lavatory," which involved wrapping a variety of ingredients in skin and placing the skin pouch on the sick man's neck.[84] While this base text does not specify the kind of skin to be used, the commentator defined the material as "a goat's *šipku*-skin," which was considered well suited for the purpose of a poultice. He went on to explain that the goat "is complement to" or represents the *rābiṣu*-demon, and that the healing procedure required ingredients to be wrapped up in a skin that symbolized the agent responsible for the sickness.[85] In this instance, it is difficult to say for sure how the *rābiṣu*-demon ended up being associated with the goat, though several have noted links between goats and epilepsy in the ancient world.[86] Our Sa-gig commentaries, however, demonstrate how such complementary relationships can be posited, often based on only one or a few points of correspondence, which are nonetheless treated as the defining characteristic(s) of both parties in the context at hand. It was apparently not a serious objection that, apart from these points of connection indicated by IGI, not every feature in one entity necessarily corresponded to some counterpart in the other.

Excerpt 428: Comm. Sa-gig 4A, obv. 11–13 (§11.1.9)

… : SA[G].KI-*šú šá* 15 G[U$_7$-*š*]*ú* ŠU ^{d}UTU TIN / [SAG.KI-*šú šá* 1]50 GU$_7$-*šú* ŠU ⸤^{d}⸥15 TIN : ⸢IGI⸣ 15 : ^{d}15 : IGI 150 : ^{d}UTU / [SAG.KI.2-*šú* (?) : ^{d}]UTU *u* ^{d}15 1-*ma* : …

… "His right temple hurts him; Hand of the god Šamaš, he will live." "His left [temple] hurts him; Hand of the goddess Ištar, he will live." **Complement to** the right *is* the goddess Ištar. **Complement to** the left *is* the god Šamaš. ["Both his temples (hurt him)" (?) *means*] Šamaš and Ištar at the same time. …

Excerpt 428 addresses a couple of diagnostic entries in the base text Sa-gig 4: 25–26, which ascribe pain in the patient's right temple to the "Hand of the god

former is probably the supposed sense of the root *šapāku* (< *šipku*) "to introduce medications into the urethra, vagina, rectum, or other parts of the body" (*CAD* Š 1, 417–418 §2b).

84 For the therapeutic base text, see *SpTU* 1, 46 obv. 6–15, edited and translated in Frahm (2011a: 397–399).

85 For astrological applications of this healing principle, see tablets BM 76483 (and perhaps *SpTU* 11, 49), BM 77971, BM 33535, and BM 56605, discussed with detailed references in Wee (2016b: 151 n. 33).

86 Stol (1993: 149–150); Gabbay (2016: 99).

Šamaš," and pain in his left temple to the "Hand of the goddess Ištar." Because terms for "Ištar" and the "right" side both could be written in cuneiform as the number 15, this goddess became associated with the right temple.[87] Relying on the principle of *pars familiaris* versus *pars hostilis*, which was widely applied in liver extispicy, astrology, and other fields of Mesopotamian omen divination,[88] the commentator argued that Ištar would not harm her own side, and that her agency manifested itself instead as the hurting left temple.[89] Conversely, the god Šamaš was complement to the left side and therefore directed pain to the patient's right temple. In this excerpt, complementary entities imagined as "facing" (IGI) each other are clearly "opposite" in the sense of being mutually referential rather than antagonistic, since the deity complement to one side of the head was responsible for harm inflicted on the other side.

We would also notice that the strength of association between Ištar and the right side is not quite symmetrical with that between Šamaš and the left side. While the orthographic similarities of "Ištar" (written ᵈ15) and "right" (written 15) are persuasive, Šamaš seems to be connected to the left side primarily by default, i.e., because the right side was already assigned to his divine sister Ištar. One possible explanation involves assonance of the name *Šamaš* with the Akkadian word *šumēlu* ("left"). This, however, begs the question why "Šamaš" (written as the logogram ᵈUTU) and "left" (written as the logogram 150) were not both expressed syllabically so as to emphasize their assonantal resemblances. The proposal by Gabbay, involving numerical manipulation typical of "mystical and mythological explanatory works" (cf. Livingstone 1986), is much too fanciful and does not persuade me.[90] In the end, perhaps we should not expect all complementary relationships in a commentary's argument to be

87 The cuneiform writing 15 for both "Ištar" and "right" results in the less common situation whereby a female (i.e., the Other in patriarchal culture and society) is not associated instead with the "left" side (i.e., the Other with respect to prevalent right-handedness).

88 Jeyes (1991–1992: 35) and (1978: 209); Starr (1983: 15–16); Koch-Westenholz (2000: 38–40) and (1995: 98); cf. Heeßel (2010c: 183–184).

89 It should be noted that this commentator's rule was not uniformly followed elsewhere. In a Middle Assyrian diagnostic tablet from Assur (VAT 11122) that seems to focus on conditions attributable to the goddess Ištar, there are several descriptions involving ailments on the "right"—rather than "left"—side of the patient's body (obv. 2–4, 10).

90 "One may speculate whether Šamaš, whose number is 20, was associated with the left (written 150), in the following way: the number for 'left,' 150, is written 2,30. These two elements, 2 and 30, when multiplied are 60 (2 × 30 = 60) or 3,600 (2 × 60 × 30 = 3,600). Šamaš is written 20, but the king, who is also written 20, can also be written 200 (3,20), the same two elements as in the writing for 'left,' 3 and 20, resulting in 60 (or 3,600) when multiplied, but in reverse order." Gabbay (2016: 95–96 n. 62); cf. Labat (1965: 259–260); Nougayrol (1972: 96, no. 12).

founded on equally compelling grounds, in order for the argument as a whole to be valid.

Excerpt 429: Comm. Sa-gig 1A, obv. 26–27 (§ 11.1.1)

... [EME$_3$ *pa-an* GIG] / ANŠE *pa-an mu-tú šá-kin lì*[*b-bu-ú* ...]

... [The jenny is **complement to** the sick man.] The donkey is **complement to** death. ...

Excerpt 430: Comm. Sa-gig 1B, rev. 7–9 (§ 11.1.2)

... : ANŠE EME$_3$ U$_5$-*ma* IGI GIG BI / [*mu-tú*] *u šu-ú ik-tap-pi-lu* : ... / [*kit-pu-lu pa*]-*ni* ANŠE *šá-niš pa-ni* MUŠ ...

... "(If) he sees a donkey mount a jenny, that sick man and [death] are intertwined." ... ["To become intertwined"][91] is **complement to** a donkey; secondly, it is **complement to** a snake. ...

Excerpts 429 and 430 represent two different ways of responding to an omen encountered by a healer en route to his patient's house: "If he sees a donkey mount a jenny, that sick man and death are intertwined" (Sa-gig S1: 22). Excerpt 429 apparently mirrors the rhetoric we saw earlier in Excerpt 428, whereby complementary pairs are first identified in symbolic relationships—i.e., "donkey" symbolizes "death," while "jenny" symbolizes the "sick man"—before they are portrayed antagonistically against one another—i.e., the "donkey–death" pair versus the "jenny–sick man" pair. The logic for the pairing is not entirely clear. One possibility is to interpret the donkey as a husband who "mounts" his wife (i.e., the jenny), thus setting up the scene for wordplay between "husband" (*mutu*) and "death" (*mūtu*).[92] In this view, the jenny becomes a visual representation of the sick man held in the firm grasp

91 My restoration here differs from [x x *pa*]-*ni* ANŠE *šá-niš pa-ni* MUŠ, "[...] a donkey's face, alternatively, a snake's face" in George (1991: 148–149); as well as [*mu-tú*(?) *pa*]-*ni* ANŠE *šá-niš pa-ni* MUŠ, "[death(?) corresp]onds to(?) the donkey; alternatively, corresponds to(?) a snake" in Gabbay (2016: 97), despite my proposed restoration [*kit-pu-lu*] (Comm. Sa-gig 1B = *SpTU* I, 27 rev. 9 in § 11.1.2) already in Wee (2012: 516, 522, 530).

92 This wordplay may also be operative in the following literary descriptions of "death" in the bedroom: *mūtu ina bēt eršēya iḫlula ḫillūtu* ("then to our bedroom stealthy Death did creep"; K 890, rev. 20) in *Elegy for a Woman Who Died in Childbirth*, translated by George (2010: 211, 213); *ina bīt mayyālīya ašib mūtu* ("in my bed-chamber Death does abide") in the Standard Babylonian *Epic of Gilgamesh* XI, 245, translated by George (2003: 718). For possibly the opposite situation where the woman does the mounting, see [DIŠ ... D]AM-*sà ir-kab* (K 9169, line 9′) in Oppenheim (1969: 157).

of death. The verb *šakin* ("it is set") in Excerpt 429 was also employed earlier in Excerpt 427, but not in Excerpts 428 and 430. In the latter instances, *šakin* may nonetheless be understood as present in ellipses: X *pān*(*i*) Y (*šakin*) means "X (is positioned as a) complement to Y."

Excerpt 430 supplies an alternative interpretation of the omen, which focuses on a different aspect of the scenario. Here, the verb "to become intertwined" (*kitpulu*) is described as complement, not only to the observed "donkey," but also to a "snake" that is nowhere mentioned in the base text. This verb, in fact, appears in numerous other depictions of the more common behaviors of snakes and lizards.[93] The life-threatening implications of a snake and snake venom suggest that intertwinement—even if enacted by merely a donkey—constitutes a negative portent for the sick man. Commentators of the two excerpts above were united in their use of the notation IGI / *pāni* to express how everyday realia were "complement to" deeper meanings beyond the obvious or observable, even if the nature of such complementary relationships was rather loosely defined. In contrast to how reciprocal numbers constitute an exclusive pair (whose product is 1) in modern mathematics, Excerpt 430 recalls the broader definition of reciprocity in cuneiform mathematics—where a single number can be part of a reciprocal pair in multiple ways, so long as the product is a power of 60—by employing the language of reciprocity for relationships between a single entity ("to become intertwined") and multiple referents ("donkey" and "snake").

93 For the numerous instances whereby the verb *kitpulu* describes intertwining snakes, see K 12851:[6′] (*CT* 11, 35); Recip. Ea Section F, 15′ (*MSL* XIV, 532); *CT* 38, 10: 27; 11: 44; 34: 20′; *CT* 39, 14: 24; K 8038, 2′ (*CT* 40, 24); *KAR* 384 obv. 4; 389 obv. [ii 18]; *STT* 321 i 11′.

"(Points) to" (*ana*)

From early on, von Soden already noticed a couple of cases where the preposition *ana* ("to, towards") conveys the meaning "abzuleiten von (der Wurzel x)" in cuneiform commentaries.[94] In Gabbay's view, "the preposition *ana* is used relatively often in lexical contexts—usually but not exclusively in lexical commentaries—to associate a verbal or nominal form with an etymological cognate, frequently a noun but most commonly the infinitive."[95] At least among the Sa-gig commentaries, however, inquiries into lexical derivation are answered in the vast majority of cases without the preposition *ana*, and the identified dictionary root is expressed also in the form of the Akkadian Infinitive (§1.2.3.1.4)—which begs the question what additional significance the notation *ana*[96] was supposed to communicate. In other words, if basic lexical identities are already elucidated by statements such as "'His tongue is *ebi*' *derives from the dictionary root* to become thick (*ebû*),"[97] what special conditions or circumstances could have led a commentator to reframe his rhetoric as *"'His tongue is *ebi*' (points) to becoming thick (*ebû*)"?[98]

As the examples suggest, the so-called lexical connections that are alleged by *ana* not infrequently result in superficial or even pseudo- etymologies. So, for instance, the claim that "a strewn offering (*sisqu*) **(points) to** *sasqu*-flour ... Secondly, a strewn offering (*sisqu*) **(points) to** scattering (*sarāqu*)"[99] puts forth two separate etymologies for "strewn offering" that cannot both be correct. In

94 *AHw*, 48 §15. These cases occur in a commentary on the *Babylonian Theodicy*: *ed-lu-tú* : *ana e-de-lu* (BM 76506, rev. 10′) and *ri-pi-it-tum* : *ana ra-pa-du* (BM 76506, rev. 11′). See Lambert (1960: 82 (commentary to lines [208–209] and 212), pl. 26). Lambert's edition of the *Babylonian Theodicy* commentary consisted of only the fragments BM 66882 + 76506, but it can now be supplemented with the additional unpublished fragments BM 76009 + 76832 + 83044 + 83045 + 83046. See *CBT* VII, 189–190; Frahm (2011a: 120).

95 Gabbay (2016: 134–135).

96 In reference to its specialized meanings in commentarial contexts (see below), I refer to *ana* as a "notation" and not merely a "preposition."

97 ⌜EME⌝-*šú* ⌜*e-bi*⌝ : *e-bu-ú* (Comm. Sa-gig 7Ca, obv. 2′ in §11.1.15).

98 *EME-*šú e-bi* : *ana e-bu-ú*.

99 *si-is-qu* : *ana sa-as-qu-u* ... / *šá-niš si-is*^{iš}*-qu* : *ana sa-ra-qu* (Aa III/1 Comm. A, obv. 14–15 in *MSL* XIV, 323). The first of the two equations was regarded as a spurious attempt at etymology by Frahm (2011a: 68) and Gabbay (2016: 135); cf. Lambert (1999b: 223).

 | DOI:10.1163/9789004417564_037

fact, *sisqu* represents one of the byforms of *sirqu* ("strewn offering"),[100] which is nonetheless associated with the similarly sounding "*sasqu*-flour," presumably because the latter is or resembles an ingredient used in the offering, and not because the alleged etymology is genuine. Along the same lines are claims such as "*pašallu* (an alloy of gold) *refers to* gold, *or* **(points) to** crawling (*pašālu*)"[101] and "URUDU *means* copper (*erû*), *which* **(points) to** being pregnant (*arû*)."[102] Earlier, I suggested that the difficult statement "BA **(points) to** (?) guarding"[103] could depict a pseudo-etymological link between the terms *nušurrû* ("diminution, decrease"; logogram BA) and *naṣāru* ("guarding").

Excerpt 431: Comm. Sa-gig 4B, obv. 1–2 (§ 11.1.10)

[DIŠ SAG.KI *ḫe-si*] ... / [...]x : ^{d}30 : SAG.KI : *ana na-ka$_4$-pu* : *qar-ra-du šá ki-ma* ^{d}30 *qar-nu* DÙ-*ú* : [...]

["If he (feels) covered up in the temple."] ... the moon-god Sîn. "The temple" **(points) to** butting (with horns). "The hero who has grown horns like the moon-god Sîn." ...

Excerpt 431 constitutes part of a lengthy commentary entry on the base text Sa-gig 4:1: "If he (feels) covered up in the temple." The lines here suggest that the moon-god Sîn is responsible for this medical condition. The commentator first associated the "temple" (*nakkaptu*) with the action of "butting (with horns)" (*nakāpu*), and then employed a quotation from the myth *Lugale* (IV, 8)—"the hero who has grown horns like the moon-god Sîn"—to show the connection between the moon-god and horns. By implication, the moon-god Sîn is therefore linked to ailments of the sick man's temple.

The use of the notation *ana* here is revealing because, unlike the examples surveyed above, a good case can be made that "temple" (*nakkaptu*) and "butting (with horns)" (*nakāpu*) are actual etymological cognates. That being said, it would have been strange to define a person's "temple" primarily as the part of the head he might use to "butt" against another object! In fact, disparities in the logographic forms SAG.KI ("temple") and DU$_7$ ("butting") suggest that etymology played a relatively minor role in the way that these terms were

100 *CAD* S, 316 s.v. *sirqu* A "an offering (of aromatics or foodstuffs)," with acknowledged byforms *širqu*, *sisqu*, and *sišqu*.

101 Frahm (2011a: 68 n. 320) suggested this is a quotation from *Malku* 5, 168: "*pa-šal-lu* | *ḫu-ra-ṣu*"; *CAD* P, 233 s.v. *pašallu* (an alloy of gold); cf. Gabbay (2016: 136).

102 Gabbay (2016: 137).

103 Comm. Sa-gig 4B, obv. 7 (§ 11.1.10).

generally conceived.[104] The decision to link these two terms together using the notation *ana* ("(points) to") likely expressed the distance felt between their respective meanings.

Excerpt 432: Comm. Sa-gig 4B, obv. 9 (§11.1.10)
[ŠÀ.MEŠ-*šú*] ⸢al⸣-du^{tu} : *dan-nu* : *ana na-pa-ḫu šá* ŠÀ : …

"[His innards] al-du," (read as the syllable signs) *al-ṭù, means* they are hard, *which* **(points) to** inflaming, in the case of the belly. …

Excerpt 433: Comm. Sa-gig 10 & 11, rev. 7′ (§11.1.18)
[…]x x : ⸢*te-eḫ*⸣*-si-ma* : *ana ka-ba-su* […]

… "You cover up (the sick nail)" **(points) to** putting on a *kubšu*-cap …

In Excerpts 432 and 433, there is no longer the semblance that items linked by *ana* have actual or plausible lexical relationships. On the contrary, it can now be more clearly seen that extra-linguistic considerations are what connect them together. The damaged beginning of Excerpt 432 contains a quotation from the base text "His innards al-du (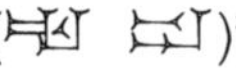)" (Sa-gig 4: 2). Although the logogram DU usually stands for the verb "to move" (*alāku*), the commentator considered such movement to be incongruous with the stative sense of the Sumerian al-prefix, and understood the signs instead as *al-ṭù* (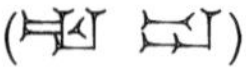) meaning "they are stiff," which describe innards that "are hard" (*dannū*).[105] However, since "hard" was not the usual way that medical texts describe the patient's belly or innards, a more appropriate description "inflaming" (*napāḫu*) was used to clarify the belly's condition.

The base text (Sa-gig 11 rev. 60) for Excerpt 433 is not well preserved, but can be restored with the help of the commentary as: "If the nail is sick, (and) you cover (it) up …"[106] According to the commentator, "covering up" the sick nail involves "putting on (it) a *kubšu*-cap," which probably refers to some kind of a protective or therapeutic covering over a sick nail that is sensitive to touch.

---

104 The "temple" (SAG.KI) was envisioned primarily as a part of the "head" (SAG), while the action of "butting" (DU_7) was applied in mathematical contexts to describe how one might "make encounter" ($DU_7.DU_7$) geometrical forms. Høyrup (2002: 44).

105 The same interpretation may be found in Comm. Sa-gig 4C, obv. 4′ (§11.1.11).

106 DIŠ UMBIN GIG *te-eḫ-*[*si-ma* …] (Sa-gig 11 rev. 60).

Excerpt 434: Mul-apin II, iii 33 MS HH[107]

DIŠ $^{mul_5.d}$EN.URU.AN.NA KUR$_4$-*ma* ILLU *u* ŠÈG : ^{d}TIR.AN.NA U$_4$ ḪÉ.NUN MU-*šú*

If Jupiter is bright, flood and rain : the name of the rainbow is Day of Abundance.

Excerpt 435: Mul-apin II, iii 33 MS E[108]

DIŠ ^{d}EN.GIŠGAL.AN.NA KUR$_4$-*ma* ŠÈG *u* ILLU *ana* ^{d}TIR.AN.NA U$_4$ ḪÉ.NUN MU.NE

If Jupiter is bright, rain and flood, **(points) to the fact that** the name of the rainbow is Day of Abundance.

Excerpts 434 and 435 do not actually come from commentaries, but include very similar types of explanations. These represent two independent variants of the astral compendium Mul-apin (II, iii 33), each of which consists of a short omen on the planet Jupiter, followed by a short comment on the omen.[109] Whereas one manuscript (MS HH) has a disjunction sign separating the omen from its comment (Excerpt 434), the other manuscript (MS E) has the notation *ana* in place of the disjunction marker (Excerpt 435). Earlier, we saw that implications expressed by *libbû* can be drawn, not only from individual elements of an argument, but also from the logical way that these elements relate to each other (§11.2.4.4). The same can be said for the notation *ana*, which relies here on the link between Jupiter—commonly known as the "white" (BABBAR, 𒌓) star—and rain symbolizing abundance, so that the rainbow resulting from the situation can be named "Day (U$_4$, 𒌓) of Abundance."[110]

107 VAT 9412+11279, iii 33.

108 AO 7540 + LKU 113 + W 18003f, v 11.

109 See Mul-apin II, iii 33 in Hunger and Steele (2019: 104); cf. Hunger and Pingree (1989: 112); with discussion in Watson and Horowitz (2011: 62).

110 A similar omen with comment occurs in *Sîn ina tāmartīšu* 1: 123 (Koch 1999: 161; with collations by Gabbay 2016: 89): [DIŠ 30 TÙR U]$_4$ ḪÉ(!).NUN(!) NIGIN$_2$(!) AN.MI ^{d}TIR.AN.NA U$_4$ ḪÉ.NUN MU.NI TÙR BABBAR NIGIN$_2$-*ma* ŠÈG SUR ..., "'[If the moon] is surrounded [by a halo] of a Day of Abundance, Eclipse.' The name of the rainbow is Day of Abundance. It is surrounded by a white halo and rain falls." In both cases, the element "Abundance" is associated with "rain." Whereas the element "Day" (U$_4$, 𒌓) derives from the "white" (BABBAR, 𒌓) halo in the *Sîn ina tāmartīšu* entry, it alludes to Jupiter's status as the "white" (BABBAR, 𒌓) star in Mul-apin II, iii 33.

"The Usual (Meaning)" (*kayyān*)

The term *kayyān* (written SAG.UŠ) appears only once in our Sa-gig commentaries, but several other examples have been collected and discussed by Gabbay.[111] Excerpt 436 below concerns a "kiln-fired brick" (*agurru*) in the base text Sa-gig U1: 39b. As is also the practice elsewhere, *kayyān* takes pride of place as the very first comment, indicating that any understanding of *agurru* should begin with its "usual" meaning or the plain meaning one assumes in prosaic communication,[112] i.e., that of a "kiln-fired brick." What follow are erudite arguments that interpret the components of *agurru* = A + gur in various ways, which I explore more thoroughly in my Notes to this commentary. In this commentary entry and others like it, such arguments serve to extend the applicability of omens by reading beyond the "usual (meanings)" of objects or persons recorded in the omen. In other words, the sick man's death is portended not only by the sight of a kiln-fired brick, but also by observing a "man who returned from the river ordeal" or a "pregnant woman."

Excerpt 436: Comm. Sa-gig 1B, rev. 21–23 (§11.1.2)

… : DIŠ SIG_4.AL.ÙR.RA IGI GIG ÚŠ : SAG.ÚS *šá-niš* LÚ *š*[*á ina ḫur-šá-a*]*n i-tu-ra* / [A : *me-e*] : GUR : *ta-a-*⸢*ra šal*⸣*-šiš* MUNUS.$PEŠ_4$: A : *ma-ru* : $^{ki\text{-}ir}$gu[r_4(KÌR) : *ka-ra-ṣ*]*a* / [*šá-niš*] ⸢A⸣ : *ma-ri* : *gur* : *na-šú-u* ⸢:⸣ …

… "If he sees a kiln-fired brick, (that) sick man will die." **The usual (meaning).** Secondly, the man who returned [from the river] ordeal. [A *means* water.] GUR *means* to return. Thirdly, a pregnant woman. A *means* son. The cuneiform sign gur_4 as the logogram KÌR [*means* to pinch] off. [Secondly], A *means* son. /*gur*/ *means* to carry. …

An analogous discussion on the "kiln-fired brick" (*agurru*) in another commentary (Comm. Sa-gig 1A) employs very similar arguments as the ones in Excerpt 436, but omits the initial mention of *kayyān* altogether.[113] This poses the question whether *kayyān* was viewed as redundant—i.e., it goes without

111 Gabbay (2016: 182–194).
112 The plain meaning of a word or expression does not always correspond to its literal meaning or to its etymology.
113 See Comm. Sa-gig 1A, obv. 11–13 (§11.1.1).

 | DOI:10.1163/9789004417564_038

saying that words have their "usual (meanings)"—or whether, in this other commentary, alternative interpretations of *agurru* were considered substitutes instead of additions to the "usual (meaning)." The instinct to treat *kayyān* as redundant is probably correct, since the term is absent from the vast majority of commentarial arguments, and it is highly unlikely that commentators were advocating so extensive a change in the "usual (meanings)" of words. Furthermore, there are several other examples in which the commentator sought to extend an omen's applicability, not by reinterpreting the name of an object in the original omen, but by including other objects associated with it in lexical lists (see §1.2.2.1).

Still, this is not to say that the substitution and replacement of plain meaning had no role in Mesopotamian hermeneutics. Particularly relevant to medical contexts is the use of *Decknamen* or secret names that appear to describe "especially disgusting and smelly substances" (*Dreckapotheke*), in order to conceal the real identities of *materia medica* from the uninitiated or from frauds.[114] Commentaries on therapeutic texts provide substitute identities for these names:

Excerpt 437: Uruk Therapeutic Comm. 11 = MLC 1863, obv. 5[115]

A.RI.A NAM.LÚ.LU$_{18}$.LU : ^{u_2}*maš-ta-kal* : *áš-šú* ^{u_2}A.RI.A : ^{u_2}*maš-ta-kal šá-niš* A.RI.A : *ri-ḫu-ut*

"A.RI.A NAM.LÚ.LU$_{18}$.LU" *refers to maštakal*-plant. Because ^{u_2}A.RI.A *refers to maštakal*-plant. Secondly, A.RI.A *refers to* semen.

Excerpt 437 asserts that the ingredient labeled A.RI.A NAM.LÚ.LU$_{18}$.LU (lit. "human semen") should be understood as a secret reference to the common plant *maštakal*, rather than accepted with its plain meaning. As a matter of fact, contrary to the practice of listing *kayyān* ("the usual (meaning)") as the very first comment in an argument, the possibility that "A.RI.A *refers to* semen"

114 Köcher (1995: 204); Geller (2010a: 53) and (2010b: 70); Chalendar (2016: 100). "There are a number of instances of secret names for *materia medica* in the Talmudic medical handbook (Git. 68b–70a), usually given as excrement or blood of various animals, and these ingredients are usually mentioned with an appended note to be 'cautious' (*nzdhr*), since *Dreckapotheke* can cause harm." Geller (2004a: 27, 48 n. 199). For *Decknamen* in Greek magical papyri from Egypt, see Dieleman (2003: 224ff.). Kinnier Wilson (2005: 49) cautions against viewing all alternative names of *materia medica* as *Decknamen*: "it might seem that many of the *Decknamen* were riddles, or belong generally to that category, such being a known component of scribal education. Other items ... were perhaps only popular names ..."

115 See also edition by Geller (2010a: 168–176), from whose syntax my translation differs.

is conceded only as a second interpretation. In this case and others like it, commentators affirmed that the plain meanings of *Decknamen* were not to be taken at face value, and needed to be understood primarily as coded references to other medical ingredients.

Other Notations

Other notations do not occur frequently enough in the Sa-gig commentaries for me to discern their special nuances, but the meanings and uses of some of them have been discussed by Gabbay. These include the terms: GABA.RI = *miḫru* ("that is"),[116] *aššu* ("because (of)"),[117] and KI or *kī*.[118]

116 Comm. Sa-gig 1A, obv. 7 (§11.1.1); Comm. Sa-gig 1B, obv. 6′ (§11.1.2); Comm. Sa-gig 1C, obv. 5 (§11.1.3).

117 Comm. Sa-gig 1A, line 38 (§11.1.1); Comm. Sa-gig 1C, rev. 7′ (§11.1.3); [Comm. Sa-gig 1D, rev. 13′ (§11.1.4)]; Comm. Sa-gig 5, line 27 if *aššu* here is not part of the base text (§11.1.12). See discussion in Gabbay (2016: 144–165).

118 Comm. Sa-gig 39, obv. 6. See discussion in Gabbay (2016: 229 n. 120).

 | DOI:10.1163/9789004417564_039

Photographs

Plate 1	Comm. Sa-gig 1A	Tablet AO 17661 obverse
Plate 2	Comm. Sa-gig 1A	Tablet AO 17661 reverse
Plate 3	Comm. Sa-gig 1B	Tablet W 22307/6 obverse
Plate 4	Comm. Sa-gig 1B	Tablet W 22307/6 reverse
Plate 5a	Comm. Sa-gig 1B	Tablet W 22307/6 bottom edge
Plate 5b	Comm. Sa-gig 1B	Tablet W 22307/6 right edge
Plate 6	Comm. Sa-gig 1C	Tablet W 22307/24 reverse
Plate 7a	Comm. Sa-gig 1C	Tablet W 22307/24 right edge
Plate 7b	Comm. Sa-gig 3A	Tablet W 22307/71 reverse
Plate 8a	Comm. Sa-gig 3B	Tablet Joins BM 43854+43938 obverse
Plate 8b	Comm. Sa-gig 3B	Tablet Joins BM 43854+43938 obverse to bottom edge
Plate 9a	Comm. Sa-gig 3B	Tablet Joins BM 43854+43938 bottom edge to reverse
Plate 9b	Comm. Sa-gig 3B	Tablet Joins BM 43854+43938 reverse
Plate 10	Comm. Sa-gig 4A	Tablet Joins W 22307/60+79+80 obverse
Plate 11a	Comm. Sa-gig 4A	Tablet Joins W 22307/60+79+80 reverse
Plate 11b	Comm. Sa-gig 4A	Tablet Joins W 22307/60+79+80 right edge
Plate 12a	Comm. Sa-gig 4A	Tablet Fragment W 22307/75 obverse
Plate 12b	Comm. Sa-gig 4A	Tablet Fragment W 22307/75 reverse
Plate 13	Comm. Sa-gig 4B	Tablet Joins BM 66965+76508 obverse
Plate 14	Comm. Sa-gig 5	Tablet W 22307/16 obverse
Plate 15	Comm. Sa-gig 5	Tablet W 22307/16 reverse
Plate 16a	Comm. Sa-gig 7A	Tablet W 22307/2 obverse
Plate 16b	Comm. Sa-gig 7A	Tablet W 22307/2 reverse
Plate 17	Comm. Sa-gig 7B	Tablet W 22307/10 reverse
Plate 18	Comm. Sa-gig 10 & 11	Tablet DT 87 obverse
Plate 19	Comm. Sa-gig 10 & 11	Tablet DT 87 reverse
Plate 20a	Comm. Sa-gig 13+	Tablet GCBC 766 obverse
Plate 20b	Comm. Sa-gig 13+	Tablet GCBC 766 right edge
Plate 21a	Comm. Sa-gig 13+	Tablet GCBC 766 bottom edge

 | DOI:10.1163/9789004417564_040

Plate 21b	Comm. Sa-gig 13+	Tablet GCBC 766 reverse
Plate 22	Comm. Sa-gig 14	Tablet W 22307/20 obverse
Plate 23	Comm. Sa-gig 14	Tablet W 22307/20 reverse
Plate 24	Comm. Sa-gig 18	Tablet BM 66873 reverse
Plate 25a	Comm. Sa-gig 18	Tablet BM 66873 top edge
Plate 25b	Comm. Sa-gig 18	Tablet BM 66873 right edge
Plate 26	Comm. Sa-gig 21 & 22a	(unnumbered) Tablet obverse
Plate 27	Comm. Sa-gig 21 & 22a	(unnumbered) Tablet reverse
Plate 28a	Comm. Sa-gig 29	Tablet BM 38375 obverse
Plate 28b	Comm. Sa-gig 29	Tablet BM 38375 reverse
Plate 29	Comm. Sa-gig 36	Tablet Joins W 22307/23+74 reverse
Plate 30	Comm. Sa-gig 39	Tablet W 22311 obverse
Plate 31	Comm. Sa-gig 40A	Tablet W 22308a obverse
Plate 32a	Comm. Sa-gig 40A	Tablet W 22308a right edge
Plate 32b	Comm. Sa-gig 40B	Tablet W 22307/73 reverse

Much appreciation goes to the following persons and institutions for their generous permission to use the above photographs in this publication:

Prof. Dr. Hermann Hunger	Plates 3, 4, 5a–b, 6, 7a–b, 10, 11a–b, 12a–b, 14, 15, 16a–b, 17, 22, 23, 29, 30, 31, and 32a–b
By courtesy of the Trustees of the British Museum,	
Photographer: John Z. Wee	Plates 8a–b, 9a–b, 13, 24, and 25a–b
Photographer: Jonathan Taylor	Plates 18, 19, and 28a–b
The Yale Babylonian Collection	Plates 20a–b and 21a–b
The Free Library of Philadelphia,	
Photographer: Joseph Shemtov	Plates 26 and 27
Musée du Louvre, Dist. RMN-Grand Palais / Raphaël Chipault / Art Resource, NY	Plates 1 and 2

For Plate 26, the photograph includes not only the obverse of Comm. Sa-gig 21 & 22a, but also part of a different non-Sa-gig commentary. Broken edges of the two tablets were artificially shaved in modern times to give the impression that they could be joined as a single cuneiform tablet (see Leichty 1973: 78–86). For the Sa-gig commentary tablets or fragments whose photographs are not provided in print in this volume, some images remain restricted, while the photographs of others are already available in digital formats online (listed under Digital Resources).

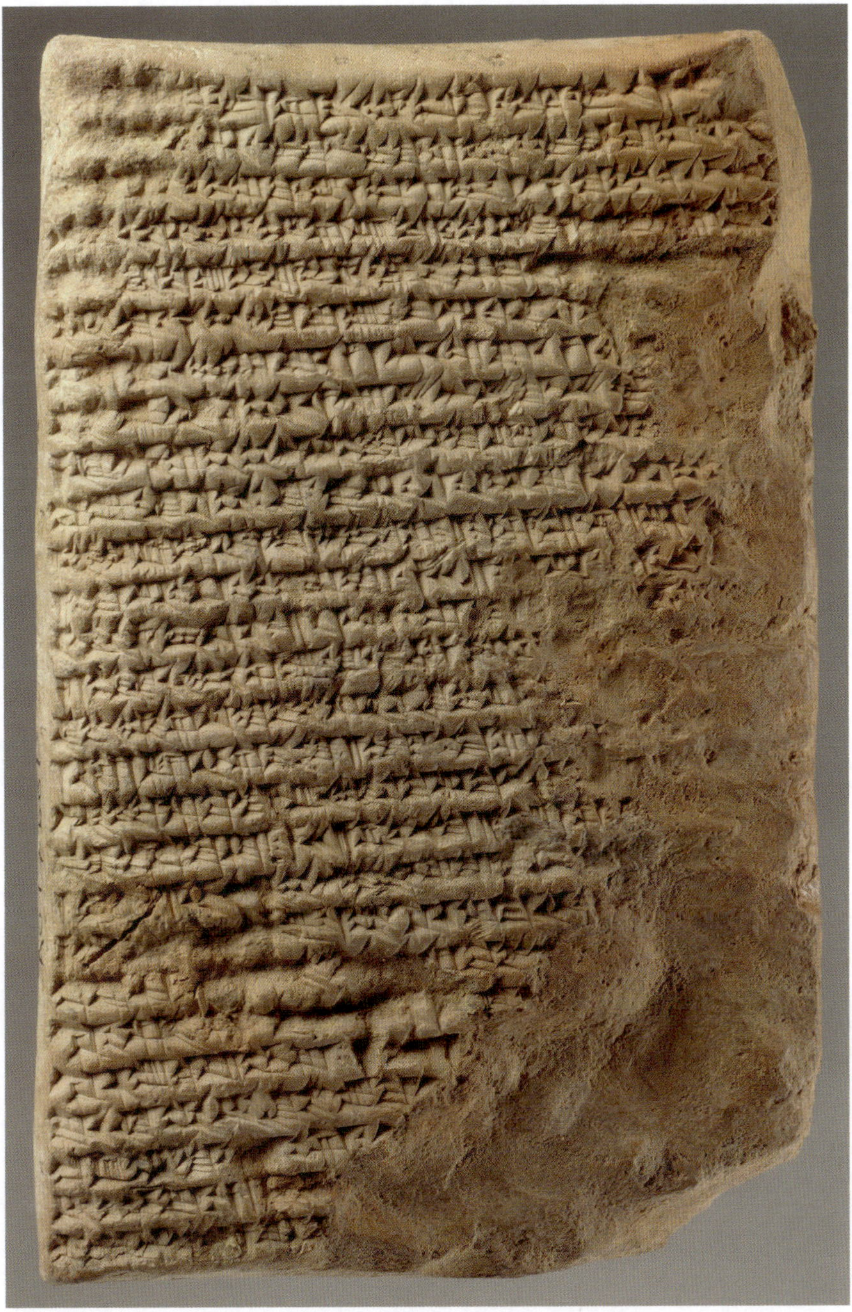

PLATE 1

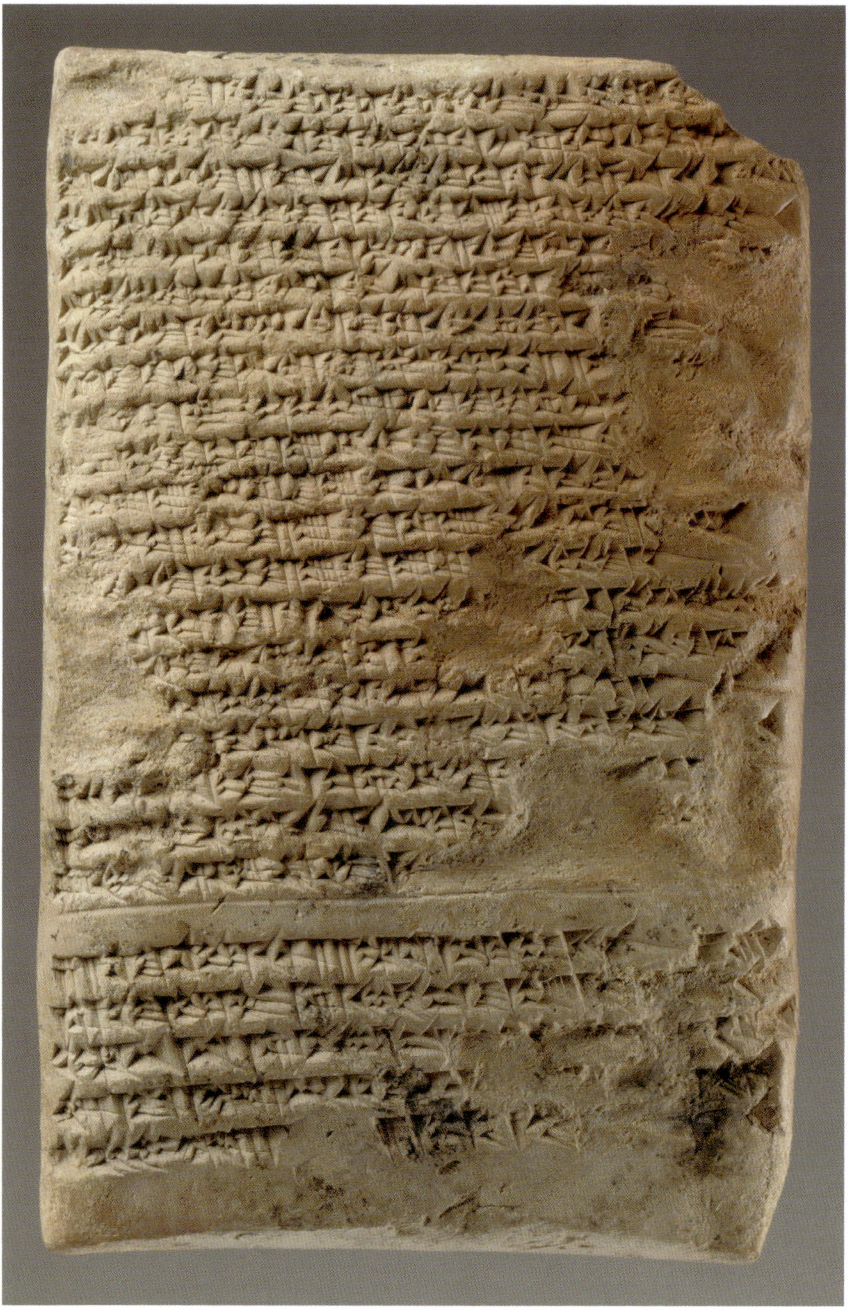

PLATE 2

PLATE 3

PLATE 4

PLATE 5A

PLATE 5B

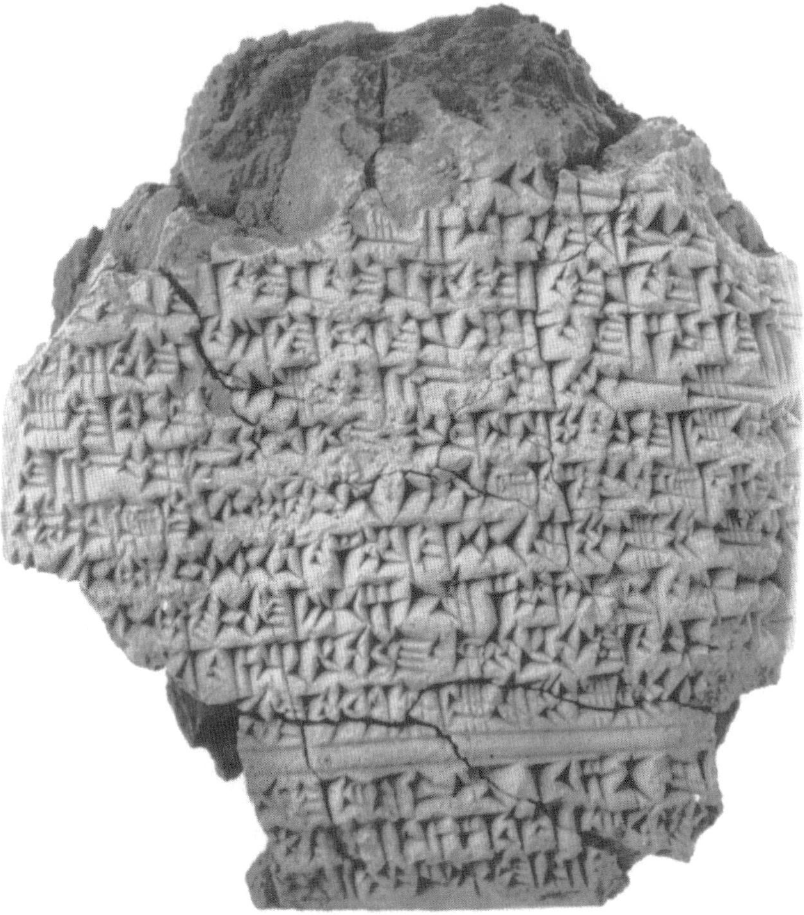

PLATE 6

PLATE 7A

PLATE 7B

PLATE 8A

PLATE 8B

PLATE 9A

PLATE 9B

PLATE 10

PLATE 11A

PLATE 11B

PLATE 12A

PLATE 12B

PLATE 13

PLATE 14

PLATE 15

PLATE 16A

PLATE 16B

PLATE 17

PLATE 18

PLATE 19

PLATE 20A

PLATE 20B

PLATE 21A

PLATE 21B

PLATE 22

PLATE 23

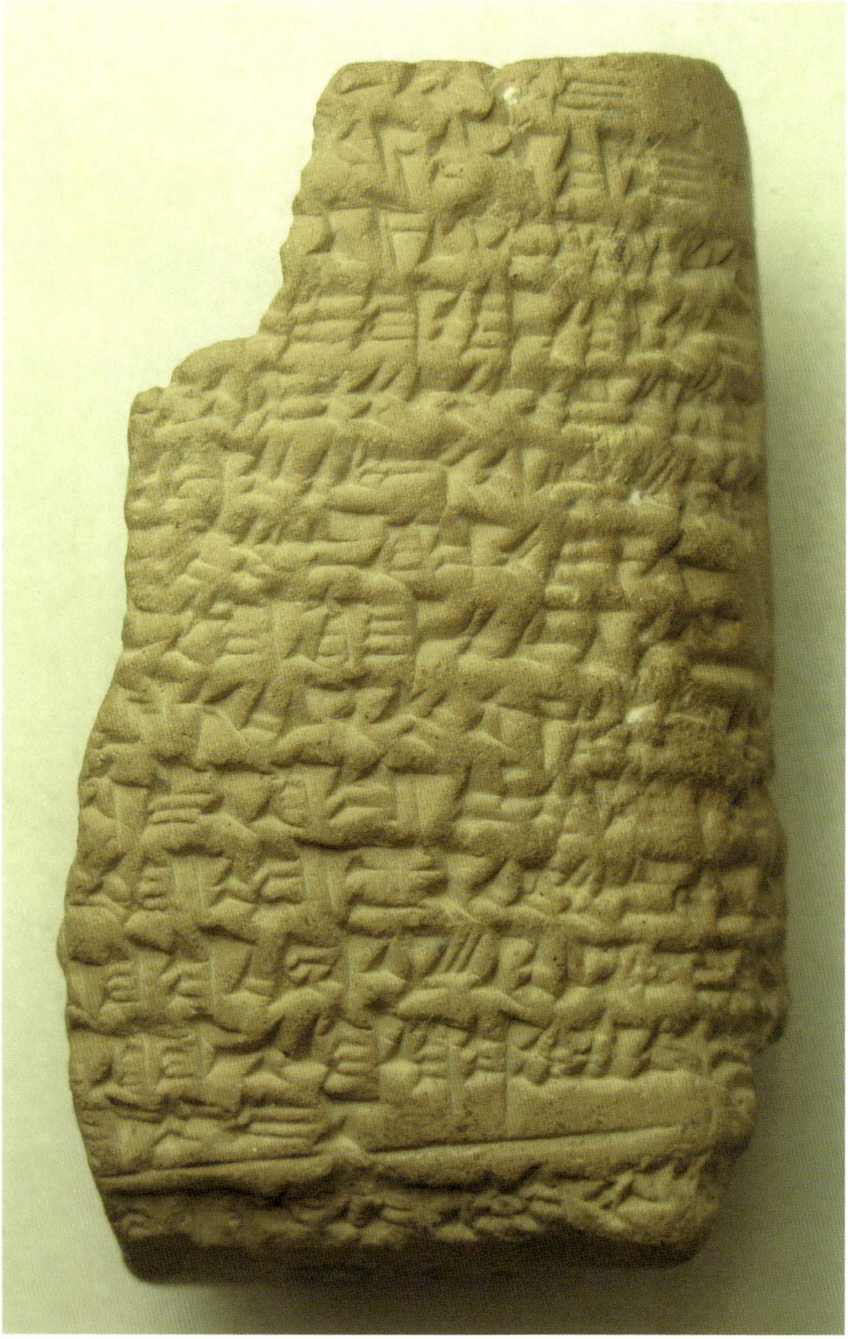

PLATE 24

PLATE 25A

PLATE 25B

PLATE 26

PLATE 27

PLATE 28A

PLATE 28B

PLATE 29

PLATE 30

PLATE 31

PLATE 32A

PLATE 32B

Bibliography

Printed Publications

bibliographical abbreviations are listed in
Volume 20 (U and W) of the *Chicago Assyrian Dictionary* (*CAD*) vii–xxxii

Aaboe, Asger

1965 "Some Seleucid Mathematical Tables: Extended Reciprocals and Squares of Regular Numbers." *JCS* 19/3, pp. 79–86.

Abusch, I. Tzvi

1974 "Mesopotamian Anti-Witchcraft Literature: Texts and Studies Part I: The Nature of Maqlû: Its Character, Divisions, and Calendrical Setting." *JNES* 33/2, pp. 251–262.

2007 "Witchcraft, Impotence, and Indigestion." Pp. 146–159 in *Disease in Babylonia*. Edited by Irving L. Finkel and Markham J. Geller. CM 36. Leiden: Brill.

2016 *The Magical Ceremony Maqlû*: A Critical Edition. AMD 10. Leiden: Brill.

Abusch, I. Tzvi, and Daniel Schwemer

2011 *Corpus of Mesopotamian Anti-Witchcraft Rituals, Volume One*. AMD 8/1. Leiden: Brill.

Adamson, P. B.

1981 "Anatomical and Pathological Terms in Akkadian: Part III." *JRAS* 113/2, pp. 125–132.

1990 "Some Anatomical and Pathological Terms in Akkadian." *RA* 84, pp. 27–32.

1993 "An Assessment of Some Akkadian Medical Terms." *RA* 87, pp. 153–159.

Al-Rawi, Farouk, and Jeremy Black

2000 "A balbale of Ninurta, god of fertility." *ZA* 90, pp. 31–39.

Al-Rawi, Farouk, and Andrew R. George

2006 "Tablets from the Sippar Library XIII: *Enūma Anu Ellil* XX." *Iraq* 68, pp. 23–57.

Al-Rawi, Farouk and Michael Roaf

1984 "Ten Old Babylonian Mathematical Problems from Tell Haddad, Himrin." *Sumer* 43, pp. 175–218.

Alster, Bendt

1995 "Halt or Dwarf: The Meaning of ba-za = *pessû*." Pp. 1–6 in *Vom alten Orient zum alten Testament. Festschrift für Wolfram Freiherrn von Soden zum 85. Geburtstag am 19. Juni 1993*. Edited by M. Dietrich and O. Loretz. AOAT 240. Kevelaer: Verlag Butzon & Bercker.

1997 *Proverbs of Ancient Sumer: The World's Earliest Proverb Collections*. 2 Vols. Bethesda, Maryland: CDL Press.

2005 *Wisdom of Ancient Sumer*. Bethesda, Maryland: CDL Press.

Alster, Bendt and Takayoshi Oshima

2006 "A Sumerian Proverb Tablet in Geneva: With Some Thoughts on Sumerian Proverb Collections." *OrNs* 75, pp. 31–72.

Ambos, Claus

2007 "Types of Ritual Failure and Mistakes in Ritual in Cuneiform Sources." Pp. 25–47 in *When Rituals Go Wrong: Mistakes, Failure, and the Dynamics of Ritual.* Edited by Ute Hüsken. Numen Book Series 115. Leiden: Brill.

Arnaud, Daniel

1985 *Recherches au Pays d'Aštata Emar VI/1. Textes sumériens et accadiens.* Planches, Paris.

1986 *Recherches au Pays d'Aštata Emar VI/3. Textes sumériens et accadiens.* Recherche sur les Grandes Civilisations, Synthèse 18. Paris: Éditions Recherche sur les Civilizations.

1987 *Recherches au Pays d'Aštata Emar VI/4. Textes de la bibliothèque. Transcriptions et traductions.* Recherche sur les Grandes Civilisations, Synthèse 28. Paris: Éditions Recherche sur les Civilizations.

1994 *Texte aus Larsa, Die epigraphischen Funde der 1. Kampagne in Senkereh-Larsa 1933.* Berliner Beiträge zum Vorderer Orient Texte 3. Berlin.

Aro, J.

1961 Review of M. Birot, *Textes administratifs de la salle 5 du Palais. OLZ* 56, pp. 603–605.

Attinger, Pascal

1993 *Eléments de linguistique sumérienne: La construction de du$_{11}$/e/di «dire».* OBO, Sonderband. Fribourg, Suisse: Editions Universitaires.

2008 "La médecine mésopotamienne." *JMC* 11 & 12, pp. 1–96.

Bácskay, András

2018 *Therapeutic Prescriptions Against Fever in Ancient Mesopotamia.* AOAT 447. Münster: Ugarit-Verlag.

Bácskay, András, Réka Esztári, and Krisztián Simkó

2014 "Some Remarks on Sa-gig I and Its Commentaries." *JMC* 24, pp. 1–10.

Baker, Heather D., ed.

2000 *The Prosopography of the Neo-Assyrian Empire. Volume 2, Part I: Ḫ–K.* The Neo-Assyrian Text Corpus Project. Finland: Vammalan Kirjapaino Oy.

Beaulieu, Paul-Alain

1995 "An Excerpt from a Menology with Reverse Writing." *ASJ* 17, pp. 1–14.

2000 "The Descendants of Sîn-lēqi-unninni." Pp. 1–16 in *Assyriologica et Semitica: Festschrift für Joachim Oelsner anläßlich seines 65. Geburtstages am 18. Februar 1997.* Edited by J. Marzahn and H. Neumann. AOAT 252. Münster.

2003 *The Pantheon of Uruk During the Neo-Babylonian Period.* CM 23. Leiden: Brill.

2007 "The Social and Intellectual Setting of Babylonian Wisdom Literature." Pp. 3–19 in *Wisdom Literature in Mesopotamia and Israel.* Edited by R. J. Clifford. SBL Symposium Series 36. Atlanta: Society of Biblical Literature.

2013 "Aspects of Aramaic and Babylonian Linguistic Interaction in First Millennium BC Iraq." *Journal of Language Contact* 6, pp. 358–378.

2014 "An Episode in the Reign of the Babylonian Pretender Nebuchadnezzar IV." Pp. 17–26 in *Extraction & Control: Studies in Honor of Matthew W. Stolper.* Edited by M. Kozuh, W. F. M. Henkelman, C. E. Jones, and C. Woods. SAOC 68. Chicago: University of Chicago.

Beckman, Gary, and Benjamin R. Foster

1988 "Assyrian Scholarly Texts in the Yale Babylonian Collection." Pp. 1–26 in *A Scientific Humanist: Studies in Memory of Abraham Sachs.* Edited by Erle

Leichty, Maria de J. Ellis, and Pamela Gerardi. Occasional Publications of the Samuel Noah Kramer Fund 9. Philadelphia.

Berlejung, Angelika

2009 "Innovation als Restauration in Uruk und Jehud: Überlegungen zu Transformationsprozessen in vorderorientalischen Gesellschaften." Pp. 71–111 in *Reformen im Alten Orient und der Antike: Programme, Darstellungen und Deutungen*. Edited by Ernst-Joachim Waschke. Orientalische Religionen in der Antike 2. Tübingen: Mohr Siebeck.

Berzon, Ecaterina M.

2014 "The Titulature of a Co-Ruler in the Seleucid Kingdom." *Antiqvitas Aeterna: The Volga Region Journal of Classical Studies* 4, pp. 105–118.

Bezold, C.

1896 *Catalogue of the Cuneiform Tablets in the Kouyunjik Collection of the British Museum.* Volume IV. Printed by Order of the Trustees of the British Museum.

Biggs, Robert D.

1967 *ŠÀ.ZI.GA: Ancient Mesopotamian Potency Incantations*. TCS 2. New York: J. J. Augustin.

1968 "An Esoteric Babylonian Commentary." *RA* 62/1, pp. 51–58.

1990 "Medizin. A. In Mesopotamien." RLA 7, pp. 623–629.

Bilbija, J.

2008 "Interpreting the Interpretation: Protasis-Apodosis-Strings in the Physiognomic Omen Series Šumma Alamdimmû 3.76–132." Pp. 19–27 in *Studies in Ancient Near Eastern World View and Society Presented to Marten Stol on the Occasion of His 65th Birthday, and His Retirement from the Vrije Universiteit Amsterdam.* Edited by R. J. van der Spek. Bethesda, Maryland: CDL Press.

Böck, Barbara

2000a *Die babylonisch-assyrische Morphoskopie*. BAfO 27. Vienna.

2000b "'An Esoteric Babylonian Commentary' Revisited." *JAOS* 120/4, pp. 615–620.

2009a "On Medical Technology in Ancient Mesopotamia." Pp. 105–128 in *Advances in Mesopotamian Medicine from Hammurabi to Hippocrates*. Edited by Annie Attia and Gilles Buisson. CM 37. Leiden: Brill.

2009b "Diagnose im Alten Mesopotamien. Überlegungen zu Grenzen und Möglichkeiten der Interpretation keilschriftlicher diagnosticher Texte." *OLZ* 104/4–5, pp. 381–398.

2010 "2.8 Fieberkrankheiten." Pp. 78–84 in *Texte zur Heilkunde*. Edited by B. Janowski and D. Schwemer. TUAT 5. Gütersloh: Gütersloher Verlagshaus.

2013 *The Healing Goddess Gula: Towards an Understanding of Ancient Babylonian Medicine*. CHANE 67. Leiden: Brill.

Boissier, Alfred

1894 *Documents assyriens relatifs aux présages*. Tome premier. Paris: Librairie Émile Bouillon.

Boiy, Tom

2002 "Royal Titulature in Hellenistic Babylonia." *ZA* 92, pp. 241–257.

Borger, Rykle

1969 "Die erste Teiltafel der zi-pà-Beschwörungen (ASKT 11)." Pp. 1–22 in *Lišān mitḫurti: Festschrift Wolfram Freiherr von Soden zum 19.VI.1968 gewidmet von Schülern und Mitarbeitern.* Edited by M. Dietrich and W. Röllig. AOAT 1. Kevelaer: Verlag Butzon & Bercker.

1969–1970 "Bemerkung zu den akkadischen Kolophonen." *WO* 5, pp. 165–171.
1971 "Geheimwissen." RLA 3, pp. 188–191.
1975 *Handbuch der Keilschriftliteratur, Band II*. Berlin: de Gruyter.
2010 *Mesopotamisches Zeichenlexikon*. AOAT 305. Münster: Ugarit-Verlag. 2nd revised ed.

Bottéro, Jean
1985 *Mythes et rites de Babylone*. Paris: H. Champion.

Bottéro, Jean, and Samuel Noah Kramer
1989 *Lorsque les dieux faisaient l'homme: Mythologie mésopotamienne*. Paris: Éditions Gallimard.

Brinkman, J. A.
1964 "Merodach-Baladan II." Pp. 6–53 in *Studies Presented to A. Leo Oppenheim, June 7, 1964*. Chicago: University of Chicago Press.

Brown, David
2000 *Mesopotamian Planetary Astronomy-Astrology*. CM 18. Groningen: Styx.
2006 "Astral Divination in the Context of Mesopotamian Divination, Medicine, Religion, Magic, Society, and Scholarship." Pp. 69–126 in *Special Issue in Honor of Prof. Ho Peng Yoke's 80th Birthday*. Edited by H. U. Vogel. East Asian Science, Technology, and Medicine 25. Tübingen: International Society for the History of East Asian Science, Technology, and Medicine.
2008 "Increasingly Redundant: The Growing Obsolescence of the Cuneiform Script in Babylonia from 539 BC." Pp. 73–101 in *The Disappearance of Writing Systems: Perspectives on Literacy and Communication*. Edited by John Baines, John Bennet, and Stephen Houston. London: Equinox.

Bruins, E. M.
1954 "Some Mathematical Texts." *Sumer* 10, pp. 55–61.

Buccellati, Giorgio
1996 *A Structural Grammar of Babylonian*. Wiesbaden: Harrassowitz Verlag.

Bullough, Vern L.
1971 "Attitudes toward Deviant Sex in Ancient Mesopotamia." *The Journal of Sex Research* 7/3, pp. 184–203.

Burstein, Stanley M.
1978 *The Babyloniaca of Berossus*. SANE 1/5. Malibu: Undena.

Cabezón, José Ignacio
1994 *Buddhism and Language: A Study of Indo-Tibetan Scholasticism*. New York: State University of New York Press.
1998 Editor of *Scholasticism: Cross-Cultural and Comparative Perspectives*. New York: State University of New York Press.

Cagni, Luigi
1969 *L'Epopea di Erra*. StSem 34. Roma: Istituto di Studi del Vicino Oriente.

Campbell Thompson, Reginald
1904 *The Devils and Evil Spirits of Babylonia, Vol. 2*. London: Luzac & Co.
1923 *Assyrian Medical Texts from the Originals in the British Museum*. London.
1924 "Assyrian Medical Texts." *PRSM* (Sect Hist Med) 17, pp. 1–34.
1931 *The Prisms of Esarhaddon and Ashurbanipal Found at Nineveh, 1927–8*. London: British Museum.
1934 "Assyrian Prescriptions for Diseases of the Urine, etc." *Bab* 14, pp. 57–151.
1949 *A Dictionary of Assyrian Botany*. London: Stephen Austin & Sons.

Cavigneaux, Antoine

1980 "Die Fragmente der sumerisch-akkadischen Wortliste „Erimhuš" im Vorderasiatischen Museum zu Berlin." *FuB* 20–21, pp. 259–270.

1982 "Remarques sur les commentaries à Labat TDP 1." *JCS* 34, pp. 231–241.

1983 "Lexikalische Listen." RLA 6/7–8, pp. 609–641.

1987 "Aux Sources du Midrash: l'herméneutique babylonienne." *AuOr* 5, pp. 243–255.

1994 Review of E. von Weiher, *Spätbabylonische Texte aus Uruk, Teil III*. *WO* 25, pp. 138–143.

1996 *Uruk: Altbabylonische Texte aus dem Planquadrat Pe XVI–4/5*. AUWE 23. Mainz am Rhein: Verlag Philipp von Zabern.

2015 Review of N. P. Heeßel, *Divinatorische Texte II*, *Syria* 92, pp. 454–456.

Cavigneaux, Antoine, and Farouk Al-Rawi

1993 "New Sumerian Literary Texts from Tell Haddad (Ancient Meturan): A First Survey." *Iraq* 55, pp. 91–105.

Chalendar, Vérène

2016 "What Reality for Animals in the Mesopotamian Medical Texts? Plant vs Animal." *Anthropozoologica* 51/2, pp. 97–103.

Charpin, Dominique

1983/1984 Review of L. Cagni, *Briefe aus dem Iraq Museum* (*TIM II*). *AfO* 29/30, pp. 103–108.

2010 *Reading and Writing in Babylon*. Translated by J. M. Todd. Cambridge, Massachusetts: Harvard University Press.

Civil, Miguel

1960 "Prescriptions médicales sumériennes." *RA* 54, pp. 57–72.

1961 "Une nouvelle prescription médicale sumérienne." *RA* 55, pp. 91–94.

1974 "Medical Commentaries from Nippur." *JNES* 33/3, pp. 329–338.

1976 "Lexicography." Pp. 123–157 in *Sumerological Studies in Honor of Thorkild Jacobsen on his Seventieth Birthday*. Edited by S. J. Lieberman. AS 20. Chicago: University of Chicago Press.

1984 "On Some Terms for 'Bat' in Mesopotamia." *AuOr* 2, pp. 5–9.

1985 "Sur les 'Livres d'écolier' à l'époque paléo-babylonienne." Pp. 67–78 in *Miscellanea Babylonica, Mélanges offerts à Maurice Birot*. Edited by J.-M. Durand and J.-R. Kupper. Paris: Editions Recherche sur les Civilisations.

1987 "Feeding Dumuzi's Sheep: The Lexicon as a Source of Literary Inspiration." Pp. 37–55 of *Language, Literature, and History: Philological and Historical Studies Presented to Erica Reiner*. Edited by Francesca Rochberg-Halton. AOS 67. New Haven: American Oriental Society.

1989 "The Texts from Meskene-Emar." *AuOr* 7, pp. 5–21.

1994 *The Farmer's Instructions: A Sumerian Agricultural Manual*. AuOrS 5. Barcelona: Editorial AUSA.

2000 "From the Epistolary of the Edubba." Pp. 105–118 in *Wisdom, Gods and Literature: Studies in Assyriology in Honour of W. G. Lambert*. Edited by A. R. George and I. L. Finkel. Winona Lake, Indiana: Eisenbrauns.

2007 "Early Semitic Loanwords in Sumerian." Pp. 11–33 in *Studies Presented to Robert D. Biggs, June 4, 2004*. Edited by Martha T. Roth, et al. From the Workshop of the Chicago Assyrian Dictionary 2. Chicago: The Oriental Institute.

Clancier, Philippe

2005 "Les bibliothèques en Babylonie au 1er millénaire av. J.-C." Ph.D. diss., Université Paris 8, Vincennes-Saint-Denis.

2009 *Les bibliothèques en Babylonie dans la deuxième moitié du 1er millénaire av. J.-C.* AOAT 363. Münster: Ugarit-Verlag.

2010 "Formation and Administration of the Collections of Literary and Scholarly Tablets in First Millennium Babylonia." Pp. 3–35 of *Looking at it from Asia: The Processes that Shaped the Sources of History of Science.* Edited by Florence Bretelle-Establet. Boston Studies in the Philosophy and History of Science 265. Dordrecht: Springer.

2014 "Teaching and Learning Medicine and Exorcism at Uruk During the Hellenistic Period." Pp. 41–66 of *Scientific Sources and Teaching Contexts Throughout History: Problems and Perspectives.* Edited by Alain Bernard and Christine Proust. Boston Studies in the Philosophy and History of Science 301. Dordrecht: Springer.

Cohen, Eran

2003–2004 "Paronomastic Infinitive in Old Babylonian." *JEOL* 38, pp. 105–112.

2006 "The Old Babylonian Paronomastic Infinitive in *-am*." *JAOS* 126/3, pp. 425–432.

Cohen, Yoram, and Sivan Kedar

2011 "Teacher-Student Relationships." Pp. 229–247 in *The Oxford Handbook of Cuneiform Culture.* Edited by Karen Radner and Eleanor Robson. Oxford: Oxford University Press.

Collins, Timothy J.

1999 "Natural Illness in Babylonian Medical Incantations." 2 Vols. Ph.D. diss., University of Chicago.

Conti, Giovanni

2000 "A proposito di Gibil, dio del fuoco." Pp. 125–134 in *Studi sul Vicino Oriente antico dedicati alla memoria di Luigi Cagni*, Vol. 1. Edited by S. Graziani. Napoli: Istituto Universitario Orientale.

Cooper, Jerrold

2008 "Redundancy Reconsidered: Reflections on David Brown's Thesis." Pp. 103–108 in *The Disappearance of Writing Systems: Perspectives on Literacy and Communication.* Edited by John Baines, John Bennet, and Stephen Houston. London: Equinox.

Couto-Ferreira, M. Érica

2009 "Etnoanatomía y partonomía del cuerpo humano en sumerio y acadio: El léxico Ugu-mu." Ph.D. diss., Universitat Pompeu Fabra.

2014 "She will Give Birth Easily: Therapeutic Approaches to Childbirth in 1st millennium BCE Cuneiform Sources." *Dynamis* 34/2, pp. 289–315.

2017 "From Head to Toe: Listing the Body in Cuneiform Texts." Pp. 43–71 in *The Comparable Body: Analogy and Metaphor in Ancient Mesopotamian, Egyptian, and Greco-Roman Medicine.* Edited by John Z. Wee. Studies in Ancient Medicine 49. Leiden: Brill.

Crisciani, Chiara

1990 "History, Novelty, and Progress in Scholastic Medicine." *Osiris, 2nd Series* 6, pp. 118–139.

Cross, Frank Moore, and John Huehnergard

2003 "The Alphabet on a Late Babylonian Cuneiform School Tablet." *OrNS* 72, pp. 223–228.

Da Riva, Rocío, and Eckart Frahm

1999/2000 "Šamaš-šumu-ukīn, die Herrin von Ninive und das babylonische Königssiegel." *AfO* 46–47, pp. 156–182.

Dalley, Stephanie
1989 *Myths from Mesopotamia: Creation, the Flood, Gilgamesh, and Others*. Oxford: Oxford University Press.
Danzig, David
2013 "Name Word Play and Marduk's Fifty Names in *Enūma Eliš*." M.A. thesis, Yale University.
Daxelmüller, Christoph, and Marie-Louise Thomsen
1982 "Bildzauber im alten Mesopotamien." *Anthropos* 77, pp. 27–64.
De Zorzi, Nicla
2009 "Bird Divination in Mesopotamia: New Evidence from BM 108874." *Kaskal* 6, pp. 85–135.
2014 *La serie teratomantica Šumma izbu: Testo, tradizione, orizzonti culturali*. 2 vols. HANEM 15. Padova: S.A.R.G.O.N. Editrice e Libreria.
Dean-Jones, Lesley Ann
1994 *Women's Bodies in Classical Greek Science*. Oxford: Clarendon Press.
Deimel, Anton
1947 *Šumerisches Lexikon*. Part I, 3rd ed. Rome: Pontificium Institutum Biblicum.
Deller, Karlheinz
1959 "Lautlehre des Neuassyrischen." Ph.D. diss., Universität Wien.
Deller, Karlheinz, Werner R. Mayer, and Joachim Oelsner
1989 "Akkadische Lexikographie: *CAD* Q." *OrNS* 58, pp. 255–282.
Di Vito, Robert A.
1993 *Studies in Third Millennium Sumerian and Akkadian Personal Names: The Designation and Conception of the Personal God*. StPohl, Series Maior 16. Rome: Pontifical Biblical Institute.
Dieleman, Jacco
2003 "Reading Magic: Social and Cultural Contexts of Two Demotic-Greek Magical Handbooks." Ph.D. diss., Leiden University.
Dougherty, R. P.
1923–1933 *Goucher College Cuneiform Inscriptions*. New Haven.
Durand, J.-M.
1979 "Un commentaire à *TDP* I, AO 17661." *RA* 73, pp. 153–170.
1981 *Textes babyloniens d'époque récente*. Paris.
Ebeling, Erich
1931 *Tod und Leben nach den Vorstellungen der Babylonier*. Berlin-Leipzig: de Gruyter.
1949 "Beschwörungen gegen den Feind und den bösen Blick aus dem Zweistromlande." *ArOr* 17/1, pp. 172–211.
Edzard, Dietz Otto
1975 "Ḫursagkalama. A. Philologisch." RLA 4, pp. 519–520.
1990 "Selbstgespräch und Monolog in der akkadischen Literatur." Pp. 149–162 in *Lingering Over Words: Studies in Ancient Near Eastern Literature in Honor of William L. Moran*. Edited by T. Abusch, J. Huehnergard, and P. Steinkeller. HSS 37. Atlanta, Georgia: Scholars Press.
2003 *Sumerian Grammar*. HdO I, 71. Leiden: Brill.
Elat, Moshe
1982 "Mesopotamische Kriegsrituale." *BiOr* 39, pp. 5–25.
Elman, Yaakov
1975 "Authoritative Oral Tradition in Neo-Assyrian Scribal Circles." *JANES* 7, pp. 19–32.

Falkenstein, Adam

1931a *Literarische Keilschrifttexte aus Uruk.* Berlin.

1931b *Die Haupttypen der sumerischen Beschwörung literarisch untersucht.* LSS NS 1. Leipzig: J. C. Hinrichs.

1959 *Das Sumerische.* HdO I, 2/1–2. Abschnitt, Lieferung 1. Leiden: Brill.

Farber, Walter

1975 "Sagḫulḫaza *mukīl rēš lemutti.*" *ZA* 64, pp. 87–95.

1977 *Beschwörungsrituale an Ištar und Dumuzi: Attī Ištar ša Ḫarmaša Dumuzi.* Akademie der Wissenschaften und der Literatur, Veröffentlichungen der orientalischen Kommission 30. Wiesbaden: Franz Steiner Verlag GmbH.

1983 "Lamaštu." RLA 6/5–6, pp. 439–446.

1987a "Lilû, Lilītu, Ardat-lilî." RLA 7/1–2, pp. 23–24.

1987b "Neues aus Uruk: Zur 'Bibliothek des Iqīša.'" *WO* 18, pp. 26–42.

1989a "(W)ardat-lilî." *ZA* 79, pp. 14–35.

1989b "Lamaštu, Enlil, Anu-ikṣur: Streiflichter aus Uruks Gelehrtenstuben." *ZA* 79, pp. 223–241.

1989c "Vorzeichen aus der Waschschüssel: Zu den akkadischen Bade-Omina (*Šumma ālu*, 43. *nisḫu*)." *OrNS* 58, pp. 86–101.

1993 "'Forerunners' and 'Standard Versions': A Few Thoughts about Terminology." Pp. 95–97 in *The Tablet and the Scroll: Near Eastern Studies in Honor of William W. Hallo.* Edited by M. E. Cohen, D. C. Snell, and D. B. Weisberg. Bethesda, Maryland: CDL Press.

2014 *Lamaštu: An Edition of the Canonical Series of Lamaštu Incantations and Rituals and Related Texts from the Second and First Millenniua B.C.* MC 17. Winona Lake, Indiana: Eisenbrauns.

Fawzi, R.

1978 "Crows: A Means to Tell the Future." *Sumer* 34, pp. 40–65 (Arabic Section).

Fincke, Jeanette C.

2000 *Augenleiden nach keilschriftlichen Quellen.* Untersuchungen zur altorientalischen Medizin. Würzburger medizinhistorische Forschungen Band 70. Würzburg: Verlag Königshausen & Neumann GmbH.

2003/2004 "The Babylonian Texts of Nineveh: Report on the British Museum's *Ashurbanipal Library Project.*" *AfO* 50, pp. 111–149.

2009 "Cuneiform Tablets on Eye Diseases: Babylonian Sources in Relation to the Series DIŠ NA IGIII-*šú* GIG." Pp. 79–104 in *Advances in Mesopotamian Medicine from Hammurabi to Hippocrates.* Edited by Annie Attia and Gilles Buisson. CM 37. Leiden: Brill.

2011a "Spezialisierung und Differenzierung im Bereich der altorientalischen Medizin: Die Dermatologie am Beispiel der Symptome *simmū matqūtu*, *kalmātu* (*matuqtu*), *kibšu*, *kiṣṣatu* und *gurištu.*" Pp. 159–190 in *The Empirical Dimension of Ancient Near Eastern Studies.* Edited by Gebhard J. Selz. Wiener Offene Orientalistik 6. Wien: Lit Verlag GmbH & Co.

2011b "Neue Erkenntnisse zur 21. Tafel der diagnostischen Omenserie SA.GIG und zur Überlieferung diagnostischer Omentexte in *Hattuša.*" *BiOr* 68, pp. 472–476.

2013 "[d]*Šaggāšu* ('Murderer'), The Demon from the Steppe." *BiOr* 70, pp. 17–24.

Finkbeiner, Uwe

1993 *Uruk: Analytisches Register zu den Grabungsberichten Kampagnen 1912/13 bis 1976/77.* Unter Mitarbeit von Manfred Robert Behm-Blancke. Berlin: Gebr. Mann Verlag.

Finkel, Irving L.

1988 "Adad-apla-iddina, Esagil-kīn-apli, and the Series SA.GIG." Pp. 143–159 in *A Scientific Humanist: Studies in Memory of Abraham Sachs*. Edited by Erle Leichty, Maria de J. Ellis, and Pamela Gerardi. Occasional Publications of the Samuel Noah Kramer Fund 9. Philadelphia.

1993 "Bilingual Proverbs: An Instructive Join." *NABU* 1993/15.

1994 "On TDP Tablets XXIX and XXXI, and the Nature of SA.GIG." *JCS* 46, pp. 87–88.

1999 "Magic and Medicine at Meskene." *NABU* 1999/30.

2000 "On Late Babylonian Medical Training." Pp. 137–223 in *Wisdom, Gods and Literature: Studies in Assyriology in Honour of W. G. Lambert*. Edited by A. R. George and I. L. Finkel. Winona Lake, Indiana: Eisenbrauns.

2005 "No. 69: Explanatory Commentary on a List of Materia Medica." Pp. 279–283 in *Literary and Scholastic Texts of the First Millennium B.C.* Edited by Ira Spar and W. G. Lambert. CTMMA 2; New York: Metropolitan Museum of Art.

2006 "On an Izbu VII Commentary." Pp. 139–148 in *If a Man Builds a Joyful House: Assyriological Studies in Honor of Erle Verdun Leichty*. Edited by Ann K. Guinan, et al. CM 31; Leiden: Brill.

2007 "On the Rules for the Royal Game of Ur." Pp. 16–32 in *Ancient Board Games in Perspective: Papers from the 1990 British Museum Colloquium, with Additional Contributions*. Edited by I. L. Finkel. London: British Museum.

2014a "Remarks on Cuneiform Scholarship and the Babylonian Talmud." Pp. 307–316 in *Encounters by the Rivers of Babylon: Scholarly Conversations between Jews, Iranians, and Babylonians in Antiquity*. Edited by U. Gabbay and Sh. Secunda. Texts and Studies in Ancient Judaism 160. Tuebingen: Mohr Siebeck.

2014b *The Ark Before Noah: Decoding the Story of the Flood.* New York: Doubleday.

2018 "On Three Tablet Inventories." Pp. 25–41 in *Assyrian and Babylonian Scholarly Text Catalogues*. Edited by Ulrike Steinert. Die babylonisch-assyrische Medizin in Texten und Untersuchungen 9. Berlin: de Gruyter.

Foster, Benjamin R.

1991 "On Authorship in Akkadian Literature." *Annuario del Istituto Orientale di Napoli* 51, pp. 17–32.

2005a *Before the Muses: An Anthology of Akkadian Literature*. Bethesda, Maryland: CDL Press, 3rd ed.

2005b "Transmission of Knowledge." Pp. 245–252 in *A Companion to the Ancient Near East.* Edited by Daniel C. Snell. Malden: Blackwell Publishing.

Foster, Benjamin R. and Emmanuelle Salgues

2006 "'Everything Except the Squeal': Pigs in Early Mesopotamia." Pp. 283–291 in *De la domestication au tabou: le cas des suidés dans le Proche-Orient ancien.* Edited by B. Lion and C. Michel. Paris: De Boccard.

Fox, Joshua

2003 *Semitic Noun Patterns*. HSS 52. Winona Lake, Indiana: Eisenbrauns.

Frahm, Eckart

1997 *Einleitung in die Sanherib-Inschriften*. BAfO 26. Horn, Austria: Ferdinand Berger & Söhne.

1999 "Nabû-zuqup-kēnu, das Gilgameš-Epos und der Tod Sargons II." *JCS* 51, pp. 73–90.

2001 "Ein krypto-sumerischer Text König Adad-apla-iddinas aus Uruk." *Bagh. Mitt.* 32, pp. 175–199, Tafeln 1–4.

2002 "Zwischen Tradition und Neuerung: Babylonische Priestergelehrte im achämenidenzeitlichen Uruk." Pp. 74–108 in *Religion und Religionskontakte im Zeitalter der Achämeniden*. Edited by R. G. Kratz. VWGTh 22. Gütersloh: Chr. Kaiser.

2003 "New Sources for Sennacherib's 'First Campaign.'" Pp. 129–164 in *Assur und sein Umland: Im Andenken an die ersten Ausgräber von Assur*. Edited by P. A. Miglus and J. M. Córdoba. ISIMU 6. Madrid: Servicio de Publicaciones Universidad Autónoma de Madrid.

2004 "Royal Hermeneutics: Observations on the Commentaries from Ashurbanipal's Libraries at Nineveh." *Iraq* 66, pp. 45–50.

2005 "On Some Recently Published Late Babylonian Copies of Royal Letters." *NABU* 2005/43.

2010a "Kommentare zu medizinischen Texten." Pp. 171–176 in *Texte zur Heilkunde*. Edited by B. Janowski and D. Schwemer. TUAT NF 5. Gütersloh.

2010b "Counter-texts, Commentaries, and Adaptations: Politically Motivated Responses to the Babylonian Epic of Creation in Mesopotamia, the Biblical World, and Elsewhere." *Orient: Reports of the Society for Near Eastern Studies in Japan* 45 (special issue: Conflict, Peace and Religion in the Ancient Near East, ed. A. Tsukimoto), pp. 3–33.

2010c "The Latest Sumerian Proverbs." Pp. 155–184 in *Opening the Tablet Box: Near Eastern Studies in Honor of Benjamin R. Foster*. Edited by Sarah Melville and Alice Slotsky. CHANE 42. Leiden: Brill.

2011a *Babylonian and Assyrian Text Commentaries: Origins of Interpretation*. GMTR 5. Münster: Ugarit-Verlag.

2011b "Keeping Company with Men of Learning: The King as Scholar." Pp. 508–532 in *The Oxford Handbook of Cuneiform Culture*. Edited by Karen Radner and Eleanor Robson. Oxford.

2012 "Headhunter, Bücherdiebe und wandernde Gelehrte: Anmerkungen zum altorientalischen Wissenstransfer im 1. Jahrtausend v. Chr." Pp. 15–30 in *Wissenskultur im Alten Orient: Weltanschauung, Wissenschaften, Techniken, Technologien*. Edited by H. Neumann. CDOG 4. Wiesbaden: Harrassowitz Verlag.

2014 "Traditionalism and Intellectual Innovation in a Cosmopolitan World: Reflections on Babylonian Text Commentaries from the Achaemenid Period." Pp. 317–334 in *Encounters by the Rivers of Babylon: Scholarly Conversations between Jews, Iranians, and Babylonians in Antiquity*. Edited by U. Gabbay and Sh. Secunda. Texts and Studies in Ancient Judaism 160. Tuebingen: Mohr Siebeck.

2018 "The Exorcist's Manual: Structure, Language, *Sitz im Leben*." Pp. 9–47 in *Sources of Evil: Studies in Mesopotamian Exorcistic Lore*. Edited by G. van Buylaere, et al. AMD 15. Leiden: Brill.

Frahm, Eckart and Enrique Jiménez

2015 "Myth, Ritual, and Interpretation: The Commentary on *Enūma eliš* I–VII and a Commentary on Elamite Month Names." *Hebrew Bible and Ancient Israel* 4/3, pp. 293–343.

Frame, Grant, and Andrew R. George

2005 "The Royal Libraries of Nineveh: New Evidence for King Ashurbanipal's Tablet Collecting." *Iraq* 67/1, pp. 265–284.

Frantz-Szabo, G.

1977 "Išḫara." RLA 5, pp. 177–178.

Frechette, C. G.
2012 *Mesopotamian Ritual-prayers of 'Hand-lifting' (Akkadian Šuillas): An Investigation of Function in Light of the Idiomatic Meaning of the Rubric*. AOAT 379. Münster: Ugarit-Verlag.

Freedman (née Moren), Sally M.
1978 "The Omen Series *Šumma Ālu*: A Preliminary Investigation." Ph.D. diss., University of Pennsylvania.
1998 *If a City Is Set on a Height: The Akkadian Omen Series Šumma Alu ina Mēlê Šakin, Volume 1: Tablets 1–21*. Occasional Publications of the Samuel Noah Kramer Fund 17. Philadelphia: University of Pennsylvania Museum.
2006 *If a City Is Set on a Height: The Akkadian Omen Series Šumma Alu ina Mēlê Šakin, Volume 2: Tablets 22–40*. Occasional Publications of the Samuel Noah Kramer Fund 19. Philadelphia: University of Pennsylvania Museum.
2017 *If a City Is Set on a Height: The Akkadian Omen Series Šumma Alu ina Mēlê Šakin, Volume 3: Tablets 41–63*. Occasional Publications of the Samuel Noah Kramer Fund 20. Winona Lake, Indiana: Eisenbrauns.

French, Roger
1994 "Astrology in Medical Practice." Pp. 30–59 in *Practical Medicine from Salerno to the Black Death*. Edited by L. García-Ballester, et al. Cambridge: Cambridge University Press.
2001 *Canonical Medicine: Gentile da Foligno and Scholasticism*. Leiden: Brill.

Freydank, Helmut
1991 *Beiträge zur mittelassyrischen Chronologie und Geschichte*. SGKAO 21. Berlin: Akademie Verlag.

Friberg, Jöran
2005 "Nos. 72–77: Mathematical Texts." Pp. 288–314 in *Literary and Scholastic Texts of the First Millennium B.C.* Edited by Ira Spar and W. G. Lambert. CTMMA 2. New York: Brepols.
2007 *A Remarkable Collection of Babylonian Mathematical Texts: Manuscripts in the Schøyen Collection, Cuneiform Texts I*. New York: Springer.

Friberg, Jöran, and Farouk N. H. Al-Rawi
2016 *New Mathematical Cuneiform Texts*. Switzerland: Springer.

Frymer Kensky, Tikva Simone
1977 "The Judicial Ordeal in the Ancient Near East." Ph.D. diss., Yale University.

Gabbay, Uri
2006 "Emesal Passages Cited in Commentaries." *NABU* 2006/81.
2009a "Deciphering Cuneiform Texts through Ancient and Modern Conceptions of Literal Meaning." Pp. 161–169 in *Le sens littéral des Écritures*. Edited by O.-T. Venard. Paris.
2009b "Some Notes on an Izbu Commentary." *NABU* 2009/53.
2012 "Akkadian Commentaries from Ancient Mesopotamia and Their Relation to Early Hebrew Exegesis." *Dead Sea Discoveries* 19, pp. 267–312.
2014 "Actual Sense and Scriptural Intention: Literal Meaning and Its Terminology in Akkadian and Hebrew Commentaries." Pp. 335–370 in *Encounters by the Rivers of Babylon: Scholarly Conversations between Jews, Iranians, and Babylonians in Antiquity*. Edited by U. Gabbay and Sh. Secunda. Texts and Studies in Ancient Judaism 160. Tuebingen: Mohr Siebeck.
2015 "Specification as a Hermeneutical Technique in Babylonian and Assyrian Commentaries." *Hebrew Bible and Ancient Israel* 4/3, pp. 344–368.

2016 *The Exegetical Terminology of Akkadian Commentaries.* CHANE 82. Leiden: Brill.

2017 "Levels of Meaning and Textual Polysemy in Akkadian and Hebrew Exegetical Texts." Pp. 76–95 in *Jewish Cultural Encounters in the Ancient Mediterranean and Near Eastern World.* Edited by M. Popović, M. Schoonover, and M. Vandenberghe. Leiden: Brill.

Gabbay, Uri, and Enrique Jiménez

2019 "Cultural Imports and Local Products in the Commentaries from Uruk. The Case of the Gimil-Sîn Family." Pp. 53–88 in *Scholars and Scholarship in Late Babylonian Uruk.* Edited by C. Proust and J. Steele. Why the Sciences of the Ancient World Matter 2. Switzerland: Springer.

Gadotti, Alhena, and Marcel Sigrist

2011 *Cuneiform Texts in the Carl A. Kroch Library, Cornell University.* CUSAS 15. Bethesda, Maryland: CDL Press.

Gantzert, Merijn

2011 "The Emar Lexical Texts, Parts I–IV." Ph.D. diss., Leiden University.

Gehlken, Erlend

2012 *Weather Omens of Enūma Anu Enlil: Thunderstorms, Wind and Rain (Tablets 44–49).* CM 43. Leiden: Brill.

Geller, Markham J.

1990 "Astronomy and Authorship." *BSOAS* 53/2, pp. 209–213.

1995 "The Influence of Ancient Mesopotamia on Hellenistic Judaism." Pp. 43–54 in *Civilizations of the Ancient Near East.* Edited by J. M. Sasson. New York: Charles Scribner's Sons.

1997 "The Last Wedge." *ZA* 87, pp. 43–95.

1997–2000 "The Aramaic Incantation in Cuneiform Script (AO 6489 = TCL 6,58)." *JEOL* 35/36, pp. 127–146.

2000 "Incipits and Rubrics." Pp. 225–258 in *Wisdom, Gods and Literature: Studies in Assyriology in Honour of W. G. Lambert.* Edited by A. R. George and I. L. Finkel. Winona Lake, Indiana: Eisenbrauns.

2001–2002 "West Meets East: Early Greek and Babylonian Diagnosis." *AfO* 48/49, pp. 50–75.

2004a "Akkadian Healing Therapies in the Babylonian Talmud." Preprint 259. Max Planck Institute for the History of Science.

2004b "Anus and Kidneys." *JMC* 4, pp. 1–8.

2005 *Renal and Rectal Disease Texts.* Edited by Robert D. Biggs and Martin Stol. BAM 7. Berlin: de Gruyter.

2006 "Les maladies et leur causes, selon un texte médical paléobabylonien." *JMC* 8, pp. 7–12.

2007a *Evil Demons: Canonical* Utukkū Lemnūtu *Incantations.* SAACT 5. Finland: Vammalan Kirjapaino Oy.

2007b "Médicine et magie: l'*asû*, l'*âšipu* et le *mašmâšu*." *JMC* 9, pp. 1–8.

2007c "Charlatans, médicins et exorcistes." *JMC* 9, pp. 9–15.

2007d "Textes médicaux du Louvre, nouvelle édition: AO 11447, AO 7760 et AO 66774 [*sic*]: Première partie." *JMC* 10, pp. 4–18.

2009 "Textes médicaux du Louvre, nouvelle édition: AO 11447, AO 7760 et AO 6774: Deuxième partie: AO 6774." *JMC* 14, pp. 28–43.

2010a *Ancient Babylonian Medicine: Theory and Practice.* United Kingdom: Wiley-Blackwell.

2010b *Look to the Stars: Babylonian Medicine, Magic, Astrology and Melothesia.* Max-Planck-Institut für Wissenschaftsgeschichte. Preprint 401.

2011a "Die theoretische Grundlage der babylonische Heilkunde." Pp. 153–157 in *Babylon: Wissenkultur in Orient und Okzident.* Edited by E. Cancik-Kirschbaum, M. van Ess, and J. Marzahn. Topoi, Berlin Studies of the Ancient World 1. Berlin: de Gruyter.

2011b Review of N. P. Heeßel, *Divinatorische Texte I: Terrestrische, teratologische, physiognomische und oneiromantische Texte. WO* 41, pp. 118–121.

2014 *Melothesia in Babylonia: Medicine, Magic, and Astrology in the Ancient Near East.* STMAC 2. Berlin: de Gruyter.

2016 *Healing Magic and Evil Demons: Canonical Udug-hul Incantations.* BAM 8. Berlin: de Gruyter.

2018 "A Babylonian Hippocrates" and "The Exorcist's Manual (KAR 44)." Pp. 42–54 and 292–312 in *Assyrian and Babylonian Scholarly Text Catalogues.* Edited by Ulrike Steinert. Die babylonisch-assyrische Medizin in Texten und Untersuchungen 9. Berlin: de Gruyter.

Geller, Markham J., and Strahil V. Panayotov

2019 *Mesopotamian Eye Disease Texts: The Nineveh Treatise.* BAM 10. Berlin: de Gruyter.

Genty, Thomas

2010a "Les commentaires dans les textes cunéiformes assyro-babyloniens." M.A. thesis.

2010b "Les Commentaires a TDP 3–40, Première Partie." *JMC* 16, pp. 1–38.

George, Andrew R.

1991 "Babylonian Texts from the Folios of Sidney Smith – Part Two: Prognostic and Diagnostic Omens, Tablet I." *RA* 85, pp. 137–163 and figs. 1–5.

1992 *Babylonian Topographical Texts.* OLA 40. Leuven: Peeters.

1993a *House Most High: The Temples of Ancient Mesopotamia.* MC 5. Winona Lake, Indiana: Eisenbrauns.

1993b "Ninurta-Pāqidāt's Dog Bite, and Notes on Other Comic Tales." *Iraq* 55, pp. 63–75.

2003 *The Babylonian Gilgamesh Epic: Introduction, Critical Edition and Cuneiform Texts.* 2 Volumes. Oxford: Oxford University Press.

2005 "On Babylonian Lavatories and Sewers." *Iraq* 77, pp. 75–106.

2009 *Babylonian Literary Texts in the Schøyen Collection.* CUSAS 10. Bethesda, Maryland: CDL Press.

2010 "The Assyrian Elegy: Form and Meaning." Pp. 203–216 in *Opening the Tablet Box: Near Eastern Studies in Honor of Benjamin R. Foster.* Edited by Sarah Melville and Alice Slotsky. CHANE 42. Leiden: Brill.

2013 *Babylonian Divinatory Texts Chiefly in the Schøyen Collection.* CUSAS 18. Bethesda, Maryland: CDL Press.

Gesche, Petra D.

2001 *Schulunterricht in Babylonien im ersten Jahrtausend v. Chr.* AOAT 275. Ugarit-Verlag.

Gibson, McGuire

1975 "Ḫursagkalama. B. Archäologisch." RLA 4, pp. 520–521.

Glassner, Jean-Jacques

2004 *Mesopotamian Chronicles.* SBLWAW 19. Atlanta: Society of Biblical Literature.

Goetze, Albrecht
1947 *Old Babylonian Omen Texts.* YOS 10. New Haven: Yale University Press.
1955 "An Incantation against Diseases." *JCS* 9/1, pp. 8–18.
1957 "Reports on Acts of Extispicy from Old Babylonian and Kassite Times." *JCS* 11/4, pp. 89–105.

Gong, Yushu
2000 *Die Namen der Keilschriftzeichen.* AOAT 268. Münster: Ugarit-Verlag.
2003 "The Names of Cuneiform Signs." *JAC* 18, pp. 1–22.

Goodnick Westenholz, Joan
2006 "The Brain, Marrow, and the Seat of Cognition in Mesopotamian Tradition." *JMC* 7, pp. 1–10.

Gössmann, Felix
1950 *Planetarium Babylonicum oder die sumerisch-babylonischen Stern-Namen.* Šumerisches Lexikon 4/2. Rome: Verlag des Päpstlichen Bibelinstituts.

Grayson, A. Kirk
1980 "Königslisten und Chroniken. B. Akkadisch." RLA 6/1–2, pp. 86–135.
1991 "Old and Middle Assyrian Royal Inscriptions – Marginalia." Pp. 264–266 in *Ah Assyria...: Studies in Assyrian History and Ancient Near Eastern Historiography Presented to Hayim Tadmor.* Edited by M. Cogan and I. Eph'al. Scripta Hierosolymitana 33.
2000 "Murmuring in Mesopotamia." Pp. 301–308 in *Wisdom, Gods and Literature: Studies in Assyriology in Honour of W. G. Lambert.* Edited by A. R. George and I. L. Finkel. Winona Lake, Indiana: Eisenbrauns.

Groneberg, Brigitte
1971 "Untersuchungen zum hymnisch-epischen Dialekt der altbabylonischen literarischen Texte." Ph.D. diss., Universität Münster.

Gurney, O. R.
1956 "The Sultantepe Tablets (Continued). V. The Tale of the Poor Man of Nippur." *AnSt* 6, pp. 145–164.

Gurney, O. R., and J. J. Finkelstein
1957 *The Sultantepe Tablets.* Volume 1. Occasional Publications of the British Institute of Archaeology at Ankara 3. London: Lund Humphries London and Bradford.

Gurney, O. R., and P. Hulin
1964 *The Sultantepe Tablets.* Volume 2. Occasional Publications of the British Institute of Archaeology at Ankara 7. London: Percy Lund, Humphries and Co. Ltd.

Güterbock, Hans Gustav
1963 *Vermischte Texte.* KBo 14; Wissenschaftliche Veröffentlichung der Deutschen Orientgesellschaft 79. Berlin: Gebr. Mann Verlag.

Halbertal, Moshe
1997 *People of the Book: Canon, Meaning, and Authority.* Cambridge, Massachusetts: Harvard University Press.

Hall, Mark G.
1985 "A Study of the Sumerian Moon-god, Nanna/Suen." Ph.D. diss., University of Pennsylvania.

Hallo, William W.
1969 "The Lame and the Halt." *Eretz-Israel* 9, pp. 66–70.
1972 "The House of Ur-Meme." *JNES* 31, pp. 87–95.

1990 "Proverbs Quoted in Epic." Pp. 204–217 in *Lingering Over Words: Studies in Ancient Near Eastern Literature in Honor of William L. Moran*. Edited by T. Abusch, J. Huehnergard, and P. Steinkeller. HSS 37. Atlanta, Georgia: Scholars Press.

1991 "The Concept of Canonicity in Cuneiform and Biblical Literature: A Comparative Appraisal." Pp. 1–19 in *The Biblical Canon in Comparative Perspective*. Edited by K. L. Younger, Jr., W. W. Hallo, and B. F. Batto. Ancient Near Eastern Texts and Studies 11. Lewiston, New York: Edwin Mellen Press.

Hämeen-Anttila, Jaakko

2000 *A Sketch of Neo-Assyrian Grammar*. SAAS 13. Finland: Vammalan Kirjapaino Oy.

Hasselbach, Rebecca

2013 *Case in Semitic: Roles, Relations, and Reconstruction*. Oxford Studies in Diachronic and Historical Linguistics 3. Oxford: Oxford University Press.

Hecker, Karl

1968 *Grammatik der Kültepe-Texte*. Analecta Orientalia 44. Rome.

1977 "Tradition und Originalität in der altorientalischen Literatur." *Archiv Orientální* 45, pp. 245–258.

Heeßel, Nils P.

2000 *Babylonisch-assyrische Diagnostik*. AOAT 43. Münster: Ugarit-Verlag.

2001/2002 "'Wenn ein Mann zum Haus des Kranken geht …': Intertextuelle Bezüge zwischen der Serie *šumma ālu* und der zweiten Tafel der Serie SA.GIG." *AfO* 48/49, pp. 24–49.

2004 "Diagnosis, Divination and Disease: Towards an Understanding of the *Rationale* Behind the Babylonian *Diagnostic Handbook*." Pp. 97–116 in *Magic and Rationality in Ancient Near Eastern and Greco-Roman Medicine*. Edited by H.F.J. Horstmanshoff and M. Stol. Studies in Ancient Medicine 27. Leiden: Brill.

2007 "The Hands of the Gods: Disease Names, and Divine Anger." Pp. 120–130 in *Disease in Babylonia*. Edited by Irving L. Finkel and Markham J. Geller. CM 36. Leiden: Brill.

2010a "Neues von Esagil-kīn-apli. Die ältere Version der physiognomischen Omenserie *alamdimmû*." Pp. 139–187 in *Assur-Forschungen: Arbeiten aus der Forschungsstelle » Edition literarischer Keilschrifttexte aus Assur « der Heidelberger Akademie der Wissenschaften*. Edited by Stefan M. Maul and Nils P. Heeßel. Wiesbaden: Harrassowitz Verlag.

2010b "1.3 Aus dem älteren diagnostischen Handbuch." Pp. 12–15 in *Texte zur Heilkunde*. Edited by B. Janowski and D. Schwemer. TUAT 5. Gütersloh: Gütersloher Verlagshaus.

2010c "Rechts oder links – wörtlich oder dem Sinn nach? Zum Problem der kulturellen Gebundenheit bei der Übersetzung von medizinischen Keilschrifttexten." Pp. 175–188 in *Writings of Early Scholars in the Ancient Near East, Egypt, Rome, and Greece: Translating Ancient Scientific Texts*. Edited by A. Imhausen and T. Pommerening. Beiträge zur Altertumskunde 286. Berlin: de Gruyter.

2011 "'Sieben Tafeln aus sieben Städten': Überlegungen zum Prozess der Serialisierung von Texten in Babylonien in der zweiten Hälfte des zweiten Jahrtausends v. Chr." Pp. 171–195 in *Babylon: Wissenkultur in Orient und Okzident*. Edited by E. Cancik-Kirschbaum, M. van Ess, and J. Marzahn. Topoi, Berlin Studies of the Ancient World 1. Berlin: de Gruyter.

2012 *Divinatorische Texte II: Opferschau-Omina*. WVDOG 139. Wiesbaden: Harrassowitz Verlag.

Held, Moshe
1961 "A Faithful Lover in an Old Babylonian Dialogue." *JCS* 15/1, pp. 1–26.
Henderson, John B.
1998 "Neo-Confucian Scholasticism." Pp. 159–175 in *Scholasticism: Cross-Cultural and Comparative Perspectives*. Edited by José Ignacio Cabezón. New York: State University of New York Press.
Hilprecht, H. V.
1906 *Mathematical, Metrological and Chronological Tablets from the Temple Library of Nippur*. Babylonian Expedition of the University of Pennsylvania, Series A: Cuneiform Texts 20/1. Philadelphia.
Hoffner, Harry A., Jr.
1996 "From Head to Toe in Hittite: The Language of the Human Body." Pp. 247–259 in *"Go to the Land I Will Show You": Studies in Honor of Dwight W. Young*. Edited by Joseph E. Coleson and Victor H. Matthews. Winona Lake, Indiana: Eisenbrauns.
Holm, Tawny L.
2005 "Literature." Pp. 253–265 in *A Companion to the Ancient Near East*. Edited by Daniel C. Snell. Malden: Blackwell Publishing.
Holtz, Shalom E.
2009 *Neo-Babylonian Court Procedure*. CM 38. Leiden: Brill.
Horowitz, Wayne
1998 *Mesopotamian Cosmic Geography*. MC 8. Winona Lake, Indiana: Eisenbrauns.
2014 *The Three Stars Each: The Astrolabes and Related Texts*. BAfO 33. Horn: Ferdinand Berger & Söhne.
Høyrup, Jens
1990 "Algebra and Naive Geometry: An Investigation of Some Basic Aspects of Old Babylonian Mathematical Thought." *AF* 17, pp. 27–69, 262–354.
2002 *Lengths, Widths, Surfaces: A Portrait of Old Babylonian Algebra and Its Kin*. Sources and Studies in the History of Mathematics and Physical Sciences. New York: Springer.
Hrůša, Ivan
2010 *Die akkadische Synonymenliste malku = šarru: Eine Textedition mit Übersetzung und Kommentar*. AOAT 50. Münster: Ugarit-Verlag.
Hruška, Blahoslav
1969 "Das spätbabylonische Lehrgedicht 'Inannas Erhöhung.'" *ArOr* 37, pp. 473–522.
Huehnergard, John
2011 *A Grammar of Akkadian*, 3rd ed. Harvard Semitic Museum Studies 45. Winona Lake, Indiana: Eisenbrauns.
Hulin, P.
1963 "A Table of Reciprocals with Sumerian Spellings." *JCS* 17/3, pp. 72–76.
Hunger, Hermann
1968 *Babylonische und assyrische Kolophone*. AOAT 2. Neukirchen-Vluyn: Butzon & Bercker Kevelaer.
1975 "Zur Ordnung der diagnostischen Omenserie." *ZA* 65, pp. 63–68.
1976 *Spätbabylonische Texte aus Uruk I*. ADFU 9. Berlin.
1981 "Kolophon." RLA 6/3–4, pp. 186–187.
1992 *Astrological Reports to Assyrian Kings*. SAA 8. Helsinki: Helsinki University Press.

Hunger, Hermann, and David Pingree
1989 *MUL.APIN: An Astronomical Compendium in Cuneiform.* BAfO 24. Horn, Austria: Ferdinand Berger & Söhne.
1999 *Astral Sciences in Mesopotamia.* HdO I, 44. Leiden: Brill.

Hunger, Hermann, and John Steele
2019 *The Babylonian Astronomical Compendium MUL.APIN.* London and New York: Routledge.

Hurowitz, Victor A.
1999 "Canon and Canonization in Mesopotamia – Assyriological Models or Ancient Realities?" Pp. 1*–12* in *Proceedings of the Twelfth World Congress of Jewish Studies. Division A: The Bible and Its World.* Edited by R. Margolin. Jerusalem: World Union of Jewish Studies.

Izre'el, Shlomo
1997 *The Amarna Scholarly Tablets.* CM 9. Groningen: Styx.

Jagersma, Bram
2010 "A Descriptive Grammar of Sumerian." Ph.D. diss., Universiteit Leiden.

Jean, Cynthia
2006 *La magie néo-assyrienne en contexte: Recherches sur le métier d'exorciste et le concept d'āšipūtu.* SAAS 17. Finland: Vammalan Kirjapaino Oy.

Jeyes, Ulla
1978 "The 'Palace Gate' of the Liver: A Study of Terminology and Methods in Babylonian Extispicy." *JCS* 30/4, pp. 209–233.
1991–1992 "Divination as a Science in Ancient Mesopotamia." *JEOL* 32, pp. 23–41.

Jiménez, Enrique
2013 "La imagen de los vientos en la literatura babilónica." Ph.D. diss., Universidad Complutense de Madrid.
2016a "Loose Threads of Tradition: Two Late Hemerological Compilations." *JCS* 68, pp. 197–227.
2016b "May the Reader Not Withhold the Tablet! On a Formula in Late Babylonian Colophons." Pp. 227–239 in *Babel und Bibel 9: Proceedings of the 6th Biennial Meeting of the International Association for Comparative Semitics and Other Studies.* Edited by L. Kogan, et al. Winona Lake, Indiana: Eisenbrauns.
2017 *The Babylonian Disputation Poems.* CHANE 87. Leiden: Brill.

Jiménez, Enrique, and Eric Schmidtchen
2017 "Explaining Diagnosis: Two New Commentaries on the Diagnostic Series *Sa-gig.*" *WO* 47, pp. 216–241.

Joannès, Francis
1992 "Les archives de Ninurta-aḫḫê-bulliṭ." Pp. 87–100 in *Nippur at the Centennial.* Edited by M. De Jong Ellis. CRRAI 35. Philadelphia: The University Museum.

Johnson, J. Cale
2013 "The Origins of Scholastic Commentary in Mesopotamia: Second-Order Schemata in the Early Dynastic Exegetical Imagination." Pp. 15–59 in *Visualizing Knowledge and Creating Meaning in Ancient Writing Systems.* Edited by Shai Gordin. Gladbeck: PeWe-Verlag.
2014 "Towards a Reconstruction of SUALU IV: Can We Localize K 2386+ in the Therapeutic Corpus?" *JMC* 24, pp. 11–38.
2017 "The Stuff of Causation: Etiological Metaphor and Pathogenic Channeling in Babylonian Medicine." Pp. 72–121 in *The Comparable Body: Analogy and*

Metaphor in Ancient Mesopotamian, Egyptian, and Greco-Roman Medicine. Edited by John Z. Wee. Studies in Ancient Medicine 49. Leiden: Brill.

2018 "Towards a New Perspective on Babylonian Medicine." Pp. 55–88 in *Assyrian and Babylonian Scholarly Text Catalogues.* Edited by Ulrike Steinert. Die babylonisch-assyrische Medizin in Texten und Untersuchungen 9. Berlin: de Gruyter.

2020 *Gastrointestinal Disease and Its Treatment in Ancient Mesopotamia: An Edition of the Medical Prescriptions Dealing with the Gastrointestinal Tract.* BAM 11. Berlin: de Gruyter.

Johnson, J. Cale, and Markham J. Geller

2015 *The Class Reunion – An Annotated Translation and Commentary on the Sumerian Dialogue Two Scribes.* CM 47. Leiden: Brill.

Jordan, Julius, and Albert Schott

1930 *Erster vorläufiger Bericht über die von der Notgemeinschaft der deutschen Wissenschaft in Uruk-Warka unternommenen Ausgrabungen: Nebst den inschriftlichen Quellen zur Geschichte Eannas.* Abhandlungen der Preussischen Akademie der Wissenschaften, Philosophish-historische Klasse 7. Berlin: Verlag der Akademie der Wissenschaften.

Jursa, Michael

1996 "Akkad, das Eulmaš und Gubāru." *WZKM* 86, pp. 197–211.

2005 *Neo-Babylonian Legal and Administrative Documents: Typology, Contents and Archives.* GMTR 1. Münster.

Karahashi, Fumi

2000 "Sumerian Compound Verbs with Body-Part Terms." Ph.D. diss., University of Chicago.

Karner, Gerhard

2009 "Elemente ritueller Handlungen in den Elija-Elischa-Erzählungen." Dr. theol. diss., Universität Wien.

Kataja, Laura

1987 "A Neo-Assyrian Document on Two Cases of River Ordeal." *SAAB* 1/2, pp. 65–68.

King, Leonard W.

1896 *Babylonian Magic and Sorcery.* London: Luzac and Co.

Kinnier Wilson, J. V.

1956 "Two Medical Texts from Nimrud." *Iraq* 18/2, pp. 130–146.

1962 "The Nimrud Catalog of Medical and Physiognomic Omina." *Iraq* 24/1, pp. 52–62.

2005 "Notes on the Assyrian Pharmaceutical Series URU.AN.NA." *JNES* 64/1, pp. 45–51.

2007 "Infantile and Childhood Convulsions." Pp. 62–66 in *Disease in Babylonia.* Edited by Irving L. Finkel and Markham J. Geller. CM 36. Leiden: Brill.

Kinnier Wilson, J. V., and Irving L. Finkel

2007 "On *būšānu* and *di'u*, or why Nabonidus went to Tema." *JMC* 9, pp. 16–22.

Kinnier Wilson, J. V., and E. H. Reynolds

2007 "On Stroke and Facial Palsy in Babylonian Texts." Pp. 67–99 in *Disease in Babylonia.* Edited by Irving L. Finkel and Markham J. Geller. CM 36. Leiden: Brill.

Kleinerman, Alexandra

2011 *Education in Early 2nd Millennium BC Babylonia: The Sumerian Epistolary Miscellany.* CM 42. Leiden: Brill.

Koch(-Westenholz), Ulla S.

1995 *Mesopotamian Astrology: An Introduction to Babylonian and Assyrian Celestial Divination*. CNIP 19. Copenhagen: Museum Tusculanum Press.

1999 "The Astrological Commentary *Šumma Sîn ina tāmartīšu* Tablet 1." Pp. 149–165 in *La sciences des cieux: Sages, mages, astrologues*. Edited by R. Gyselen. ResOr 12. Bures-sur-Yvette: Groupe pour l'étude de la civilisation du Moyen-Orient.

2000 *Babylonian Liver Omens: The Chapters Manzāzu, Padānu, and Pān Tākalti of the Babylonian Extispicy Series Mainly from Aššurbanipal's Library*. CNIP 25. Copenhagen: Museum Tusculanum Press.

2005 *Secrets of Extispicy: The Chapter Multābiltu of the Babylonian Extispicy Series and Niṣirti bārûti Texts mainly from Aššurbanipal's Library*. AOAT 326. Münster: Ugarit-Verlag.

2015 *Mesopotamian Divination Texts: Conversing with the Gods*. GMTR 7. Münster: Ugarit-Verlag.

Köcher, Franz

1953 *Literarische Texte in akkadischer Sprache*. Keilschrifturkunden aus Boghazköi 37. Deutsche Akademie der Wissenschaften zu Berlin. Institut für Orientforschung.

1963–1980 Die babylonisch-assyrische Medizin in Texten und Untersuchungen, Vols. 1–6. Berlin: de Gruyter.

1978 "Spätbabylonische medizinsche Texte aus Uruk." Pp. 17–39 in *Medizinische Diagnostik in Geschichte und Gegenwart: Festschrift für Heinz Goerke zum Sechzigsten Geburtstag*. Published by Christa Habrich, et al. München: Werner Fritsch.

1995 "Ein Text medizinischer Inhalts aus dem neubabylonischen Grab 405." Pp. 203–217 in *Uruk: Die Gräber*. Edited by R. M. Boehmer, F. Pedde, and B. Salje. Mainz am Rhein: Verlag Philipp von Zabern.

Köcher, Franz, A. L. Oppenheim, and H. G. Güterbock

1957–1958 "The Old Babylonian Omen Text VAT 7525." *AfO* 18, pp. 62–80.

Koehler, Ludwig, Walter Baumgartner, Johann J. Stamm, et al.

1994–2000 *The Hebrew and Aramaic Lexicon of the Old Testament*. 5 Volumes. Leiden: Brill.

Kolev, Rumen K.

2013 *The Babylonian Astrolabe: The Calendar of Creation*. SAA 22. Winona Lake, Indiana: Eisenbrauns.

Kouwenberg, N. J. C.

1997 *Gemination in the Akkadian Verb*. Studia Semitica Neerlandica 33. Assen: Van Gorcum.

2005 "Reflections on the Gt-Stem in Akkadian." *ZA* 95/1–2, pp. 77–103.

2010 *The Akkadian Verb and Its Semitic Background*. Winona Lake, Indiana: Eisenbrauns.

Kraus, Fritz Rudolf

1936 "Ein Sittenkanon in Omenform." *ZA* 43/1–4, pp. 77–113.

Krebernik, Manfred

2010 "dŠID." RLA 12/5–6, p. 451.

2015 "Uraš. A." RLA 14/5–6, pp. 401–406.

Krecher, Joachim and Vladimir Souček

1957–1971 "Glossen." RLA 3, pp. 431–440.

Kuhrt, Amélie

1995 *The Ancient Near East c. 3000 – 330 BC*. 2 Vols. Routledge History of the Ancient World. London and New York: Routledge.

Labat, René

1933 *Commentaires assyro-babyloniens sur les présages*. Bordeaux: Imprimerie-Librairie de l'Université.

1951 *Traité akkadien de diagnostics et pronostics médicaux*. Paris: Academie Internationale d'Histoire des Sciences.

1954 Review of A. Salonen, *Notes on Wagons and Chariots in Ancient Mesopotamia*. *OLZ* 49, p. 40.

1956 "Une nouvelle tablette de pronostics médicaux." *Syria* 33, pp. 119–130.

1965 "Jeux numériques dans l'idéographie susienne." Pp. 257–260 in *Studies in Honor of Benno Landsberger on His Seventy-Fifth Birthday, April 21, 1965*. Edited by H. G. Güterbock and T. Jacobsen. AS 16. Chicago: University of Chicago Press.

Laessøe, J.

1953 "Literary and Oral Tradition in Ancient Mesopotamia." Pp. 205–218 in *Studia orientalia Ioanni Pedersen septuagenario A.D. VII id. nov. anno MCMLIII a collegis discipulis amicis dicata*. Edited by F. Hvidberg. Hauniae: E. Munksgaard.

Lambert, Wilfred G.

1954–1956 "An Address of Marduk to the Demons." *AfO* 17, pp. 310–321.

1957 "Ancestors, Authors, and Canonicity." *JCS* 11/1, pp. 1–14.

1957–1958 Review of F. Gössmann, *Das Era-Epos*. *AfO* 18, pp. 395–401.

1959–1960 "An Address of Marduk to the Demons: New Fragments." *AfO* 19, pp. 114–119.

1960 *Babylonian Wisdom Literature*. Oxford: Clarendon Press.

1962 "A Catalogue of Texts and Authors." *JCS* 16/3, pp. 59–77.

1967 "Enmeduranki and Related Matters." *JCS* 21, pp. 126–138.

1969 "A Middle Assyrian Medical Text." *Iraq* 31, pp. 28–39.

1970 "Fire Incantations." *AfO* 23, pp. 39–45.

1977a "Išḫara." RLA 5, pp. 176–177.

1977b "Karašul." RLA 5, p. 408.

1981 "Kūbu." RLA 6/3–4, p. 265.

1984 "Studies in Marduk." *BSOAS* 47/1, pp. 1–9.

1987 "Lugal-urubarra, Lugal-urušagga." RLA 7, p. 154.

1995 Review of Robert A. Di Vito, *Studies in Third Millennium Sumerian and Akkadian Personal Names: The Designation and Conception of the Personal God*. *OrNS* 64/2, pp. 131–136.

1999a "Marduk's Address to the Demons." Pp. 291–296 in *Mesopotamian Magic: Textual, Historical, and Interpretative Perspectives*. Edited by T. Abusch and K. van der Toorn. AMD 1. Groningen: Styx.

1999b "Babylonian Linguistics." Pp. 217–231 in *Languages and Cultures in Contact: At the Crossroards of Civilizations in the Syro-Mesopotamian Realm*. Edited by K. van Lerberghe and G. Voet. CRRAI 42. Leuven: Peeters.

2013 *Babylonian Creation Myths*. MC 16. Winona Lake, Indiana: Eisenbrauns.

Landsberger, Benno

1934 *Die Fauna des alten Mesopotamien nach der 14. Tafel der Serie ḪAR-RA = ḫubullu*. Der Abhandlungen der philologisch-historischen Klasse der sächsischen Akademie der Wissenschaften 6. Leipzig: S. Hirzel.

1935–1936 "Studien zu den Urkunden aus der Zeit des Ninurta-tukul-Aššur." *AfO* 10, pp. 140–159.

1964 "Einige unerkannt gebliebene oder verkannte Nomina des Akkadischen." *WO* 3, pp. 48–79.

1967a "Über Farben im Sumerisch-Akkadischen." *JCS* 21, pp. 139–173.

1967b *The Date Palm and Its By-products According to the Cuneiform Sources.* BAfO 17. Graz: Weidner.

Lanfranchi, Giovanni B.

1989 "Scholars and Scholarly Tradition in Neo-Assyrian Times: A Case Study." *SAAB* 3/2, pp. 99–114.

Langdon, S.

1916 "Assyrian Grammatical Texts." *RA* 13, pp. 27–34.

Lauinger, Jacob

2012 "Esarhaddon's Succession Treaty at Tell Tayinat: Text and Commentary." *JCS* 64, pp. 87–123.

Leichty, Erle

1964 "The Colophon." Pp. 147–154 in *Studies Presented to A. Leo Oppenheim, June 7, 1964.* Edited by R. D. Biggs and J. A. Brinkman. Chicago: University of Chicago Press.

1970 *The Omen Series Šumma Izbu.* TCS 4. New York: J. J. Augustin.

1973 "Two Late Commentaries." *AfO* 24, pp. 78–86.

1986 *Catalogue of the Babylonian Tablets in the British Museum, Volume VI: Tablets from Sippar 1.* London: British Museum Publications.

2011 *The Royal Inscriptions of Esarhaddon, King of Assyria (680–669 BC).* RINAP 4. Winona Lake, Indiana: Eisenbrauns.

Leichty, Erle, and Albert Kirk Grayson

1987 *Catalogue of the Babylonian Tablets in the British Museum, Volume VII: Tablets from Sippar 2.* London: British Museum Publications.

Lenzen, Heinrich J., et al.

1959 *XV. vorläufiger Bericht über die von dem Deutschen Archäologischen Institut und der Deutschen Orient-Gesellschaft aus Mitteln der Deutschen Forschungsgemeinschaft unternommenen Ausgrabungen in Uruk-Warka, Winter 1956/57.* Abhandlungen der Deutschen Orient-Gesellschaft 4. Berlin: Gebr. Mann Verlag.

Lenzi, Alan

2008 "The Uruk List of Kings and Sages and Late Mesopotamian Scholarship." *JANER* 8/2, pp. 137–169.

Lieberman, S. J.

1990 "Canonical and Official Cuneiform Texts: Towards an Understanding of Assurbanipal's Personal Tablet Collection." Pp. 305–336 in *Lingering Over Words: Studies in Ancient Near Eastern Literature in Honor of William L. Moran.* Edited by T. Abusch, J. Huehnergard, and P. Steinkeller. HSS 37. Atlanta, Georgia: Scholars Press.

Litke, Richard L.

1998 *A Reconstruction of the Assyro-Babylonian God-Lists, AN: ᵈA-nu-um and AN: Anu šá amēli.* Texts from the Babylonian Collection 3. New Haven: Yale Babylonian Collection.

Livingstone, Alasdair

1986 *Mystical and Mythological Explanatory Works of Assyrian and Babylonian Scholars.* Oxford: Clarendon Press.

1989 *Court Poetry and Literary Miscellanea.* SAA 3. Helsinki: Helsinski University Press.

2007 "Ashurbanipal: Literate or Not?" *ZA* 97, pp. 98–118.

2013 *Hemerologies of Assyrian and Babylonian Scholars.* CUSAS 25. Bethesda, Maryland: CDL Press.

Lloyd, G. E. R.

1992 "Methods and Problems in the History of Ancient Science: The Greek Case." *Isis* 83/4, pp. 564–577.

Luckenbill, Daniel D.

1924 *The Annals of Sennacherib.* OIP 2. Chicago: University of Chicago Press.

Luiselli, Michela

2003 "The Colophons as an Indication of the Attitudes towards the Literary Tradition in Egypt and Mesopotamia." Pp. 343–360 in *Basel Egyptology Prize: Junior Research in Egyptian History, Archaeology, and Philology.* Edited by Susanne Bickel and Antonio Loprieno. Ægyptica Helvetica 17. Basel: Schwabe.

Luukko, Mikko

2004 *Grammatical Variation in Neo-Assyrian.* SAAS 16. Finland: Vammalan Kirjapaino Oy.

2007 "The Administrative Roles of the 'Chief Scribe' and the 'Palace Scribe' in the Neo-Assyrian Period." *SAAB* 16, pp. 227–256.

Machinist, Peter, and Hayim Tadmor

1993 "Heavenly Wisdom." Pp. 146–151 in *The Tablet and the Scroll: Near Eastern Studies in Honor of William W. Hallo.* Edited by M. E. Cohen, D. C. Snell, and D. B. Weisberg. Bethesda, Maryland: CDL Press.

Makdisi, George

1990 *The Rise of Humanism in Classical Islam and the Christian West: With Special Reference to Scholasticism.* Edinburgh: Edinburgh University Press.

Mayer, Werner R.

1976 *Untersuchungen zur Formensprache der babylonischen "Gebetsbeschwörungen."* StPohl, Series Maior 5. Rome: Pontifical Biblical Institute.

Mayer, Werner R., and Wilfred H. van Soldt

1991 "Akkadische Lexikographie: *CAD* S." *OrNS* 60, pp. 109–120.

Maul, Stefan M.

1988 *'Herzberuhigungsklagen': Die sumerisch-akkadischen Eršaḫunga-Gebete.* Wiesbaden: Otto Harrassowitz.

2003 "Omina und Orakel. A. Mesopotamien." RLA 10/1–2, pp. 45–88.

2005 "Nos. 2–18: Bilingual (Sumero-Akkadian) Hymns from the Seleucid-Arsacid Period." Pp. 11–116 in *Literary and Scholastic Texts of the First Millennium B.C.* Edited by Ira Spar and W. G. Lambert. CTMMA 2; New York: Metropolitan Museum of Art.

2010 "Aleuromantie: Von der altorientalischen Kunst, mit Hilfe von Opfermehl das Mass göttlichen Wohlwollens zu ermitteln." Pp. 115–130 in *Von Göttern und Menschen: Beiträge zu Literatur und Geschichte des Alten Orients, Festschrift für Brigitte Groneberg.* Edited by D. Shehata, F. Weiershäuser, and K. V. Zand. Cuneiform Monographs 41. Leiden: Brill.

McDowell, A. G.

1999 *Village Life in Ancient Egypt: Laundry Lists and Love Songs.* Oxford: Oxford University Press.

McGrath, William

2016 "The Diagnostic Series SA.GIG: Ancient Innovations and Adaptations." M.A. thesis, University of Toronto.

Meier, Gerhard
1937–1939 "Kommentare aus dem Archiv der Tempelschule in Assur." *AfO* 12, pp. 237–246.
1939 "Ein akkadisches Heilungsritual aus Boğazköy." *ZA* 45, pp. 195–215.
Meissner, Bruno
1937 *Studien zur assyrischen Lexicographie III*. MAOG 11/1–2. Osnabrück: O. Zeller Verlag, reprint 1972.
Melchert, H. Craig
1993 *Cuneiform Luvian Lexicon*. Lexica Anatolica 2; Chapel Hill, NC.
Meyer, Rudolf
1992 *Hebräische Grammatik*. Berlin: de Gruyter.
Michalowski, Piotr
1992 "The Early Mesopotamian Incantation Tradition." Pp. 305–326 in *Literature and Literary Language at Ebla*. Edited by Pelio Fronzaroli. Quaderni di Semitistica 18. Florence: University of Florence.
2003 "The Libraries of Babel: Text, Authority, and Tradition in Ancient Mesopotamia." Pp. 105–129 in *Cultural Repertoires: Structure, Function and Dynamics*. Edited by G. J. Dorleijn and H. L. J. Vanstiphout. Groningen Studies in Cultural Change 3. Leuven: Peeters.
Michel, Cécile
1962 "Une incantation paléo-assyrienne contre Lamaštum." *OrNS* 66/1, pp. 58–64.
Mirelman, Sam
2008 "*Tuḫru* 'Achilles' Tendon'?" *NABU* 2008/65.
2017 "A New Manuscript of Lugal-e, Tablet IV." *Iraq* 79, pp. 155–162.
Mirelman, Sam, and Walther Sallaberger
2010 "The Performance of a Sumerian Wedding Song." *ZA* 100, pp. 177–196.
Moss, Ann
2003 *Renaissance Truth and the Latin Language Turn*. Oxford: Oxford University Press.
Murdoch, John E.
1974 "Philosophy and the Enterprise of Science in the Later Middle Ages." Pp. 51–74 in *The Interaction Between Science and Philosophy*. Edited by Y. Elkana. Atlantic Highlands, N.J.: Humanities Press.
1975 "From Social into Intellectual Factors: An Aspect of the Unitary Character of Late Medieval Learning." Pp. 271–348 in *The Cultural Context of Medieval Learning: Proceedings of the First International Colloquium on Philosophy, Science, and Theology in the Middle Ages – September 1973*. Edited by J. E. Murdoch and E. D. Sylla. Boston Studies in the Philosophy of Science 26. Dordrecht and Boston: D. Reidel Publishing Company.
1979 "Propositional Analysis in Fourteenth-Century Natural Philosophy: A Case Study." *Synthese* 40, pp. 117–146.
1981 "*Scientia Mediantibus Vocibus:* Metalinguistic Analysis in Late Medieval Natural Philosophy." Pp. 73–106 in *Sprache und Erkenntnis im Mittelalter: Akten des VI. internationalen Kongresses für mittelalterliche Philosophie der Société internationale pour l'étude de la philosophie médiévale, 29. August – 3. September 1977 in Bonn*. Edited by Jan P. Beckmann, et al. Berlin: de Gruyter.
Myhrman, David W.
1902 "Die Labartu-Texte: Babylonische Beschwörungsformeln nebst Zauberverfahren gegen die Dämonin Labartu." *ZA* 16, pp. 141–200.

Nauert, Charles G.
1998 "Humanism as Method: Roots of Conflict with the Scholastics." *The Sixteenth Century Journal* 29/2, pp. 427–438.
Neugebauer, Otto
1952 *The Exact Sciences in Antiquity*. New Jersey: Princeton University Press.
Neugebauer, Otto, and Abraham Sachs
1945 *Mathematical Cuneiform Texts*. AOS 29. New Haven: American Oriental Society and American Schools of Oriental Research.
Nielsen, John P.
2009 "Trading on Knowledge: The Iddin-Papsukkal Kin Group in Southern Babylonia in the 7th and 6th Centuries B.C." *JANER* 9/2, pp. 171–182.
2011 *Sons and Descendants: A Social History of Kin Groups and Family Names in the Early Neo-Babylonian Period, 747–626 BC*. CHANE 43. Leiden: Brill.
Nougayrol, Jean
1950 "Textes hépatoscopiques d'époque ancienne conservés au Musée du Louvre (III)." *RA* 44, pp. 1–44.
1963 "Aleuromancie babylonienne." *OrNS* 32/4, pp. 381–386.
1972 "Notes brèves no. 12." *RA* 66, p. 96.
Nurullin, Rim
2014 "An Attempt at *Šimâ milka* (Ugaritica V, 163 and Duplicates). Part I: Prologue, Instructions II, III, IV." *Babel und Bibel* 7, pp. 175–229.
Nutton, Vivian
2013 *Ancient Medicine*, 2nd edition. London and New York: Routledge.
Oelsner, Joachim
1982 "Spätachämenidische Texte aus Nippur." *RA* 76/1, pp. 94–95.
1983 Review of H. Hunger, *Spätbabylonische Texte aus Uruk*, Teil I. *OLZ* 78, pp. 246–250.
1995 Review of E. von Weiher, *Spätbabylonische Texte aus dem Planquadrat U 18*, Teil IV. *OLZ* 90, pp. 381–391.
2002 "Babylonische Kultur nach dem Ende des babylonischen Staates." Pp. 49–73 in *Religion und Religionskontakte im Zeitalter der Achämeniden*. Edited by R. G. Kratz. VWGTh 22. Gütersloh: Chr. Kaiser.
2003 "BM 54609, Rs. 1–9: ein Abschnitt der Sternliste von Ḫḫ Tafel XXII." *NABU* 2003/82.
Oelsner, Joachim, Bruce Wells, and Cornelia Wunsch
2003 "Mesopotamia: Neo-Babylonian Period." Pp. 911–974 in *A History of Ancient Near Eastern Law, Volume Two*. Edited by Raymond Westbrook. HdO I, 72/2. Leiden: Brill.
Oppenheim, A. Leo
1962 "On the Observation of the Pulse in Mesopotamian Medicine." *OrNS* 31, pp. 27–33.
1964 *Ancient Mesopotamia: Portrait of a Dead Civilization*. Chicago: University of Chicago Press.
1969 "New Fragments of the Assyrian Dream-Book." *Iraq* 31/2, pp. 153–165.
1974 "A Babylonian Diviner's Manual." *JNES* 33/2, pp. 197–220.
Ossendrijver, Mathieu
2010 "Evidence for an Instrumental Meaning of *ina libbi*, 'by means of.'" *NABU* 2010/44.

2011 "Science in Action: Networks in Babylonian Astronomy." Pp. 213–221 in *Babylon: Wissenskultur in Orient und Okzident*. Edited by Eva Cancik-Kirschbaum, Margarete van Ess, and Joachim Marzahn. Berlin: de Gruyter.

2012 "A New Join Between Fragments of MUL.APIN from Uruk." *NABU* 2012/73.

Panayotov, Strahil V.

2017 "Eye Metaphors, Analogies and Similes within Mesopotamian Magico-Medical Texts." Pp. 204–246 in *The Comparable Body: Analogy and Metaphor in Ancient Mesopotamian, Egyptian, and Greco-Roman Medicine*. Edited by John Z. Wee. Studies in Ancient Medicine 49. Leiden: Brill.

2018 "Notes on the Assur Medical Catalogue with Comparison to the Nineveh Medical Encyclopedia." Pp. 89–120 in *Assyrian and Babylonian Scholarly Text Catalogues*. Edited by Ulrike Steinert. Die babylonisch-assyrische Medizin in Texten und Untersuchungen 9. Berlin: de Gruyter.

Parpola, Simo

1970 *Letters from Assyrian Scholars to the Kings Esarhaddon and Assurbanipal. Part I: Texts*. AOAT 5/1. Kevelaer: Verlag Butzon & Bercker.

1983 *Letters from Assyrian Scholars to the Kings Esarhaddon and Assurbanipal. Part II: Commentary and Appendices*. AOAT 5/2. Kevelaer: Verlag Butzon & Bercker.

1993 *Letters from Assyrian and Babylonian Scholars*. SAA 10. Helsinki: Helsinki University Press.

Pearce, Laurie E.

1982 "Cuneiform Cryptography: Numerical Substitutes for Syllabic and Logographic Signs." Ph.D. diss., Yale University.

1993 "Statements of Purpose: Why the Scribes Wrote." Pp. 185–193 in *The Tablet and the Scroll: Near Eastern Studies in Honor of William W. Hallo*. Edited by M. E. Cohen, D. C. Snell, and D. B. Weisberg. Bethesda, Maryland: CDL Press.

Pearce, Laurie E., and L. Timothy Doty

2000 "The Activities of Anu-bēlšunu, Seleucid Scribe." Pp. 331–341 in *Assyriologica et Semitica: Festschrift für Joachim Oelsner anläßlich seines 65. Geburtstages am 18. Februar 1997*. Edited by J. Marzahn and H. Neumann. AOAT 252. Münster.

Pedersén, Olof

1985–1986 *Archives and Libraries in the City of Assur: A Survey of the Material from the German Excavations*. Parts I and II. Sweden: Uppsala.

1998 *Archives and Libraries in the Ancient Near East 1500–300 BC*. Bethesda, Maryland: CDL Press.

Peled, Ilan

2014 "*assinnu* and *kurgarrû* Revisited." *JNES* 73/2, pp. 283–297.

Perreiah, Alan R.

1982 "Humanistic Critiques of Scholastic Dialectic." *The Sixteenth Century Journal* 13/3, pp. 3–22.

2014 *Renaissance Truths: Humanism, Scholasticism and the Search for the Perfect Language*. Surrey, England: Ashgate Publishing Company.

Peterson, Jeremiah

2009 *God Lists from Old Babylonian Nippur in the University Museum, Philadelphia*. AOAT 362. Münster: Ugarit-Verlag.

Piepkorn, Arthur C.

1933 *Historical Prism Inscriptions of Ashurbanipal I: Editions E, B_{1-5}, D, and K*. AS 5. Chicago: University of Chicago Press.

Postgate, J. Nicholas
1976 *Fifty Neo-Assyrian Legal Documents*. Warminster: Aris & Phillips.
Potts, D. T.
2005 "Before Alexandria: Libraries in the Ancient Near East." Pp. 19–33 in *The Library of Alexandria: Center of Learning in the Ancient World*. Edited by R. MacLeod. London: I. B. Tauris.
Powell, M. A.
1987 "Maße und Gewichte." RLA 7, pp. 457–530.
Prioreschi, Plinio
2003 *A History of Medicine. Volume V, Medieval Medicine*. Omaha: Horatius Press.
Proust, Christine
2012 "Interpretation of Reverse Algorithms in Several Mesopotamian Texts." Pp. 384–422 in *The History of Mathematical Proof in Ancient Traditions*. Edited by K. Chemla. Cambridge: Cambridge University Press.
Radner, Karen
2011 "Royal Decision-Making: Kings, Magnates, and Scholars." Pp. 358–379 in *The Oxford Handbook of Cuneiform Culture*. Edited by Karen Radner and Eleanor Robson. Oxford: Oxford University Press.
Rawlinson, Henry C.
1884 *The Cuneiform Inscriptions of Western Asia, Vol. V*. London.
Reiner, Erica
1958 *Šurpu: A Collection of Sumerian and Akkadian Incantations*. BAfO 11. Graz.
1960 "Fortune-Telling in Mesopotamia." *JNES* 19/1, pp. 23–35.
Reiner, Erica, and David Pingree
1981 *Babylonian Planetary Omens, Part Two, Enuma Anu Enlil, Tablets 50–51*. BiMes 2/2. Malibu: Undena.
Reiner, Erica, Janet H. Johnson, and Miguel Civil
1994 "Linguistics in the Ancient Near East." Pp. 61–96 in *History of Linguistics. Volume 1, The Eastern Traditions of Linguistics*. Edited by Giulio Lepschy. Longman Linguistics Library 1. London: Longman.
Reisner, G. A.
1894 "The Berlin Vocabulary V.A.Th. 244." *ZA* 9, pp. 149–164.
Reynolds, F.
2010 "A Divine Body: New Joins in the Sippar Collection." Pp. 291–302 in *Your Praise is Sweet: A Memorial Volume for Jeremy Black from Students, Colleagues and Friends*. Edited by H. D. Baker, E. Robson, and G. Zólyomi. London: British Institute for the Study of Iraq.
Riondato, Ezio, and Luigi Olivieri, eds.
1985 *Pietro d'Abano, Conciliator. Ristampa fotomeccanica dell'edizione Venetiis apud Iuntas 1565*. I Filosofi Veneti. Sezione II, Ristampe I. Padova: Editrice Antenore.
Robson, Eleanor
1999 *Mesopotamian Mathematics, 2100–1600 BC: Technical Constants in Bureaucracy and Education*. OECT 14. Oxford: Clarendon Press.
2002a "Guaranteed Genuine Originals: The Plimpton Collection and the Early History of Mathematical Assyriology." Pp. 245–292 in *Mining the Archives: Festschrift for C. B. F. Walker on the Occasion of His 60th Birthday*. Edited by C. Wunsch. Dresden: ISLET.
2002b "More than Metrology: Mathematics Education in an Old Babylonian Scribal School." Pp. 325–365 in *Under One Sky: Mathematics and Astronomy in the*

Ancient Near East. Edited by J. M. Steele and A. Imhausen. AOAT 297. Münster: Ugarit-Verlag.

2008a *Mathematics in Ancient Iraq: A Social History.* Princeton: Princeton University Press.

2008b "Mesopotamian Medicine and Religion: Current Debates, New Perspectives." *Religion Compass* 2/4, pp. 455–483.

2011a "The Production and Dissemination of Scholarly Knowledge." Pp. 557–576 in *The Oxford Handbook of Cuneiform Culture.* Edited by Karen Radner and Eleanor Robson. Oxford: Oxford University Press.

2011b "Empirical Scholarship in the Neo-Assyrian Court." Pp. 603–629 in *The Empirical Dimension of Ancient Near Eastern Studies.* Edited by Gebhard J. Selz. Wiener Offene Orientalistik 6. Wien: Lit Verlag GmbH & Co.

Rochberg(-Halton), Francesca

1984 "Canonicity in Cuneiform Texts." *JCS* 36/2, pp. 127–144.

1987 "The Assumed 29th aḫû Tablet of Enūma Anu Enlil." Pp. 327–350 in *Language, Literature, and History: Philological and Historical Studies Presented to Erica Reiner.* Edited by F. Rochberg-Halton. AOS 67. Locust Valley, New York.

1988 *Aspects of Babylonian Celestial Divination: The Lunar Eclipse Tablets of Enūma Anu Enlil.* BAfO 22. Horn, Austria: Verlag Ferdinand Berger & Söhne.

1998 *Babylonian Horoscopes.* TAPS 88, Part I. Philadelphia: American Philosophical Society.

2000 "Scribes and Scholars: The *ṭupšar Enūma Anu Enlil.*" Pp. 359–375 in *Assyriologica et Semitica: Festschrift für Joachim Oelsner anläßlich seines 65. Geburtstages am 18. Februar 1997.* Edited by J. Marzahn and H. Neumann. AOAT 252. Münster.

2004 *The Heavenly Writing: Divination, Horoscopy, and Astronomy in Mesopotamian Culture.* Cambridge: Cambridge University Press.

2010 *In the Path of the Moon: Babylonian Celestial Divination and Its Legacy.* AMD 6. Leiden: Brill.

2016a "Canon and Power in Cuneiform Scribal Scholarship." Pp. 217–229 in *Problems of Canonicity and Identity Formation in Ancient Egypt and Mesopotamia.* Edited by K. Ryholt and G. Barjamovic. Carsten Niebuhr Institute Publications 43. Copenhagen: Museum Tusculanum Press.

2016b *Before Nature: Cuneiform Knowledge and the History of Science.* Chicago: University of Chicago Press.

Römer, Willem H. P.

2007 Review of A. Schaffer, *UET* 6/3, *BiOr* 64, pp. 180–182.

Roth, Martha T.

1997 *Law Collections from Mesopotamia and Asia Minor,* 2nd ed. SBLWAW 6. Atlanta: Scholars Press.

2010 "How We Wrote the Chicago Assyrian Dictionary." *JNES* 69/1, pp. 1–21.

Rummel, Erika

1995 *The Humanist-Scholastic Debate in the Renaissance and Reformation.* Cambridge, Massachusetts: Harvard University Press.

Rutz, Matthew T.

2011 "Threads for Esagil-kīn-apli: The Medical Diagnostic-Prognostic Series in Middle Babylonian Nippur." *ZA* 101, pp. 294–308.

2013 *Bodies of Knowledge in Ancient Mesopotamia: The Diviners of Late Bronze Age Emar and Their Tablet Collection.* AMD 9. Leiden: Brill.

Sachs, Abraham J.
1952 "Babylonian Horoscopes." *JCS* 6/2, pp. 49–75.
Sachs, Abraham J., and Hermann Hunger
1988 *Astronomical Diaries and Related Texts from Babylonia. Volume I: Diaries from 652 B.C. to 262 B.C.* Denkschriften der philosophisch-historischen Klasse 195. Wien: Verlag der Österreichischen Akademie der Wissenschaften.
1989 *Astronomical Diaries and Related Texts from Babylonia. Volume II: Diaries from 261 B.C. to 165 B.C.* Denkschriften der philosophisch-historischen Klasse 210. Wien: Verlag der Österreichischen Akademie der Wissenschaften.
Sack, Ronald H.
1994 *Cuneiform Documents from the Chaldean and Persian Periods.* London and Toronto: Associated University Presses.
Salin, Silvia
2015 "When Disease 'Touches', 'Hits', or 'Seizes' in Assyro-Babylonian Medicine." *KASKAL* 12, pp. 319–336.
2016 "Transmission and Interpretation of Therapeutic Texts. *Šumma amēlu muḫḫašu umma ukāl*: a Case Study." *Distant Worlds Journal* 1, pp. 117–131.
2017 "'Stinging Pain' in Assyro-Babylonian Medical Texts: Some Considerations." *JMC* 29, pp. 35–48.
Sallaberger, Walther
1993/1994 "Keilschrifttexte einer Privatsammlung." *AfO* 40/41, pp. 52–63.
San Nicolò, M.
1933 "Parerga Babylonica X–XI." *ArOr* 5, pp. 284–302.
Scheil, V.
1916 "Notules. XIX. Tablette scolaire d'Uruk avec gloses et vocabulaire." *RA* 13, pp. 137–138.
1921 "Catalogue de la collection Eugène Tisserant." *RA* 18, pp. 1–33.
Schmidtchen, Eric
2018 "Esagil-kīn-apli's Catalogue of *Sakikkû* and *Alamdimmû*" and "The Edition of Esagil-kīn-apli's Catalogue of the Series *Sakikkû* (SA.GIG) and *Alamdimmû*." Pp. 137–157 and 313–333 in *Assyrian and Babylonian Scholarly Text Catalogues.* Edited by Ulrike Steinert. Die babylonisch-assyrische Medizin in Texten und Untersuchungen 9. Berlin: de Gruyter.
Schramm, Wolfgang
1979 Review of H. Hunger, *Spätbabylonische Texte aus Uruk, Teil I. WO* 10, pp. 121–124.
Schretter, Manfred
1986 "Zum Examenstext A, Zeile 14." Pp. 231–236 in *Im Bannkreis des Alten Orients: Studien zur Sprach- und Kulturgeschichte des Alten Orients und seines Ausstrahlungsraumes, Karl Oberhüber zum 70. Geburtstag gewidmet.* Edited by W. Meid and H. Trenkwalder. Innsbrucker Beiträge zur Kulturwissenschaft 24. Innsbruck.
2002 Review of Y. Gong, *Die Namen der Keilschriftzeichen. ZA* 92, pp. 156–157.
Schwemer, Daniel
2009 "Washing, Defiling, and Burning: Two Bilingual Anti-witchcraft Incantations." *OrNS* 78/1, pp. 44–68.
2010a "Therapeutische Texte aus Ḫattuša und Emar." Pp. 38–45 in *Texte zur Heilkunde.* Edited by B. Janowski and D. Schwemer. TUAT NF 5. Gütersloh.
2010b "'Forerunners' of Maqlû: A New Maqlû-Related Fragment from Assur." Pp. 201–220 in *Gazing on the Deep: Ancient Near Eastern, Biblical, and Jewish Studies*

in Honor of Tzvi Abusch. Edited by J. Stackert, B. N. Porter, and D. P. Wright. Bethesda, Maryland: CDL Press.

2014 "'Form follows function?' Rhetoric and Poetic Language in First Millennium Akkadian Incantations." *WO* 44/2, pp. 263–288.

Scurlock, JoAnn

1999 "Physician, Conjurer, Magician: A Tale of Two Healing Professionals." Pp. 69–79 in *Mesopotamian Magic: Textual, Historical and Interpretive Perspectives*. Edited by T. Abusch and K. van der Toorn. AMD 1. Groningen: Styx.

2004 "The Hippocratic Treatise *Humors*, Chapter 1: A Humorous Student Commentary." *Ktema* 29, pp. 255–257.

2005 "Ancient Mesopotamian Medicine." Pp. 302–315 in *A Companion to the Ancient Near East*. Edited by Daniel C. Snell. Malden: Blackwell Publishing.

2006 *Magico-Medical Means of Treating Ghost-Induced Illnesses in Ancient Mesopotamia*. Ancient Magic and Divination III. Leiden: Brill Academic Publishers.

2007 "A Stroke of Luck." *JMC* 10, pp. 45–46.

2009 "Corrections and Suggestions to Geller, BAM VII, Part I: Urinary Tract Texts." *JMC* 13, pp. 38–48.

2014 *Sourcebook for Ancient Mesopotamian Medicine*. SBLWAW 36. Atlanta: Society of Biblical Literature.

Scurlock, JoAnn, and F. Al-Rawi

2006 "A Weakness for Hellenism." Pp. 357–382 in *If a Man Builds a Joyful House: Assyriological Studies in Honor of Erle Verdun Leichty*. Edited by Ann K. Guinan, et al. CM 31; Leiden: Brill.

Scurlock, JoAnn, and B. R. Andersen

2005 *Diagnoses in Assyrian and Babylonian Medicine*. Urbana and Chicago: University of Illinois Press.

Silver, Morris

2006 "Temple/Sacred Prostitution in Ancient Mesopotamia Revisited." *UF* 38, pp. 631–663.

Sinclair, Cameron

1970 "A Linguistic Analysis of Neo-Assyrian Syntax." Ph.D. diss., The Dropsie College for Hebrew and Cognate Learning, Philadelphia.

Siraisi, Nancy G.

1986 "Pietro d'Abano and Taddeo Alderotti: Two Models of Medical Culture." *Medioevo* 11, pp. 139–162.

Sjöberg, Å. W.

1975 "Der Examenstext A." *ZA* 64, pp. 137–176.

1976 "The Old Babylonian Eduba." Pp. 159–179 in *Sumerological Studies in Honor of Thorkild Jacobsen on his Seventieth Birthday*. Edited by S. J. Lieberman. AS 20. Chicago: University of Chicago Press.

1996 "UET VII, 73: An Exercise Tablet Enumerating Professions." Pp. 117–139 in *Tablettes et images aux pays de Sumer et d'Akkad. Mélanges offerts à Monsieur H. Limet*. Edited by Ö. Tunca and D. Deheselle. Association pour la Promotion de l'Histoire et de l'Archéologie Orientales, Mémoires, 1. Liège: Université de Liège.

Sollberger, Edmond

1952 *Le système verbal dans les inscriptions 'royales' présargoniques de Lagaš*. Genève: E. Droz.

Sommerfeld, Walter

1985 Review of L. Cagni, *Briefe aus dem Iraq Museum* (*TIM II*). *OrNS* 54, pp. 505–508.

Stadhouders, Henry

2011 "The Pharmacopoeial Handbook *Šammu šikinšu* – An Edition." *JMC* 18, pp. 3–51.

Starr, Ivan

1983 *The Rituals of the Diviner*. BiMes 12. Malibu: Undena.

Steele, John M.

2011 "Astronomy and Culture in Late Babylonian Uruk." Pp. 331–341 in *Archaeoastronomy and Ethnoastronomy: Building Bridges between Cultures, Proceedings of the 278th Symposium of the International Astronomical Union and 'Oxford IX' International Symposium on Archaeoastronomy, held in Lima, Peru.* Edited by Clive L. N. Ruggles. Cambridge: Cambridge University Press.

Stein, Peter

2000 *Die mittel- und neubabylonischen Königsinschriften bis zum Ende der Assyrerherrschaft: Grammatische Untersuchungen.* Jenaer Beiträge zum Vorderen Orient 3. Wiesbaden: Harrassowitz Verlag.

Steinert, Ulrike

2012 *Aspekte des Menschseins im Alten Mesopotamien: Eine Studie zu Person und Identität im 2. und 1. Jt. v. Chr.* CM 44; Leiden: Brill.

2017 "Concepts of the Female Body in Mesopotamian Gynecological Texts." Pp. 275–357 in *The Comparable Body: Analogy and Metaphor in Ancient Mesopotamian, Egyptian, and Greco-Roman Medicine.* Edited by John Z. Wee. Studies in Ancient Medicine 49. Leiden: Brill.

2018 "Introduction," "Catalogues, Texts and Specialists," and "The Assur Medical Catalogue." Pp. 7–21, 158–200, and 203–291 in *Assyrian and Babylonian Scholarly Text Catalogues.* Edited by Ulrike Steinert. Die babylonisch-assyrische Medizin in Texten und Untersuchungen 9. Berlin: de Gruyter.

Stol, Marten

1991–1992 "Diagnosis and Therapy in Babylonian Medicine." *JEOL* 32, pp. 42–65.

1993 *Epilepsy in Babylonia.* CM 2. Groningen: Styx.

1998 "Einige kurze Wortstudien." Pp. 343–352 in *Festschrift für Rykle Borger zu seinem 65. Geburtstag am 24. Mai 1994.* Edited by Stefan M. Maul. CM 10. Groningen: Styx.

2000 *Birth in Babylonia and in the Bible: Its Mediterranean Setting.* CM 14. Groningen: Styx.

2007a "Fevers in Babylonia." Pp. 1–39 in *Disease in Babylonia.* Edited by Irving L. Finkel and Markham J. Geller. CM 36. Leiden: Brill.

2007b "Remarks on Some Sumerograms and Akkadian Words." Pp. 233–242 in *Studies Presented to Robert D. Biggs, June 4, 2004.* Edited by Martha T. Roth, et al. From the Workshop of the Chicago Assyrian Dictionary 2. Chicago: The Oriental Institute.

2009a "'To be ill' in Akkadian: The Verb *salāʾu* and the Substantive *siliʾtu*." Pp. 29–46 in *Advances in Mesopotamian Medicine from Hammurabi to Hippocrates.* Edited by Annie Attia and Gilles Buisson. CM 37. Leiden: Brill.

2009b "Insanity in Babylonian Sources." *JMC* 13, pp. 1–12.

2016 *Women in the Ancient Near East.* Berlin: de Gruyter.

Strassler, Robert B. (ed.), and Andrea L. Purvis (trans.)

2009 *The Landmark Herodotus: The Histories.* New York: Anchor Books.

Streck, Maximilian
1916 *Assurbanipal und die letzten assyrischen Könige bis zum Untergang Nineveh's.* VAB 7. Leipzig: J. C. Hinrichs.

Streck, Michael P.
1999 *Die Bildersprache der akkadischen Epik.* AOAT 264. Münster: Ugarit-Verlag.
2010 "Notes on the Old Babylonian Hymns of Agušaya." *JAOS* 130/4, pp. 561–571.

Striker, Gisela
2009 *Aristotle: Prior Analytics Book I.* Clarendon Aristotle Series. Oxford: Clarendon Press.

Tammuz, Oded
2017 "The Evolution of the Boomerang: On Some Meanings of GIŠ.RU." *ANES* 54, pp. 91–101.

Testen, David
2001 "Cognates to Two Babylonian Terms Referring to Oral Anatomy." *NABU* 2001/95.

Thomsen, Marie-Louise
1984 *The Sumerian Language: An Introduction to Its History and Grammatical Structure.* Mes. 10. Copenhagen: Akademisk Forlag.

Thureau-Dangin, François
1921 "Rituel et Amulettes contre Labartu." *RA* 18, pp. 161–198.
1938 *Textes mathématiques babyloniens.* Leiden: Brill.

Tsukimoto, Akio
1999 "'By the Hand of Madi-Dagan, the Scribe and *Apkallu*-Priest' – A Medical Text from the Middle Euphrates Region." Pp. 187–200 in *Priests and Officials in the Ancient Near East: Papers of the Second Colloquium on the Ancient Near East – the City and its Life held at the Middle Eastern Culture Center in Japan (Mitaka, Tokyo).* Edited by K. Watanabe. Heidelberg: Universitätsverlag C. Winter.

Ungnad, A.
1944 "Besprechungskunst und Astrologie in Babylonien." *AfO* 14, pp. 251–284.

Van De Mieroop, Marc
2016 *Philosophy Before the Greeks: The Pursuit of Truth in Ancient Babylonia.* Princeton: Princeton University Press.

van der Toorn, Karel
1985 *Sin and Sanction in Israel and Mesopotamia: A Comparative Study.* Assen/Maastricht: Van Gorcum.

van Dijk, J. J. A.
1957 *Tabulae Cuneiformes a F. M. Th. de Liagre Böhl Collectae, Leidae Conservatae II (TLB II). Textes Divers.* Leiden: Nederlands Instituut voor het Nabije Oosten.
1962 "Die Inschriftenfunde." Pp. 39–62 in *Vorläufiger Bericht über die Ausgrabungen in Uruk-Warka* 18. Berlin: Abhandlungen der Deutschen Orient-Gesellschaft.
1983 *LUGAL UD ME-LÁM-bi NIR-GÁL: le récit épique et didactique des Travaux de Ninurta, du Déluge et de la Nouvelle Création.* 2 Volumes. Leiden: Brill.

van Dijk, J. J. A., A. Goetze, and M. I. Hussey
1985 *Early Mesopotamian Incantations and Rituals.* YOS 11. New Haven: Yale University Press.

van Soldt, Wilfred H.
1995 *Solar Omens of Enuma Anu Enlil: Tablets 23 (24) – 29 (30).* PIHANS 73. Holland: Nederlands Historisch-Archaeologisch Instituut te Istanbul.
2003–2005 "Ordal. A. Mesopotamien." RLA 10, pp. 124–129.

Vanstiphout, H. L. J.

1995 "On the Old Babylonian Eduba Curriculum." Pp. 3–16 in *Centres of Learning: Learning and Location in Pre-Modern Europe and the Near East.* Edited by J. W. Drijvers and A. A. MacDonald. Brill's Studies in Intellectual History 61. Leiden: Brill.

2003 *Epics of Sumerian Kings: The Matter of Aratta.* SBLWAW 20. Leiden: Brill.

Vedeler, H. Torger

2002 "The ḪAR.GUD Commentary and Its Relationship to the ḪAR-ra=*ḫubullu* Lexical List." M.A. thesis, Yale University.

Veldhuis, Niek

1991 "The Reading of GISSU in Ophthalmological Context." *NABU* 1991/106.

1992 "Corrections to « The Reading of GISSU in Ophthalmological Context »." *NABU* 1992/32.

1997 "Elementary Education at Nippur. The List of Trees and Wooden Objects." Ph.D. diss., University of Groningen.

1998 "TIN.TIR = Babylon, The Question of Canonization and the Production of Meaning." *JCS* 50, pp. 77–85.

2003 "Mesopotamian Canons." Pp. 9–28 in *Homer, the Bible, and Beyond: Literary and Religious Canons in the Ancient World.* Edited by M. Finkelberg and G. G. Stroumsa. Jerusalem Studies in Religion and Culture 2. Leiden: Brill.

2004 *Religion, Literature, and Scholarship: The Sumerian Composition Nanše and the Birds, with a Catalogue of Sumerian Bird Names.* CM 22. Leiden: Brill.

2009 "BAM 7, 51: An Alternative Reading." *JMC* 14, pp. 44–48.

2014 *History of the Cuneiform Lexical Tradition.* GMTR 6. Münster: Ugarit-Verlag.

Verderame, Lorenzo

2002 *Le Tavole I–VI della serie astrologica Enūma Anu Enlil.* Nisaba 2. Rome: Di.Sc.A.M.

Villard, Pierre

1997 "L'éducation d'Assurbanipal." *Ktema* 22, pp. 135–149.

Vogelzang, M. E.

1988 *Bin šar dadmē: Edition and Analysis of the Akkadian Anzu Poem.* Groningen: Styx.

1995 "Learning and Power During the Sargonid Period." Pp. 17–28 in *Centres of Learning: Learning and Location in Pre-Modern Europe and the Near East.* Edited by J. W. Drijvers and A. A. MacDonald. Brill's Studies in Intellectual History 61. Leiden: Brill.

Voigt, Rainer M.

1988 *Die infirmen Verbaltypen des Arabischen und das Biradikalismus-Problem.* Akademie der Wissenschaften und der Literatur zu Mainz, Veröffentlichungen der Orientalischen Kommission 39. Stuttgart: Franz Steiner Verlag.

von Soden, Wolfram

1938a "Altbabylonische Dialektdichtungen." *ZA* 44, pp. 26–44.

1938b Review of Fr. X. Kugler, *Sternkunde und Sterndienst in Babel. ZA* 44, pp. 310–306.

1955 "Zum akkadischen Wörterbuch. 67–80." *OrNS* 24, pp. 377–394.

1961 Review of H. H. Figulla, *Cuneiform Texts from Babylonian Tablets in the British Museum,* Part XLII. *BiOr* 18, pp. 71–73.

1966 Review of O. R. Gurney and P. Hulin, *The Sultantepe Tablets II. OLZ* 61, pp. 560–565.

1977 Review of *CAD* L. *OLZ* 72, pp. 27–30.

von Weiher, Egbert

1983 *Spätbabylonische Texte aus Uruk II*. ADFU 10. Berlin.

1988 *Spätbabylonische Texte aus Uruk III*. ADFU 12. Berlin.

1993 *Spätbabylonische Texte aus Uruk IV*. AUWE 12. Mainz am Rhein.

1998 *Spätbabylonische Texte aus Uruk V*. AUWE 13. Mainz am Rhein.

Waetzoldt, Hartmut

1992 "Zum Verb ga_6 (ÍL)." *NABU* 1992/16.

Wasserman, Nathan

1996 "An Old-Babylonian Medical Text against the *Kurārum* Disease." *RA* 90/1, pp. 1–5.

1997 "An Old-Babylonian Medical Text against the *Kurārum* Disease: Addition." *RA* 91/1, pp. 31–32.

2003 *Style and Form in Old-Babylonian Literary Texts*. CM 27. Leiden: Brill.

2007 "Between Magic and Medicine—Apropos of an Old-Babylonian Therapeutic Text against *Kurārum* Disease." Pp. 40–61 in *Disease in Babylonia*. Edited by Irving L. Finkel and Markham J. Geller. CM 36. Leiden: Brill.

Waswo, Richard

1987 *Language and Meaning in the Renaissance*. Princeton, New Jersey: Princeton University Press.

Watson, Rita, and Wayne Horowitz

2011 *Writing Science before the Greeks: A Naturalistic Analysis of the Babylonian Astronomical Treatise MUL.APIN*. CHANE 48. Leiden: Brill.

Wee, John Z.

2012 "The Practice of Diagnosis in Mesopotamian Medicine: With Editions of Commentaries on the Diagnostic Series Sa-gig." Ph.D. diss., Yale University.

2014a "Lugalbanda Under the Night Sky: Scenes of Celestial Healing in Ancient Mesopotamia." *JNES* 73/1, pp. 23–42.

2014b "Grieving with the Moon: Pantheon and Politics in the Lunar Eclipse." *JANER* 14/1, pp. 29–67.

2015a "Phenomena in Writing: Creating and Interpreting Variants of the Diagnostic Series Sa-gig." Pp. 247–287 in *In the Wake of the Compendia: Infrastructural Contexts and the Licensing of Empiricism in Ancient and Medieval Mesopotamia*. Edited by C. Johnson. Science, Technology, and Medicine in Ancient Cultures 3. Berlin: de Gruyter.

2015b "Discovery of the Zodiac Man in Cuneiform." *JCS* 67, pp. 217–233.

2016a "A Late Babylonian Astral Commentary on Marduk's Address to the Demons." *JNES* 75/1, pp. 127–167.

2016b "Virtual Moons Over Babylonia: The Calendar Text System, Its Micro-Zodiac of 13, and the Making of Medical Zodiology." Pp. 139–229 in *The Circulation of Astronomical Knowledge in the Ancient World*. Edited by J. M. Steele. Time, Astronomy, and Calendars 6. Leiden: Brill.

2017 "Pan-astronomical Hermeneutics and the Arts of the Lamentation Priest." *ZA* 107/2, pp. 236–260.

2018 "Five Birds, Twelve Rooms, and the Seleucid Game of Twenty Squares." Pp. 829–872 in *Mesopotamian Medicine and Magic: Studies in Honor of Markham J. Geller*. Edited by S. V. Panayotov and L. Vacín. Ancient Magic and Divination 14. Leiden: Brill.

In press "A Systemic Etiology of Sicknesses from Ancient Iraq: Organ Systems and the Functional Holism of the Babylonian Body." In *Ancient Holisms: Contexts, Forms and Heritage*. Edited by C. Thumiger. Cambridge, UK: Cambridge University Press.

Weeden, Mark

2011 "Adapting to New Contexts: Cuneiform in Anatolia." Pp. 597–617 in *The Oxford Handbook of Cuneiform Culture*. Edited by Karen Radner and Eleanor Robson. Oxford: Oxford University Press.

Weidner, Ernst F.

1941–1944 "Die astrologische Serie Enûma Anu Enlil." *AfO* 14, pp. 172–195 and 308–318.

1959/1960 "Ein astrologischer Sammeltext aus der Sargonidenzeit." *AfO* 19, pp. 105–113.

1966 "Ein Kommentar zu den Schlangen-Omina." *AfO* 21, p. 46, pl. IX–X.

1967 *Gestirn-Darstellungen auf babylonischen Tontafeln*. Österreichische Akademie der Wissenschaften, Philosophisch-historische Klasse Sitzungsberichte 254/2. Wien: Hermann Böhlaus Nachf.

Weidner, Ernst F., and Dietrich Opitz

1935–1936 "Aus den Tagen eines assyrischen Schattenkönigs." *AfO* 10, pp. 1–52.

Weitemeyer, Mogens

1956 "Archive and Library Technique in Ancient Mesopotamia." *Libri* 6/3, pp. 217–238.

Westendorf, Wolfhart

1999 *Handbuch der altägyptischen Medizin*. Two Volumes. HdO I, 36. Leiden: Brill.

Weszeli, M.

2011 "Stall. A. In Mesopotamien. Philologisch." RLA 13, pp. 98–101.

Wiggermann, Frans A. M.

1992 *Mesopotamian Protective Spirits: The Ritual Texts*. CM 1. Groningen: Styx.

1993 "Mischwesen. A." RLA 8, pp. 222–246.

2000 "Lamaštu, Daughter of Anu. A Profile." Pp. 217–252 in Marten Stol, *Birth in Babylonia and in the Bible: Its Mediterranean Setting*. CM 14. Groningen: Styx.

2003 "Pāšittu." RLA 10, pp. 363–364.

2010 "Dogs, Pigs, Lamaštu, and the Breast-Feeding of Animals by Women." Pp. 407–414 in *Von Göttern und Menschen. Beiträge zu Literatur und Geschichte des Alten Orients. Festschrift für Brigitte Groneberg*. Edited by Dahlia Shehata, Frauke Weiershäuser, and Kamran V. Zand. CM 41. Leiden: Brill.

2018 "The Göttertypentext as a Humanistic Mappa Mundi: An Essay." Pp. 351–370 in *Sources of Evil: Studies in Mesopotamian Exorcistic Lore*. Edited by G. van Buylaere, et al. AMD 15. Leiden: Brill.

Wilcke, Claus

2000 *Wer las und schrieb in Babylonien und Assyrien: Überlegungen zur Literalität im Alten Zweistromland*. Bayerische Akademie der Wissenschaften, Sitzungsberichte 2000/6. München.

Wilhelm, Gernot

1991 *Literarische Texte in sumerischer und akkadischer Sprache*. KBo 36. Berlin: Gebr. Mann Verlag.

1994 *Medizinische Omina aus Ḫattuša in akkadischer Sprache*. StBoT 36. Wiesbaden: Harrassowitz Verlag.

Willemen, Charles, Bart Dessein, and Collett Cox

1998 *Sarvāstivāda Buddhist Scholasticism*. HdO II, 11. Leiden: Brill.

Winitzer, Abraham

2011 "Writing and Mesopotamian Divination: The Case of Alternative Interpretation." *JCS* 63, pp. 77–94.

Wiseman, Donald J., and Jeremy A. Black
1996 *Literary Texts from the Temple of Nabû*. CTN 4. British School of Archaeology in Iraq.
Woods, Christopher
2008 *The Grammar of Perspective: The Sumerian Conjugation Prefixes as a System of Voice*. CM 31. Leiden: Brill.
Worthington, Martin
2009 "Schankwirt(in)." RLA 12, pp. 132–134.
2012 *Principles of Akkadian Textual Criticism*. Studies in Ancient Near Eastern Records 1. Germany: de Gruyter.
Yakubovich, Ilya S.
2008 "Sociolinguistics of the Luvian Language." Ph.D. diss., University of Chicago.
Zamazalová, Silvie
2011 "The Education of Neo-Assyrian Princes." Pp. 313–330 in *The Oxford Handbook of Cuneiform Culture*. Edited by Karen Radner and Eleanor Robson. Oxford: Oxford University Press.
Zettler, Richard
1984 "The Genealogy of the House of Ur-Me-me: A Second Look." *AfO* 31, pp. 1–9.
Zonta, Mauro
2006 *Hebrew Scholasticism in the Fifteenth Century: A History and Source Book*. Amsterdam Studies in Jewish Thought 9. Dordrecht: Springer.

Digital Resources

all online sources last accessed 1 July 2017

Cuneiform Commentaries Project, ed. E. Frahm, E. Jiménez, M. Frazer, and K. Wagensonner, 2013–2017
Frahm, Eckart, Mary Frazer, and Enrique Jiménez
2013 "Commentary on Sagig 1 (*CCP* 4.1.1.A.a)" at http://ccp.yale.edu/P348843. DOI: 10079/4qrfjkk.
2013 "Commentary on Sagig 1 (*CCP* 4.1.1.A.b)" at http://ccp.yale.edu/P461308. DOI: 10079/0zpc8k4.
2013 "Commentary on Sagig 1 (*CCP* 4.1.1.B)" at http://ccp.yale.edu/P348448. DOI: 10079/w9ghxgg.
2013 "Commentary on Sagig 1 (*CCP* 4.1.1.C)" at http://ccp.yale.edu/P348449. DOI: 10079/rjdfngo.
2013 "Commentary on Sagig 1–3 (and perhaps 4) (*CCP* 4.1.1.D)" at http://ccp.yale.edu/P338717. DOI: 10079/msbccff.
2013 "Commentary on Sagig 4 (*CCP* 4.1.4.A)" at http://ccp.yale.edu/P348451. DOI: 10079/c866tdc.
2013 "Commentary on Sagig 5 (*CCP* 4.1.5)" at http://ccp.yale.edu/P348452. DOI: 10079/3r228cc.
2013 "Commentary on Sagig 7 (*CCP* 4.1.7.A)" at http://ccp.yale.edu/P348453. DOI: 10079/02v6x8k.
2013 "Commentary on Sagig 7 (*CCP* 4.1.7.B)" at http://ccp.yale.edu/P348454. DOI: 10079/v9s4n88.

2013 "Commentary on Sagig 14 (*CCP* 4.1.14)" at http://ccp.yale.edu/P348457. DOI: 10079/b8gtj64.

2013 "Commentary on Sagig 19 (*CCP* 4.1.19)" at http://ccp.yale.edu/P348450. DOI: 10079/2v6wx2v.

2013 "Commentary on Sagig 21 and 21a (*CCP* 4.1.21)" at http://ccp.yale.edu/P461062. DOI: 10079/z34tn2j.

2013 "Commentary on Sagig 36 (*CCP* 4.1.36)" at http://ccp.yale.edu/P348460. DOI: 10079/f1vhjod.

2013 "Commentary on Sagig 39 (*CCP* 4.1.39)" at http://ccp.yale.edu/P348461. DOI: 10079/98sf7zx.

2013 "Commentary on Sagig 40 (*CCP* 4.1.40.A)" at http://ccp.yale.edu/P348462. DOI: 10079/5mkkww3.

2016 "Commentary on Sagig 4 (*CCP* 4.1.4.C)" at http://ccp.yale.edu/P461193. DOI: 10079/ngf1vwj.

Geller, Markham J., and Eric Schmidtchen

2016 "Commentary on Sagig 3 (*CCP* 4.1.3.C)." at http://ccp.yale.edu/P461216. DOI: 10079/tb2rc1z.

Jiménez, Enrique

2014 "Commentary on *Ālu* 22–23 (*CCP* 3.5.22.A.b)" at http://ccp.yale.edu/P461301. DOI: 10079/zgmsbr9.

2014 "Commentary on Sagig 4 (*CCP* 4.1.4.C.b)" at http://ccp.yale.edu/P461199. DOI: 10079/n02v78t.

2014 "Commentary on Sagig 10–11 (*CCP* 4.1.10)" at http://ccp.yale.edu/P461113. DOI: 10079/qjq2c7p.

2015 "Commentary on Sagig 7 (*CCP* 4.1.7.C.b)" at http://ccp.yale.edu/P481113. DOI: 10079/9s4mwkh.

2015 "Commentary on Sagig 13 and 12 (*CCP* 4.1.13.B)" at http://ccp.yale.edu/P294665. DOI: 10079/g1jwt6m.

2015 "Commentary on Sagig 18 (*CCP* 4.1.18)" at http://ccp.yale.edu/P461278. DOI: 10079/6hdr85n.

2015 "Commentary on Sagig 23 (*CCP* 4.1.23)" at http://ccp.yale.edu/P270807. DOI: 10079/pkop31d.

2015 "Commentary on Sagig 29 (*CCP* 4.1.29)" at http://ccp.yale.edu/P461169. DOI: 10079/jsxktow.

2015 "Commentary on Sagig 34 (*CCP* 4.1.34)" at http://ccp.yale.edu/P348644. DOI: 10079/pnvxoz5.

2015 "Commentary on Sagig 40 (*CCP* 4.1.40.B)" at http://ccp.yale.edu/P348463. DOI: 10079/1vhhmvk.

2016 "Commentary on Sagig 3 (*CCP* 4.1.3.A)" at http://ccp.yale.edu/P348450. DOI: 10079/h1893dw.

2016 "Commentary on Sagig 3 (*CCP* 4.1.3.B)" at http://ccp.yale.edu/P461263. DOI: 10079/x95x6pp.

2016 "Commentary on Sagig 4 (*CCP* 4.1.4.B)" at http://ccp.yale.edu/P285998. DOI: 10079/7h44jcv.

2016 "Commentary on Sagig 7 (*CCP* 4.1.7.C.a)" at http://ccp.yale.edu/P461244. DOI: 10079/prr4xvx.

2016 "Commentary on Sagig 7 (?) (*CCP* 4.1.7.C.c)" at http://ccp.yale.edu/P470057. DOI: 10079/70rxws6.

Geography of Knowledge in Assyria and Babylonia Project, ed. E. Robson, S. Tinney, et al., 2007–2012

Clancier, Philippe

2009 "SpTU 1, 027 [Sakikku 01 commentary]" at http://oracc.org/cams/gkab/P348448.

2009 "SpTU 1, 028 [Sakikku 01 commentary]" at http://oracc.org/cams/gkab/P348449.

2009 "SpTU 1, 029 [Sakikku 03 commentary]" at http://oracc.org/cams/gkab/P348450.

2009 "SpTU 1, 030 [Sakikku 04 commentary]" at http://oracc.org/cams/gkab/P348451.

2009 "SpTU 1, 031 [Sakikku 05 commentary]" at http://oracc.org/cams/gkab/P348452.

2009 "SpTU 1, 032 [Sakikku 07 commentary]" at http://oracc.org/cams/gkab/P348453.

2009 "SpTU 1, 033 [Sakikku 07 commentary]" at http://oracc.org/cams/gkab/P348454.

2009 "SpTU 1, 036 [Sakikku 14 commentary]" at http://oracc.org/cams/gkab/P348457.

2009 "SpTU 1, 038 [Sakikku 19–20 commentary]" at http://oracc.org/cams/gkab/P348459.

2009 "SpTU 1, 039 [Sakikku 36 commentary]" at http://oracc.org/cams/gkab/P348460.

2009 "SpTU 1, 040 [Sakikku 39 commentary]" at http://oracc.org/cams/gkab/P348461.

2009 "SpTU 1, 041 [Sakikku 40 commentary]" at http://oracc.org/cams/gkab/P348462.

2009 "SpTU 1, 042 [Sakikku 40 commentary]" at http://oracc.org/cams/gkab/P348463.

2009 "SpTU 2, 039 [Šaziga commentary]" at http://oracc.org/cams/gkab/P348644.

2009 "SpTU 5, 256 [Sakikku 01 commentary]" at http://oracc.org/cams/gkab/P348843.

The British Museum's Ashurbanipal Library Project, 2003–

Fincke, Jeanette C.

Database of Babylonian Nineveh Texts at http://www.fincke-cuneiform.com/nineveh/babylonian/index.htm

Index of Excerpts
(Two Volumes)

Excerpt numbers (not page numbers) indexed here run consecutively across the two companion volumes: *Knowledge and Rhetoric in Medical Commentary* (CM 49/1 = §I) includes Excerpts 1–372, while *Mesopotamian Commentaries on the Diagnostic Handbook Sa-gig* (CM 49/2 = §II) includes Excerpts 373–437.

Commentaries on the Diagnostic Handbook Sa-gig

(§II.1.1) *Comm. Sa-gig 1A*
Tablet AO 17661
obv. 3–5 417
obv. 3–6 247
obv. 6–10 408
obv. 11–13 285
obv. 13–14 348
obv. 17 289
obv. 26–27 223, 429
lines 29–30 170
lines 31–32 377
lines 32–34 163
lines 35–38 174
lines 38–39 234
line 41 241, 395

(§II.1.2) *Comm. Sa-gig 1B*
Tablet W 22307/6 = IM 74357
Editio princeps SpTU I, 27
obv. 1′–5′ 173
obv. 6′–7′ 165
obv. 10′ 108
obv. 10′–11′ 7, 271, 425
obv. 11′–12′ 140, 265
obv. 12′–15′ 179, 407
obv. 13′, 16′–17′ 83
obv. 17′–18′ 411
obv. 19′–21′ 284
obv. 20′–21′ 198, 399
obv. 24′–25′ 160, 246
obv. 24′–28′ 409
obv. 24′–29′ 164
obv. 26′–27′ 275
rev. 4 385
rev. 5 406
rev. 6–7 419
rev. 7–8 267
rev. 7–9 224, 430
rev. 9 420
rev. 12–13 274
rev. 13–17 171, 410
rev. 21–23 436
rev. 26–27 276

(§II.1.3) *Comm. Sa-gig 1C*
Tablet W 22307/24 = IM 74374
Editio princeps SpTU I, 28
obv. 7 8, 384
obv. 9–10 404
rev. 4′–5′ 381
rev. 8′ 141, 290, 422

(§II.1.4) *Comm. Sa-gig 1D*
Tablet W 22666/1c
Editio princeps SpTU V, 256
– –

(§II.1.5) *Comm. Sa-gig 1–3*
Tablet S.U. 51/70
Hand Copy STT II, 403
obv. 17 349
obv. 18 350
obv. 19 13
obv. 20 371
obv. 23–25 84
obv. 24–25 263
obv. 27 187
obv. 28 264
lines 31–48 340
line 35 351
lines 37–39 167
line 43 107
line 45 1
line 47 219
line 50 352
lines 52–53 237

(§II.1.6) ***Comm. Sa-gig 3A***
Tablet W 22307/71
Editio princeps SpTU I, 29
rev. 5′–6′ 233

(§II.1.7) ***Comm. Sa-gig 3B***
Tablet BM 43854 + 43938
obv. 2′–4′ 168
obv. 3′–5′ 383
obv. 7′–8′ 273
rev. 1–6 341
rev. 2–3 118
rev. 5–6 228

(§II.1.8) ***Comm. Sa-gig 3C***
Tablet BM 55491
obv. 1–3 231
obv. 4 258, 361
obv. 5 244
obv. 5–7 412
obv. 5–8 369

(§II.1.9) ***Comm. Sa-gig 4A***
Tablet W 22307/60+79+80(+)75
Editio princeps SpTU I, 30
obv. 2–3 9
obv. 3 374
obv. 4 353
obv. 6 190
obv. 6–7 283
obv. 6–8 288
obv. 9 119
obv. 11–13 139, 222, 428
obv. 13 227
obv. 14 226
obv. 14–17 181
obv. 16–18 415

(§II.1.10) ***Comm. Sa-gig 4B***
Tablet BM 66965 + 76508
obv. 1 261
obv. 1–2 431
obv. 2 175, 206
obv. 5–6 280
obv. 7 178, 400
obv. 7–8 180
obv. 9 245, 432
obv. 9–10 10, 202
obv. 11 266, 401
obv. 12 225, 364
obv. 13 193, 209
obv. 13–14 5
obv. 15 252
obv. 16 211, 388

(§II.1.11) ***Comm. Sa-gig 4C***
Tablet BM 40837 + 41252
rev. 8′ 362

(§II.1.12) ***Comm. Sa-gig 5***
Tablet W 22307/16
Editio princeps SpTU I, 31
obv. 8 208
line 24 254
line 25 373
line 26 207
line 27 116
lines 28–29 423
lines 31–32 424

(§II.1.13) ***Comm. Sa-gig 7A***
Tablet W 22307/2
Editio princeps SpTU I, 32
rev. 1–2 268, 363
rev. 2 376
rev. 4 183
rev. 7–8 182
rev. 11–12 405
rev. 11–13 220, 253
rev. 5–6 255

(§II.1.14) ***Comm. Sa-gig 7B***
Tablet W 22307/10
Editio princeps SpTU I, 33
rev. 2′–3′ 11
rev. 3′–4′ 189, 242
rev. 8′–12′ 135

(§II.1.15) **Comm. Sa-gig 7Ca**
Tablet BM 48727 + 48741
– –

(§II.1.16) ***Comm. Sa-gig 7Cb***
Tablet BM 48729
line 5′ 281

(§II.1.17) ***Comm. Sa-gig 7Cc (?)***
Tablet BM 49044
obv. 8′ 354

(§II.1.18) ***Comm. Sa-gig 10 & 11***
Tablet DT 87
obv. 1 103, 243
obv. 2–3 212, 229, 389
obv. 2–10 342
obv. 10 113
rev. 5′ 200
rev. 7′ 433

(§II.1.19) ***Comm. Sa-gig 13+***
Tablet GCBC 766
Hand Copy GCCI II, 406
obv. 1 99
obv. 3 104
obv. 8 196
obv. 9 115, 355
line 10 394
line 13 114

(§II.1.20) ***Comm. Sa-gig 14***
Tablet W 22307/20
Editio princeps SpTU I, 36
obv. 2–10 343
obv. 4 109, 356
obv. 5 117, 203, 248
obv. 5–6 213
obv. 6–7 3, 368, 418
obv. 8–9 214
obv. 8–10 88
obv. 10 386
obv. 14 387
obv. 15–16 396
obv. 19 110
obv. 22–23 188
obv. 23 414
obv. 23–24 156
obv. 24 398
obv. 25 357, 421
obv. 27 192

(§II.1.21) ***Comm. Sa-gig 18***
Tablet BM 66873
– –

(§II.1.22) ***Comm. Sa-gig 19***
Tablet W 22307/32
Editio princeps SpTU I, 38
obv. 11 105, 194
obv. 12 112
obv. 12–13 205, 230
obv. 13 375
obv. 15–16 378
obv. 15–17 413
obv. 18 251
obv. 19 257, 365

(§II.1.23) ***Comm. Sa-gig 21 & 22a***
obv. 1–2 197, 278
obv. 3–4 216, 402
obv. 5–6 101
obv. 8 218, 397
obv. 9 256
obv. 10 111
obv. 11 186, 260
obv. 18–19 367

(§II.1.24) ***Comm. Sa-gig 23***
Tablet RMC 193
obv. 1–2 106, 259

(§II.1.25) ***Comm. Sa-gig 29***
Tablet BM 38375
obv. 6–7 379

(§II.1.26) ***Comm. Sa-gig 34***
Tablet W 22730/2
Editio princeps SpTU II, 39
obv. 1–2 366
obv. 4 358
rev. 6′–7′ 204

(§II.1.27) ***Comm. Sa-gig 36***
Tablet W 22307/23+74
Editio princeps SpTU I, 39
rev. 4′–5′ 215
rev. 5′ 16
rev. 9′–12′ 169, 277
rev. 10′–11′ 382

(§II.1.28) ***Comm. Sa-gig 39***
Tablet W 22311
Editio princeps SpTU I, 40
obv. 2–3 380

obv. 2–4 155, 279
obv. 2–7 370
obv. 7–8 191
obv. 8–9 217, 403
obv. 9–11 240
obv. 11–12 185, 235
obv. 11–13 210

(§11.1.29) ***Comm. Sa-gig 40A***
Tablet W 22308a
Editio princeps SpTU 1, 41
obv. 2–5 286, 426
obv. 2–12 344
obv. 6 282
obv. 7 250
obv. 7, 10 195
obv. 8–9 2
obv. 12 176
obv. 13 96, 249, 359
obv. 14 201

(§11.1.30) ***Comm. Sa-gig 40B***
Tablet W 22307/73
Editio princeps SpTU 1, 42
rev. 3′ 184, 360
rev. 6′ 199

Other Cuneiform Medical Genres

The Diagnostic Handbook Sa-gig

Sa-gig S1: 6 72
Sa-gig (S1: 7–8)
U1: 10–11 82
Sa-gig S1: 12 59
Sa-gig S1: 13 64
Sa-gig S1: 16 60
Sa-gig U1: 10–11
(S1: 7–8) 82
Sa-gig U1: 38 77
Sa-gig 3: 13–14 14
Sa-gig 3: 27–31b 337
Sa-gig 3: 35, 41–80 345
Sa-gig 3: 41–42 166
Sa-gig 3: 45–46 272
Sa-gig 3: 64 303
Sa-gig 3: 88 236
Sa-gig 3: 98 304
Sa-gig 3: 98–99 232
Sa-gig 4: 1 46
Sa-gig 4: 10 43
Sa-gig 4: 11 305
Sa-gig 4: 13 27
Sa-gig 4: 20–21 287
Sa-gig 9: 31 306
Sa-gig 9: 35 55
Sa-gig 9: 50 307
Sa-gig 9: 50 65
Sa-gig 9: 69 28
Sa-gig 9: 74 308
Sa-gig 10: 1–2 102
Sa-gig 10: 1–24 346
Sa-gig 10: 8 309
Sa-gig 10: 11 MS A 89
Sa-gig 10: 11 MS B 90
Sa-gig 10: 28 78
Sa-gig 10 B rev. 8–10 310
Sa-gig 10 B rev. 18 311
Sa-gig 11: 9 312
Sa-gig 11 rev. 36 313
Sa-gig 12: 6 MS A 22
Sa-gig 12: 73″ 79
Sa-gig 12: 85″ 314
Sa-gig 12: 125″ 315
Sa-gig 12: 132″ 316
Sa-gig 13: 2 98
Sa-gig 13: 23–24 317
Sa-gig 13: 35 66
Sa-gig 13: 46 73
Sa-gig 13: 68 67
Sa-gig 13: 79 318
Sa-gig 13: 89 68
Sa-gig 13: 138 56
Sa-gig 14: 25–28 338
Sa-gig 14: 68 MS C 20
Sa-gig 14: 106–108 319
Sa-gig 14: 112 320
Sa-gig 14: 257′ 47
Sa-gig 15: 30′ 57
Sa-gig 15: 40′ 321
Sa-gig 15: 41′ 34
Sa-gig 15: 43′ 322
Sa-gig 15: 50′ 323
Sa-gig 15: 91′ 69
Sa-gig 16: 10 44
Sa-gig 16: 12 324

Sa-gig 16: 46′ 325
Sa-gig 16: 60′ 51
Sa-gig 16: 83′–84′ 326
Sa-gig 16: 88′ MS B 74
Sa-gig 17: 8–9 327
Sa-gig 17: 26 70
Sa-gig 17: 43 MS E 75
Sa-gig 17: 62 52
Sa-gig 17: 72 53
Sa-gig 17: 105 29
Sa-gig 18: 38′ 76
Sa-gig 19/20: 13′ 54
Sa-gig 19/20: 17′ 61
Sa-gig 19/20: 95′ 25
Sa-gig 19/20: 103′ 35
Sa-gig 19/20: 119′ 62
Sa-gig 19/20: 120′ 63
Sa-gig 21: 17 100
Sa-gig 22: 22 36
Sa-gig 22: 25–26 12
Sa-gig 22: 40 MS A 48
Sa-gig 22: 52 MS E 71
Sa-gig 23: 1 328
Sa-gig 23: 6 49
Sa-gig 23: 7 37
Sa-gig 26: 14′ MS B 45
Sa-gig 26: 23′ 80
Sa-gig 26: 28′–29′ MS A 24
Sa-gig 26: 28′–29′ MS B 23
Sa-gig 26: 29′ 38
Sa-gig 26: 29′ MS B 50
Sa-gig 26: 48′–49′ 40
Sa-gig 26: 86′–87′ 329
Sa-gig 27: 32–34 330
Sa-gig 27: 33–34 41
Sa-gig 29: 6–7 331
Sa-gig 31: 1–14, 19′–22′ 335
Sa-gig 31: 9–11 332
Sa-gig 33: 80 30
Sa-gig 33: 96 31
Sa-gig 33: 96 MS A 91
Sa-gig 36: 4 81
Sa-gig 36: 5 26
Sa-gig 36: 65 58
Sa-gig 37: 19 39
Sa-gig 37: 21 42
Sa-gig 40: 3–43 347
Sa-gig 40: 24 32
Sa-gig 40: 48 33
Sa-gig 40: 116 333

Other Diagnostic Texts
2N-T 336 334
CBS 12580, obv. 5 21
CBS 12580, obv. 6 19
STT 89: 192–195 (Stol 1993: 97) 94

Therapeutic Texts
AMT 77/1++, i 1–16 336
BAM 66, obv. 1–28, rev. 4′–16′ 295
BAM 145 299
BAM 146, lines 8′–20′, 29′–48′ 297
BAM 147, obv. 1–5, 13–15; rev. 5′–16′, 20′–25′ 298
BAM 186 300
BAM 480, ii 19–22, 26–27; iii 22–31 296
BM 42298, obv. 21–22 (Finkel 2000: 181–182) 127
H 170 293
Tablet of Madi-Dagan, obv. 1–15, 20–36, 98 294
YBC 4592 (*YOS* 11, 28), obv. 1–6 292

Commentaries on Therapeutic Texts
BM 59607, obv. 13 391
CTMMA II, no. 69, obv. 1 390
MLC 1863, obv. 5 437
SpTU I, 47 obv. 13–14 427

Pharmacopoeic Texts
BAM 1 i 42–58 302
Šammu šikinšu I §45′ and II §19 301

Medical or Physiognomic Fragment
AMT 94/8: 2′–3′ 339

Other Cuneiform Commentaries

Commentary on the Babylonian Creation Myth, Enūma eliš
Comm. Z on *Enūma eliš* III, 53 (Lambert 2013: 82; cf. 135, 138) 6

Commentary on Extispicy (bārûtu)
Koch-Westenholz (2000: 136–137, no. 19, §26) 138

Commentaries on the Terrestrial Omen Series, Šumma ālu
K 36+2917, obv. 13′; rev. 1 and 9 129
K 2895, obv. 11; rev. 9′–10′, 16′ 128

Principal Commentary to the Teratological Omen Series, Šumma izbu
on *Izbu* II, 54′ (De Zorzi 2014: 392, lines 29–30) 269
on *Izbu* IV (De Zorzi 2014: 440, line 33) 97

Other Commentaries on Šumma izbu
Finkel (2006: 147, Fig. 1), obv. 10–11 416
Finkel (2006: 147, Fig. 1), rev. 35–36 121
K 1913, obv. 5′–8′ 85

Commentary on the Physiognomic Omen Series, Alamdimmû
SpTU I, 83 rev. 28–29 142

Commentary on Astronomical and Physiognomic Omens
SpTU I, 84 obv. 19 17

Commentary on the Astronomical Omen Series, Enūma Anu Enlil
BM 47447, rev. 31–34 136

Commentaries on the Composition Marduk's Address to the Demons
Ass. 13955fx (A 163), obv. 9′–14′ 148
BM 47529 + 47685, obv. 12–15 (Wee 2016a: 136–137, §5–6) 87
BM 47529 + 47685, obv. 16–18 (Wee 2016a: 136–137, §7a–f) 161

Commentary on Maqlû and Šurpu Rituals and Incantations
KAR 94 obv. 14′–15′ 86

The Esoteric Babylonian Commentary
obv. 5–7 and rev. 1–8 (Wee 2017: 245–246) 125

Lexical Texts

Aa (MSL XIV*)*
Aa iii/4, 220 (*MSL* XIV, 342) 239
Aa v/2, 22–26 (*MSL* XIV, 416) 393

Antagal (MSL XVII*)*
Antagal VIII, 109–112 (*MSL* XVII, 173) 392

Erimhuš (MSL XVII*)*
Erimhuš II, 197–198 (*MSL* XVII, 37) 270
Erimhuš V, 211–214 (*MSL* XVII, 76) 262

ḪAR-gud (MSL V–XI*; Vedeler 2002)*
Hg. A I, 203 (Vedeler 2002: 45) 172
Hg. D III, 330 (Vedeler 2002: 95) 221

ḪAR-ra = ḫubullu (MSL V–XI*)*
Hh. xviii, 3–5 (*MSL* VIII/2, 96) 162

Igituh
Igituh I, 40–57
(VAT 10270, obv.) 120

Lu (= ša) (MSL XII)
Lu iii i 17′–19′
(*MSL* XII, 123) 159

Nabnitu (MSL XVI)
Nabnitu A, 274–275
(*MSL* XVI, 67) 157
Nabnitu XXVII, 255–265
(*MSL* XVI, 236–237) 126

Syllabary B (MSL III)
S^b ii, 236
(*MSL* III, 144) 238

Lexical Text similar to Idu
CT 12, 29 rev. 5 158

Divinatory Genres

Extispicy
SpTU IV, 158 rev. 12′
(Koch 2005:
457–458, no. 95) 154
VAT 13798, obv. 3–5
in Heeßel (2012:
244, no. 73) 153

Terrestrial Omen Series, Šumma ālu
CT 38, 26: 24–27
(*Šumma ālu*
XIX, 45′–48′) 95

Bird Omens
IM 74500, rev. 32
(Fawzi 1978: 50, 62) 93

Remedial-Apotropaic Genres

Fire Incantation
Fire Incantation, lines 5–7
(Lambert 1970: 40) 4

Anti-Witchcraft Tablet
STT 256 obv. 1–11 92
(Tzvi and Schwemer 2011: 138, 144)

'Evil Spirits' (Utukkū Lemnūtu) Incantation Series
Lunar Eclipse Myth, lines 1–2
(in *Utukkū Lemnūtu*
Tablet 16) 177

Rituals against Sexual Impotency
Šà-zi-ga Ritual
(*AMT* 65/7: 2′–3′
in Biggs 1967: 51) 15

Myths

Myth of Ninurta's Exploits, Lugale
VI, 32–33 (van Dijk
1989: 1,85; 2,89;
lines 268–269) 372

Lunar Eclipse Myth
lines 1–2
(Geller 2016: 501) 177

On Astronomy and Astrology

The Astral Compendium Mul-apin
Mul-apin II,
iii 33 MS E 435
Mul-apin II,
iii 33 MS HH 434

Astrological Discussions by Scholars and the Assyrian King
SAA VIII no. 82,
rev. 3–5
(Hunger 1992: 49) 122
SAA VIII no. 147
(Hunger 1992:
89–90) 147
SAA VIII no. 158,
obv. 4–rev. 5
(Hunger 1992: 93) 145
SAA VIII no. 454,
rev. 1–6
(Hunger 1992: 255) 150

SAA x no. 8,
obv. 21–rev. 22
(Parpola 1993: 9–10) 146, 291

On Scribal Education and Scholarship

Discourses on Scribal Education
Edubba D, lines 11–14
(Civil 1985: 69) 123
Examenstext A,
lines 8–14
(Sjöberg 1975: 140) 137

On the Scholar Esagil-kīn-apli
Esagil-kīn-apli's Manifesto,
A 51–71 // B 18′–33′ 18
Exorcist's Manual
(*KAR* 44, rev. 14) 124
on "series … of Esagil-kīn-apli"

On Scholars and the Antediluvian Sages
K 2486++ (on Enmeduranki;
Lambert 1967: 132) 143
List of Kings and
Sages/Scholars 144

Scholarly Credentials and the Assyrian Court
SAA x no. 160,
obv. 36–45
(Parpola 1993: 122) 151
SAA x no. 160,
rev. 28–34
(Parpola 1993: 124) 134
SAA x no. 182,
rev. 24–28
(Parpola 1993: 146–147) 152

Colophons and Scribal Notes

BAM 106 rev. 9′–12′ 132
BM 38413, obv. 1–4 //
rev. 17′–20′ 130
CBS 1516 = PBS 1/2
no. 106, rev. 30 149
Comm. Sa-gig 7B,
rev. 8′–12′
(§II.1.14) 135
CT 41, 21, rev. 42 133
Esoteric Babylonian
Commentary, rev. 6–8
(Wee 2017: 245–246) 125
K 36+2917, obv. 13′;
rev. 1 and 9 129
K 2895, obv. 11;
rev. 9′–10′, 16′ 128
YBC 11407, rev. 13
(Frahm 2010c:
159, 166–168) 131